INTRODUCTION TO

COMPUTING USING C++ AND OBJECT TECHNOLOGY

WILLIAM H. FORD
WILLIAM R. TOPP

University of the Pacific

An Alan R. Apt Book

Prentice Hall, Upper Saddle River, NJ 07458

Library of Congress Cataloging–in–Publication Data

Ford, William H.
   Introduction to computing using C++ and object technology. /
  William H. Ford, William R. Topp
     p.   cm.
  Includes index.
  ISBN 0-13-268152-8
   1. C++ (Computer program language) 2. Object-oriented methods
(Computer science) I. Topp, William R., II. Title.
  QA76.73.C153F68   1999
  005. 13'3—dc21
                                       99-31759
                                       CIP

Publisher: Alan Apt
Acquisitions Editor: Laura Steele
Editor-in-Chief: Marcia Horton
Art Director: Heather Scott
Assistant to Art Director: John Christiana
Production Coordinator: Wanda España/WEE DESIGN GROUP
Vice President Director of Production and Manufacturing: David W. Riccardi
Director of Creative Services: Paula Maylahn
Associate Creative Directors: Amy Rosen
Managing Editor: Bayani Mendoza de Leon
Cover Designer: Marjorie Dressler
Interior Designer: Donna Wickes, Judith Matz-Coniglio
Manufacturing Buyer: Donna Sullivan
Compositor: Progressive Information Technologies Inc.
Art Studio: Marita Froimson

©1999 by Prentice-Hall, Inc.
Simon & Schuster/A Viacom Company
Upper Saddle River, New Jersey 07458

Printed in the United States of America

10 9 8 7 6 5 4 3 2 1

ISBN   0-13-268152-8

Prentice-Hall International (UK) Limited, *London*
Prentice-Hall of Australia Pty. Limited, *Sydney*
Prentice-Hall Canada Inc., *Toronto*
Prentice-Hall Hispanoamericana, S.A., *México*
Prentice-Hall of India Private Limited, *New Delhi*
Prentice-Hall of Japan, Inc., *Tokyo*
Simon & Schuster Asia Pte. Ltd., *Singapore*
Editora Prentice-Hall do Brasil, Ltda., *Rio de Janeiro*

To our support team:

Our families who provide love and patiently accept our endless work
Our university who gave us time, support and resources
Our colleagues who gave us suggestions, encouragement and some humor
Our students who gave us a laboratory, feedback and sometimes confused stares
Our publisher who gave us expertise, patience and a finished product

Preface

This book is designed for a first course in computing using the C++ programming language and the principles of object technology. The goal is to teach problem solving using a computer. Using objects, we develop design principles and techniques that allow a programmer to manage data for real world situations. We assume no prior programming experience or mathematics beyond high school algebra. We ask only that students jump into the modern world of object technology and learn to use the methods of object-oriented programming and the powerful C++ language. We introduce objects from page one and blend design and language topics so that students master the fundamentals of C++ object oriented programming in one-semester. If students already have programming background, some of the language concepts and syntax can be covered more rapidly leaving time for advanced topics. The later chapters introduce modern features of object technology including templates, function and operator overloading, container classes, iterators, and inheritance. The material provides excellent special topics in a first course or a transition to follow-up courses in data structures and algorithms.

Importance of Objects

Objects and their types, called classes, are not a merely a topic in C++ but rather are the core of the language. They provide a paradigm for problem solving. Learning object-oriented analysis (OOA), object-oriented design (OOD), and object-oriented programming (OOP) is the primary goal for students seeking to program in the modern world of object technology. From the beginning, students are introduced to class descriptions that define both the data and the operations of an object. The authors provide a wide variety of pre-written classes that can be used in complete C++ programs to solve interesting problems. Students can early-on use objects without having to understand the technical details of class implementations and underlying C++ syntax. After introducing the primitive C++ number and character types in Chapter 2 and the prototype of a function in Chapter 3, students are able to understand the formal declaration of a C++ class. By Chapter 5, the book has covered simple conditional and loop control structures that enable students to design and implement their own classes to solve problems. The remaining chapters are then able to develop language constructs such as arrays, object composition, operator overloading, dynamic memory and inheritance.

Learning the principles of object technology with C++ takes time and a growing familiarity the syntax and structures of the language. The book supports this effort by providing hundreds of examples and complete programs that motivate the concepts and then use them in the design and implementation of algorithms to solve problems.

Design of the Book

The book is organized around problem solving using objects and classes. Each chapter introduces one or more topics in the style of object technology. This often includes class description, declaration, and implementation. In the process, we develop the C++ language constructs that describe algorithms for the handling of objects.

Chapter Descriptions

Chapter 1

The chapter blends principles of object technology with specific problem solving situations. In the process, we develop class descriptions and write several complete C++ programs that run on a computer. The chapter also introduces the UML (Unified Modeling Language) description of an object. The programs let you anticipate the direction of the book and explore the specifics of your particular C++ programming environment.

Chapter 2

The chapter defines the C++ primitive number and character types that are the building blocks for all data in a program. These types give us numbers like 2, −16, 3.14 and the standard keyboard characters such as 'A'. We develop the C++ operators that apply to the primitive types. This allows us to create arithmetic expressions, assignment statements and stream input and output that are key components in any application program. In addition to the primitive types, we introduce String objects. They allow us to use words, labels, and descriptive phrases as simple data items in our programs.

Chapter 3

Chapter 1 introduces the concept of a class description that provides an informal specification for object attributes and operations. The primary new C++ language construct introduced in this chapter is the function and its prototype. The function implements class operations. After expanding the class description to include function prototypes, the chapter introduces class declarations that are the C++ specification of an object type. We give new examples of classes and provide prewritten code for use in applications. The UML notation is expanded to assist in the specification of a class. The chapter concludes with a discussion of the prototype and implementation of free functions that are not associated with any class. Such functions are necessary in C++ programming.

Chapter 4

The chapter begins to develop the more sophisticated tools of programming logic. We first introduce the concept of logical expressions that evaluate to true or false. Logical expressions are the building blocks for control structures consisting of selection and looping statements. These control structures enable us to design algorithms for challenging and realistic applications. We revisit control structures in Chapter 6 and further extend the programming constructs available to algorithms.

Chapter 5

Chapter 3 discusses the structure of a class using the C++ class declaration. The problem of class implementation is deliberately delayed to this chapter so that we can focus on the use of classes in writing programs. We are now in a position to build our own classes. With an understanding of free function implementations from Chapter 3 and with the syntax for control structures from Chapter 4, we can implement the member functions of a class. In the process, we learn how to create header files that contain the class declaration and the C++ statements that implement the member functions.

Chapter 6

This chapter expands our understanding of control structures and gives us many important C++ tools for implementing algorithms. The chapter includes nested if/else statements, switch statements, and flexible for statements that generalize the control structures of the while loop. For good program design, C++ provides enumeration types that allow programs to assign meaningful names to integer values. Pass by reference arguments are discussed. This mechanism allows a function to modify its the run-time arguments. Since many applications store data on disk, we introduce C++ text file objects. Their member functions are used with loops to handle large volumes of character, string, or numeric data.

Chapter 7

This chapter develops the syntax for one-dimensional arrays and uses them in a variety of object-oriented algorithms. For example, the FinanceCenter class has an array as a data member. We develop classical algorithms that search for a key in a list and sort a list in ascending order. The generation of random numbers plays a very important role in the creation of computer games and in event simulation. The class, RandomNumber, generates random integer and floating point numbers. The class is used in an interesting technique that estimates π and in simulating dice tosses and creating a bar graph. We define String objects in Chapter 2 and have used them for names, labels, and other text information. In this chapter we revisit the String type and use array operations to access the individual characters in the string. We also introduce a wide variety of String member functions that do pattern matching and string editing. These operations make a string class one of the most powerful and important object types for applications.

Chapter 8

With background from the previous chapters, students have a good understanding of computer problem solving using objects. The chapter extends this understanding by introducing object composition that promotes code reuse and is one of the more important principles of object technology. We introduce the object-oriented program development cycle, which includes analysis, design, program implementation, and testing. We formally show how the program cycle is used by developing an application that displays a full-year calendar. The chapter concludes with C++ rules that specify the scope and lifetime of an object and a study of recursion that provides an alternative to iteration (looping). Using simple examples, we develop the structure of recursive algorithms and their implementation as recursive functions.

Chapter 9

The chapter introduces function and operator overloading. Function overloading is particularly important for constructors that are operations to initialize the attributes of an object. Operator overloading is an extension of function overloading and allows programs to use class objects in essentially the same way number and character objects are used in arithmetic and logical expressions. It is a powerful tool in object technology. To illustrate operator overloading, we develop the Rational class whose objects represent familiar fractions. To generalize the data that can be used by functions and classes, C++ defines templates. The concept is developed in detail in the chapter and greatly extends the power of C++ in programming applications.

Chapter 10

The chapter looks at a new object type, called a pointer, that allows a program to access an object through its address in memory. Its most important use is managing dynamic memory that allows a program to request memory at run-time and then deallocate it when no longer needed. The chapter discusses the destructor, copy constructor, and overloaded assignment operator that must be implemented when dynamic memory is used. We develop a template-based Vector class that provides a powerful tool for handling lists of data in an application. The chapter concludes with a discussion of C++ strings. Historically, C++ strings were developed in the C programming language and are used in millions of lines of C and C++ code worldwide. Despite the fact that the String class can be used for most applications, the programmer must have some familiarity with C++ strings to extend and maintain existing application software.

Chapter 11

In Chapter 10, we develop the Vector class as a template-based storage structure. The Vector class is an example of a container class that is used to store, retrieve and modify data. This chapter develops a container class, List, that implements a sequential list. The structure allows insertion, deletion, and updates at any point of the list. The access to list elements is facilitated by using an iterator that is a generalized pointer. Iterators are important in a general study of containers. Linked lists are a basic implementation tool for programmers and are used in the implementation of the List class. A linked list is a storage structure that allows for efficient insertion and removal of data. Understanding how to create and maintain a linked list is a critical programming skill. We develop linked lists over two sections in the chapter. The chapter concludes by showing how a linked list is used to implement the List class.

Chapter 12

The subject of inheritance combines with object composition to create the primary techniques for reusing software. This chapter develops the key features of inheritance using a simple Employee hierarchy as a demonstration model as well as examples from graphics programming. Inheritance can be used to extend the functionality of an existing class. We use inheritance to develop an ordered list class from the List class. Polymorphism adds an extra dimension to the use of inheritance and is implemented in C++ using virtual member functions. Polymorphism is developed in the chapter and used in a program that draws colored shapes simulating a kaleidoscope. The chapter concludes with a discussion of virtual destructors and a study of abstract base classes that are used to specify the design of a class that is likely to have different implementations.

Using the Text in the Classroom

The book is ideally suited for a first course in computing (CS1). Most instructors will want to cover the material in Chapters 1–7 and, as time permits, the topics of object composition and the object-oriented programming life cycle from Chapter 8. Simple concepts of inheritance are available in Sections 12.1 through 12.2 and require no advanced C++ programming constructs. Topics on overloading and templates from Chapter 9 and pointers and dynamic memory from Chapter 10 can be used as special topics.

The material in Chapters 9–11 can be used as a supplement to a course in data structures or for self-study. The material is presented with the same care as the early material in the book.

The organization of the book supports instructors who wish to delay class implementations. Chapter 5 can be covered after Chapters 6 and 7, since all class implementations in those chapters are confined to separate sections. If Chapter 5 is covered at the end of the course, students can easily find the implementation details for the classes in earlier chapters.

Graphics Classes

Creating graphical figures and animation on a drawing surface provides an excellent example of object-oriented programming. The book feature a series of graphics classes for lines, circles, rectangles, polygons, and text. They are woven into most of the chapters and are used to illustrate relevant C++ language constructs and algorithms. For instance, loops are used to create animation for a jack-in-the-box and a shooting star. The graphics classes are used to illustrate the concept of inheritance in Chapter 12 and a kaleidoscope is implemented using virtual functions and polymorphism. Except for system dependent technical details, the book allows students to analyze the design and implementation of each of the graphics classes.

Software Design Tools and UML

Object technology has prompted the creation of software-development tools for program design. One of the powerful features of these tools is visual modeling that uses graphical specifications to assist in object and program design. The book gives you some experience with these tools using the Unified Modeling Language (UML). In the process, the reader is introduced to the object-oriented analysis and design methods that were developed by Grady Booch, Ivar Jacobson, and James Rumbaugh.

HTML Help System

A Web-based documentation for each class and free function library in the book is available in the software supplement. Using a browser, students may explore the description, declaration, and implementation of each class or function library. The documentation provides an on-line support system that can be used while students study programs in the text or work on written and programming exercises.

Highlighted Sections

Key points in each chapter are emphasized using shading. The highlighted sections include:

Syntax: A formal definition of the form and action of a C++ construct. One or more examples is included to illustrate the syntax.

Class Description: An informal listing of a class with its attributes and operations. A description of each operation includes a brief description of its action and its input arguments, return value, and C++ function prototype.

Class Declaration: A formal specification of the private and public members of the class.

Programming Note: A discussion of programming style and the identification of instruction sequences that can lead to runtime errors.

Technical Note: A system or language note that provides additional technical information about a topic in the chapter.

Exploring Concepts: Interesting problems that can be used to stimulate class discussion. Answers are often open-ended.

Exercise Sets

Each chapter includes review exercises that cover the basic topics. Complete answers are provided in the book so that the exercises can be used a chapter pre-test. The written exercises support and extend the basic text material and provide a range of difficulties from routine to challenging. In many cases the Programming exercises implement classes and algorithms developed in the written exercises. The programming project involves more difficult programming and substantially more algorithm development.

Supplements

The HTML documentation and complete source code listings for the classes and programs in the book are on the CD-Rom accompanying the book. They are also available through the Internet at the following locations:

http://www.uop.edu/~fordtopp

http://www.prenhall.com

The CD-Rom and the Internet sites also include a demo version of the Rational Rose object design tools and graphics software for Windows 95, Windows 3.1/DOS, and Macintosh.

Readers may contact the authors directly to make comments on the book. Email to "billf@uop.edu".

The Instructors Guide offers teaching tips for each chapter, answers to most written exercises and sample tests. The guide features solutions to many of the programming exercises and is available from Prentice Hall.

Appendices

The book includes six appendices that are written in a tutorial fashion with examples and complete programs. They can be used to supplement key topics in the book.

Appendix A Computer Data Storage
Supplements the discussion of primitive numeric and character types by showing how data is represented in a computer.

Appendix B Character Codes
Provides a full discussion of the ASCII character set. It also briefly discusses the Unicode and EBCDIC character sets.

Appendix C Operator Precedence
Gives a chart that specifies the precedence and associativity of each C++ operator.

Appendix D Stream Formatting
Provides a detailed discussion of format options for number and character data.

Appendix E The C++ Preprocessor
Introduces the #include, #define and conditional compilation directives.

Appendix F Namespaces and the ANSI/ISO C++ Standard Library
Introduces the namespace construct of ANSI/ISO C++ and gives a basic description of the standard library and show how to access its components in a program.

Acknowledgements

The authors have been supported by friends, students, and colleagues in the preparation of the book. The University of Pacific has generously provided resources and support to complete the project. Prentice-Hall offered a superb team of dedicated and talented professionals who handled the book design and production. We are especially grateful to our publisher Alan Apt, computer science editor Laura Steele, and development editor Sondra Chavez who collectively provided insight, encouragement, and resources to complete the project. To pass from manuscript to final book, we were greatly aided by a quality production staff that included the production manager Bayani DeLeon, production editor Wanda Espana, art director Heather Scott, artist Morita Froimson, and manufacturing buyer Donna Sullivan. The creativity and dedication to detail by all members of the Prentice Hall team has produced a book that we hope is attractive, easy to use, and an effective vehicle for learning the material.

Students have offered valuable criticism of the manuscript by giving us explicit feedback or unsolicited blank stares. Our reviewers offered invaluable guidance in the development of the manuscript. They provided detailed comments on both the content and the pedagogical approach. We took most of their recommendations into account. Special thanks go to Robert Holloway (University of Wisconsin - Madison), Robert Langser and Fred Harris (University of Nevada - Reno), Frank Dolinar (Michigan State University), Adair Dingle (Seattle University), Ted Christopher (University of Rochester), Erlan Wheeler (Carthage College), Robert Caviness (University of Delaware), David Finkel (Worchester Polytechnic Institute), Karl Klee (Jamestown Community College), and Dimtri Khijniak (Wayne State University). Two colleagues, Ralph Ewton at the University of Texas, El Paso and Joseph Liauw at the University of the Pacific made extensive contributions by a detailed reading of the manuscript. Their insights and support were invaluable to the authors and greatly improved the final contents of the book.

Brief Contents

1   *Introduction to Object Technology* *1*

2   *Basic C++ Types and Programs* *35*

3   *Describing and Declaring Classes*. *92*

4   *Basic C++ Control Structures*. *146*

5   *Developing Your Own Classes*. *204*

6   *Additional C++ Control Structures*. *250*

7   *Arrays*. *339*

8   *Program Design and Algorithms*. *441*

9   *Operator Overloading and Templates* *511*

10   *Pointers and Dynamic Memory* *576*

11   *Containers and Linked Lists* *654*

12   *Inheritance and Virtual Functions* *712*

Appendix A Computer Data Storage *A-1*

Appendix B Character Representations *B-1*

Appendix C C++ Operator Summary. *C-1*

Appendix D Stream Formatting. *D-1*

Appendix E The C++ Preprocessor. *E-1*

Appendix F Namespaces and the ANSI/ISO Standard Libraries. *F-1*

Index *I-1*

Contents

1   Introduction to Object Technology *1*

    1.1   Elements of Problem Solving   **2**
           Problem Solving and Objects   **3**
    1.2   Computers and Problem Solving   **4**
    1.3   Describing Computer Objects   **7**
           Initializing Object Attributes   **9**
           Visual Model of Object Types   **9**
    1.4   Programming with C++ Objects   **10**
           Language Identifiers   **11**
           Declaring and Using Objects   **11**
           A First C++ Program   **12**
           The C++ Programming Environment   **16**
    1.5   Exploring Rectangle Objects   **17**
    1.6   Drawing Figures: Rectangles   **20**
    1.7   The C++ Programming Language   **23**
    Chapter 1 Summary   **24**
           Object Types (Classes) in the Chapter   **24**
           Key Terms   **24**
    Review Exercises   **25**
           Answers to Review Exercises   **27**
    Written Exercises   **28**
    Programming Exercises   **31**
    Programming Project   **33**

2   Basic C++ Types and Programs *35*

    2.1   Integer Objects and Simple Expressions   **36**
           Declaring Integer Objects   **37**
           Basic Integer Operators   **39**
           Assignment Operators   **41**
    2.2   C++ Input and Output   **42**
           Sending Output to the Screen   **42**
           Formatting the Output   **44**
           Reading from the Keyboard   **46**
           Initializing Objects during Program Execution   **49**

2.3   Character Objects   **50**
      Escape Codes   **51**
      Character I/O   **52**
      Representing Character Data   **54**
      Character Operations   **56**
2.4   Real Number Objects   **58**
      C++ Real Number Types   **59**
      Exploring Real Numbers in Linear Equations   **62**
      Named Constants   **64**
2.5   Working with C++ Operators   **66**
      Operator Precedence   **66**
      Operator Associativity   **67**
      Type Conversion   **67**
2.6   Extending Arithmetic Operators   **71**
      Compound Assignment Operators   **71**
      Increment Operators   **72**
2.7   The String Type   **73**
      String Object Declaration   **73**
      String Input/Output   **74**
      String Operations   **75**
Chapter 2 Summary   **78**
      Object Types (Classes) in the Chapter   **79**
      Key Terms   **79**
Review Exercises   **80**
      Answers to Review Exercises   **82**
Written Exercises   **82**
Programming Exercises   **87**
Programming Projects   **90**

3   *Describing and Declaring Classes* *92*
3.1   Class Descriptions   **93**
      Describing Operations As Functions   **94**
      Constructor   **95**
      The StudentAccount Class: Formal Description   **95**
3.2   Declaring and Using Objects   **96**
      Calling Member Functions   **97**
      Application: Student Account Transactions   **98**
3.3   Describing the Rectangle Class   **101**
3.4   A Visual Model of Classes   **103**

3.5   The C++ Class Declaration   **104**

Moving from Description to Declaration   **107**

3.6   Classes and Problem Solving   **107**

3.7   Function Prototypes with Default Values   **111**

The GradeRecord Class   **113**

3.8   Drawing Circle Figures   **116**

3.9   Free Functions   **118**

Pure Object-Oriented Design   **118**

Structured Design   **119**

Program Design Using C++   **120**

Building C++ Programs with Objects and Free Functions   **121**

Exploring the Math Library   **122**

The Drawing Functions   **124**

Application: Using Graphics Functions and Objects   **125**

3.10 Defining Free Functions in a Main Program   **127**

Chapter 3 Summary   **131**

Classes in the Chapter   **132**

Key Terms   **132**

Review Exercises   **133**

Answers to Review Exercises   **135**

Written Exercises   **137**

Programming Exercises   **141**

Programming Project   **144**

4   *Basic C++ Control Structures*..*146*

4.1   Algorithms and Flow Control   **146**

Selection   **147**

Looping   **149**

4.2   Logical Expressions   **150**

Relational Operators   **150**

Logical Operators   **152**

Precedence of Arithmetic and Logical Operators   **154**

Short-Circuit Evaluation   **154**

Interpreting the OR Operation   **155**

4.3   Selection Statements   **155**

One-way Selection Using the if Statement   **155**

Grouping Statements in a Block   **156**

Two-Way Selection Using the if /else Statement   **158**

Multiple Selection Using Nested if/else   **161**

The Roots of a Quadratic Equation   **163**

4.4   The Boolean Type in C++   **165**
Checking Graduation Requirements   **167**
Integers As Logical Values   **169**

4.5   Loop Structures   **170**
The while Statement   **171**
Counter and Event-Controlled Loops   **173**
The do/while Statement   **179**
Loops and Numeric Palindromes   **180**

4.6   Animation with Loops   **185**
Jack in the Box Animation   **186**

Chapter 4 Summary   **190**
Classes in the Chapter   **190**
Key Terms   **190**

Review Exercises   **192**
Answers to Review Exercises   **193**

Written Exercises   **194**
Programming Exercises   **201**
Programming Project   **203**

5   *Developing Your Own Classes* *204*

5.1   Implementing Classes   **204**
Illustrating Member Function Implementations   **205**
Implementing the Constructor   **206**
Implementing the Rectangle Class   **208**

5.2   Organizing Program Source Code   **210**
Building A Class Header File   **210**
Building the Main Program   **211**
Building and Using the Accumulator Class   **213**
Alternative Source Code Design (Optional)   **215**

5.3   Error Checking in Class and Program Design   **217**

5.4   Private Member Functions   **219**
The Time24 Class   **219**
Time24 Class Declaration and UML   **221**
Implementation of the Time24 Class   **223**

5.5   Member Functions with Loops: the Loan Class   **225**
The Loan Class   **226**
Implementing the Loan Class   **228**

5.6   Inline Code   **230**
The Circle Class Using Inline Code   **230**

Implementing Inline Code   **232**
Application: Enclosing Maximum Area   **232**
Inline Code for Free Functions (Optional)   **234**
Chapter 5 Summary   **235**
Classes in the Chapter   **236**
Key Terms   **236**
Review Exercises   **237**
Answers to Review Exercises   **238**
Written Exercises   **240**
Programming Exercises   **246**
Programming Project   **248**

6   Additional C++ Control Structures *250*

6.1   Multiple Selection: Nested If Statements   **251**
The "Dangling" Else   **253**
6.2   Multiple Selection: Switch Statement   **255**
6.3   Enumeration Types   **261**
Properties of Enumeration Types   **263**
6.4   Building an Enumeration Class   **265**
Implementation of the Days class   **267**
6.5   The Date Class   **269**
Date Class Implementation   **272**
6.6   The For Loop   **275**
6.7   For Loop Applications   **278**
Number Theory: Exploring Factors   **279**
Approximating a Circle   **280**
6.8   Advanced Loop Concepts   **283**
Designing Nested Loops   **283**
Generalized For Loops   **286**
Loop Break and Continue Statements   **288**
6.9   Argument Passing   **292**
Pass by Value   **292**
Pass by Reference   **294**
6.10   Constant Function Arguments   **302**
6.11   Conditional Expressions (OPTIONAL)   **303**
6.12   Text File I/O   **306**
C++ Stream Classes   **307**
Creating File Stream Objects   **308**
Reading and Writing File Data   **310**
File Error Checking   **311**

Streams as Function Arguments (OPTIONAL) **316**
Stream States and Errors (OPTIONAL) **319**
Chapter 6 Summary **319**
Classes in the Chapter **320**
Key Terms **320**
Review Exercises **323**
Answers to Review Exercises **324**
Written Exercises **326**
Programming Exercises **334**
Programming Projects **337**

7 *Arrays* *339*

7.1 Introducing Arrays **340**
Application: Weather Statistics **344**
7.2 Array Storage **346**
Array Bounds Checking **349**
7.3 Initializing Arrays **349**
Array Initialization in the Date Class **352**
7.4 Arrays as Arguments **353**
The Statistics Class **357**
7.5 Arrays Of Objects **361**
Default Constructor **361**
Application: Painter's Job Schedule **364**
7.6 Random Numbers **367**
Estimating π **372**
7.7 Sequential Array Algorithms **374**
Sequential Search **374**
Removing a List Element **376**
Application: Removing Duplicates **377**
7.8 Arrays as Class Data Members **380**
Const Member Functions **382**
Application: Using the FinanceCenter Class **383**
Implementing the FinanceCenter Class **385**
7.9 Graphing Dice Tosses **387**
Graphing Dice Probabilities **391**
7.10 Array Sorting Algorithm **395**
7.11 String Objects **398**
The Index Operator [] **399**
String I/O **399**

7.12 Additional String Member Functions (OPTIONAL)   **404**
    String Search Functions   **405**
    Copying Substrings   **406**
    Modifying a String   **407**
    Analyzing File Names   **407**
7.13 Multidimensional Arrays   **409**
    Two-dimensional Array Arguments   **413**
    The SqMatrix Class   **414**
    The Storage of Two Dimensional Arrays (OPTIONAL)   **421**
Chapter 7 Summary   **422**
    Classes in the Chapter   **423**
    Key Terms   **423**
Review Exercises   **425**
    Answers to Review Exercises   **428**
Written Exercises   **429**
Programming Exercises   **436**
Programming Projects   **439**

8 *Program Design and Algorithms* *441*

8.1 Object Composition   **442**
    The Employee Class   **443**
    UML Representation for Composition   **446**
    The Constructor in Composition   **446**
    The Triangle Class   **448**
8.2 Object and Program Design Principles   **451**
    Object-Oriented Analysis   **451**
    Object-Oriented Design   **452**
    Object-Oriented Programming   **453**
8.3 Creating a Full Year Calendar   **455**
    Designing the Calendar Class   **456**
    Declaring the Calendar Class   **459**
    Implementing the Member Functions   **461**
    The Calendar Application   **465**
8.4 Accessing and Storing Objects   **466**
    Scope   **466**
    Storage Class   **471**
8.5 Recursive Algorithms   **475**
    Finding Recursive Algorithms   **477**
    Developing Recursive Functions   **478**

Tracing a Recursive Function   **481**
8.6   Recursion and Problem Solving   **482**
The Tower of Hanoi Puzzle   **482**
Traversing a Maze   **486**
Comparing Recursive and Iterative Algorithms   **494**
Chapter 8 Summary   **495**
Classes in the Chapter   **496**
Key Terms   **496**
Review Exercises   **498**
Answers to Review Exercises   **500**
Written Exercises   **503**
Programming Exercises   **508**
Programming Projects   **509**

9   *Operator Overloading and Templates* *511*

9.1   Function Overloading   **512**
Overloading Class Member Functions   **515**
9.2   The Rational Number System   **518**
Defining Rational Numbers   **518**
Rational Number Arithmetic   **519**
Number Systems (OPTIONAL)   **519**
The Rational Class   **520**
9.3   Operator Overloading   **522**
Defining Overloaded Operators   **523**
The Rational Class (Extended)   **526**
Overloading the Stream I/O Operators   **527**
9.4   Member Function Overloading   **530**
9.5   Converting Rational Numbers   **532**
Mixed Numbers   **537**
9.6   Template Functions   **540**
Template Syntax   **542**
Template Expansion   **542**
Template-based Selection Sort   **544**
9.7   Generalized Searching   **546**
Binary Search   **548**
Comparing Search Algorithms (OPTIONAL)   **552**
9.8   Template Classes   **555**
Constructing a Template Class   **556**
Declaring Template Class Objects   **558**

Chapter 9 Summary   **559**
   Classes in the Chapter   **560**
   Key Terms   **560**
Review Exercises   **562**
   Answers to Review Exercises   **565**
Written Exercises   **566**
Programming Exercises   **572**
Programming Projects   **573**

10 Pointers and Dynamic Memory *576*

10.1 C++ Pointers   **577**
   Declaring Pointer Objects   **578**
   Assigning Values to Pointers   **579**
   Accessing Data with Pointers   **580**
10.2 Arrays and Pointers   **583**
   Pointer Arithmetic   **583**
   Arrays As Pointer Arguments   **585**
   Pointers and Class Types   **588**
10.3 Dynamic Memory   **590**
   The Memory Allocation Operator new   **590**
   Dynamic Array Allocation   **592**
   Dynamically Allocated Class Objects   **593**
   The Memory Deallocation Operator delete   **595**
10.4 Classes Using Dynamic Memory   **599**
   The DynamicDemo Class   **600**
10.5 The Assignment Operator and Copy Constructor   **605**
   The Assignment Operator for DynamicDemo Objects   **606**
   The Class this Pointer   **610**
   The Copy Constructor for DynamicDemo Objects   **611**
10.6 Building a Vector Class   **616**
   Declaring the Vector Class   **617**
   Applications Using Vectors   **620**
   Implementing the Vector Class   **624**
10.7 C++ Strings   **629**
   C++ String I/O   **631**
   C++ String Handling Functions   **634**
   Implementing the String Class   **636**
Chapter 10 Summary   **638**
   Classes in the Chapter   **639**

Key Terms   **639**
Review Exercises   **640**
Answers to Review Exercises   **643**
Written Exercises   **645**
Programming Exercises   **650**
Programming Projects   **651**

11   *Containers and Linked Lists* *654*

11.1 The List Container   **655**
Creating List Objects   **656**
Accessing General List Elements   **659**
General Insert and Erase Operations   **663**
Application: Removing Duplicates   **665**
Iterators   **668**
11.2 Linked Lists   **667**
Describing a Linked List   **668**
Computer Representation of a Linked List   **669**
The Node Class   **670**
Building a Linked List   **674**
11.3 Building Linked Lists with Nodes   **675**
Creating a Node   **676**
Inserting at the Front of a List   **676**
Deleting at the Front of a List   **677**
Inserting a Node at the Rear of a List   **678**
Clearing a List   **679**
Removing a Target Node   **681**
11.4 Implementing the List Class   **684**
UML Representation for the List Class   **684**
List Class Private Members   **685**
List Iterators   **687**
Selected Member Functions   **690**
The General List Insertion Member Function   **693**
Chapter 11 Summary   **695**
Classes in the Chapter   **696**
Key Terms   **696**
Review Exercises   **697**
Answers to Review Exercises   **700**
Written Exercises   **702**

Programming Exercises   **707**
Programming Project   **709**

12   Inheritance and Virtual Functions.. 712

12.1 Inheritance in C++   **713**
    Declaring Derived Classes   **715**
    Delcaring the Graphics Hierarchy   **717**
    Constructors And Derived Classes   **720**
12.2 An Employee Hierarchy   **721**
12.3 Ordered Lists   **726**
    Application: List Insertion Sort   **728**
    Ordered List Class Implementation   **730**
12.4 Polymorphism and Virtual Functions   **730**
    Virtual Functions in an Inheritance Hierarchy   **732**
    Application: Painting Houses using Polymorphism   **734**
12.7 Geometric Figures And Virtual Functions   **737**
    Implementation of the PolyShape Class   **739**
    Application: Building a Kaleidoscope   **742**
12.8 Advanced Inheritance Topics   **746**
    Virtual Functions And The Destructor   **746**
    Abstract Base Classes   **749**
Chapter 12 Summary   **751**
    Classes in the Chapter   **752**
    Key Terms   **752**
Review Exercises   **753**
    Answers to Review Exercises   **756**
Written Exercises   **757**
Programming Exercises   **765**
Programming Project   **766**

Appendix A   Computer Data Storage A-1

Binary Numbers   **A-1**
Converting Binary and Decimal Numbers   **A-2**
Storing and Retrieving Numbers in a Computer   **A-3**
Primitive Data Types   **A-5**
    The Object Type char   **A-5**
    The Object Type short   **A-5**
    The Object Type long   **A-5**

The Storage of Real Numbers   **A-5**
The C++ size of Operator   **A-7**

Appendix B   Character Representations *B-1*

ASCII Character Set   **B-1**
Control Codes   **B-2**
Printable Characters   **B-2**
EBCDIC Character Set   **B-3**
Unicode Character Set   **B-4**

Appendix C   C++ Operator Summary *C-1*

Appendix D   Stream Formatting *D-1*

Format Flags   **D-1**
Handling Format Flags   **D-2**
One Argument Form of setf()   **D-3**
Two Argument Form of setf()   **D-3**
Clearing Flags with unsef()   **D-5**
Accessing Flag Values   **D-5**
Adjusting the Width of Output   **D-6**
Adjusting the Fill Character   **D-6**
Setting Decimal Point Precision   **D-6**
I/O Manipulators   **D-7**
Width Manipulator: setw(n)   **D-8**
Precision Manipulator: setprecision(n)   **D-8**

Appendix E   The C++ Preprocessor *E-1*

#include Directive   **E-1**
#define Directive   **E-2**
#Conditional Compilation   **E-4**

Appendix F   Namespaces and the ANSI/ISO C++ Standard Library *F-1*

The Keyword using   **F-2**
The C++ Standard Library   **F-3**

Chapter 1
Introduction to Object Technology

CHAPTER CONTENTS

1-1 ELEMENTS OF PROBLEM SOLVING
Problem Solving and Objects

1-2 COMPUTERS AND PROBLEM SOLVING

1-3 DESCRIBING COMPUTER OBJECTS
Initializing Object Attributes
Visual Model of Object Types

1-4 PROGRAMMING WITH C++ OBJECTS
Language Identifiers
Declaring and Using Objects
A First C++ Program
The C++ Programming Environment

1-5 EXPLORING RECTANGLE OBJECTS

1-6 DRAWING FIGURES: RECTANGLES

1-7 THE C++ PROGRAMMING LANGUAGE
Written Exercises

A computer is a problem-solving tool that handles input of data, carries out high-speed calculations, and provides output of the results. Its actions are controlled by a series of instructions, called a *program,* that can perform a wide variety of tasks such as monitoring automated assembly lines, managing databases, and creating graphic designs. Through the Internet, a computer provides electronic mail, World Wide Web access to newspapers, stock averages, and sports scores, and brings on-line shopping to our home. Computers impact most of the practical areas of our everyday life.

In this chapter, we discuss design principles and programming techniques that allow us to manage data for real world situations. Our approach uses modern principles of object technology, including objects and their types. Our approach defines these terms using a variety of examples. To implement this approach, we introduce C++, a widely used programming language that features most of the modern object-oriented constructs.

The chapter blends principles of object technology with problem-solving. This enables us to look at both object-oriented design and programming. In the process, we develop several complete C++ programs that run on a computer. The programs let you anticipate the direction of the book and explore the specifics of your particular C++ programming environment.

In an introductory chapter, you can get only a partial understanding and an intuitive grasp of object-technology concepts. Technical details and deepened understanding will follow from the work in subsequent chapters. Nevertheless, the topics in this chapter provide an important starting point for our study. Work through the ideas and examples carefully since they apply to the material in later chapters.

1-1 ELEMENTS OF PROBLEM SOLVING

Every day, people are confronted with a variety of tasks that have to be done. Some are simple, like setting an alarm clock or eating breakfast; others are more complex like baking a cake, replacing a faucet, or building a patio in the back-yard. These more complex tasks represent a challenge that requires problem-solving skills. A closer look at each of the tasks reveals general problem-solving principles. Let's start by looking at a recipe to bake a cake. A recipe describes ingredients and processes that illustrate most of the concepts that are involved in effective problem solving.

Some cooks bake a cake "from scratch." However, most people start with a cake mix and use the recipe that specifies the baking process. The recipe lists the ingredients, pan size, temperature, and so forth. Table 1-1 gives a recipe for a German chocolate cake.

The baking involves ingredients, pans, a mixer, oven, and timer. Once we decide on the type of cake, each of the items can be specified and the cake can be made. For instance, a bundt cake uses

Bundt Cake

pan:	greased and lightly-floured bundt pan
oven:	set to 350°
timer:	set to 45 minutes
ingredients:	cake mix, water, and oil
beater:	set to high speed

The recipe specifies what items are needed and gives step-by-step instructions on how to put them together. When the recipe is followed, the cake is properly cooked. The product manufacturer has solved the problem of baking a cake. The recipe is the end product of the problem-solving process. You will learn to analyze problems and solve them by creating your own recipes.

Replacing a kitchen faucet is a more difficult task. Typically, there is no simple recipe that sets out the parts and tools and no step-by-step guide to do the job. This lack of structure forces the plumber to do some important preplanning and then decide what materials are needed and how the job should be done. Before starting, the plumber must decide on either a faucet with separate hot and cold spouts or a single spout with controls to mix water temperatures. The connections to the hot and cold water sources can be flexible pipe or rigid copper tubing. These decisions are part of the preliminary *problem analysis*. Once the task is defined, the plumber must enter the *problem design* phase of the process. He must decide on tools such as a pipe cutter, soldering torch, pipe,

Table 1-1 Recipe for a Cake

What You Need	Oven 350°	Water 1 Cup	Oil 1/3 Cup	Beat 2 minutes
Prep	Preheat oven to 350°. Grease pan with shortening.			
Mix	Mix cake, water, and oil in a large bowl. Beat 2 minutes at high speed			
Bake	13x9 inch 30-40 minutes	Two 8 inch 30-40 minutes	Bundt Pan 40-50 minutes	24-30 cupcakes 15-20 minutes

or Crescent wrench, and so forth and the steps that must be followed to remove the old unit and install a new one.

Problem Solving and Objects

The components in problem solving are called *objects*. They are the building blocks and tools that interact to produce the final outcome. We view an object in terms of its *attributes* that describe what it is, and its *actions* that describe what it can do. For instance, with the cake, a pan is an object whose attributes are shape (circle, rectangle, bundt), depth (2″, 3″, 6″) and surface material (aluminum, non-stick teflon, glass). The oven is an object with actions to control the temperature and the source of heat. The following is a general description of an oven. The format uses separate categories for the attributes and actions and lists the common features that apply to any oven object.

DESCRIPTION: OVEN OBJECT ▬▬▬▬▬▬▬▬▬▬▬▬▬▬▬

Attributes:
 Size, temperature level,
 heat source (top = broil, bottom = bake)
Actions:
 Turn the oven on or off
 Select the heat source (bake, broil)
 Set the temperature level

To install a new faucet—the type of unit, the connecting pipes, and wrenches are critical objects. Each has attributes and actions that are part of the plumbing repair. For instance, the wrench has a style (pipe, Crescent, etc.), weight, handle length, and jaw size. As an action, its jaw openings are adjusted to fit different size pipes.

Once objects are specified, problem solving must identify an *agent* who organizes the interaction among the objects to accomplish the task. Picture a baker, who is the agent for making a cake. He preheats the oven, greases the pan, mixes the batter, and sets the timer. A plumber is the agent who removes the old faucet, cuts connecting pipes, and installs the new unit with washers, solder, and so forth.

Object technology views problem solving from the perspective of objects. Preliminary analysis identifies objects as the elements of the problem-solving process. The final analysis creates a master plan or recipe that allows an agent to coordinate the action of the objects.

EXAMPLE 1.1 ━━━━━━━━━━━━━━━━━━━━━━━━━━

Let's look at some real-world situations that involve objects and problem solving.

1. Late Night Studying
   You are in your room late at night with an assignment to read and outline Chapter 1 of this book. The problem requires a series of objects. You'd better have the book, a light, paper, and a pencil.

   You are the agent who must turn on the light, open the book, and organize the writing of the outline.

2. TV Remote Control Unit
   A remote control unit solves a lot of problems for the TV viewer. A unit has a keypad and an operation that controls the volume.

   The TV watcher is the agent with the responsibility to turn on the set, select a channel, and adjust the volume.   ■

Exploring Concepts

Highway patrol officers have specially-equipped cars to assist motorists. What are some of the objects at their disposal? Describe the objects in terms of their attributes and actions. Which of the objects are used by an officer to catch a speeding driver?

Modern self-service gas stations have become so automated that a motorist can get gas, make a payment, and leave without seeing another human being. What objects are involved?

You are working during the Super Bowl and would like to video tape the game for later viewing. What objects would you need? Describe the actions that must be done to get the game taped.

1-2   COMPUTERS AND PROBLEM SOLVING

With real-world problem solving, an agent physically handles the objects. When a computer is involved, the process changes to accommodate the nature of the machine. A computer is a computational tool that works with number and character data. It acts like a high-speed calculator that features memory to hold data and the results of calculations, a keypad to enter data, buttons to carry out operations, and a display to view the results (Figure 1-1). Unlike a simple calculator, however, a computer is a device that can be set up with instructions that are designed to handle a variety of different situations. Computer processes are designed to handle a flow of information where data is input to memory, calculations are performed, and the results are provided as output data (Figure 1-2). When a computer is involved in problem solving, we need to focus our attention

FIGURE 1-1
Calculator.

on objects whose attributes are data and whose actions are operations that access and manage the data.

Modeling Real World Objects. Computer objects represent abstract models of the real world. They isolate only the data that is relevant to a problem situation. Student records at a university are a classical illustration of this idea. In the real world, a student is a complex entity with a variety of physical attributes (sex, age, hair color), demographic information (local address, hometown), academic records (major, gpa), and so forth. When the student enters the university, he or she makes contact with the registrar, the finance office, the office of student life, and perhaps the athletic department. Each contact involves different data handling and different problem situations for a computer. Each contact involves very specific data and requires us to create different models of a student. For instance,

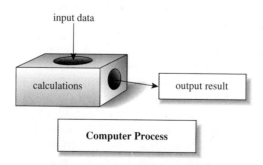

FIGURE 1-2
Input, Calculations, and Output in Computer Processes.

the finance office typically does not care about the student's age, hair color, sex, or major. Rather the office is interested in a student identification number, billing address, and the current account balance. The sex and age of the student are attributes of interest to the housing office or the athletic department while the major and gpa is relevant data for the registrar and the student's academic department.

To describe a student at a university, we create a series of objects whose attributes model the interaction between the student and the different offices and departments. For instance,

> Student Account:
>   Attributes: student ID, name, balance
> Student Major:
>   Attributes: student ID, major, gpa
> Student Housing:
>   Attributes: student ID, sex, age

Here are characteristics of a student, Mari Winters

59-1420	Mari Winters	3.45	-2650.00	history	female	21
studentID	studentName	gpa	balance	major	sex	age

These characteristics are distributed into the different types of objects as follows:

> Student Account:
>   student ID   59-1420
>   name   Mari Winters
>   balance   − $2650.00
> Student Major:
>   student ID   59-1420
>   major   history
>   gpa   3.45
> Student Housing:
>   student ID   59-1420
>   sex   female
>   age   21

The objects must model not only the attributes but also the operations that describe the interactions between a student and the offices or departments. Consider, for example, the finance office that deals with a student using a Student Account object. During the school year, a student makes charges and payments to his or her account. These are operations that update the balance. On a regular basis, the office sends a billing statement to the parents, listing any recent transactions and the amount owed. The finance office supplies the operation getBalance that allows other units in the university to access the current balance. For instance, the registrar checks the account before releasing a final diploma to the student. The following is a summary of operations for a student account.

charge: Debit an amount from the current balance

payment: Credit an amount to the current balance

getBalance: Get the value of the current balance

getID: Get the student identification number

getName: Get the student name

writeAccount: Output information that summarizes the current state of the account.

Exploring Concepts

An incoming college student is skilled with the drums. Which organizations on campus would find this music skill to be a relevant attribute?

Which student attributes and which operations are relevant to the alumni office?

1-3 DESCRIBING COMPUTER OBJECTS

A problem-solving situation uses specific objects. A finance office handles an account for Mari Winters (studentName) with ID number 59-1420 (studentID) and current balance of −$2650 (balance). Her account can be given a credit of $1,000 by using the payment operation. Nevertheless, the action of the finance office is not limited to this account. The studentName, student ID and balance attributes and the account update operations are common to all accounts maintained by the finance office. They define a template that is the form or structure of any StudentAccount object. The template acts like a cookie pattern that enables us to press out dozens of cookies (objects) of the same form. Object technology refers to an object template as an *object type*. A specific object is called an *instance* of its object type.

> **Definition** An *object type* is a template that describes the attributes and operations available to any object.

EXAMPLE 1.2

The example distinguishes between a student account object type and its objects which are specific instances (examples) of the object type. The finance office creates objects mWinters and dHuey as specific student accounts containing personal identification information and a balance. ∎

59-1420	Mari Winters	-2650.00

student account object: mWinters

99-1243	David Huey	0.00

student account object: dHuey

In this book, we develop a format for describing computer object types. Our approach not only lists the attributes but also describes the structure and action of each operation. An object type description is divided into three parts and begins with a title that gives the name and a brief statement of its purpose. The StudentAccount type illustrates the ideas.

DESCRIPTION: StudentAccount OBJECT TYPE ▬▬▬▬▬

A StudentAccount object maintains records for a student's financial transactions.

The second component of the object type description lists the attributes. Their names are chosen to indicate that they describe a real person or thing. The StudentAccount object type has three attributes that identify the student and maintain a record of the current balance. The character sequence "//" indicates that the remainder of the line is a descriptive comment.

Attributes
    studentID   // student's identification number
    studentName   // student's name
    balance   // balance in the student's account

The last part of an object-type description includes the actions, which we now call *operations*. These are the most detailed elements in the description. We view operations as tasks that are required by an agent using the object. To describe an operation, we first look at any information that must be supplied by the agent when using the operation. For instance, the bookstore supplies an amount before posting a charge to the student's account; a parent sends a check that indicates the amount of payment to the account. A value that is passed to an operation is called an *argument*. The value is provided to the operation before it begins execution and may be used by the operation in any of its calculations. For instance, amount is an argument for the charge and payment operations.

Operation   *Argument*
    charge   amount   (used to debit the account)
    payment   amount   (used to credit the account)

Some object type operations are used to return information to the agent. For instance, the getBalance operation identifies the current balance and makes it available as a *return value.*

The description for an operation includes reference to its arguments, its action, and its return value. The following describes the operations in the StudentAccount object type.

Operations:
    charge: The amount of the new charge is passed as an argument and the value is subtracted from the current balance. There is no return value.

                   new balance = current balance − amount

payment:	The amount of deposit is given as an argument and the value is added to the current balance. There is no return value.

$$\text{new balance} = \text{current balance} + \text{amount}$$

getBalance:	Returns the current balance in the StudentAccount object.
getID:	Returns the student identification number.
getName:	Returns the name of the student.
writeAccount:	Provides a formatted listing of the account information. The output simulates a billing statement and includes the studentID, studentName, and the current balance.

Initializing Object Attributes

Computer object types have an operation called the *constructor* that initializes the attributes of an object. The operation may have arguments that specify initial values for the attributes. The constructor is called when an object is created, and it copies the arguments to the corresponding attributes. For instance, when a student agrees to attend a university, the finance office creates a Student-Account object. The constructor gets initial values for the studentID, the studentName, and the starting balance and copies them to the object attributes. In most cases the starting balance is $0.00 unless some scholarship funds were granted in the financial aid package. In an object-type description, the constructor is assigned the name of the type.

StudentAccount:	The constructor has initial values for the studentID, studentName, and balance. The values are copied to the attributes in the object.

Visual Model of Object Types

The growth of object technology has prompted the creation of software-development tools for *program design*. One of the powerful features of these tools is visual modeling that uses graphical specifications to assist in object and program design. Visual modeling is used extensively by software companies to create large application systems.

A detailed study of visual modeling lies beyond the scope of this book. Nevertheless, we want to give you some experience with the tools and an appreciation of their power. Our limited study will help you understand the design and structure of object types. We use the *Unified Modeling Language (UML)* to give a graphical representation of an object type. The software product Rational Rose C++[1] implements the creation of UML models.

---

[1] Rational Rose is the visual modeling software application from Rational Software Corporation. The object-oriented analysis and design methods were developed by Grady Booch, Ivar Jacobson, Jim Rumbaugh from the unification of a number of methodologies.

The UML representation follows the format of an object type description. The figure is divided into three compartments that include the name, attributes, and operations. The notation "()" that follows the name of each operation indicates that an action is performed. Figure 1-3 gives the UML representations for the StudentAccount object type.

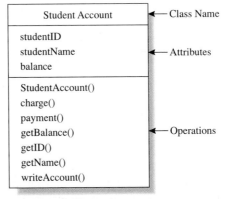

UML view of StudentAccount

FIGURE 1-3
UML Representation of StudentAccount

1-4 PROGRAMMING WITH C++ OBJECTS

Computer programs are powerful tools for problem solving. Their development begins by analyzing the problem and creating a series of steps that lead to a solution. This sequence of steps is called an *algorithm*. In this book, we implement the steps using precise C++ statements.

> **Definition** An *algorithm* is a sequence of instructions that leads to a solution of a problem in a finite amount of time.

Computer problem solving is provided by algorithms that are implemented by a program. To design a program, we first identify the objects that must store and handle the data. Once the objects are selected, we need to develop a main program whose algorithm provides any necessary input, coordinates the interaction of the objects, and writes output to the screen. Using our analogy from real-world problem solving, the main program is the agent for the computing task.

In this book, we implement programs using C++. The language has built-in object types for numbers and characters. The language also allows the development of programmer-defined object types such as StudentAccount. In C++, these types are called *classes*.

Programs are initially written as a sequence of C++ statements and are then translated to instructions that execute at the electronic level. These are called *machine instructions.* Computers run a program by executing the machine instructions. Different types of computers have different machine instructions. For instance, a PC with an Intel processor has different machine instructions than a system running a Motorola processor. A translator, called a *compiler,* is responsible for converting C++ statements into machine instructions. Depending on the computer, compiler, and other local features, readers will have a variety of environments for creating and executing a program.

In this section, we introduce the C++ programming language and give you some experience with your local programming environment. You do not need any prior background in the language since each program will be fully documented with a detailed explanation of most instructions. The exercises include other complete programs that you can enter and run. In this chapter, we focus on object descriptions and their use in problem solving. All object types have been implemented in C++ by the authors.

Language Identifiers

Computer programs must define objects and their types using *identifiers.* Like all programming languages, C++ uses restrictive naming conventions. A C++ identifier consists of a sequence of letters ('a' . . . 'z,' 'A' . . . 'Z'), digits ('0' . . . '9'), or underscore '_'. An identifier must begin with a letter or underscore. The other characters, if any, may be a letter, digit, or underscore. C++ is *case-sensitive,* meaning that it distinguishes between equivalent upper and lowercase letters. Good programming practice uses descriptive names; although practical considerations and restrictions of your computing environment may limit the length of an identifier.

EXAMPLE 1.3 ▬▬▬▬▬▬▬▬▬▬▬▬▬▬▬▬▬▬▬▬▬▬▬▬▬▬▬▬

1. The following names are valid C++ identifiers:

count	n1	salesTax
sales_tax	DaysOfWeek	_code

2. These are not valid C++ identifiers:

2over	(begins with a number)
Ten%	('%' is not a valid identifier character)
split Word	(contains a blank character)

3. Although PI, Pi, and pi are all different identifier names, it is not good practice to use more than one of them in a program.

4. Compound names can be created with an uppercase or an underscore separator. The identifiers "salesTax" and "sales_tax" use these conventions. In this book, we normally use an uppercase separator. ■

Declaring and Using Objects

In a C++ program, an object is created in a declaration statement that includes its type and its name. For some programmer-defined classes such as StudentAccount, the declaration requires initial values in parentheses immediately following the object name. These values are arguments for the constructor. They are given as a list separated by commas.

```
ClassName    object(value₁, value₂,...);
```

For a StudentAccount object, the declaration contains initial values for the studentID, studentName, and the starting balance. The following declaration creates the object mySon.

```
StudentAccount mySon("23-9812","Lee, Bob",0.0);
```

Once an object is declared, the program may execute any of its operations by using a format that includes the object name and the operation name separated by a '.' (period). The action of executing an operation is also described by the term *calling an operation*. The operation name is followed by a pair of parentheses containing a comma-separated list of arguments. For instance, a program may execute a charge or a getBalance operation with the StudentAccount object mySon. The first operation requires an amount as an argument. Despite the fact that getBalance does not require an argument, the operation must still include the parentheses.

```
mySon.charge(400)   (operation subtracts 400 from the balance)
mySon.getBalance()  (operation returns the current balance)
```

A First C++ Program

The science of programming is learned by first watching and then doing. Start by typing in programs that are written by others and running them on your system. Gradually, you'll gain the necessary skills and confidence. This section describes the structure of a C++ program that uses StudentAccount objects. The basic structure includes a *main* program unit that contains object declarations and C++ statements that input data, perform operations, and output results. Besides the structure of a program, this section also discusses how your computer system provides an environment to execute the program.

APPLICATION 1-1 BASIC C++ PROGRAM STRUCTURE

The program features the single StudentAccount object called student. For input, the program requests the user to enter a bookstore charge and a fee payment. The requests are given in the form of a *prompt*. The input values provide arguments for transactions that use the operations student.charge() and student.payment(), respectively. The program features output from two different sources. The operation student.getBalance() is used to display the current balance after the program posts the bookstore charge. A final account summary is provided by the student.writeAccount() operation. We assume that the StudentAccount class is implemented in the file **studacct.h.**

In the program listing, the numbers in brackets are used only to reference points in our discussion. They are not part of the program.

```
[1]    /*
           PROGRAM DEMO: This program illustrates the structure of
           a simple C++ program.
       */

[2]    // declares the input/output operations
[3]    #include <iostream.h>

[4]    // file containing declaration of StudentAccount class
[5]    #include "studacct.h"

[6]    int main()
[7]    {
[8]        double bookCharge, feePayment;     // keyboard input
[9]        // student Bob Lee has starting balance of $250
[10]       StudentAccount student("23-9812","Lee, Bob",250.0);

[11]       cout << "Enter a bookstore charge: ";
[12]       cin >> bookCharge;
[13]       student.charge(bookCharge);
[14]       cout << "After charge, balance is "
                   << student.getBalance() << endl;

[15]       cout << "Enter a fee payment: ";
[16]       cin >> feePayment;
[17]       student.payment(feePayment);
[18]       cout << "Current account information:" << endl;
[19]       student.writeAccount();

[20]       return 0;
[21]   }

[22]
```

```
Run:

Enter a bookstore charge: 175
After charge, balance is 75
Enter a fee payment: 500
Current account information:
ID:       23-9812
Name:     Lee, Bob
Balance:  $575.00
```

Program Explanation

(A) A *comment* contains information about the C++ program and does not become part of the final machine code. All good programs should contain ample comments since they document the design and coding of the problem. C++ allows two styles of program comments. Lines [2], [4], and [8] illustrate the single line comment that starts with "//" and continues only to the end of the line. For the multiline comment on line [1], C++ brackets the text with the character pairs "/*" and "*/." The form is useful for writing long documentation notes. This book will use the "//" comment for most program documentation.

(B) An "#include" statement identifies program statements *(source code)* that will be inserted into the program from a separate file. The statement begins with a '#' in column 1 and contains a file name surrounded by brackets [3] or double-quotes [5]. The include files typically reference system or programmer defined C++ statements. In [3], the file `iostream.h` defines the `cin` and `cout` stream objects that handle input from the keyboard and output to the screen. System files are enclosed in angle brackets (< . . . >) and programmer-defined files are enclosed in double quotes (" . . . "). In [5], the file `studacct.h` references the C++ implementation of the StudentAccount class with its attributes and operations. A file that is accessed with a #include statement normally ends with the suffix ".h" and is called a *header file.*

(C) Your specific computer will control program execution by creating a *runtime environment* and executing the program statements. On some systems, this environment includes a graphical window that displays program activity, while other systems use a simple display screen. After completing execution of the program, the computer shuts down the run-time environment and continues its previous activities. The run-time environment begins execution of the program in the unit named main. The unit is identified by the phrase `"int main()"` in [6]. The word *int* indicates that the program returns an integer value specifying its status at termination. The identifier int is called a *reserved word* or *keyword*. This means that the word is part of the C++ language and cannot be used for any purpose other than that determined by C++. As the book progresses, you will learn many other keywords such as *while, for, return* and *class.*

(D) The body of the main program is blocked off using braces. Between the left brace "{" at [7] and the right brace "}"at [21], the main program includes object declarations and statements that carry out its actions.

(E) The main program unit declares three objects. The declarations at [8] include double objects associated with the bookstore charge (`bookCharge`) and the payment (`feePayment`). The identifier double is a C++ type that indicates the objects will be assigned real numbers, which have a whole and a fractional part. For instance, 2.8 and –19.85 are real numbers. In [10], the StudentAccount object student is declared with the identification number "23-9812" as the studentID, "Lee, Bob" as the studentName, and $250 as the starting balance.

(F) Program execution begins with an output statement (cout) at [11] that prompts for a bookstore charge. The statement (cin) at [12] inputs the value for bookCharge from the keyboard.

(G) Statement [13] causes the charge operation to execute with bookCharge as its argument. The balance is updated and its new value is output in [14]. The "cout" statement includes three components separated by "<<". We follow the phrase "After charge, balance is" by the current balance that is returned from the operation get-Balance. The output sequence terminates with "endl" that causes the next output to occur on a new line. After completing statement [14], the run-time window looks like

```
Enter a bookstore charge: 175
After charge, balance is 75
```

(H) The sequence of statements [15]–[16] prompt for a payment. After the program inputs the value feePayment from the keyboard, the balance is updated at [17] by the payment operation of object student. A summary of the account is output with the operation writeAccount. After completing statement [19], the run-time window looks like

```
Enter a bookstore charge: 175
After charge, balance is 75
Enter a fee payment: 500
Current account information:
ID:       23-9812
Name:     Lee, Bob
Balance:  $575.00
```

(I) The statement at [20] returns the integer value 0 to the system that launched the program. The value indicates that the program terminates normally. A return value greater than 0 indicates that the program terminates in an error state.

(J) A run of the program is included at [22]. The text was captured from the output window and then included as a shaded box. This is the format used in the book for all program runs.

The C++ Programming Environment

A number of steps must take place before Application 1.1 can be run on a computer system.

Step 1: C++ program statements are entered into a file using an *editor.* The editor allows you to enter the text and make alterations to it. Editors contain convenient tools for text manipulation, such as cut, copy, and paste.

Step 2: A translation process converts the program statements into machine code that can execute on the system. Anticipating the translation to machine code, programmers refer to the C++ statements as *source code.* The translation process begins by having a program called the C++ *preprocessor* read the source code and implement the #include statements. The expanded source code is converted by the C++ *compiler* into *object code* that consists of machine instructions corresponding to the source code.

Step 3: Object code from the translation process is normally incomplete, since it would be inefficient and impractical to require that a programmer write C++ statements for everything the program does. C++ allows programs to access prewritten machine code that is stored in separate files called *object libraries.* For instance, input and output is typically executed from code found in libraries. The separate code is merged into the compiled object code using an application called a *linker* that creates *executable code.*

Step 4: A run-time system is responsible for program execution. It loads the linked code and begins execution in the program unit main. The run-time system may provide a *debugger* that assists in locating any execution errors that may occur.

The different stages in the preparation and execution of a C++ program is reflected in Figure 1-4.

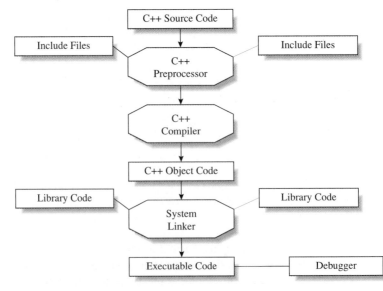

FIGURE 1-4
Entering and Running a C++ Program.

Your local system may support program development in a *command line environment* or an *integrated development environment* (IDE). With a command line environment, the editor is run as a separate application. After the source code is prepared, a single command normally runs the preprocessor, compiler, and linker. The debugger is run as a separate application. For instance, the GNU C++ compiler is a command line environment on a Unix system. With an integrated development environment, the editor, preprocessor, compiler, run-time system, and debugger are provided as one application. As an example, the Borland C++ and Microsoft Visual C++ compilers provide an IDE environment on a PC. The CodeWarrior compiler provides a C++ IDE environment on both a PC and a Macintosh system.

1-5 EXPLORING RECTANGLE OBJECTS

Up to this point in the chapter, our discussion of objects has focused on the StudentAccount class. A second example, featuring rectangles, provides many useful applications involving measurement. Rectangles help us to determine the amount of paint needed to cover a wall. Commercial buildings are rented by the square foot, a value that is computed by finding the area of each room. The perimeter (distance around the outside) determines the cost of fencing a backyard.

As a measurement figure, a rectangle is determined by its length and width. These are the two attributes in a Rectangle object. The operations area and perimeter use the length and width of the rectangle to compute the surface area and the distance around the outer edge (Figure 1-5).

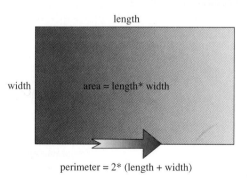

perimeter = 2* (length + width)

FIGURE 1-5
Measurement Operations with a Rectangle.

The following is a formal description of the Rectangle object type. The description includes the constructor (Rectangle) that initializes the length and width attributes of an object and access operations to update the attributes or retrieve their current value. The icon next to the description indicates that the C++ code corresponding to the Rectangle type is found in the file **rect.h.**

rect.h

DESCRIPTION: Rectangle OBJECT TYPE ▬▬▬▬▬▬▬

A Rectangle object is a measurement tool that identifies the length, width, area, and perimeter of a rectangle figure.

Attributes:
  length
  width

Operations:

Rectangle	Takes initial values l and w as arguments and assigns them as the length and width of the rectangle
area	Computes length * width and returns the value as the area
perimeter	Computes 2 * (length + width) and returns the value as the perimeter
setSides	Takes values l and w as arguments and updates the attributes length and width to have values l and w respectively
getLength	Returns the current value of length
getWidth	Returns the current value of width

The Rectangle object type describes the features of each Rectangle object. The description says that any Rectangle object has a length and a width as attributes, a constructor and five operations including area and perimeter. A particular Rectangle object—say one with length = 2 and width = 3—is an instance of the Rectangle object type. The object has an area of 6 and a perimeter of 10.

In Figure 1-6, we present a UML graphical representation for the Rectangle object type. The keyword double is included with the attributes to indicate they are real numbers. Types, like double and int, are discussed in Chapter 2.

Rectangle
length: double width: double
Rectangle() area() perimeter() setSides() getLength() getWidth()

FIGURE 1-6
*UML Representation
for Rectangle.*

Building a Swimming Pool. Objects of Rectangle type are used to compute the cost of finishing a swimming pool. City building code requires that a 3-foot wide concrete walkway must surround the pool edge and the entire area must be enclosed by a 6-foot fence. As a problem-solving situation, we want to determine the amount and cost of the materials.

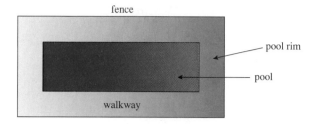

In the program design, we define the pool and its surrounding rim as two Rectangle objects called pool and poolRim, respectively. The poolRim object is 6 feet longer and 6 feet wider than the pool to accommodate the walkway around the pool. To simplify the problem, we assume the cost of fencing is $10.00 per linear foot, and the cost of concrete is $0.80 per square foot. The area and perimeter operations of the two objects determine the amount and cost of materials. The program uses the number objects `fenceLength` and `concreteArea` to contain the length of the fence and the area of the concrete walkway. The amount of fencing is determined by the perimeter of the poolRim.

$$fenceLength = poolRim.perimeter()$$

The amount of concrete for the walkway is computed by subtracting the area of the pool object from the area of the poolRim object.

$$concreteArea = poolRim.area() - pool.area()$$

The cost of the fence is fenceLength * 10 and the cost of the concrete is concreteArea * 0.80.

APPLICATION 1-2   FINISHING THE SWIMMING POOL

The program computes the amount of materials and their cost for both a concrete walkway and a fence around the pool. Separate listings for the fencing and concrete are output along with labels. To simplify the program, we assume the pool has fixed dimensions of 40 by 15 feet. As noted in its description, the C++ code for Rectangle is found in file **rect.h.**

```
#include <iostream.h>

#include "rect.h"     // use Rectangle class

int main()
{
   // declare the 40' x 15' pool object and the outer pool rim
   Rectangle pool(40,15), poolRim(40+6,15+6);

   // objects contain amount of needed fencing and concrete
   double fenceLength, concreteArea;
```

```
            // compute the amount of fencing and concrete
            fenceLength = poolRim.perimeter();
            concreteArea = poolRim.area() - pool.area();

            // for each material, output its amount and cost
            cout << "The fence requires " << fenceLength
                << " feet costing $" << fenceLength * 10.00
                << endl;

            cout << "The concrete covers " << concreteArea
                << " square feet costing $" << concreteArea * .80
                << endl;

            return 0;
        }
```

```
    Run:

    The fence requires 134 feet costing $1340
    The concrete covers 366 square feet costing $292.8
```

1-6   DRAWING FIGURES: RECTANGLES

This book features software to draw a range of figures including lines, circles, rectangles, regular polygons, and text. The figures provide good examples of objects and C++ code structures. They also find a rich variety of uses in computer applications. The figures are basic tools in any drawing or painting package.

This section uses the RectShape object type to draw rectangles. Unlike Rectangle objects that are measurement tools, a RectShape object is a tool for sketching rectangles on a drawing surface. In addition to length and width attributes, a RectShape object has a base point that locates the rectangle on the surface and a color that fills the interior of the rectangle.

The base point specifies the location of the upper left-hand corner of the rectangle in the drawing surface. Horizontal coordinates are positive moving to the right, and vertical coordinates are positive moving downward. We assume the surface is approximately a 10×8 unit coordinate system. In Figure 1-7, the rectangle has dimensions given by length and width with its upper left-hand corner fixed at point (x,y). The interior of the rectangle has a color attribute whose value is given by the object type `ShapeColor`. In Figure 1-7, the rectangle has color "blue."

By its nature, the RectShape object type is more complex than the Rectangle object type since it requires the base-point attribute to locate the figure and a separate attribute for the color. The constructor must initialize the base point, color, length, and width. The draw operation places the object on the drawing surface.

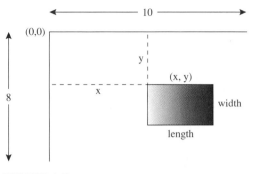

FIGURE 1-7
Drawing a Rectangle.

DESCRIPTION: RectShape OBJECT TYPE ━━━━━━

A RectShape object describes a rectangle on a drawing surface.

Operations:

RectShape   The arguments are coordinates x, y for the base point, l,w for the
              dimensions, and c for the color. The arguments are copied to the
              corresponding attributes. The color is chosen from the list.

white	blue	teal	green
turquoise	darkgrey	brown	purple
lightblue	lightgrey	gold	red
orange	pink	yellow	black

draw   Draws the rectangle at the base point with the given color.

rectsh.h

Drawing a Swimming Pool. Application 1.2 uses Rectangle objects to determine
the cost of materials for a swimming pool fence and concrete walkway. The program assumed a 40×15-foot pool surrounded by a 3-foot walkway. This program uses RectShape objects to create a graphic that represents the swimming
pool and the pool rim. The lengths in feet must be scaled to fit on a 10×8 surface. Assuming that the actual pool dimensions are 40×15 feet and the extended walkway dimensions are 46 by 21 feet, the picture dimensions can be
scaled by a factor of 5. This is done by dividing each dimension by 5.0.

	Actual Dimension	Scaled Dimension
Pool Length	40	40/5.0 = 8
Pool Width	15	15/5.0 = 3
Walkway Length	46	46/5.0 = 9.2
Walkway Width	21	21/5.0 = 4.2

APPLICATION 1-3 DRAWING A SWIMMING POOL

The program draws a swimming pool by declaring two RectShape objects, `poolDraw` and `poolRimDraw`. The larger object, `poolRimDraw`, is drawn in lightgray with its upper left-hand corner at (.5,.5) on the drawing surface and its length and width scaled to 9.2 and 4.2. The interior poolDraw object represents the swimming pool that is offset from the rim by the 3-foot walkway. In the drawing, the poolDraw object has color blue. Its upper left-hand corner is offset by the walkway that scales to $3/5.0 = 0.6$ units in both the x and y direction.

poolRimDraw: point(.5,.5), length = 9.2, width = 4.2

poolDraw: point(1.1,1.1), length = 8, width = 3

To use a RectShape object, the run-time system must create a drawing surface on the screen and provide graphics-handling tools. While these processes are system dependent, the authors have defined the operations openWindow, viewWindow, and closeWindow to carry out the tasks. These operations are called utilities. They are not associated with objects but stand alone to support program development. The supplemental software implements the operations for Windows, DOS and Macintosh systems.

openWindow():   Opens a window as the drawing surface.
viewWindow():   Pauses the program until a key is pressed.
closeWindow():   Removes the window from the screen.

The openWindow operation must be called before any drawing task is requested.

```
#include "rectsh.h"    // use RectShape class

int main()
{

    // declare the two RectShape objects using scaled units
    RectShape poolRimDraw(.5, .5, 9.2, 4.2, lightgray),
            poolDraw(1.1, 1.1, 8, 3, blue);

    // open the drawing window
    openWindow();

    // draw the pool rim object;
    poolRimDraw.draw();

    // draw the pool object
    poolDraw.draw();

    // pause to view the drawing
    viewWindow();
```

```
// close the drawing window
closeWindow();

    return 0;
}
```

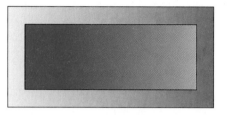

1-7 THE C++ PROGRAMMING LANGUAGE

This book introduces the reader to object-oriented programming using C++. While a number of languages are available, C++ has developed a preeminence due to its origins in the popular C programming language.

The languages C and C++ were developed at the AT&T Bell Laboratories. In 1969, Ken Thompson began the design and implementation of UNIX, a small general-purpose time-sharing system that was used to support research and development at Bell Labs. One of the early users, Dennis Ritchie, designed and wrote a compiler for the C programming language. In 1973, Ritchie and Thompson rewrote most of UNIX in C, breaking with the tradition of the day that system software be written in *assembly language,* which is a language that uses mnemonics that directly represent machine instructions for a particular computer. Their choice of C made it possible to more quickly implement UNIX on a wide variety of machines. Owing to outstanding support from AT&T, the elegance of UNIX, and the availability of inexpensive compilers, C became a favorite in colleges and universities. Its impact was felt in the development of system software and a multitude of application packages.

In the late 1970s, programmers began to look toward object-oriented programming languages to support the new object technology. Given the great popularity of C, a Bell Labs group headed by Bjarne Stroustrup, set out to add object constructs to C and make the new language easier to use. The development on top of C meant that the new language C++ did not have to be developed from scratch and its relation to C gave it a vast audience of quality programmers. The language C++ was originally called "C with Classes" and was made available to programmers in the early 1980s. Translators were written to convert the C with Classes source code to C source code before calling the C compiler to create the machine code. The name C++ was coined by Rick Mascitti in the summer of 1983. He used the C increment operator "++" to reflect both the language's origins in C and its extensions to C.

Groups have questioned whether C++ should retain compatibility with C, particularly as C++ develops powerful new constructs and facilities not present in C. As a practical matter, the language will probably continue to be an extension of C. The amount of existing C software will force developers of C++ to retain the strong tie to the C language. The definition of C++ continues to ensure that common C and C++ constructs have the same meaning in both languages.

CHAPTER 1 SUMMARY

This chapter introduces problem solving with objects that represent physical entities with attributes and actions. For problem solving, like taping a football game, you identify objects such as a clock, a TV, and a video recorder and use them as building blocks of the solution. Once the objects are identified, problem-solving must develop a set of instructions that coordinate the interaction among the objects to carry out the task.

Computer objects and their object type are the main focus of the chapter. A computer object type represents an abstract model of the real world and consists of attributes (data) that are relevant to a problem situation. The actions of the computer object are operations that manage the data. By looking at a university student interact with the finance office, the registrar, housing, and so forth, we are able to define a variety of object types that use relevant data from a student profile. Our discussion of object types is informal. A format is developed for an object type description that specifies the attributes and highlights the arguments, action, and return value for each operation. A UML representation provides a graphical view of an object type.

Computer problem solving is implemented with C++ programs that consist of a series of instructions to input data, carry out calculations, and output results. We ask you to jump in and start programming with StudentAccount, Rectangle, and RectShape objects. Don't worry about details since the object types are available in the supplemental software. The entire book will explore C++ syntax and programming algorithms. Just get used to your local environment and begin to understand the power and simplicity of programming with objects.

Object Types (Classes) in the Chapter

Name	Implementation File
StudentAccount	studacct.h
Rectangle	rect.h
RectShape	rectsh.h

KEY TERMS

Algorithm
A sequence of instructions that leads to a solution of a problem in a finite amount of time.

Compiler
A translator that is responsible for converting C++ statements into machine instructions.

Constructor

An operation within an object type that initializes the attributes of an object.

Include

A statement in a C++ program that provides access to a file that implements an object type or supplies utility operations.

Object Type

A template that describes the attributes and operations available to its objects.

Preprocessor

A component of the programming environment that reads the source code and implements the #include statements.

Program Environment

A command line or integrated development system (IDE) that supplies an editor, preprocessor, compiler, and linker to enter a source level program and translate it into machine instructions. A debugger may be available to assist in program development.

REVIEW EXERCISES

1. The following questions look at physical objects:
   (a) Indicate the attributes and operations that would specify a digital alarm clock. What additional attributes and operations would be required if the clock had a snooze alarm?
   (b) In an automobile, an automatic transmission has an attribute called "in Park" that indicates whether the transmission is locked in the park position or not. Describe two actions for the transmission that would use this attribute. How would this attribute affect using the ignition key?
   (c) An automatic change maker takes a $1 bill as input and returns change in quarters. What are several attributes that the machine has? Assume that the change maker is attached to a soda machine and returns change from a purchase. What additional attributes does this object need?
   (d) Describe the operation `buySoda` that would be used by the change machine. Your analysis should include its argument(s), action, and return value.

2. You are a scorekeeper at a soccer game. Design a computer object that would allow you to keep track of the score. Indicate the attributes and the operations that you would need.

3. In computer objects, what is the purpose of the constructor?

4. For a bank savings account, describe its data attributes and operations. What would be the action of the constructor for the object?

5. A radio is an example of an object type.
   (a) What attributes and operations specify the type?
   (b) An object is an instance of an object type. Give several examples of radio objects

6. What is the meaning of the acronym "UML" and what is the purpose of a UML representation?

7. (a) In a C++ program, why include comments? What is the difference between a "/* . . . */" comment and a "//" comment.
   (b) The declarations and instructions in the main section are enclosed by _____ .

8. The run-time environment begins execution of a program in the unit called _____.

9. (a) Using an editor, you type in a program that is called the _____ .
   (b) The C++ program is translated into machine code by a complex piece of software called the _____ .

10. (a) Code from _____ libraries is combined with the code for the main program by the _____ .
    (b) During run time, program errors can be dealt with by using a _____ .
    (c) Source code can be placed in _____ files and then brought into the program by the _____ directive.

11. Linear measurement is simulated by the object type Length. The object type has the single attribute lenValue that is the numerical value for the length of the object. For operations, the constructor initializes lenValue, the operation addLength adds some length (plus or minus) to the attribute lenValue, and getLength returns the value of lenValue.
    (a) Give an object specification for the operation, addLength, that includes the argument(s), action, and return value.
    (b) Give a UML listing of the Length object type.

12. Which of the following are valid C++ identifier names. If the name is invalid, correct it to make it a valid identifier.
    (a) McDonald   (b) don't   (c) 4_Score   (d) largest_int

13. A pipe is modeled as a Length object. The pipe's length can be changed by connecting and disconnecting pieces. The following C++ program controls the actions of the pipe. Identify the C++ statements that correspond to parts (a)–(e).

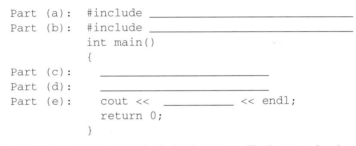

```
Part (a):    #include _____
Part (b):    #include _____
             int main()
             {
Part (c):        _____
Part (d):        _____
Part (e):        cout << _____ << endl;
             return 0;
             }
```

(a) Which C++ statement includes the system file that contains the operations for input (cin) and output (cout)?
(b) The attributes and operations for the Length object type are declared in file *length.h*. Which C++ statement will access the declaration of the object type.
(c) How would we declare the pipe object with initial length of 100?
    (i) Length(100) pipe   (ii) Length pipe(100)
    (iii) Length(pipe) = 100   (iv) Length(ruler) = 100
(d) Which instruction would add 20 to the length of the pipe?
    (i) Length.addLength(20)   (ii) pipe(addLength(20))
    (iii) pipe(Length,20)   (iv) pipe.addLength(20)
(e) Write a statement that prints the current length of the pipe.

14. (a) High-level languages like C++ are now used to write system software. Originally, such software was written in _____, which is just one step above machine language.

(b) The Unix operating system is written in the _____ programming language that is the predecessor of C++.

Answers to Review Exercises

1. (a) Attributes: number of hours, minutes, seconds for the time display, hours and minutes for the alarm setting and an alarm switch that is ON/OFF.

Operations: displayTime, setTime, setAlarmTime, turnAlarmOn, turnAlarmOff

For the snooze, there must be an ON switch.

(b) putInPark—place the transmission into park

putInGear—move the transmission out of park to a gear

Cannot remove the key unless the transmission is in park.

(c) An attribute for holding quarters and a mechanism for recognizing that a dollar bill is entered into the machine. If the change maker is used in a soda machine, attributes must be added for dimes and nickels.

(d) buySoda—The argument is the cost of the soda. The operation computes the difference between $1 and the input amount. The return value is the change that is returned from the purchase.

2. Attributes: score for home team; score for visiting team

Operations `incrementScore` with team as an argument

3. The constructor builds an object by giving values to its attributes. Often these initial attribute values are passed as arguments to the constructor.

4. Attributes: balance

Operations: deposit, withdraw, getBalance

The constructor initializes the starting account balance.

5. (a) Attributes: volume control, channel changer, AM/FM switch, ON/OFF switch

Operations: turnOn, turnOff, adjustVolume, selectStation, selectAM_FM

(b) portable radio, car radio, stereo receiver

6. "Universal Modeling Language." UML pictures the attributes and operations of an object type. UML also is used to show the relationship of object types to each other.

7. (a) Comments document the purpose of a program and how it works. It allows programmers to more effectively update the application in the future. The "//" comment extends from "//" to the end of the line and is the most commonly used C++ comment. The "/* ... */" comes from the C-programming language and allows a comment to extend over several lines. This type of comment is often used in a paragraph that describes the overall action of the program.

(b) braces "{" and "}"

8. main

9. (a) source code   (b) compiler

10. (a) object code   linker   (b) debugger   (c) header   include

11. (a) `addLength`: Take an argument len and use it to update the value of
attribute lenValue

$$lenValue = lenvalue + len$$

(b)

Length
lenValue: double
Length ( )   addLength ( ): void   getLength ( ): double

12. (a) Valid   (b) Invalid. Correction doNot or don_t
(c) Invalid. Correction fourScore or score4   (d) Valid
13. (a) <iostream.h>   (b) #include "length.h"   (c) (ii)   (d) (iv)
(e) cout << pipe.getLength() << endl;
14. (a) assembly language   (b) C

WRITTEN EXERCISES

15. Describe some attributes and operations that would specify each physical object
(a) an automatic food blender   (b) a computer monitor

16. What are attributes that would apply to
(a) a cup   (b) a bed

17. A CD player is an object that plays musical recordings. With a CD in the caddy, we
can insert and eject the disk, start and stop the music, and move the laser head to a
different piece by selecting a different track.
(a) What attributes permit the CD player to carry out these actions?
(b) Describe the operation, `setTrack`, which is used to select a song number. Your
description should include any arguments and return value.

18. A truck is an object with attributes that include vehicle ID, size, and maximum load
capacity (in weight). List several problem-solving situations that would use
(a) the vehicle ID
(b) size
(c) maximum load capacity
Could you identify a situation that would use all of the attributes?

19. A bank is asked to loan money for the purchase of a local minor league baseball
team. The bank wants to treat the team as a computer object and determine the
likely income and expenses. Identify those attributes that would be part of the
team's income and part of the team's expenses.

20. An object is an instance of an object type. Give several instances for a _____ object
type.
(a) TV   (b) phone   (c) computer

21. A baseball player is described by the Baseball object type that has attributes for the uniform number (uniformNo), the number of times at bat (atbats), the number of hits (hits), and the batting average (batavg = hits/atbats). When declaring a player object, the constructor assigns the uniformNo and sets atbats, hits, and batavg to 0. The object type has three additional operations to handle the data. The operation getBatAvg returns the current batting average, writeBattingStats outputs the current batting statistics for the player including uniform number, at bats, hits, and percentage. And updateBattingStats takes the number of times at bat and the number of hits and updates the batting average batavg. For instance,

Before operation:	atbats	5	hits	2	batavg = 0.4
Update statistics:	atbats	3	hits	2	
After operation:	atbats	8	hits	4	batavg = 0.5

(a) Describe the constructor for the Baseball object type including arguments and action.

(b) Describe the operations, getBatAvg, updateBattingStats, and writeBattingStats, including arguments, return values, and actions.

(c) Create the UML representation for Baseball

22. Use the Baseball object type from Exercise 21 to keep track of batting statistics for players henryA and babeR. The object type is implemented in the file *baseball.h*. Fill in the missing blanks to complete each C++ statement.

```
#include <iostream.h>

// provide the program access to the Baseball object type
_____

int main()
{
  // declare henryA and babeR with uniforms 44 and 3
  Baseball _____, _____;
  // henryA plays 2 games. in game 1, henryA gets 1 hit
  // in 2 times at bat. update his batting average
  _____.updateBattingStats(_____);

  // output the batting average for henryA after game 1
  cout << "After game 1:  henryA is batting "
       << _____ << endl;

  // in game 2, henryA gets 2 hits in 3 times at bat
  // in game 1, babeR gets 1 hit in 4 times at bat
  _____    // update henryA
  _____    // update babeR

  // output the batting statistics for henryA and babeR
  _____    // statistics for henryA
  _____    // statistics for babeR
  return 0;
}
```

```
Run:
After game 1:   henryA is batting 0.5
Player 44 At Bats 5   Hits 3 Average 0.600
Player  3 At Bats 4   Hits 1 Average 0.250
```

23. An ATM machine allows a bank customer 24-hour access to a savings account for withdrawing money. Describe an ATM machine as a computer object. What would be some of the operations for this object?

24. Most C++ programs use "include" statements.
    (a) What is the purpose of these statements?
    (b) Distinguish between an include statement that encloses the file name in angle brackets (< . . . >) and in double quotes (" . . . ").

25. (a) Statements such as "#include <iostream.h>" are processed by an application called the C++ _____.
    (b) Distinguish between object code and executable code.
    (c) Distingish between an IDE and a command-line environment. Which do you use?

26. The UML representation describes a circle as an object type. The constructor takes a floating point number r as an argument and uses it to initialize the radius.

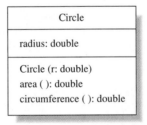

Circle
radius: double
Circle (r: double) area ( ): double circumference ( ): double

For this exercise, you are given two Rectangle objects innerR and outerR and a Circle object circ. The inner rectangle is inscribed in the circle and the outer rectangle is circumscribed about the circle. In part (1) of the figure, the shaded area is given by

```
outerR.area() - circ.area()
```

For each question, write an expression that computes the specified quantity.
(a) The area of the circle in the figure, part (1)
(b) The area of the shaded regions in the figure, part (2)
(c) The area of the unshaded regions in the figure, part (2)
(d) The distance traveled along the black line in the figure, part (3)
(e) The length of fencing that would enclose the shaded region in the figure, part(3)

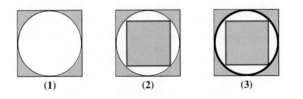

(1)   (2)   (3)

27. Which of the following are valid C++ identifier names? If the name is invalid, correct it to make it a valid identifier.
(a) mainProg   (b) A's   (c) floor12
(d) first name   (e) 7th_inning   (f) move2Left

28. A queue is an object type that describes a list of items. The operations for a queue are insert that puts an item at the rear of the list and erase that deletes an item from the front of the list. Give several objects that are instances of a queue.

29. The figure represents a tennis court. The inner section is the actual court with a clay surface. The outer rim that surrounds the court is a concrete surface.
(a) Declare a Rectangle object that represents a 100 × 50 ft. court area and a Rectangle object that represents the entire 150 × 80 ft. tennis area.
(b) Fencing around the entire tennis area costs $10 per ft. Give a C++ statement that assigns to object, fenceCost, the cost of fencing the area.
(c) Assume the cost of installing clay is $12 per square ft. and the cost of concrete is $6 per sq. ft. Give a C++ statement that assigns to object, surfaceCost, the cost of covering the clay court and surrounding concrete area.

Tennis Court

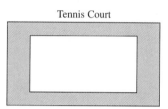

30. The C++ programming language has roots in C.
(a) What is the relationship between C and C++?
(b) Who are some of the leading figures in the development of C and C++?

31. (a) Give two reasons for the popularity of C++.
(b) The operator "++" takes an object and increases its value by 1. For instance, if n is an object with integer value 4, then n++ changes the value to 5. Explain why the language we are studying is called "C++."

PROGRAMMING EXERCISES

32. Use the Baseball object type found in Written Exercise 22. Enter the program on your local system and then run it.

```cpp
#include <iostream.h>

#include "baseball.h"

int main()        // and so forth
{
   // declare a player
   Baseball player(45);
   double startAvg, endAvg;
```

```
        player.updateBattingStats(100, 32);
        startAvg = player.getBatAvg();

        player.updateBattingStats(4,3);
        endAvg = player.getBatAvg();
        cout << "The game increased the batting average by "
             << (endAvg-startAvg) << " points" << endl;
        player.writeBattingStats();

        return 0;
    }
```

```
    Run:
    The game increased the batting average by .0165385
    points
    Player 45   At Bats 104   Hits 35   Average 0.337
```

33. A rectangular farm yard has a small pen (shaded area) in the upper-left corner of the yard. The farmer needs to fence both areas. Since the pen holds animals, fencing costs for this section is $12 per linear ft. The fencing costs for the area outside of the pen is $5 per linear ft.

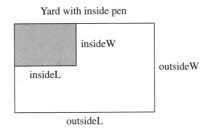

Yard with inside pen

The following program prompts for the dimensions of the two areas. With those values, a yard object and a pen object are declared and used to compute and output the cost of fencing. Type in the program and run it on your local system. As input, use dimensions 80 and 100 for the yard, and 30 and 20 for the pen.

```
#include <iostream.h>

#include "rect.h"

int main()
{
    double outsideL, outsideW;
    double insideL, insideW;
    double fenceCost;

    cout << "Enter the length and width of the yard: ";
    cin >> outsideL >> outsideW;
```

```
        cout << "Enter the length and width of the pen: ";
        cin >> insideL >> insideW;

        Rectangle yard(outsideL,outsideW), pen(insideL,insideW);

        fenceCost = (yard.perimeter()-0.5*pen.perimeter())*5 +
                    pen.perimeter()*12;
        cout << "Fence cost is $" << fenceCost << endl;

        return 0;
    }
```

```
    Run:

    Enter the length and width of the yard: 80 100
    Enter the length and width of the pen: 30 20
    Fence cost is $2750
```

PROGRAMMING PROJECT

34. A homeowner wants to put vinyl siding on a side of the house that includes a door
and two matching windows. The installer places siding on the shaded surface and
adds trim around the outer dimensions of the side, around the windows, and around
the door. Assume that the cost of the vinyl siding is $18 per sq. ft. and the cost of the
trim is $5 per linear ft. For the house, the dimensions of the side are 40 × 10 and
the dimensions of the door and windows are 4 × 8 ft. and 8 × 5 ft., respectively.
The problem is to write a program that uses Rectangle objects to compute the
total cost of the siding and the total cost of the trim. Use the following design in
your program.

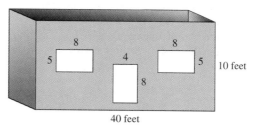

(a) Include the system file for output statements. Include the programmer-defined
file *rect.h* for the Rectangle objects.
(b) Declare objects for the side of the house, for a window, and for the door.
(c) Use the following declarations of objects that describe the area of the vinyl siding and its total cost as well as the length of trim and its total cost.

```
    double vinylArea, vinylCost, trimLength, trimCost;
```

(d) Compute values for the real number objects.

```
trimLength = _____;
trimCost = _____;

vinylArea = _____;
vinylCost = _____;
```

(e) Give the costs in separate statements.

```
cout << "Cost of trim is " << _____  << endl;
cout << "Cost of vinyl is " << _____  << endl;
```

(f) Enter the program on your local system and run it.

Chapter 2
Basic C++ Types and Programs

C H A P T E R   C O N T E N T S

2-1 INTEGER OBJECTS AND SIMPLE EXPRESSIONS
Declaring Integer Objects
Basic Integer Operators
2-2 C++ INPUT AND OUTPUT
Sending Output to the Screen
Formatting the Output
Reading from the Keyboard
Initializing Objects during Program Execution
2-3 CHARACTER OBJECTS
Escape Codes
Character I/O
Representing Character Data
Character Operations
2-4 REAL NUMBER OBJECTS
C++ Real Number Types
Exploring Real Numbers in Linear Equations
Named Constants
2-5 WORKING WITH C++ OPERATORS
Operator Precedence
Type Conversion
2-6 EXTENDING ARITHMETIC OPERATORS
Compound Assignment Operators
Increment Operators
2-7 THE STRING TYPE
String Object Declaration
String Input/Output
String Operations
Written Exercises

In Chapter 1, we introduced concepts of object technology that apply to problem analysis and program design. Using a series of objects from the StudentAccount, Rectangle, and RectShape classes, we applied the concepts in demonstration programs. The chapter did not attempt to show the C++ constructs that built the classes nor did it dwell on the C++ syntax for program statements. The concepts were initially too complex and a detailed study of C++ statements would not have been understandable.

In this chapter, we define the C++ primitive number and character types that are the building blocks for all data in a program. These types give us numbers like 2, −16, 3.14 and the standard keyboard characters such as 'A.' We develop the C++ operators that apply to the primitive types. This allows us to create arithmetic expressions, assignment statements, and stream input and output that are key components in any application program.

In C++, primitive number and character data have values and a set of familiar arithmetic operations that are used in calculations. As such, these data items are objects. There is, however, a very important difference from objects we saw in Chapter 1. A StudentAccount object is a programmer-implemented object whose object type is a class. The object type for the primitive number and character data are defined by the C++ language without the structure of a class. We will refer to the object type of these primitive data items as simply a *type*. We reserve the term class to describe programmer-defined object types.

Objects of primitive types appear in most applications. The same can be said for stream objects that provide input and output of data and string objects that introduce words, labels, and descriptive phrases in a program. Unlike the primitive language types, however, the stream and string types are user defined types with carefully defined sets of operations. This chapter looks at stream and string objects. The streams cin and cout, from the include file **iostream.h,** have operations to read numbers and characters from the keyboard and produce for-mattted output to the screen. The authors provide a String type in the header file **tstring.h** that allows programmers to use strings as simple data items.

2-1   INTEGER OBJECTS AND SIMPLE EXPRESSIONS

As infants, we start to learn numbers by counting on our fingers 1, 2, 3, and so forth. These values along with their negative counterpart provide us a first experience with a number system, called the *integers*. For their representation, integer numbers combine a sign (+ or −) and a magnitude to create constants such as +55, −7, and 3. Numbers in this form are referred to as *integer literals*. An integer literal without a sign is positive (+) *by default*. This means that without an explicit sign a positive value is implied.

Computers use integers as primitive numeric values in calculations. In the C++ language, *int* is the fundamental type for integer objects that are used to represent a person's age (in years), the page count for this book, and today's low temperature (in degrees). A corresponding geometric representation symmetrically positions the integers on the number line at unit intervals on each side of 0.

As an object, an integer has an attribute that is its value and associated arithmetic operations such as add(+) and subtract(−), which we discuss later in this section.

The Short and Long Integer Types. Computers store all data in computer memory using a series of switches in the ON or OFF positions. These alternative positions represent the digits 1 and 0. Numbers stored in this fashion are called *binary numbers*. For instance, the data value 10011101 consists of eight digits, called *bits,* and represents the decimal number 157. A computer stores data using a fixed number of bits (Figure 2-1). If more bits are allocated, larger numbers can be declared. This can be important if the program wants to reference the population of China that now exceeds 1.2 billion. However, only a few bits are needed to distinguish the days in the week (1−7) or the months in the year (1−12). The radically different sizes of these values points out a need to use a variety of storage sizes for integers. C++ provides this flexibility by declaring

8-bit Binary Number (157)

FIGURE 2-1
*Number Represented by a Fixed Number
of Binary Bits.*

two additional integer types called *short* and *long*. As the terms indicate, short integers provide values in a more restricted range, usually 16 bits, while long integers apply to a wider range of numbers and are usually 32 bits.

Integer Types	Range of Values
short	-32768 to 32767
long	-2147483648 to -2147483647

<table>
<tr><td>*Technical
Note*</td><td>The range of values for an int varies from compiler to compiler and system to system, but normally matches either the short or long range. For now, we will use only int data, since it is the most commonly used integer type. The other types of integer data are reserved for specific applications. Appendix A provides an extended discussion of data storage on a computer.</td></tr>
</table>

Declaring Integer Objects

For computer programs to use integer objects, they must first be declared. The format of a declaration statement includes an integer type and an object-identifier-list that is a series of one or more object names separated by commas. The statement allocates computer storage for each object.

SYNTAX ▪▪

Integer Object Declarations

Form: `int  object-identifier-list;`
            `short object-identifier-list;`
            `long object-identifer-list;`

Action: Object-identifier-list is a comma separated list of C++ identifiers. The computer system allocates data storage for each object in the identifier list. The size of the storage depends on the integer type (int, short, long). The semicolon (;) is mandatory and serves as the *terminator* for the declaration.

Example: `int  daysInMonth, daysInYear;`
            `short smInt;`
            `long bigInt;`

The process does not, however, automatically assign an initial value to the object. By default, the declaration creates an *uninitialized object* that should not be used in a calculation until it is given a value.

int daysInYear;

```
      ??
```
daysInYear

With primitive types such as integers, C++ provides very simple and direct *initialization*. Place the symbol "=" after the object name and follow it with the value. The compiler generates machine instructions to do the initialization.

int fieldWidth = 60;
int fieldLength = 100;

```
      50
```
fieldWidth

```
     100
```
fieldLength

Initialization can be done for any or all of the objects in the declaration. For instance, the following declaration creates three int objects, one, two, and three. The objects one and two are given initial data values 1 and 2 while object three is uninitialized.

```
int one = 1, two = 2, three;
```

Programming Note

Having multiple objects in one declaration eliminates a seemingly redundant use of the type name, such as "int" or "long." Use this shortcut sparingly, however, since each object has its own role in the program. When combining objects in a single declaration, make sure they have some common function that warrants their grouping. For instance, the following declaration is valid but confusing.

```
int i, count = 0, score, j, seriesSum = 0, population, k;
```

EXAMPLE 2.1

1. Object maxEnrollment describes the maximum number of students that can enroll in a course. The object currEnrollment is an uninitialized object indicating the actual number of students in the course.

    int maxEnrollment = 45, currEnrollment;

2. A programmer may place the suffix "L" after an integer literal to indicate that it is of type long. The object sunDistance, describes the distance from the earth to the sun. The short integer, shuttleCrew, is an uninitialized object.

```
long sunDistance = 93000000L;   // 93 million miles
short shuttleCrew:               // no initial value  ■
```

Technical Note

Integer literals such as 355, 27516, −789 are considered to be of type int in C++. If the literal value exceeds the range allotted to an int, the compiler will generate a warning message and convert the value to an int. The result may not be correct. For instance, if an int is represented using 16 bits and the declaration for sunDistance is given by

```
long  sunDistance = 93000000;
```

the compiler will output a warning message and will use a value of −12544 for sunDistance. Avoid this problem by placing "L" immediately after the literal value.

Basic Integer Operators

In the C++ programming language, the integer types int, short, and long describe computer objects that have attributes and operations. You are familiar with the operations and the standard operator symbols for addition (+), subtraction (−), multiplication (*), and negation (−) from your early training in arithmetic. Assuming that a, b, c are declared as integer objects, Table 2-1 lists the C++ operators along with sample computations.

TABLE 2-1   C++ Operators and Examples.

int a = 3, b = 5, c = 6;			
Operation	**C++ Operator**	**Integer Computation**	**Value**
addition	+	a + 5	3 + 5 = 8
subtraction	-	b - 2	5 - 2 = 3
multiplication	*	a * b	3 * 5 = 15
negation	-	-c	-6

We have deliberately delayed discussing division since this operation needs special attention. With integers, the division operation is integer division yielding two answers, the quotient and remainder. For instance, 14 "divided by 4" translates into the integer division problem

$$
\begin{array}{r} 3 \\ 4\overline{)14} \\ 12 \\ \hline 2 \end{array} \quad \text{or} \quad \begin{array}{r} 3 \\ 4\overline{)14} \end{array} \ \text{R2}
$$

C++ provides separate operators to compute the two values. The quotient is identified by the "/" operator and the remainder by the "%" operator.

```
quotient:   14/4      // value 3
remainder:  14 % 4    // value 2
```

Table 2-2 lists the quotient and remainder operators. Note that the value of the computation m % n falls in the range 0 to n − 1. For instance, when dividing by 4, the remainder always falls in the range 0 to 3.

TABLE 2-2 Quotient and Remainder Operations.

int m = 33, n = 7;			
Operation	**C++ Operator**	**Integer Computation**	**Value**
quotient	/	m/n	33/7 = 4
remainder	%	m % n	33 % 7 = 5

EXAMPLE 2.2

1. Assume that m = 33 and n = 7. The operations n/m and n % m correspond to the integer division $33\overline{)7}$.

$$\text{n/m (quotient) is } 0 \qquad \text{n \% m (remainder) is } 7$$

2. Integer division is used with measurement to convert among units.
   Length in Feet and Inches
   A line is 76 inches long. To convert to feet and inches use

$$76 / 12 = 6 \qquad 76 \% 12 = 4$$

   The line length is 6 feet, 4 inches.
   Time in Hours and Minutes
   140 minutes can be broken into hours and minutes.

$$140 / 60 = 2 \qquad 140 \% 60 = 20$$

   140 minutes is 2 hours and 20 minutes.

3. When dividing an integer by 2, the remainder is 0 or 1. The result 0 occurs when the integer is even and 1 occurs when the integer is odd. Put another way, an integer is even if it is divisible by 2 and odd if it is not divisible by 2.
   20 is an even integer since 20 % 2 is 0.
   23 is an odd integer since 23 % 2 is 1.

4. A number m is divisible by n provided m % n is 0.
   15 is divisible by 5 since 15 % 5 = 0 ∎

The operators +, −, *, /, and % are *binary operators* since they work with two data values *(operands)*. Negation is a *unary operator* since it changes the sign of a single operand.

Assignment Operator

Assignment ("=") is one of the most important operators for any data type. Its syntax assumes there is an expression on the right and an object on the left.

> **Definition** An **expression** may be a single constant or non-constant object or it may involve objects that combine with operators and parentheses.
> *Example:*
>
> 4 (constant object)   m (integer object)   5 + m   (m + 5) * n

The assignment operator copies the value of the right-hand side into the object on the left-hand side. Any object on the right-hand side is unchanged.

SYNTAX ▬▬▬▬▬▬▬▬▬▬▬▬▬▬▬▬▬▬▬▬▬▬▬

Assignment Operator

Form: object = expression
Action: The value of the expression is assigned to the object. The original value in the object is destroyed.
Example: Assume int m = 100, n = 30, p;

```
m = 35;
```

Before	After
100	35
m	m

```
p = m * n;
```

3000	100	*	30
p	m		n

With assignment, the right-side expression may combine several terms but the operand on the left of "=" must be a simple object. The assignment to p + 7 is invalid since this is an expression and not an object.

```
p + 7 = m + 2;    // invalid; must assign to an object
```

At first contact, you may mistakenly think of "=" as a simple arithmetic equals sign and not a C++ operator that does something. Don't be deceived! The assignment operator initiates a physical operation that directs the computer system to store a new value in an object. Consider the following statement that makes no sense as a mathematical identity.

$$n = n + 1;$$

As a computer statement, n is used as a *counter.* The assignment operator adds 1 to the current value of n.

If two or more objects need the same value, *multiple assignment operators* can be used. For instance, the statement

$$n = m = 100;$$

assigns 100 into object m and then takes the new value in m and copies it to object n.

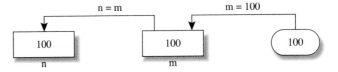

Exploring Concepts

If n is an int object, give two values for n such that n % 12 has value 7. What is the smallest positive value of n for which this is true? Can you develop a process that will generate all positive numbers n for which n % 12 is 7?

If the range of a short integer is -32768 to 32767, what value do you think is assigned to the short object n by the statement

short n = 32768L;

2-2   C++ INPUT AND OUTPUT

Now that we have familiarity with integer objects, we can use them in complete C++ programs. Any realistic example assumes, however, that we can enter new data at run time and output the results of our calculations. This section begins a formal look at *input* and *output (I/O)* in a C++ program. The topic is covered in stages throughout the chapter as we introduce new types. Basic I/O is handled by the C++ objects, *cin* and *cout,* that control data input from the keyboard and output to the screen. These are called *stream objects* and are part of an extensive C++ stream I/O system.

Sending Output to the Screen

The object *cout* represents the screen. Output is done by using the operator "<<" that writes a series of data items to the screen in the order of left to right. For instance, assuming that size = 100, the statement

```
cout << "The size is " << size;
```

outputs the description "The size is " and the value of object size to the screen.

```
The size is 100
```

The description is a string literal that consists of a sequence of characters surrounded by double quotes. Descriptions are often included to clarify the meaning of the output.

C++ associates the term stream with its input and output objects since they provide flow of data in and out of a program. For cout, think of each item as entering the stream and flowing toward the screen (Figure 2-2).

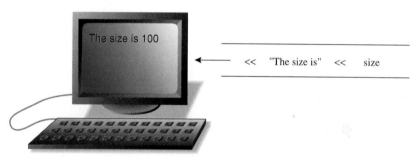

FIGURE 2-2
The Output Stream cout.

SYNTAX ▬▬▬▬▬▬▬▬▬▬▬▬▬▬▬▬

Output Operator << (Insertion Operation)

Form: cout << expression₁ << expression₂ << . . .;

Action: From left to right, each successive expression in the list is evaluated and its value is sent to the screen as output. An expression may be a string as well as a numeric expression. Space between the outputs can be created by using a C++ string literal " " consisting of one or more blank spaces.

Example: Assume m = 25, n = 40.

```
cout << m << " and " << n;
   Output: 25 and 40
cout << "Sum/Difference " << m + n << " " << m - n;
   Output: Sum/Difference 65 - 15
```

From an output statement, data is continuously written on the same line unless the program explicitly interrupts the flow and moves output to the next line. To provide this change, C++ provides the stream manipulator *endl* (abbreviation for "end line"). A *stream manipulator* is an operation that changes stream characteristics. The endl manipulator causes subsequent output to occur on the next line. The following sequence of statements output results from integer division of 17 by 4. Since each statement contains an endl, output in the screen window is on separate lines (Figure 2-3).

```
cout << "Divide 17 by 4" << endl;
cout << " Quotient = " << 17/4 << endl;
cout << " Remainder = " << 17 % 4 << endl;
```

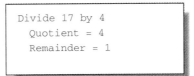

```
Divide 17 by 4
   Quotient = 4
   Remainder = 1
```

FIGURE 2-3
Illustrating the Manipulator endl.

A cout statement may contain any number of expressions. When the list exceeds the line length, the programmer may simply continue to the next line or may start a new output statement. The following are equivalent forms:

Continuing to the Next Line

```
cout << "The height is " << feetLength << " ft and "
     << inchCount << " in";
```

Separate Statements

```
cout << "The height is " << feetLength << " ft and ";
cout << inchCount << " in";
```

Programmers prefer to continue the output statement on the next line, since this format indicates a single stream of output.

Technical Note

A program may split a string between two lines. A double quote (") terminates the partial string on the first line and begins the remainder of the string on the next line. The string terminates with a double quote.

```
cout << "This is a long string that continues "
        "onto the next line";
```

Formatting the Output

For most output, a program can separate values on a line by using a string of blanks. In some cases, however, output should be organized into fixed columns. In a word processor, this organization is accomplished with tabs. In our C++

programs, we use the stream manipulator, `setw(n)` ("set width"), that causes output in fixed blocks (fields) on the line. The manipulator specifies that the next value is output in a field whose width is at least n character positions. In case the value requires less than n positions, the output is *right justified* in the field by default. If the value requires more than n positions, the field is extended to hold the entire value. Note that `setw()` affects only the next output value. Unless the manipulator is used again, data values are output with no justification.

Each of the following statements includes the set width manipulator in the cout stream. In listing the output, the symbol □ represents a space.

```
int i = 10, j = 29463;
// field for i is 5 characters; for j is 7 characters
cout << setw(5) << i << setw(7) << j << endl;
  Output: □□□10□□□29463

// string "i+j =" uses 5 chars; field i+j uses 10 chars
cout << "i+j =" << setw(10) << (i+j) << endl;
  Output: i+j =□□□□□29473

// field for i+j expands to 5 chars (size of value)
cout << "i+j =" << setw(1) << (i+j) << endl;
  Output: i+j =29473
```

The manipulator `setw` is declared in the system file **iomanip.h.** When used, standard programming practice places "#include" directives for iostream.h and iomanip.h as the first statements in a program.

```
#include <iostream.h>
#include <iomanip.h>
```

EXAMPLE 2.3 ▬▬▬▬▬▬▬▬▬▬▬▬▬▬▬▬▬▬▬▬▬

1. With setw(), the two lines of output organize the data in columns (Figure 2-4).

```
long area1 = 3200L, area2 = 56000L;
long population1 = 75000L, population2 = 1225000L;

cout << "Area/Population:" << setw(10) << area1
     << setw(9) << population1 << endl;
```

```
Area/Population:      3200       75000
Area/Population:     56000     1225000
```

FIGURE 2-4
Using setw( ) to Line Up Data in Columns.

```
cout << "Area/Population:" << setw(10) << area2
     << setw(9) << population2 << endl;
```

2. The `setw()` manipulator applies to C++ string literals. The symbol □ represents a space.

```
cout << setw(4) << "one" << setw(6) << "one";
  Output: □one□□□one
```

3. The `endl` manipulator can be used to create blank lines.

```
// insert two blank lines
cout << endl << endl;

// second endl creates a blank line
cout << "Some text" << endl << endl;     ■
```

Reading from the Keyboard

C++ defines the object *cin* as a stream of characters coming from the keyboard. The object, along with the stream operator "`>>`", provides data input to a program. The general form of the operator combines the stream cin and one or more data objects. During execution, data is input from the keyboard and stored in the objects in the order of left to right. For instance, assume that m and n are declared as integer objects. The statement

```
cin >> m >> n;
```

inputs consecutive integers from the keyboard and stores their values in the objects m and n respectively (Figure 2-5).

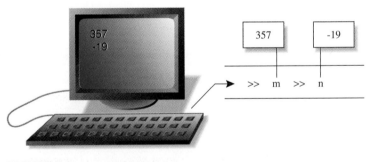

FIGURE 2-5
Reading Two Integer Values from the cin Stream.

Handling data input requires some knowledge of how C++ reads characters from the keyboard. The data is *buffered* (stored in computer memory) before it flows into objects. The buffered data is released only when the *enter key* (also called the *return key*) is pressed. The data is partitioned into blocks of characters that are separated by blank spaces, tabs, and the end-of-line (*newline*) character. These separator characters, called *whitespace*, allow us to enter multiple data items on one line. On the other hand, the input data can be spread over two or more lines by typing a return at the end of each line. Assume □ represents a space and ¶ the newline character. We can input integer values for objects m and n using either of the following methods.

input statement

```
cin >> m >> n;        // enter two integer values
```

method 1: Place data on separate lines

```
Input:   387¶
         -19¶
Result: m is 387 and n is -19
```

method 2: Separate data with whitespace

```
Input:   387□-19¶
Result: m is 387 and n is -19
```

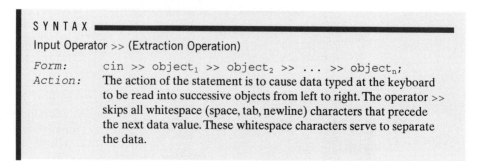

SYNTAX ━━━━━━━━━━━━━━━━━━━━━━━━━━━━━━━━━

Input Operator >> (Extraction Operation)

Form: cin >> object$_1$ >> object$_2$ >> ... >> object$_n$;
Action: The action of the statement is to cause data typed at the keyboard to be read into successive objects from left to right. The operator >> skips all whitespace (space, tab, newline) characters that precede the next data value. These whitespace characters serve to separate the data.

Example: Assume □ is a space and ¶ is a return (enter).

```
int m, n;
long p;
```

Input statement.

```
  cin >> m >> n >> p;
```

Input 1: Separate each data item with whitespace.

  Input: 23□5799□□653557¶
          <Assign> m=23, n=5799, p=653557

Input 2: No input occurs until the enter key is
         pressed.
  Input: 23□5799□□653557
                    <Assign> m = ??, n = ??, p = ??

Input 3: Data is input from separate lines

  Input: 23□653¶
          5799¶   <Assign> m=23, n=653, p=5799

PROGRAM 2.1

To illustrate integer division and input/output, the program reads the length of a movie in minutes and outputs its length in hours and minutes. Note that the prompt in the cout statement has a blank space after the ":" and does not terminate with a newline. This allows the user to enter data on the same line as the prompt.

```cpp
#include <iostream.h>

int main()
{
   int movieLength;

   cout << "Enter the length of the movie in minutes: ";
   cin >> movieLength;

   cout << "Movie length is " << movieLength /60
        << " hr. and " << movieLength %60 << " min." << endl;

   return 0;
}
```

Run:

Enter the length of the movie in minutes: 168
Movie length is 2 hr. and 48 min.

Enter and run this short program

```cpp
#include <iostream.h>

int main()
{
    short number1;
    int number2;
    long number3;

    cin >> number1 >> number2 >> number3;
    cout << number1 << "   " << number2
         << "   " << number3 << endl;

    return 0;
}
```

Discuss runs of the program using the following input. The size of the integer objects come into play.

```
Input 1:   456□6341□□□3451235
Input 2:   33000□6341□□□-345
Input 3:   -6□70000□□□4000000000
```

Exploring Concepts

Initializing Objects during Program Execution

Data can be stored in memory in three different ways: through compile time initialization, through assignment to an object, or through an input statement.

```cpp
int m = 35;     // compile time initialization of m
m = 56;         // run time assignment of m
cin >> m;       // input m from the keyboard
```

In any application, the programmer must insure that an object has a value before it is used in a computation. Most C++ compilers will give a warning message indicating that the program is attempting to use an object before it is defined.

```cpp
int x, y;

y = x * 2;      // Warning!! x is used before it is defined
```

While an input statement assigns an initial value to an object, it should be used only when the program must rely on the user for data. In most cases, objects are not assigned initial values from the keyboard. For instance, asking a user to input a value for PI is unnecessary and could lead to inaccurate results.

PROGRAM 2.2

The program takes the digits in a two digit integer and creates a new number with the digits reversed. We include this example to illustrate all of the different ways of assigning values to an object. Data for the object value is read from the keyboard.

```cpp
cin >> value;
```

The integer base10 is initialized to 10 by the compiler.

```
int base10 = 10;        // assign an initial value
```

Data for all other objects are initialized by assignment statements. Expressions with the integer base10 compute the ones digit and tens digit of value.

```
unitValue = value % base10;
tenValue = value / base10;

// to reverse 45,  reverseInt = 54 = 5 * 10 + 4
reverseValue = unitValue * base10 + tenValue;
```

```
#include <iostream.h>

int main()
{
    int base10 = 10;            // assign an initial value

    int value;                  // user supplied value

    int reverseValue;           // assigned as the final result
    int unitValue, tenValue;    // assigned in intermediate calculations


    cout << "Enter a two digit integer: ";
    cin >> value;

    unitValue = value % base10;    // unit's digit in the number
    tenValue = value/ base10;      // ten's digit in the number
    reverseValue = (unitValue * base10) + tenValue;

    cout << "The reverse value is " << reverseValue << endl;

    return 0;
}
```

```
Run:

Enter a two digit integer: 45
The reverse value is 54
```

2-3   CHARACTER OBJECTS

A variety of integer objects provide our first example of primitive C++ types. Of equal importance is character data that consists of letters, digits, and other special symbols. Characters are used to create names, addresses, labels, and so forth and find important applications as data for printers and keyboards.

A C++ character object has type *char*. The different values are divided into *printable characters* and *control characters* that are used in data communications. The printable characters consist of familiar uppercase and lowercase letters, digits, and punctuation marks such as comma, period, and so forth. Among control characters, you will recognize the tab, backspace, and enter key characters. For initialization and assignment of printable characters, we use *literals* that consist of a character enclosed in single quotes. For instance:

```
'A'   'w'    5'    '?'   '"'   ' '
```

The usual rules for declaring objects and initializing them apply to the char type.

```
// declare char object ch and quitCh with initial values
char ch = 'T', quitCh = 'q';

// declare unitialized char objects digitCh and otherCh.
// use assignment to give them an initial value
char digitCh, otherCh;

digitCh = '8';     // assign with char literal '8'
otherCh = quitCh;  // assign with other char object
```

Escape Codes

C++ permits the programmer to represent printable characters by enclosing them in single quotes. In general, this option is not available for control characters. An exception is made for a small set of commonly used control codes that are represented by special notation called *escape codes*. The code uses the backslash (\) and a descriptive character as a pair to represent a control character. For instance, the character transmitted with the enter key is called the newline character and is represented by \n. Table 2-3 lists important escape codes in C++.

TABLE 2-3 C++ Escape Codes.

Character Name	C++ Representation	Description
newline	\n	When the new line is sent to the screen, the cursor moves down one line and over to the left-hand margin.
horizontal tab	\t	Moves the cursor to the next tab setting on the current line.
backspace	\b	Moves the cursor back one character. The system usually deletes the preceding character.
backslash	\\	Since the backslash is used in the escape code notation, \\ references the backslash character.
single quote	\'	Since the single quote is used to designate a character literal, type '\'' to reference ' as a character literal.

EXAMPLE 2.4 ▬▬▬▬▬▬▬▬▬▬▬▬▬▬▬▬▬▬▬▬▬▬▬▬▬

The examples feature control characters. For initialization and run-time assignment to a char object, escape codes are enclosed in single quotes. Within a string literal, the codes are not enclosed in quotes.

1. Declare character objects

```
char middleInitial = 'R', tab = '\t', backslash = '\\';
```

2. When the string `"x\tF(x)"` is output, the F begins at the next tab setting.

```
Output: x  F(x)
```

3. As a carryover from C, you will find output strings using \n for newline. For instance, the following statement outputs "C++" followed by two newline characters. The result is an extra blank line.

```
cout << "C++\n\n"
```

Placing \n in an output string is very similar to using the "endl" manipulator. In each case, a newline character is inserted into the output stream. However, during execution, the manipulator has the addition effect of flushing the output buffer which causes all pending output characters to be displayed. For this effect, we consistently use endl in the book.

```
cout << "End of line" << '\n'; // use escape code for newline
cout << "End of line" << endl; // use manipulator for newline   ■
```

Character I/O

The C++ stream operator `"<<"` (output) was introduced for integer objects. All of its actions apply to characters. The same applies to the >> stream operator for input. After skipping whitespace, the `">>"` operator reads the next character in the stream. Consider the example of char objects ch1 and ch2. The cin and cout statements input two character values from the keyboard and then output them to the screen. Three different input formats are used. In each case, the same output is created. Figure 2.6 illustrates the case where T and x are separated by the whitespace character blank.

```
cin >> ch1 >> ch2;
cout << "First char is " << ch1 << " Second char is " << ch2
     << endl;

<input: adjacent characters>    Tx¶

<input: space separators>       T□□x¶

<input: newline separator>      T¶
                                x¶
```

```
T X
First char is T   Second char is X
```

FIGURE 2-6
Character Input with Whitespace.

Some care must be used when the input mixes integer and character data. Recall that an integer begins with an optional `+/-` that is followed by a sequence of digits 0 to 9. To understand how the operator `">>"` works with integer and character data, think of cin as a stream of characters with a pointer identifying the current character in the stream. When reading an integer object, leading whitespace is skipped and the operation extracts successive digits from the stream until the pointer reaches the first nondigit character. When reading a character object, leading whitespace is skipped, the character is input, and the stream pointer is positioned at the next character. The following illustrates input of an integer followed by a character value. Assume that the keyboard input includes two blanks followed by the integer 578 and the character 'T'. After assigning the value 578 to object m, the stream pointer is positioned at the letter 'T' which is the first non-digit in the stream after the integer digits '5', '7', and '8'. After extracting the letter from the stream, the pointer is positioned at the blank, waiting for an input request.

```
cin >> m >> ch; // input 578 for int m and 'T' for char ch
```

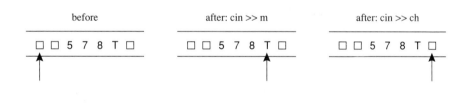

EXAMPLE 2.5 ████████████████████████████

Two different cin statements input characters ch1 and ch2 and integer m. A cout statement outputs the values to the screen. For input, assume □ represents a space and ¶ the newline character.

```
1. cin >> ch1 >> m >> ch2;
     <keyboard input>  342□M¶
   cout << ch1 << endl << m << ch2;
     Output:    3
                42M
```

```
2. cin >> ch1 >> ch2 >> m;
     <keyboard input>   34□¶
                          280¶
   cout << ch1 << " " << ch2 << " " << m << endl;
     Output:    3 4 280   ■
```

Character Input: `cin.get`. The input operator `">>"` skips whitespace when reading data. As a result, it prevents the programmer from identifying the presence of whitespace characters in the stream. Some applications, like word processors, must recognize these characters and take appropriate action. Consider the problem of stopping further output until the user types the newline (enter) character. The delay allows the user to leisurely view the contents of the screen. Up to now, we have only the `">>"` operator for input.

```
cout << "Type <Enter> to continue";    // input request
cin >> ch;                              // read a character
```

The action fails since typing the "enter" key places the newline character in the stream and the `">>"` operator ignores it as whitespace. In order to read the newline character, we need a cin operation that extracts each character in the input stream, including whitespace. The action is provided by the *get* operation.

SYNTAX ▄▄▄▄▄▄▄▄▄▄▄▄▄▄▄▄▄▄▄▄▄▄▄▄▄▄▄▄▄▄▄▄

The get() Operation

Form: `cin.get(ch);`   // ch is an object of type char
Action: The operation extracts the next character ch from the input stream,
            even if it is a whitespace character.
Example: Declare m and n as int objects and ch as a char object. The input
            statements extract three data values from the stream. Assume □ represents a blank and ¶ the newline character.

```
<input statements>
cin >> m;           // read integer m
cin.get(ch);        // read the next character
cin >> n;           // read the next integer

1.Input: 25W53¶ // m is 25, ch is W, n is 53
2.Input: 25□53¶ // m is 25, ch is blank, n is 53
3.Input: 25¶    // m is 25, ch is the newline
         53¶    // character '\n', and n is 53
```

Representing Character Data

Since the memory of a computer contains only binary numbers, numeric values must be used to represent characters such as 'A.' To create some standardization, the computer industry adopted the *ASCII representation* (American Standard Code for Information Interchange) for characters. An *ASCII code* stores a character as an 8-bit *(byte)* number.

▌ **Definition** The ASCII code for a character is an integer value that represents the character.

The different codes are divided into 95 printable characters and 33 control characters. Table 2-4 shows the printable ASCII character set and their numeric values. A full list of characters is given in Appendix B. The blank character, represented by □, is the first printable character and has ASCII code 32. The code for each character is given with the tens digit along the row and the ones digit along the column. For instance, the character 'T has ASCII code 84.

TABLE 2-4 Printable ASCII Character Set.

Left Digit	Right Digit									
	0	1	2	3	4	5	6	7	8	9
3			□	!	"	#	$	%	&	'
4	(	)	*	+	,	-	.	/	0	1
5	2	3	4	5	6	7	8	9	:	;
6	<	=	>	?	@	A	B	C	D	E
7	F	G	H	I	J	K	L	M	N	O
8	P	Q	R	S	T	U	V	W	X	Y
9	Z	[	\	]	^	_	`	a	b	c
10	d	e	f	g	h	i	j	k	l	m
11	n	o	p	q	r	s	t	u	v	w
12	x	y	z	{	|	}	~			

EXAMPLE 2.6 ■■■■■■■■■■■■■■■■■■■■■■■■■■■■■■■■■■

1. The ASCII representation for characters in the string "C++" is given by

    67   43   43

2. Using ASCII codes, we can create a dictionary ordering for words.

    "house" precedes "mountain"   (h (ASCII 104) < m (ASCII 109))

    "Zelda" precedes "aardvark"   (Z (ASCII 90) < a (ASCII 97))   ■

Within the ASCII character set, control characters, decimal digits, and alphabetic characters fall within well-defined ranges. Control codes with integer values 00–31 and "Del" with value 127 lie at the extreme ends of the ASCII range. The range for digit and alphabetic characters is described in Table 2-5.

TABLE 2-5 ASCII Character Ranges.

ASCII Characters	Decimal
Decimal digits ('0'–'9')	48–57
Uppercase ('A'–'Z')	65–90
Lowercase ('a'–'z')	97–122

Technical Note

While ASCII is the primary representation used for characters, other representations exist. The EBCDIC character set (Extended Binary Coded Decimal Interchange Code) places the code for a blank space at 64 and the value for "A" at 193. A full listing of EBCDIC codes is given in Appendix B. Note that the EBCDIC codes are scattered throughout the range 64 to 249, whereas the ASCII codes use the range 0 to 127. With supporting hardware, applications can use the ASCII codes in the range 128 to 255. These codes can represent graphical characters, foreign language characters, and special symbols. The Unicode character set is a 16-bit code that defines characters for a variety of languages such as Arabic and Chinese. Unicode characters have importance for Internet communication.

Character Operations

A character object is represented by an integer value and so a program can freely mix character and integer objects in expressions. The operations take place using the ASCII code. For instance, addition and subtraction can generate other characters in the ASCII range. Assume ch = 'S'.

```
ch = ch + 1;    // ch increases by 1; ch = 'T'
ch = ch - 3;    // ch decreases by 3; ch = 'P'
```

The range of uppercase and lowercase letters begin with ASCII code 65 and 97 respectively. Each corresponding uppercase and lowercase letter differs by 32 (97 − 65). This fact can be used to change the case of a character.

Add 32 to change a letter from uppercase to lowercase.

```
ch = 'E';       // uppercase 'E' is ASCII 69
ch = ch + 32;   // lowercase 'e' is ASCII 101 = 69 + 32
```

Subtract 32 to change a letter from lowercase to uppercase.

```
ch = 't';       // lowercase 't' is ASCII 116
ch = ch - 32;   // uppercase 'T' is ASCII 84 = 116 - 32
```

The ASCII code for '0' is 48. Since all of the decimal digits are ordered in the range 48 to 57, a program may switch between a digit and its corresponding numeric value by using addition and subtraction. For instance, digit '3' has ASCII code 51 (48 + 3). The corresponding numerical value is obtained by subtracting '0' (ASCII 48).

```
Numeric Value: 3 = '3' - '0' = 51 - 48
```

Adding 48 to an integer value in the range 0 to 9 produces the corresponding character digit.

```
Character: 5 + 48 = 53 = '5'
```

PROGRAM 2.3

When reading an integer value, the input operator ">>" is responsible for converting a sequence of characters from the keyboard into an integer that can be stored in the object. The process is called *input conversion*. This program illustrates the conversion that occurs in the operation

```
cin >> m;    // m is an int object
```

Figure 2.7 Extract '8' '2' From Input Stream and Store Integer 82 in m

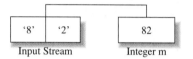

'8'	'2'		82

Input Stream   Integer m

FIGURE 2-7

The program reads the two digit number as two characters chTen and chUnit. For instance, chTen is '8' and chUnit is '2' In order to compute the corresponding integer value, each character must be converted to the digit in the range 0 to 9. This is done by subtracting 48 ('0') from the ASCII value of the character.

```
valueTen = chTen - '0';  // '8' - '0' is 8
valueUnit = chUnit - '0';  // '2' - '0' is 2
```

To create the integer value for m, the positional value of each digit must be used. In this case, multiply valueTen by 10.

```
m = valueTen * 10 + valueUnit;  // m = 8*10 + 2 = 82

#include <iostream.h>

// illustrate character and integer objects
int main()
{
   char chTen, chUnit;              // digit characters
   int valueTen, valueUnit, value;  // numeric values

   cout << "Enter a two digit number: ";
   cin >> chTen >> chUnit;

   valueTen = (chTen - '0') * 10;   // 10's digit
   valueUnit = (chUnit - '0');      // 1's digit

   value = valueTen + valueUnit;    // value of number
   cout << "Numeric value is " << value << endl;

   return 0;
}
```

```
Enter a two digit number: 82
Numeric value is 82
```

*Technical
Note*

The previous program performs input conversion for two-digit integers by reading each digit as a separate character. This process is used for all numeric input, since the operator ">>" can extract only characters from the keyboard. We say that the input operator reads integers. In fact, this is not technically correct. The operator reads characters and uses a conversion process to store the numeric value in the object.

*Exploring
Concepts*

1. You are given the declarations

   ```
   char ch;
   int intCh;
   ```

   If intCh is 115 and the assignment statement

   ```
   ch = intCh;
   ```

   is executed, what is the value of ch? What is the value of ch after the statement

   ```
   ch = (ch + 5) - 32;
   ```

2. Twenty-six control characters can be typed at the keyboard by pressing the <Ctrl> key and one of the keys 'A' through 'Z.' In each case, the code sent by the keyboard is the remainder after dividing the character value by 32. For instance,

   ```
   Control Character    ASCII Value        Function
   <Ctrl>g              103 % 32 = 7       terminal bell
   <Ctrl>J              74  % 32 = 10      newline
   ```

   The ASCII codes for backspace and tab are 8 and 9, respectively. How can you transmit these codes by using the Ctrl key?

2-4 REAL NUMBER OBJECTS

Integer and char types, which are referred to as *discrete types,* represent data values that can be counted, e.g., $-2, -1, 0, 1, 2, 3$, and so forth.

Many applications require numbers that have fractional values, such as 3.14159 and 6.02×10^{23}. These numbers, called *real numbers,* are represented with a whole and a fractional part and occupy a continuum on the number line.

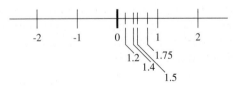

Real number objects are represented with two different formats. The *fixed point* format represents the value as a pure decimal number that contains a whole part and a fraction part. The whole part is a signed integer and the fraction part is a series of digits preceded by a decimal point.

```
Fixed point format   <whole part>.<fraction part>
  -12.452      // whole part = -12  fraction part = .452
  2625.4       // whole part = 2625 fraction part = .4
  +18.23       // + sign is optional
```

The *floating point* format represents the number in *scientific notion* that includes a *mantissa* and an *exponent* that is a power of 10. The format uses the character 'e' to separate the parts of the number.

```
Floating point format   <mantissa>e<exponent>
  -6.02e23   // the value -6.02 x 10²³ in scientific notation
             // mantissa = -6.02 exponent = 23
  4.3e0      // the fixed point form is 4.3
  2.7853e3   // the fixed point form is 2785.3
```

C++ Real Number Types

C++ supports three real types, *float, double* and *long double*. Like the distinction between short and long, the various real types provide different levels of accuracy. The real type *float* is normally implemented as a 32-bit number and *double* as a 64-bit number. The double type is used when greater accuracy is required. All real literals, such as 3.5 and $-9.5e8$ are considered to be double values. Although the type *long double* is available, it has application only when extreme accuracy or size is required.

Objects of real type use the standard C++ declaration format and can be initialized.

float x = 0.1, y, z;

double pi = 3.14159, avagadro = 6.02e23;

Real number objects are used as operands with the familiar arithmetic operators: addition($+$), subtraction($-$), multiplication($*$), division($/$) and negation($-$).

float x = 2.5, y = 5, z;

```
z = x + y;      // z = 7.5
z = x * y;      // z = 12.5
z = -x/y;       // z = -.5
```

Real number division must be contrasted with integer division. With real numbers, "fractional division" is used and gives a single decimal result. For instance, $5.0/2 = 2.5$, whereas integer division produces the result $5/2 = 2$ with a remainder of 1. Real objects cannot be used with the % operator that is restricted to integers only.

```
int m = 2.5 % 3;   // invalid operation; 2.5 is a real number
```

EXAMPLE 2.7 ▬▬▬▬▬▬▬▬▬▬▬▬▬▬▬▬▬▬▬▬▬▬▬▬

Declare

```
double x = 2.5, y = 3.1e2, z;
int n;
```

```
1. z = x*x + y;    // y is 310; z = 2.5 * 2.5 + 310 = 316.25
2. n = 12/5;       // integer division: n = 2
3. z = 12.0/5.0;   // real division: z = 2.4  ■
```

Technical Note

The storage of real numbers typically uses a format that represents the sign, exponent, and mantissa. The format is more complicated than the integer or character representation and is discussed in Appendix A. The following indicates the ranges for float and double objects that are used on most systems.

	Negative Numbers	*Positive Numbers*
float	$-1.7 \times 10^{+38}$ to -0.29×10^{-38}	0.29×10^{-38} to $1.7 \times 10^{+38}$
double	$-0.9 \times 10^{+308}$ to -0.86×10^{-308}	0.86×10^{-308} to $0.9 \times 10^{+308}$

Real Number Stream I/O. Real number objects can be used with the cin and cout I/O streams. For input, whitespace is used to separate two or more values on the same line. The following program prompts for the length and width of a rectangle and outputs its area.

PROGRAM 2.4 ▬▬▬▬▬▬▬▬▬▬▬▬▬▬▬▬▬▬▬▬▬▬▬▬

The program inputs the length and width of a rectangle, computes the area and then outputs the result.

```cpp
#include <iostream.h>

int main()
{
  double length, width, area;

  cout << "Input the length and width of a rectangle: ";
  cin >> length >> width;
  area = length * width;
  cout << "The area of the rectangle is " << area << endl;

  return 0;
}
```

```
Run:

Input the length and width of a rectangle: 2.5  6.25
The area of the rectangle is 15.625
```

Input can mix integer, character, and real objects. Depending on the fixed or floating point form of a real number, the decimal point '.' and exponent 'e' can be read as part of the number. Look at two situations where the order of input for int, char, and double objects is shuffled. For each case, assume the declaration

```
double x;
int n;
char c;

Input: 6.8
  cin >> n >> x;        // n = 6, x = .8
  cin >> n >> c >> x; // n = 6, c = '.', x = 8.0
```

Using the floating point form of a real number, the input must reconize both the decimal point '.' and the exponent 'e'.

```
Input: 6.3e4 27
  cin >> n >> x >> c; // n = 6, x = 0.3e4 (3000), c = '2'
  cin >> n >> c >> x; // n = 6, c = '.', x = 3e4 (30000)
  cin >> x >> c >> n; // x = 6.3e4 (63000), c = '2', n = 7   ∎
```

Output Format for Real Objects. There are three modes for output of real values, *default, scientific* and *fixed.* Default mode chooses between using fixed-point format or scientific notation, depending on the size of the number. Typically C++ systems will use scientific notation if the magnitude of the number gets too large or too small. The following list illustrates the default output format for various real numbers. Don't worry about the details since we will shortly define a manipulator that allows you to control output if you do not want to accept the default mode.

```
cout << 123456.0 << endl;      // Output: 123456
cout << 0.123456 << endl;      // Output: 0.123456
cout << 1234567000.0 << endl;  // Output: 1.23457e+09
cout << .00000012345 << endl;  // Output: 1.2345e-07
```

Formatted output for real numbers is more complicated than similar format for integers and characters. Not only do we need to worry about the number of output positions, but also the mode (fixed, scientific) and the decimal place precision. A detailed study of format rules is given in Appendix D. For our work, the authors have provided a manipulator setreal that is declared in the header file **textlib.h** of the software supplement. The manipulator takes integer arguments w and p where w gives the number of output positions and p the number of decimal places. For instance, with $w = 8$ and $p = 3$, the real number is output in 8 character positions with three decimal point accuracy. The decimal point is included among the 8 positions.

```
cout << setreal (8, 3) << realValue;
```

The manipulator causes all subsequent real output to be in fixed mode with p decimal places. Trailing zeros are added, if necessary, so p decimal places are displayed. The argument w applies only to the next item in the stream and specifies that the output is written into a field of w positions. By using □ to represent a space, the following examples illustrate setreal.

```
cout << setreal(10,3) << 23.476;   // Output: □□□□23.476

cout << setreal(8,2) << 3.567;     // Output: □□□□3.57

cout << setreal(1,5) << 163.567;   // Output: 163.56700
cout << setreal(1,1) << 163.567;   // Output: 163.6
```

Exploring Real Numbers in Linear Equations

A nonvertical line in a plane is determined by two points (x_1, y_1) and (x_2, y_2) with $x_1 \neq x_2$. Mathematics provides a point-slope equation for the line. The slope (m) of the line is given by

$$m = \frac{y_2 - y_1}{x_2 - x_1}$$

and the general equation of the line is $y = mx + b$, where $(\varnothing, b)$ is the point of intersection of the line and the y-axis. The point b is called the y-intercept of the line.

$$b = y_1 - mx_1 \quad \text{(Figure 2-8)}$$

On the line, the distance between the two points (x_1, y_1) and (x_2, y_2) is given by the formula $d = \sqrt{(x_2 - x_1)^2 + (y_2 - y_2)^2}$ (Figure 2-8). In C++, the square root is evaluated by the function (operation) sqrt that is declared in the system file **math.h**. This library of mathematical functions is discussed more fully in Chapter 3.

C++ Function sqrt:
$$d = sqrt((x_2 - x_1) * (x_2 - x_1) + (y_2 - y_1) * (y_2 - y_1));$$

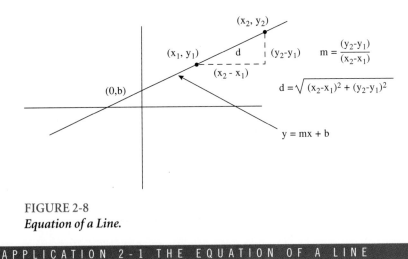

FIGURE 2-8
Equation of a Line.

The program uses two points on a plane to compute the length of the line segment connecting the points and the equation of the line. For input, the two numbers are entered in the form (x,y). The parentheses and comma are read and then discarded. We assume that the two points have different x-coordinates and thus do not lie on a vertical line.

The distance of the line segment is output with three decimal places. The setreal manipulator specifies the format for the different real number values. The program then outputs the equation of the line in the format

$$y = mx + b$$

where the slope is displayed with two decimal places, and the y-intercept b is displayed with one decimal place.

```
#include <iostream.h>
#include <math.h>        // use mathematical function sqrt(x)

#include "textlib.h"  // use manipulator setreal(w,p)

int main()
{
   // coordinates of the two points on the line
   double x1, y1, x2, y2;

   // distance between the points, the slope and y-intercept
   // of the line
   double d, m, b;

   // use char objects to read and discard '(', ',' and ')'
   char paren, comma;

   // prompt for the points
   cout << "Enter the point (x1,y1) and (x2,y2): ";
   cin >> paren >> x1 >> comma >> y1 >> paren
       >> paren >> x2 >> comma >> y2 >> paren;

   // compute and output the distance between the two points
   d = sqrt( (x2-x1)*(x2-x1) + (y2-y1)*(y2-y1) );
   cout << "The distance between the points is "
        << setreal(1,3) << d << endl;

   // compute slope m and y-intercept b of the line between
   // the points
   m = (y2-y1)/(x2-x1);
   b = y1 - m * x1;

   // output the equation of the line
   cout << "y = " << setreal(1,2) << m << "x + "
        << setreal(1,1) << b << endl;

   return 0;
}
```

```
Run 1:

Enter the point (x1,y1) and (x2,y2): (4,6) (3,5)
```

```
The distance between the points is 1.414
y = 1.00x + 2.0

Run 2:

Enter the point (x1,y1) and (x2,y2): (2,4) (6,7)
The distance between the points is 5.000
y = 0.75x + 2.5
```

Named Constants

Applications often use specific numeric or character values in the program design. For instance, the constant $\pi = 3.14159265\,\ldots$ is a component of many mathematical formulas. An accounting program may use the current state sales tax in its calculations. To introduce these values, C++ allows the program to associate a name with a value. The reference is called a *named constant* and may be used in the body of the program whenever the constant value is needed. This makes the program more readable and simpler to update.

SYNTAX ━━━━━━━━━━━━━━━━━━━━━━━━━━━━━━━━━━━━━━━

Named Constant Declaration

Form: `const type objectName = value;`
Action: The compiler associates the value with the name. In a program, whenever the name is used, the compiler substitutes the constant value.
Example: `const double TAXRATE = 0.05;`
             `const double PI = 3.14159265;`
             `const int SIZE = 10;`

In a program that computes the tax on an item, the named constant TAXRATE would be used

$$tax = itemCost * TAXRATE;$$

By programming convention, we define all named constants with uppercase letters. The use of a constant associates a meaningful name with a specific value and simplifies code modification when the value must be changed. For instance, assume the state changes its tax rate. A single change to the constant TAXRATE changes all statements that need the value.

EXAMPLE 2.8 ━━━━━━━━━━━━━━━━━━━━━━━━━━━━━━

1. With the constant double object PI = 3.14159265, the area and circumference of a circle with radius r are computed by

   area = PI * r * r;

   circumference = 2 * PI * r;

2. A named constant object cannot be changed while the program runs. Any at-

tempt to assign a new value will result in a compilation error. For instance, this assignment statement will generate an error:

TAXRATE = 0.05; ■

The program illustrates named constants by defining the conversion factor between inches and centimeters (2.54 cm = 1 inch).

const double INCH2CM = 2.54;

  The program prompts for a person's height in feet (feetHeight) and inches (inchHeight). After converting the feet to inches, the height measurement (in inches) is shifted to metric using the conversion factor. Both the height in centimeters (cmHeight) and the height in meters (mHeight) are output as formatted real numbers using setreal.

```
#include <iostream.h>

#include "textlib.h"

int main()
{
   // conversion factor from inches to centimeters
   const double INCH2CM = 2.54;

   // height of a person in feet and inches
   double feetHeight, inchHeight;
   // height of the person in centimeters. height in meters
   double cmHeight, mHeight;

   cout << "Enter the height in feet and inches: ";
   cin >> feetHeight >> inchHeight;

   // height in centimeters. multiply height in inches by CMPERINCH
   cmHeight = (feetHeight*12 + inchHeight)*INCH2CM;

   // height in centimeters
   mHeight = cmHeight/100;

   // output of the height in centimeters and meters
   cout << "height " << setreal(1,0) << cmHeight << " cm or "
        << setreal(1,2) << mHeight << " m" << endl;

   return 0;
}
```

```
Run:

Enter the height in feet and inches: 6  2
height 188 cm or 1.88 m
```

1. Specify the setreal manipulators that will produce the following output. Assume □ is a space.

```
cout << setreal(_,_) << 2.5748;    // output 2.6
cout << setreal(_,_) << 842.823;   // output □□□□842.82300
```

2. Since a fixed number of bits are used to represent a double object, the real number representation on a computer is granular, which means there are gaps where no numbers fall. Enter the following program and run it several times using values d = 0.001, 0.00001, 0.0000001 and so forth. Verify that eventually, 1 + d = 1. What does this tell you about the real numbers in the vicinity of 1?

Exploring Concepts

```
#include <iostream.h>

int main()
{
    double d;

    cin >> d;

    cout << (1.0+d) << endl;

    return 0;
}
```

2-5 WORKING WITH C++ OPERATORS

Up to this point in the chapter, we have used simple arithmetic expressions that involve a single operator and operands of a single type (int, char, float). The C++ language allows a programmer to work with multiple arithmetic operators and different number types. For instance, the expression 6 + 3.6/3 combines both addition and division of int and double types. We need to understand which operator, '+' or '/' is done first and how C++ handles the mixture of int and double values. This understanding is obtained by studying operator precedence and type conversion operations.

Operator Precedence

The *precedence* of an operator determines its order of evaluation when it is combined in an expression with other operators. Higher precedence operators execute first. C++ defines precedence for all of its operators. The following three rules apply.

1. A parenthesized expression is evaluated as a separate term.
2. For the arithmetic operators, negation has the highest precedence, followed by multiplication and division and then addition and subtraction.

Highest: — (negation)

       * / %

Lowest: + —

For instance:

```
3 + 2 * -6 = 3 - 12 = -9    // multiply first, then add
(3 + 2) * 4 = 5 * 4 = 20    // compute (3 + 2) first
```

Operator Associativity

All operators at the same precedence follow an associativity rule. In the case of the arithmetic operators, operations of the same precedence are *left associative,* meaning that they evaluate in order left to right. For instance:

```
2 - 7 + 3 = -5 + 3 = -2     // first subtract, then add
```

Some operators, like assignment, execute from right to left and are referred to as *right-associative.*

```
n = m = 5;                  // order is m = 5 then n = m
```

EXAMPLE 2.9 ■■■■■■■■■■■■■■■■■■■■■■■■■■■■■■■■■■■■■■

Use the declaration

```
int a = 8, b = 5, c;
```

```
1. c = a*b / 3;     // execute *, / left to right: c = 40/3 = 13
2. c = 9 + a%b ;    // execute % then +: c = 9 + 3 = 12
3. c = 10/3*(2+b);  // execute /, compute (2+b) and then execute *
                    // c = 10/3 * 7 = 3 * 7 = 21
4. c = b/a*9;       // execute /, * left to right: c = 0 * 9 = 0  ■
```

Operator precedence and associativity will be discussed throughout the book as additional operators are introduced. A listing of the precedence and associativity for all C++ operators is providing in Appendix C.

Type Conversion

Computers perform arithmetic operations with data of the same size and type. For instance, if two 16-bit integer numbers are to be added, a machine instruction for adding integers is used. When the operation involves data of different size or type, some form of data conversion is required since the data uses different internal storage representations. Integers use simple binary representation, while real numbers use a more complex storage representation involving a mantissa and exponent. When an operator is used, the language converts the less complex operand to the type of the more complex operand and applies the corresponding operator. This is called *implicit conversion.* For instance:

```
short + int     (executed with int addition)
int * long      (executed with long multiplication)
double - long   (executed with double subtraction)
```

Arithmetic expressions that contain operands of different data types are called *mixed type* expressions. In some cases, conversions in mixed type expressions are implicitly handled by the language while other cases involve explicit program supplied conversion. Consider the addition of a 16-bit integer m = 2 and a 32-bit float y = 3.0, with the result assigned to a float z.

$$z = m + y;$$

Since the two objects m and y have different types, the language converts the integer to a real number. The first step of the process involves converting m to an equivalent temporary 32-bit float value. Next, the machine instruction for float objects performs the addition of the temporary object and y (Figure 2-9).

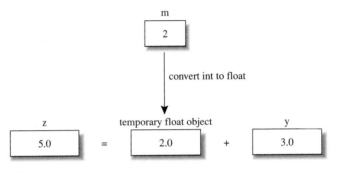

FIGURE 2-9
Temporary Objects in Type Conversion.

After assigning the result to z, the temporary object is destroyed since it is no longer needed.

$$z = m + y;   // 5.0 = 2.0 + 3.0$$

EXAMPLE 2.10 ▬▬▬▬▬▬▬▬▬▬▬▬▬▬▬▬▬▬▬▬▬▬▬

1. float floatA = 12.5;
   double doubleS = 3.123456;

   ```
   floatA * doubleS // convert floatA to double and multiply
   ```

2. Mixing precedence and conversion can be tricky. Consider the expression

   4.5 + 7/2

   Since 7 and 2 are integer operands, the integer division 7/2 = 3 is performed first and the result is promoted to a floating-point value. The result is 7.5 and not 8.

   4.5 + 7/2 = 4.5 + 3 = 7.5 ■

Explicit Conversion. Rather than letting the language control conversions, the program can perform *explicit type conversion.* The process involves attaching the type to the object.

double(9) converts the integer 9 to the double 9.0

char(65) converts the integer 65 to the char 'A'

int(6.7) converts the double 6.7 to the int 6

In C++, any primitive type can be used for conversion.

S Y N T A X ━━━━━━━━━━━━━━━━━━━━━━━━━━━

Explicit Type Conversion

Form: `T(v) where T is type and v is an object`

Action: Explicit conversion is provided by an operator that takes a value v and returns a value with type T.

Example: `double d = 12.78`
```
float x;
int k;
```

   Conversion:

```
k = int(d);      // k is assigned int value 12
x = float(d);    // x is a float with less precision
d = double(k);   // k is upgraded to a double
```

Type conversion can isolate the whole and fraction part of a real number.

```
double z = 7.56;
int wholePart = int(z);
double fractionPart = z - wholePart;
```

When dividing two integer operands, the compiler will choose integer division by default. If a real number result is required, the programmer must explicitly specifies one of the operands to be a real number. After the conversion, the system then promotes the operation to real division. For instance, compare the results:

```
int m = 10, n = 4, r;
double x;

r = m/n;          // r = 2 = 10/4 (integer division)
x = double(m)/n;  // x = 2.5 = 10.0/4 = 2.5 (real division)
```

Technical Note

C++ allows another format for type conversion, called a *type cast,* that encloses the type in parentheses. The format has origins in the C language and is used in some advanced programming situations.

```
(int)x     // equivalent to int(x)
(char)h    // equivalent to char(v)
```

Type casting should not be used as an alternative for type conversion unless it is absolutely necessary. This condition occurs with type char * that defines a pointer type (Chapter 10). We must use a type cast since the type consists of two words.

```
(char *)t  // char *(t) is not valid syntax
```

Exploring
Concepts

What is the action of the following conversions?

```
short h;   int n;   double x;   char ch;

n = int(x + 0.5);
h = short(50000L);
ch = char(int(ch) + 1);
```

Assignment Conversion. When assigning a value to an object, the compiler adjusts the precision of the value to match the type of the left-hand side. The action is a form of implicit type conversion that we will refer to as *assignment conversion*. For instance, the same double value is assigned to both a double and a float object. The assignment to floatB reduces the precision of the stored value.

```
float floatA, floatB;
double doubleA, doubleB;

doubleB = floatA * doubleA   // stored with double precision
floatB = floatA * doubleA    // stored with float precision
```

When assigning a float or double value to an int object, the value of the right-hand side is truncated(chopped) to an integer and the fractional part is discarded.

EXAMPLE 2.11 ████████████████████████████████████

For each example, use the object declarations

```
float floatVal;
double obj1 = 2.8, obj2 = .123456789, doubleVal;
int intVal;
```

1. The assignment statement

```
doubleVal = obj1 * obj2;
```

performs the multiplication using double arithmetic with the result 0.3456790092. The following assignment statement stores the result in floatVal with less precision, such as 0.345679.

```
floatVal = obj1 * obj2;
```

2. Floating point or integer *overflow* will occur if you attempt to assign a value from the right-hand side that is too large in magnitude. On most systems, the following statements result in overflow. When integer overflow occurs, the C++ run-time system normally allows the program to run with incorrect values. When floating point overflow occurs, the symbol INF (infinity) is output if the object is placed in an output stream.

```
intVal = 3.1e50;     // double value overflows int range
floatVal = 3.1e50;   // double value overflows float range
```

3. This assignment statement appears to assign 25000 to intVal.

```
intVal = 25000*2/2;
```

However, intVal actually has the rather surprising value –7768 when an int is stored using 16 bits. This is caused by the internal representation of integer numbers. Since "*" and "/" are left associative, the product 25000*2 = 50000 is done first, followed by the division. The product exceeds 32767, the maximum positive value for a 16-bit int object and overflow occurs. ■

2-6 EXTENDING ARITHMETIC OPERATORS

When introducing the different number types, we looked at the standard arithmetic operations +, –, *, and /. We now develop additional operators that find use in specific applications. As the book progresses, we will find that C++ supports a wide range of operators. In this section, we present compound assignment operators that update number objects and also discuss the very useful increment/decrement operators.

Compound Assignment Operators

Assignment is one of the most important operations in a programming language. For specific applications, C++ allows the simple assignment operator = to combine with an arithmetic operator to form a *compound assignment operator*. The arithmetic operator comes before the assignment operator without any separating blank. The right-hand side may be any applicable expression.

SYNTAX ▬▬▬▬▬▬▬▬▬▬▬▬▬▬▬▬▬▬▬▬▬▬▬▬▬▬▬▬▬▬

Compound Assignment Operator

Form: object op= expression   // operator op precedes "="

Action: A compound assignment statement is equivalent to a simple assignment statement. The operator is applied with the current value of the object as the left operand and the expression as the right operand. The result is copied back to the object. Its action is equivalent to the statement.

        object = object op (expression)

Example: The following is a series of examples that include most of the arithmetic operators.

```
 Assume sum = 100, score = 15, and n = 47.

 Compound Operator      Equivalent Operation
 sum += score           sum = sum + score (sum = 115)
 n -= 1;                n = n - 1 (n = 46)
 sum *= 2               sum = sum * 2 (sum = 200)
 n /= 10                n = n /10 (n = 4)
 n += score*3           n = n + (score*3) (n = 92)
```

EXAMPLE 2.12 ────────────────────────────────

1. At the cash register, each item has 5% tax added to its cost.

```
cost += cost*0.05;    // cost = cost + cost*0.05
```

2. Divide the number x in half

```
x /= 2;
```

3. Convert a lowercase letter to uppercase.

```
ch -= 32;         // ch = ch - 32  ■
```

Increment Operators

Programs frequently use counters to maintain a record of the number of times that an event occurs. The counter begins at 0 and moves through the range 1, 2, 3, 4, and so forth, as successive events occur. If the counter is an integer object, an increment could be done with a simple assignment or a compound assignment statement.

count = count + 1;   *or*   count += 1;

Since the operation is so common, C++ provides a unary operator "++" for this purpose. Place the "++" immediately after an integer object and the value of the object is incremented by 1. The operator −− decrements the value of an object by 1.

```
count++;    // add 1 to count
```

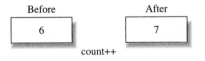

```
count--;    // subtract 1 from count
```

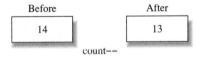

Note: The increment operators have an alternative form that places the ++ and −− symbols before the object. The forms, called predecrement and preincrement, are discussed in Chapter 11 when the operations have applications. For now, we use "++" or "−−" only on the right-hand side of an object.

EXAMPLE 2.13 ────────────────────────────────

Add the values t1, t2, and t3 to sum and then compute the average. In each statement, the integer count identifies the number of data values that contribute to the sum.

```
double sum = 0.0;
int count = 0;

sum += t1;        count++;
sum += t2;        count++;
sum += t3;        count++;

average = sum/count;   ■
```

Consider the integer objects

```
int a = 76, b = 37, c;
```

Assume that the following instructions are executed in order. What are the values for a, b, and c after each statement?

Exploring
Concepts

```
c = b % a * 9;
a++;
b--;
c += a+b;
c %= 2*5;
c++;
```

2-7   THE STRING TYPE

Strings are important objects in many nonnumerical computing problems. They are used for business applications, pattern matching, and programming language compilers. In Section 2.2, we introduced C++ string literals, such as "Hello World," as a sequence of ASCII characters enclosed in double quotes. We now look at the user-defined object type String and develop methods for string handling. The object type is declared in the header file **tstring.h.**

Like numbers, String objects have basic operations that allow a user to declare constant objects, implement assignment statements, combine objects, and perform I/O. We introduce the String type through a series of simple examples and conclude with a program that demonstrates basic String operations. The String type is expanded throughout the book as we develop language constructs and applications.

String Object Declaration

Like any object declaration, the statement begins with the type *String* followed by a list of object names separated by commas. For instance, this declaration creates String objects message and name:

```
String message, name;
```

A String object, declared this way, has no characters and is referred to as a *NULL string*. The declaration can specify an initial value by using the "=" operator followed by a C++ string literal or another String object that is previously declared.

```
String greeting = "Have a nice day!",
       cityName = "New York";

// initialize with String cityName
String mailingLocation = cityName;
```

String Input/Output

Like number and character data, String objects can be used with the >> and << operators in an I/O stream. For input, whitespace is used to separate the objects. Be careful of this fact when you try to read two words like a full name (first-name, lastname). Your input must use separate Strings. The following reads a title followed by the full name.

```
String firstname, lastname;
cin >> title >> firstname >> lastname;
    Input: Mr John Doe
       Result: title= "Mr" firstname = "John", lastName = "Doe"
```

Using the output operator >>, the String is output in the next character position on the line. The setw() manipulator may be used to set the field width for a String.

```
String countryName = "Great Britain," name = "dinosaur";
int n = 235;

cout << countryName << endl;
cout << setw(13) << name << setw(6) << n << endl;
```

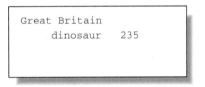

```
Great Britain
       dinosaur    235
```

---

*Technical
Note*

The String type is implemented as a C++ class and in the header file **tstring.h.** Some newer C++ compilers supply an object type, string, whose operations conform to international C++ standards. If you have this resource on your system, you may access the class from a system file that is described in Appendix F. In this book, you may exclusively use the String class that is developed by the authors. The class corresponds to the C++ standards but is limited to those operations used in the book.

PROGRAM 2.5

The program declares a series of objects of different types. The objects teamName and coach are strings while the teamID is an integer and the competitionLevel is a character. Information on a team is read as input and then organized into descriptive output.

```
#include <iostream.h>
#include <iomanip.h>

#include "tstring.h"
#include "textlib.h"

int main()
{
    String teamName, coach;
    int teamID;      // league assigns teamID number
    char level;      // teams play at levels A, B, C

    cout << "Enter team name, id, level and coach: ";
    cin >> teamName >> teamID >> level >> coach;

    cout << "Team: " << teamName << endl;
    cout << setw(10) << teamID << " (ID)" << endl;
    cout << setw(10) << level << " (Level)" << endl;
    cout << setw(10) << coach << " (Coach)" << endl;

    return 0;
}
```

```
Run:

Enter team name, id, level and coach: Stringers 415 B
Donagal
Team: Stringers
       415 (ID)
         B (Level)
   Donagal (Coach)
```

String Operations

The String type provides a powerful set of operations for string handling. We develop the operations in context throughout the book. In this section we look at the simple assignment operator, the length operation, and concatenation that joins together separate strings into a single object.

String Assignment. The assignment operator applies to String objects. The operation allows either a String object or a C++ string literal on the right-hand side. Both forms of assignment are used in applications. For instance, consider the problem of identifying the different parts of a file name.

```
String fileName, fileExtension, f;
```

To the fileExtension string, we assign the C++ literal that identifies it as a header file.

```
fileExtension = ".h";
```

The string f is read with a simple input statement and its value is assigned to the object fileName.

```
cin >> f;        // input string f
fileName = f;    // assign f to fileName
```

String Length. The *length operation* returns the number of characters in the string. This value is important in string applications. From the declaration

```
String s = "four";
```

the length is defined by s.length() with value 4.

EXAMPLE 2.14 ■■

1. Sample strings:

```
String state = "Arizona";        // state.length() is 7
String humorist = "Will Rogers";
cout << humorist.length();       // Output: 11
```

2. The length operation can combine with setw() to output strings in columns (Figure 2-10).

```
Minnesota
Arizona       MST Zone
Minnesota     CST Zone
```

FIGURE 2-10

```
String northState, weststate = "Arizona";
cin >> northState;  // <input Minnesota>

// output each line so states and time zones line up
cout << weststate << setw(20-weststate.length())
     << "MST Zone" << endl;
cout << northState << setw(20-northState.length())
     << "CST Zone"<< endl;  ■
```

String Concatenation. The appending of one string onto the end of another is called *concatenation*. The operation is modeled after addition and is represented by the binary operator +. For instance, assume the string declaration for objects s, t, u, and v.

```
String s = "Object", t = "C++, u = "Oriented", v ;
v = s + t;                 // v is "ObjectC++"
```

The concatenation operation allows the program to join two or more strings that may be either String objects or C++ string literals. This flexibility greatly expands the power and usefulness of strings.

```
v = s + "-" + u;          // v = "Object-Oriented"
v = "String " + s;        // v = "String Object"
```

The compound assignment operator += appends the string on the right to the string on the left.

```
s += t;                   // s ="ObjectC++"
t += " Programming";      // t = "C++ Programming"
```

APPLICATION 2-3 USING STRING OBJECTS

The program illustrates basic String operations. The user is asked to enter a first and last name as separate objects. Using concatenation, the objects are combined to create a full name (e.g., "John Doe") and an alphabetic name in the format "Doe, John."

A second part of the program focuses on I/O. The user enters a date using the long format ("May 5, 1977"). The month is read as a string and the day and year as integers. The comma after the day is read from the stream as a character and discarded. For output, we write the date corresponding to the 50th anniversary of the event.

```cpp
#include <iostream.h>

#include "tstring.h" // use String objects

int main()
{
  // define the String objects dealing with the name
  String firstname, lastname, fullname, alphaname;
  String month;    // month in a date
  char comma;      // read the comma in the date
  int day, year;   // day and year in the date

  cout << "Enter a first and a last name: ";
  cin >> firstname >> lastname;

  // use concatenation to form "First Last" and "Last, First"
  fullname = firstname + " " + lastname;
  alphaname = lastname + ", " + firstname;
  cout << "The full name is " << fullname << endl;
  cout << "The alphabetic name is " << alphaname
       << endl << endl;

  cout << "Enter a date in the format MONTH DAY, YEAR: ";
  cin >> month >> day >> comma >> year;
  // output the date 50 years later
```

```
        cout << "The 50th anniversary of the event is "
              << month << " " << day << ", " << (year+50) << endl;

      return 0;
    }
```

```
    Run:

    Enter a first and a last name: Joe Carlson
    The full name is Joe Carlson
    The alphabetic name is Carlson, Joe

    Enter a date in the format MONTH DAY, YEAR: May 5, 1977
    The 50th anniversary of the event is May 5, 2027
```

Consider the string declaration

```
    String s = "C++", t;
```

What is t after the statement

```
    t += s;
```

The String concatenation operators "+" and "+=" will accept a single character
as the right operand and add the character to the end of the string. What is the
output of this sequence of statements for the input line "May 5"?

Exploring
Concepts

```
    String s;
    int d;
    char cd;

    cin >> s >> d;

    cd = '0' + d;
    s += " ";
    s += cd;
    cout << s << endl;
```

CHAPTER 2 SUMMARY

The chapter focuses on C++ primitive number and character types that are the building
blocks for all data in a program. The types are defined by the C++ language and include
the familiar arithmetic operators. We also introduce the programmer-defined type, String,
whose objects provide text (strings of characters) and the type stream whose objects `cin`
and `cout` are used for the input and output of data.

Now that the chapter is completed, you should feel comfortable working with
primitive types. This involves understanding how a computer defines the short, int, and
long type to handle integers of different sizes. It also implies that you are familiar with
the operations +, -, *, and integer division (/,%). The same understanding applies to real

numbers that are declared as float or double type to differentiate size and accuracy. Computers distinguish between real number and integer operations. This chapter gives a detailed analysis of implicit and explicit conversion for expressions with objects of mixed number types.

Characters provide important data in a program. They can be used as values for objects of char type or as components of strings. The chapter discusses basic computer handling of characters including their ASCII representation, escape codes, operations, and input/output. Strings are introduced as a programmer-defined object type with operations for input and output, length, and concatenation (+). The String type is more fully developed in Chapter 7.

Assignment is the single most important operation for a computer program. The subject is treated extensively in this chapter. You are introduced to simple assignment, multiple assignment, compound assignment and assignment conversion.

The C++ file system defines stream objects for input and output of data. The stream cin provides input from the keyboard using the >> and get operators. The get operator allows the program to input any character from an input stream, including even whitespace. The cout stream is used with the operator << for output to the screen. Using manipulators like setw, setreal, and endl, we can format output.

Object Types (Classes) in the Chapter

Name	Implementation File
String	tstring.h

KEY TERMS

ASCII Code:
An integer code that represents a character. The code standardizes the representation of characters as an 8-bit (byte) number.

Assignment Operation:
An operation that copies the value of an expression that is the right-hand operand into an object that is the left-hand operand.

Division:
With integer objects, the operation is called integer division and produces a quotient with the / operator and a remainder with the % operator. With real objects, the / operation is fractional division with the result given with a whole and fractional part.

Escape Codes:
A set of control characters that a C++ program references with the format '\<char>'. For instance, '\t' is the tab character.

Initializing Objects:
The process of assigning an initial value to an object. The process can involve compile time initialization that assigns a value when the object is declared, the assignment operator that copies data to the object as a left-hand operand or input from a file stream.

Integer Types:
Object types short, int, and long that describe numbers like 20, −15, and so forth. Short integer objects are 16-bit values while long integers are typically 32-bit values. The size of an int object is system dependent.

Manipulator (stream output):
A stream operation that inserts format directives into the output stream. The directives specify characteristics such as the number of character positions to use for output, decimal places, justification, and so forth.

Named Constant:
An object literal whose value is associated with a name. The compiler substitutes the constant value for the name whenever it appears.

Real Number Types:
Object types float and double that describe numbers like 20.5 and $-15.45e2$. For input and output, the numbers can be represented in fixed or scientific notation. The type double provides greater range of values and accuracy.

String:
A type whose objects consist of a sequence of characters that are interpreted as a single item. String objects may be used with the << and >> operators for I/O. The concatenation operator + and the length operation apply to String objects.

REVIEW EXERCISES

1. Write declarations for the following:
   (a) an integer object n with initial value 2453
   (b) two integer objects p and q. p is uninitialized and q has initial value 455

2. Compute
   (a) 32 / 6   (b) 32 % 6   (c) 6 / 32   (d) 6 % 32

3. Assume m = 8 and n = 5. Compute the following:
   (a) m * n + 8   (b) m/n   (c) m % n   (d) −m * n

4. Indicate all values of n such that n % 5 = 2 where n = _____.
   (a) 71   (b) 12   (c) 2   (d) 55   (e) 502

5. How would you describe all integers n where n % 2 = 0?

6. Write declarations for the following:
   (a) a character c whose initial value is lowercase t
   (b) a character nl whose initial value is the newline character

7. Which string is represented by the following ASCII code sequence?

   66   121   116   101

8. Assume the declarations

   ```
   char    ch1 = 'c',    ch2 = '5',    ch3;
   int     k = 5, n;
   ```

   (a) ch3 = ch1 − 32;   (b) n = ch2 − '0';
       ch3 = _____   n = _____
   (c) n = ch1;   (d) ch3 = char(k * 10);
       n = _____   ch3 = _____

9. What character or string is represented by
   (a) '\\'   (b) "\\t"

10. The grid [(a)–(c)] contains output from three separate statements. From each

group of output statements, select the cout statement that provides the output in the grid. Assume the declarations:

int i = 100;   double x = 8.25;   char c = 't';

(a)	1	0	0				1	0	0
(b)		8	.	2	5	0		8	. 3
(c)	A		=		3	2			t

```
(a) cout << setw(6) << i << i;
    cout << i << setw(6) << i;
(b) cout << setreal(6,3) << x << setreal(4,1) << x;
    cout << setreal(5,3) << x << setreal(3,1) << x;
    cout << setreal(2,3) << x << setreal(2,1) << x;
(c) cout << "A = " << i - 68 << " " << t;
    cout << "A = " << i - 68    << c;
    cout << "A = " << i - 68 << " " << c;
```

11. Compute each of the following expressions:
(a) 2.4/3   (b) int(6.4/2)   (c) int(6.4)/2

12. Check each statement for syntax. If valid, indicate "valid"; otherwise, identify the errors and show how they could be changed to be valid.
(a) char ch = "t";   (b) int n = 'c';
(c) int n = 45.5 % 6;   (d) float x = 3.45e7.8;

13. Define as named constants.
(a) a tax rate of 7.75%   (b) the string "JANUARY"

14. Describe the value of each object after completing the input statement. Assume ¶ is a newline and □ is a space.

```
int          i, j;
double       x;
char         ch1, ch2;

cin >> i >> ch1 >> x;
cin.get(ch2);
cin >> j;
```

(a) Input: 23□14.6¶ // i = __ j = __ x = __ ch1 = __ ch2 = __
            8t¶
(b) Input: 23.14t¶ // i = __ j = __ x = __ ch1 = __ ch2 = __
            95.1¶

15. Indicate what implicit type conversions take place in each expression. Give the resulting value for the object on the left-hand side. Assume the declarations

double x = 23.57, y;
float z = 4.5;
int i;
short s = 5;

(a) y = 2 * z;   (b) i = s * 3;   (c) z = x/s;

16. Consider the strings:

```
String s("john"), t("son"), v;
```

For each operation, give the resulting string and its length.
(a) `v = s+t;`   (b) `s += s+t;`   (c) `v = t + " of " + s;`

Answers to Review Exercises

1. (a) int n = 2453;   (b) int p, q = 455;
2. (a) 5   (b) 2   (c) 0   (d) 6
3. (a) 48   (b) 1   (c) 3   (d) −40
4. (b) 12   (c) 2   (e) 502
5. n is an even integer
6. (a) char c = 't';   (b) char nl = '\n';
7. Byte
8. (a) c3 = 'C'   (b) n = 5   (c) n = 99   (d) c3 = '2'
9. (a) \   (b) \t
10. (a) `cout << i << setw(6) << i;`
    (b) `cout << setreal(6,3) << x << setreal(4,1) << x;`
    (c) `cout << "A = " << i-68 << " " << c;`
11. (a) .8   (b) 3   (c) 3
12. (a) Invalid   (b) Valid   (c) Invalid   (d) Invalid
    char ch = 't';   int n = 45%6;   float x = 3.45e8;
13. (a) `const float TAXRATE = .0775;`
    (b) `const String FIRST_MONTH = "JANUARY";`
14. (a) i = 23   j = 8   x = 4.6   ch1 = '1'   ch2 = '\n'
    (b) i = 23   j = 95   x = 14   ch1 = '.'   ch2 = 't'
15. (a) The integer 2 is converted to float and 2*z is done using float arithmetic. The result is converted to double and assigned to y, whose value is 9.0.
    (b) Since the literal 2 is an int, the short object s is converted to int and the multiplication is done using int arithmetic. The product is assigned to i, whose value is 15.
    (c) The short object s is converted to double and x/s is done using double arithmetic. The double value is rounded to float and assigned to z, whose value is 4.714.
16. (a) johnson (`v.length()` is 7)   (b) johnjohnson (`s.length()` is 11)
    (c) son of john (`v.length()` is 11)

WRITTEN EXERCISES

17. Write declarations for the following:
(a) a "small size" integer object m with initial value 5
(b) a "large size" integer k with initial value 600055
(c) three integers p, q, and r. p is uninitialized, q has initial value 200, and r has a value twice that of q.

18. Assume $m = 27$ and $n = 8$. Compute the following:

(a) $m * n + 8$ (b) m/n (c) $m \% n$
(d) $-m * n$ (e) n/m (f) $n \% m$

19. For each integer n, give the value for $a = n /10$ and $b = n \% 10$;
(a) $n = 2935$ $a =$ _____ $b =$ _____
(b) $n = 82$ $a =$ _____ $b =$ _____

20. Compute the value of each of the following expressions. Assume declarations:

int $x = 27, y = 4$;

(a) x/y (b) y/x (c) $x \% y$ (d) $y \% x$

21. Indicate all values of n such that $n \% 9 = 6$ where $n =$ _____
(a) 65   (b) 96   (c) 24   (d) 56   (e) 6

22. How would you describe all integers n that are divisible by 4?

23. Write declarations for the following
(a) a character with initial value uppercase J
(b) a character with initial value equal to a tab

24. Give the ASCII decimal code for each character
(a) 'G'   (b) '6'   (c) '!'   (d) '~'

25. What is the difference between the number 0 and the character '0'?

26. Which string is represented by the following ASCII code sequence?

49   50   51   32   71   111   33

27. What character or string is represented by
(a) "\\n"   (b) "\\\\"   (c) "\\\n"
(d) '"'   (e) '\''

28. Write the real numbers in the specified format:
(a) x = 738.2914 using floating-point format
(b) x = 12.294e5 using fixed-point notation

29. Equate the fixed and floating-point number values
(a) 23.51e4 = _____ (fixed)
(b) 814.92 = _____ e2 (float)
(c) 9713.2761 = 9713276.1e_____ (float)

30. What is the meaning of the manipulators `setw` and `setreal`?

31. What is the manipulator that stands for a '\n' in an output stream?

32. Use the grid to create output from the following statements:

```
int i = 45, j = 8945;
double x = 3.17;
char c = 't';
```

```
(a) cout << "i = " << i << " " << j << c << endl;
(b) cout << setw(5) << i << setw(2) << j << endl;
(c) cout << i+j << setreal(6,3) << x << setreal(4,1) << x;
```

33. Fill in the grid to indicate the result of these output statements:

```
double x = 57.89;

cout << setw(7) << x << setw(1) << x << endl;
cout << setw(7) << "Go" << setw(12) << "String" << endl;
cout << setreal(8,4) << x << setreal(1,1) << x << endl;
```

34. Give the output for each statement:
    (a) cout << setw(3) << 5 << setreal(4,2) << 3.14159265;
    (b) cout << setw(8) << 23.45 << " " << 3.5355;
    (c) cout << setw(5) << "abc" << setw(3) << "de" << endl;

35. The input statement reads integer and character data. Give the resulting value for integers m and n and character ch for each keyboard input.

```
cin >> m >> n >> ch;
```

    (a) Input: 28 33 4¶
    (b) Input: 28 33¶
                 J¶
    (c) Input: 28 33T¶
                 173¶

36. An integer, a character, and a real number are input in different orders.

```
int n;    char ch;    float x;
```

    Input order:

```
(I)   cin >> n >> ch >> x;    (II) cin >> x >> ch >> n;
(III) cin >> n >> x >> ch;    (IV) cin >> ch >> x >> n;
```

    For the following input, give the value of the three objects that result from the different input orders (I)–(IV)

```
Input:   28.34¶
         17.3¶
```

    Order I: n = _____   ch = _____   x = _____
    Order II: n = _____   ch = _____   x = _____
    Order III: n = _____   ch = _____   x = _____
    Order IV: n = _____   ch = _____   x = _____

37. Assume the declarations

```
char ch1 = 't', ch2 = '5', ch3;
int  k = 5, m, n;
```

    (a) n = ch1 - 5;   // n = _____
    (b) n = ch2 - '1' + k;   // n = _____

(c) `ch3 = 'M' + 32;`   `// ch3 = _____`
(d) `ch3 = char(k * 20); // ch3 = _____`

38. Compute each of the following expressions
(a) int(0.6/0.2)   (b) int(0.6)/0.2

39. Each statement uses type conversion. Give the value assigned to *x*.
(a) int *x*;   (b) int *x*, *y* = 20;
   x = int(3.8);   *x* = int(3.8 * *y*);
(c) char *x*;   (d) int *x*, *y* = 20;
   x = char(65);   *x* = int(3.8) * *y*;
(e) char ch = 'F';
   int *x*;
   x = ch;

40. Indicate the implicit type conversions for each expression. Assume the declarations

$$\text{double } x, y; \quad \text{float } z; \quad \text{int } i; \quad \text{short } s; \quad \text{char ch};$$

(a) $z = 2 * i;$ (b) $z += s;$ (c) $s = ch + 2;$
(d) $z = y;$ (e) $y = l + z;$ (f) $z = 4.0/s;$

41. Assume *i* = 38 and *j* = 11. In each case, give the values for *i* and for *j*.
(a) *i*++;   (b) *i* += *j*;   (c) *j* = *i* *= 5;   (d) *i*++; *j* = *i* − 6;

42. Assume *i* = 35 and *j* = 8. In each case, give the values for *i* and *j*.
(a) *i*++;   (b) *j*−−;   (c) *i* += *j*;   (d) *i* *= 5;
         i += *j*   *j*++;

43. Fill in the values for the objects a and b in the program.

```
#include <iostream.h>

int main()
{
    int a, b;

    a = 20;
    a -= 4;        // a = _____

    a = 20;
    b = 4;
    a += b;        // a = _____
    b *= a;        // b = _____
    a %= b+6;      // a = _____

    a = 35;
    b = 88;
    a++;           // a = _____
    b--;           // b = _____

    return 0;
}
```

44. Given the typical size of short and long integers on a computer system, indicate whether the operation would result in overflow.

short t = 20000, u = 15000, v;
long d;

(a) v = 60000 /2;   (b) $v = t + u$;   (c) d = long(t*4) * 100;
(d) d = double(4e25);   (e) t += 25000;   (f) $u = t \% 50000$;
(g) $d = 2*t/2$;

45. Consider the strings

String S("good"), T("bye"), V;

For each operation, give the resulting string
(a) V = S + T;
(b) S += S + T;
(c) S += "y"; V = S += " ";

46. Trace the code in a main program segment and indicate the output from the cout statement.

(a)
```cpp
int main()
{
    int v;
    float a, x;

    cin >> a;    // input real number a
    v = int(a);
    x = a - v;
    cout << v << " and " << x;

    return 0;
}
```

```
For input    345.62      output is:
For input    21.187      output is:
```

(b)
```cpp
int main()
{
    int v;
    char ch1, ch2;

    cin.get(ch1);
    cin.get(ch2);
    v = 10 * (ch2 - '0') + (ch1 - '0');
    cout << >> a;        // input real number a
    cout << v;

    return 0;
}
```

```
For input    78      output is:
For input    24      output is:
```

47. Trace the code in a main program segment and indicate the output from the cout statement.

(a)
```cpp
int main()
{
    int v;
```

```
    float a, x;

    cin >> a;        // input real number a
    v = int(a);
    x = a - v;
    cout << v << " and " << x;

    return 0;
}
```

```
For input   345.62     output is:
For input    21.187    output is:
```

PROGRAMMING EXERCISES

Formatting of output is an important feature of the chapter. Many of the exercises require that output be given with a specified number of decimal places. The notation xxx.xx indicates fixed-point output with two decimal places, whereas xxx.xxx indicates output with three decimal places.

48. Write a program that reads an integer n, squares it, and creates the output line

```
<n> squared is <n²>
```

Run the program three times with values of $n = 5, 15,$ and -9.

49. Write a program that asks the user to enter two integer values m and n. Output $m + n, m - n, m*n, m/n$ and $m\%n$ in the format represented by the following run:

```
Run:
Enter integer m: 35
Enter integer n: 9
m+n = 44
m-n = 26
m*n = 315
m/n = 3
m%n = 8
```

50. Write a program that inputs three long integers from the keyboard and outputs the sum, average, and product of the numbers. Compute the average as a real number and output it using the default format. Here is a sample run.

```
Run:
Enter three integer values: 25   67   36
Sum is 128
Average is 42.6667
Product is 60300
```

51. Write a program that creates the following table:

```
1995          12345
1996            456
1997           4326
1998          41785
1999             45
```

Each line must be generated by a single cout statement using the setw manipulator.

52. Write a program that uses a series of cout statements to form the string "C++" using block letters:

53. Write program that inputs a three-digit positive integer, extracts the individual digits, and outputs them as distinct digits separated from each other by two blanks. The following run illustrates the required format:

```
Run:
Enter a three digit positive integer: 537
5  3  7
```

54. A boat motor requires that the oil and gasoline be mixed in the ratio of 50 units of gasoline to 1 unit of oil. Given that there are 128 ounces per gallon, write a program that inputs the number of gallons of gasoline to be placed in a gasoline can and outputs the number of ounces of oil that must be added. Use one decimal place accuracy for the number of ounces of oil. Use the format demonstrated by the following run.

```
Run:
Enter the number of gallons of gasoline: 4
Add 10.2 ounces of oil
```

55. In metric, a pound is 0.45 kilograms. Write a program that defines the conversion factor as the named constant LB2KILO and declares objects lbWeight and kgWeight. The program should prompt for the weight in pounds and output the weight in kilograms. Use manipulators to create the following output with two decimal places.

weight is xxx.xx kg

Run the program three times with input values of 10, 16, and 55 pounds.

56. Create a test program that illustrates basic C++ expression evaluation. Declare integer objects a and b with initial values 10 and 12, respectively. Illustrate that "*" has a higher precedence than "+" by assigning the value of the expression 8 + a*b to object x and by assigning the value of expression (8+a)*b to object y. Output x and y.

A second calculation should directly output 9/5*9 and 9/(5*9) in separate cout statements to verify that multiplication and division are left-associative.

57. Write a program that reads three characters and outputs both the characters and their ASCII codes. Run the program three times using input characters

```
    A a 0    9 ? %    & H ~
```

Check your results by looking up the codes in the ASCII chart in Appendix B.

58. Recall that the hypotenuse of a right triangle is the square root of the sum of the squares of the other two sides. Prompt for two real numbers *a* and *b* and output the hypotenuse in the following format:

For a = xxx.xx and b = xxx.xx, the hypotenuse is xxx.xx.

Run the program with the input data a = 3, b = 4 (c = 5).

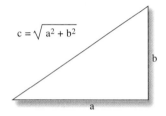

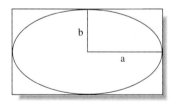

59. Write a program that inputs the radius of a circle and outputs its circumference and area. Use a prompt for the input and labels to indicate the meaning of each output statement. Define PI as a named constant where PI = 3.14159265.

60. An ellipse or oval is determined by a circumscribing rectangle whose dimensions are 2a by 2b.

The numbers a and b are called the semi-axes of the ellipse. An ellipse whose semi-axes are the same length is a circle. The area of an ellipse is πab.
Prompt for the semi-axes and output the area of the corresponding ellipse using a descriptive label. Define PI as a named double constant with value 3.141592653589793.

61. Temperatures are given in Fahrenheit and Celsius units. The conversion equation is

$$\text{celsiusValue} = 5/9(\text{fahrenheitValue} - 32)$$

Write a complete program that prompts for input of a Fahrenheit temperature and outputs the equivalent Celsius value.
   Sample:
     Input: Enter Fahrenheit temperature, 98.6
     Output: Celsius temperature is 37.0

62. Write a program that is designed to test for overflow with short, long, and int data. Declare objects

```
short shint1 = 25000, shint2 = 15000, shint3;
long  lint;
```

Execute the following statements and output the values of shint3 and lint.

```
shint3 = shint1 + shint2;
lint = long(shint1) + long(shint2);
```

63. Declare two Strings, str1 and str2, that have initial values "Monday" and "12/25/2000." Print the day and date in the format

```
The starting day is <day>
The starting date is <date>
```

By using the value of str1 and the String "Tuesday," apply the operator "+" to assign str1 the value "MondayTuesday" and output the value. Use the operator "+=" to assign " MondayTuesdayMondayTuesday" to str1 and output the value.

64. Write a program that outputs the value of the integer object m three times to produce

```
Run:
25
125
126
```

Use compile time initialization to obtain $m = 25$. Obtain the value 125 using a compound assignment operator and the value 126 using an increment operator.

65. Read a string and use the manipulator setw and the String operation length() to output it centered in a field of 30 spaces between two 'x' characters. For example, if the input is "string," the output should be

                          x   string   x

PROGRAMMING PROJECTS

66. A cash register uses an automated coin machine to help make change. We assume that a clerk is handed money to pay for purchases. For change, the clerk returns to the customer any paper money and directs the coin machine to distribute any change less than $1. In this exercise, you are to simulate the action of the clerk and the machine.

Problem Analysis

At the cash register, we need access to the purchase price and the payment. The change, which is the difference between the payment and the purchase price, is a real number. The whole part represents the change in dollars and the fractional part is the change in cents that is returned in quarters, dimes, nickels, and pennies. For instance, with a payment of $10 to cover purchases of $3.08, the required change is

$6.92. The clerk hands out $6 and the coin machine distributes 3 quarters, 1 dime, 1 nickel, and 2 pennies for the 92 cents.

$$92 = 3(25) + 1(10) + 1(5) + 2$$

Program Design

Use real-number objects that identify the purchase price, the amount of payment, and the change. The main program computes the amount of change and partitions it into dollars, quarters, dimes, nickels, and pennies.

Input: Prompt for the purchase price and payment that are entered as real numbers in the following format:

Enter the purchase total and payment: 3.08   10.00

Processing: Develop the change algorithm using the example of paying $10.00 to cover a purchase of $3.08 — the change is $6.92. Using a specific example to think about a process is often good strategy as long as the example can be generalized into an algorithm.

Change is the difference between the payment and the purchase price.

$$change = 10.00 - 3.08$$

The dollar amount is the whole part of the change.

$$int(6.92) = 6$$

The coin amount is the fractional part of the change converted to an integer value.

$$\$0.92 \ = \ > 92 \text{ cents } (int((change - dollar) * 100))$$

Start returning coins with the largest coins (quarters) and then proceed in order through dimes, nickels, and pennies.

$$quarters = coinChange/25 = 92/25 = 3$$
$$coinChange = coinChange \% 25 = 92 \% 25 = 17$$

quarters = 3

25	25	25	10	5	1	1

coinChange = 17

Output: Print the amount of the purchase, the payment, and the amount of change that must be returned as real numbers. Then indicate the number of dollars, quarters, dimes, nickels, and pennies that make up the change total. Use the following output format:

Purchase Total	3.08
Payment	10.00
Change	6.92
Dollars	6
Quarters	3
Dimes	1
Nickels	1
Pennies	2

Chapter 3
Describing and Declaring Classes

CHAPTER CONTENTS

3-1 CLASS DESCRIPTIONS
Describing Operations As Functions
Constructor

3-2 DECLARING AND USING OBJECTS
Calling Member Functions
Application: Student Account
Transactions

3-3 DESCRIBING THE RECTANGLE CLASS

3-4 A VISUAL MODEL OF CLASSES

3-5 THE C++ CLASS DECLARATION
Moving from Description to
Declaration

3-6 CLASSES AND PROBLEM SOLVING

3-7 FUNCTION PROTOTYPES WITH DEFAULT
VALUES
The GradeRecord Class

3-8 DRAWING CIRCLE FIGURES

3-9 FREE FUNCTIONS
Pure Object-Oriented Design
Structured Design
Program Design Using C++
Building C++ Programs with Objects
and Free Functions
Exploring the Math Library
The Drawing Functions
Application: Using Graphics Func-
tions and Objects

3-10 DEFINING FREE FUNCTIONS IN A MAIN
PROGRAM
Using Free Functions in Program
Design
Written Exercises

Chapter 1 introduced the concept of a programmer-defined object type called a class, and illustrated it by developing the StudentAccount, Rectangle, and Rect-Shape classes. To understand classes, we presented an informal specification for attributes and operations. We also introduced UML notation as a graphical representation for classes. While objects were used in several demonstration programs, we did not give a formal declaration of their classes. Beginning that study is the primary topic of this chapter. We first present an expanded class description format that associates C++ types with each attribute. In the description, we develop function notation, which is the C++ language for operations. This leads to the formal declaration of a C++ class.

In a C++ program, most of the tasks are handled by the operations of objects. For applications, C++ also allows the programmer to design operations that are independent of an object. The tasks, called free functions, are important tools in good C++ program design. The topic is introduced at the end of the chapter.

The StudentAccount and Rectangle classes from Chapter 1 provide examples as we develop the main concepts of this chapter. We also introduce the new classes Dorm-Room, MealBill, GradeRecord, and Circle-Shape and use them in applications. Code for all of the classes is provided in the supplemental software. We encourage you to print a copy of each class and look at its format. Don't worry if you cannot understand many of the details. Very soon you will find a pattern and the pieces will begin to fit together. Most importantly, learn how to use classes as tools in program applications. A discussion of C++ class implementation is left for Chapter 5.

3-1   CLASS DESCRIPTIONS

In this section, we develop a format to describe the attributes and operations of a class. The format is used by professional programmers to document a class. Our approach views a class description as three separate components that provide a title, a listing of attributes, and a listing of operations. We intersperse a general discussion of each component with specific illustrations from the StudentAccount class.

The class description begins with a title that gives the class name and a brief statement of its purpose. In this book, we begin all class names with an uppercase letter.

```
DESCRIPTION: ClassName CLASS ━━━━━━━━━━

<A brief statement of the purpose>
```

The StudentAccount class is designed for the finance office to handle charges, payments, and inquiries into a student account at a university. Putting this as a title in a formal description of the class, we have

```
DESCRIPTION: StudentAccount CLASS ━━━━━━━━

A Student Account object maintains an account record for a student.
```

In a class, attributes are listed with their name and data type. We now have access to the primitive C++ number and character types from Chapter 2 along with the String type for groups of characters. As we develop additional types, we can greatly expand the kind of attributes in a class.

Attributes
```
<a list of the attributes and their types>
```
The StudentAccount class identifies a student using an ID and name. These values are String objects and the balance is a floating-point number. Comments may further clarify the meaning of an attribute.

Attributes for Student Account
```
String studentID;        // ID in the form ##-####
String studentName;      // student name
double balance;          // account balance
```

Describing Operations As Functions

An operation represents a task that can be performed by an object. In the context of a programming language, an operation is referred to as a *function*. To understand a class operation as a function, we must see it as a process that can accept data values (arguments), carry out calculations, and return a value. These features are incorporated into a declaration that is called a *function prototype*.

A function prototype specifies the function name, an argument list enclosed within parentheses, and a return type. A prototype often includes a comment that explains the action of the function.

S Y N T A X ▬▬▬▬▬▬▬▬▬▬▬▬▬▬▬▬▬▬▬▬▬▬▬▬▬▬▬

Function Prototype

Form: `// description of the function`
              `returnType  functionName (argument list);`
Action: The prototype is a statement that terminates with a semi-colon (;)

The *argument list* includes zero or more *formal argument* declarations separated by commas. Each argument must have an associated data type.

> `Formal Argument  List:`
>   `type`$_1$ `arg`$_1$`,   type`$_2$ `arg`$_2$`, . . . , type`$_n$ `arg`$_n$

The parentheses must be present even if the function has no arguments. The returnType can be any valid C++ type. When the function does not return a value, the keyword *void* is used as the return type.

Example: In the StudentAccount class, the function charge has an argument list has the single item amount with no return value

> `void charge(double amount);`

The function getBalance has an empty argument list and a return type of double

> `double getBalance();`

Using the language of function prototypes, we can now specify how operations are defined as part of a class description. Each operation has a brief statement that includes information on its arguments and return type and a description of its action. The information concludes with the function prototype. In this book, all function names begin with a lowercase letter. Uppercase letters are used when the function name is a compound word.

Operations:
    functionName: Describe the action, arguments, and return type of the function
                     returnType functionName (argument list);

Look at the following three operations in the StudentAccount class. They illustrate different function prototypes.

Operations:

payment: Take the amount as an argument and use its value to credit the balance in the account

     void payment(double amount);

getID: Return the value of studentID

     String getID();

writeAccount: Give a summary of the current account information

     void writeAccount();

The items in a class are called *members*. The attributes are referred to as *data members* and the operations are referred to as *member functions*. In general, we will use the term member function when referring to an operation of a class. From this point on in the book, any reference to an operation in explanatory text will append double parentheses "()" to the name. The notation indicates that the function performs an action. For instance, a reference to the payment function in the StudentAccount class is given by payment().

Constructor

A class has a special function that initializes the attributes. The function, called the *constructor,* may have an argument list that contains the initial values of the object's attributes. In C++, the constructor is given the name of the class and is automatically called when an object of the class type is created. The constructor has no return type specified, not even void.

ClassName: The constructor is an operation with the same name as the class. It has no return value and an argument list that contains values to initialize the class attributes.

     ClassName (argument list of initial values);

The constructor for the StudentAccount class has three items in its argument list. The items initialize the studentID, studentName, and balance attributes. The type of each formal argument corresponds to the data type of the associated attribute.

StudentAccount: The constructor initializes the 3 attributes of the class

     StudentAccount(String ID, String name, double initbal);

The StudentAccount Class: Formal Description

Now that we have developed the three components of a class description, let's combine them into a complete description of the StudentAccount class. While most of the elements have been included in previous examples, you should see the class description as a single unit.

studacct.h

DESCRIPTION: StudentAccount CLASS ━━━━━━━

A StudentAccount object maintains an account record for a student

Attributes:
```
String studentID;        // ID in the form ##-####
String studentName;      // student name
double balance;          // account balance
```

Operations:

StudentAccount:	Use ID, name, and initbal arguments to initialize the attributes of the object.
	StudentAccount(String ID, String name, double initbal);
getID():	Return the value of studentID
	String getID();
getName():	Return the value of studentName
	String getName();
getBalance():	Return the value of current balance
	double getBalance ();
charge:	Take the amount as an argument and use its value to debit the balance in the account
	void charge(double amount);
payment:	Take the amount as an argument and use its value to credit the balance in the account
	void payment(double amount);
writeAccount:	Give a summary of the current account information
	void writeAccount();

Note the icon **studacct.h** next to the class description. This identifies the header file that implements the StudentAccount class. The file is available in the software supplement. Within the limit of eight characters, the name of the file is derived from the class name. By using only eight characters, the file names are compatible with current operating systems.

━━━━━━━━━━

3-2   DECLARING AND USING OBJECTS

Now that we have a format to describe the attributes and operations of a C++ class, we can draw on the information to declare objects and use them in a program. To declare any object, give the class name followed by the object name. Any initial values that are required by the constructor are included in an argument list following the object name. The initial values may be constants or previously defined objects. For instance, a StudentAccount object must be passed initial string values for the ID and name, and a real number for the balance.

```
// arguments using constant values
StudentAccount  student("45-8712", "Tom Vale", 2000.00);
```

```
// arguments using previously declared objects
String SSNo = "37-5629", name = "Holly McGrath";
double startBal = 500.00;
StudentAccount student(SSNo, name, startBal);
```

Calling Member Functions

A program statement may execute a member function by using the object name and the function name separated by a period. The process is referred to as *"calling the function."* In case the member function has arguments, the calling statement includes a comma-separated list of values in parentheses that correspond to the objects in the formal argument list. The values are termed *run-time arguments.*

```
// call payment() for the StudentAccount object student:
student.payment(500);      // 500 is a run-time argument

// output the current balance for object student:
cout << student.getBalance();
```

Figure 3-1 illustrates the interaction between the calling statement and the member function. The process involves three separate steps. When the calling statement is executed, the run-time arguments are "passed" to the corresponding formal arguments in the function (Step 1). Each formal argument assumes the value of the corresponding run-time argument. Program control is then given to the member function that carries out its task. During execution of the function, the formal arguments may be used in any calculation (Step 2). Upon completion of the operation, the function returns to the calling statement with its value, if any (Step 3). After the return, the calling expression has a value that may then be used for assignment, I/O, and so forth.

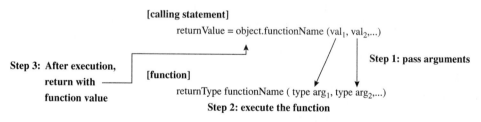

FIGURE 3-1
Calling a Member Function.

In a function call, there is a one-to-one correspondence linking each run-time argument in the member function call with the corresponding formal argument in the argument list. The corresponding pair must be of the same type or the compiler must be able to apply type conversion to the run-time argument. For instance, the formal argument for the function charge() is a real number. Hence the run-time argument must be convertible to a double value.

```
student.charge(500.00);      // pass double constant 500.00

int n = 15;
student.charge(n);           // convert int n to a double

student.charge("amount");    // invalid since "amount" is a string
```

Exploring
Concepts

The prototype for member function f of a class CL is

```
double f(double x);
```

What value is passed to the formal argument x in each call to f?

```
CL obj;
double y;
char digit = '5';


y = obj.f(3.89);
y = obj.f('A');
y = obj.f(digit - '0');
y = obj.f(100000L);
```

Application: Student Account Transactions

We illustrate the use of objects in an application using the StudentAccount class, and a new class named DormRoom. We introduce the DormRoom class by giving its class description. Carefully read each part, since the information includes the data stored by a DormRoom object and the functions that manage the data. From the description you will understand what a DormRoom object is and what it does.

dormroom.h

DESCRIPTION: DormRoom CLASS ▬▬▬▬▬▬▬

A DormRoom object maintains housing office information.

Attributes:
```
int roomNumber;     // room number
int roomCount;      // number of students in the room
double roomCost;    // cost of the room
```

Operations:

DormRoom:	Initialize the room number and the room count (number of occupants). The room cost is set by the constructor at a rate of $2700 for a double and $3500 for a single *DormRoom(int roomNo, int number);*
getRoomNumber:	Return the room number. *int getRoomNumber()*
getRoomCount:	Return the number of occupants in the room *int getRoomCount()*

getRoomCost:	Return the cost of the room for each occupant
	double getRoomCost()
setRoomCount:	Use the argument number to set the number of occupants in the room and update the room cost.
	void setRoomCount(int number);

APPLICATION 3-1 STUDENT ACCOUNT TRANSACTIONS

The program looks at student Tom Walker who has ID "62-3174" and an initial account balance of $5000.00. These values are given as arguments to the constructor when the StudentAccount object tomW is declared.

```
StudentAccount tomW ("62-3174", "Walker, Tom", 5000.00);
```

Tom will live on campus in dormitory room number 355 and will have a roommate. The room number and the number of room occupants (2) are supplied as arguments to the constructor for the DormRoom object tomWRoom.

```
DormRoom tomWRoom(355,2);
```

To simulate account and housing office transactions, the program prompts for the cost of the yearly tuition (tuitionCharge). The cost of Tom's housing contract (roomCharge) is determined by using the member function getRoomCost() for DormRoom object tomWRoom.

```
// prompt for and input Tom's tuition
cout << "Enter cost for tuition: ";
cin >> tuitionCharge;

// get Tom's room cost
roomCharge = tomWRoom.getRoomCost();
```

The sum of the objects tuitionCharge and roomCharge are used as the argument for a charge() to object tomW. We output the result of the operation using functions getID() and getBalance().

```
tomW.charge(tuitionCharge + roomCharge);
cout << "Balance for account " << tomW.getID()
     << " is " << tomW.getBalance() << endl;
```

A second prompt asks for the amount of the September payment which is used as an argument for the payment() function. After a call to payment(), the status of the account is output using writeAccount().

```
tomW.payment(septPayment);
tomW.writeAccount();
```

The following is the source code for the program. We include the header files, **studacct.h** and **dormroom.h,** that contain the implementation for StudentAccount and DormRoom classes, respectively.

```
#include <iostream.h>

#include "studacct.h"
#include "dormroom.h"

int main()
{
    // declare StudentAccount, DormRoom objects for Tom Walker
    StudentAccount tomW ("62-3174", "Walker, Tom", 5000.00);
    DormRoom tomWRoom(355,2);
    // objects used to contain Tom's costs and payment
    double tuitionCharge, roomCharge;
    double septPayment;

    // prompt for and input Tom's tuition
    cout << "Enter cost for tuition: ";
    cin >> tuitionCharge;

    // get Tom's room cost
    roomCharge = tomWRoom.getRoomCost();
    cout << "Cost of Tom's room: " << tomWRoom.getRoomCost()
         << endl;

    // charge Tom's tuition and room and debit the account
    tomW.charge(tuitionCharge + roomCharge);
    cout << "Balance for account " << tomW.getID()
         << " is " << tomW.getBalance() << endl;

    // prompt for September payment, credit account and write
    // account status
    cout << "Enter a September payment: ";
    cin >> septPayment;
    tomW.payment(septPayment);
    tomW.writeAccount();

    return 0;
}
```

```
Run:

Enter cost for tuition: 6500
Cost of Tom's room: 2700
Balance for account 62-3174 is -4200
Enter a September payment: 1000
ID:        62-3174
Name:      Walker, Tom
Balance:   $-3200.00
```

3-3   DESCRIBING THE RECTANGLE CLASS

A Rectangle object is a measurement tool that has attributes length and width and the operations area() and perimeter(). Its constructor, Rectangle(), has real number arguments l and w that initialize the length and width. Like many classes, Rectangle has operations to access (get) the current values of its attributes and to update (set) their values. The dimensions of the Rectangle object can be modified with the operation setSides() and the current value of the attributes can be retrieved with the operations getLength() and getWidth(). The following is a formal description of the class.

rect.h

DESCRIPTION: Rectangle CLASS ▬▬▬▬▬▬▬

A Rectangle object is a measurement tool that identifies the length, width, area, and perimeter of a rectangle figure.

Attributes:
  double length;
  double width;

Operations:

Rectangle:	Create a rectangle with initial length = l and width = w *Rectangle(double l, double w);*
getLength:	Return the length of the rectangle *double getLength();*
getWidth:	Return the width of the rectangle *double getWidth();*
setSides:	Set the length and width to l and w respectively *void setSides(double l, double w);*
area:	Return the area = length * width *double area();*
perimeter:	Return the perimeter = 2*(length + width) *double perimeter();*

EXAMPLE 3.1 ▬▬▬▬▬▬▬

The statements declare and use Rectangle objects.

1. The box is a Rectangle object with length 4 and width 5

```
Rectangle box(4,5);

// double the dimensions of the box
box.setSides(box.getLength()*2, box.getWidth()*2);
```

2. After reading the length and width, the declaration creates two Rectangle objects. The larger figure has a length and width that is 3 units larger than the smaller figure.

```
double len, wid;
cin >> len >> wid; // input length and width

Rectangle smBox(len,wid);        // smaller Rectangle

Rectangle lgBox(len+3, wid+3);   // larger Rectangle
```

Object smBox is placed inside of lgBox to create an outer rim region (shaded section in the accompanying figure). The area and perimeter of the rim region is

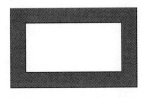

```
rimArea = lgBox.area() - smBox.area();
rimPerimeter = lgBox.perimeter() + smBox.perimeter();   ■
```

PROGRAM 3.1

A standard sheet of paper is a rectangle with dimensions 8.5 × 11″, having a perimeter of 39 inches. When used with a modern laser printer, the surface of a sheet is partitioned into a series of dots. With a 600 dpi (dots per inch) printer, each square inch is comprised of 600 × 600 = 360,000 dots. The program declares the Rectangle object stdPage and outputs the total number of dots on the page. The dimensions of the object are modified to allow for 1.5 inch margin at the top and 1 inch margin on the other three sides. For output, we include the perimeter of the reduced page and the total number of dots on the surface.

```
#include <iostream.h>

#include "textlib.h"
#include "rect.h"

int main()
{
   // declare a standard sheet of paper
   Rectangle stdPage(8.5,11);

   // new dimensions after page resized to account for margins
   double newLength, newWidth;

   // every square inch contains 600 x 600 pixels
   const long PIXELS_PER_INCH = 360000L;

   // pixels on page
   long dots;

   // compute and output number of pixels on a sheet of paper
```

```
dots = long(stdPage.area() * PIXELS_PER_INCH);
cout << "The number of dots on a standard sheet is  "
     << dots << endl;

cout << "Margins cut 1.5 inch from top, 1 inch elsewhere"
     << endl;
// resize the page by eliminating the margins
newLength = stdPage.getLength()-2.5;
newWidth = stdPage.getWidth()-2.0;
stdPage.setSides(newLength, newWidth);

// output the perimeter and the number of pixels on the
// resized page
cout << "   Perimeter of the reduced page is "
     << stdPage.perimeter() << endl;
dots = long(stdPage.area()*PIXELS_PER_INCH);
cout << "   Number of dots on the reduced page is "
     << dots << endl;

return 0;
}
```

```
Run:

The number of dots on a standard sheet is  33660000
Margins cut 1.5 inch from top, 1 inch elsewhere
   Perimeter of the reduced page is 30
   Number of dots on the reduced page is 19440000
```

3-4 A VISUAL MODEL OF CLASSES

In Chapter 1, we introduced the UML graphical representation for a class. We can now refine this representation to include the object type for each attribute along with the return type and arguments for each operation. The UML figure is divided into three components that include the class name, attributes, and function prototype for each operation. Note the similarity between a class description and its UML graphical representation. A UML representation is a compact and efficient view of the class description.

The following is the UML representation of the Rectangle class (Figure 3-2). The tool places the object type after the name for the attributes and the formal arguments. The return type of an operation follows the argument list. This is a variation from C++, where the type name is given first.

UML Format	*C++ Format*
objName : ObjType	ObjType objName
function(arguments) : ObjType	ObjType function(arguments)

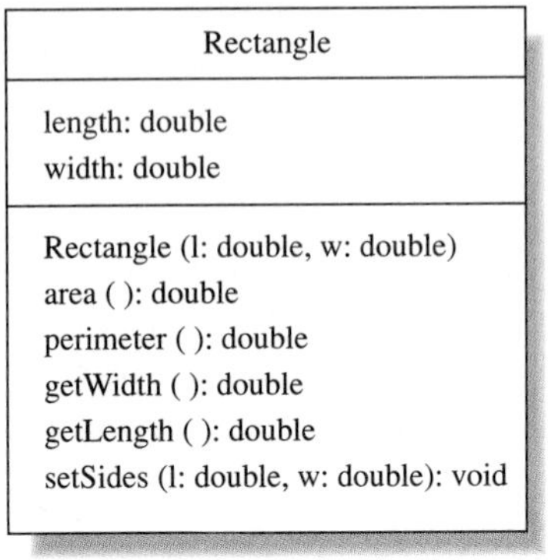

Rectangle
length: double width: double
Rectangle (l: double, w: double) area ( ): double perimeter ( ): double getWidth ( ): double getLength ( ): double setSides (l: double, w: double): void

FIGURE 3-2
Rectangle Class UML.

*Exploring
Concepts*

A class, called Length, has an attribute len that maintains a measurement in inches. For operations, the function addLength() adds a value in inches to len and the function getLength() retrieves the value of the current length. The operation writeLength() outputs the length in feet and inches. What would be a UML representation for the Length class?

3-5 THE C++ CLASS DECLARATION

A class description is an informal view of a class. We are now in a position to give a formal description of a class called the C++ *class declaration.* Our work is done in stages as we first describe the overall structure of a class declaration and then discuss each of its parts.

A class declaration begins with the *class header* that consists of the reserved word *class* followed by the name of the class.

```
class ClassName       // ClassName identifies the class type
```

The rest of the declaration is called the *class body.* It is enclosed in braces and terminates with a semicolon (";"). The body is partitioned into distinct sections that are labeled *private* and *public*[1]. The sections hold the attribute declarations and the function prototypes for the operations of the class. Note that a colon ":" terminates the section labels.

---

[1] A class may place members in a third section, called *protected.* This concept is related to class inheritance and is discussed in Chapter 12.

DECLARATION: ClassName CLASS ▬▬▬▬▬▬▬

clname.h

```
class ClassName
{
    private:
        // <private data members>
        // <private member function prototypes>
        . . . . . . . .

    public:
        // <public member function prototypes>
        . . . . . . . .
};
```

In object-oriented programming, it is not customary to place data members in the public section of a class. Data is normally placed in the private section of the class and only member functions are used to update and access the data.

Let's use the StudentAccount class as an example of a class declaration. The implementation is contained in the file **studacct.h.**

DECLARATION: StudentAccount CLASS ▬▬▬▬▬▬

studacct.h

```
// maintains student account records
class StudentAccount
{
    private:
        // private data members
        String studentID;    // ID in the form ##-####
        String studentName;  // student name
        double balance;      // account balance

    public:
        // constructor initializes the attribute list
        StudentAccount(String ID, String name, double initbal);

        // update the balance with a charge or payment
        void charge(double amount);
        void payment(double amount);

        // return the current values of the attributes
        String getID();
        String getName();
        double getBalance();
```

```
        // output account information
        void writeAccount();
};
```

Private and Public Sections. The public and private sections in a class declaration allow program statements different access to the class members. The private section contains the attributes and any internal operations that are exclusively used to implement the class. Private members can be accessed only by C++ statements that implement a member function. A public member of an object can be accessed by any statement in the main program that declares the object or by any member function of the object. Public members of a class are the interface of an object to the main program (Figure 3-3). As we learn more about C++, we will identify program units other than the main program. In these units, a programmer can declare objects and use their public member functions.

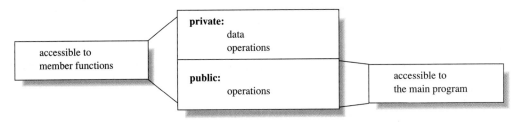

FIGURE 3-3
Public and Private Sections of a Class.

For a practical understanding of public and private members, consider the StudentAccount class. The attribute, balance, is a private data member, which means that it can be accessed only by operations of the class. The balance is updated only by the public member functions charge() and payment() that debit and credit the balance. The main program can access the current value of the balance only by calling the function getBalance().

```
StudentAccount student("54-9876","John Doe", 1000.00);

// access the balance
cout << student.getBalance();
```

A program statement cannot directly access the balance. For instance, the following statement attempts to credit the account with $500.00.

```
student.balance += 500.00;
```

The statement is invalid. A credit can be given only by using the public member function payment().

```
student.payment(500.00);
```

*Technical
Note*

Programming language designers have long understood the danger of "indiscriminate access" to application data. Languages like Modula2 and Ada restricted access to data by adding modules and packages, respectively. Object-oriented languages like C++ and Java use classes, whose declarations typically place data members in the private section. This restriction of access to the private data is a carefully considered principle of software engineering and is known as **information hiding.**

Moving from Description to Declaration

Section 3-2 presents a description for the DormRoom class. We will use it to demonstrate the typical process of translating a class description to its equivalent declaration. The DormRoom class has three attributes, roomNumber, roomCount, and roomCost that maintain housing information. The operations include a series of "get" functions to access the attribute values and a single "set" function, setRoomCount(), that updates the number of occupants and the room cost. In the class declaration, place the attributes in the private section of the class and place the function prototypes in the public section of the class declaration. The declaration should include comments to enhance understanding of the attributes and member function prototypes..

dormroom.h

```
DECLARATION: DormRoom CLASS

class DormRoom
{
    private:
        int roomNumber;        // room number
        int roomCount;         // number of students in the room
        double roomCost;       // cost of the room
    public:
        // constructor
        DormRoom(int roomNo, int number);

        // functions retrieve value of attributes
        int getRoomNumber();
        int getRoomCount();
        double getRoomCost();

        // change number of room occupants and update cost
        void setRoomCount(int number);
};
```

3-6 CLASSES AND PROBLEM SOLVING

The design of classes is the most essential part of object-oriented problem solving. Class attributes and operations are identified in the problem analysis and their objects are used in the problem solution. As an example, we look at an enterprising company called Restaurant Products, Inc. that wants to produce small machines for use by waiters in a restaurant. Each machine is initialized with the name of the restaurant and the local sales tax rate. When a customer has finished eating, the waiter enters the cost of the meal and has the machine output a bill in the following form:

```
Bill
   Meal cost    xx.xx
   Tax          xx.xx
   Tip          xx.xx
   Total cost   xx.xx
```

The bill automatically adds a 15% tip to the cost. The machine is again used when the customer is ready to pay. The waiter enters the amount paid by the customer and outputs a receipt that includes the cost of the meal, the customer payment, the change that is due, and a thank you note from the restaurant in the following form:

```
Receipt
   Total cost   xx.xx
   Payment      xx.xx
   Change       xx.xx

   Thank you for dining at <restaurant name>
```

To produce the machine, Restaurant Products Inc. contracts with a C++ programmer to implement the machine's software. We simulate this work with the MealBill class.

For attributes, a machine needs the name of the restaurant and the local sales-tax rate. In addition, it must compute and retain the total cost of the meal, including the sales tax and tip. This value is also used for customer payment since the change is computed as the difference between the amount of the customer's payment and the total cost of the meal.

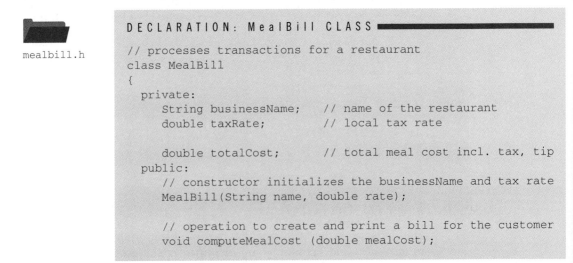

mealbill.h

```
DECLARATION: MealBill CLASS ━━━━━━━━━━
// processes transactions for a restaurant
class MealBill
{
  private:
     String businessName;    // name of the restaurant
     double taxRate;         // local tax rate

     double totalCost;       // total meal cost incl. tax, tip
  public:
     // constructor initializes the businessName and tax rate
     MealBill(String name, double rate);

     // operation to create and print a bill for the customer
     void computeMealCost (double mealCost);
```

```
    // receive payment and print a receipt
    void handlePayment(double amountPaid);

    // return the amount of the meal, tip and tax
    double getTotalCost();
};
```

When a program declares a MealBill object, it must include the name of the restaurant as a String object and the local sales tax rate as a floating-point number. For instance,

```
// Brown Dog restaurant. local sales-tax rate is 4%
MealBill brownDog("Brown Dog", .04);
```

To create a bill, use the member function computeMealCost() with the amount of the meal as an argument. The function computes the total cost by summing the cost of the meal, the sales tax and a 15% tip and assigns the sum to totalCost. The function concludes with output of a bill.

```
// a customer at the Brown Dog Restaurant spends $65.00
brownDog.computeMealCost(65);

Bill
    Meal cost      65.00
    Tax             2.60
    Tip             9.75
    Total cost     77.35
```

The member function handlePayment() takes the payment as an argument, determines the amount of change that is owed and outputs a receipt. For instance, with a payment of $80.00, the machine produces the following receipt.

```
// accept payment of $80 for the bill. output the receipt
brownDog.handlePayment(80);

Receipt
    Total cost     77.35
    Payment        80.00
    Change          2.65

Thank you for dining at Brown Dog
```

The class has a "get" member function getTotalCost() that can be used to retrieve the total cost. Assume the bill at Brown Dog is charges for a party of three. The average meal cost is:

```
double avgCost = brownDog.getTotalCost()/3;
```

The University Summit Restaurant allows a student Tom Monroe to charge the cost of a meal to his student account. Records are stored in the StudentAccount object tomM that has a current balance of $200.00. The Summit implements billing by creating a MealBill object which is set to charge 6% sales tax.

```
StudentAccount tomW("68-4938", "Monroe, Tom", 200.00);
MealBill summit ("University Summit", 0.06);
```

The program prompts for the cost of the meal and stores this result in the real number object tomBill. This value is used as an argument for computeMeal-Cost() to output the bill.

```
summit.computeMealCost(tomBill);
```

With getTotalCost(), we access the total cost of the meal and use this value to charge Tom's student account.

```
tomM.charge(summit.getTotalCost());
```

A receipt is output using handlePayment(). The StudentAccount member function writeAccount(), displays the current status of Tom's account.

```
summit.handlePayment(summit.getTotalCost());

cout << endl << "Current status of Tom's account:" << endl;
studTom.writeAccount();
```

The program includes the header files, **mealbill.h** and **studacct.h** to access the class implementations for the MealBill and StudentAccount classes.

```
#include <iostream.h>

#include "mealbill.h"
#include "studacct.h"

int main()
{
    // restaurant name "University Summit," sales-tax rate 6%
    MealBill summit("University Summit",0.06);
    StudentAccount tomW("68-4938", "Monroe, Tom", 200.00);
    double tomBill;

    cout << "Amount of Tom's bill: ";
    cin >> tomBill;
    cout << endl;

    // enter bill into machine and print a summary
    summit.computeMealCost(tomBill);
    cout << endl;
```

```
    cout << "Charge the meal to Tom's account" << endl << endl;
    // charge the meal and output the receipt
    tomW.charge(summit.getTotalCost());
    summit.handlePayment(summit.getTotalCost());

    cout << endl << "Current status of Tom's account:" << endl;
    tomW.writeAccount();

    return 0;
}
```

```
Run:

Amount of Tom's bill: 12.25

Bill
    Meal cost     12.25
    Tax            0.73
    Tip            1.84
    Total cost    14.82


Charge the meal to Tom's account

Receipt
    Total cost    14.82
    Payment       14.82
    Change         0.00
Thank you for dining at University Summit


Current status of Tom's account:
ID:         68-4938
Name:       Monroe, Tom
Balance:    $185.18
```

3-7 FUNCTION PROTOTYPES WITH DEFAULT VALUES

Computer applications often predefine initial values for attributes. These values, called *default values*, are employed unless the user explicitly defines a different value. For instance, a word processor uses default values for page margins, tab stops, fonts, and so forth. A World Wide Web browser defaults the home page to the location of the company that created the application. The idea of default values carries over to C++ member functions where it is not necessary for the calling statement to pass a run-time value for every argument in the argument list. A programmer can provide a member function with default values by assigning initial values to one or more arguments at the tail of the argument list. When the corresponding run-time argument is missing in a function call, the default value is used.

SYNTAX

Function Prototype with Default Values

Form:
```
returnType name(T arg₁, . . . ,T arg_{k-1},
                T arg_k=value_k, . . . ,T arg_n=value_n);
```

Action: In the argument list, default values are available for all objects in the range k to n. Once an argument is defined with a default value, all subsequent arguments in the list must also be defined with default values.

In the function call, run-time values must be passed to the first k-1 arguments. Other values are optional. If provided, they are assigned to the arguments in the order k, k+1, and so forth.

Example: The constructor in class DemoCL has 3 arguments with 2 default values.

```
DemoCL (int a, int b = 20, int c = 30);
```

When declaring DemoCL objects, 1-3 values may be passed to the constructor.

```
DemoCL object1(1);          // a=1, b=20, c=30
DemoCL object2(1,2);        // a=1, b=2, c=30
DemoCL object3(1,2,3);      // a=1, b=2, c=3
```

Be careful to follow the rules for default values when constructing a member function prototype. For instance, the following constructor is incorrect.

```
// since b has a default value, so must c
DemoCL (int a, int b = 30, int c);
```

Once argument b is given a default value, argument c must also have a default value.

EXAMPLE 3.3

The Accumulator class describes objects that maintain running totals. In the class, the constructor has a default argument of 0.0, and the addValue() member function adds a value to the total. If the argument is omitted, the default value of 1.0 is used.

1. The following is the declaration for the Accumulator class.

accum.h

DECLARATION: Accumulator CLASS

```
class Accumulator
{
   private:
      // total accumulated by the object
      double total;
```

```
   public:
      Accumulator(double value = 0.0);   // constructor
      double getTotal();                 // return total
      void addValue(double value = 1.0);// add value to total
};
```

2. Object one is declared with argument 5. Its constructor uses the argument to initialize the value of total. Object two uses the default value of 0.0 to initialize the value of total.

```
Accumulator one(5), two;

one.addValue();           // adds +1 by default
cout << one.getTotal();   // output is 6

two.addValue(8);          // adds 8. total is now 8   ■
```

The GradeRecord Class

The GradeRecord class maintains student records for the registrar. Its attributes include the studentID along with the total number of units attempted and the total grade points earned (Figure 3-4). To determine grade points, we assume grades are given on the scale A(4), B(3), C(2), D(1), and F(0).

```
4-unit course with grade B:   grade points = 4 * 3 = 12
2-unit course with grade D:   grade points = 2 * 1 = 2
```

67-9251	100	345
studID	units	gradepts

gpa = double (gradepts) / units = 3.45

FIGURE 3-4
Student Grade Record.

The attributes units and gradepts are used to compute the student's grade point average (gpa).

```
gpa = double(gradepts)/units;     // gpa = 345.0/100 = 3.45
```

The constructor accepts arguments corresponding to the student ID and the number of units and grade points earned. The number of units and grade points default to 0 (GPA 0.0), corresponding to a new student. The class has the member function gpa() that computes and returns the GPA, and the member function writeGradeInfo() that outputs student information in the form:

Student: 67-9251   Units: 100   GradePts: 345   GPA: 3.45

Each semester, the registrar updates student records with grades from recently completed courses. The operation, updateGradeInfo(), adds the new units and grade points to the existing data. For instance, assume student "67-9251" completed a semester in which he or she earned 16 units and 58 grade points. The units and gradePts are increased to 116 and 403 respectively.

```
student.updateGradeInfo(16,58);
cout << student.gpa();              // <output> 3.47
```

Figure 3-5 displays the UML representation for the GradeRecord class. The prototype for the constructor indicates that the arguments gpts and gunits have 0 as the default value.

GradeRecord
studentID: String gradepts: int units: int
GradeRecord (ID: String, gunits: int = 0, gpts: int = 0) gpa ( ): double printGradeInfo ( ): void updateGradeInfo (newunits: int, newgpts: int): void

FIGURE 3-5
The UML Representation of the GradeRecord Class.

DECLARATION: GradeRecord CLASS ━━━━━━

graderec.h

```
class GradeRecord
{
    private:
        String studentID;      // ID in the form ##-####
        int units;             // total units earned
        int gradepts;          // total grade points accumulated
    public:
        // constructor initializes the attributes
        GradeRecord(String ID, int gunits = 0, int gpts = 0);

        // compute and return the student gpa
        double gpa();

        // output student ID and grade information
        void writeGradeInfo();

        // update record to account for new course work
        void updateGradeInfo(int newunits, int newgpts);
};
```

Since the constructor specifies default values of 0 for the initial number of grade points and number of units, a GradeRecord object can be declared by passing a single argument containing the student name. This situation corresponds to the registrar setting up records for a beginning freshman. This is illustrated in Program 3.2.

PROGRAM 3.2

The program declares Bob as a new freshman. We indicate this by calling the member function gpa() that outputs Bob's initial grade point average as 0.0. The program prompts for the grade points and units that Bob earns in the first semester. These values, stored as integer objects newUnits and newGradePts, are used as arguments for the member function updateGradeInfo(). Bob's record at the end of the first semester is output using the function writeGradeInfo().

```cpp
#include <iostream.h>

#include "graderec.h"
#include "textlib.h"

int main()
{
    // Bob is a new freshman
    GradeRecord bob("18-8127");
    int newUnits, newGradePts;

    // output grade records for Bob
    cout << "Bob's GPA is " << setreal(1,2)
         << bob.gpa() << endl;

    cout << "Bob's 1st semester grade points and units: ";
    cin >> newUnits >> newGradePts;
    bob.updateGradeInfo(newUnits, newGradePts);
    bob.writeGradeInfo();

    return 0;
}
```

```
Run:

Bob's GPA is 0.00
Bob's 1st semester grade points and units: 18 55
Student:  18-8127  Units:  18  GradePts: 55  GPA:  3.06
```

3-8 DRAWING CIRCLE FIGURES

Chapter 1 introduced the drawing class RectShape that displays a colored rectangle on a drawing surface. This book has other drawing classes for lines, circles, polygons, and text. This section develops the CircleShape class that draws circles using a center point and radius.

We have an opportunity to look at the fill color in a graphical figure. Each of the drawing classes has a color attribute of enumeration type ShapeColor. The value of the attribute can be set by the class constructor or changed with the member function setColor(). The CircleShape class contains the list of colors available to all of the drawing classes.

We present CircleShape using its class description. Note that the member functions of the class use the same name as the functions in the RectShape class.

circlesh.h

DESCRIPTION: CircleShape CLASS ▬▬▬▬▬▬▬

A CircleShape object describes a circle on a drawing surface.

Attributes: double radius;
double baseX, baseY;   //center at (baseX, baseY)
ShapeColor color;   // color that fills the circle

The color is chosen from the list:

white	blue	teal	green
turquoise	darkgray	brown	purple
lightblue	lightgray	gold	red
orange	pink	yellow	black

Operations:
CircleShape: Construct a circle with center at (x,y) having radius r. The default values define a circle with center at $(0,0)$ radius of 0, and fill color darkgray.
     CircleShape(double x = 0.0, double y = 0.0,
             double r = 0.0, ShapeColor c = darkgray);
getRadius: Return the radius of the circle
     double getRadius();
setRadius: Set the radius of the circle to r.
     void setRadius(double r);
setColor: Set the color of the circle to c.
     void setColor(ShapeColor c);
draw: Draw the circle in the current color.
     void draw();

The Drawing Surface. For all graphics applications, we assume the drawing surface is 10 units wide. The height depends on the resolution of the monitor. Normally the height is 8 units. Horizontal coordinates are positive moving to the right and vertical coordinates are positive moving downward. The accompanying figure has two circles with radius r = 1. Circle C1 has a center at P = (x,y) while circle C2 has a center P = (x′,y′) = (x + 4,y − 4). Note that x increases as P moves to the right on the surface and y decreases as P moves toward the top of the surface.

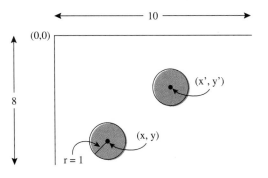

A series of operations, declared in **graphlib.h,** control the drawing surface. Their implementation is available in the supplemental software for Windows, Macintosh, or DOS systems.

```
openWindow():    // opens a window as the drawing surface
viewWindow():    // pauses drawing until a key is pressed
closeWindow():   // removes the window from the screen
```

The openWindow() operation must be called before any drawing task is requested. Before completing the program, use the closeWindow() operation to close the drawing window.

APPLICATION 3-3   DRAWING A BULL'S-EYE

The program uses the capabilities of CircleShape to draw a bull's-eye which is formed from an outer ring, a middle ring and an inner circle. Drawing a ring can be accomplished by drawing two circles of different radius at the same center point. The larger circle provides the color of the ring.

Three CircleShape objects are used to draw the bull's-eye. The center of each circle is (2, 2) and the radii are ordered in descending length from the outer to the middle and finally the inner circle. The bull's-eye is created when the circles are drawn in that order.

```
#include "circlesh.h"          // use the CircleShape class

int main()
{
   // declare three CircleShape objects for the bull's-eye.
   // have decreasing radii, different colors, same center
   CircleShape outer(2,2,1.0,blue),
               middle(2,2,0.6,white),
               inner(2,2,0.2,darkgray);

   openWindow();                // open the drawing window

   // draw the circles that form the bull's-eye
   outer.draw();
   middle.draw();
   inner.draw();

   viewWindow();                // pause to view the bull's-eye

   closeWindow();               // close the window and terminate

   return 0;
}
```

3-9 FREE FUNCTIONS

A program can be viewed as a collection of data and operations that interact to solve a problem. Historically, programs have been organized using different design methodologies that vary depending on the relationship between data and operations. The design depends partially on the bias of the programmer and partially on the underlying structure of the language.

Pure Object-Oriented Design

In pure object-oriented program design, all data and operations are designed as components of objects. The operations are implemented as member functions since they are associated with some object. Even the main program execution is organized as an object that is defined as the program administrator. The main object imports the necessary program components and then launches the application. Figure 3-6 illustrates a pure object-oriented program design and includes the run-time interaction between the main object and the other objects in the program.

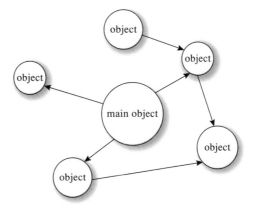

FIGURE 3-6
Pure Object-Oriented Program Design.

To illustrate this design technique, consider a checkout register at a modern grocery store. In the object-oriented design view (Figure 3-7), the checker acts like an administrator, working with a bar-code scanner object, a database to determine the cost of an item, a cash register object, and an automatic teller machine (ATM) object for payment. Each of the objects has its own operations that are designed to handle its role in the checkout process. For instance, the scanner reads the bar-code ID and notifies the cash register that an item must be processed. With the bar-code ID, the register accesses the store's database that includes the cost of the item. The cash register reads price information from the database and maintains a list of items that are purchased. For payment, the customer may use an ATM machine that must interact with both a bank and the cash register. From both a design and implementation strategy, the checkout register involves an interaction among objects.

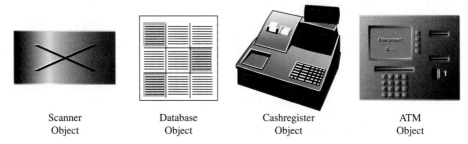

| Scanner | Database | Cashregister | ATM |
| Object | Object | Object | Object |

FIGURE 3-7
Grocery Store Checkout Objects.

Structured Design

Object-oriented design is a relatively new approach to program design. Historically, most program design strategies have separated the data and the operations. With this approach, operations are performed by *non-member* or *free functions.* Rather than starting with objects, the design focuses on the main program that is responsible for identifying critical data and setting out the tasks that must be done to solve the problem. The approach uses the contractor–subcontractor model for building a house. The main program is the contractor with the set of blueprints that define the application. The contractor is responsible for the overall project but calls on subcontractors to handle many of the subtasks. The design technique is known as *structured analysis* and requires that the programmer design and create a hierarchy of tasks that are implemented by free functions (Figure 3-8).

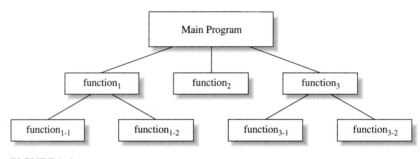

FIGURE 3-8
Free Functions and a Structure Chart.

Program Design using C++

Languages like Java or Smalltalk are pure object-oriented programming languages and require the programmer to use pure-object design. On the other hand, a C programmer will use structured program design, since the language does not implement classes. All operations in a C program are free functions. The language provides a vast collection of such functions to support string handling **(string.h),** mathematical operations **(math.h),** and so forth.

The C++ language is an object-oriented language that retains compatibility with C and, as such, is not a pure object-oriented language. Good C++ programming will primarily focus on objects but will make selective use of free functions. Free functions enable a program to use the *principle of code simplicity,* when working with long statement sequences. Such sequences of code are intrinsically complex and can challenge the human limits to manage information. Complex code can resemble travel directions volunterred by a local resident.

> *"Travel on Burris Avenue one block past the third stop light until you reach Bridge Circle. Five roads intersect in the circle. Take the third road traveling counterclockwise, and drive past the park entrance, . . ."*

After a while, you get information overload and stop listening. Imagine the problem when conditions are added.

> *"If Burris has construction, take the \next street, called Jones, which skips the circle. . . ."*

When code gets too complex, the principle of *code simplicity* directs the programmer to organize some of the statements as a task and isolate them in a free function.

Building C++ Programs with Objects and Free Functions

In this section, we introduce some principles of C++ program design. Up to this point, we have focused on how to create and use objects in a program. Now we want to introduce free functions. They enable us to organize the main program and to carry out supplemental calculations. Our introduction to free functions starts with the mathematical operations in **math.h**. As the book progresses, we will find a range of good examples where a free function can perform a calculation or handle I/O. Free functions will simplify program logic and make code more efficient. We want you to feel comfortable with their use as a C++ programming tool. However, object design will remain our primary focus.

Free Function Description and Prototype. Like a member function, a free function may have formal arguments and a return value. When it is called, the function takes run-time arguments, performs a calculation, and then returns a result. Member functions and free functions share the same description and prototype format, including the format for default arguments. The following example illustrates the description and prototype for the free functions sqrt() and pow() in the system file **math.h**.

EXAMPLE 3.4

1. The square root of a number x is defined as the value y such that y * y = x. The calculation of y is done by the sqrt() function. The function takes a nonnegative real number as an argument and returns the square root.

   sqrt: The function is defined only for a nonnegative real number x and returns the positive number y such that y * y = x
                   double sqrt (double x);

2. In the math library, the function, pow(), computes x^y.

   pow: computes and returns x^y
                   double pow(double x, double y);   ■

Calling Free Functions. A statement calls a function by referencing its name along with the necessary run-time arguments. Since a free function is not associated with any object, only the function name is used without "objName." preceding it. The run-time arguments are passed to the function, with conversion performed when necessary.

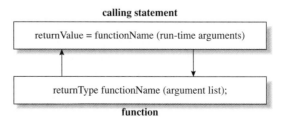

Consider the functions sqrt() and pow().

```
double a = 7.5, b, t = 3;
b = sqrt(a);         // b = 2.7386

cout << pow(t,2);    // output 9 = 3²

b = pow(5,t);        // b = 125 = 5³
```

Exploring the Math Library

C++ provides an extensive mathematics library for scientific calculations. The operations can be readily used by any program that requires scientific, engineering, or statistical calculations. The prototypes for the library functions are found in the header file **math.h.** Typically, you do not have access to the actual function source code. This code is compiled and placed in a system object code library.

We give a partial listing of **math.h,** using C++ syntax for the function prototypes. You will find a somewhat different versions of the function prototypes in your system file, since they are written to be compatible with both C and C++. In most cases, the arguments and return type are double. In our listing, the entries are partitioned into trigonometric, exponential/logarithmic, power, and real to whole number conversion functions.

Trigonometric Functions:
```
double cos(double x);             // trigonometric cosine
double sin(double x);             // trigonometric sine
```
Exponential and Logarithmic Functions:
```
double exp(double x);             // exponential function eˣ
double log(double x);             // natural logarithm of x
```
Power Functions:
```
double pow(double x, double y);   // power function xʸ
double sqrt(double x);            // square root
```
Real to Integer Conversion Functions:
```
double ceil(double x);            // smallest integer ≥ x
double floor(double x);           // largest integer £  x
```

We will have limited opportunity to use the trigonometric and exponential/logarithmic functions from **math.h**. The following example illustrates the action of the power and integer bound functions.

EXAMPLE 3.5 ━━━━━━━━━━━━━━━━━━━━━━━━━━━━

1. The pow() function computes x^y where both x and y may be real numbers.

```
double x = 3.0, y;
y = pow(x,4);         // y = x⁴ = 3.0⁴ = 81.0
y = pow(2,20);        // y = 2²⁰ = 1,048,576
y = pow(x,0.5);       // x¹/² = sqrt(x)
```

2. The floor() and ceil() functions return the nearest integer above (ceil) and below (floor) a real value.

```
ceil(5.6) = 6        // smallest integer ≥ 5.6
floor(5.6) = 5       // largest integer ≤ 5.6

ceil(-3.2) = -3      // smallest integer ≥ -3.2
floor(-3.2) = -4     // largest integer ≤ -3.2  ■
```

APPLICATION 3-4 EVALUATING AN ANNUITY

An annuity is a popular investment tool for retirement. One type of annuity has the owner invest an amount of money (principle) at a fixed interest rate (rate). The amount is allowed to grow over a period of time (nyears). The value of the annuity after nyears is given by

$$annuity = principle * (1 + rate)^{nyears}$$

This calculation is performed using the function pow() from **math.h**.

The program begins by prompting the user for the principle, the annual interest rate and the number of years to maturity. The output gives the future value of the annuity using the format:

After _____ years, $_____ grows to _____

We run the program with principle = \$10,000, interest rate = 10% and the length of time = 25 years.

```
#include <iostream.h>
#include <math.h>        // uses mathematical function pow()

#include "textlib.h"     // uses manipulator setreal()

int main()
{
    // principle invested and interest earned per year
    double principle, interestRate;

    // number of years for the annuity
    int nyears;

    // final value of the annuity
    double annuityValue;

    cout << "Enter the principle, rate, and number of years: ";
    cin >> principle >> interestRate >> nyears;

    // compute value of annuity using function pow()
    annuityValue = principle * pow(1+interestRate, nyears);

    // output a summary of the information
```

```
        cout << "After " << nyears << " years, $" << setreal(1,2)
             << principle << " grows to $" << setreal(1,2)
             << annuityValue << endl;

        return 0;
    }
```

Run:

Enter the principle, rate, and number of years: 10000
0.1 25
After 25 years, $10000.00 grows to $108347.06

Exploring
Concepts

Mathematics defines a series of exponential and logarithmic identities. Use functions from **math.h** to demonstrate the identities by evaluating and outputting each side of the equation using specific values of x.

```
log(x/y) = log(x) - log(y), where log is the natural
     logarithm of x.
```
$$e^{x+y} = e^x * e^y$$
$$e^{\log(x)}) = x$$
$$\log(e^x) = x$$

The Drawing Functions

For the drawing classes, like RectShape and CircleShape, we provide a series of free functions in **graphlib.h** that handle the screen. In Chapter 1, we used them intuitively as operations for graphical applications. Now we want to use our understanding of free functions and their prototypes, to give a full description of these screen-handling operations.

The functions openWindow(), eraseWindow() and closeWindow() create the drawing surface, erase it, and shut it down. The library provides two additional functions that support the drawing of figures. The operation viewWindow() causes the program to wait until a key is pressed, while delayWindow() suspends execution for a specified amount of time. The function delayWindow() can be used with draw () and erase () functions to implement simple animation.

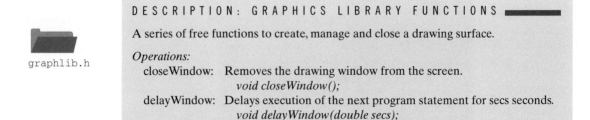

DESCRIPTION: GRAPHICS LIBRARY FUNCTIONS ━━━━

A series of free functions to create, manage and close a drawing surface.

graphlib.h

Operations:
closeWindow: Removes the drawing window from the screen.
        void closeWindow();
delayWindow: Delays execution of the next program statement for secs seconds.
        void delayWindow(double secs);

eraseWindow: Clears all drawing from the window.
                void eraseWindow();

viewWindow: Delays execution of the next program statement until a key is pressed.
                void viewWindow();

openWindow: Creates an empty drawing window on the screen.
                void openWindow();

A typical drawing program will have the following structure:

```
int main()
{
    <declare drawing and other objects>
    openWindow();     // create drawing surface

    <execute drawing operations>
    viewWindow();     // wait until key is pressed
    closeWindow();    // close drawing surface

    return 0;
}
```

Note: The program may use delayWindow() instead of viewWindow() when the viewing period is timed. The function eraseWindow() is used when the programmer wishes to create a clear drawing surface.

Application: Using Graphics Functions and Objects

To illustrate CircleShape drawing objects and the use of free functions from **graphlib.h**, we create an application that draws three separate pictures. The example uses each of the free functions and also introduces a new TextShape class for writing text on the drawing surface. Before we introduce the application, let's describe this class. It features a constructor that determines the text, its location and its color. The actual writing of the text in the window is accomplished by the member function draw(). To change the text, we can use the member function setText().

textsh.h

DESCRIPTION: TextShape CLASS ▬▬▬▬▬▬▬

Operations:

TextShape: Identify a point (x,y), the text, and the color of the text.
        TextShape(double x = 0.0, double y = 0.0,
                    String s = "", ShapeColor c = darkgray);

setText: Assign new text to the object
        void setText(String s);

setColor: Set the color of the text to c.
        void setColor(ShapeColor c);

draw: Display the text starting at the point (x,y)
        void draw();

After creating the drawing surface with `openWindow()`, the program draws two overlapping circles. The first circle, with radius 1.5, appears at the point (4,4) with blue color.

```
// declare the CircleShape object
CircleShape circ(4,4,1.5,blue);

openWindow();              // open the drawing window

circ.draw();               // draw the circle
```

The function `delayWindow()` causes a 2 second delay before drawing a light blue circle with the same size but located to the right one unit at (5,4).

```
delayWindow(2);            // wait 2 seconds

circ.setColor(lightblue);  // circle is lightblue
circ.move(5,4);            // move to the right
circ.draw();               // draw the circle
```

For the last picture, the program delays 3 seconds, clears the window using `eraseWindow()` and then draws the text "That's all folks!" using a TextShape object.

```
TextShape folks(5,4,"That's all folks!");

delayWindow(3);            // wait 3 seconds

eraseWindow();             // erase the screen

folks.draw();              // display the text
```

The program terminates with calls to `viewWindow()` and `closeWindow()`.

```
#include "circlesh.h"       // use the CircleShape class
#include "textsh.h"         // use the TextShape class

int main()
{
   // declare a CircleShape object, radius 1.5,
   // center at (4,4) and color blue
   CircleShape circ(4,4,1.5,blue);

   // declare the text we want to display at (5,4).
   // the text is drawn in orange
   TextShape folks(5,4,"That's all folks!",orange);

   openWindow();             // open the drawing window

   circ.draw();              // draw the circle
   delayWindow(2);           // wait 2 seconds
```

```
circ.setColor(lightblue);    // circle is lightblue
circ.move(5,4);              // move to the right
circ.draw();                 // draw the circle
delayWindow(3);              // wait 3 seconds

eraseWindow();               // erase the screen

folks.draw();                // display the text

viewWindow();                // wait for a keystroke
closeWindow();               // close the window

return 0;
}
```

That's all folks!

3-10   DEFINING FREE FUNCTIONS IN A MAIN PROGRAM

Up to this point in the chapter, we have used free functions that are given in **math.h** or were developed by the authors (**textlib.h**, **graphlib.h**). We now want to involve you in the writing of free functions to expand your ability as a programmer.

A C++ free function prototype includes the return type, function name and argument list. The same components are part of the *function definition* that actually contains the code. In this book, we refer to the function definition as the *function implementation.* In the implementation, the ";" in the prototype is replaced by a program unit called the *function body* that consists of declarations and statements delimited by the braces "{" and "}".

Free Function Prototype:
```
returnType functionName(argument list);
```

Free Function Implementation:
```
returnType functionName(argument list)
{
    object declarations

    C++ statements
    <return statement>
}
```
⎤
⎥ function body
⎦

The return statement causes exit from the function. The form includes an expression when a non-void return type is specified. If the return type is void, C++

permits the programmer to omit the return statement. In this case, an exit occurs after executing the last statement in the function body.

SYNTAX ▬▬▬▬▬▬▬▬▬▬▬▬▬▬▬▬▬▬▬▬▬▬▬▬▬

The return Statement

Form: `return;`
            `return <expression>;`

Action: The return statement without an expression is used when the function has a void return type. If the function has a non-void return type, the program evaluates the expression and returns its value. The compiler will make the usual conversion of primitive number types.

Example: Consider the function cube() that takes a single real argument x and returns x^3.

    Prototype:
```
double cube(double x);
```
    Implementation:
```
double cube(double x)
{
    return x*x*x;    // compute and return value
}
```

In a program, we separate the function prototype from the function implementation. The prototype occurs immediately after the included header files while the implementation is given after the main program. Splitting a function prototype and implementation simplifies the reading of the source code. The prototype enables the compiler to check the type of each argument and the type of the return value when the function is called from the main program. The implementation can be studied after the main program is understood.

PROGRAM 3.3

A program uses the cube() function in both an assignment statement and an output statement. The free function prototype for cube() is given immediately after including **iostream.h**. The function implementation is given after the main program.

```
#include <iostream.h>

// compute and return x cubed
double cube (double x);

int main()
{
    double x, y;

    x = 3;
    // compute x-cubed and assign result to y
    y = cube(x);
```

```
    // output result of the two computations
    cout << x << " cubed = " << y << endl;
    cout << 2 << " cubed = " << cube(2) << endl;

    return 0;
}

// function implementation
double cube (double x)
{
    return x*x*x;
}
```

```
Run:

3 cubed = 27
2 cubed = 8
```

Using Free Functions in Program Design

Application 3-4 computes the future value of an annuity using only the main program. Suppose we want to write a more complete version of the program that includes a banner to advertise the name of the annuity company. If this new code is added to the main program, the code sequence is both longer and more complex because it has to create a banner and compute the value of the annuity. Using the principle of code simplification, we can create a free function to generate the banner and a free function to compute the value of the annuity. The main program is then left with the responsibility of declaring objects, inputting values, and calling the free functions. The following listing implements two free functions `companyBanner()` and `annuity()`. The function `companyBanner()` outputs a promotional banner that identifies the company and its financial specialty.

```
*****************************************************
*          Creative Investment Corporation         *
*                Annuity Specialists               *
*****************************************************

// output a promotional banner
void companyBanner();
```

The `annuity()` function takes the principle, rate, and number of years and returns the value of the annuity.

```
// compute value of an annuity
double annuity(double principle, double rate, int nyears);
```

After displaying the banner, the program computes the value of a $10,000 annuity that is held for 25 years at 10% interest and outputs the value.

```cpp
#include <iostream.h>
#include <math.h>          // use mathematical function pow()

#include "textlib.h"    // use manipulator setreal()

// output a promotional banner
void companyBanner();

// compute value of an annuity
double annuity(double principle, double rate, int nyears);

int main()
{
   // principle amount and fixed annual interest rate
   double principle;        // single payment to the annuity
   double interestRate;     // fixed annual interest rate
   int nyears;              // number of years for the annuity
   double annuityValue;     // final value of the annuity

   // output the banner by calling function companyBanner()
   companyBanner();

   cout << "Enter the principle, rate, and number of years: ";
   cin >> principle >> interestRate >> nyears;

   // compute value of annuity using function annuity
   annuityValue = annuity(principle, interestRate, nyears);

   // output a summary of the information
   cout << "After " << nyears << " years, $" << setreal(1,2)
        << principle << " grows to $" << setreal(1,2)
        << annuityValue << endl;

   return 0;
}

void companyBanner()
{

   cout << "****************************************" << endl;
   cout << "*    Creative Investment Corporation    *" << endl;
   cout << "*          Annuity Specialists          *" << endl;
   cout << "****************************************" << endl;
   cout << endl;
}
```

```
double annuity(double principle, double rate, int nyears)
{
    // compute and return principle*(1+rate)^nyears
    return principle * pow(1+ rate, nyears);
}
```

```
Run:

*******************************************
*       Creative Investment Corporation   *
*               Annuity Specialists        *
*******************************************

Enter the principle, rate, and number of years: 10000
0.1 25
After 25 years, $10000.00 grows to $108347.06
```

CHAPTER 3 SUMMARY

A C++ class defines the data type of a programmer-defined object. The class constructor and its arguments indicate how to declare an object. The member functions specify how a program uses an object in an application. From this chapter, you have your first formal introduction to the structure of a class. Implementation details are left to Chapter 5.

We start with a class description that is an efficient listing of the attributes and operations in the class. It lets you know the action and prototype of each operation so that you can use it in a C++ program. A member function prototype specifies the run-time arguments that must be used in a calling statement and the return value that is provided by the function.

This chapter also introduces the UML representation for a class—it is the graphical equivalent of a class description. Additional capabilities of UML will be discussed throughout the book.

A class declaration includes the C++ syntax that defines a class structure. The format separates members into private and public sections that provides for information hiding. The importance of a declaration will become clearer in subsequent chapters when you will implement your owns classes and be introduced to private member functions, composition, and inheritance.

Since objects are the centerpiece of problem solving, you must learn how to design and describe classes as part of overall problem solving. This chapter provides a rich set of examples including the DormRoom, GradeInfo, and MealBill classes. We also look at geometric problems with the Rectangle measurement class and introduce you to a variety of drawing classes that draw circles and text in a window. This is only the beginning. Subsequent chapters will add to your experiences with classes and deepen your understanding of how they are used in problem solving.

In this chapter, most of our discussion of functions and their prototypes relate to class operations. The concepts apply to both member functions and free functions that are independent of an object. The chapter introduces free functions as a tool in program design. While C++ has most of the features of pure object-oriented language, it uses free functions for code simplification in program development.

Classes in the Chapter

Name	Implementation File
Accumulator	accum.h
CircleShape	circlesh.h
DormRoom	dormroom.h
GradeRecord	graderec.h
MealBill	mealbill.h
Rectangle	rect.h
StudentAccount	studacct.h
TextShape	textsh.h

KEY TERMS

Arguments:
Used to pass data from the calling statement to a function. A formal argument is specified by its data type and name. Each formal argument corresponds to the run-time argument that is passed when the function is called. The compiler may use type conversion if the type of the run-time argument does not correspond to that of the formal argument.

Class Declaration:
Begins with the class header that consists of the reserved word class followed by the name of the class. The rest of the declaration is called the class body. It is enclosed in braces and terminates with a semicolon (";"). The body is partitioned into distinct sections that are labeled private and public. The sections hold the attribute declarations and the function prototypes for the operations of the class. Private members can be accessed only by C++ statements in a member function. A public member can be accessed by any statement in the main program that declares an object and by a member function. Public members of a class are the interface of an object to the main program.

Class Description:
A format that describes the attributes and operations of a class. The class description begins with a title that gives the class name and a brief statement of its purpose. Attributes are listed with their name and data type. Each operation has a brief statement of its action followed by the C++ function prototype.

Constructor:
A special function that initializes the attributes. It may have an argument list that contains the initial values of the object's attributes. The function has the same name as the class and is automatically called when an object of the class type is created. It has no return type, not even void.

Default Arguments:
Initial values provided for one or more arguments at the tail of a function argument list. When the corresponding run-time argument is missing in a function call, the default value is used.

Free Function:
Operations that are independent of an object. A free function may have arguments and has a return value. For its action, the function takes the arguments and uses

them in a calculation and then returns the result. Member functions and free functions share the same description and prototype format, including the format for default arguments. Large libraries of free functions, such as **math.h**, are available to the C++ programmer.

Function Implementation (Definition):
Specifies the code for the function. The ";" in the function prototype is replaced by a program unit called the function body that consists of declarations and statements delimited by the braces "{" and "}".

Function Prototype:
Specifies the function name, an argument list enclosed within parentheses, and a return type. A prototype often includes a comment that explains the action of the function.

Information Hiding:
Placing data members in the private section of a class and operations in the public section. This avoids inadvertent modification of attributes. Access to the private data members is typically done using "get" and "set" member functions.

Member of a Class:
An attribute or operation of a class.

Program Design:
The organizational structure that a program uses. In pure object-oriented program design, all data and operations are designed as components of objects. The operations including the main program are implemented as member functions. With structured analysis, the data and the operations are separated. Operations are independent of an object and are performed by free functions that implement a hierarchy of tasks. C++ allows a programmer to use both design strategies.

Return Statement:
Causes exit from a function. Its form includes an expression when a non-void return type is specified. C++ permits the programmer to omit the return statement when the return type is void. In this case, an exit occurs after executing the last statement in a function body.

UML Representation:
A graphical design tool that can be used to describe a class. The class name appears in the first compartment; the attributes are placed in the second compartment; and the third compartment contains the member functions. The tool places the data type after the object name for the attributes and the formal function argument declarations. The return type of an operation follows the argument list.

REVIEW EXERCISES

1. What is a function prototype?

2. (a) The free function `append()` takes as arguments the String object `str` and the character `ch`. It appends `ch` to the end of the String and returns the modified String. Give the function prototype for "f".

   (b) Declare the String `str` having value "WOW." Fill in the missing part of the cout statement that uses `append()` and produces the output "WOW!."

   ```
   cout << _____ << endl;
   ```

3. Use the StudentAccount class in the following sequence of statements.

   (a) The program inputs a positive value into the real number object startBalance. In the missing statement, declare the StudentAccount object, studentGS, with ID "56-5345," name "Sanders,George" and startBalance as the constructor arguments.

```
        cin >> startBalance;
        _____              // declare object studentGS
```

(b) Assume the balance for studentGS is positive. Fill in statements that withdraw 20 percent of the balance.

```
    withdrawAmount = _____   // determine amount to withdraw
    _____                 // deduct funds from account
```

4. The object type, GasPump, handles pricing for the purchase of gas. The data member, pricePerGallon is a double and stores the cost for one gallon of gas. This value is initialized by the constructor. The operation `pumpGas()` takes the number of gallons pumped as argument of type double and returns the total cost of the purchase.
   (a) Give a description for the class, listing the attributes and the function prototypes.
   (b) From (a), give the UML graphical representation of the class.
   (c) From (a) and (b), give a C++ declaration for the class GasPump.
   (d) Declare a GasPump object, gasBill, that sets the cost of gas at $1.35 per gallon.
   (e) Using gasBill, write a "cout statement" that outputs the cost of purchasing 18 gallons.

5. The following is a UML graphical representation for a class:

ReviewCL
value: int
ReviewCL (v: int =0) getValue ( ): int setValue (v: int): void add (obj: ReviewCL): ReviewCL

Give the class declaration for ReviewCL.

6. Indicate any syntax errors in each of the function prototypes. Revise the syntax to remove the errors.
   (a) `int g(int a, double b = 2.8, double c);`
   (b) `void f(int a, b, c);`
   (c) `g(a:int, b:int = 3, c:int = 0): int;`
   (d) `g(int a, int b);`

7. Identify syntax errors in the C++ class declarations. There may be several in each example.

   (a)
   ```
   class DemoCL
   {
       private
          int t;
       public
          DemoCL(initValue : int);
   }
   ```

   (b)
   ```
   class DemoCL
   {
       private:
          int p, q;
          void DemoCL(int n, m)
   };
   ```

8. (a) Give the prototype for the free function f() that takes a real number x and an integer n and returns the product n * x.

(b) Give the implementation for f().

9. What is the value of the mathematical operations?
(a) pow(5,3)   (b) ceil(8.2)   (c) floor(−7.8)
(d) Give values for x and y such that $z = pow(x,y)$ would have the same value as $z = \sqrt{27}$

10. How does the programmer create and close the drawing window when using the RectShape and CircleShape classes?

Answers to Review Exercises

1. A function prototype is the C++ declaration that specifies the name, arguments and return type of a function. The prototype ends with a semicolon. It is appropriate to include a comment describing the process executed by the function.

2. (a) `// return the string with ch appended to the end of str`
`   String append(String str, char ch);`
(b) `String str = "WOW";`
`   cout << append(str,'!') << endl;`

3. (a) `StudentAccount studentGS("56-5345","Sanders,George",`
`                               startBalance);`
(b) `withdrawAmount = studentGS.getBalance() * 0.20;`
`   studentGS.charge(withdrawAmount);`

4. (a)

DESCRIPTION: GasPump CLASS ▬▬▬▬▬▬

A GasPump object determines the cost of pumping gas.

Attributes:
   double pricePerGallon; // price per gallon of gasoline
Operations:
   GasPump Initialize pricePerGallon
               GasPump(double cost);
   pumpGas Compute cost of pumping gas (pricePerGallon * gallons) and return the result.
               double pumpGas(double gallons);

(b)

GasPump
🔒 pricePerGallon: double
◇ GasPump (cost: double) ◇ pumpGas (gallons: double): double

(c)
```
class GasPump
{
    private:
        double pricePerGallon;
    public:
        GasPump(double cost);
        double pumpGas(double gallons);
};
```

(d)
```
GasPump gasBill(1.35);
```

(e)
```
cout << gasBill.pumpGas(18) << endl;
```

5.
```
class ReviewCL
{
    private:
        int value;
    public:
        ReviewCL(int v = 0);
        int getValue();
        void setValue(int v);
        ReviewCL add(ReviewCL obj);
};
```

6. (a) c must be given a default value also or the default argument must be last one.

```
int g(int a, double b = 2.8, double c = 0.0);
```

or

```
int g(int a, double c, double b = 2.8);
```

(b) The type must precede each argument.

```
void f(int a, int b, int c);
```

(c) UML is a generic notation and does not apply to C++.

```
int g(int a, int b = 3, int c = 0);
```

(d) A function must have a return type or a default of `int` is assumed. You should never accept this default. Always specify `int` if the function does return an `int` and void if there is no return value.

```
void g(int a, int b);
```

7. (a)
```
class DemoCL
{
    private:                    // add colon:
        int t;
    public:                     // add colon:
        DemoCL(int initValue);  // invalid argument
};                              // add;
```

(b)
```
class DemoCL
{
    private:
        int p, q;
    public:                      // constructor in public section
        DemoCL(int n, int m);    // invalid form for C++ argument
};                               // no return value for
                                 // constructor
```

8. (a) double f(double x, int n);

   (b) double f(double x, int n)
   ```
   {
       return n * x;
   }
   ```

9. (a) 125   (b) 9   (c) −8   (d) $z = pow(27,.5)$;

10. To create the drawing window, call the free function `openWindow()`. When the program is done with drawing operations, use `closeWindow()`.

    ```
    openWindow();
    ... drawing operations ...
    closeWindow();
    ```

WRITTEN EXERCISES

11. Mary Taylor resides in dormitory room number 367. Her roommate moves out and Mary decides to keep the room as a single. Declare a DormRoom object, maryT-Room, that represents Mary's initial housing situation. Using `getRoomCost()` and `setRoomCount()`, update her housing status and print the extra charge that Mary will be required to pay.

    ```
    _____                  ; declare MaryTRoom

    currentCost = _____    ; obtain current room cost
    _____                  ; update Mary's housing status
    newCost = _____        ; obtain new room cost
    cout << _____          ; output extra charge
    ```

12. Give the prototype for function `f()` that takes two integers *m* and *n* and a character `ch` as arguments and returns an integer.

13. Use the Accumlator class from Section 3.7. Determine the result of each output statement.

    ```
    #include <iostream.h>
    #include "accum.h"

    int main()
    {
        Accumulator obj;
    ```

```
        cout << obj.getTotal() << endl;          // output: _____
        obj.addValue();
        obj.addValue(3);
        obj.addValue(obj.getTotal()+3);
        cout << obj.getTotal() << endl;          // output: _____

        // build a temporary object with constructor argument 8
        Accumulator val(8);
        obj = val;
        obj.addValue();
        cout << obj.getTotal() << endl;          // output: _____
        return 0;
    }
```

14. Distinguish between the public and private sections of a class. How does the private section contribute to information hiding?

15. This exercise uses the GradeRecord class of Section 3.7.
(a) The student, Glenn Roberts, has the following grade data:

4981	100	345
studentID	units	gradepts

Declare a corresponding GradeRecord object, studentGR.
(b) Fill in the statement that determines Glenn's GPA.

```
    gpa = _____
```

(c) After completing a semester with 16 units and 60 grade points, fill in the statement that updates Glenn's grade information.

```
    _____          // update Glenn's grade records
```

(d) Output the updated grade information.

```
    _____          // output grade information
```

16. Consider the UML representation for the class Mileage. The attribute miles stores a distance measured in miles. The constructor has an argument m that initializes the atrribute miles. The operations allow a program to access distance in either miles or kilometer units. A program can use objects to convert between miles and kilometer measures.

```
┌──────────────────────────────────┐
│            Milage                 │
├──────────────────────────────────┤
│  🔒 miles: double                 │
├──────────────────────────────────┤
│  ◇ Mileage (m: double = 0)        │
│  ◇ getMiles ( ): double           │
│  ◇ getKilometers ( ): double      │
│  ◇ setMiles (m: double): void     │
│  ◇ setKilometers (k: double): void│
└──────────────────────────────────┘
```

(a) Declare the constructor, Mileage, with a function prototype.

(b) Give the function prototypes for the operations

    (i) `getKilometers()`   (ii) `setKilometers()`

(c) Determine the action of the following statements:

```
Mileage odometer(65);
cout << odometer.getKilometers() << endl;
```

(d) In the Olympics, the 1500 meter race covers a little less than a mile. Using the conversion 1000 meters = 1 kilometer, what do the following statements indicate?

```
double meterDistance = 1500;
Mileage olympicRace;

olympicRace.setKilometers(mDistance/1000);
cout << "Race is " << olympicRace.getMiles()
     << " miles" << endl;
```

(e) In track, a 200 meter and a 220 yard race are very close to the same length. Using the Mileage object mDistance, determine the number of yards in a 200 meter race. Note that 1760 yards = 1 mile.

```
Mileage mDistance;

// set mDistance to store 200/1000 = .2 km
_____;
// get number of miles in 200 meters
milesIn200m = _____;
// convert miles to yards
yardsIn200m = _____;
```

17. In the stock market, a company is listed by a symbol (e.g., "IBM"). The class Stock has attributes for the symbol, for the starting price of the stock, and for the closing price of the stock. The constructor has arguments sym and price that initializes the symbol and the starting price. The operation, change() takes the day's final price of the stock as an argument and returns the amount of change in the price for the day. For instance, if "IBM" starts at 150.00 and closes at 153.00, change()returns the value 3.00.

(a) Give the declaration for the Stock class.

(b) What is the declaration statement that creates the object IBMStock with symbol "IBM" and starting price 150.00?

(c) Complete the following statement that would output "Price change for the day is $3.00"

```
cout << _____ << _____;
```

(d) Can you recommend the addition of any "get" functions to the class? If so, add them to the declaration.

18. A company builds 4 foot high chain link fences, whose cost depends on the length of the fence and the number of gates. Each gate is 3 feet wide and costs $75. The chain link portion of the fence costs $12 per foot. To handle customers, we design the Fence class with integer attribute numberOfGates and real number attributes fenceLength and totalCost. The length of the fence includes the width of the gates. The constructor takes as arguments the total fence length and the number of gates and uses them to initialize the attributes. It is assumed that the fence is long enough to accommodate the requirred number of gates. The member function, getTotalCost(), returns the total cost of the fence.

(a) Give the prototype for the constructor.

(b) Give the prototype for the function getTotalCost().

(c) Develop a declaration for the Fence class.

(f) Create the corresponding UML.

19. An object of type CashRegister simulates handling transactions in a small business.

DESCRIPTION: CashRegister CLASS ━━━━━━━━━━━━━━

Provides an employee with tools to enter the price of an item, deducts any storewide discount that is in effect, and displays the amount owed by the customer.

Attributes:

double discountRate;   // storewide discount

double price;   // marked price of item

double discountPrice;   // reduced price of item

Operations:

CashRegister   Use storewide discount to initialize discountRate.
                CashRegister(double discount = 0.0);

enterPrice   Update the price and discountPrice attributes.
                (discountPrice = (1.0 − discountRate)*price
                void enterPrice(double itemCost);

getPrice   Return the current value of discountPrice.
                double getPrice();

billingInfo   Output billing information as indicated by the following example.

    Marked Price   40.00
    Discount: 10%
    Discount Price: 36.00
        void billingInfo();

(a) Give a declaration for the CashRegister class.

(b) A storewide discount of 40 percent is in effect. Declare a CashRegister object called coat. Then create a list of C++ statements that would execute the following tasks for the coat object.

Set the price of the coat at $125.00.

Using "cout," indicate discounted price of the coat

Output the customer's bill.

20. (a) Give the UML graphical representation for the class, DemoType, which has the following components:

Attributes: Integer objects valueA and valueB

Operations:

A constructor that has arguments *a* and *b* to initialize the attributes. The value for *b* has the default 100. The operation f() has an integer and a character argument and returns an integer value.

(b) Give the C++ class declaration for DemoType.

21. Identify syntax errors in the C++ class declarations. There may be several in each
example.

(a)
```
CL class
   private
   {
      int p, q;
   }
   public
   {
      void CL();
      setData(int a, int b):void;
   }
```

(b)
```
class CL
{
   private;
      int t;
   public;
      int CL(int initValue)
      void printCL();
};
```

22. The class DemoCL has the following data members:

Integer objects mValue, nValue, pValue

(a) Give a function prototype for the constructor that has three formal arguments,
m, n, and p. The arguments n and p have default values of 1 and 0, respectively.

(b) Give the values for mValue, nValue and pValue in each of the following objects.

DemoCL obj1(1,2,5), obj2(5,6), obj3(8);

23. Give the value of the mathematical operations:

(a) pow(2,5)   (b) ceil(−3.8)   (c) floor(7.1)

(d) Using the pow() function, give the C++ expression for the mathematical equation

$$y = (1 + x^5)^{1/4}$$

24. (a) Write a prototype for a function rem5() that takes an integer value n and returns the remainder when n is divided by 5.

(b) Give the implementation for rem5().

25. (a) Give the prototype for function fracPart() that takes a real number argument x, computes the fractional part of x and returns the result of the calculation.

(b) Give an implementation for fracpart().

(c) Write a cout statement that uses fracpart() and outputs the fractional value
.68 for the real number 7.68.

26. (a) The function linkNames() takes String objects name1 and name2 and separator character ch. It concatenates the Strings in the form <name2><ch><name1>
and returns the new String. Give the prototype for linkNames().

(b) Give an implementation for the function.

(c) Declare the Strings str1 and str2 having values "Barney" and "Betty," respectively. Fill in the following statement that uses linkNames() and produces the
output "Barney&Betty."

```
cout << _____ << endl;
```

PROGRAMMING EXERCISES

27. In the student center, the housing office maintains a special suite of three rooms
with numbers, 1–3. Input the number of students in each room and then declare
three DormRoom objects, specialA, specialB, and specialC. Compute and output

the total funds collected by the housing office for this set of rooms. Remember that `getRoomCount()` determines the number of students in a room, and `getRoomCost()` returns the cost per student for the room.

28. Use the GradeRecord class from Section 3.7. Write a program that declares these objects:

> GradeRecord studentAnn("45-2791", 49, 14), studentBob("67-5803", 50, 25);

Output the grade data for Ann and Bob. Assume Ann takes four units and gets an A (16 grade points). Update her data. Prompt the user to input units and grade points for Bob and update his GPA. Output the new grade information for each student.

29. Bruno's Italian Restaurant uses the MealBill machine to handle purchases. An adult dinner costs $9.95 per person, and the price for a child is $5.95. In the program, the costs should be declared as named constants. Create a MealBill object, brunos, with local tax of 5 percent. Write a program that inputs the number of adults and children and outputs the bill. Complete the program by reading the payment and writing the receipt.

30. A designer builds custom windows that include both stained and clear glass in various patterns. The cost for stained glass is $.75 per square inch and the cost for clear glass is $.40 per square inch. One pattern begins with a square frame whose sides are of length s. The midpoints of each side are joined to form a square that contains clear glass. The remainder of the frame contains stained glass.

Write a program that enters side s and uses it to declare a Rectangle object that represents the frame. Declare a second Rectangle object that corresponds to the clear glass. Note that each side of the interior square has length $\dfrac{s}{\sqrt{2}}$. Output the total cost of the window.

31. Write a program that uses the RectShape class to draw a nested sequence of three colored rectangles. From outer to inner, the colors are to be dark gray, white, and blue. Model the program after Application 3.3.

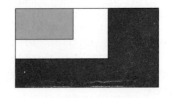

32. (a) Write a complete C++ program that declares a TextShape object and then draws the string "C++" beginning at (1,1).

(b) Modify the program to write "C++" as three separate strings (make each character a string). After drawing a character, delay two seconds and then clear the screen.

33. In mathematics, it is known that

$$x^y = e^{y*\log(x)}$$

where log is the natural logarithm of x. Write a program that inputs real values x and y. Output x^y using `pow()` and $e^{y*\log(x)}$ using the functions `log()` and `exp()` from math.h. This experimentally verifies the mathematical equality.

34. Roofing materials are sold in bundles that cover 22 square feet. Write a program that inputs the area of the roof and outputs the number of bundles that must be purchased; also, figure the amount of roofing materials left over in square feet. Use `ceil()` from math.h.

35. In the main program, declare the following String objects:

```
String algsDat = "Algorithms + Data Structures",
       programs = " Programs",
       title;
```

Using the function `linkNames()` defined in Written Exercise 3.26, the program should assign to title to the String

$$\text{Algorithms + Data Structures = Programs}$$

and output it.

36. Home owners are familiar with mortgages. Each month, a payment is made that covers the interest owed and allots a portion to debt reduction. The amount of the monthly payment is determined by the principle amount borrowed (p), the monthly interest rate (r), and the number of months for which payments are made (n). The minimum payment is determined by the following formula:

$$\text{minimumPayment} = \left(\frac{r(1 + r)^n}{(1 + r)^n - 1}\right)p$$

For instance, assume a family obtains a $100,000 mortgage with a yearly interest rate of 7.5 percent and a payment period of 25 years. The monthly interest rate is $r = .075/12 = .00625$, and the number of payments is $n = 25*12 = 300$, so the minimum monthly payment is

$$\text{minimumPayment} = \left(\frac{.00625(1 + .00625)^{300}}{(1 + .00625)^{300} - 1}\right)100000 = 738.99$$

Over the 25 years, the payments total 738.99*300 = $221,697.

(a) Develop an implementation for the free function `payment()` that computes the minimum monthly payment for a mortgage. Use `pow()` from **math.h**.

$$\text{double payment(double p, double r, int n);}$$

(b) Write a program that inputs the amount of a home loan, the yearly interest rate, and the length of the loan in years. Use `payment()` to output the monthly payment for the mortgage. The program should also output the ratio of the total of all payments to the cost of the house. Run the program three times using the example for the first run.

PROGRAMMING PROJECT

37. The following is a description for the RealNumber class.

DESCRIPTION: RealNumber CLASS ▬▬▬▬▬▬▬▬

A RealNumber object provides conversion operations for a nonnegative (≥ 0.0) real number.

Attributes:
  double realValue;   // the nonnegative real number

Operations:

RealNumber	Initializes realValue.
	RealNumber(double x = 0.0);
round	Return realValue rounded to the nearest integer.
	long round();
wholePart	Return the integer part of realValue.
	long wholePart();
fracPart	Return the fractional part of realValue.
	double fracPart();
getReal	Return realValue.
	double getReal();
setReal	Change realValue.
	void setReal(double x);

(a) Develop the UML representation for RealNumber.
(b) Give the declaration for RealNumber.
(c) You are asked to develop the implementation for the class. You will do this using a technique called in-line code that is formally discussed in Chapter 5. Modify the declaration by replacing each member function prototype by its function implementation. For example, the following is the implementation for round().

```
class RealNumber
{
    ...
    int round()
    {
        return int(x+0.5);
    }
    ...
};
```

Place the class implementation in the header file "realnum.h."

(d) Write a program that enters a real number and uses it to declare a RealNumber object, realObj. Create a series of three statements to output the rounded, whole, and fractional values of the real number. Develop a statement that doubles the value held by realObj and outputs the same data.

Chapter 4
Basic C++ Control Structures

C H A P T E R   C O N T E N T S

4-1 *ALGORITHMS AND FLOW CONTROL*
   Selection
   Looping
4-2 *LOGICAL EXPRESSIONS*
   Relational Operators
   Logical Operators
   Precedence of Arithmetic and Logical
   Operators
   Short-Circuit Evaluation
   Interpreting the OR Operation
4-3 *SELECTION STATEMENTS*
   One-way Selection using the if
   Statement
   Grouping Statements in a Block
   Two-Way Selection using the if /else
   Statement
   Multiple Selection Using Nested if/else
   The Roots of a Quadratic Equation
4-4 *THE BOOLEAN TYPE IN C++*
   Application: Checking Graduation
   Requirements
   Integers as Logical Values
4-5 *LOOP STRUCTURES*
   The while Statement
   Counter and Event-Controlled Loops
   The do/while Statement
   Loops and Numeric Palindromes
4-6 *ANIMATION WITH LOOPS*
   Jack-In-The-Box Animation
Written Exercises

U p to this point in the book, our focus has been on objects and their types as the building blocks of an application. In Chapter 2, we introduced the C++ primitive number and character types and then used them in Chapter 3 to declare programmer-defined classes. Our efforts have created a rather impressive variety of objects. The applications, however, have been relatively simple since they have used only I/O and assignment statements.

In this chapter, we begin to develop the tools of programming logic using control structures. We introduce the concept of logical expressions that evaluate to true or false. Logical expressions are the building blocks for simple selection and loop statements. These are control structures that enable us to design algorithms for more challenging and realistic applications. We include examples of such algorithms to determine a palindrome and to create graphics animations. These are reasonably challenging problems that will enable you to use many of the concepts we have developed in the book.

4-1   ALGORITHMS AND FLOW CONTROL

Recall that an algorithm is a set of statements that are designed to carry out a task. The logic of the algorithm creates a *flow of control* that specifies the order in which the computer executes the statements. For a simple algorithm, the computer executes statements one after another in the order they are written. For instance, the following four statements implement a simple algorithm that reads two numbers, computes their average, and outputs the value.

```
float    x, y, avg;                  // declaration

cout << "Enter two numbers: ";       // prompt for input
cin >> x >> y;                       // read two values
avg = (x + y)/2;                     // compute average
cout << "Average is " << avg;        // output the result
```

More interesting algorithms involve logic that alters the flow of control. In a programming language, this is most frequently accomplished by selection and looping constructs that are basic flow control structures.

Selection

Selection occurs when the flow of an algorithm encounters alternative choices. Based on a test of the condition, the program selects one action when the result is true and another action when the result is false. For example, a bank will process a check only when the customer has sufficient funds. To handle the transaction, program logic tests the condition "accountBalance ≥ check-Amount". When the condition is true, the bank deducts funds and when it is false the bank posts overdraft charges.

To illustrate the flow of logic in a program, we use a *flowchart* that is a graphical representation of program actions. A flowchart uses symbols such as rectangles, diamonds, and connecting arrows as its components. The rectangle specifies actions that the program executes, while the diamond is a decision symbol that tests a condition. Figure 4-1 is a flowchart that illustrates the flow of control in the check-cashing algorithm.

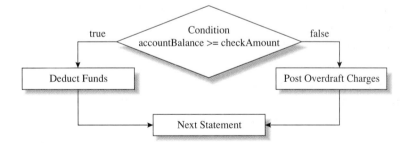

FIGURE 4-1
Flowchart for Check Cashing (two-way selection).

The bank example is a selection process in which the computer chooses between two alternative actions, depending on whether the condition is true or false. We call this *two-way selection*. In some cases, an algorithm is faced with a simple choice of doing or not doing a specific action. For instance, suppose a company agrees to pay a salesperson a 2% bonus when the monthly sales exceed 100 units. The algorithm that computes the salary must test for the number of units sold and add the bonus when the condition "unitsSold > 100" is true. The decision involves simple or *one-way selection* (Figure 4-2).

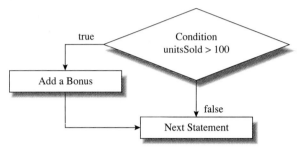

FIGURE 4-2
Flowchart for Salary Bonus (one-way selection).

One- and two-way selection are the most common selection statements. At times, an algorithm involves more than two alternatives. Such an algorithm must use *multiple selection.* For instance, a GUI application must monitor the location of the mouse click in a windowing system. When a mouse click occurs, the program performs actions that depend on the current location of the mouse. If it is in a scroll bar, the text view must be adjusted. If the click is in the title bar, the user may drag the window, and if it is in the close box, the system must shut down the window. A GUI windowing system uses multiple selection to handle mouse clicks (Figure 4-3).

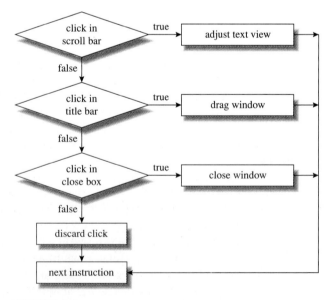

FIGURE 4-3
GUI Mouse Selection (multiple selection).

Looping

Selection is only one type of flow control structure. Many algorithms involve a set of statements that are repeated over and over again to handle a series of similar cases. For instance, a fast food restaurant may use a payroll package to generate salary information. For each employee, the net salary is based on the number of hours worked, the hourly pay rate, and the amount withheld for taxes. The following set of statements handle one employee.

```
Salary code for an employee
   cin >> ssno >> payRate >> hoursWorked;

   // earnings before taxes are withheld
   grossEarnings = payRate * hoursWorked;

   // net earnings after tax deducted
   taxesWithheld = grossEarnings * taxRate;
   netEarnings = grossEarnings - taxesWithheld;
   cout << "Employee: " << ssno << endl;
   cout << "Gross earnings: " << grossEarnings << endl;
   cout << "Taxes Withheld: " << taxesWithHeld << endl;
   cout << "Net earnings: " << netEarnings << endl;
```

Assuming that the company has 100 employees, the program would not want to duplicate the code to handle the company payroll.

```
Code for employee1:
   .  .  .  .
Code for employee12:
   .  .  .  .
Code for employee100:
   .  .  .  .
```

A more efficient solution has the program creating a *loop structure* that repeats execution of the same salary code over and over again until the payroll is generated. A loop structure directs flow of control back to previously executed statements. For instance, after computing earnings for one employee and outputting salary information, the loop structure directs flow of control back to the input statement that reads the ssno, payRate and hoursWorked for the next employee.

The process is monitored by a test condition that determines whether another employee should be processed. An integer, loopCount, maintains a count of the number of employee that have been paid. Once the condition "loopCount > numberOfEmployees" is true, the payroll is complete and the looping process terminates. Program control then continues with the next statement that follows immediately after the repeated code (Figure 4-4).

This Chapter develops the C++ syntax for selection and looping statements. Each of the constructs rely on decision logic that tests whether a condition is true or false. The analysis of these conditions is the starting point of our study.

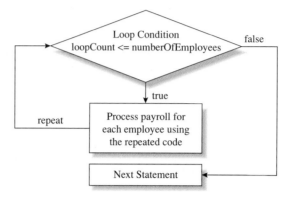

FIGURE 4-4
Salary Loop Algorithm

4-2   LOGICAL EXPRESSIONS

The C++ programming language provides *logical expressions* that have a value of *true* or of *false*. These expressions are important components of algorithms. For instance, the following are logical expressions

In a rectangle, the lengths of the two diagonals are equal (true).

The number 35 is an even integer (false).

A US president can serve three consecutive terms in office (false).

Much of the development of logical expressions owes its origins to George Boole, a nineteenth century British mathematician who authored a pioneering work on logic. The book, called *The Mathematical Analysis of Logic,* is a cornerstone in the development of digital computers. In your readings, you will see the terms "Boolean" and "logical" used interchangeably in phrases like Boolean expression, Boolean constant, and so forth.

In this chapter, we will learn a variety of ways of creating a logical expression. We will look at the literals true and false, a logical object of type bool, and more complex expressions that combine objects and constants with comparison and logical operators. For now, we start with relational operators that compare numeric values. These operators use your knowledge of arithmetic and provide the most common form of logical expressions.

Relational Operators

Mathematics defines a set of relational operators such as $<$ and $\geq$ that compare numeric values. In each case, the operation creates a logical expression since it evaluates to true or false. For instance, assume a $= 3$ and m $= 9$

```
a < 5  is true       // comparison: 3 < 5
m * 5 > 50 is false  // comparison: 9 * 5 = 45 > 50
```

> **Definition** A relational operator is an operator that compares two values. C++ defines the six relational operators ==, !=, <, <=, >, >= (Table 4.1). A *relational expression* is an expression that combines operands with a *relational operator*. If the relationship is valid, the expression is true; if not, the expression is false.

TABLE 4-1 Relational Operators.

int age = 23, value = -5, year = 1999;			
C++ Operator	Meaning	Relational Expression	Value
==	equal to	(year + 1) == 2000	true
!=	not equal to	value != (3 - 8)	false
<	less than	age < 21	false
<=	less than or equal	value <= 0	true
>	greater than	(23/5) > 4	false
>=	greater than or equal	year >= 1776	true

EXAMPLE 4.1

1. A person under the age of 18 is called a minor. This classification is determined by the relational expression that compares the age of a person with 18.

```
age < 18     // check if the person is a minor
```

For age = 14, the expression is true and the person is a minor; for age = 32, the expression is false and the person is not a minor.

2. In an interactive dialog, the program asks the user to respond "Yes" or "No" by entering the character 'Y' or 'N'.

```
cout << "Enter a 'Y' or 'N': ";
cin  >> response;
```

The following "==" comparison checks for the "Yes" response.

```
response == 'Y'
```

The "!=" comparison looks for any response other than 'Y'

```
response != 'Y'  // response interpreted as "No"
```

3. An integer n is even, provided it is divisible by 2. This fact is determined by checking whether the remainder (n % 2) is equal to 0.

```
n % 2 == 0    // expression is true when n is even
```
■

In arithmetic, the "=" operator stands for logical equality. For instance

$$5 * 3 = 20 - 5 \qquad 5 \% 3 = 2 \qquad 100/4 = 25$$

Programming
Note

In C++, the "=" operator is the assignment operator and involves copying the value of an expression into an object in memory. The logical equality operator is "==". Be careful, these are quite separate operations.

a = 5;   (assigns the value 5 to a)

a == 5   (asks the question: does a have the value 5?)

Logical Operators

Logical expressions can be used as operands with the operators "(AND)," (OR), and !(NOT) to produce more complex logical expressions. Like the symbols + and − for addition and subtraction, C++ defines symbols to represent the logical operations.

Operator && (AND)

An expression with the binary && operator is true only if both operands are true; otherwise it is false.

Example: An integer is in the range 10 to 99 if it greater than or equal to 10 and less than 100. The object value is a two-digit number provided both conditions are true in an expression that uses the logical && (AND) operator.

```
(value >= 10) && (value < 100)
```

Operator || (OR)

An expression with the binary || operator is true if either of the operands is true; otherwise it is false.

Example: A theater gives half price admission to youngsters under 12 years of age and to senior citizens (age >= 65). A movie-goer gets a reduced admission provided one of the conditions is true in an expression that uses the logical || (OR) operator.

```
(age < 12) || (age >= 65)
```

Operator ! (NOT)

An expression with the unary ! operator is true if the operand is false and is false if the operand is true.

Example: The ! operator tests whether a logical expression is false. The following expression is true for all years other than 2000.

```
!(year == 2000)
```

Table 4-2 describes the operators and their actions. The symbols p and q represent logical expressions that are true or false. The four rows indicate all possible alternatives when combining the two values.

TABLE 4-2 C++ Logical Operators

p	*q*	*p && q (AND)*	*p ‖ q (OR)*	*!p (NOT)*
true	true	true	true	false
true	false	false	true	—
false	true	false	true	true
false	false	false	false	—

EXAMPLE 4.2

1. The logical expressions test the character ch
   Use && to determine if ch is a digit ('0', '1', '2', . . . , '9')

   ```
   (ch >= '0') && (ch <= '9')
   ```

   Use ‖ to determine if ch is an uppercase T or a lowercase t

   ```
   (ch == 'T') || (ch == 't')
   ```

   Use ! and ‖ to test whether ch is not a vowel

   ```
   !( (ch == 'a')||(ch == 'e')||(ch == 'i')
            ||(ch == 'o')||( ch == 'u'))
   ```

2. An insurance company gives school-age drivers a "good driver" discount if they have not had a accident and their gpa is 3.0 or above. A test for this discount uses the && operator.

   ```
   (numberOfAccidents == 0) && (gpa >= 3.0)
   ```

3. The NCAA disqualifies student-athletes from competition if their gpa falls below 2.0 or they do not make progress toward graduation (average 24 units per year). A test for disqualification uses the ‖ operator.

   ```
   (gpa < 2.0) || (totalUnits/yearsInSchool < 24)   ■
   ```

1. Assume that x, y, and rainfall are real number objects. Develop logical expressions for

   "x is at least three times larger than y"
   "it never rains more than 30 inches per year"

2. Create a logical expression that describes the situation. Use relational and logical operators and the real number objects x and y.

   (a) x lies strictly between 9.2 and 14 (x cannot equal 9.2 or 14)
   (b) both x and y are negative
   (c) the difference between x and y is greater than 15.

3. Select all values for s = −2, 0, 2, 4, or 6 that give the logical expression the specified value.

   (a) !(s-4 <= 0) has value false
   (b) s != 2 && s != 4 has value true

*Exploring
Concepts*

Precedence of Arithmetic and Logical Operators

The relational, logical, and arithmetic operators follow rules of precedence that indicate the order in which operations are performed. In general, arithmetic operators have the highest precedence, followed by the relational operators, and finally the logical operators. The exception is the unary operator NOT that binds immediately to the operand and is performed first. Table 4-3 gives the order of precedence for the arithmetic and logical operators. The precedence of all C++ operators is given in Appendix C.

Using the table, we can trace the order of operations for some logical expressions.

```
2 + 3 < 4
    (operation 1)   addition        // 2 + 3 is 5
    (operation 2)   relational <    // 5 < 4 is false

!(8 < 20) || 7 > 25
    (operation 1)   relational <    // 8 < 20 is true.
    (operation 2)   logical !       // !true is false
    (operation 3)   relational >    // 7 > 25 is false
    (operation 4)   logical ||      // false || false is false
```

Short-Circuit Evaluation

C++ uses a highly efficient algorithm to determine the value of a logical expression. To understand this algorithm, let's look at some examples.

> (a) a == b || a > 30   (b) a < 5 && b % 2 == 0

With expression (a), the "||" operator has relational expressions "a == b" and "a > 30" as operands. The result of the || operation is true if either operand is true. With *short-cut evaluation,* the computer evaluates the operands from left to right and stops as soon as the logical value of the entire expression is known. If the left-hand operand "a == b" is true, the || expression is true and the right-hand operand "a > 30" is not evaluated. In (b), the "&&" operator is false if either of the operands is false. Using short-cut evaluation, the computer evaluates the left-hand operand "a < 5" and stops if its result is false. In this case, the && expression is false and the right-hand operand "b % 2 == 0" is not evaluated.

TABLE 4-3 Precedence Levels from high to low

Operator	Operations
! −	logical NOT and urinary minus
* / %	multiplication and division
+ −	addition and subtraction
< <= > >=	logical comparison
== !=	logical equals and not-equals
&&	logical AND
||	logical OR

> **Definition** The process that evaluates the operands of a logical expression in the order left to right and stops as soon as the value of the expression can be determined is called *short-circuit evaluation.*

```
// 5 > 3 is true; hence the || expression is true
5 > 3 || 3 == 8

// 8/3 == 1 is false; hence the && expression is false
8/3 == 1 && 2 == 2

// if x is 0, x != 0.0 is false, '20/x < 1' is not evaluated
x != 0.0 && 20/x < 1
```

Interpreting the OR Operation

When you tell someone you are going to dinner OR going to a movie, the ordinary language meaning of OR implies that you are going to either dinner or to a movie but not both. This is the *"exclusive-OR"* interpretation of the word OR that is familiar in ordinary language. In contrast, if the || operator were used for the OR

```
going to dinner || going to a movie
```

the statement would be true if you go to dinner, go to a movie or do both. This is the *"inclusive-or"* interpretation of OR.

C++ does not have a logical exclusive-or operator. If the operation is required, a programmer must combine the operators &&, || and !. Assume p and q are logical expressions. The exclusive-or of p and q is given by

```
(p && !q) || (q && !p)
```

To understand the logic, consider the two operands. The expression (p && !q) is true only when p is true and q is false. Likewise, the expression (!p && q) is true only when p is false and q is true. Since one of the operands must be true for an || expression to be true, the exclusive-or expression is true only when p and q have different logical values.

4-3 SELECTION STATEMENTS

Now that we have introduced logical expressions, we can use them to develop the C++ selection control structures. We start with the C++ *if statement* that implements one-way selection.

One-way Selection Using the if Statement

The C++ if statement includes a condition that is given as a logical expression and statements that are executed when the condition is true. The notation, Statement$_T$, represents a set of one or more statements that is executed when the condition is true.

SYNTAX ▬▬▬▬▬▬▬▬▬▬▬▬▬▬▬▬▬▬▬▬▬▬▬▬▬▬▬

The if Statement for Simple Selection

Form: if (condition)

```
Statement_T;      // execute if condition true
```

Action: The condition is first tested. If the result is true, Statement_T is executed; otherwise, program control passes to the next statement. The condition is given as a logical expression and must be included in parentheses.

Example: When unitsSold exceeds 100 units, the salesperson gets a 2% bonus added to the salesTotal.

```
int unitsSold;
double salesTotal;          // earnings from sales

if (unitsSold > 100)
    salesTotal *= 1.02;     // add 2% bonus
```

If ch is an uppercase letter, convert it to lowercase (add 32).

```
char ch;

if (ch >= 'A' && ch <= 'Z')
    ch += 32;
```

Figure 4-5 is a flowchart for the simple if statement. Program control passes to Statement_T when the condition is true. Otherwise, control continues with the "next statement" that is the first statement following the if statement.

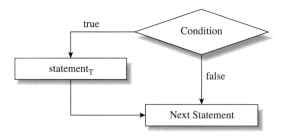

FIGURE 4-5
Flow Diagram for the if Statement.

Grouping Statements in a Block

Like most programming languages, C++ collects a variety of constructs under the general heading of "statement". *Simple statements* implement input/output, function calls, and assignment operations. *Declaration statements* create and initialize objects. Each type of statement is terminated by a semicolon. With selection and looping constructs, we need to define a *block statement* that consists of zero or more statements enclosed in braces { and }. A block sets aside a sequence of statements that are executed as a unit. There is no semicolon after a block since the "}" terminates the construct.

SYNTAX ▬▬▬▬▬▬▬▬▬▬▬▬▬▬▬▬▬▬▬▬▬▬▬▬▬▬▬▬▬▬▬▬▬▬▬

Block Statement

Form:
```
{
    statement₁
    statement₂
    .   .   .   .
    statementₙ
}
```

Action: The statements are executed as a group in the order $statement_1, \ldots,$ $statement_n$.

Example:
```
if (sum > 100)
{
    cout << sum << endl;  // block with 2 simple
                          // statements
    sum = 0;
}
```

While technically a single statement can be placed in a block, this is not common programming practice. For example, you would not see a statement such as the following in a typical C++ program.

```
if (i <= 5)
{
    sum += i;
}
```

A block may contain declarations. Note that when we defined free functions in Chapter 3, the body of the function was a block, perhaps containing declarations.

```
// function returns totalCost with tax included
// the function body is a block with 3 statements
double totalCost(double cost, double taxRate)
{
    double tax;               // declaration statement

    tax = cost * taxRate;     // 2 simple statements
    return cost + tax;
}
```

Since a block is a set of statements that is treated as a single unit, we want to make careful use of indenting to increase program readability. By indenting the statements several spaces, they become organized as sub-statements within the larger block.

In this book, we set off a block in an if statement by placing the brackets directly below the word "if."

Programming Note

```
if (condition)
{
    statement;   // indented statement
    . . .
}                    // line up ending "}" under the "{"
```

Some programmers use a different format that places the left bracket after the condition in the if statement.

```
if (condition) {
    statement;      // indented statement
    . . .
}                      // bracket to indicate end of block
```

EXAMPLE 4.3

```
Assume int a, b = 0, c = 0;

   cin >> a;      // input a value for int a

   if (a < 10)    // block with two statements
   {
      b = a * 2;
      c = a - 20;
   }

   Input:  5
      The condition 5 < 10 is true. Execute the block.
      Result: b = 10, c = -15

   Input:  30
      The condition 30 < 10 is false. Skip the block
      Result: b = 0, c = 0  ■
```

Two-Way Selection Using the if/else Statement

In many algorithms, we must test a condition and then choose between alternative actions depending on whether the result of the test is true or false. In C++, this control structure is implemented by the if/else statement, whose flowchart is given in Figure 4-6. For the definition of the if/else statement, the notation Statement$_T$ and Statement$_F$ indicate the choice of statements that will execute depending on the value of the condition.

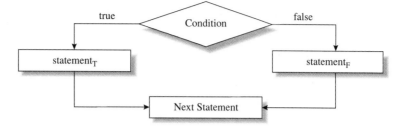

FIGURE 4-6
Flow Diagram for the if/else Statement.

S Y N T A X

The if/else Statement for Two-Way Selection

Form:
```
if (condition)
    Statement_T;   // execute when condition is true
else
    Statement_F    // execute when condition is false
```

Action: The condition is tested. If the result is true, Statement_T is executed and program control passes to the next statement after the if/else. If the condition is false, Statement_F is executed. The condition is given as a logical expression and must be included in parentheses.

Example: For integer n, the if statement indicates whether n is even or odd.

```
if (n % 2 == 0)
    cout << n << " is even" << endl;
else
    cout << n << " is odd" << endl;
```

The absolute value of a real number is its magnitude. For instance, the absolute value of 2 is 2 while the absolute value of −5 is 5. The if/else statement determines the absolute value of x.

```
if (x >= 0)
    abs = x;      // x is positive
else
    abs = -x;     // x is negative
```

E X A M P L E   4 . 4

1. Input a student's grade on a test. Output "Pass" or "Fail" using the selection criteria that a pass is a grade of 70 or higher.

```
cin >> score;
if (score >= 70.0)
    cout << "PASS" << endl;
else
    cout << "FAIL" << endl;
```

2. A company contributes to an employee retirement fund based on total earnings. For the first $50,000, the company contributes 5% and then reduces the amount to 3% for earnings above $50,000. Given the total salary of an employee, an if/else statement computes the amount of money contributed to the retirement fund.

```
if (earnings <= 50000)
   contribution = earnings * 0.05;
else
   // contribute $2500 for the first $50000 of earnings
   contribution = 2500 + (earnings - 50000) * 0.03.   ■
```

PROGRAM 4.1

Hourly workers are paid time and a half for overtime (work beyond 40 hours). Given the total number of hours worked and the hourly pay rate, the program uses an if/else statement to computes the number of regular hours and the number of overtime hours that are worked. These values are used to output the weekly salary for the worker.

```
#include <iostream.h>

#include "textlib.h"

int main()
{
   double hoursWorked, regularHours, overtimeHours;
   double payRate, salary;

   cout << "Enter hours worked and hourly pay rate: ";
   cin >> hoursWorked >> payRate;

   // condition checks for no overtime
   if (hoursWorked <= 40)
   {
      // all hours are regular with no overtime hours
      regularHours = hoursWorked;
      overtimeHours = 0;
   }
   else
   {
      // worked beyond 40 hours; some overtime occurs
      regularHours = 40;
      overtimeHours = hoursWorked - 40;
   }

   // compute salary with time and a half for overtime
   salary = regularHours*payRate + 1.5*overtimeHours*payRate;
   cout << "Working " << hoursWorked << " hours at $"
        << setreal(1,2) << payRate << " per hour, the "
        << "salary is $" << setreal(1,2) << salary << endl;

   return 0;
}
```

2. The example handles a student account transaction. If the transaction amount is negative, post a charge to the account; otherwise, credit the account.

```
StudentAccount fred("45-3357", "Flintstone, Fred",-200.0);
double transactionAmount;

cin >> transactionAmount;
if (transactionAmount < 0)
    fred.charge (-transactionAmount);
else
    fred.payment (transactionAmount);
```

Multiple Selection Using Nested if/else

A program often uses an algorithm that makes decisions involving more than two alternatives. For instance, an instructor uses a student's final average to select a letter grade. In the following table, students with an average of 70 and above pass with an A, B, or C grade. An average below 70 results in a failing (F) grade.

Final Average	Grade
score >= 90	A
80 <= score < 90	B
70 <= score < 80	C
score < 70	F

Unlike a PASS/FAIL grade, a single if/else statement cannot assign all letter grades since more than two alternatives are available. If the grade is not an A, we must still select from among the choices B, C, and F. After determining that it is not a B, the choice of C, or F remains. The algorithm requires a series of tests that allow the computer to select from a list of alternative grades. To highlight this *multiple selection,* we combine the "else" and following "if" condition on a single line. The resulting statement is called the *"else if"* construct.

```
if (score >= 90)        // if condition: score in A range
    grade = 'A';
else if (score >= 80)   // else if condition: score in B range
    grade = 'B';
else if (score >= 70)   // else if condition: score in C range
    grade = 'C';
else                    // final else
    grade = 'F';
```

SYNTAX ━━━━━━━━━━━━━━━

Nested if/else Statements for Multiple Selection

```
Form:     if (condition₁)
              statement₁
          else if (condition₂)
              statement₂
```

```
          else if (condition₃)
              statement₃
              . . .
          else
              statementₙ
```

Action: Select among the alternatives $condition_1$, $condition_2$, $condition_3$, ..., $condition_n$. If $condition_1$ is true, execute $statement_1$. Otherwise, if $condition_2$ is true, execute $statement_2$.... Otherwise, if $condition_n$ is true, execute $statement_n$. Once a statement is executed, program control passes to the next statement after the alternative conditions. Note that each succeeding if-statement represents an alternative selection for the previous if-statement.

Example: The integer n can be strictly positive(> 0), zero($== 0$), or negative(< 0).

```
          if (n < 0)
              cout << n << " is negative";
          else if (n == 0)
              cout << n << " is zero";
          else
              cout << n << " is strictly positive";
```

EXAMPLE 4.5

1. Nested if statements allow selection from among a series of options. In many cases each option involves testing a range of values. Ranges within the ASCII character set serve as a good example. A character ch can be alphabetic ('A' to 'Z', 'a' to 'z'), numeric ('0' to '9'), whitespace (' ', '\t', '\n'), or other type. Nested if statements identify the character's type.

```
if (ch >= 'a' && ch <= 'z' || ch >= 'A' && ch <= 'Z')
    cout << "alphabetic" << endl;
else if (ch >= '0' && ch <= '9')
    cout << "numeric" << endl;
else if (ch == ' ' || ch == '\t' || ch == '\n')
    cout << "white space" << endl;
else
    cout << "other" << endl;
```

2. Basketball allows a player to score from 1 to 3 points, depending upon the situation and the length of the shot.

```
int score;

if (score == 3)
    cout << "3-pointer";
else if(score == 2)
    cout << "field goal";
else if(score == 1)
    cout << "free throw";          ■
```

The Roots of a Quadratic Equation

In mathematics, a *quadratic equation* has the form $ax^2 + bx + c = 0$ where $a \neq 0$, b, and c are real number coefficients and x is a variable. A *root* of the equation is a value r, such that $ar^2 + br + c = 0$. Each quadratic equation has exactly two roots that are given by the quadratic formula.

$$\text{root1} = \frac{-b + \sqrt{b^2 - 4ac}}{2a} \qquad \text{root2} = \frac{-b - \sqrt{b^2 - 4ac}}{2a}$$

The expression $b^2 - 4ac$ is called the *discriminant* and distinguishes the different types of roots for the equation.

> *Case 1:* discriminant < 0 : two complex roots
>
> Example: $x^2 + 2x + 4 = 0$
>
> discriminant $= 2^2 - 4 * 1 * 4 = -12$
>
> *Case 2:* discriminant $== 0$: two equal roots
>
> $$\text{root1} = \text{root2} = \frac{-b}{2a}$$
>
> Example: $x^2 + 2x + 1 = 0$
>
> discriminant $= 2^2 - 4 * 1 * 1 = 0$
>
> root1 $= -1$, root2 $= -1$
>
> *Case 3:* discriminant > 0 : two distinct real roots
>
> Example: $x^2 - x - 6 = 0$
>
> discriminant $= (-1)^2 - 4 * 1 * (-6) = 25$
>
> $$\text{root1} = \frac{1 + \sqrt{(-1)^2 - 4(1)(-6)}}{2(1)} = 3,$$
>
> $$\text{root2} = \frac{1 - \sqrt{(-1)^2 - 4(1)(-6)}}{2(1)} = -2$$

APPLICATION 4-1 FINDING THE ROOTS OF A QUADRATIC EQUATION

The program implements the algorithm for computing the roots of a quadratic equation. An input prompt asks the user to enter the coefficients a $\neq$ 0, b, and c. The discriminant is evaluated as a free function:

```
// function computes the discriminant for a quadratic equation
double discriminant(double a, double b, double c)
{
    return b*b - 4*a*c;
}
```

The program outputs the roots of the quadratic equation or indicates that they are complex numbers.

```cpp
#include <iostream.h>
#include <stdlib.h>      // for exit()
#include <math.h>        // for sqrt()

// compute the discriminant for the quadratic equation
// a*x*x + bx + c = 0
double discriminant(double a, double b, double c);

int main()
{
    double a, b, c;        // coefficients
    double root1, root2;   // the two roots
    double d;              // use to determine root structure

    cout << "Enter the coefficients for the polynomial: ";
    cin >> a >> b >> c;

    d = discriminant(a,b,c);

    // handle three cases with discriminant < 0, == 0, and > 0
    if (d < 0)
    {
        cout << "Discriminant = " << d << endl
             << "Equation has only complex roots" << endl;
    }
    else if (d == 0)
    {
        root1 = -b/(2 * a);
        cout << "Discriminant = " << d << endl
             << "Equation has two equal roots x = " << root1
             << endl;
    }
    else
    {
        root1 = (-b + sqrt(d))/(2 * a);
        root2 = (-b - sqrt(d))/(2 * a);
        cout << "Discriminant = " << d << endl
             << "Two roots are x = " << root1 << " and x = "
             << root2 << endl;
    }

    return 0;
}
/* implementation of discrimant() is given in the application
discussion */
```

Run 1:

Enter the coefficients for the polynomial: 1 -6 9

```
Discriminant = 0
Equation has two equal roots x = 3

Run 2:

Enter the coefficients for the polynomial: 6 -48 90
Discriminant = 144
Two roots are x = 5 and x = 3

Run 3:

Enter the coefficients for the polynomial: 4 1 8
Discriminant = -127
Equation has only complex roots
```

4-4 THE BOOLEAN TYPE IN C++

Up to this point, we have dealt with the Boolean expressions that are built using relational and logical operators. We now define a Boolean object whose value is either *true* or *false*. For these objects, C++ defines the logical type *bool*. In applications, objects may be declared with the bool type and given initial values.

```
bool  logicalObj = true;
bool  isSeniorCitizen;
```

To see how a bool object can be used in a calculation, consider a video store that gives a free movie to a customer who has had an account for at least three months and has rented at least 20 movies.

```
int monthsAsMember, totalMovies;
bool freeMovie;

// assign logical expression to the bool object
freeMovie = (monthsAsMember >= 3) && (totalMovies >= 20);
```

A bool object can be part of a condition within a selection statement.

```
// boolean is true when weather is severe
extremeTemperature = temp > 120 || temp < -20;
// cancel game is weather is severe
if (extremeTemperature)
   cout << "Cancel the game";
```

EXAMPLE 4.6 ▬▬▬▬▬▬▬▬▬▬▬

Like numbers and characters, bool objects may be used as arguments and return values in functions.

1. The function, inRange(), takes real values a, b, and x and determines whether x lies in the interval between a and b.

```
bool inRange(double a, double b, double x);// prototype
                 . . .
bool inRange(double a, double b, double x) // implementation
{
    return x >= a && x <= b;
}
```

2. The function, price(), takes the cost of an item and the bool object isTaxable. The return value gives the price after adding a tax of 5% when appropriate.

```
double price(double cost, bool isTaxable); // prototype
                 . . .
double price(double cost, bool isTaxable)  // implementation
{
    if (isTaxable)
        return cost * 1.05;
    else
        return cost;
}
```

3. The Boolean expression that evaluates the exclusive-or of two logical values is included in the free function eor() that takes two bool objects as arguments and returns a bool value

```
bool eor(bool p, bool q)
{
    return (p && !q) || (q && !p);
}  ■
```

1. Declare bool objects p, q, and r and give them initial values.

```
bool p = true, q = false, r = false;
```

   What is the logical value for the expression

```
(p || !q) && (!p || q).
```

2. What logical values for bool objects p and q would make
   (a) `p && !q` false
   (b) `p || (p != q)` true

*Exploring
Concepts*

3. Are the following logical expressions equivalent? If not, assign the values true or false to the object so that you can show the expressions are not equivalent.
   (a) `p != q` `!(p && q)`
   (b) `p != q` `(p || q) && !(p && q)`

4. What is the value of the bool object bexp after each assignment statement?

```
bexp = false != true;
bexp = !false;
```

Application: Checking Graduation Requirements

To graduate, the university requires that a student have a gpa of at least 2.0 and no outstanding bills at the finance office. To check on the graduation status of a student, we declare a free function, validGraduate(), that takes a Student-Account object and a GradeRecord object as arguments and returns a bool value that indicates whether a student is eligible to graduate. In the function, the bool object eligibleToGraduate maintains the graduation status of the student as the gpa and balance conditions are tested. Initially, eligibleToGraduate is set to true and becomes false only when a graduation condition fails.

```
// verify student has at least a 2.0 GPA and no balance due
// return value indicates whether student may graduate
bool validGraduate(GradeRecord sGrade,StudentAccount sAcct)
{
    bool eligibleToGraduate = true;

    // check the gpa
    if (sGrade.gpa() < 2.0)
    {
        cout << "GPA below 2.0 requirement" << endl;
        eligibleToGraduate = false;
    }

    // check account balance
    if (sAcct.getBalance() < 0.0)
    {
        cout << "Student must pay off the balance owed" << endl;
        eligibleToGraduate = false;
    }
    return eligibleToGraduate;
}
```

APPLICATION 4-2 MEETING GRADUATION REQUIREMENTS

The application uses the function validGraduate() to look at the graduation status for student Bob Lee. The GradeRecord object studentRec contains grade information and the StudentAccount object studentAcct contains account balance information. The function validGraduate() is first called during Bob Lee's final semester to access his graduation status. It indicates that he currently fails both the gpa and account balance criteria.

```
// student gpa = 1.96
GradeRecord studentRec("35-8264",100,216);

// student owes $80.00
StudentAccount studentAcct("35-8264","Lee,Bob",-80.00);
```

At the end of the semester, the grade record is updated by the registrar who adds the last semester of academic work (14 units, 36 grade points) using the

GradeRecord member function updateGradeInfo(). The StudentAccount member function getBalance() specifies the amount of money that Bob Lee still owes. The finance office receives payment for this amount and credits the account using the member function payment(). The program concludes by displaying the final grade and account information using the member functions write-GradeInfo() and writeAccount() and then makes a second call to the free function validGraduate() to verify that Bob will graduate.

```cpp
#include <iostream.h>

#include "studacct.h"    // StudentAccount class
#include "graderec.h"    // GradeRecord class
#include "textlib.h"     // access setreal()

// verify student has at least a 2.0 GPA and no balance due
// return value indicates whether student may graduate
bool validGraduate(GradeRecord sGrade,StudentAccount sAcct);

int main()
{
    // student is down 4 grade points
    GradeRecord studentRec("35-8264",110,216);

    // student owes $80.00
    StudentAccount studentAcct("35-8264","Bob Lee",-80.00);

    bool willGraduate;
    double finalPayment;

    cout << "Preliminary assessment" << endl;
    willGraduate = validGraduate(studentRec, studentAcct);
    if (willGraduate == true)
        cout << endl << "Student is on track for graduation";
    else
        cout << endl << "Student has deficiencies";
    cout << endl;

    // update registrar's data with last semester grades
    cout << "Add last semester grades: 14 units, 36 gradepts"
         << endl;
    studentRec.updateGradeInfo(14,36);

    // pay off balance of the account
    if (studentAcct.getBalance() < 0)
    {
        finalPayment = -studentAcct.getBalance();
        cout << "Student makes payment of $" << setreal(1,2)
             << finalPayment << endl;
        studentAcct.payment(finalPayment);
        cout << endl;
    }
```

```
    // output a summary of grade and financial data
    cout << "Final information from Registrar" << endl;
    studentRec.writeGradeInfo();
    cout << endl;

    cout << "Final information from Finance Office" << endl;
    studentAcct.writeAccount();
    cout << endl;

    // output records and final status
    willGraduate = validGraduate(studentRec, studentAcct);
    if (willGraduate == true)
        cout << "The student will graduate" << endl;

    return 0;
}
/* implementation of validGraduate() is given in the program
discussion.*/
```

```
Run:

Preliminary assessment
GPA below 2.0 requirement
Student must pay off the balance owed

Student has deficiencies
Add last semester grades: 14 units, 36 gradepts
Student makes payment of $80.00

Final information from Registrar
Student:   35-8264   Units:   124   GradePts: 252 GPA: 2.03
Final information from Finance Office
ID:        35-8264
Name:      Bob Lee
Balance:   $0.00

The student will graduate
```

Integers As Logical Values

The C programming language does not have the bool type. It associates logical values with numeric values. Each C numeric expression has the logical value *true* when the value of the expression is non-zero (value != 0) and *false* when the value of the expression is zero (value == 0). For instance, the following numeric expressions have a logical value:

35 % 7 is false, since the value of the expression is 0

5.6 is true, since the value of the literal is not 0

To maintain its historical roots in C, the C++ language allows a programmer to use the int type for logical objects and expressions. While any non-zero numeric expression has a logical value of true, programmers customarily use 0 for false and 1 for true. By language definition, relational and logical operators return the values 0 for false and 1 for true.

```
int honorStudent = 1;          // value 1 represents true
int isMinor = age < 16;        // isMinor has value 0 or 1

// divisibleBy5 has value 0 when n is divisible by 5
int divisibleBy5 = n % 5 == 0;
```

In this book, we assume your compiler supports bool as a primitive type. If this is not the case, we provide a programmer-defined version of the data type in the file "bool.h" from the supplemental software. The file equates the type bool with the int type and defines as constant integers the identifiers true and false.

```
const int true = 1;
const int false = 0;
```

By simply including "bool.h" as a program header file, you may define bool objects and use the constants true and false just as though the type were part of the language.

E X A M P L E   4 . 7

Since C++ associates a logical value with all numeric expressions, programmers can accidentally produce a subtle error that nullifies the condition test in a selection statement. The relational equals operator "==" must be distinguished from "=" that represents assignment. Look at this programming error.

```
// test is incorrect
if (age = 13)
     cout << "You are starting the teenage years";
```

In the condition, the assignment statement always executes and age becomes 13. Since the value of age is non-zero, the logical value of the condition is always true and the output statement executes. Unfortunately, a baby at age 2 would be "starting the teenage years" as would an elderly person at age 100.

```
// valid test
if (age == 13)
     cout << "You are starting the teenage years";   ■
```

4-5   LOOP STRUCTURES

Selection statements allow a program to make choices among alternative actions. This is only one type of flow control structure. Many programs are designed around algorithms that repeat a task over and over again. The repetition is provided by a control structure called a loop. This section introduces the while and do/while statements that define basic C++ loops. We draw on our understanding of logical expressions and conditions for the syntax. Loops greatly extend the power of algorithms. In Chapter 6, we discuss other constructs that provide generalized looping capabilities.

The while Statement

The *while statement* defines a basic loop structure. The statement includes a logical expression that tests whether the loop should continue and a *loop body* that defines a task that is repeated. The logical expression is called the *loop test*.

SYNTAX ▬▬▬▬▬▬▬▬▬▬▬▬▬▬▬▬

while Statement

Form: while (logical expression)   // loop test

            <loop body>

Action: At the start of the while statement, the logical expression is evaluated. If the condition is true, the code in the loop body is executed and then program control automatically returns to again evaluate the logical expression. If the condition is false, the loop process terminates and program control passes to the next statement that is the first statement after the loop.

Example: A while loop assigns a PASS/FAIL grade to 4 students. A score of at least 70 is required for a pass.

```
studentNo = 1;
while (studentNo <= 4)
{
    // read a score and give a grade
    cin >> score;
    if (score >= 70)
        cout << "PASS" << endl;
    else
        cout << "FAIL" << endl;

    // update the value of studentNo
    studentNo++;
}
```

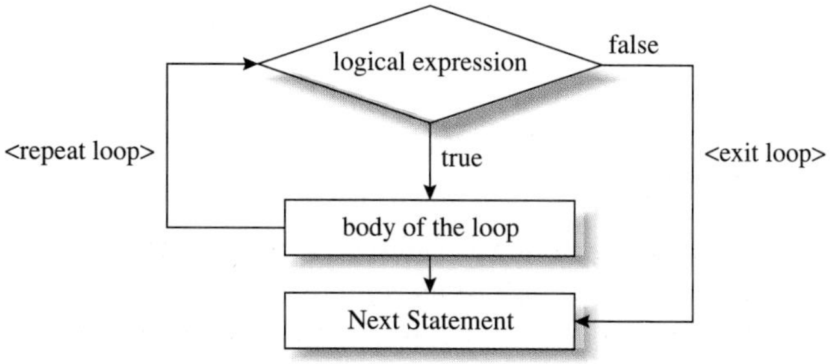

FIGURE 4.-7
Flow Diagram for the while Statement.

Figure 4-7 illustrates the flow of control in a while statement. Note that the while loop has a built-in mechanism that returns control from the end of the loop body back to an evaluation of the logical expression.

A loop is designed to repeatedly carry out a task. Each execution of the loop body is called an *iteration* of the loop. At the heart of a loop is a set of one or more *loop control objects* whose values are used to determine the number of iterations. These control objects are used in the construction of the logical expression and their values are updated in the loop body. For instance, the grading example uses studentNo as a loop control object to monitor the number of the student being processed. The loop test checks the condition "studentNo <= 4".

```
while (studentNo <= 4)  // loop test condition
{
    <read score and grade student number "studentNo">
    studentNo++;   // update control object
}
```

We can begin to understand the dynamics of a while loop by tracing the grading example. The loop test is performed before each iteration. This fact highlights an important issue. A program must initialize its loop control objects before the loop begins. The grade program assigns studentNo an initial value of 1. The loop test acts like a gatekeeper that indicates whether the next iteration should be performed. If the condition is true (studentNo <= 4), we enter the loop body and carry out the task of reading the score and giving a grade. Since loop control automatically returns to the loop test, we are faced with another important issue. The loop body must update the loop control objects prior to the next test. The grade example increments by 1 the value of studentNo. From this repeated update process, the value of studentNo becomes 2 then 3, and finally 4. After the fourth iteration, the value of studentNo is updated to 5 and the loop terminates. Table 4-4 traces each iteration by indicating the value for studentNo at the loop test and after the update. The table emulates the loop task by including a score and a grade.

In the design of a loop algorithm, a programmer must be aware of the value of control objects outside of the loop structure. The values of the control objects before the first iteration are called the *preloop conditions* and the state of the objects after exiting the loop are called the *postloop conditions*. In the

TABLE 4-4   Tracing the Grading Loop

Iteration	studentNo (at loop test)	Score	Grade	studentNo (after update)
1	1	74	PASS	2
2	2	60	FAIL	3
3	3	95	PASS	4
4	4	45	FAIL	5

grade example, the preloop conditions specify that studentNo has value 1 and the postloop conditions determine that studentNo has value5.

```
<preloop conditions>       // initialize control objects

while (loop test)
{
    <loop task>
    <update one or more control objects>
}

<postloop conditions>      // control objects after loop
```

Counter and Event-Controlled Loops

Applications feature two major types of loops that depend on the loop test conditions. A *counter-controlled loop* performs a fixed number of iterations. The exact number of iterations is known before beginning the loop. In contrast, an *event-controlled loop* performs an indefinite number of iterations. The loop test looks at an event condition that specifies when the loop should terminate. The number of iterations depends on run-time conditions.

Counter-Controlled Loops. When a loop executes a fixed number of iterations, control is managed by a counter that is initialized as part of the preconditions. The loop test uses a relational expression that checks whether the counter is within range. Consider a while statement that sums the first 10 integers.

```
sum = 1 + 2 + 3 + 4 + 5 + 6 + 7 + 8 + 9 + 10     // sum is 55
```

The integer counter, i, controls the number of iterations. The object sum starts with initial value 0 and maintains the running total. The loop test determines whether the counter i is less than or equal to 10. For each iteration, the loop body adds the current value of i. A loop control statement increments the counter.

```
int i = 1;                 // loop control object i has value 1
int sum = 0;

while (i <= 10)            // loop test i <= 10
{
    sum += i;              // add the current value of i to sum
    i++;                   // increment counter i by 1
}
cout << sum << endl;   // output the total 55
```

This simple while statement illustrates the efficiency of loops. Suppose the problem is modified to sum the first 100 integers.

```
sum = 1 + 2 + 3 + ... + 99 + 100 = 5050
```

The loop test statement must simply increase its limit from 10 to 100.

```
while (i <= 100)    // loop test i <= 100
```

The execution of the loop provides 100 iterations and a sum of 5050.

PROGRAM 4.2

During a rocket launch, the program uses a while to emulate a count down to BLAST OFF!!!. The counter-controlled object, count, begins with value 5 and passes through the range 5, 4, 3, 2, and 1. At count = 0, BLAST OFF!!! occurs.

```cpp
#include <iostream.h>

int main()
{
    int count = 5;     // counter-control object starts at 5

    cout << "Start countdown sequence" << endl;
    // loop test determines whether count has reached 0
    while(count > 0)
    {
        cout << count << endl;
        count--;                    // decrement the count
    }
    cout << "BLAST OFF!!!" << endl;

    return 0;
}
```

```
Run:

Start countdown sequence
5
4
3
2
1
BLAST OFF!!!
```

Using Loops for Weather Statistics. Weather statistics include yearly rainfall data for a region. We use a while loop to compute the average rainfall for a period of n years. The calculation uses an Accumulator object called rainfall that maintains a running total of the rainfall over the n years. As the counter control object ranges from 1 to n, we use the member function addValue() to add the rainfall for the year to the total.

APPLICATION 4-3 COMPUTING AVERAGE RAINFALL

The program implements the algorithm to compute the average rainfall. The number of iterations for the while loop is controlled by the integer object year = 1, 2, . . . , n. In the loop body, read the amount of yearly rainfall and add this to the total in the Accumulator object rainfall. The total rainfall over the n year period is given by the total rainfall (`rainfall.getTotal()`) divided by n.

```cpp
#include <iostream.h>

#include "accum.h"        // for Accumulator class
#include "textlib.h"      // for setreal()

int main()
{
    // nyears is number of years,
    // year is the loop control object
    int nyears, year;

    // object to hold the yearly rainfall amount
    double yearlyRainfall;

    // object maintains record of total rainfall
    Accumulator rainfall;

    // input nyears as the number of years for data
    cout << "Enter the number of years for rainfall data: ";
    cin >> nyears;

    cout << "Enter rainfall data for " << nyears
         << " years:" << endl;

    // run loop for year = 1, 2, ..., nyears
    year = 1;
    while (year <= nyears)
    {
        // input a yearly rainfall and add to total rainfall
        cin >> yearlyRainfall;
        rainfall.addValue(yearlyRainfall);
        // increment loop control object year
        year++;
    }

    cout << "The average rainfall over" << nyears

         << "years is" << setreal(1,2)
         << rainfall.getTotal()/nyears << endl;

    return 0;
}
```

```
Run:

Enter the number of years for rainfall data: 10
Enter rainfall data for 10 years:
20 18.7 15.8 22.3 19.5 23.5 15.7 18.5 16.5 20.7
The average rainfall over 10 years is 19.12
```

Event-controlled Loops. In an event-controlled loop, the test identifies criteria under which the loop should continue. The process terminates when a run-time event occurs that invalidates the criteria. For instance, a customer may use an ATM machine for a series of bank transactions. A simple prompt asks whether the customer wishes to continue.

```
<ATM Prompt>  "Process another transaction "Yes" or "No"?
```

A "Yes" response initiates another transaction. Only when the customer indicates "No" does the machine terminate transactions and return the customer's card. To simulate the running of an ATM, we define the bool object, continueATM, as a loop control object. Its initial value is set to true.

```
bool continueATM = true           // continueATM to true

char customerResponse;            // response to ATM prompt

while (continueATM)               // test value of continueATM
{
    . . . <transaction> . . .

    // prompt customer for response
    cout << " Process another transaction (Y or N): ";
    cin >> customerResponse;
    if (customerResponse == 'N')
       continueATM = false;       // set criteria to false
}
```

Having the customer respond with 'N' creates the run-time event that changes the criteria (continueATM becomes false) and the loop terminates.

PROGRAM 4.3

We can implement integer division (n/divisor, n % divisor) using repeated subtraction. The process continues as long as the subtraction does not produce a negative number. The number of iterations is the quotient and the last value of n is the remainder. For instance, consider n = 26 and divisor = 7.

```
Integer division:  quotient = 3, remainder = 5

            3  R5
        7√26
```

Repeated Subtraction: quotient (number of subtractions) = 3
                        remainder (last non-negative result) = 5

```
    n (26)         26      19      12       5
    divisor(7)     -7      -7      -7      -7
                   ----    ----    ----    ----
    difference     19      12       5     <neg>
```

The program inputs a number and its divisor and then uses repeated subtraction to compute the quotient and remainder. A while loop uses the event criteria

```
n-divisor >= 0    // continue if the difference is non-negative
```

to indicate whether another subtraction should be performed.

```
#include <iostream.h>

int main()
{
   int n, divisor, quotient, remainder;

   cout << "Input a number and a divisor: ";
   cin >> n >> divisor;

   // quotient = 0 before counting subtractions
   quotient = 0;

   // continue while result is non-negative
   while (n - divisor >= 0)
   {
      n -= divisor;  // carry out the next subtraction
      quotient++;    // increment the quotient count
   }
   remainder = n;

   cout << "The quotient is " << quotient
        << " and the remainder is " << remainder << endl;

   return 0;
}
```

```
Run:

Input a number and a divisor: 155 8
The quotient is 19 and the remainder is 3   ■
```

Application: Raising Band Funds. As an application of event-controlled loops, consider a school band that needs $10,000 to make a trip to Disneyland. Local groups have committed to raise the funds, and the director accepts contributions until the goal is attained. An event-controlled while loop monitors the amount of contributions. The loop terminates when the band reaches the goal.

APPLICATION 4-4 RAISING FUNDS FOR A BAND TRIP

The program uses the real number objects contribution and totalFunds. For each iteration, we input the contribution and update totalFunds and then output the funds collected and the amount needed to reach the goal. The loop continues as long as the condition "totalFunds < goal" is true

In the program the goal is $10,000 and groups make contributions of $1500, $3000, $1800, $2400, and $1750. We trace the loop for each contribution.

Iteration	loop test totalFunds < goal	Contribution	Total Funds	Amount to Goal
1	true	1500.00	1500.00	8500.00
2	true	3000.00	4500.00	5500.00
3	true	1800.00	6300.00	3700.00
4	true	2400.00	8700.00	1300.00
5	true	1750.00	10450.00	Goal Reached
6	false			

```cpp
#include <iostream.h>

#include "textlib.h"

int main()
{
   const double goal = 10000.00;
   double contribution, totalFunds = 0;

   // has the total reached the goal?
   while (totalFunds < goal)
   {
      cin >> contribution;        // input next contribution
      totalFunds += contribution; // update the total

      // output current state of the fund-raising project
      cout << "Contribution: " << setreal(9,2) << contribution
           << "  Total: " << setreal(9,2) << totalFunds;
      if (totalFunds < goal)
         cout <<  "  Amount to goal: " << setreal(9,2)
              << (goal - totalFunds);
      else
         cout << "  Goal reached";
      cout << endl;
   }

   return 0;
}
```

```
Run:

1500 3000 1800 2400 1750
Contribution: 1500.00  Total: 1500.00  Amount to goal:
8500.00
Contribution: 3000.00  Total:  4500.00  Amount to goal:
5500.00
Contribution: 1800.00  Total:  6300.00 Amount to goal:
3700.00
```

```
Contribution: 2400.00  Total:  8700.00  Amount to goal:
1300.00
Contribution: 1750.00  Total: 10450.00  Goal reached
```

1. Design a loop that reads 10 characters from the keyboard and output the lowercase equivalent for each uppercase letter.

2. Compute sum = 10 + 9 + ... + 2 + 1 by using a loop control object that decreases from 10 to 1.

3. The following table gives the value of n and the specific output for each iteration of a while loop. Using the table, construct the event-driven loop.

Exploring Concepts

Iteration	Loop Control (n)	Output
1	10	100
2	8	64
3	6	36
4	4	16
5	2	4
6	0	(loop terminates)

The do/while Statement

In a while statement, the loop test is performed before entering the loop body. As an alternative loop structure, C++ provides a *do/while statement* that places the loop test at the end of the loop body.

SYNTAX

The do/while Statement

Form:
```
do
      <loop body>
while (logical expression);  // loop test
```

Action: After executing the statements in the loop body, the logical expression is evaluated. If the result is true, program control returns to the first statement in the loop body; otherwise, program control passes to the next statement. Since the test is performed after executing the loop body, at least one iteration must occur.

Example: A user must enter the password, "SYSTEM", to gain access to the main server. A do/while loop allows for repeated attempts to log in until the correct password is entered.

```
        String    password;

        do
        {
            cout << "Enter the password: ";
            cin >> password;
        }
        while (password != "SYSTEM");    // test password
```

Figure 4-8 is the flow diagram for the do/while statement. While it has obvious similarities to the while statement, a do/while loop tends to be used less frequently. A primary application for the do/while loop is with problems involving numeric conversion.

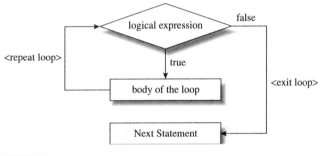

FIGURE 4-8
The do/while Statement.

EXAMPLE 4.8

Sum the first 20 integers, $1 + 2 + 3 + \ldots + 20$ using a do/while loop.

```
int sum = 0, i = 1;
do
{
    sum += i;
    i++;
} while (i <= 20);    ■
```

Loops and Numeric Palindromes

An integer N is a *palindrome* if its digits read the same forward and backward. For instance, 232 and 184481 are palindromes. In the fascinating world of number theory, addition can be used to take any nonnegative integer N and create a palindrome. The algorithm relies on a function called reverseInt() that takes an integer N and returns another integer with the digits of N in reverse order. The design and implementation of this function is given after Application 4-5.

reverseInt(2358) = 8532

reverseInt(17) = 71

reverseInt(232) = 232

To create a palindrome based on the integer N, repeat the following process over and over again until success occurs. Begin each iteration by calling reverseInt(N) and compare the result with N. If they are equal, then N is a palindrome and the process terminates. If they are not equal, update N by adding reverseInt(N) to its current value and use the new value of N for the next iteration.

Update N for next iteration: N = N + reverseInt(N)

Table 4-5 illustrates the steps for N = 155.

TABLE 4-5 Building a Palindrome from 155

Step	Current N	reverseInt(N)	N is a palindrome	Updated N (if test false)
1	155	551	false	706 = 155 + 551
2	706	607	false	1313 = 706 + 607
3	1313	3131	false	4444 = 1313 + 3131
4	4444	4444	true	

Technical Note

For some numbers, success occurs quickly, while others require a great many iterations and produce palindromes with hundreds or even thousands of digits. The number N = 484 is a palindrome that is identified in the first iteration. More typically, the number N = 287 yields the palindrome 233332 after 7 steps while N = 89 does not produce a palindrome after 35 steps.

The Palindrome Function. We define a free function, `createPalindrome()`, that implements the algorithm to create a palindrome. A long integer, intN, is the single argument and the function executes at most 15 iterations of the algorithm in an attempt to derive a palindrome. If the process terminates within the 15 iterations, the resulting palindrome is returned; otherwise –1 is the return value. The function terminates after 15 iterations since the size of intN would exceed the range of a long integer.

```
// start with intN; within 15 steps, attempt to create a
// palindrome. if successful, return the palindrome;
// otherwise, return -1
long createPalindrome(long intN)
. . . .
{
    const int ATTEMPTS = 15;            // max reversals allowed

    bool isPalindrome = false;          // is palindrome found?
    long reverseN;                      // value from reverseInt()
```

```
    int   step = 0;

    // perform an iteration and continue until we have a
    // palindrome or have performed ATTEMPTS reversals
    do
    {
        reverseN = reverseInt(intN);   // get the reverse of intN

        // is intN a palindrome?  if yes, set the Boolean value
        if (reverseN == intN)
            isPalindrome = true;
        else
        {
            // no palindrome yet. add reverseN and increment step
            intN += reverseN;
            step++;
        }
    } while (isPalindrome == false && step < ATTEMPTS);

    if (isPalindrome)
        return  intN;
    else
        return -1;
}
```

APPLICATION 4-5 CREATING A PALINDROME NUMBER

The program implements the algorithm to create a palindrome using the free functions createPalindrome() and reverseInt(). In the main program, a while loop reads five integers in the range 50 to 500. For each input, a call to the function, createPalindrome(), attempts to create a palindrome within 15 steps. If the function is successful, we output the palindrome. Otherwise, we indicate that additional steps are needed.

```
#include <iostream.h>

// return number whose digits are the reverse of intN
long reverseInt (long intN);

// start with intN; within 15 steps, attempt to create a
// palindrome. if successful, return the palindrome;
// otherwise, return -1
long createPalindrome(long intN)

int main()
{
    long number;       // read 5 integer values into number
    long palindrome;   // result value of createPalindrome()
    int i = 1;         // loop control object
```

```
      cout << "Enter 5 integers in the range 50 to 500: ";
      while (i <= 5)
      {
         // input a number and look for a palindrome
         cin >> number;
         palindrome = createPalindrome(number);
         cout << "For N = " << setw(3) << number;
         if (palindrome != -1)
            cout << ", palindrome is " << palindrome << endl;
         else
            cout << ", requires more than 15 steps" << endl;
         i++;
      }

      return 0;
   }

   long reverseInt(long intN)
   {
      long reverseN = 0, rightDigit; // reverseN starts at 0

      do
      {
         rightDigit = intN % 10;      // get right-most digit

         // shift reverseN left one position and add new digit
         reverseN = 10 * reverseN + rightDigit;

         // isolate remaining digits of the number
         intN /= 10;
      }
      while (intN != 0);                  // quit when quotient is 0

      return reverseN;
   }

   long createPalindrome(long intN)
   {
      const int ATTEMPTS = 15;        // max reversals allowed

      bool isPalindrome = false;      // is palindrome found?
      long reverseN;                  // value from reverseInt()
      int  step = 0;

      // perform an iteration and continue until we have a
      // palindrome or have performed ATTEMPTS reversals
      do
      {
         reverseN = reverseInt(intN); // reverse of intN

         // is intN a palindrome?  if yes, set Boolean value
```

```
            if (reverseN == intN)
               isPalindrome = true;
            else
            {
               // if no, add reverseN and increment count
               intN += reverseN;
               step++;
            }
      } while (isPalindrome == false && step < ATTEMPTS);

      if (isPalindrome)
         return  intN;
      else
         return -1;
}
```

```
Run:

Enter 5 integers in the range 50 to 500: 155 89 232 287
447
For N = 155, palindrome is 4444
For N = 89, requires more than 15 steps
For N = 232, palindrome is 232
For N = 287, palindrome is 233332
For N = 447, palindrome is 5115
```

The Reverse Digits Function. To create a number, reverseN, that consists of the digits of N in reverse order, we use integer division by 10. The remainder, N % 10, returns the right most digit of the number while the quotient, N/10, gives the other digits. By repeatedly dividing by 10, we can extract the digits of N in reverse order. Let us look at the process for N = 365. We extract the digits in the order 5, 6, and 3. To create reverseN, we take these digits and use multiplication by 10 to position them from left to right. Start by setting reverseN to 0.

Step 1: Extract digit 5 from N using the % operator (365 % 10 = 5). Multiply reverseN by 10 (reverseN * 10 = 0) to maintain compatibility with subsequent steps. Add 5 as the new ones digit in reverseN. Update the value of N with the / operator.

$$\begin{array}{ll} \text{reverseN} = \text{reverseN} * 10 + N \% 10 & N = N / 10 \\ = 0 * 10 + 5 & = 365 / 10 \\ = 5 & = 36 \end{array}$$

Step 2: Extract digit 6 from N (36 % 10 = 6). Shift the digits of reverseN to the left one position by multiplying by 10. Then add 6 as the new ones digit in reverseN. Update N.

$$\begin{array}{ll} \text{reverseN} = \text{reverseN} * 10 + N \% 10 & N = N / 10 \\ = 5 * 10 + 6 & = 36 / 10 \\ = 56 & = 3 \end{array}$$

Step 3: Extract digit 3 from N (3 % 10 = 3). Shift the digits of reverseN to the left one position by multiplying by 10. Then add 3 as the new ones digit in reversed. The updated N is 0 and the process terminates.

$$\begin{aligned} \text{reverseN} &= \text{reverseN} * 10 + \text{N} \% 10 & \text{N} &= \text{N} / 10 \\ &= 56 * 10 + 3 & &= 3 / 10 \\ &= 563 & &= 0 \end{aligned}$$

The following is a definition of the free function, reverseInt(). The do/while loop is ideal for the code since at least one iteration must be performed. In fact, exactly one iteration occurs for a one digit number such as 5.

```
// return number whose digits are the reverse of intN
long reverseInt(long intN)
{
    long reverseN = 0, rightDigit;    // new number starts at 0

    do
    {
        rightDigit = intN % 10;       // get right-most digit

        // shift reverseN left one position and add new digit
        reverseN = 10 * reverseN + rightDigit;

        // isolate remaining digits of the number
        intN /= 10;
    }
    while (intN != 0);                // quit when quotient is 0

    return reverseN;
}
```

4-6 ANIMATION WITH LOOPS

We introduced the RectShape and CircleShape classes in Chapters 1 and 3 and use their draw() operations to display simple figures. In this section we describe other operations of the classes including erase(), move(), and the base-point access functions getX() and getY(). With this full set of operations and looping constructs, we can perform simple animation. The basic idea is this. Draw a figure at a location on the screen and hold it at that position for a short time. Then erase the figure and move it to another location, and repeat the process. Each individual snapshot is called a *frame*. A sequence of frames gives the illusion that an object is moving across the screen.

To implement a delay, we use the graphics function delayWindow() that causes a delay for a specified number of seconds. To erase a graphic object and draw it at a new point, we must introduce some additional features of the drawing classes. Each RectShape or CircleShape object has the following member functions. Recall that the base point for a circle is its center and the base point for a rectangle is its upper left-hand corner.

erase	Erase the shape from the window. Do not confuse this with erase-Window() that clears the entire drawing surface. void erase();
getX	Return the x-coordinate of the shape's base point. double getX();
getY	Return the y-coordinate of the shape's base point. void getY();
move	Locate the base point of the shape at (x,y). void move(double x, double y);

Jack in the Box Animation

To illustrate graphical animation, we simulate a jack-in-the-box with a circle and a rectangle. The box is a square drawn at the point (4,3) with sides of length 1. The jack is a blue circle that rises out of the box and moves to the top of the screen and then descends back into the box (Figure 4-10).

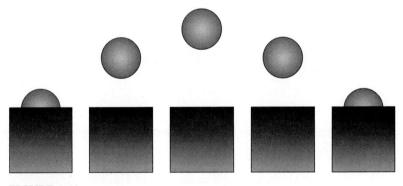

FIGURE 4-10
Jack in the box frames.

The action of the jack is provided by the free function `jackInTheBox()` that takes the box as an argument. The function creates a CircleShape object, jack, whose center, (jackX, jackY), is at the center of the box and whose radius, jackRadius, is $^1/_4$ of the box width.

```
void jackInTheBox(RectShape box);
```

Movement of the jack is controlled by an event-loop that creates a series of frames to lift the jack to the top of the screen. This occurs while the condition "jackY < jackRadius" is true. The motion stops when the jack touches the top of the screen. The figure illustrates the position of the jack (circle) at the top of the screen.

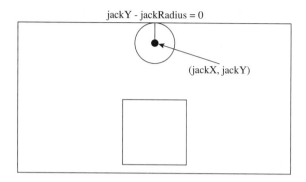

The structure of the loop that moves the jack is as follows:

```
while (jackY >= jackRadius)
{
    <draw the jack>
    <wait 1/20 of a second>
    <erase the jack>
    <move the jack upward>
}
```

Each frame is held on the screen for 1/20th of a second using delayWindow() and then the center of the jack moves upward .1 units for the next frame.

```
jackY -= .1;   // move the jack upward
jack.move(jackX,jackY);
```

To make the animation simulate a jack-in-the-box, we do not want the jack to appear until it begins to leave the top of the box. To accomplish this, the jack is not drawn until its upper edge appears (Figure 4-11 (a)).

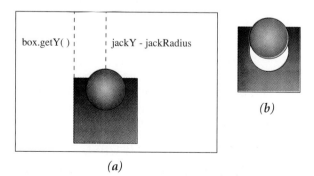

(b)

(a)

FIGURE 4-11
Handling the jack when it overlaps the box.

```
// condition that the jack appears
jackY - jackRadius < box.getY().
```

As the jack begins to leave the box, there is a short period in which the frame must redraw both the jack and the box. Otherwise, a portion of the box is erased and would leave white space (Figure 4-11(b)). The following statement refreshes the screen by re-drawing the box.

```
// redraw the box as long as the jack overlaps it
if (jackY+jackRadius >= box.getY())
    box.draw();
```

As the jack ascends, we count the number of iterations (frames) using the integer object numIterations. This value is used in a counter-controlled loop to create the same number of frames as the jack falls. The descent uses a smaller delay of 1/40th of a second. The only differences between the ascent and descent loops is the delay factor and the fact that the jack moves down (jackY increases).

```
jackY += .1;  // move the jack downward
jack.move(jackX,jackY);
```

The following is a complete listing of the function jackInTheBox(). The previous discussion has isolated the main logic of the function. The listing lets you see how the various elements fit together in the C++ implementation.

```
// simulate a jack in the box
void jackInTheBox(RectShape box)
{
    // number of iterations as jack comes down
    int numIterations = 0, i;
    double jackX, jackY, jackRadius; // jack attributes

    // center of the jack is the center of the box
    jackX = box.getX() + box.getLength()/2;
    jackY = box.getY() + box.getWidth()/2;
    // radius of jack is 1/4 width of the box
    jackRadius = box.getLength()/4;

    // declare the jack and make it blue
    CircleShape jack(jackX,jackY,jackRadius, blue);

    // jack moves upward until it touches top of the screen.
    // event-controlled loop
    while (jackY >= jackRadius)
    {
        numIterations++;  // count number of iterations required

        if (jackY-jackRadius < box.getY())
        {
            jack.draw();              // draw the jack
            // redraw the box as long as the jack overlaps it
            if (jackY+jackRadius >= box.getY())
                box.draw();
```

```
                // wait 1/20th second and then erase the jack
                delayWindow(.05);
                jack.erase();

            }
            jackY -= .1;  // move the jack upward
            jack.move(jackX,jackY);
        }

        // move the jack back into the box. we counted the number
        // of iterations required to move up, so moving back down
        // is a counter-controlled loop
        i = 1;
        while (i <= numIterations)
        {
            if (jackY-jackRadius < box.getY())
            {
                jack.draw();                // draw the jack
                // re-draw the box as long as the jack overlaps it
                if (jackY+jackRadius >= box.getY())
                    box.draw();

                delayWindow(.025);
                jack.erase();

            }
            jackY += .1;  // move the jack downward
            jack.move(jackX,jackY);
            i++;
        }

        viewWindow();  // pause to view the box
    }
```

APPLICATION 4-6 THE JACK IN THE BOX

The program uses the function jackInTheBox() for animation. The main program declares a dark gray rectangle as the box and draws it. The function does all of the animation and then returns control to the main program in order to close the graphics window

```
#include "rectsh.h"      // use RectShape class
#include "circlesh.h"    // use CircleShape class

// simulate a jack in the box
void jackInTheBox(RectShape box);

int main()
```

```
    {
        // declare a box with color darkgray
        RectShape box(4,3,1,1, darkgray);

        openWindow();                    // open the drawing window
        box.draw();                      // draw the box
        jackInTheBox(box);               // draw the jack in the box
        closeWindow();                   // close the drawing window
    } return 0;
    /* implementation of jackInTheBox() is given in the program
    discussion */
```

Figure 4-10 shows a sequence of frames as the jack moves up and then down.

CHAPTER 4 SUMMARY

This chapter switches emphasis from the structure of classes to the logic of algorithms. With the introduction of logical expressions, we have the tools to develop control structures that are essential components of most algorithms.

Selection statements allow a programmer to chose from among alternative actions. The chapter includes a thorough discussion of one-way, two-way, and multiple selection using the if, if/else, and nested if/else statements. Loops are a second form of control structure. We cover the while and do/while loops that are the prototype of general loop structures. We cover key terms such as loop test, loop body, and loop control objects.

C++ defines the logical type bool. While the chapter discusses how logical objects can be defined as integers, we use the bool type exclusively in this book. Such objects are used as function arguments and return values.

This chapter presents a number of interesting computer applications using loops. The applications include reversing the digits of a number, discovering palindromes, and creating animation for a jack-in-the-box.

With control structures, we have powerful new tools to create problem solving algorithms. In addition, we have tools to implement your own functions and classes. That becomes the task of the next chapter.

Classes in the Chapter

Name	*Implementation File*
Accumulator	accum.h
CircleShape	circlesh.h
GradeRecord	graderec.h
RectShape	rectsh.h
StudentAccount	studacct.h

KEY TERMS

Block:
Consists of zero or more statements enclosed in braces { and }. A block group a sequence of statements that are executed as a unit. There is no semicolon after a block since the '}' terminates the construct.

bool type:

A C++ primitive type having the logical values true and false, which are key words. In applications, objects may be declared with the bool type and given initial values.

do/while loop:

Evaluates the loop test after executing the statements in the loop body. If the result is true, program control returns to the loop body; otherwise, program control passes to the next statement. Since the test is performed after the loop body, at least one iteration must always occur.

Flow of control:

Specifies the order in which the computer executes the instructions. In some cases, the computer executes statements one after another in the order they are written in the program. Most interesting algorithms involve logic that modifies the normal execution of statements by using selection and looping.

Logical expression:

An expression that evaluates to true or false. Such expressions are used to make the decisions involved with selection and looping statements.

Logical operator:

The operators && (AND), ǁ (OR), !(NOT). The operators have operands that are logical expressions and evaluate to true or false. The operator && is true only if both operands are true; whereas ǁ is true if either of the operands is true. An expression with the unary ! operator is true if the operand is false and is false if the operand is true.

Looping:

Executing a set of instructions that are repeated over and over again to handle a series of similar cases. A loop statement includes a logical expression called a loop test that tests whether the loop should continue and a loop body that defines a task that is repeated. Loop control objects are used to define the conditions in the loop test and their values are updated in the loop body. A counter-controlled loop performs a fixed number of iterations, which are determined before beginning the loop. An event-controlled loop performs an indefinite number of iterations. The loop test looks at an event condition that specifies when the loop should terminate. The number of iterations depends on run-time conditions in the program.

Relation Expression:

An expression that involves a relational operator. If the relationship is valid, the expression is true; if not, the expression is false.

Relational operator:

An operator that compares two values. C++ defines the six relational operators ==, !=, <, <=, >, >=.

Selection:

Choosing from a set of one or more alternative actions. When the program chooses among two alternative actions, we call this two-way selection. With one-way selection, program logic chooses one alternative action when the condition is true; multiple selection is used when the algorithm must select from three or more of alternative actions.

Short-circuit evaluation:

A method by which the computer evaluates the operands in a logical expression from left to right and stops as soon as the value of the entire expression is known.

While loop:

Evaluates the loop test at the start of each loop iteration. If the condition is true, the code in the loop body is executed and then program control automatically returns once more to reevaluate the logical expression. If the condition is false, the loop process terminates and program control passes to the next statement after the loop.

REVIEW EXERCISES

1. Assume that x, y, and z are real number objects. For each description, give the logical expression.
   (a) x is not equal to $y - 5$.
   (b) x lies strictly between 9.2 and 14.

2. Trace the statement for each value of a.

   ```
   if (a < 6);
       cout << "a is less than 6" << endl;
   else
       cout << "a is greater than or equal to 6" << endl;
   ```

   (a) $a = 15$ (b) $a = 6$ (c) $a = 3$

3. Assume a, b, and c are integer objects with $a = 0, b = 6, c = -4$. Give the logical value for each of the following expressions.
   (a) $a\ != 0$ (b) $b\ != 0$ (c) $!(c >= 0)$ (d) $b - 6 < c + 6$

4. The human body cannot exist in extreme temperatures without support. For the example, assume that extreme heat is above $122°$ and extreme cold is below $-45°$. Write a logical expression that assigns the bool object extremeTemp true if conditions are extreme and false otherwise.

5. What is the value of the float object y for each value of x? Why are we protected from division by 0 in case $x = 5$?

   ```
   if (x != 5 && 1.0/(x-5) > 0)
       y = 1;
   else
       y = 2;
   ```

   (a) $x = 8$ (b) $x = 5$ (c) $x = 4$

6. A university student graduates with "highest honors" when the gpa is 3.8 and above, with "high honors" when the gpa is above 3.6, and with "honors" when the gpa is above 3.4. Write a nested if statement that takes a gpa and outputs the kind of honors available to a student. The statement should indicate when no honors are earned.

7. The while loop produces output 1   4   9   16   25. What is the logical expression in the loop test and the cout statement in the loop body?

   ```
   i = 1;
   while (<loop test>)                 // logical expression _____
   {
       cout << _____ << "  ";        // output statement _____
       _____;                          // update statement _____
   }
   ```

8. Trace the loop instructions and give the resulting value for n, which is initially set to 0.

   ```
   (a) i = 1;                    (b) year = 1980;
       while (i < 8)                 while(year <= 1989)
       {                             {
           n += i;                       if (year % 4 == 0)
           i += 2;                           n++;
       }                                 year++;
                                     }
   ```

9. Loop statements can contain some tricky syntax or logical errors that cause them not to compile or to run correctly. Look at the following statements and identify problems as being syntax or logical errors. In each case explain the problem.

(a)
```
i = 1;
   while (i <= 5);
   {
      cout << i << endl;
      i++;
   }
```

(b)
```
i = 9;
   do
      cout << i << end;
      i--
   while (i > 0);
```

10. Trace the do/while loop and give the output for statements in loop block A and loop block B.

```
i = 5;
do
{
   <loop block>
} while (i > 0);
```

(a)
```
Loop Block A:
   cout << i * i << "   ";
   i--;
```

(b)
```
Loop Block B:
   i--;
   cout << i * i << "   ";
```

11. Explain how simple animation can be done using a class like RectShape or Circle-Shape.

Answers to Review Exercises

1. (a) $x != (y-5)$. Since the precedence of "$-$" is higher than the precedence of "$!=$", the expression can also be written $x != y - 5$.
   (b) $x > 9.8 \&\& x < 14.0$

2. (a) a is greater than or equal to 6.
   (b) a is greater than or equal to 6.
   (c) a is less than 6.

3. (a) false   (b) true   (c) true   (d) true

4. Let temp be a float object specifying the current temperature.
```
extremeTemp = temp > 122 || temp < -45;
```

5. (a) $y = 1$ (b) $y = 2$ (c) $y = 2$
   Shortcut Boolean expression evaluation is used. When x = 5, the sub-expression "x != 5" is false and so the expression is false. The division is not done.

6.
```
float gpa;

cin >> gpa;

if (gpa >= 3.8)
   cout << "Highest honors" << endl;
else if (gpa >= 3.7)
   cout << "High honors" << endl;
else if (gpa >= 3.5)
   cout << "Honors" << endl;
```

```
       else
           cout << "No form of honors awarded" << endl;
```

7.
```
    i = 1;
    while (i <= 5)
    {
        cout << i*i << "   ";
        i++;
    }
```

8. (a) 16   (b) 3

9. In (a), the semicolon (;) after (i <= 5) terminates the while by creating a NULL statement that does nothing. Since i <= 5 is true, the statement executes forever, creating an infinite loop. In (b), the body of the do/while contains two statements and a block must be used.

(a)
```
    i = 1;
    while (i <= 5)
    {
        cout << i << endl;
        i++;
    }
```

(b)
```
    i = 9;
    do
    {
        cout << i << end;
        i--;
    }
    while (i > 0);
```

10. (a) 25 16 9 4 1   (b) 16 9 4 1 0

11. Draw a shape at a location on the screen and hold it at that position for a short time using the free function `delayWindow()`. Then use the `erase()` member function to erase the figure and move it to another location using `move()`. Repeat the process. The sequence of frames gives the illusion that an object is moving across the screen.

WRITTEN EXERCISES

12. Fill in the value of the logical expressions.

```
    const int VAL = 35;
    int n = -5;
```

Expression	Result	Expression	Result
VAL + 3 == 38	_____	n < 0	_____
VAL * 3 > 120	_____	VAL/n + 8 <= 0	_____
VAL - 30 < n + 10	_____	VAL % 2 != 0	_____

13. Write logical expressions that correspond to each phrase below.
(a) integer m is greater than 10.
(b) integers a, b, and c are all even.
(c) at least one of integers $a, b,$ and c are even.
(d) ch is a digit character (i.e., ch is '0', '1', . . . , '9').

14. Object ch is a character. Write logical expressions that correspond to each phrase below.
(a) ch is not a lowercase letter.
(b) ch is an uppercase letter in the word MISSISSIPPI.

15. Use integers *m* and *n* to create logical expressions.
(a) neither *m* nor *n* is odd.
(b) *m* is no more than 5 units larger than *n* .
(c) both *m* and *n* are even.
(d) exactly one of *m* and *n* is even.

16. Assume that *x*, *y*, and *z* are real number objects. For each description, give the logical expression.
(a) both *x* and *y* are positive.
(b) *x* is equal to neither *y* nor *z*.

17. Integer objects *m* and *n* are used in logical expressions. Assume that $m = 4$ and that *n* has one of the following values: $-2, 0, 2, 4, 6$. For each problem, list all values for *n* that give the logical expression the value in the parentheses.
(a) $n == 0$ (false)   (b) $m != n$ (false)   (c) $n < 0$ (true)
(d) $n < m$ (false)   (e) $!(m == n)$ (true)   (f) $m > n + 3$ (true)
(g) $m - n$ (false)

18. Assume that *p*, *q*, and *r* are objects of type bool. What is the logical value for each expression?

p = true; q = false; r = false;

(a) `!r`   (b) `r && p`
(c) `!(r || q) && p`   (d) `(r && !r) || (p && !p);`
(e) `(p && !q) || (!p && q);`   (f) `(r || !r) && (p || !p);`

19. The following logical expressions assign a value to bool object boolValue. Give values for *p*, *q*, and *r* (where appropriate) that would result in boolValue having the specified value. When multiple answers are possible, give at least two different sets of values for *p*, *q*, and *r*.
(a) `boolvalue = !p || q`   `boolvalue = false;`
(b) `boolvalue = p && !q`   `boolvalue = true;`
(c) `boolvalue = p && (q || !r)`   `boolvalue = true;`
(d) `boolvalue = (p && !q) || (!p && r)`   `boolvalue = false;`

20. Trace the statement for the given input.

```
float salary = 30000.00, sales;

cin >> sales;
if (sales >= 50000.00)
    salary *= 1.05;
cout << salary << endl;
```

(a) 45000   (b) 67000   (c) 50000

21. (a) Trace the statement:

```
if (a == 6)
    cout << "a is 6" << endl;
else
    cout << "a is not 6" << endl;
```

(i) $a = 15$ (ii) $a = 6$ (iii) $a = 3$

(b) Trace the statement.

```
if (a = 6)
    cout << "a is 6" << endl;
else
    cout << "a is not 6" << endl;
```

(i) $a = 15$ (ii) $a = 6$ (iii) $a = 3$

22. Trace the code and give the output for each of the input values.

```
char testchar, ch;

cin >> testchar;
if (testchar <= 'k')
    ch = ch + 1;
else
    ch = ch - 2;
cout << ch << endl;
```

(a) Input: testchar = 'e'   Output:
(b) Input: testchar = 'm'   Output:
(c) For what input value would the output be x?
(d) For what input value would the output be f?
(e) Which two input values would give the same output?

23. Each of the following situations involve logical expressions. Declare objects that serve as operands for the expression and a bool object whose name describes the expression. Give the expression. For instance, a student gets a car insurance discount if his or her gpa is 3.0 or above.

```
float gpa;                   // object to hold grade point data
bool  getsStudentDiscout; // indicates if discount applies

if (gpa >= 3.0)
    getsStudentDiscout = true;
else
    getsStudentDiscout = false;
```

(a) The company classifies a part-time worker as one who works less than 20 hours per week.
(b) A car is said to be fuel efficient if its miles per gallon (mph) in the city is at least 22.
(c) In the region, normal rainfall total is in the range $9.0 \leqslant rain < 14.0$.
(d) When looking at the number of goals scored by the opposing soccer teams, we describe a close game as one in which the scores differ by at most 1 goal.

24. Write an if/else sequence that looks at the following situation.
First prompt the user:

```
String responseString;
cout << "Do you want to continue"
cin >> responseString;
```

The if statement should allow for input of "Y," "Yes," or "y" and output "The program continues." For input "N," "No," or "n," print "The program terminates." For all other input print "Bad input."

25. Trace the statements.

```
char c;
int n, m;

cin >> n;
cin.get(c);
if (c == ':')
{
    cin >> m;
    n += m;
}
else if (c == ' ')
    m = 0;
else
{
    m = 2;
    cin >> n;
}
cout << m << " " << n;
```

What values are output for *m* and *n* for each of the following input?
(a) 3:5   (b) 5 !   (c) 7?1

26. Objects *n* and *m* are integers. After input of *n*, *m* is assigned a value that depends on *n* as follows:

n is 1:	*m* is *n*
n is 3:	*m* is *n*n*
n is 4:	*m* is *n*n*n*
n is 7:	*m* is 1
all other values of *n*:	*m* is 0

Write a nested if/else sequence that assigns the value of *m* .

27. In GUI programming, multiple selection must be used to determine where a mouse click occurs. Depend on the location, some appropriate action is taken. Assume the programmer has access to the following set of six free functions. A comment describes the action of each function when it returns a value true. Assume that the following free functions are available to the program.

```
bool inCloseBox();        // void closeWindow();
bool inMaximize();        // void maximizeWindow();
bool inMinimize();        // void minimizeWindow();
bool inMenuBar();         // void handleMenus();
bool inScroll();          // void handleScroll();
bool inContent();         // void handleContent();
```

Develop a nested if/else sequence that will handle a mouse click.

28. Assume the program has double objects *x1*, *y1*, *x2*, and *y2* representing two points *P1* = (*x1,y1*) and *P2* = (*x2,y2*) in a plane. The program also has objects double *r1* and *r2* representing the radius for two circles centered at *P1* and *P2* respectively. Write an if statement that tests whether the two circles intersect.

29. Define the function:

    ```
    bool inSequence(double x, double y, double z);
    ```

    that returns true when $x \leqslant y \leqslant z$ and false otherwise.

30. (a) Define the function:

    ```
    char toLower(char c);
    ```

    If *c* is an uppercase character, the function returns the corresponding lowercase character. If the character is lowercase or a nonalphabetic character, it returns *c*.
    (b) Define the function:

    ```
    bool isIdChar(char c);
    ```

    that returns true if *c* can be the first character of a C++ identifier.

31. Write the definition of the function

    ```
    bool isSum(int a, int b, int c);
    ```

    that returns true if any of the arguments is the sum of the other two (e.g., $b + c == a$) and false otherwise.

32. (a) Write the definition for the function:

    ```
    String min2(String s, String t);
    ```

    that returns the string appearing first in alphabetical order.
    (b) Write the definition for the function:

    ```
    String min3(String s, String t, String u);
    ```

    that returns the string appearing first in alphabetical order. Use the function min2() from part (a).

33. What is the output of each code sequence?
    (a) int sum = 0, i = 1;

    ```
    while (i <= 10)
    {
        if (i % 2 == 0)
            sum += i;
        i++;
    }
    cout << sum << endl;
    ```

(b) int fact = 1, i = 1;

```
do
{
    fact *= i;
    i++;
} while (i < 6);
```

34. Write a while loop that uses the counter-control object index to output the numbers from 10 to 100, each on a separate line.

35. Write the following while statement as a do/while loop.

```
balance = 100;  i = 1;
while (balance > 0)
{
    balance -= i*i;
    i--;
}
```

36. What is the output of the following statements?

(a) int i = 1;

```
while (i <=8)
{
    cout << i << "   ";
    i += 2;
}
```

(b) int i = 4, k;

```
do
{
    k = 2*i;
    cout << k << "   ";
    i--;
} while (i >= 0);
```

37. Trace the statements and give the resulting value for *n*. Assume *n* is initially set to 0.

(a) i = 5;

```
while (i > 0)
{
    n += 2 * i;
    i--;
}
```

(b) i = 1;

```
do
{
    n += 10;
    i++;
} while (i <= 5);
```

38. What is the output of the following statements?

(a) t = 6;

```
while (t > 3)
{
    cout << t << endl;
    t--;
}
cout << t << endl;
```

(b) t = 6;

```
do
{
    cout << t << endl;
    t--;
} while (t > 3);
cout << t << endl;
```

39. Create loops that implement each of the algorithms.

(a) With a while loop, add the even integers between 2 and 20 and print the sum.

(b) With a do/while loop, add the integers 1, 2, 3, until the sum 1 + 2 + 3 + _ exceeds 500. Print the sum.

(c) The while loop begins with *n* = 10 and prints the squares of 10, 8, . . . ,2.

(d) A school band sets out to collect $5,000. Write a sequence of statements that reads the individual contribution and outputs the cumulative sum to that point. Continue until the $5,000 is raised. Print the total amount of money collected and the amount of the largest contribution.

40. Two versions of a while loop are used to create output 14 16 18 20 22. Fill in the missing statements for each version.

(a) i = 14;
```
while (_____)
{
    cout << . . .
    _____;
}
```

(b) i = 7;
```
while (_____)
{
    cout << . . .
    _____;
}
```

41. Create a loop that implements the algorithm.
   (a) With a while statement, use `cin.get(ch)` to read a sequence of letters. Stop on the first newline character and print the number of characters read. Do not include the newline character in your count.
   (b) Repeat the algorithm for part (a) using a do/while statement. Print the number of characters read, including the newline character.

42. The exercise creates two statement blocks that input a sequence of alphabetic characters until an "X" is read. The character input may be in upper or lowercase. Convert each lowercase character to uppercase. The statements should print each character.
   (a) For statement block A, use a while loop that terminates immediately after reading the "X" without printing the stopping character.
   (b) For statement block B, use a do_while loop that terminates after reading and printing the stopping character.

43. C++ loops can be tricky, so stay alert. Trace the code and indicate what is output.

```
int i;
bool stop = false;
```

(a) while (stop = false)
```
{
    cin >> i;
    if (i != 7)
        cout << i*i << endl;
    else
        stop = true;
}
```

(b) i = 10;
```
while (i > 0)
{
    cout << i << endl;
    i++;
}
```

44. Trace the code and identify the output. Assuming ¶ represents the newline character, the input is

```
2aZ?zv¶
```

```
cin.get(c);
while (c != '\n')
{
    if (c == 'Z' || c == 'z')
        c = '*';
    else if (c >= 'A' && c < 'Z' || c >= 'a' && c < 'z')
        c++;
}
```

```
        cout << c;
        cin.get(c);
    }
```

45. The function `countBits()` returns the number of 1-bits in the binary representation of *n*. For instance, the binary representation for $n = 21$ is 10101 and the function returns 3. Fill in the missing loop components.

```
int countBits(int n)
{
    int count=0, bit;

    do
    {
        bit = _____;
        if (bit == 1)
            count++;
        n /= _____;
    } while (_____);=;

    return count;
}
```

46. Write the function:

```
double power(double x, int n);
```

that uses a while loop to compute and return x^n. Hint: Initialize double tempPower = 1 and use it in the loop body.

PROGRAMMING EXERCISES

47. Write a program that uses strings to read a person's first name and last name and a character "f" or "m" to read the sex. Output the name with the title "Ms" for female and "Mr" for male. Run the program three times using as input:

```
Tom McCarthy      m
Jeri Dong         f
<your name>       <your sex>
```

48. Declare three (3) string objects str1, str2, and str3. Write a program that inputs three names and outputs the one that comes first in alphabetical order using the function `min3()` from Written Exercise 4.32.

```
input:    sam    dick    harry
output:   dick
```

49. A textile company employs managers with fixed yearly wages, hourly workers, and piece workers who are paid by the unit. Write a program that enters a character "m," "h," and "p" to indicate the type of worker. Use a nested if/else sequence whose instruction blocks handle the different types of workers. Within each block, use instructions that prompt for critical information and then output the weekly salary. The following critical information should be input.

manager:	yearlySalary
hourly worker:	hourlyPayRate, hoursWorked (pay the hourlyPayRate for the first 40 hours and time and a half for all overtime hours)
piece worker:	unitPayRate, numberOfUnits

Run the program three times using the input data

m	52000
h	12.50 50
p	0.75 700

50. Test your function inSequence() from Written Exercise 4.29 by developing a complete program. Prompt for three double input values and output whether they are in numeric order.

51. Use your solution to Written Exercise 4.28 in a complete program. Prompt for the two points $(x1,y1)$, $(x2,y2)$ and the radii $r1$ and $r2$. Output whether the two circles intersect.

52. The program enters a sequence of integers, stopping with 0. Handle the positive and negative values separately. For output, print the average of the positive numbers and the average of the negative numbers.

53. Write a program that prompts the user for an integer $n \le 0$ and then displays the powers of 2 from 2^0 to 2^n using the function power() developed in Written Exercise 4.46.

54. Use the function countBits() from Written Exercise 4.45 in a complete program. Input an integer value and output the number of 1-bits in the binary representation. Run the program five times, including the values:

$n = 7$ (number of 1-bits = 3)
$n = 32767$ (number of 1-bits = 15)

55. Using the function reverseInt() from Section 4.5 as a guide, write a function:

```
long reverseBin(long intN);
```

that returns the integer whose binary digits are in the reverse order of those for intN. For example, the binary representation for intN = 25 is 11001 and reverseBin() returns the integer value 19 with binary representation 10011.

Use reverseBin() in a program that prompts for intN and uses the functions reverseInt() and reverseBin() to output the reverse decimal and binary values.

56. Write a complete program that implements the loop in Written Exercise 4.39(d). Input the individual contributions from the keyboard.

57. In the Fibonacci the first two values are 1. For $n \ge 3$, each term in the sequence is the sum of the previous two terms.

$$F_1 = 1, \qquad F_2 = 1, \qquad F_n = F_{n-1} + F_{n-2}, \qquad n \ge 3$$

Write a complete program that prompts for the value n and then prints the first n terms of the Fibonacci sequence. Use long integer objects. Hint: the first seven terms are 1,1,2,3,5,8,13.

58. A floating-point object can only assume a finite number of values since it is stored using a fixed number of bits. For the double object, d, the term $1 + d$ eventually is stored as 1 when d takes on decreasing values $1/10, 1/100, 1/1000, \ldots, 1/10^n$. Write a complete program that uses a loop to evaluate $1 + d$ as n increases. Terminate the loop when $1 + d == 1.0$. Output the final value of n.

59. This exercise performs a simple animation. Create a loop that draws a sequence of squares whose upper left-hand corners are at the point (5,4) and whose sides are of length $2, 1, \frac{1}{2}, \frac{1}{4}$ and $\frac{1}{8}$. Hold each square on the screen for $\frac{1}{4}$ second before erasing it and beginning a new loop iteration. Each square is to have a different color. At the conclusion of the loop, pause two seconds, clear the window, and draw a red circle at (5,4) with radius 3.

PROGRAMMING PROJECT

60. Write a complete program that uses the StudentAccount class and an event-driven loop. Initially, input a starting balance and use it to declare an object fredAcct for the student Fred Barnes having identification number "33-6531." To simulate account activity, create a nested if/else sequence that handles different transactions in a loop. For loop control, use a character that is input from the keyboard. The possible values of the character are:

"C": prompt for the amount of the charge, debit the account, and then output the resulting balance.

"P": prompt for the amount of the payment, credit the amount, and then output the resulting balance.

"D": display the current balance.

"Q": output the message "done" and terminate the program

For all other input, output an error message. Run the program with the following input data:

```
<starting balance>        -550.0
<char input>              C
    <charge amount>       300
<char input>              D
<char input>              P
    <payment amount>      850
<char input>              Q
```

Run the program again with your own data. Make sure to include improper input.

Chapter 5
Developing Your Own Classes

CHAPTER CONTENTS

5-1 IMPLEMENTING CLASSES
Illustrating Member Function
Implementations
Implementing the Constructor
Implementing the Rectangle class

5-2 ORGANIZING PROGRAM SOURCE CODE
Building A Class Header File
Building the Main Program
Building and Using the Accumulator
Class
Alternative Source Code Design
(Optional)

**5-3 ERROR CHECKING IN CLASS AND
PROGRAM DESIGN**

5-4 PRIVATE MEMBER FUNCTIONS
The Time24 Class
Time24 Class Declaration and UML
Implementation of the Time24 class

**5-5 MEMBER FUNCTIONS WITH LOOPS: THE
LOAN CLASS**
The Loan Class
Implementing the Loan Class

5-6 INLINE CODE
The Circle Class Using Inline Code
Implementing Inline Code
Application: Enclosing Maximum
Area
Inline Code for Free Functions
(Optional)
Written Exercises

Chapter 3 discusses the structure of a C++ class using the class description, UML graphical representation, and formal class declaration. For examples, we used a series of predefined classes whose implementations are found in header files in the supplementary software. The problem of class implementation was deliberately delayed until this chapter so that you could focus on using classes.

You are now in a position to build your own classes. With an understanding of free function implementations from Chapter 3 and with the control structures from Chapter 4, you can implement the member functions of a class. In the process, you will learn how to create header files that contain the class declaration and the C++ statements that implement the member functions.

5-1   IMPLEMENTING CLASSES

To implement a class, we start with its declaration that specifies the data members and gives the prototype for the member functions. The rest of the process involves writing C++ statements that implement the member functions. The resulting C++ code for each operation is called a *member function definition* or a *member function implementation*. In this book, we use the term "implementation" to describe the code for the member functions.

Member function implementations are placed after the class declaration. Their C++ format is modeled after the syntax for free functions. One major difference is that the tag `"ClassName::"` precedes the member function name. The symbol `"::"` is the *scope resolution operator* that signals the compiler that the function is a member of the class. By using the operator, the statements in the function body may access all of the members of the class, even the private data members. For instance, consider a member function from each of the StudentAccount, Rectangle, and CircleShape classes. The first line of each implementation includes the `"::"` operator to associate the function with the class.

```
// payment is a member function in StudentAccount class.
void StudentAccount::payment(double amount)
{ <function body> }

// update function is associated with the Rectangle class
void Rectangle::setSides(double l, double w)
{ <function body> }

// this access function is associated with CircleShape
double CircleShape::getRadius()
{ <function body> }
```

By adding the scope resolution operator, we obtain the implementation format for a non-constructor member function.

SYNTAX ▬▬▬▬▬▬▬▬▬▬▬▬▬▬▬▬▬▬▬▬▬▬▬▬

Member Function Implementation (non-constructor)

Form: `returnType ClassName::functionName(argument list)`
```
{
    <C++ statements>
}
```

Action: The operation functionName() is a member function of the class called ClassName. The scope resolution operator :: associates the function with the class. In all other respects, a member function is coded like a free function.

Example: The member function getLength() of the Rectangle class simply returns the attribute length of a Rectangle object.

```
double Rectangle::getLength()
{
    return length;
}
```

Illustrating Member Function Implementations

To illustrate the implementation of class member functions, we look at the operations `getBalance()` and `writeAccount()` in the StudentAccount class. We give a partial declaration of the StudentAccount class that includes all of the data members, the constructor and the function prototypes for our selected operations. The implementation of the constructor introduces special syntax and is covered in the next section.

studacct.h

```
DECLARATION: StudentAccount CLASS ━━━━━

class StudentAccount
{
   private:
       String studentID;      // ID in the form ##.####
       String studentName;    // student name
       double balance;        // account balance
   public:
       // constructor that initializes the data attributes
       StudentAccount(String ID, String name, double initbal);
            . . . .
       double getBalance();   // return current balance
       void writeAccount();   // output account information
};
```

The member functions are implemented outside of the class declaration. The scope resolution operator links the external function implementation with the private members in the class declaration. This allows each member function to access the data members in the StudentAccount class. The `getBalance()` operation returns the current balance of the account.

```
// return current value of private data member balance
double StudentAccount::getBalance()
{
   return balance;
}
```

The `writeAccount()` member function displays the three attributes, one per line.

```
// output account information along with labels
void StudentAccount:: writeAccount()
{
   cout << "ID:        " << studentID << endl;
   cout << "Name:      " << studentName << endl;
   cout << "Balance:   " << '$' << setreal(1,2)
        << balance << endl;
}
```

Implementing the Constructor

A constructor in a class declaration is a special member function with the same name as the class. Its task is to initialize the attributes of an object. The function prototype has no return type.

```
ClassName(T₁ arg₁, T₂ arg₂, …);   // Tᵢ are argument types
```

For its implementation, the constructor must use the scope resolution operator like any other member function. As a result, we find the seemingly redundant syntax

```
ClassName::ClassName(T₁ arg₁, T₂ arg₂, …)
{. . .}
```

The first reference to ClassName identifies the constructor as a member function in the class. The second reference to ClassName is the actual name of the member function. For instance, the implementation of the StudentAccount constructor begins with

```
StudentAccount::StudentAccount(String ID, String name,
                                double initbal)
{. . .}
```

To implement a constructor, C++ allows the programmer to use an *initialization list* to assign initial values to the data members. The initialization list is separated from the argument list by a ":" and includes data members followed by their initial value enclosed in parentheses. The items in the list are separated by commas. The following syntax describes the general format for implementing a constructor with an initialization list.

SYNTAX ▬▬▬▬▬▬▬▬▬▬▬▬▬▬▬▬▬▬▬▬▬▬▬

Constructor Implementation with Initialization List

Form:
```
ClassName::ClassName(...,Tₘ argₘ,...,Tₙ argₙ,...):
         dataₓ (argₘ),data_y (argₙ),...
    {
        <statements initialize remaining data members>
    }
```

Action: From the initialization list, data member data$_x$ is assigned the value arg$_m$, data$_y$ is assigned the value arg$_n$, and so forth. The list may initialize only selected data members. The remaining data members are assigned initial values in the body of the constructor.

Example: The constructor for StudentAccount has three arguments that initialize the student ID, the student name, and the beginning account balance. The action of the function is carried out by the initialization list. The function body is empty since no other statements are required.

```
StudentAccount::StudentAccount(String ID,
            String name, double initbal):
      studentID(ID), studentName(name), balance(initbal)
   {}
```

The body of a constructor may contain declarations and statements that supplement the action of the initialization list. In this case, the action of the initialization list is performed before the statements in the constructor body. With simple constructors, all data members are given values by the initialization list and the function body is empty (`"{}"`).

Initializing the data members can be done in the constructor body rather than with an initialization list. For instance, the StudentAccount constructor implementation can be written as follows:

Technical Note

```
// implementation constructor without initialization list
StudentAccount::StudentAccount(String ID, String name,
                               double initbal)
{
    studentID = ID;
    studentName = name;
    balance = initbal;
}
```

The use of an initialization list is sometimes required for the implementation of class inheritance, constants, and references in advanced C++ programming. In this book, we will use the initialization list whenever applicable.

Implementing the Rectangle class

In the previous sections, we introduced the syntax to implement the member functions of a class. Now let us put all of the ideas together to create a complete implementation of the Rectangle class that was introduced in Chapter 1. We begin with a declaration of the class that lists the data members in the private section and the constructor and other member functions in the public section.

```
class Rectangle
{
    private:
        // length and width of the Rectangle object
        double length,width;
    public:
        // constructor
        Rectangle(double l = 0.0, double w = 0.0);

        // compute rectangle measurements
        double perimeter();
        double area();

        // data access functions
        double getLength();                     // return length
        double getWidth();                      // return width

        // data update function
        void setSides(double l, double w);   // update dimensions
};
```

The implementation of each member function is given outside of the class declaration. By using the scope resolution operator " :: ", we associate a member function with the class and allow the C++ statements in its implementation to access the data members length and width.

Constructor:

The constructor arguments specify the initial dimensions for a Rectangle object. An initialization list assigns the arguments to the length and width attributes.

```
// implementation of the Rectangle constructor
Rectangle::Rectangle(double l, double w) : length(l), width(w)
{}
```

Access Functions:

The class provides two "get" functions that access the values of the data members length and width.

```
// return the value of the length attribute
double Rectangle::getLength()
{
    return length;
}

// return the value of the width attribute
double Rectangle::getWidth()
{
    return width;
}
```

Update Function:

The values of length and width are initially set by the constructor. Their values can be updated during run-time by using the member function set-Sides() that has new values for the data members as arguments. Since an initialization list is available only to the constructor, the new values must be assigned in the body of the function.

```
// assign new values for the length and width
float Rectangle::setSides(double l, double w)
{
    length = l;
    width = w;
}
```

Measurement Functions:

The Rectangle class features the measurement functions area() and perimeter(). For each implementation, we use the length and width to compute the measurement and return the result.

```
// the area is the product of the length and width
double Rectangle::area()
{
    return length * width;
}
```

```
// the perimeter is twice the sum of the length and width
double Rectangle::perimeter()
{
    return 2 * (length + width);
}
```

5-2   ORGANIZING PROGRAM SOURCE CODE

In this book, we develop program source using a series of separate files. Corresponding to each class, there is a header file that contains its declaration and implementation. In some cases, we also use free function utility libraries such as "**textlib.h**". These files contain both the prototype and implementation of the functions. The main program is contained in a ".cpp" file that #includes the header files and may implement its own free functions. In the following sections, we show you how to build the class header files and the main program file.

Building A Class Header File

A class header file consists of the class declaration and its implementation. The file ends in ".h" and should have a name that is descriptive of the class. For instance, the StudentAccount class header file is "studacct.h" and the Rectangle class header file is "rect.h". In order to be compatible with current operating systems, we restrict the file names to 8 characters. The following is the structure of a class header file. In case the implementation needs access to other C++ header files, they can be brought in with include statements at the beginning of the source code.

```
SYNTAX ═══════════════════════════════════

Class Header File  "clname.h"

Form:      // include files
           #include <C++ system header files>
           #include "programmer-defined header files>

           // class declaration
           class ClassName
           {
               private:
                   . . . .
               public:
           . . . .
           };

           //   class implementation
```

```
                        // constructor implementation
                        ClassName::ClassName ( . . .)  : . . .
                        { . . . }

                        returnType ClassName::memberFunction(. . .)
                        { . . .}
```

Action: The header file contains the declaration and implementation of the class. By including the file, a programmer may declare objects of the class type and use their member junctions.

Example: The inclusion of other header files depends on the class declaration and implementation. For instance, the StudentAccount class contains data members of type String and the writeAccount() function uses "cout" statements to list the values of the data members. For the header file studacct.h, we include the C++ system file **iostream.h** and the programmer-defined header file **tstring.h.**

```
    #include <iostream.h>  // access to cout
    #include "tstring.h"   // access to String

    // class declaration
    class StudentAccount
    {
        . . .
    };

    // class implementation
    . . .
```

Building the Main Program

The source code for the main program is located in a single ".cpp" file. Its structure begins with a series of include statements that specify system and programmer-defined header files. The main program file must include the function `main()` that specifies the starting point for execution. The compiler will generate object code for the main program. The system linker merges the compiled object code and system object code libraries to create a single executable code file. Figure 5-1 illustrates the action of the compiler and linker for the main program file "program.cpp" and a single class header file "clname.h".

PROGRAM 5.1

The program declares a 4.5 by 8.2 rectangle and outputs its area and diagonal length. In the design of the program, we use the mathematical function sqrt() to compute the diagonal

```
    diagonal = sqrt(length² + width²)
```

and the manipulator setreal() to output the real numbers with two decimal place preci-

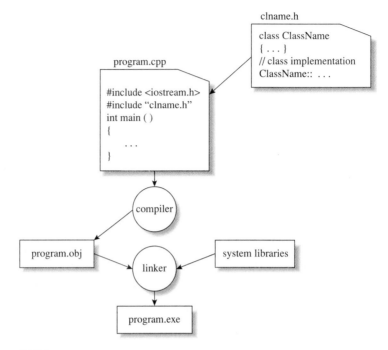

FIGURE 5-1
Compiling and Linking Files.

sion. To support these operations and to declare a Rectangle object, the main program, "prog5_1.cpp", includes four header files. The final executable file is "prog5_1.exe".

```
#include <iostream.h>
#include <math.h>     // access sqrt function

#include "rect.h"     // access Rectangle class
#include "textlib.h" // access manipulator setreal()

int main()
{
    double diagonal;

    Rectangle rect(4.5,8.2);
    cout << "Area is " << setreal(5,2) << rect.area() << endl;

    diagonal = sqrt(rect.getLength()*rect.getLength() +
                    rect.getWidth()*rect.getWidth());
    cout << "Diagonal is" << setreal(5,2) << diagonal << endl;

    return 0;
}
```

```
Run:

Area is 36.90
Diagonal is 9.35
```

Building and Using the Accumulator Class

We illustrate the building of a header file and a main program file using the C++ Accumulator class that was introduced in Section 3.7. The class has a single data member, total, that contains the cumulative value of the object. The constructor has an argument that initializes the total. The argument has a default value of 0.0. For member functions, getTotal() returns the current cumulative total in the object and addValue() updates the total by adding a new value. This example revisits most of the introductory concepts in the chapter and illustrates how you would build a class and then use it in an application.

Start by building the class header file "accum.h" to contain the declaration and implementation of the Accumulator class.

class Declaration:

```cpp
class Accumulator
{
   private:
      double total;                           // cumulative total
   public:
      Accumulator(double value = 0.0);        // initialize total
      double getTotal();                      // return total
      void addValue(double value = 1.0);      // add to total
};
```

Class Implementation:

The class implementation follows the declaration of the class in accum.h.

```cpp
// implement the constructor with an initialization list
// initialize total
Accumulator::Accumulator(double value): total(value)
{}


// implement the member function getTotal()
// return the current total
double Accumulator::getTotal()
{
   return total;
}
```

```
// implement the update member function addTotal()
// add value to total
void Accumulator::addValue(double value)
{
   total += value;
}
```

The program uses Accumulator objects intValue, posValue and negValue to maintain a series of totals. Input consists of a sequence of integers that terminate when a 0 is read. The Accumulator objects maintain totals for the entire set of integers, for the positive integers, and for the negative integers. Their final values are output using the member function getTotal(). The main program is contained in the source file apl5_1.cpp that is found in the software supplement.

```
#include <iostream.h>

#include "accum.h"

int main()
{
   Accumulator intValue, posValue, negValue;
   int value;

   cin >> value;
   while (value != 0)
   {
      intValue.addValue(value);
      if (value < 0)
         negValue.addValue(value);
      else
         posValue.addValue(value);
      cin >> value;
   }
   cout << "Total input value is " << intValue.getTotal()
        << endl;
   cout << "Total negative value is " << negValue.getTotal()
        << endl;
   cout << "Total positive value is " << posValue.getTotal()
        << endl;

   return 0;
}
```

```
Run:

8 4 -3 -7 -5 6 -2 -10 0
```

```
Total input value is -9
Total negative value is -27
Total positive value is 18
```

In our design, each program source file may use include statements that provide access to other classes and free functions. With multiple header files, it is possible that the same class declaration may be included more than once. For instance, the drawing classes **rectsh.h** and **circlesh.h** both rely on a Shape class found in the file **shape.h.** If the main program includes both the rectangle and circle drawing classes, the Shape class will be included twice.

```
program.cpp          rectsh.h              circlesh.h
. . .                      . . .                    ...
#include "rectsh.h"   #include "shape.h"    #include "shape.h"
#include "circsh.h"
```

Technical Note

A program is not permitted multiple declarations of classes. The problem is solved by using the preprocessor directive `"#ifndef"` in the file shape.h. This allows the compiler to disregard a class declaration if the information was already provided by another include statement. We illustrate the use of this directive for **shape.h.** The flag GEOMETRIC_FIGURES_BASE indicates the file has already been included. To understanding the technical details, see Appendix E for a discussion of `"#ifndef"` and other preprocessor directives.

```
#ifndef GEOMETRIC_FIGURES_BASE   // test if flag is set
#define GEOMETRIC_FIGURES_BASE   // if not, set the flag


. . . .                          // class declaration
. . . .                          // class implementation
#endif   // end of GEOMETRIC_FIGURES_BASE header file
```

Alternative Source Code Design (Optional)

In this book, we design a class header file to contain both the class declaration and implementation. This is only one approach to designing program source code. In this section we discuss two alternative methods that are quite different.

One method places the class declaration and implementation in the main program file. This creates a single source unit that can be compiled and run. While simple, the approach complicates the ability to reuse software, that is one of the most important benefits of object-oriented programming. To reuse the class, a programmer must copy the declaration and implementation from one main program to another. Figure 5-2 illustrates a single source unit, program.cpp. The first part of the unit consists of include statements and a declaration of the ClassName class. The other parts of the source unit consist of the main() function and the implementation of class member functions.

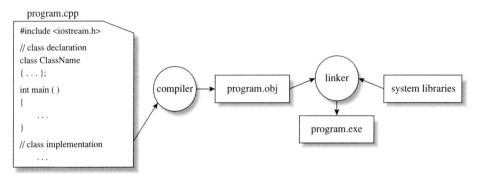

FIGURE 5-2
Placing a Class in the Main Program Source File.

Commercial software distribution is often done with separately compiled object code libraries. This is done by a second method that splits the class declaration and implementation into separate files. The declaration is placed in a header file (clname.h). The implementation is placed in a source file (clname.cpp), compiled, and then inserted into an object code library. When a program needs the class, it includes the header file **clname.h** so that the compiler knows the structure of the class. Figure 5-3 displays three separate source files for the class declaration, implementation, and main program. The header file **clname.h** and the implementation file **clname.cpp** are compiled to create an

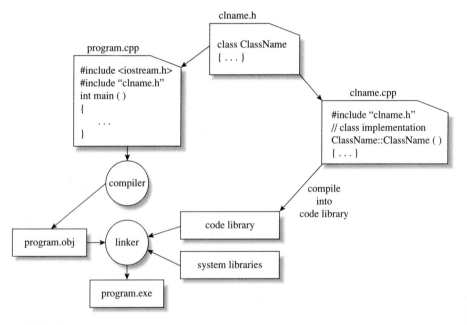

FIGURE 5-3
Linking from an Object Code Library.

object file **clname.obj** that is included in the code library. A separate compilation creates a program object file **program.obj.** The linker combines the appropriate code and system libraries with the program object file to create the executable file **program.exe.**

Using code libraries has several important advantages. Large blocks of code can be precompiled into libraries and do not have to be compiled with the main program. Most commercial software distributions do not provide the source code for the class and free function implementations. The classes and free functions declared in **iostream.h** and **math.h** are an example. Programs must link from the corresponding code libraries to use the functions in an application.

5-3 ERROR CHECKING IN CLASS AND PROGRAM DESIGN

In designing an application, a programmer must be aware that the final product will execute in a run-time environment that includes not only the computer system but also a user. Errors can occur that cause the program to malfunction or produce inaccurate results. For instance, a user may enter incorrect data that is accepted by the program and produces invalid results. Computer people refer to this as the "GIGO" (garbage-in garbage-out) principal. With a GUI operating system, a program may mismanage memory and cause other executing programs to fail as well. Good program design attempts to anticipate errors and create code that can maintain the integrity of the program and the system as a whole. We look at error checking in function implementation. For large applications, C++ allows more advanced error handling using exceptions. We discuss this approach briefly in a technical note.

In a function implementation, error checking is provided by a selection statement that indicates when there are invalid run-time arguments or when the current state of the object does not support the operation. For instance, the charge() operation in the StudentAccount class must have a positive amount for its argument. An attempt to charge a negative amount does not make sense and indicates a logical problem in the program. When such an error is identified, the operation must take some form of remedial action.

The function may output an error message and return control to the calling calling statement, thereby allowing the program to continue execution. This strategy assumes the calling statement may reasonably continue and perhaps repeat the function call. Often this approach is accomplished by returning a logical flag that indicates whether an error occurs. For instance, the charge() function could return a bool value of true when no error occurs and a value of false when an error is detected.

```
bool StudentAccount::charge(double amount)
{
   // if amount negative, indicate error. return false
   if (amount < 0)
```

```
    {
        cerr << "Charge must not be negative" << endl;
        return false;
    }
    else
    {
        // debit the balance and return true
        balance -= amount;
        return true;
    }
}
```

The error message uses the C++ stream "cerr" that is an output stream distinct from cout. Since some applications may want to equate cout with a disk file, C++ provides the object cerr that always sends output to the screen.

Some errors indicate that the run-time environment is in an unrecoverable condition or can produce incorrect results. We handle these errors, called *fatal errors*, by using the *exit()* operation from the system file **stdlib.h.**

SYNTAX ▬▬▬▬▬▬▬▬▬▬▬▬▬▬▬▬▬▬▬▬▬▬▬▬▬▬▬▬▬▬▬▬

The exit Statement

Form: void exit(int status);

Action: The function causes the program to terminate, and program control returns to the run-time system that initiated execution. The value of status is used by the run-time system to evaluate the state of the program upon termination. A value of 0 indicates that the program terminated normally; a value greater than 0 indicates that the program terminated abnormally. In this book, we use exit(1) to terminate the program when a fatal error occurs.

Example: cerr << "Fatal error. Program terminates";
            exit(1);

This is the approach we use with the `charge()` function in the Student-Account class. A negative amount as the argument is identified as a fatal error and the `exit()` statement terminates the program. The same error checking is used in `payment()` when the amount is negative.

```
// make sure amount is positive. if not, terminate the
// program; otherwise debit the amount from the balance
void StudentAccount::charge(double amount)
{
    if (amount < 0)
    {
        cerr << "Charge must be positive" << endl;
        exit(1);
    }
    balance -= amount;
}
```

Technical
Note

In large systems applications, a program may use *C++ exceptions* to handle errors. To illustrate the concept, we picture an application that implements a chain of function calls. For instance, a word processor calls a grammar checker that calls a spell checker. Before initiating a call to the grammar checker, the word processor marks the code that will execute if an error occurs in the chain of operations of the grammar or spell checker. Figure 5-4 illustrates how exceptions enable an application to recover from "distant" errors.

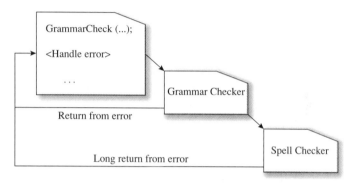

FIGURE 5-4
C++ Exceptions.

Exploring
Concepts

The formula $z = x^{1/n}$ finds the nth root of x. The operation is not valid when n is zero or when n is even and x is a negative number. For instance, $(-3)^{1/2}$ is not a real number. Describe an error checking algorithm that outputs a message and terminates the program when the conditions are invalid.

5-4 PRIVATE MEMBER FUNCTIONS

Up to this point in the book, all of the class operations have been public member functions. These operations provide an interface to the object and allow a calling statement to access the data members of the object. As our experience with classes increases, we identify examples where some operations are used locally in support of the class implementation. These operations are *private member functions* that are not available to the calling statement. Similar to free functions in an application, these private functions make the class implementation more efficient and easier to read.

The Time24 Class

People typically measure time with twelve-hour periods that break the day into AM and PM hours. For computer applications, time is more conveniently measured in a single 24-hour block. For instance, an update to a file at 7:30 PM stamps the last modification time as 19:30. With the 24-hour clock, hours are given in the range of 0 to 23 and minutes in the range of 0 to 59. We illustrate private member functions with the Time24 class whose objects store time in 24-hour format.

The class has hour and minute as integer data members. These values are initialized by the constructor whose arguments have a default value of 0. Thus, by default, a Time24 object is set to 0:00 or midnight. For input and output, the class has member functions, called `readTime()` and `writeTime()` that enter time in the form "<hour>:<minute>" and output it with the same format. The class also includes two member functions, `getHour()` and `getMinute()`, that access the private data members. For updating the time, the class features a member function, called `addTime()`, that takes a time interval in minutes and adds it to the current time. For instance,

```
Time24 t;          // object is initially set to 0:00

t.readTime();      // Input: 15:50  (3:50 PM)
t.addTime(150);    // add 150 minutes = 2 hours 30 minutes
t.writeTime();     // Output:  18:20
```

The constructor and operations, `readTime()` and `addTime()`, make sure that the values for the private data members fall within the 24-hour and 60-minute time ranges respectively. At times this means adjusting the minutes and hour, a process that is called normalizing the time. For instance,

Original Time	*Normalized Time*	
14 hours 80 minutes	15 hours 20 minutes	
27 hours 15 minutes	3 hours 15 minutes	(next day)
22 hours 150 minutes	0 hours 30 minutes	(150 = 2 hours 30 minutes)

Within the class, normalization of the time is executed by a private member function `normalizeTime()`. A private member function is referred to as a utility function, since it is a tool that is used by other member functions. (Figure 5-5).

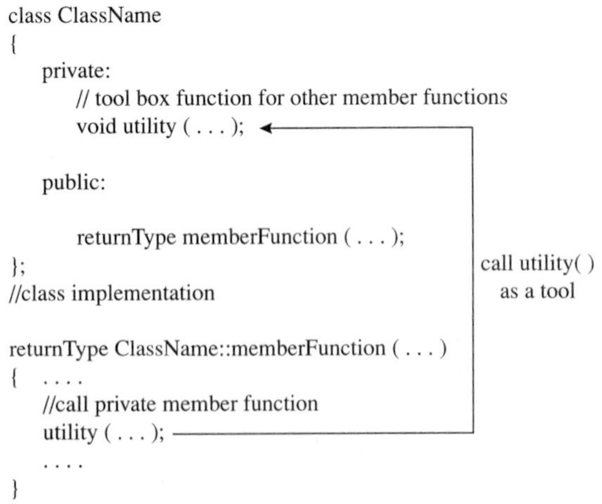

```
class ClassName
{
    private:
        // tool box function for other member functions
        void utility ( . . . );   ◄─────────────┐

    public:

        returnType memberFunction ( . . . );
};                                              call utility( )
//class implementation                          as a tool

returnType ClassName::memberFunction ( . . . )
{   . . . .
        //call private member function
        utility ( . . . ); ────────────────────┘
        . . . .
}
```

FIGURE 5-5
Private Member Function.

Time24 Class Declaration and UML

Before giving the declaration for Time24, we display the UML representation of the class (Figure 5-6). Note that normalizeTime() is adorned with the lock symbol 🔒. This highlights the fact that it is a private member function. We will give a detailed description of normalizeTime() when we implement the class.

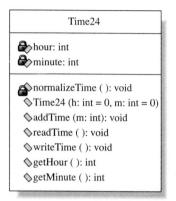

FIGURE 5-6

UML Representation of the Time24 Class.

The following is a declaration of the class along with examples that illustrate its use.

time24.h

```
DECLARATION: Time24 CLASS

class Time24
{
    private:
        int hour, minute;       // data members
        void normalizeTime();   // put time units in range
    public:
        // constructor with starting time
        Time24(int h = 0, int m = 0);

        // update time by adding m minutes
        void addTime(int m);

        // input/output of time
        void readTime();
        void writeTime();

        // access member functions
        int getHour();
        int getMinute();
};
```

EXAMPLE 5.1

1. The normalizeTime() function is used by the member functions to adjust the time.

```
Time24 t(5,90);    // 90 minutes normalized to 1 hour 30 minutes
t.writeTime();     // Output:  6:30

t.readTime();      // Input:   30:15
t.writeTime();     // Output:  6:15

t.addTime(75);     // add 1 hour 15 minutes
t.writeTime();     // Output:  7:30
```

2. The Time24 objects gameStart and gameLength record the starting time of a game and its length respectively. They are used to determine the time when the game ends (gameEnd). The functions getMinute() and getHour() are used to convert the game length to minutes.

```
Time24 gameStart(19,30);            // game starts 7:30 PM
Time24 gameLength(2,45);            // game length 2:45
Time24 gameEnd = gameStart:         // equate times

int  lengthInMinutes = gameLength.getHour() * 60
                     + gameLength.getMinute();
gameEnd.addTime(lengthInMinutes);   // update gameEnd

gameEnd.writeTime();                // Output: 22:15  ■
```

APPLICATION 5-2 TIME AROUND THE WORLD

The program compares time for San Francisco (USA), Melbourne (Australia), and Frankfort (Germany). If San Francisco is the base time, Frankfurt is 9 hours ahead and Melbourne is 17 hours ahead. An hour represents a time zone. The program declares three Time24 objects corresponding to the cities. After reading a time for San Francisco, the program equates the time objects and then uses the function addTime() to determine the time in Frankfurt (add 9 * 60 minutes) and Melborne (add 17 * 60 minutes). The member function writeTime() displays the times.

```
#include <iostream.h>

#include "time24.h"      // use Time24 class

int main()
{
   // declare time objects
   Time24 sanfrancisco, melbourne, frankfurt;

   // read the current time
   cout <<  "Enter the current time in San Francisco: ";
   sanfrancisco.readTime();
```

```
    // assign melbourne and frankfurt the current time
    melbourne = frankfurt = sanfrancisco;
    // melbourne is 17 hours ahead. frankfurt is 9 hours ahead
    melbourne.addTime(17*60);
    frankfurt.addTime(9*60);

    cout << "The time in Frankfurt is ";
    frankfurt.writeTime();
    cout << endl;
    cout << "The time in Melbourne is ";
    melbourne.writeTime();
    cout << endl;

    return 0;
}
```

```
Run:

Enter the current time in San Francisco: 6:00
The time in Frankfurt is 15:00
The time in Melbourne is 23:00
```

Implementation of the Time24 class

This section gives a partial implementation for the Time24 class including the constructor and the public member function `addTime()`. Using an example, we first illustrate the algorithm for the private member function normalizeTime() that is called by both the constructor and addTime(). Consider the Time24 object t that is initially set to 22 hours and 210 minutes.

```
    Time24    t(22,210);        // 22 hours and 210 minutes
```

The normalizing process uses integer division by 60 to adjust the minutes and then division by 24 to adjust the hours. Start with the 210 minutes. The quotient 210/60 defines the number of extra hours that can be extracted from the original 210 minutes.

```
    ExtraHour = 210/60       // ExtraHour =3
```

Use the remainder operator "%" to shift the minute value into the range of 0 to 59.

```
    minute = 210 % 60;       // minute  = 30
```

Add the extra hours to hour and adjust its value using integer division by 24. The remainder puts hour within the range of ot.23. All extra full days (24 hours) are discarded.

```
    hour =  (hour + ExtraHour) % 24;
         =  (22 + 3) % 24
         =  25 % 24              // hour = 1
```

normalizeTime:

```
// set minute and hour within proper range
void  Time24::normalizeTime()
{
    int extraHours = minute / 60;

    // set minute in range 0 to 59
    minute %= 60;

    // update hour, set in range 0 to 23
    hour = (hour + extraHours) % 24;
}
```

The constructor sets hour and minute using the initialization list. Since we allow both hour and minute to be assigned any positive value, it may be necessary to normalize hour and minute. This task is performed by calling the private function `normalizeTime()`.

```
// assign starting time using initialization list
Time24::Time24(int h, int m) : hour(h), minute(m)
{
    // put hour and minute in correct range
    normalizeTime();
}
```

The member function `addTime()` takes a time interval in minutes and uses the value to update the current time. The operation simply adds the value of the argument to the data member minute and calls `normalizeTime()`.

```
// add m minutes to the time
void Time24::addTime(int m)
{
    // add m to minute. minute may exceed 59, so normalize
    minute += m;
    normalizeTime();
}
```

Private Member Functions and Code Duplication. In many applications, a particular output or calculation is repeated at different locations in the program, perhaps with different data values. Unless the code is relatively brief, the program should not repeat identical blocks of code at several locations. The *principle of code duplication* suggests that the operation be abstracted into a function and executed by function calls. The function normalizeTime() demonstrates this principle.

Using a private member function to display error messages is another example of the principle. Often two or more member functions in a class do error checking. Rather than having each function display an error message and terminate the program, a programmer can develop a single error function that takes an argument identifying the error. The function handles the message and program termination.

```
void error(int err);
```

This approach not only reduces code duplication but also places the error messages in one location. See Review Exercise 5.5 for an example.

Exploring Concepts

Assume the Time24 class has the member function subTime() that subtracts minutes for the current time. Investigate the algorithm that would implement this function.

5-5 MEMBER FUNCTIONS WITH LOOPS: THE LOAN CLASS

This chapter provides a number of different classes that illustrate implementation techniques. With the Loan class, we have a member function that uses a loop.

Most of us have experience with loans and loan repayment. Each month, a payment is made that covers the interest owed and allots a portion to debt reduction. The amount of the monthly payment is determined by the size of the loan (principal), the interest rate (per month), and the length of the loan (in months). The following calculations look at a single payment and determine the amount that is allocated to interest, the amount that is allocated to loan reduction, and the balance that is still owed.

```
// compute the interest owed for the month
interest = loanBalance * rate;

// portion of the payment used to reduce the balance
loanReduction = payment - interest;

// compute the new balance of the loan
loanBalance = loanBalance - loanReduction;
```

EXAMPLE 5.2

A new car owner obtains a 4 year loan of $20,000 at 8% iterest. The loan is repaid in 48 monthly equal payments where the interest rate is 0.08/12. The minimum monthly payment is calculated to be

```
payment  =  $488.26   (required minimum payment)
```

1. For the first payment, the following loan information is used.

```
interest = loanBalance * rate
         = 20000 * 0.08/12 =  133.33
loanReduction = payment - interest
              = 488.26 - 133.33 = 354.93
loanBalance = loanBalance - loanReduction
            = 20000 - 354.93 = 19645.07
```

2. For the second payment, the monthly loan rate is applied to a current balance of $19,645.07. Over time, the balance is continually reduced and less of the payment goes to interest and more goes to loan reduction. The following graphs compare these amounts for each month of the loan. ∎

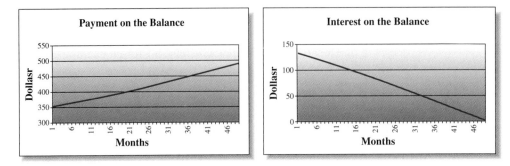

The Loan Class

The Loan class is designed to handle simple interest loans that are repaid with a fixed number of payments. Home mortgages and car loans are typical examples. The class contains three data members, loanBalance, interestRate, and payment-Periods, that specify the key components of the loan. Other data members record necessary loan information, such as the minimum monthly payment that is required to retire the debt. The member functions in the class deal with payments and loan statistics. Before we look at these functions in detail, we give a formal declaration of the class.

loan.h

```
DECLARATION: Loan CLASS

class Loan
{
    private:
        double   loanBalance;      // current amount owed
        double   interestRate;     // interest per payment period
        int      paymentPeriods;   // number of payment periods

        double   minPayment;       // minimum payment per period
        double   interestPmt;      // interest paid in last
                                   // payment
        double   principalPmt;     // principal paid in last
                                   // payment
    public:
        // constructor
        Loan(double principal, double rate, int periods);

        // return the minimum loan payment
        double minimumPayment();

        // make minimum payment + extraAmount
        void makePayment(double extraAmount = 0.0);

        // output loan statistics for current and future
        // payments; argument allows for extra
```

```
        // payment over the minimum
        void writePaymentInfo();
        void writeLoanInfo(double extraAmount = 0.0);
};
```

The constructor initializes the loan amount, the interest rate per payment period, and the number of payments. The information is necessary to compute the minimum monthly payment, `minPayment`, which is the return value for the member function `minimumPayment()`. The calculation of the minimum payment is done by the constructor. Consider, for instance, the car loan in Example 5.2.

```
Loan  carLoan(20000, 0.08/12, 48);   // loan specifications
cout << carLoan.minimumPayment();    // Output: 488.26
```

The function `makePayment()` applies a payment to the loan balance. The function applies the minimum payment, that is determined by the constructor. The borrower may make an additional payment that is passed as a run-time argument extraAmount. By default, the argument is 0.0. Consider the carLoan object. A call to `makePayment()` represents a payment of $488.26. If the borrower wishes to pay $550.00 on the loan, the extra amount would be $61.74.

```
carLoan.makePayment();        // simple payment of 488.26
carLoan.makePayment(61.74);   // payment of 550.00
```

The member function `writePaymentInfo()` pertains only to the most recent payment. It outputs the amount of that payment and the remaining loan balance. The information also includes the amount of the payment applied to interest and the amount applied to loan reduction. The member function `writeLoanInfo()` provides loan statistics that can be used by the borrower to determine future loan statistics. The function assumes the minimum payment plus an additional amount that is passed as a run-time argument. By default, the additional amount is 0.0. The function outputs the total number of payments necessary to retire the loan and the total amount of interest paid. With this information, the borrower can judge the interest savings that occur when "balloon payments" are made on a loan.

PROGRAM 5.2

The program illustrates the use of the Loan class for the car loan described in Example 5.2. After determining the minimum payment, we project a loan history based on this level of payment. We also project a loan history based on paying $550.00 per month. The program concludes by actually making a minimum payment and then displaying the current status of the loan.

```
#include <iostream.h>

#include "loan.h"
```

```
int main()
{
   // a $20,000 car loan at 8% (APR) for 48 months
   Loan carLoan(20000.0,.08/12, 48);

   cout << "Minimum loan payment " << setreal(1,2)
        << carLoan.minimumPayment() << endl << endl;

   // what happens if loan is paid off with minimum payments
   cout << "Loan history assuming minimum payment" << endl;
   carLoan.writeLoanInfo();
   cout << endl;

   // what happens with payments of $550.00 per month
   cout << "Loan history assuming payment of $550.00" << endl;
   carLoan.writeLoanInfo(550.0-carLoan.minimumPayment());
   cout << endl;

   carLoan.makePayment();          // make the first payment
   cout << "Loan status after first minimum payment" << endl;
   carLoan.writePaymentInfo();  // current loan status

   return 0;
}
```

```
Run:

Minimum loan payment 488.26

Loan history assuming minimum payment
   Current    Monthly    Total       Total
   Balance    Payment    Payments    Interest
   20000.00   488.26        48        3436.41

Loan history assuming payment of $550.00
   Current    Monthly    Total       Total
   Balance    Payment    Payments    Interest
   20000.00   550.00        42        2981.19

Loan status after first minimum payment
   Payment      Interest      Principal     Balance
    488.26       133.33        354.93        19645.07
```

Implementing the Loan Class

We give a partial implementation of the Loan class that includes the constructor and the member functions makePayment() and writeLoanInfo(). These functions include the key algorithms of the class implementation.

Constructor

The constructor initializes the class data members, including the minimum payment for the loan. The payment is determined by a formula that we provide without explanation.

For principle p, number of payments n, and interest rate r

$$\text{minPayment} = p * \left(\frac{r(1 + r)^n}{(1 + r)^n - 1} \right)$$

All of the data members except minPayment are set by the initialization list. The calculation of `minPayment` uses the mathematical function `pow()` from **math.h**.

```
// constructor. initialize data members
Loan::Loan(double principal, double rate, int periods)
    :loanBalance(principal), interestRate(rate),
     paymentPeriods(periods), interestPmt(0.0),
     principalPmt(0.0)
{
   // compute minimum payment
   double term = pow(1+interestRate, paymentPeriods);

   minPayment = interestRate*term*loanBalance/(term-1);
}
```

makePayment

The function assumes a payment of `minPayment+extraAmount` dollars. The operation computes the interest and the amount applied to loan reduction. The results are assigned to data members `interestPmt` and `principalPmt`, respectively. These values are listed as part of the output from `writePaymentInfo()`. The function reduces the amount of the loan by `principalAmt`.

```
// make a payment of payment+extraAmount
void Loan::makePayment(double extraAmount)
{
   // compute the interest and payment on the balance.
   // update the balance
   interestPmt = interestRate*loanBalance;
   principalPmt = minPayment + extraAmount - interestPmt;
   loanBalance -= principalPmt;
}
```

writeLoanInfo

The `writeLoanInfo()` function uses a while loop that starts with the current loan balance and simulates payments of `minPayment+extraAmount` dollars per period until the loan is paid off (balance ≤ 0). In reality, the last payment of a loan is reduced so the balance is exactly 0.00. The loop accumulates the total interest from the payments. A series of output statements list the current balance, the number of required payments, and the total accumulated interest.

```
// assume payments of minPayment+extraAmount, output
// total payments necessary to retire the loan and
// the total amount of interest paid.
void Loan::writeLoanInfo(double extraAmount)
{
    double balance = loanBalance, interest,
                        totalInterest = 0.0;
    int paymentNumber = 0;

    // loop while money is owed
    while (balance > 0)
    {
        // make a payment
        paymentNumber++;
        // compute interest and reduce the balance
        interest = balance * interestRate;
        totalInterest += interest;
        balance = balance - (minPayment+extraAmount-interest);
    }
    cout << "  Current    Monthly    Total      Total" << endl;
    cout << "  Balance    Payment    Payments   Interest"
         << endl;
    cout << setreal(10,2) << loanBalance
         << setreal(9,2) << (minPayment+extraAmount)
         << setw(7) << paymentNumber
         << setreal(13,2) << totalInterest << endl;
}
```

5-6 INLINE CODE

In our implementation of classes, we create a header file that first gives the class declaration and then is followed by the implementation of the member functions. The format allows a programmer to separate the class declaration from the implementation details. While this separation is appealing, C++ allows a programmer to declare and implement a member function inside the class declaration. The process creates *inline code* that we illustrate for member functions in the Circle class.

The Circle Class Using Inline Code

Like a rectangle, a circle has measurement properties such as area and perimeter (circumference). Its objects are identified by a single data member called the radius that is used with the constant π to compute the measurements. In designing the Circle class, we include a constructor that initializes the radius with a default value of 0.0. The class also has two public member functions, called getRadius() and setRadius(), that access the private data member radius and allow a programmer to perform a run-time update of its value. Figure 5-7 displays the UML representation for the Circle class.

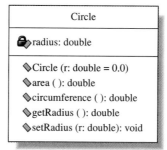

FIGURE 5-7
*The UML Representation of
the Circle Class.*

The following version of the class implementation uses inline code for the member functions. Note that each ";" that normally terminates the function prototype is replaced by the function body.

circle.h

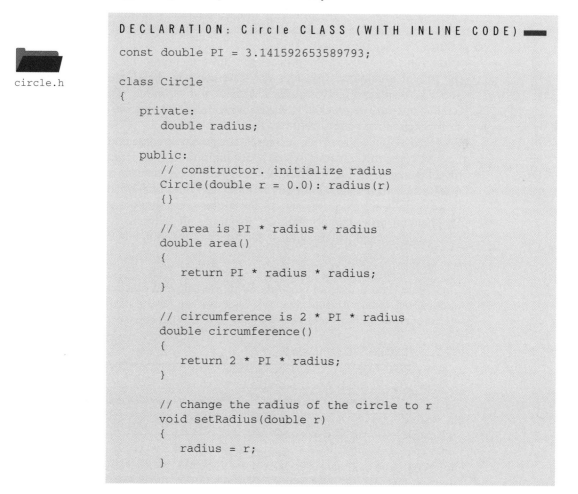

```
DECLARATION: Circle CLASS (WITH INLINE CODE)
const double PI = 3.141592653589793;

class Circle
{
    private:
        double radius;

    public:
        // constructor. initialize radius
        Circle(double r = 0.0): radius(r)
        {}

        // area is PI * radius * radius
        double area()
        {
            return PI * radius * radius;
        }

        // circumference is 2 * PI * radius
        double circumference()
        {
            return 2 * PI * radius;
        }

        // change the radius of the circle to r
        void setRadius(double r)
        {
            radius = r;
        }
```

```
        // return the radius of the circle
        double getRadius()
        {
            return radius;
        }
};
```

Since the constructor uses a default value of 0.0 for the initial radius, a Circle object can be declared without a constructor argument.

```
Circle c1(40), c2;                    // c1.radius = 40, c2.radius = 0;

rimSize = c1.circumference();  // rimSize is 2*π*40 (251.327)
c2.setRadius(5);               // radius = 5
cout << c2.area();             // output is π*5² (78.5398)
```

Implementing Inline Code

C++ handles inline code differently than it handles standard functions. Instead of generating code that passes arguments, transfers control to the function, and returns a value, the compiler replaces the function call with all of the statements in the function body. In the process, the run-time arguments are substituted for the formal arguments. Consider the statements in the Circle class discussion. Table 5-1 displays a C++ program statement and its "inline" expansion. The class scoping operator is attached to the radius to further define the substitution.

Since inline code substitutes the function body for each function call, the total size of the source code increases. If a function consists of only a very few lines of code, this increase in size is not important. Under these circumstances, the elimination of the function call and return mechanism makes inline code more efficient. If a function body requires 100 lines of code and three separate function calls are made, the size of the source code would expand by 300 lines. Professional programmers measure the trade-off between code size and run-time efficiency and will use inline code for small function blocks.

Application: Enclosing Maximum Area

The Circle class is used to illustrate an interesting and practical problem that is understood by farmers and ranchers. Suppose you have a fixed amount of fencing to enclose animals and you want to design a pen that provides the largest

TABLE 5-1 Inline Code.

C++ Source Code Statement	Compiler Interpreted Substitution
rimSize = c1. circumference ( );	rimSize = 2 * PI * c1::radius
c2.setRadius (5);	c2::radius = 5;
cout << c2.area ( );	cout << PI * c2::radius * c2::radius;

amount of area (Figure 5-8). Your best solution is a circle, a fact that can be proved using mathematical analysis. Our problem looks at squares as an appealing alternative. Rectangular objects with equal length and width define the squares.

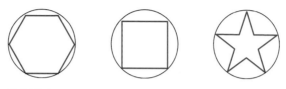

FIGURE 5-8
Comparing Closed Figures with the Same Perimeter.

APPLICATION 5-3 MAXIMIZING AREA

The program prompts for the perimeter (size of the pen) and declares a circle and square having that perimeter. The arguments used to initialize the objects are determined from the mathematical relationships:

Perimeter perim:

$$\text{radius of the corresponding circle: } \frac{\text{penPerimeter}}{2\pi}$$

$$\text{side of the corresponding square: } \frac{\text{penPerimeter}}{4}$$

The program outputs the ratio of the area of the square to the area of the circle (`square.area()/circle.area()`). The ratio is less than 1 since the area of a circle is the maximum.

```
#include <iostream.h>

#include "circle.h"          // use Circle class
#include "rect.h"            // use Rectangle class

int main()
{
    double penPerimeter;     // perimeter of the pen
    double radius;           // measurement for circle
    double side;             // measurement for rectangle

    cout << "Enter the perimeter of the pen: ";
    cin >> penPerimeter;

    // compute radius of circle and sides of the square
    radius = penPerimeter/(2*PI);
    side = penPerimeter/4;

    // declare the circle and square objects
```

```
      Circle circ(radius);
      Rectangle square(side, side);

      cout << "Ratio of area of square to area of circle is "
           << square.area()/circ.area() << endl;

      return 0;
}
```

```
Run:

Enter the perimeter of the pen: 4
Ratio of area of square to area of circle is 0.785398
```

Exploring Concepts

Note that the ratio of the area of the square to the area of the circle is .785398. Will all runs of the program output the same ratio? If your answer is "yes", can you prove your assertion?

Inline Code for Free Functions (Optional)

Inline code may also be used for free functions. The keyword *inline* must precede the return type in the function implementation. For instance, the following is an inline version of the cube() function.

```
// return the value x cubed; inline is a required keyword
inline double cube(double x)
{
    return x*x*x;
}
```

The resulting code removes the overhead of passing arguments, transfering control to the function, and returning a value. Each call to the function is replaced by the expression "x * x * x" where x is the run-time argument. When used selectively, inline code can significantly reduce execution time.

In the program design, we depart from the practice of declaring a function before the main program and then giving its implementation after the main program. With inline code, the function implementation must precede the main program. The following program listings implement a 5-million iteration loop that calls the cube() function. The two versions were run on an author's system. The running time for the inline version drops 2.75 seconds from 7.86 to 5.11 seconds, a 35% improvement in efficiency.

<u>Inline Version</u>
```
// compute x cubed
inline double cube(double x)
```

<u>Noninline Version</u>
```
// compute x cubed
double cube(double x)
```

```
{
    return x*x*x;
}

int main()
{   double a = 1.0, b;

    // call cube() 5000000 times
    while (a <= 5000000.0)
    {
        b = cube(x);
        a += 1.0;  // increment a
    }
    return0;
}
```

```
int main()
{
    double a = 1.0, b;

    // call cube() 5000000 times
    while (a <= 5000000.0)
    {
        b = cube(x);
        a += 1.0;  // increment a
    }
    return0;
}

double cube(double x)
{
    return x*x*x;
}
```

A look at the code indicates why the inline version is more efficient. To execute in noninline code, the run-time system must pass an argument x, transfer to the function, and handle the return value 5,000,000 times. Contrast that overhead to the simple execution in the loop of the statement b = a * a * a, that is the inline expansion of the call to the cube() function.

Programming Note

When dealing with class member functions or free functions, inline code should be used only for short functions. In this case, we obtain the benefit of increased execution speed but also maintain the type checking that is associated with the function argument-passing mechanism. We also maintain the modularity that is provided by breaking a program into classes and free functions.

CHAPTER 5 SUMMARY

In previous chapters, you learned how to use a class by reading a class description, a class declaration or viewing the UML representation. All of the classes have been predefined and are available through include files with no reference to their implementation. This chapter introduces you to the process of implementing classes.

The implementation of a member function is very similar to that used for a free function. The scope resolution operator associates the function with a class, and the constructor initialization list assists in initializing values for the data members.

To build a class, we create a header file that includes the class declaration followed by the member function implementations. This is a simple scheme that allows any application to use the class. Alternatively, the class declaration may be placed in a header file and the class implementation compiled separately and placed in a library. This technique is used for most system-supplied classes such as those declared in **iostream.h**.

The chapter develops two major classes. The Time24 class introduces the concept of a private member function. Such a function simplifies class design and is an example of the general principle of code duplication. The Loan class is useful for financial calculations and introduces the use of a loop in the implementation of a member function.

Inline code is used to make class member functions and free functions more efficient. When used, the function call and return mechanism is bypassed, since the compiler replaces the function call with all of the statements in the function body. In the process, the run-time arguments are substituted for the formal arguments. Use inline code only for short functions, since its indiscriminate use can increase the size of an application appreciably.

Classes in the Chapter

Name	Implementation File
Accumulator	accum.h
Circle	circle.h
Loan	loan.h
Rectangle	rect.h
StudentAccount	studacct.h
Time24	time24.h

KEY TERMS

Class header file:
Consists of the class declaration followed by its implementation. The file ends in ".h" and should have a name that is descriptive of the class.

Constructor initialization list:
Syntax by which the constructor can assign initial values to the data members. The initialization list is separated from the constructor argument list by a ":" and includes data members followed by their initial value enclosed in parentheses. The items in the list are separated by commas.

Exit function:
Function whose prototype is declared in the system header file **stdlib.h.** It causes the program to terminate, and program control returns to the runtime system that initiated execution. The value of argument is used by the runtime system to evaluate the state of the program upon termination. A value of 0 indicates that the program terminated normally. A value greater than 0 indicates that the program terminated abnormally.

Inline code:
Allows a programmer to declare and implement a member function inside the class declaration. The process saves execution time, since it eliminates the need to pass arguments, transfer control to the function, and return a value. A free function can also be declared inline by placing the keyword inline before the return type in the implementation. When inline code is used, the compiler replaces the function call with all of the statements in the function body. In the process, the runtime arguments are substituted for the formal arguments.

Member function implementation:
C++ statements that implement a member function. The C++ format for a member function implementation is modeled after the syntax for free functions.

Principle of code duplication:

Used in an application when a particular output or calculation is repeated at different locations in the program, perhaps with different data values. Unless the redundancy is removed, the program contains identical blocks of code at several locations. Abstract the operation into a function and execute it using function calls.

Private member function:

Operations used locally in support of a class implementation. These operations are not available to a calling statement. Like free functions in an application, these private functions make the class implementation more efficient and easier to read.

Scope resolution operator:

Used to specify that a function belongs to a particular class. When implementing a member function, the operator:: is combined with the class name as a prefix to the function name using the format "ClassName::". By using the scope resolution operator, the function implementation is linked to a class and statements in the function body can access all the private and public members of the class.

REVIEW EXERCISES

1. (a) What is an initialization list? What is its role in implementing a class constructor?
   (b) The demoCL class has three integer attributes called value1, value2, and value3. The constructor is given by

   ```
   demoCL(int a, int b);
   ```

   In the constructor, arguments a and b are initial values for value1 and value2 while value3 must be assigned 0.

   Give the initialization list for demoCL and use it to implement the constructor.

2. You have developed a class named List that maintains a collection of items. It is designed to be used in any program that does list handling. Explain how the class is made available to a program.

3. Review exercise 3.4 deals with the class GasPump that handles pricing for the purchase of gas.
   (a) Give the code for the gasPump constructor.
   (b) Give the code for the member function fillTank.

4. Review exercise 3.5 gives the UML graphical representation for the class ReviewCL. In addition to the access member functions getValue() and setValue(), the class features the function add() that takes another ReviewCL object, obj, as an argument. It returns a ReviewCL object whose value attribute is the sum of that for the current object and obj.

ReviewCL
🔒 value: int
◆ ReviewCL (v: int = 0)   ◆ getValue ( ): int   ◆ setValue (v: int): void   ◆ add (obj: ReviewCL): ReviewCL

Give the implementation for the member functions setValue() and add().

5. In the StudentAccount class, the member functions charge() and payment() each separately verify that the amount is not negative. This task can be performed by a private member function. Add the following private member function to the StudentAccount class.

```
// output an error message and terminate the program.
// if whichOne == 1, error is in change(),
// if whichOne == 2, error is in payment()
void errorCheck(double amount, int whichOne);
```

The member functions charge() and payment() call errorCheck(). If the call returns, adjust the balance appropriately.
   (a) Give the UML for the modified class, showing only the attributes, the constructor, errorCheck(), charge() and payment().
   (b) Give the implementation for errorCheck(), charge() and payment().

6. Declare a Time24 object t that has initial time of 8:30 PM. Use member functions to update the time by 3 hours and 5 minutes and output the result.

7. You have a 10% college loan of $10,000 that must be repaid in 4 years.
   (a) Declare a Loan object, myLoan, which represents your loan.
   (b) Use a class member function to output the minimum monthly payment.
   (c) Write a code segment that makes the first 12 payments on your loan.
   (d) You decide to pay an additional $50 per month. How do you output the interest savings that result from the additional payment?

8. What are the advantages of inline code? What are the disadvantages?

9. Give a declaration of the Accumulator class that includes inline code.

Answers to Review Exercises

1. (a) The initialization list is a comma separated sequence of items in the format

```
<class data member name>(initialValue)
```

   The initialization list follows a ":" after the constructor argument list. Each value in the list becomes the initial value of the corresponding class data member. A value is normally a constructor argument but can be a constant such as 0.
   (b) `demoCL::demoCL(int a, int b): value1(a), value2(b),`
                                                    `value3(0)`
       `{ }`

2. Create a header file "list.h" that contains the class declaration followed by the implementation of the member functions. Any program needing the List class includes "list.h".

3. (a) `GasPump::GasPump(double cost): pricePerGallon(cost)`
       `{ }`

   (b) `double GasPump::pumpGas(double gallons)`
       `{`
          `return pricePerGallon * gallons;`
       `}`

4.
```
void ReviewCL::setValue(int v)
{
    value = v;
}

ReviewCL ReviewCL::add(ReviewCL obj)
{
    ReviewCL tmp;
    temp.value = value + obj.value;
    return tmp;
}
```

5. (a)

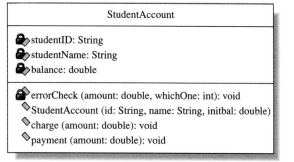

(b)
```
void StudentAccount::errorCheck(double amount,
                                int whichOne)
{
    // if amount is not negative, just return
    if (amount >= 0)
        return;

    // error. output the appropriate message
    if (whichOne == 1)
        cerr << "Charge must not be negative" << endl;
    else
        cerr << "Payment must not be negative" << endl;

    // terminate the program
    exit(1);
}

void StudentAccount::charge(double amount)
{
    // call errorCheck with whichOne = 1
    errorCheck(amount, 1);

    balance -= amount;
}

void StudentAccount::payment(double amount)
```

```
        {
            // call errorCheck with whichOne = 2
            errorCheck(amount, 2);

            balance += amount;
        }
```

6.
```
Time24 t(20,30);
t.add(185);
t.writeTime();
```

7. (a) `Loan myLoan(10000,.10/12,4*12);`

(b) `cout << myLoan.minimumPayment() << endl;`

(c)
```
for(i=0;i < 12;i++)
    myLoan.makePayment();    // make minimum payment
```

(d) `myLoan.writeLoanInfo(50); // see effect of extra $50/month`

8. Advantages: The program does not have to pass arguments, transfer control to the function, and return a value. The run-time arguments are inserted in place of the formal arguments and the expanded code replaces the function call. Disadvantages: Unless the function is short, multiple calls to the function significantly increase the size of the machine code. Use inline code only for functions having a small number of statements.

9.
```
class Accumulator
{
    private:
        // total accumulated by the object
        double total;
    public:
        // constructor. initialize total
        Accumulator(double value = 0.0): total(value)
        {}

        // return the current total
        double getTotal()
        { return total; }

        // add value to total
        void addValue(double value = 1.0)
        { total += value; }
};
```

WRITTEN EXERCISES

10. Declare the Time24 objects, time and oldTime.

```
// time represents 8:00 AM, oldTime midnight
Time24 time(8,0), oldTime;
```

Write a while loop that enters a series of 5 increasing times in the range 8:01 AM to

11:59 PM. Indicate the number of minutes between time intervals. Use the following statements to input a new time.

```
oldTime = time;
time.readTime();
```

11. Write a free function isLater() that takes two Time24 objects and determines if the first time is later than the second.

```
bool isLater(Time24 t1, Time24 t2);
```

For instance, assume `time1 is 8:15 AM` and `time2 is 5:25 AM`
```
        Time24 time1(8,15), time2(5,25);
```
```
        if (isLater(time1, time2)) // condition true
```

12. (a) The Accumulator class does not have a member function that will change the total. Create a modified class by giving the implementation for a new member function setTotal().

```
void setTotal(double value = 0);   // update total
```

(b) Declare the object

```
Accumulator sumTo100;
```

that begins with a total of 0.0. Write a while loop that prompts for a new value and adds it to object sumTo100 using the member function addValue(). If the resulting value of the data member total in sumTo100 exceeds 100, use setTotal() to reduce the value of total by 100. For instance, if sumTo100.getTotal() is 120, the new total is 20 after the total is reduced. Each loop iteration should output the current value of total. Terminate the loop when 0 is input. Here is an example of input and the resulting output:

```
Input:    20  80   70  90  100   5   3  0
Output:   20  100  70  60   60  65  68
```

13. Modify the Accumulator class so that it can compute and return the average of the numbers that form the total. Do this by adding a new data member, count, that is initialized to 1 by the constructor. The value of count is increased by 1 at each execution of addValue(). A new member function, average(), returns total/count.

```
class Accumulator
{
    private:
        // total accumulated by the object
        double total;
        // number of values accumulated in total
        int count;
    public:
        // constructor. initialize total and assign count = 1
        Accumulator(double value = 0);

        // return total
        double getTotal();

        // add value to total and increment count
        void addValue(double value = 1);
```

```
                // return total/count
                double average();
        };
```

(a) Implement the constructor.
(b) Implement addValue().
(c) Implement average().
(d) The following program uses a while loop to enter 10 numbers and output their average. Complete the statements.

```
        int main()
        {
            int i;
            double value;

            Accumulator sum;

            i = ____;
            while (i <= 10)
            {
                cin >> value;
                sum.addValue(____);

                ____;
            }
            cout << _____ << endl;    // output the average

            return 0;
        }
```

14. (a) At most schools, a student can petition to remove an F grade from the transcript. Of course, this will improve the GPA. To implement this, we can add the member function

```
        void removeFGrade(int gunits);
```

to the GradeRecord class. The function subtracts gunits from the class data member units. Give the implementation for the member function.

(b) The student, J. B. Clemson, has the following grade data.

```
        GradeRecord ("3456-64", 100, 196);
```

Unfortuntely, J.B. failed Chemistry 101, which is a 4 unit course. Since he has changed majors, the University agrees to drop the F from his transcript. Write statements that output his current GPA and the GPA after dropping the F.

15. This exercise extends the Rectangle class in **rect.h.**
(a) Take the declaration of the Rectangle class and add the member function, diagonal(), which returns the length d. Give the prototype for the new function.

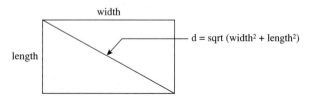

(b) Give an implementation for the member function diagonal().

16. This exercise extends the Circle class in **circle.h.** Recall that Circle is given using in-line code. To the class, add the member function,

```
double sector();
```

that returns the area of a sector defined by the angle theta measured in degrees. The area of a sector is given by the formula

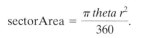

$$sectorArea = \frac{\pi\ theta\ r^2}{360}.$$

Sector

theta

Implement the member function sector()

17. The Salary class maintains the status of an employee for a pay period. The informa-tion includes the employee ID, a Boolean object that indicates whether the em-ployee is full time, the pay rate per hour, and the number of hours worked per pe-riod. For a full time employee, the company contributes 5% of the monthly salary to a retirement fund. The following is the class declaration.

```
class Salary
{
    private:
        // initialized from constructor arguments
        String id;
        bool isFullTime;
        double payRate;
        int hoursWorked;

        // computed by constructor from data members.
        // retirementBenefit is 0.0 for part time employee
        double salary, retirementBenefit;

    public:
        // constructor
        Salary(String empID, bool status, double rate,
                int hours);

        // access member functions
        double getSalary();
        double getRetirementBenefit();

        // print formatted employee information
        void printInformation();
};
```

The employee information is output using the following format.

```
ID: XXX-XX-XXXX
Salary is $XXX.XX        Retirement benefit is $XX.XX
```

(a) Declare two Salary objects, florence having ID "457-45-2345" and tom with ID "578-29-1890". Both employees receive $15.00 per hour, and florence is full time, but tom is part time. During the last week, florence worked 44 hours and tom worked 30 hours.

(b) Using the objects of part (a), show how to output just the salary and retirement benefit for Florence.

(c) Using the objects of part (a), show how to output salary information for Tom.

(d) Is the following implementation for the constructor correct? If not, correct it.

```
Salary::Salary(String empID,bool status, double rate,
        int hours): id(empID), isFullTime(status),
        payRate(rate), hoursWorked(hours)
{
    salary = payRate * hoursWorked;
    retirementBenefit = salary * .05;
}
```

(e) Implement the member function getSalary().

(f) Implement the member function printInformation().

18. Consider the UML representation for the class Mileage that was introduced in Written Exercise 3.16. The attribute, miles, stores a distance measured in miles. The constructor gives the attribute an initial value. The operations allow a program to access distance in either miles or kilometer units.

(a) Implement the constructor whose argument specifies the number of miles.

(b) Give the implementation for the access function getMiles()

(c) Implement the update function setMiles().

(d) Conversion between miles and kilometers use the constants

$$miles = 1.61 \text{ kilometers} \qquad kilometers = 0.62 \text{ miles}$$

Give the implementation for the operations
(i) getKilometers()   (ii) setKilometers()

19. The Temperature class holds information on high and low temperature readings. The two readings are maintained using the Fahrenheit scale in the two private

double objects highTemp and lowTemp. The updateTemp() function takes a new data value in Fahrenheit and updates one of the extreme temperature values in the object. If the value marks a new low, then lowTemp is revised. Similarly, a new high will change highTemp. The following is a declaration for the class that includes comments describing the action of the member functions.

```
const char F = 'F', C = 'C';

class Temperature
{
    private:
        // current high and low readings in Fahrenheit
        double highTemp, lowTemp;
    public:
        // constructor. argument temperatures in
        // Fahrenheit. low temperature is lTemp, and high
        // temperature is hTemp
        Temperature (double lTemp, double hTemp);

        // functions to retrieve temperature data.
        // Celsius value returned if tempType is C;
        // otherwise, a Fahrenheit temperature is returned
        double getLowTemp (char tempType = F);
        double getHighTemp (char tempType = F);

        // update the current low or high. reading is in
        // Fahrenheit
        void updateTemp (double temp);
};
```

For instance, assume the low temperature is 50 and the high temperature is 85.

```
Temperature temp(50, 85);

// 30 degrees updates lowTemp
temp.updateTemp(30);
cout << temp.getLowTemp();      // 30

// 98.6 degrees updates highTemp
cout << updateTemp(98.6);
cout << temp.getHighTemp(C);   // 37 in Celsius
```

(a) Water freezes at 32° Fahrenheit and boils at 212°. Declare a Temperature object, water, that specifies these extremes and develop output statements that display the temperatures in Celsius.

(b) Implement the constructor.

(c) Conversion from Fahrenheit to Celsius is done with the following formula:

$$C = \frac{5}{9}(F - 32)$$

Implement the access function getHighTemp().

(d) Implement the update function updateTemp().

PROGRAMMING EXERCISES

20. (a) Write a program that declares a Time24 object, clock, that is initially set to 9:00 AM. In a loop, enter a sequence of minutes values. Use each to increment time and output the new value. Terminate the loop when clock exceeds 5:00 PM and output the final time.

   (b) Rewrite the program to use the free function, isLater(), developed in Written Exercise 5.11 to determine if the time exceeds 5:00 PM.

21. (a) A concert starts at 8:00 PM and is finished at 10:45 PM. Write a program that creates Time24 objects for the starting time and for the finishing time of the concert. Output the length of time for the concert in minutes.

   (b) Modify the program by creating a free function named duration() that takes as arguments two Time24 objects, earlyTime and lateTime, and returns an integer that specifies the length of time between the objects.

```
int duration (Time24 earlyTIme, Time24 lateTime);
```

22. This exercise investigates the savings involved when a home mortgage is paid over a shorter time. Input the price of a home and the interest rate. Declare Loan objects, home15 and home25. The object home15 represents a mortgage paid over 15 years, and home25 is paid over 25 years. Output the minimum payment in each case. Using the member function writeLoanInfo(), display the amount of interest that is paid over the lifetime of both loans.

23. Write a program that declares a Loan object representing a $10,000 principle at 10% yearly interest paid over 10 years. Create a loop with the following structure:

```
while(done == false)
{
   . . .

   cout << "Are you satisfied with the result: ";
   cin >> answer;
   if (answer == 'Y')
      done = true;
}
```

In the loop body, input an additional payment per month that you think will pay off the loan in 5 years. Use the member function writeLoanInfo() to determine how close you are. The loop should continue until the additional payment will retire the loan within 3 months of 5 years. After leaving the loop, output the total monthly payment.

24. Implement the Accumulator class as described in Written Exercise 5.12 and place it in the header file **accum1.h.** Write a program that solves the problem described in part (b) of the written exercise. Run the program with the data specified in the problem description.

25. Implement the Accumulator class as described in Written Exercise 5.13 and place it in the header file **accum2.h.** Run the program given in part (d) of the written exercise with the data 1, 2, 3, 4, 5, 6, 7, 8, 9, 10, whose average is 5.5.

26. Implement the modified GradeRecord class as described in Written Exercise 5.14

and place it in the header file **xgradrec.h.** Implement the problem given in part (b) of the written exercise in a complete program.

27. From the supplemental software, create file **xrect.h** as a copy of **rect.h** and add the diagonal() member function described in Written Exercise 5.15 to the class. Write a program that declares a Rectangle object, rect, with length = 5 and width = 3. Output the diagonal and area of the rectangle.

28. From the supplemental software, create file **xrect.h** as a copy of **rect.h** and add the diagonal() member function described in Written Exercise 5.15 to the class. Write a complete C++ program that uses the new class to compute a series of values for a combination of Circle and Rectangle objects. The program inputs a radius r that is used to declare the Circle object innerCircle. With this radius, declare a square, called innerSquare, that circumscribes the circle. A third object, outerCircle, circumscribes the square.

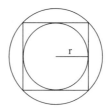

Output the ratio of the perimeter of the outer circle to the inner square. Also output the ratio of the area of the inner square to the inner circle.

29. (a) From the supplemental software, create file **xcircle.h** as a copy of **circle.h** and add the sector() member function described in Written Exercise 5.16 to the class. Write a program that uses the new class to solve the following problem:

    A bakery sells pies that are 9 inches in diameter and that are 12 inches in diameter. You decide you would cut the larger pie into 8 equal pieces and the smaller pie into 6 equal pieces. After declaring two objects, lgpie and smlpie, for the different size pies, output the sector area for a piece from each pie.

    (b) We now try to find methods of cutting the pies that will make the sector areas approximately equal. Modify your program for part (a) so it enters the number of pieces m into which object lgpie is cut and the number of pieces n into which object smlpie is cut. Output the two sector areas. Run the program several times until you find the best cutting strategy.

30. Place the implementation of the class Salary discussed in Written Exercise 5.17 in the file **salary.h.** All company employees are paid $18.00 per hour. Write a program that inputs the number of hours worked by the full time employee Fred Barnes and the number of hours worked by the part time employee Sandy Rose. Declare the Salary objects fred and sandy that represent these employees. Output just the salary and retirement benefit information for Fred and complete salary information for Sandy.

31. This exercise uses the results of Written Exercise 5.18. Complete the implementation of the class in the file **mileage.h.** Write a program that uses it to solve the problems posed in Written Exercises 3.16(d) and (e) of Chapter 3.

32. Implement the Temperature class of Written Exercise 5.19 in the file **temp.h.** Write a program that prompts the user to enter the low and high Fahrenheit temperatures in New York City and create the Temperature object newyork. Similarly, prompt the user for the low and high readings in Zurich and create the object zurich. Compare the low in each city using the function getLowTemp() with the Celsius scale, and output the lowest of the two readings. If the low is in New York, the temperature is output in Fahrenheit; otherwise, it is output in Celsius. Next, compare the two high readings in Fahrenheit and output the highest reading using the appropriate scale.

33. This exercise uses the modified Rectangle class created in Written Exercise 5.15, which is assumed to be implemented in the file **xrect.h.** When building doors for a shed, a carpenter often uses a Z-frame. The door is constructed by connecting three boards in a Z-pattern. A collection of wood slats are then attached to the frame. Input the dimensions of the door in inches (length, width) from the keyboard and assume 4″ slats are used. Declare two Rectangle objects gate and slat. The object gate is of dimensions length × width, and slat is of dimensions width × 4. The number of slats we must cut is the nearest integer value greater than or equal to the real number `door.area()/slat.area()`. For instance, if the computation gives 7.3, we must cut 8 slats. If the computed value is exactly 7, we must cut 7 slats. Use the C++ function ceil() from the mathematical library <math.h> for this computation. Determine the number of inches of wood and the number of slats that must be cut.

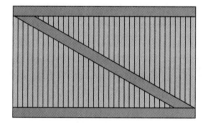

PROGRAMMING PROJECT

34. Define a class Geometry that contains two (2) data items measure1 and measure2 of type double. The constructor has 2 formal arguments that correspond to the data members. The second argument has the default value 0.0 that allows a Geometry object to be declared with a single run-time argument. When measure2 is 0.0, the figure is a circle; otherwise, it is a rectangle.

```
// represent a circle of radius 1 and a rectangle with
// dimensions 3 x 5
Border circ(1), rect(3,5);
```

The function border() returns the perimeter of the object. The functions area() and diagonal() return the area and diagonal of the object, respectively. The UML representation of Geometry is given as follows.

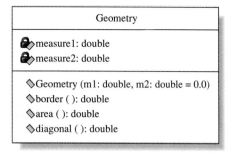

Implement the Geometry class in the file "geometry.h" and develop the following application.

Input the radius of a circle and declare a Geometry object that represents it. Use this radius to declare a square that circumscribes the circle. Declare a circle which circumscribes the square. Output the area and perimeter of each figure.

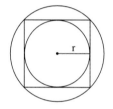

Chapter 6
Additional C++ Control Structures

CHAPTER CONTENTS

6-1   MULTIPLE SELECTION: NESTED IF STATEMENTS

The "Dangling" Else

6-2   MULTIPLE SELECTION: SWITCH STATEMENT

6-3   ENUMERATION TYPES

Properties of Enumeration Types

6-4   BUILDING AN ENUMERATION CLASS

Implementation of the Days class

6-5   THE DATE CLASS

Date Class Implementation

6-6   THE FOR LOOP

6-7   FOR LOOP APPLICATIONS

Formatting Output
Number Theory—Exploring Factors
Approximating a Circle

6-8   ADVANCED LOOP CONCEPTS

Designing Nested Loops
Generalized For Loops
Loop Break and Continue Statements

6-9   ARGUMENT PASSING

Pass by Value
Pass by Reference

6-10 CONSTANT FUNCTION ARGUMENTS

6-11 CONDITIONAL EXPRESSIONS (OPTIONAL)

6-12 TEXT FILE I/O

C++ Stream Classes
Creating File Stream Objects
Reading and Writing File Data
File Error Checking
Streams as Function Arguments
(Optional)
Stream States and Errors (Optional)

Written Exercises

Chapter 4 introduced control structures including basic selection and loop statements. This chapter expands our understanding of these structures and gives us important new C++ tools for implementing algorithms.

Basic selection uses the if statement to allow a programmer to chose from among alternative actions. Depending on the number of alternatives, we use various forms of the if statement to implement one-way, two-way, or multiway selection. In this chapter we introduce additional selection methods that use more complex if/else statements. We also discuss the C++ switch statement that is an efficient way to handle multiway selection when a control object can direct the program to choose from among alternative actions.

The while statement is the fundamental loop structure in a programming language, and its form is well-suited for event-controlled loops. C++ provides a powerful and flexible *for statement* that generalizes the while loop. In practice, a for statement is primarily used for counter-controlled loops. We develop the for loop and use it with applications in number theory and graphics.

For good program design, C++ provides enumeration types that allow programs to assign meaningful names to integer values. We introduce the types in Section 6.3 and use them in a series of multi-way selection applications, including the Date class of Section 6.5.

Selection and loop statements provide two types of control structures. We must also appreciate the importance of a function as a control structure. Whether it be a free function or a class operation, a function call takes a list of arguments, passes control to a separate block, and obtains return values. Up to this point in the book, our function calls have simply copied the arguments and derived a single return value. This is only one form of interaction between a calling statement and a function. C++ provides another mechanism that allows a function to modify the run-time arguments. The mechanism, called pass by reference, is developed in Section 6-9 and is used throughout the rest of the book.

Since many applications store data on disk, we introduce C++ text file objects in Section 6-12. Their member functions are used with loops to handle large sets of character, string, or numeric data. With files, we can expand the types of applications we discuss and deal with larger data sets.

6-1 MULTIPLE SELECTION: NESTED IF STATEMENTS

An if statement allows the program to select from alternative actions. In one-way or two-way selection, we refer to these alternatives as Statement$_T$ and Statement$_F$. In some applications, the alternative statements may involve additional selection, *creating nested if statements*.

```
if (condition)
{
    if (condition)     // if/else Statement_T
        . . .
    else
        . . .
}
else
{
    . . .
    if (condition)     // one-way if statement
        . . .
}
```

For instance, tax payers may make different levels of contribution to an individual retirement account (IRA) based on their filing status (married or single) and their level of income. Table 6-1 identifies the allowed IRA contribution limits.

TABLE 6-1 IRA Contributions.

Status	Taxable Income	IRA Limit
Single	0–40,000	2500
	40,000+	1500
Married	0–75,000	4000
	75,000+	2800

To determine IRA contribution limit for a tax payer, a program must first distinguish whether the payer is married or single.

```
if (taxStatus == 'S')
   <check income levels for a single tax payer>
else
   <check income levels for a married tax payer>
```

Each alternative involves an if/else statement to distinguish contribution limits based on income level. For instance, a single tax payer is bound by the limit of $2500 or $1500 based on the conditional test `"income <= 40000"`. The IRA contribution limit for a tax payer is thus determined by nested if statements. We illustrate the logic with the free function iraLimit() that takes taxStatus and income as arguments and returns the allowable IRA contribution.

```
// return maximum allowable IRA contribution
double iraLimit (double income, char taxStatus)
{
   double contribution;

   // initial selection tests taxStatus
   if (taxStatus == 'S')
      // test income level for single tax payer
      if (income <= 40000.00)
         contribution = 2500;
      else
         contribution = 1500;
   else
      // test income level for married tax payer
      if (income <= 75000.00)
         contribution = 4000;
      else
         contribution = 2800;

   return contribution;
}
```

APPLICATION 6-1 COMPUTING IRA CONTRIBUTIONS

The program uses the function `iraLimit()` to compute the maximum allowable IRA contribution for a tax payer. The program reads the income as a real number and the status as a character "M" (married) or "S" (single). The two values are passed as run-time arguments to the function and the return value is used in a simple output statement.

```
#include <iostream.h>

#include "textlib.h"    // access to manipulator setreal()

// return maximum allowable IRA contribution
double iraLimit (double income, char taxStatus);

int main()
{
   double taxableIncome;
   char   maritalStatus;

   cout << "Enter taxable income and marital status M or S: ";
   cin >> taxableIncome >> maritalStatus;

   // call the function to compute and return IRA limit
   cout << "Maximum IRA contribution is $" << setreal(1,2)
        << iraLimit(taxableIncome,maritalStatus) << endl;

   return 0;
}


/* iraLimit() is implemented in the program discussion */
```

```
Run 1:

Enter taxable income and marital status M or S: 25000 S
Maximum IRA contribution is $2500.00

Run 2:

Enter taxable income and marital status M or S: 100000 M
Maximum IRA contribution is $2800.00
```

The "Dangling" Else

When various combinations of if and if/else statements combine in a nested structure, it can be difficult to keep straight the if/else pairings. While indenting is important for program readability, it is not used by the compiler to match the if and else statements. This can create some nasty logical errors that are difficult to detect. The problem is often called the *dangling else*. Consider the following bank situation. Senior citizens are offered free checking accounts, while others are charged 25 cents ($0.25) per check. All customers pay $20.00 for an overdraft. To post the proper charge for a check transaction, program logic could first determine if sufficient funds are present and then look at the type of account. The following nested if statement seems to implement the algorithm.

```
// declare objects with initial checkCharge set to 0.0
double checkAmount, checkCharge = 0.0;
double acctBalance;
bool isSeniorAccount;

// check for sufficient funds to cover the check
if (checkAmount >= acctBalance)

    // non-seniors pay $.25 per check
    if (isSeniorAccount == false)
       checkCharge = .25;

// with insufficient funds, all customers charged $20
else
        checkCharge = 20.00;
```

The C++ statements compile and run without an error message. Unfortunately, the compiler uses a different set of rules to analyze the nested if statement and the bank's senior citizen customers get charged $20.00 per check. To understand how this occurs, look at the problem faced by the compiler. After identifying the conditional expression in the outer if statement

```
if (checkAmount >= acctBalance)
    < Statement_T>
```

the compiler looks for the statement that will execute when the condition is true. In this case the statement is an if/else statement. The keyword else is not indented and appears to identify the action that is taken when the check "bounces". When the compiler sees the else, however, it must match it with a corresponding if. A simple rule of syntax is applied. Match an else with the closest previous unmatched if statement. In our example, the compiler matches the else with the inner if statement that checks whether the account is owned by a senior citizen.

Compiler Interpretation

```
// check for sufficient funds to cover the check
if (checkAmount >= acctBalance)

    // if the check is good, is check cashing free?
    if (isSeniorAccount == false)
       checkCharge = .25;
    else
       checkCharge = 20.00;    // charge seniors $20
```

In order to have the else link with the outer if statement, a programmer must put Statement_T in a block. The one-way if statement is "hidden" in the block and is not seen by the compiler when it looks for a match to the else. The following is correct code for the algorithm.

Correct Code for the Algorithm

```
// check for sufficient funds to cover the check
if (checkAmount >= acctBalance)
{
    // charge $0.25 if not a senior citizen account
    if (isSeniorAccount == false)
        checkCharge = .25;
}
// else executes when account has insufficient funds
else
    checkCharge = 20.00;
```

*Exploring
Concepts*

Look at the nested if statement and use it to explore some issues.

```
if (s <= 40)
    if (s > 10)
        result = 1;
    else
        result = 2;
else
    if (s < 100)
        result = 3;
    else
        result = 4;
```

(a) give the range of values for integer s that would give result = 1; = 2; = 3; = 4.

(b) create an equivalent nested if statement that begins with the condition

```
if (s < 100)
    . . .
```

6-2 MULTIPLE SELECTION: SWITCH STATEMENT

In Chapter 4, we introduced multiple selection by using a series of "else if" statements to choose from among the alternative actions. In many applications, a selection is made from a set of discrete values. For instance, consider the Roman numeral characters I, V, X, and L that correspond to decimal numbers.

$$I = 1 \quad V = 5 \quad X = 10 \quad L = 50$$

A programmer could use multiple selection with "else if" to equate the different number values with the five Roman numeral characters. For instance, the following statements assign to object decValue the decimal value corresponding to a Roman numeral.

```
char romanNumeral;
int decValue;
```

```
if (romanNumeral == 'I')
   decValue = 1;
else if (romanNumeral == 'V')
   decValue = 5;
else if (romanNumeral == 'X')
   decValue = 10;
else if (romanNumeral == 'L')
   decValue = 50;
else
   cout << "Not a Roman numeral <= 50";
```

Note that the particular selection depends on the value of the object roman-Numeral. This value controls the selection process. For this type of situation, C++ provides the *switch statement* when the alternative actions are controlled by a selector expression.

Before giving the general syntax for the switch statement, we use it with the Roman numerals.

```
switch (romanNumeral)    // selector expression
{
    case 'I':   decValue = 1;
                break;
    case 'V':   decValue = 5;
                break;
    case 'X':   decValue = 10;
                break;
    case 'L';   decValue = 50;
                break;
    default:    cout << "Not a Roman numeral <= 50";
                break;
}
```

In the statement, the *case constants* define four char values that correspond to a Roman numeral. Associated with each constant is a *case statement* that assigns an integer value to decValue. The object romanNumeral is the *selector expression* that is used to select the option that matches the constant. A fifth option, called *default,* is selected when romanNumber does not match any of the case constants. In the statement, cases are enclosed in a block.

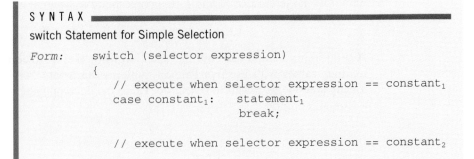

SYNTAX

switch Statement for Simple Selection

Form: switch (selector expression)
            {
                // execute when selector expression == constant₁
                case constant₁: statement₁
                                   break;

                // execute when selector expression == constant₂

```
case constant₂:     statement₂
                    break;

            .   .   .

// execute when selector expression == constantₙ
case constantₙ:     statementₙ
                    break;

// optional: execute when selector expression
// finds no match
default:            default statement
                    break;
}
```

Action: The value of the selector expression and the case constants must be of
the some *integral type.* This includes integer, character, bool, and enumeration types. The case constants are either literal or constant objects.
Execution of the switch statement begins by computing a value for the
selector expression that is used to identify the case. Program control
passes to the selected case and continues execution until a break statement is encountered or the end of the switch statement is reached. The
break statement terminates execution within the switch block and
passes control to the first statement outside the block. C++ allows an
optional default case which is selected if no case constant equals the selector value. Figure 6-1 shows the flow control of the switch statement.

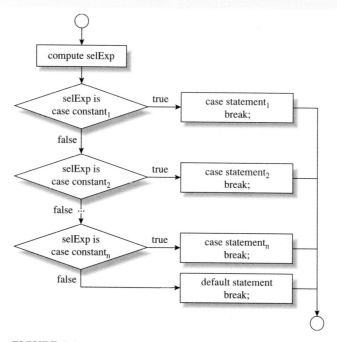

FIGURE 6-1
The Switch Statement.

```
Example: int n;

         cin >> n;
         switch(n)
         {
             case 1:    cout << "one";
                        break;
             case 2:    cout << "two";
                        break;
             case 5:    cout << "five";
                        break;
             default:   cout << "not 1, 2 or 5";
                        break;

         }
```

EXAMPLE 6.1 ▬▬▬▬▬▬▬▬▬▬▬▬▬▬▬▬▬▬▬▬▬▬▬▬▬▬

1. In American football, a team can score 1, 2, 3, or 6 points on a play, depending on how a score is made. A switch statement outputs the play(s) that can produce a given score.

```
switch(score)
{
    case 1:    cout << "extra point" << endl;
               break;
    case 2:    cout << "safety or 2-point conversion" << endl;
               break;
    case 3:    cout << "field goal" << endl;
               break;
    case 6:    cout << "touchdown" << endl;
               break;
    default:   cout << "no related scoring play" << endl;
               break;
}
```

```
(a) For score = 3, the switch statement selects case 3.
    <output> field goal
```

```
(b) For score = 7, the switch statement cannot find a match
    with a case.
    <output> no related scoring play
```

2. The world Olympic committee formerly held the winter and summer Olympics in the same year. This policy ended in 1992 when the committee decided to hold the winter Olympics in 1994 and then every four years. Dating back to 1980, we determine whether a year has both Olympics, only one type of Olympics, or no Olympics. Note that two or more case constants can refer to the same case statement.

```
switch(year)
{
   case 1980:
   case 1984:
   case 1988:
   case 1992:   cout << year << " has both Olympics";
                break;

   case 1994:
   case 1998:
   case 2002:   cout << year << " has winter Olympics";
                break;

   case 1996:
   case 2000:   cout << year << " has summer Olympics";
                break;

   default:     cout << year << " has no Olympics";
                break;
}  ■
```

Missing Breaks: In the switch statement, the execution of a case option must terminate with a break statement if the programmer wants control to pass to the next statement after the switch block. Otherwise the program executes all subsequent case options. Consider the football scoring example (6.1) but with all of the break statements removed.

```
// switch statement with breaks removed
switch(score)
{
   case 1:   cout << "extra point" << endl;
   case 2:   cout << "safety or 2-point conversion" << endl;
   case 3:   cout << "field goal" << endl;
   case 6:   cout << "touchdown" << endl;
   default:  cout << "no related scoring play" << endl;
}
```

For score = 2, execution begins at the `"case 2:"` statement and continues through all of the remaining statements in the block.

```
<output> safety or 2-point conversion
         field goal
         touchdown
         no related scoring play
```

PROGRAM 6.1

The program simulates a simple desktop calculator that can add, subtract, multiply, and divide two real numbers. Operations have the format

```
number op number
```

where *op* is one of the arithmetic operators "+", "−", "*" and "/". The operator is the selector expression in a switch statement that computes the result. Special attention is paid to division by zero, which is a fatal error. The free function exit() in stdlib.h is used to terminate the program.

```cpp
#include <iostream.h>
#include <stdlib.h>

int main()
{
    double operand1,operand2, result;
    char op;

    // enter the operation
    cin >> operand1 >> op >> operand2;

    // perform the calculation
    switch(op)
    {
        case '+':   result = operand1 + operand2;
                    break;

        case '-':   result = operand1 - operand2;
                    break;

        case '*':   result = operand1 * operand2;
                    break;

        case '/':   // make sure don't attempt division by 0
                    if (operand2 == 0.0)
                    {
                        cerr << "Cannot divide by 0" << endl;
                        exit(1);
                    }
                    else
                        result = operand1 / operand2;
                    break;
    }

    // display the result
    cout << "Result = " << result << endl;

    return 0;
}
```

```
Run 1:

45 - 56
Result = -11
```

```
Run 2:

48 / 10
Result = 4.8
```

Give the equivalent nested if statement for the switch statement

```
switch (ch)
{
    case 'm':
    case 'n':   cout << "one" << endl;
                break;
    case 'p':   cout << "two" << endl;
                break;
    default:    cout << "three" << endl;
                break;
}
```

What is the switch statement that corresponds to the nested if/else sequence.

Exploring
Concepts

```
if (ch == 'a' || ch == 'b' || ch == 'c')
    cout << "in your abc's";
else if (ch >= 'g' && ch < 'i')
    cout << "in mid alphabet";
else if (ch == 'z')
    cout << "at end of letters";
else
    cout << "other letters";
```

Can this statement be conveniently written as a switch statement?

```
if (n < 5 || n > 8)
    cout << "Range 1";
else if (n >= 5 && n <= 7)
    cout << "Range 2";
else
    cout << "Range 3";
cout << endl;
```

6-3 ENUMERATION TYPES

The primitive integer types consist of discrete numeric values. They are often used to distinguish items in a list. For instance, the date "October 4th" has a shorthand representation 10/4 since October is the tenth month in the year. If the date falls on a Tuesday, we note that it occurs on the third day of the week.

While programmers can use numeric values like 10 and 3 to indicate a month of the year or day of the week it is preferable to use meaningful names that represent numeric constants. The name October is more descriptive than 10, April is more descriptive than 4, and so forth. The names make programs more readable and algorithms easier to code. To use a list of named items, C++ allows a programmer to define a type consisting of a list of identifiers that correspond to integer constants. The declaration uses the reserved word *enum*, the type name, and a list of identifiers.

SYNTAX ▄▄

Enumeration Type

Form: `enum TypeName {item₀, item₁, item₂, . . . , itemₙ};`

Action: The enumeration type specifies a list of non-keyword identifiers that are separated by commas and enclosed in braces. The list of items corresponds to a sequence of integer values.

Example: `// four seasons of the year:`
                `enum Seasons {Winter, Spring, Summer, Fall};`
            `// primary monitor colors:`
                `enum Color {red, green, blue};`

            `// invalid since it includes keywords`
                `enum Keyterms = {class, if, else, while};`

An enumeration type can be used to declare and initialize objects.

```
Seasons schoolTerm = Fall;

Color background;
background = blue;
```

EXAMPLE 6.2 ▄▄

The file **textlib.h** defines an output manipulator, setjust(), that allows the programmer to left and right justify text in the output stream. The manipulator sets the justification for all subsequent items in the stream. In the implementation, we define an enumeration type to specify the justification.

```
// specifies left or right justification
enum Direction {Left, Right};
```

The enumeration constant Left or Right is the direction argument for the manipulator. The manipulator, setjust(Left), outputs all subsequent items left justified in their print field. To right justify output, use setjust(Right). Consider the following examples where the character □ represents a space.

```
// demo is left justified in a field of width 8
cout << setjust(Left) << setw(8) << "demo" <<endl;
```

```
// right justify constant 19.82 in a field of width 7
cout << setjust(Right) << setreal(7,2) << 19.817 << endl;
```

```
Output:
   demo□□□□
   □□19.82
```

Properties of Enumeration Types

Enumeration type associate names with integer values. While an enumeration type is distinct from the int type, it shares characteristics such as conversions, arithmetic operations and I/O. In this section, we develop these characteristics and note some problems that are unique to enumeration types. This material is critical for Section 6.4 that develops a wrapper class facilitating the use of enumeration types.

The items in an enumeration type correspond to a sequence of non-negative integers. By default, the first item corresponds to integer value 0 and subsequent items to integers 1, 2, 3, and so forth. For instance, in the enumeration type DaysInWeek, Sun corresponds to 0 and Wed to 3. The relationship with integers allows the programmer to order enumeration objects and apply relational operators.

```
enum DaysInWeek {Sun, Mon, Tue, Wed, Thu, Fri, Sat};
int  dayValue;
DaysInWeek  d = Wed;

if (d == Fri)
   cout << "Leave for vacation tomorrow";

if (d >= Mon && d <= Fri)
   cout << "A week day";
```

Since items in an enumeration list have numeric representation, we can perform conversion with int objects. An enumeration object can be freely assigned to an integer object. For instance, the assignment implicitly converts d to an integer value.

```
dayValue = d;    // dayValue= 3 since d is Wed
```

Conversion from an integer to an enumeration type must use explicit conversion to avoid a compiler error or warning message. For instance,

```
d = 3;           // compiler warning or error message

// explicit conversion of 3 to enumeration value Wed
d = DaysInWeek(3);
```

Arithmetic with Enumeration Types: Enumeration objects may be included in addition and subtraction, operations. Care must be taken so that the resulting enumeration value is in range. For instance, DaysInWeek objects must be in the range Sun to Sat with corresponding integer values 0 to 6.

```
d = DaysInWeek(d+2);    // d has value Fri (Wed + 2)

d = DaysInWeek(d+5);    // d out of range (integer value 8)
```

A programmer may use the "++" or "−−" operations to update an enumeration object to its successor or predecessor value. The operations can result in invalid results when applied at the ends of the enumeration range.

```
d = Tue;

d++;        // d advances to Wed (successor of Tue)
d--;        // d is Mon (predecessor of Tue);

d = Sat;
d++;        // d is invalid since integer value is 7
```

Technical Note

In the declaration of the enum type, the programmer may create a different internal representation of the items in the list by assigning a new initial value. For instance, we usually associate months of the year with the values 1 to 12.

```
enum MonthName = {Jan = 1,Feb,Mar,Apr,May,Jun,Jul,Aug,Sep,
                  Oct,Nov,Dec};
```

I/O with Enumeration Types: An enumeration object can be placed in an output stream. In this case, its integer representation is output. For instance:

```
DaysInWeek day = Wed;
cout << day << endl;   // Output: 3
```

A free function can be developed to associate the enumeration value with the corresponding name. For instance, the function writeDay() outputs a DaysInWeek object as a meaningful string such as Wed.

```
void writeDay(DaysInWeek d)
{
   switch(d)
   {
      case Sun:  cout << "Sun";
                 break;
      case Mon:  cout << "Mon";
                 break;
             . . .
      case Sat:  cout << "Sat";
                 break;
   }
}
```

C++ stream input is not defined for an enumeration object. The following input statement either generates a compiler error or warning message.

```
cin >> d;    // not a valid operation
```

We deal with this limitation by developing the wrapper class Days in the next section.

6-4 BUILDING AN ENUMERATION CLASS

Enumeration types have limited arithmetic and I/O capabilities. Even the available operations can result in errors. The solution is to create a *wrapper class* that contains an enumeration value as a data member. The class member functions correctly carry out operations with the enumeration value.

Wrapper classes are a key object technology concept. We illustrate them with the Days class that wraps the enumeration type DaysInWeek. The class contains the data member day of type DaysInWeek and member functions that perform arithmetic and I/O operations.

days.h

```
DECLARATION: Days CLASS
enum DaysInWeek {Sun, Mon, Tue, Wed, Thu, Fri, Sat};

class Days
{
   private:
      DaysInWeek day;
   public:
      Days(DaysInWeek d = Sun);

      // access function
      DaysInWeek getDay();

      // arithmetic operations
      void succ();          // day set to its successor
      void pred();          // day set to its predecessor

      // set day to dayAmount >= 0 days later
      void addDay(int dayAmount);

      // update function
      void setDay(DaysInWeek d);

      // I/O operations
      void readDay();
      void writeDay();
};
```

Use of the Days class facilitates the use of the enumeration type. The function getDay() accesses the current enumeration value of an object and function setDay() assigns a new enumeration value. The I/O functions readDay() and writeDay() allow the programmer to work with the names "Sun,"

"Mon," and so forth. The functions succ(), pred(), and addDay() implement arithmetic with the enumeration type.

EXAMPLE 6.3 ━━━━━━━━━━━━━━━━━━━━━━━━━━━━

1. Input and update a Days object.

```
Days d, e(Sat)      // d Sun by default

e.writeDay();       // Output: Sat

d.readDay();        // Input: Wed

// add 10 days to Wed and get Sat
d = today.addDay(10);
d.writeDay();       // Output: Sat
```

2. Looping with a Days control object.

```
d.setDay(Mon);      // assign Mon as new value

// loops outputs days from Mon to Fri
while(d.getDay() <= Fri)
{
   d.writeDay();
   cout << "  ";
   d.succ();
}
Output: Mon  Tue  Wed  Thu  Fri  ■
```

PROGRAM 6.2 ━━━━━━━━━━━━━━━━━━━━━━━━━━━━

A hotel charges $88 per night during the week and $75 on the weekend. The program inputs the day a family arrives and the number of days they will stay. Output includes the total cost for the room and the day the family departs.

```
#include <iostream.h>

#include "days.h"

int main()
{
   // represents the days in the stay
   Days hotel;
   // number of days the family stays at hotel
   int nDays;
   // total cost of the stay
   double cost = 0.0;
   int i;
   DaysInWeek d;

   cout << "What is the day of arrival? ";
   hotel.readDay();
```

```
cout << "How many days will the family stay? ";
cin >> nDays;

for (i = 1; i <= nDays; i++)
{
   // get current day
   d = hotel.getDay();
   // determine cost
   if (d == Sat || d == Sun)
      cost += 75.0;
   else
      cost += 88.0;
   // move to the next day
   hotel.succ();
 }

cout << "The family leaves on ";
hotel.writeDay();
cout << endl;
cout << "The total cost of the stay is $" << cost
      << endl;
return 0;
}
```

```
Run:

What is the day of arrival? Thu
How many days will the family stay? 5
The family leaves on Tue
The total cost of the stay is $414
```

Implementation of the Days class

This section gives a partial implementation for member functions in the Days class. The list includes `pred()`, `succ()`, `addDays()`, and `writeDay()` that illustrate many of the interesting features of the class.

pred:

The function sets the object to the previous day. It changes the object so its value is 1 less than the current value for day. Sun is a special case since the previous day is Sat.

```
// predecessor of day
void Days::pred()
{
   // handle Sun as a special case;
   // otherwise, return day before
   if (day == Sun)
      day = Sat;
```

```
        else
            day = DaysInWeek(day-1);
    }
```

succ:

The function sets the object to the next day. The enumeration value of the object becomes 1 greater than the current value for the attribute day. An exception occurs when day = Sat, since the integer value day+1 = 7 is out of range. To handle this situation, we take the remainder after dividing day+1 by 7, which falls in the range 0 to 6. Explicit conversion using DaysInWeek assigns the integer value as an enumeration value. Consider the calculation for Sat.

```
    day = Sat:  DaysInWeek( (6+1) % 7) = DaysInWeek(7 % 7)
                                       = DaysInWeek(0)
                                       = Sun
```

```
// successor of day
void Days::succ()
{
    // Sat(int value 6) goes to Sun (int value 0)
    day = DaysInWeek((day+1) % 7);
}
```

addDays:

The function sets the object to an enumeration value that is dayAmount from the current day. Like the calculation in succ(), we add dayAmount to the current value of the attribute day and take the remainder after division by 7. Explicit conversion assigns the integer value to an enumeration value. For example, suppose day = Wed and dayAmount = 8.

```
    DaysInWeek((day + 8) % 7) = DaysInWeek((3+8) % 7)
                              = DaysInWeek(11 % 7)
                              = DaysInWeek(4)
                              = Thu
```

```
// set the day to dayAmount days in the future
Days Days::addDay(int dayAmount)
{
    // add dayAmount and set result to
    // the range 0 to 6
    day = DaysInWeek((day+dayAmount) % 7);
}
```

writeDay:

Use a switch statement that associates the enumeration value of the attribute day with a statement that displays the value as a string. For instance associate Sun with the string "Sun".

```
        // output
        void Days::writeDay()
        {
            switch(day)
            {
            case Sun:   cout << "Sun";
                        break;
            case Mon:   cout << "Mon";
                        break;
            case Tue:   cout << "Tue";
                        break;
            case Wed:   cout << "Wed";
                        break;
            case Thu:   cout << "Thu";
                        break;
            case Fri:   cout << "Fri";
                        break;
            case Sat:   cout << "Sat";
                        break;
            }
        }
```

6-5 THE DATE CLASS

Date information is an important component in many database tables. For instance, student records include date of birth, high school graduation date, and so forth. An operating system maintains the creation, modification, and last access date for a disk file. A Date class is a useful addition to our collection of object-oriented tools for program development. We develop the class as an important illustration of the concepts in the chapter. The implementation makes use of nested if statements and switch statements. We suggest you study this section carefully.

A Date object contains the month, day, and year as private integer data members. When declaring an object, these values are initialized by three integer constructor arguments mm, dd, and yyyy. Error checking is performed to insure the arguments correspond to a valid date. A programmer may access and update the current value of these arguments using a series of "get" and "set" functions like getMonth() and setYear(). For output, the member function writeShortDate() outputs the date in short format (12/25/1999), while the member function writeLongDate() uses the long format (December 25, 1999). For instance, consider the Date object myBirthday.

```
    Date  myBirthday(10,24,1973);

    myBirthday.writeLongDate();    // October 24, 1973
    myBirthday.writeShortDate();   // 10/24/1973

    Date invalidDay(11,31,2000);   // November has 30 days
```

We use function descriptions and examples to illustrate the other operations in the Date class. Assume that valentine is a Date object initialized to
2/14/2000.

incrementDate:

Take an argument ndays in the range 0 to 365 and add that number of days
to the current date.

```
void incrementDate(int ndays);

Example:
   Date valentine (2,14,2000);
   // set date to 2/28/2000
   valentine.incrementDate(14);
```

daysInMonth:

Returns the number of days in the current month.

```
int daysInMonth();

Example:
   Returns 29 (2000 is a leap year)
      valentine.daysInMonth();
```

numberOfDays:

Return the number of days from January 1st to the current date. For the
1st of the year, numberOfDays() returns 1.

```
int numberOfDays();

Example:
   Returns 45 = 31(Jan) + 14
      valentine.numberOfDays();
```

EXAMPLE 6.4 ▬▬▬▬▬▬▬▬▬▬▬▬▬▬▬▬▬▬▬▬▬▬▬▬▬▬▬

The example demonstrates the Date operations for object d.

```
Date d(12,24,1991);                    // d is December 24, 1991

cout << d.getDay();                    // Output: 24
d.incrementDate(80);                   // Add 80 days;

if (d.isLeapYear())
   cout << d.getYear() << " is a leap year";
else
   cout << d.getYear() << " is not a leap year";

// Output:   73 = 31(Jan)+29(Feb)+13;
cout << d.numberOfDays();
d.writeShortDate();                    // Output: 3/13/1992  ■
```

The following is a full declaration of the Date class.

DECLARATION: Date CLASS ▬▬▬▬▬▬▬▬▬▬▬▬▬

date.h

```
class Date
{
    private:
        // private type used by Date
        enum MonthName {Jan = 1, Feb, Mar, Apr, May, Jun,
                        Jul, Aug, Sep, Oct, Nov, Dec};

        // private members that specify the date
        int month, day, year;

    public:
        // supply date in format MM/DD/YYYY
        Date (int mm=1, int dd=1, int yyyy=1600);

        // output the date in the format "MM/DD/YYYY"
        void writeShortDate ();
        // output the date in the format "Month day, year"
        void writeLongDate ();

        // add ndays to the date
        void incrementDate(int ndays);
        // return the number of days into the year
        int numberOfDays();

        // access member functions

        // return the month as integer value 1 to 12
        int getMonth();
        // return day of the month
        int getDay();
        // return the year
        int getYear();

        // update the value of an attribute
        void setMonth(int mm);
        void setDay(int dd);
        void setYear(int yyyy);

        // return number of days in the month
        int daysInMonth();

        // is the current year a leap year (true/false)
        bool isLeapYear();
};
```

Note that the class declaration includes the enumeration type, MonthName, which gives a list of names for the months of the year. The integer representation of the months is 1, 2, and so forth. Since the enumeration type is declared in the private section, only member functions may declare objects of MonthName type.

PROGRAM 6.3

In school year 2000, a university schedules May 19 as the last day of spring exams and August 28 as the first day of fall classes. After creating objects springDate(5,19,2000) and fallDate(8,28,2000), the program computes the number of days for summer vacation and outputs the result. It also computes the number of days in August that students will be back in school.

```
#include <iostream.h>

#include "date.h"

int main()
{
    Date springDate(5,19,2000), fallDate(8,28,2000);

    cout << "There are "
         << (fallDate.numberOfDays()-springDate.numberOfDays())
         << " days in the summer vacation" << endl;

    cout << "In August students are in school "
         << (fallDate.daysInMonth()-fallDate.getDay())
         << " days" << endl;

    return 0;
}
```

```
Run:

There are 101 days in the summer vacation
In August students are in school 3 days
```

Date Class Implementation

We give a partial implementation that includes the functions isLeapYear(), daysInMonth(), and the constructor. The logical function isLeapYear() uses a conditional expression to determine whether the current year is a leap year. A switch statement is used to return a value for the function daysInMonth(). The constructor initializes the month, day, and year attributes of a Date object. In the process, it uses the member function daysInMonth() for error checking to insure that the initial values are in range. In the software supplement, the function numberOfDays() is another good example of an algorithm using a switch statement and a test for leap year.

Computing Leap Year. Most of us learn that a leap year occurs every four years. The rule of thumb is usually true except for those years that are divisible by 100. At the turn of a century, the year is a leap year only if it is divisible by 400. For instance, 1700, 1800, and 1900 are not leap years. However 2000 (`2000 % 400 == 0`) is a leap year. We can organize these facts into a statement that easily translates into a logical expression.

> A year is a leap year provided it is divisible by 4 and not divisible by 100 (e.g. 1988, 2004) or it is divisible by 400 (e.g. 1600 and 2000)
>
> ```
> (year % 4 == 0  && year % 100 != 0) || year % 400 == 0
> ```

The definition of the function `isLeapYear()` evalues the logical expression and returns the value.

```cpp
bool Date::isLeapYear()
{
    if ((year % 4 == 0 && year % 100 != 0) || year % 400 == 0)
        return true;
    else
        return false;
}
```

Evaluating Days in the Month. To return the number of days in the month represented by a `Date` object, we use a switch statement whose selector expression is the data member month. Since month is an integer, we convert it to a `Month-Name` enumeration object (e.g. `MonthName(4) = Apr`). The action of the switch statement is to assign the number of days in the month to the integer object `monthLength`. The case for `Feb` checks whether the attribute year is a leap year and, if so, assigns `monthLength` the value 29. The object `monthLength` is returned as the value of the function.

```cpp
// return the number of days in the month
int Date::daysInMonth()
{
    int monthLength;

    // MonthName(month) converts integer month to the
    // equivalent MonthName object
    switch (MonthName(month))
    {
        case Jan:
        case Mar:
        case May:
        case Jul:
        case Aug:
        case Oct:
        case Dec:   monthLength = 31;    // months with 31 days
                    break;
```

```
        case Apr:
        case Jun:
        case Sep:
        case Nov:  monthLength = 30;    // months with 30 days
                   break;

        case Feb:  if (isLeapYear())    // special case of Feb
                       monthLength = 29;
                   else
                       monthLength = 28;
                   break;
    }

    return monthLength;
}
```

Constructor for the Date Class. The constructor is passed integer arguments mm, dd, and yyyy that are used to initialize the month, day, and year attributes of the object. The assigning of data to the attributes is handled by an initialization list.

```
Date::Date (int mm, int dd, int yyyy) :
            month(mm), day(dd), year(yyyy)
```

The constructor verifies that the month is given in the range 1 to 12. A value that is out of range causes the constructor to output an error message and terminate the program.

```
if (month < 1 || month > 12)
{
   // error message and program termination
   cerr << "Date constructor: " << month
        << " invalid month" << endl;
   exit(1);
}
```

The constructor next checks that the attribute day assumes a correct value. The range of possible values for the day argument depends on the month. For instance, Apr (month 4) allows a range of days from 1 to 30, so a value of day = 31 is invalid. For February, the limit on the range is 28 or 29 depending on whether the year is a leap year. The member function, daysInMonth(), accounts for leap year and returns the number of days in the month. The constructor verifies that day falls in the range $1 \leq$ day $\leq$ daysInMonth().

```
if (day <= 0 || day > daysInMonth())
{
   cerr << "Date constructor: " << day
        << " invalid day of month" << endl;
   exit(1);
}
```

For your convenience, we now list the constructor in its entirety.

```
// constructor. month, day, year given as integer
// values mm dd yyyy
Date::Date (int mm, int dd, int yyyy):
     month(mm), day(dd), year(yyyy)
{
   if (month < 1 || month > 12)
   {
      cerr << "Date constructor: " << month
           << " invalid month" << endl;
      exit(1);
   }

   if (day <= 0|| day > daysInMonth())
   {
      cerr << "Date constructor: " << day
           << " invalid day of month" << endl;
   exit(1);
   }
}
```

*Exploring
Concepts*

Assume that spring begins in any year on March 21 and ends on June 20. If you read today's date, how can you determine if that date falls in the spring?

6-6   THE FOR LOOP

Counter-controlled loops are used in applications where the number of iterations are known before starting the loop. In their design, such loops initialize a counter object, test its value, and execute a loop update statement that increments the counter. Since these kinds of loops have a well-defined structure and find frequent applications, C++ provides a for statement that is designed to implement them. For instance, to add the first five integers, the for statement is

```
int  loopCount, sum = 0;

for (loopCount = 1; loopCount <= 5; loopCount++)
   sum += loopCount;     // loop body with one statement
```

A for loop includes three separate parts separated by semicolons. The first part, called the initialization statement, executes only once, before the program enters the loop body for the first time. This serves to initialize loop control objects. The second part of the for statement is the loop test that is evaluated at the beginning of each iteration. When the condition is true, program control passes to the loop body. The third part contains the update expression that is executed at the end of each iteration and alters the loop control objects. Figure 6-2 shows the logical flow of control in the for statement.

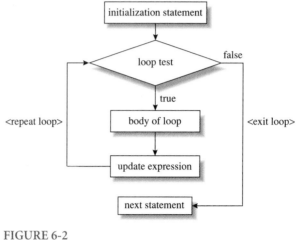

FIGURE 6-2
for Loop.

S Y N T A X

for Statement

Form: `for (init statement; loop test; update expr)`
          `<loop body>`

Action: A for statement follows a specific order of execution.

  1. Execute the initialization (init) statement.
  2. Evaluate the loop test. If the result is false, program control passes to the first statement after the loop body. Otherwise, execute the statement(s) in <loop body>.
  3. Evaluate the update expression (expr).
  4. Repeat step 2.

Example: `int i, sum = 0;`
          `// computes 1 + 2 + 3 + ... + 10`
          `for (i=1;i <= 10;i++)`
          `    sum += i;`
          `cout << sum << endl;    // outputs 55`

Some or all parts of the for statement may be omitted. We will discuss this situation in Section 6-8 when we cover generalized for loops.

The sequence of actions in a for loop are equivalent to the actions of a while loop.

```
initialization statement   // 1st part of the for statement
while (loop test)          // 2nd part of the for statement
{
   <loop body>
   update expression       // 3rd part of the for loop
}
```

A comparison between the for and while statements illustrates the common features. Take the problem of adding the first five integers. The control object i is used to control both loops.

$$sum = 1 + 2 + \cdots + 5 = 15$$

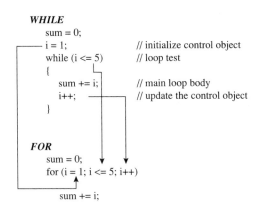

In both the for and while statements, the initialization, i = 1, occurs at the beginning. The logical expression comes next and is evaluated before each iteration. Each loop explicitly increments the counter i. A while loop typically places the statement i++ at the end of the loop body and the for loop computes the increment as its third part.

EXAMPLE 6.5 ████████████████████████████████████

1. Typically, for statements use integer counters to handle the number of iterations.

   (a) Input four test scores and compute their average.

```
int i, score, sum = 0;
float average;

for (i = 1; i <= 4; i++)
{
    cin >> score;
    sum += score;
}
average = sum/4.0;
```

   (b) The range of integer values can be adjusted to better suit the application. A car dealer compiles a record of the total number of trucks sold between 1990 and 1995. The counter is called year and is used in the input prompt.

```
int year, truckSales, totalTruckSales = 0;

for (year = 1990; year <= 1995; year++)
```

```
                    {
                        cout << "Number of trucks sold in " << year << ":";
                        cin >> truckSales;
                        totalTruckSales += truckSales;
                    }
```

2. The control object can be any discrete type. A for loop with a character control object ch outputs the lowercase letters 'a'–'z'.

```
   char ch;    // character control object (range 'a' to 'z')

   for (ch = 'a'; ch <= 'z'; ch++)
       cout << ch;
```

3. A Days object specifies a day in the week. It may be used as a control object in a for loop. The example inputs museum attendance for the weekdays Mon to Fri and maintains a record of total attendance.

```
   int totalAttendance = 0, attendance;

   Days d;

   for (d = Days(Mon); d.getDay() <= Fri; d.succ())
   {
       cin >> attendance;
       totalAttendance += attendance;
   } ■
```

Exploring Concepts

A restaurant is closed Monday and open the rest of the week. How would you create a loop that reads sales figures and computes the total sales for the week? Your loop must use the type Days and must advance from Tue through Sun. Is a for loop an appropriate statement for this problem?

Technical Note

A counter control object in a for statement may be declared for the first time in the initialization part of the statement. For example, the for statement declares and initializes the counter i. The loop sums the integers from 1 to 50.

```
   int sum = 0;
        . . .
   for (int i=1; i <= 50; i++)
       sum += i;
   cout << sum << endl;
```

In this book, we will not declare objects in a for statement.

6-7 FOR LOOP APPLICATIONS

The for loop can be used whenever you want to repeat a process a fixed number of times. We look at some algorithms that use a for loop, including problems in number theory, and geometry.

Number Theory: Exploring Factors

Number theory explores the properties of integers. Many results involve decomposing an integer into its factors.

> **Definition** Integer k is a *factor* of n provided k divides n with no remainder (n % k is 0). The equivalent multiplication expression says $n = k * x$ for some integer x. The numbers *1* and n are always factors of n.
>
> Example: 4 is a factor of 12 since 12 % 4 = 0.
> Equivalently, 12 = 4 * x where x = 3.

To find all of the factors of n, a for loop traverse the integers in the range 1 to n. Using a control object k, the remainder operation, n % k, indicates whether k is a factor.

$$\text{if } (n \% k \;=\; =\; 0)$$

$$< k \text{ is a factor of } n >$$

Actually, the algorithm can be more efficient. Since *1* and n are always factors, there is no need to test these extreme values. The loop can focus on the possible factors starting with $k = 2$. For the upper limit, we know that k is a factor only when $k * x = n$ for some integer x. Since we are not considering the factor $k = n$ ($x = 1$), we conclude that $x \geqslant 2$. If $x = 2$, then $k = n/2$, and if $x = 3$, then $k = n/3$. In general, it follows that $k \leqslant n/2$. For instance, with $n = 12$, we can immediately identify 1 and 12 as factors and then limit our testing of other possible factors to the range from 2 to $12/2 = 6$.

Factors of 12 are 1   2   3   4   6   12

PROGRAM 6.4

The program illustrates the algorithm for finding factors of an integer. The run looks at integers 36 and 7.

```cpp
#include <iostream.h>

int main()
{
    int number, k;

    cout << "Enter a positive integer: ";
    cin >> number;

    cout << "Factors of " << number << " are ";
    // output 1 which must be a factor
    cout << 1 << "   ";

    // loop testing for intermediate factors
```

```
        for (k=2; k <= number/2; k++)
            if (number % k == 0)     // test for factor
                cout << k << "   ";  // output k if it is a factor

        // list number as a factor if it is greater than 1
        if (number > 1)
            cout << number;
        cout << endl;

        return 0;
    }
```

```
Run 1:

Enter a positive integer: 36
Factors of 36 are 1  2  3  4  6  9  12  18  36

Run 2:

Enter a positive integer: 7
Factors of 7 are 1  7
```

Approximating a Circle

A regular polygon is a closed figure with n sides of equal length. For instance, a square is a regular polygon with four sides, a regular octagon has eight equal sides, and a regular decagon has 10 equal sides (Figure 6-3). These figures can be created by the PolyShape class, whose member functions are similar to those of the CircleShape and RectShape classes.

Square   Regular Octagon   Regular Decagon

FIGURE 6-3
4-sided , 8-sided and 10-sided Polygons.

In application 6-2, we use a for loop draw a series of figures to show that regular polygons with a fixed perimeter approximate a circle as the number of sides *n* increase. Before developing the application, we describe the PolyShape class. A PolyShape object is specified its center point, the number of sides, the length of each side, and the fill color. The constructor has a set of default arguments that initialize the attributes. For instance, the object equiTrangle is a darkgray equilateral triangle with sides of length 1.0 and center at (3,3).

```
PolyShape equitriangle(3.0, 3.0, 3, 1.0, darkgray);
```

The operations consist of a series of "get" and "set" functions that access the attributes along with the graphic functions `draw()` and `erase()` that sketch and remove the `PolyShape` objects. You are familiar with most of the operations from the other drawing classes.

DESCRIPTION: PolyShape CLASS ▰▰▰▰▰▰▰▰▰▰▰▰▰

A PolyShape object describes a regular polygon on a drawing surface.

Attributes:

```
double baseX, baseY;    // center of the polygon
ShapeColor color;       // color of the polygon
int n;                  // number of sides
double length;          // length of each side
```

Operations:

```
PolyShape:  Initialize a regular n-sided polygon with cen-
            ter at (x,y) and sides of length len. The de-
            fault color that fills the circle is darkgray.
                PolyShape(double x = 0.0, double y = 0.0,
                          int numsides = 4, double len = 0.0,
                          ShapeColor c = darkgray);

getLength:  Return the length of each side.
                double getLength();

setLength:  Set the length of each side to len.
                void setLength(double len);

getN:       Return the number of sides.
                int getN();

setN:       Set the number of sides to numsides.
                void setN(int numsides);

setColor:   Set the color of the polygon to c.
                void setColor(ColorShape c);

draw:       Draw the polygon in the current color.
                void draw();

erase:      Erase the polygon from the drawing surface.
                void erase();
```

EXAMPLE 6.6 ▰▰▰▰▰▰▰▰▰▰▰▰▰▰▰▰▰▰▰▰▰

1. A prompt directs the user to enter a real number P. The value is used to declare a Rectangle object sq that is a square whose perimeter is P. The length of the sides for sq is P/4.

```
cin >> P;
Rectangle sq(P/4, P/4);
```

Declare sqFigure as a PolyShape object that represents the square. Center sq-Figure at (5,3) and use blue as the fill color;

```
PolyShape sqFigure(5.0, 3.0, 4, sq.getLength(), blue);
```

2. Use PolyShape object sqFigure.

```
sqFigure.draw();              // draw the figure in the window

sqFigure.erase();             // erase figure
sqFigure.setN(6);             // figure is now a hexagon
sqFigure.setColor(green);     // fill color changed to green
sqFigure.draw();              // redraw the figure in the window  ■
```

APPLICATION 6-2 POLYGONS CONVERGING TO A CIRCLE

The program uses animation to illustrate how polygons expand into a circle as the number of sides increases. The drawing figure is a `PolyShape` object named `poly`, with center at (5,4) and with a blue fill color. After opening the window, a for loop draws a sequence of regular polygons with 3, 4, 5, . . . , and 20 sides and a fixed perimeter of 10. In each case, the length of a side is 10/n. The program ends by drawing a 120-sided polygon that "looks" like a circle (Figure 6-4).

| 3 sides | 6 sides | 8 sides | 12 sides | 120 sides |

FIGURE 6-4

Polygons Approach a Circle.

During the execution of the program, the `delayWindow()` function from the graphics library causes a momentary delay of one-half a second before the polygon is erased and the next polygon is drawn. Using viewWindow(), the 120-sided polygon remains on the screen until you type a key.

```
#include "polysh.h"    // use polygon shapes

int main()
{
    // n is number of polygon sides
    int n;
    // length of each polygon side
    double side;

    // position center of polygons at (5,4)
    PolyShape poly(5,4);

    poly.setColor(blue); // all polygons are blue
```

```
openWindow();      // open drawing window

// draw polygons with 3 to 20 sides and perimeter 10
for(n=3; n <= 20; n++)
{
    side = 10.0/n;            // length of each side
    poly.setLength(side);     // set side length
    poly.setN(n);             // number of sides is n
    poly.draw();              // draw polygon
    delayWindow(.5);          // wait 1/2 second
    poly.erase();             // erase the polygon
}

// draw 120-sided polygon
side = 10.0/120;
poly.setLength(side);
poly.setN(120);
poly.draw();
viewWindow();

closeWindow();                // shut down the window

return 0;
}
```

Run:
   (Five of the figures are drawn in Figure 6-4)

6-8   ADVANCED LOOP CONCEPTS

In a nested if construct, one if statement is contained inside another. In a similar fashion, there is no reason why a loop body cannot contain additional loops. In this section we look at the design of nested loops and use them in several applications. The section also discusses some additional loop control constructs that are available in C++. The topics include the generalized structure of a for statement and loop control break and continue statements.

Designing Nested Loops

A nested loop consists of the outer loop whose body has one or more inner loops that execute on each iteration.

```
<outer loop>
{  // outer loop body
   . . .
   <inner loop>
```

```
   {
       . . .
   }
       . . .
}
```

Drawing a number triangle illustrates nested loops. In the example, the outer loop is responsible to output the nine lines of the triangle. The inner loop is responsible to output the sequence of numbers on a line. The inner loop may access the current value of any control object defined in the outer loop. For the triangle, the inner loop uses the line number (iteration) to output the sequence 1, 2, 3, ..., line number.

```
1                               // line number = 1
1   2                           // line number = 2
1   2   3                       // line number = 3
1   2   3   4                   :
1   2   3   4   5               // .
1   2   3   4   5   6           // line number = 6
1   2   3   4   5   6   7       // .
1   2   3   4   5   6   7   8   :
1   2   3   4   5   6   7   8   9   // line number = 9
```

The following is code for the outer loop and an outline of the inner loop's task.

```
// set loop to execute with lineNumber = 1, 2, 3, ..., 9
for (lineNumber = 1; lineNumber <= 9; lineNumber++)
{
    // loop body
    <output the minilist: 1 2 ... lineNumber>
}
```

The loop body involves the output of successive integers. Table 6-2 traces the first four iterations of the outer loop. Each iteration outputs the integers from 1 to lineNumber.

TABLE 6-2 Nested Loop Triangle.

Output Loop:	Inner Loop Range:	Output:
lineNumber = 1	1 to 1	1
lineNumber = 2	1 to 2	1 2
lineNumber = 3	1 to 3	1 2 3
lineNumber = 4	1 to 4	1 2 3 4

To create the output on each line, we use an inner loop with a separate counter control object j. The range for j is always 1 to lineNumber.

Inner loop:

```
// print series of numbers 1  2  3  . . .  <lineNumber>
for (j = 1; j <= lineNumber; j++)
    cout << j << "  ";            // output numbers
cout << endl;                     // terminate with a newline
```

By combining the two loops, we have a nested structure that outputs the triangle.

Nested for loop:

```
for (lineNumber = 1; lineNumber <= 9; lineNumber++)
{
    // output integer row and a newline
    for (j = 1; j <= lineNumber; j++)
        cout << j << "  ";
    cout << endl;
}
```

EXAMPLE 6.7 ■■■■■■■■■■■■■■■■■■■■■■■■■■■■■■■■■■■■

By changing an inner loop statement, we can create a variation of the triangle. The function `starTriangle()` draws a triangle that displays stars on each of n lines. The sample is a triangle with 11 lines

```
            // draw a right triangle with stars
*           void starTriangle(int n);
**          {  // i is the line number
***            int i, j;

****           // output n lines in the triangle
*****          for(i = 1; i <= n; i++)
******         {
*******            // output i stars and a newline
********           for (j = 1; j <= i; j++)
*********             cout << '*';
**********        cout << end;
***********    }
            } ■
```

APPLICATION 6-3 DRAWING TRIANGLES USING NESTED LOOPS

The program creates the function `starRightTriangle()` that draws a triangle with the line of stars right-justified. The function has an argument n that specifies the number of lines. On each line i, n − i blanks must be output before displaying the i stars at the end of the line.

$$i: \quad \underbrace{\Box\ \Box\ \Box\ \dots\ \Box}_{n\ -\ i}\ \underbrace{*\dots**}_{i}$$

Each iteration of the outer loop contains separate loops to output the blanks and the stars respectively.

```
#include <iostream.h>

// draw the triangle with the stars right justified
void starRightTriangle(int n);
```

```
int main()
{
   starRightTriangle(7);
   return 0;
}

void starRightTriangle(int n)
{
   int i,j;

   // outer loop controls number of lines, blanks, and *'s
   for (i=1; i <= n; i++)
   {
      // output n-i leading blanks
      for (j=1; j <= n-i; j++)
         cout << ' ';

      // output i *'s on line i
      for(j=1; j <= i; j++)
         cout << '*';

      // after displaying  *'s, go to the next line
      cout << endl;
   }
}
```

```
Run:

      *
     **
    ***
   ****
  *****
 ******
*******
```

Generalized For Loops

Section 6.6 introduces the for loop using a single control object. The value of the object is set in the initialization statement and later modified by the update expression. While this is the typical format of a for loop, C++ allows the initialization and update statements to involve more general loop control logic.

The initialization statement of the for loop may contain two or more statements separated by commas. These statements are executed before the first iteration.

```
for (i = 1, j = 7; … ; … )    // initialize  i to 1 and j to 7
   . . .
```

The update part of a for loop may contain multiple expressions that allow the loop to modify more than one control object. The expressions are separated by commas and are evaluated at the end of each iteration.

```
// increment i, decrement j on each iteration
for ( … ; … ; i++, j--)
    . . .
```

We use a generalized for loop in this book only when it simplifies loop structure.

EXAMPLE 6.8

1. The for loop has integer control objects i and j. Initially i = 1 and j = 7. After each iteration, the value of i is incremented and the value of j is decremented. The process continues as long as i is less than or equal to j and produces the output 15 14 13 12.

```
for (i = 1, j=7; i <= j; i++, j--)
    cout << i+2*j << "   ";
cout << endl;
```

2. In most for loops, the control object is incremented or decremented by 1 using the operators ++ and −−. A for loop may have steps other than +1 or −1.

```
// start loop at 10 and step by 5
for (i = 10; i <= 30; i+= 5)
    cout << i << "   ";
```

```
Output is:  10  15  20  25  30 ■
```

Exploring Concepts

This form of the for statement may look strange but it works.

```
for(cin >> n; n != 0; cin >> n)
    cout << n * n << "   ";
```

What is the output if the following data items are entered on one line 5 8 −9 7 3 0?

Programming Note

Any or all of the parts in a for statement may be missing. However, both semi-colons must be present. There are two primary situations where parts may be missing. If all the control objects are already initialized, the first part of the for statement can be empty.

```
int i=1, sum = 0;

for(; i <= 10; i++)
    sum += i;
cout << sum << endl;    // Output: 55
```

It is generally clearer to initialize control objects in the first part of the for statement. In this way, someone reading the code does not have to look outside the loop to determine the initial values.

A loop can be designed to repeat indefinitely. The statement, called an *infinite loop*, is used by system software to handle service requests. For instance, a network server runs in the background on a system and handles network transactions as they arrive. The for statement can conveniently create an infinite loop as follows:

```
// the two semicolons must be included
for(;;)
{
    <wait until service is requested>
    <perform a task>
}
```

A while statement whose condition is always true may also be used.

```
while (true)
{
    . . .
}
```

Loop Break and Continue Statements

In a loop statement, a test is used to determine whether another iteration should occur. The while and for statements carry out the test before beginning an iteration and the do/while statement carries out the test after each iteration. For some applications, the test should occur at an intermediate point in the iteration, and the program should be able to alter loop control. This is particularly true when exit conditions are deeply nested within if/else statements. To handle these situations, C++ provides two special loop handling constructs, called the *break* and *continue* statements.

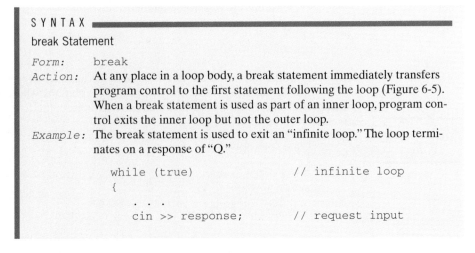

SYNTAX

break Statement

Form: break

Action: At any place in a loop body, a break statement immediately transfers program control to the first statement following the loop (Figure 6-5). When a break statement is used as part of an inner loop, program control exits the inner loop but not the outer loop.

Example: The break statement is used to exit an "infinite loop." The loop terminates on a response of "Q."

```
while (true)                // infinite loop
{
    . . .
    cin >> response;        // request input
```

```
            if (response == 'Q')    // test for Q
                break;               // exit loop
            . . .                    // continue loop body
        }
```

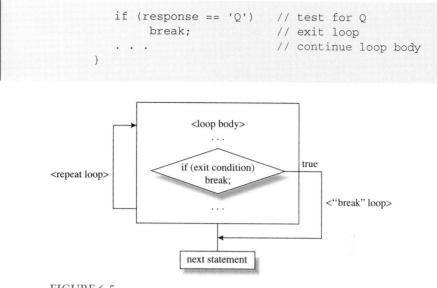

FIGURE 6-5
The Break Statement.

In a loop, the C++ break statement terminates the loop. In contrast, the continue statement causes the program to begin the next loop iteration.

SYNTAX ██

continue Statement

Form: continue

Action: The continue statement skips all remaining statements in the current iteration and begins the next iteration (figure 6-6). When continue is used in a while or do . . while statement, the next code to execute is the loop test. Note that the programmer is responsible to update control objects before executing the continue statement. In a for loop, the next code to execute is the update expression.

Example: The body of the while loop handles only positive integers.

```
        while (i < n)
        {
            . . .
            cin >> n;      // input an integer value
            if (n <0)      // test for negative n
            {
                i++;        // prepare for next iteration
                continue;   // go to next iteration
            }
                . . .       // otherwise continue loop body
        }
```

The equivalent for statement also uses continue.

```
for(i=1; i < n; i++)
{
    . . .
    if (n < 0)       // test for negative n
        continue;    // go to i++
    . . .
}
```

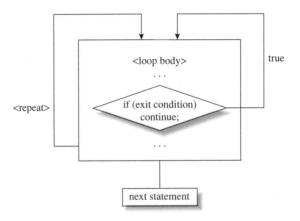

FIGURE 6-6
The Continue Statement.

Programmers can effectively use a break or continue statement when the exit conditions involve multiple logical tests imbedded in nested if/else statements. The resulting code is easier to understand and to write. Consider an infinite while loop that reads successive integers and maintains a running sum. The loop body contains a series of conditions that must be met.

Conditions:

If the input value is negative, the program simply discards the data and "continues" with the next iteration.

The positive input values are added to a running sum until the total exceeds 50. This is one "break" or stopping condition.

A loop counter triggers a second "break" condition when the number of positive integers exceeds 5.

Figure 6-7 diagrams the three loop control tests within the loop body.

APPLICATION 6-4 USING THE BREAK AND CONTINUE STATEMENTS

The conditions from Figure 6-7 are included in a complete C++ program. An infinite while loop uses control objects, value (input), sum, and count. For each positive input, the program outputs the current value of count and the

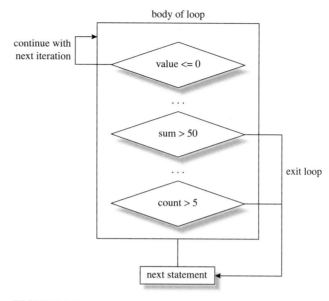

FIGURE 6-7
Multiple Loop Control Tests.

running sum. After the loop terminates, the final value for count and sum are displayed.

```cpp
#include <iostream.h>

int main()
{
    int value, sum = 0;
    int count = 1;

    while(true)              // set up an infinite loop
    {
        cin >> value;        // read a value

        if (value <= 0)      // drop 0 or negative values
            continue;        // go to next iteration

            sum += value;    // add value to sum
            cout << count << "   " << sum
                 << endl;    // output current count and sum

        if (sum > 50)        // break when sum exceeds 50
            break;
        count++;             // anticipate next positive value
        if (count > 5)       // break after 5 pos. values
            break;
    }

    // output final state of objects
```

```
            cout << "After loop: count = " << count
                 << " sum = " << sum  << endl;

        return 0;
    }
```

```
    Run 1:

    0  1 2  0 -1 -3 3 4 0 0 5
    1   1
    2   3
    3   6
    4   10
    5   15
    After loop: count = 6 sum = 15

    Run 2:

    20 0 25 9 0 4
    1   20
    2   45
    3   54
    After loop: count = 3 sum = 54
```

6-9 ARGUMENT PASSING

Up to this point in the book, all function calling statements have simply copied information to the arguments and retrieved information only from the return value. The section reviews this argument passing mechanism, called "pass by value". We also introduce a new mechanism called "pass by reference", that allows a function to return two or more values or to update the value of a run-time argument.

Pass by Value

When a function copies the value of a run-time argument into its corresponding formal argument and carries out its computations using the copy, the formal argument is called a *value argument*. The process is called *pass by value*.

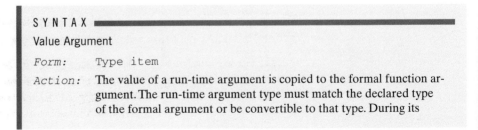

SYNTAX

Value Argument

Form: Type item

Action: The value of a run-time argument is copied to the formal function argument. The run-time argument type must match the declared type of the formal argument or be convertible to that type. During its execution, the function carries out its computation using the copy of the run-time argument. The run-time argument is not changed by the function.

Example: The char, int, and String arguments of f() are all passed by value.

```
void f(char ch, int n, String str);
```

To illustrate pass by value, consider the function, `distance()`, that computes the distance between the points (0,0) and (x,y) in the plane. The arguments x and y are value arguments.

```
double distance(double x, double y)
{
    return sqrt(x*x + y*y);
}
```

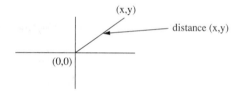

In an application using `distance()`, the calling statement must pass two data values to the arguments. Assume double object a and the literal 5 are the run-time arguments. Figure 6.8 illustrates the copying of a to x and the copying of the literal (converted to 5.0) to y. During execution, the function `distance()` does its calculations with objects x and y.

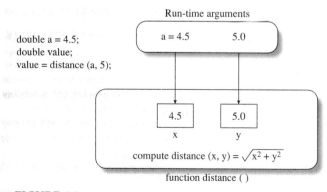

FIGURE 6-8
Illustrating Pass by Value.

A pass by value argument can be modified in the body of the function and still have no effect on the run-time argument. For instance, the function `sum()` returns $1 + 2 + 3 + \cdots n$ by using the argument n for loop control.

```
int sum(int n)
{
   int sumval = 0;

   while (n > 0)
   {
      sumval += n;
      n--;
   }
   return sumval;       // n has value 0
}

      . . .
```

In pass by value, the run-time argument is not modified. For instance

```
int m = 5;

cout << sum(m) << endl; // output is 15

// value of run-time argument m is not changed
cout << m << endl;      // output is 5
```

Pass by Reference

Simply passing arguments by value is not sufficient for some applications. At times, the function may need to return two or more values to the calling statement. This problem occurs when an input function is responsible for reading data into several run-time arguments that are supplied by the function call. In other cases, the function must be able to update run-time arguments. With pass by value arguments, there is no link between a run-time argument in the function call and a formal argument in the function, since the formal argument is only a copy of the run-time argument.

To provide greater function handling capability, C++ allows *reference arguments* that give the function direct access to a run-time argument. The process is called *pass by reference*.

SYNTAX

Reference Argument

Form: `T& item`

Action: The run-time argument that is passed by the function call must be a single object name. It cannot be a named constant, a literal, or an expression involving an operator. In the function, the corresponding formal argument is linked to the run-time argument so that the formal argument becomes another name (alias) for the run-time argument. All calculations with the formal argument use the value of the run-time argument and all assignments to the formal argument update the value of the run-time argument.

Example: The function div performs integer division of m by n and makes available the quotient and remainder to the calling statement. This is done by declaring quotient and remainder as reference arguments.

```
void div(int m, int n, int& quotient,
                       int& remainder)
{
   quotient = m/n;     // assign the quotient
   remainder = m%n;    // assign the remainder
}
```

In a main program,

```
int a = 34, b = 6, q, r;
// pass a and b by value; q and r by reference
// q is updated to 5 (quotient)
// r is updated to 4 (remainder)
div(a,b,q,r);
cout << q << "  " << r;     // output 5   4
```

The following function call is invalid, since 6 is a literal and a+b is an expression involving an operator. These are not valid run-time arguments in call by reference.

```
div(a,b,6,a+b);
```

Comparing Value and Reference Arguments. We develop an example that includes a value and a reference argument. We distinguish the argument passing mechanisms by tracing the value of the respective run-time and formal arguments. In function f(), object m is passed by value while object x is passed by reference. The main program declares objects s and t which are run-time arguments for the call to f().

```
void f(int m, double& x)
{
   m = 100;          // assign 100 to the argument m
   x = 6.75;         // assign 6.75 to the run-time argument
}

int main()
{
   int s = 50;
   double t = 4.5;
   f(s,t);           // call f with run-time arguments s, t

   return 0;
}
```

The following steps trace the execution of function f() starting with the calling statement that passes the run-time arguments, s and t. The trace continues with the two assignment statements in the function body.

Function Call:

The value of object s is copied to the formal argument m in f(). The reference argument x is associated with t. Figure 6-9(a) illustrates the relationship between the arguments by drawing a single arrow for the value argument s and a double arrow for the reference argument t.

Assignment to Value Argument m:

The statement "m = 100;" assigns the integer 100 to the object m. There is a change in the value of the formal argument m but no change in the corresponding run-time argument s (Figure 6-9(b)).

Assignment to Reference Argument x:

The statement "x = 6.75;" assigns the real number 6.75 to x which is a reference to t. The assignment changes the value of the run-time argument t (Figure 6-9(c)).

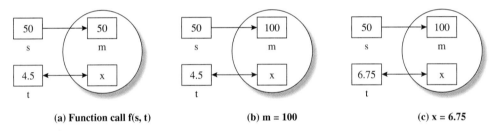

(a) Function call f(s, t)   (b) m = 100   (c) x = 6.75

FIGURE 6-9
Tracing Run-time and Formal Arguments.

Reference Arguments and Input. To illustrate how a function uses reference arguments to input values, we develop the function readRoom(). It has the value argument roomName that is a string describing the type of room. It also has the reference argument, room, of type Rectangle. The function prompts for the length and width of the room. After reading the data, the Rectangle operation setSides() updates the dimensions of the reference argument room. This has the effect of assigning new dimensions to the corresponding run-time argument in the calling statement.

```
// prompt for length and width of a room named roomName.
// use setSides() to update the Rectangle object room
void readRoom(String roomName, Rectangle& room)
{
    double length, width;
```

```
      cout << "Enter the length and width for the "
           << roomName << ": ";
      cin >> length >> width;
      room.setSides(length, width);
  }
```

PROGRAM 6.5

A main program uses the function readRoom() to input sizes for the kitchen, dining room and living room of a house. In each case, the values for the length and width are used to update the Rectangle object room. The program outputs the total area of the rooms.

```
#include <iostream.h>

#include "rect.h"
#include "tstring.h"

// prompt for length and width of a room named roomName
// use setSides() to update the rectangle object room
void readRoom (String roomName, Rectangle& room);

int main()
{
    int i;
    double totalArea = 0.0;
    Rectangle room;

    // determine the total area of three rooms in a house
    for (i = 1; i <= 3; i++)
    {
        switch(i)
        {
            case 1: readRoom("kitchen", room);
                    break;
            case 2: readRoom("dining room", room);
                    break;
            case 3: readRoom("living room", room);
                    break;
        }
        totalArea += room.area();
    }
    cout << "Total area of the rooms is "
         << totalArea << " square feet" << endl;

    return 0;
}

/* implementation of readRoom() in the program discussion */
```

```
Run:

Enter the length and width for the kitchen: 14 16
Enter the length and width for the dining room: 12 18
Enter the length and width for the living room: 20 24
Total area of the rooms is 920 square feet
```

Reference Arguments and Sorting. Sorting algorithms exchange items in a list until they create an ordering of elements from small to large or vice versa. C++ arrays that store lists are introduced in Chapter 7 along with a basic sorting algorithm. For now, we develop the function, exchange(), which is an important tool used to exchange two real numbers. Since the operation must interchange the actual run-time arguments and not their copies, reference arguments are used.

```
void exchange(double& x, double& y);
```

Assume and b are run-time arguments that are used by the exchange() call.

```
double a = 15, b = 27;
exchange(a,b);
```

Figure 6-10 uses double arrows to illustrate the relationship between the objects a and b and the corresponding reference arguments x and y. Part (a) gives the values immediately after passing the arguments. Part (b) gives the values after executing the function and carrying out the exchange.

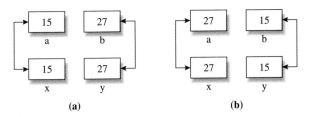

FIGURE 6-10
Run-time and Formal Arguments in exchange().

The algorithm uses a temporary object to hold the original value of x while assignment statements copy data to new locations. Parts (a)-(c) in Figure 6-11 display the data after executing the statements in the function.

```
// exchange the values of x and y
void exchange(double& x, double& y)
{
    double temp;    // used for temporary storage

    temp = x; // save value of x
```

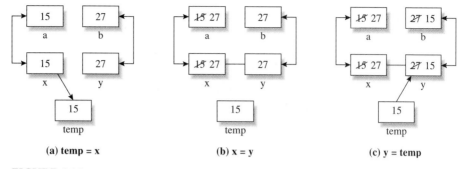

(a) temp = x   **(b) x = y**   **(c) y = temp**

FIGURE 6-11
Tracing the **exchange ( )** *Function.*

```
    x = y;    // assignment updates run-time argument
    y = temp; // assign original x. updates run-time argument
}
```

APPLICATION 6-5 SORTING A 3 ELEMENT LIST

The program illustrates the `exchange()` function by reading values for three double objects a, b, c and sorting the objects so that $a \le b \le c$. The algorithm makes any necessary exchanges to insure that a has the smallest value. We first compare a and b and then compare a and c. In each case, an exchange is made if the second object is less than a. After the two comparisons, the value of a is less than or equal to both b and c. As an illustration, use a = 9, b = 5, c = 8.

Compare a and b. Since b = 5 is less than a = 9, exchange the two objects.

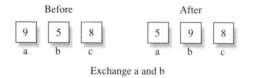

Before   After

Exchange a and b

Compare a and c. Since c = 8 is larger than a = 5, no exchange occurs.

Conclude by comparing b and c. If c is less than b, exchange the two values.

In the example, b = 9 and c = 8 so exchange b and c.

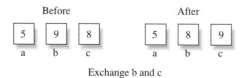

Before   After

Exchange b and c

```
#include <iostream.h>

// exchange the values of x and y
```

```
void exchange (double& x, double& y);

int main()
{
   double a, b, c;
   cout << "Enter three values: ";
   cin >> a >> b >> c;

   // store smaller value of a and b in a
   if (b < a)
      exchange(a,b);
   // store smaller value of a and c in a
   if (c < a)
      exchange(a,c);

   // smallest element is now in a;  compare b and c
   // store smaller value of b and c in b
   if (c < b)
      exchange(b,c);
   cout << "Ordered list: " << a << "   "
        << b << "   " << c << endl;

   return 0;
}

/* implementation of exchange() given in program discussion */
```

```
Run:

Enter three values: 9 5 8
Ordered list: 5   8   9
```

Reference Arguments and Screen Animation. Screen animation is produced by repeatedly drawing, erasing, and then redrawing a graphical object. Movement is created by an update function that changes the attributes of the object before it is redrawn.

APPLICATION 6-6 DRAWING A SHOOTING STAR

The program simulates a shooting star that moves up into the sky. The simulation is done by drawing a series of circles with decreasing radii and changing colors. Each circle is erased after 1/10 of a second, giving the illusion that the star is getting smaller as it moves off into the distance.

A for loop provides the movement. Initially CircleShape object circ is defined with center at (2,6), radius 2, and color blue. In the loop body, a function nextCircle() takes the object as a reference argument along with changes to the center and a scale factor. The function reduces the radius of the circle by the scale factor, shifts its center point, and changes its color. The fact that the object is passed by reference is critical since the updated CircleShape object is used for the next drawing operation.

```
// scale the radius and move the center to (x,y)
void nextCircle(CircleShape& circ, double scale,
               double dx, double dy);
```

The main program defines a for loop with 30 iterations. The loop body calls nextCircle() with a scale factor of .85 (85%). The center is positioned .1 units to the right and .3 units up. These units are passed as arguments dx and dy. The function updates the color for the next draw operation by incrementing the current color.

```
#include "circlesh.h"

// scale radius, move circle and change its color
void nextCircle(CircleShape& circ, double scale,
               double dx, double dy);
int main()
{
   // circle at (2.0, 6.0), radius 2.0, color blue
   CircleShape circ(2.0, 6.0, 2.0, blue);
   int i;                        // for loop control

   openWindow();

   // iteration produces the shooting star
   for(i=1;i <= 30;i++)
   {
      circ.draw();              // draw current circle
      delayWindow(.1);          // pause 1/10 th second
      circ.erase();             // erase the star

      // update the circle
      nextCircle(circ,.85,.1,.3);
   }

   closeWindow();

   return 0;
}

void nextCircle(CircleShape& circ, double scale,
               double dx, double dy)
{
   double newRadius = circ.getRadius();
   ShapeColor color = circ.getColor();

   newRadius *= scale;          // scaled radius
   circ.setRadius(newRadius);   // assign new radius
   // set new center
   circ.move(circ.getX()+dx,circ.getY()-dy);
```

```
      color++;                    // new color
      circ.setColor(color);       // assign new color
}
```

Run:
(Four of the stars are displayed.)

6-10 CONSTANT FUNCTION ARGUMENTS

The keyword *const* is used in the declaration of an object to indicate that its value cannot be changed. You have seen the declaration of constant objects in the main program. For instance,

```
int main()
{
    const double PI = 3.14159;
        . . .
}
```

The modifier const can also be used in the declaration of a free or member function argument. When *const* begins a formal argument declaration, the compiler prohibits any alteration of the argument during execution of the function. No assignment can be made to the argument and it cannot be passed as a reference argument to another function. The effect is to make the argument a read-only data item and is particularly effective when used with a reference argument. In this case the alias provided by the formal argument cannot be used to change the value of run-time argument. This provides an alternative to call by value. The mechanism is called *constant reference argument passing* and combines the key word const and pass by reference.

SYNTAX ▬▬▬▬▬▬▬▬▬▬▬▬▬▬▬▬▬▬▬▬▬▬▬

Constant Reference Argument

Form: const Type& obj
Action: The actual run-time argument is accessed but cannot be modified.

Example: The free function writeRectData() outputs the length, width, area and perimeter of a Rectangle object. The function uses Rectangle member functions that do not alter the object.

```
void writeRectData(const Rectangle& r)
{
    cout << "Length: " << r.getLength() << endl;
    cout << "Width: " << r.getWidth() << endl;
    cout << "Length: " << r.area() << endl;
    cout << "Length: " << r.perimeter() << endl;
}
```

Use constant reference argument passing for most formal arguments of class type when their values should not be changed. This avoids the copying of data members when pass by value is used. Pass arguments of primitive type by value.

Chapter 5 introduces the `Time24` class that maintains time using 24-hour format. The class has the member function `addTime()` that takes minutes as an argument and updates the current time. We now add a new member function `addTime24()` that takes a `Time24` object as an argument.

```
Time24 t(6,45), interval(1,15);

t.addTime24(interval);   // add 1 hour, 15 minutes to t
t.writeTime();           // 8:00
```

Since the function will only use and not modify the attributes of the argument, we can efficiently pass the object using constant reference

```
class Time24
{
        . . .
    // add time represented by t to the object
    void addTime24 (const Time24& t);
};

// convert t to minutes and use member function addTime()
void Time24::addTime24 (const Time24& t)
{
    int min = t.hour * 60 + t.minute;

    addTime(min);
}
```

6-11 CONDITIONAL EXPRESSIONS (OPTIONAL)

A programmer often finds a situation in which an object is assigned one of two alternative values depending on a condition. For instance, the if/else statement assigns to min the minimum of x and y.

```
if (x <= y)
    min = x;
```

```
else
   min = y;
```

To handle this common situation, C++ provides the operator called the *conditional expression* that uses selection to return a value. The operator contains a condition and two expressions that are delineated by separators "?" and ":", respectively.

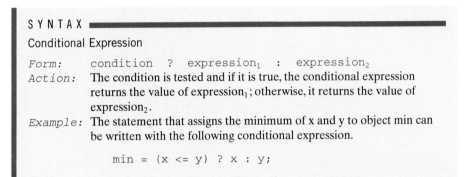

SYNTAX

Conditional Expression

Form: condition ? expression$_1$: expression$_2$

Action: The condition is tested and if it is true, the conditional expression returns the value of expression$_1$; otherwise, it returns the value of expression$_2$.

Example: The statement that assigns the minimum of x and y to object min can be written with the following conditional expression.

```
min = (x <= y) ? x : y;
```

EXAMPLE 6.9

1. A conditional expression evaluates the quotient of two real numbers y/x. When the divisor x is 0, z is assigned the value 0; otherwise, z is given the value y/x.

```
z = (x == 0) ? 0 : y/x;
```

2. For an integer n, we want to create output that specifies whether n is even or odd. A conditional expression assigns to the string, intForm, the value "is even" or "is odd."

```
intForm = ( n % 2 == 0) ? " is even" : " is odd";
cout << n << intForm;
```

3. A conditional expression can be placed directly into the output stream. Because the conditional expression has low precedence, parenthesis must surround the expression.

```
bool flag;

// evaluate flag and output TRUE or FALSE
cout << (flag ? "TRUE" : "FALSE") << endl;   ∎
```

Programming Note

The conditional expression is the only C++ operator that has three operands (a *ternary operator*). It is a substitute for the use of if/else and therefore is optional.

Conditional expressions can be nested to make complex expressions. We avoid this use since it tends to make the C++ statements confusing or prone to error. Then conditional expressions are used in the book only when they make a simple selection between two values.

PROGRAM 6-6

The program illustrates conditional expressions that find the absolute value of a number and the successor of an enumeration value of type `FlagColor`. The program outputs the integer representation for the new enumeration value.

```
#include <iostream.h>

enum FlagColor {red, white, blue};

int main()
{
    int x, z;
    FlagColor fcolor = blue;

    cout << "Enter an integer value: ";
    cin >> x;

    // compute the absolute value of x and assign it to z
    z = (x < 0) ? -x : x;
    cout << "Absolute value of " << x << " is "
         << z << endl;

    // assign to fcolor its successor
    fcolor = (fcolor == blue) ? red : FlagColor(fcolor+1);
    cout << "Integer representation = " << fcolor << endl;

    return 0;
}
```

```
Run:

Enter an integer value: -9
Absolute value of -9 is 9
Integer representation = 0
```

1. Assume x, y and z are objects of type double. Can you rewrite the statement as an if statement?

```
val = x < y && y != 0 ? 1 : 0;
```

2. Assume x, y and z are objects of type double. The conditional expression for val consists of nested expressions. Can you rewrite the statement as nested if/else statements?

```
val = x >= y && x <= z ? z-y : x < y ? 0 : 1.0e25;
```

3. Describe this situation in terms of a conditional expression.
   The cost of renting a truck is $45 or $10 plus $0.35 per mile, whichever is larger.

Exploring Concepts

6-12 TEXT FILE I/O

In C++, I/O is provided by stream objects that handle the flow of data between memory and an external device such as a keyboard, disk, or CD-ROM. For interactive I/O, the external devices are the keyboard and monitor. The cin object is the standard input stream handling data transfer from the keyboard to memory. The objects cout and cerr are standard output and error streams that write characters to the screen.

Each stream object is logically connected to a specific device *(physical file)*, which stores the information as a sequence of characters. A block of system memory, called a *buffer*, holds data going to or coming from the file. For input, the stream allows data to flow from the keyboard or disk file to the buffer. For output, the stream handles data that flows from the buffer to a monitor or disk file. The operating system provides a series of low-level operations to transfer data between the associated buffer and the device. These operations are system-dependent and are used to implement the high-level member functions that the programmer uses to transfer data.

A computer system distinguishes between text and binary files. A *text file* consists of a sequence of ASCII characters which is divided into lines by the newline character ' \n '. Text files are created by an application tool called an editor or as ASCII output from an application. For instance, the text file, "greeting," contains two lines:

```
Hello, how are you?<newline>     -- line 1
Have a nice day.<newline>        -- line 2
```

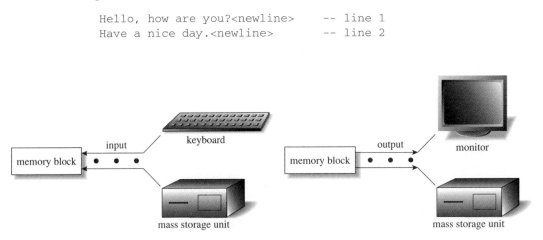

A *binary file* consists of data records that vary from a single character to more complex structures that include integers, floating point values, programmer-defined objects and so forth. Binary files are used by word processors, graphics programs, sound and video storage formats, and compilers when they generate machine code. Binary files are not discussed in this book. We develop text files since they are easier to deal with and introduce us to the critical features of file handling.

The newline character varies from system to system. On Unix systems, each line of a text file ends with the <line feed> character (ASCII code 10), whereas on a Macintosh system the newline character is <carriage return> (ASCII 13). With Microsoft Windows, the newline character '\n' is actually the two character sequence <line feed><carriage return>.

Assume the following statement is executed at the end of a line.

```
cin.get(c);    // input a char object c
```

In the Windows environment, the statement actually reads both characters from the file but returns '\n' with integer value 10 (<line feed>).

Technical
Note

C++ Stream Classes

The C++ stream I/O system is implemented using class inheritance, which can be illustrated by a hierarchy tree (Figure 6-12). Class inheritance is discussed in Chapter 12. For now, we will give a simple description of the class features for each level in the chart.

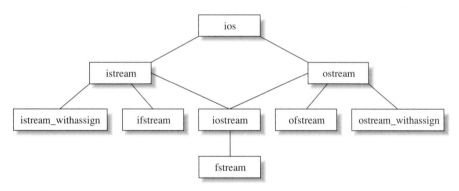

FIGURE 6-12
The C++ Stream Hierarchy.

The ios Level. At the root of the tree, the *ios class* maintains format settings and provides member functions to retrieve or modify these settings. The authors used these operations to create the manipulator setreal(). The ios class also maintains an integer status word that identifies whether an error occurs during an I/O operation. This status word provides a continuously updated report on the state of the stream. The ios class contains operations which interpret the information in the status word.

The Data Transfer Level. In the second level of the tree, the classes *istream* and *ostream* contain the data transfer operations that carry data between memory and the device. The istream class defines input operations such as the extraction operator ">>" and the get() member function. The ostream class implements the insertion operator "<<" that is used by cout and cerr. Since these classes have a common link to the parent ios class, they inherit (have access to) the data and operations of that class.

File Identification Level. The third level of the tree has classes that identify the standard keyboard, screen devices and disk files. The familiar cin and cout streams are objects of the "withassign" classes. The object cin is of the type *istream_withassign* and cout is of the type *ostream_withassign*. These classes allow the programmer to assign a general stream object to cin or cout, a feature that has important usage in some technical applications. Access to the attributes and operations of the "withassign" classes and their parent classes (istream, ostream, ios) is provided by the directive

```
#include <iostream.h>
```

For streams that are linked to disk files, additional capabilities are defined in the *ifstream* and *ofstream* classes. Objects of type ifstream are used for input; objects of type ofstream are used for output. More general streams allow both input and output. These objects are of type *fstream,* which is not discussed in this book. Access to the classes that are used for disk handling is provided by the directive

```
#include <fstream.h>
```

Creating File Stream Objects

The standard objects cin, cout, and cerr are predefined streams in the header file `iostream.h`. All other text file objects in our discussion must be explicitly declared of type ifstream for input or ofstream for output.

```
ifstream fin;      // fin is an input stream object

ofstream fout;     // fout is an output stream object
```

Opening a File. A stream object cannot be used until it is attached to a physical file. The streams cin and cout are connected to the keyboard and screen by the run-time system. For disk files, we must explicitly attach the file by *opening the stream*. The action is provided by the member function *open()* that contains the file name as an argument. For instance, the following statement attaches the stream fin to the file "namelist.dat" on a PC floppy disk (Drive a:).

```
fin.open("a:namelist.dat");
```

The `open()` operation requires that the file name be given as a C++ string, which is a sequence of characters terminated by the NULL character (ASCII code 0). C++ strings are discussed in Chapter 10. A string literal, such as `"a:namelist.dat"`, is interpreted by the compiler as a C++ string. In this book, our strings have been predominantly String objects and not C++ strings. String objects cannot be supplied as an argument in the `open()` function. For instance,

```
// filename is a String object and not a valid argument
String filename = "acctdata.out";
fout.open(filename);
```

To use a String object as a file name, it must be converted to a C++ string before being passed to open(). Fortunately, our String class has a member function called c_str() that converts a String object into a C++ string object. We can correct the previous invalid open() statement by using c_str() in the argument list.

```
fout.open(filename.c_str());
```

When opening a stream, the run-time system must be able to access the physical file. By using the full pathname as the argument, the open() statement can immediate attach the stream to the physical file. Assume

```
c:\data\table.dat
```

is the input file, the open() statement is

```
dataIN.open("c:\\data\\table.dat");
```

Technical Note

Having to always supply a full pathname is clumsy, and most compilers provide rules to simplify the filename argument for the open() operation. For instance, if you are using the GNU C++ compiler and the file is in the same directory as the C++ main program, a simple name is sufficient. Most other compilers use a project directory as the point of reference.

```
fout.open("integer.dat");   // simple file name sufficient
```

Note that the path delimiter \ is given by "\\" since \ indicates an escape sequence.

EXAMPLE 6.10

1. The following statements are used to declare a file stream object and attach it to a file "numbers.dat" for input of data.

```
ifstream fin;               // declare the file stream object
fin.open("numbers.dat");    // open the text file
```

2. Using String objects, read the name of the input file from the keyboard and then create a name for an output file by appending ".out". Use the c_str() conversion operator to open the files.

```
ifstream infile;        // an input stream object
ofstream outfile;       // an output stream object
String ifname, ofname;  // file names

// create the file names
cout << "Enter the file name: ";
cin >> ifname;
ofname = ifname + ".out";

// open the files
infile.open(ifname.c_str());
outfile.open(ofname.c_str());   ■
```

Most compilers return an error condition when open() attempts to open a non-existent file. Some, however, create a zero-length file with the specified name and do not return an error. This can cause the program to run incorrectly. To prevent this situation, use an extended form of the open().

```
fin.open(<filename>, ios::in|ios::nocreate).
```

*Programming
Note*

The second argument is a file mode expression that uses the terms "in" and "no create" that are defined in the ios class. The argument insures that whenever the input file does not exist, the system will not create an empty file. The symbol "|" is the *bitwise OR* operator that performs a logical or of corresponding bits in the operands.

An attempt to open an existing file for output causes, by default, the file to be truncated to zero length.

Closing a File: Opening a stream establishes a connection between the stream and the physical file. By *closing the stream*, the connection is broken. C++ provides the member function *close()* for this purpose.

```
outfile.close();    // detach a stream from the physical file
```

*Programming
Note*

The close() operation is particularly important for output streams. Typically, the run-time system copies the output to a buffer (memory block) which is then periodically cleared (flushed) by writing data to the file. The close() operation flushes the buffer before detaching the stream from the file. Failing to call the operation can result in a loss of data if the program terminates abnormally. It is good programming practice to explicitly close a stream when it is no longer needed by the application.

Reading and Writing File Data

Once an input stream is open, the programmer can use the extraction operator "`>>`" and the get() function to read data from the file in the same way that data is read from cin. For instance, assume fin is an input stream attached to the disk file "input.dat".

```
Input File Data:
    345   application
    6.3   80

Object Declarations:
    int n;
    float x;
    String str;
    char ch;
```

```
Input Statements:
    fin >> n >> str;    // n = 345    str = application
    fin >> x;           // skip whitespace and then x = 6.3
    fin.get(ch);        // ch = ' ' (space)
    fin >> n;           // n = 80
    fin.get(ch);        // ch = '\n' (newline)
```

Similarly, an output stream may use the insertion operator "<<" and manipulators, like setw() and setreal(), that have been defined for the cout object. Let fout be an output stream attached to the disk file "output.dat".

```
Object Declarations:
    int n = 345, x = 45.817;

Output Statements:
    fout << "Count is " << n << endl;
    fout << setw(5) << n << setreal(7,2) << x;

Resulting Output File Data:
    Count is 345
      345   45.82
```

File Error Checking

C++ monitors the state of a stream object during any open operation or any I/O operation. The results are recorded in an integer data member of the ios class. Within the integer, selected bits indicate whether the open failed or input read past end of file. The data value also contains other information that indicates whether a fatal error occurred. These topics are discussed in the optional section "Stream States and Errors" at the end of the chapter. In this section we look only at file open errors and the end of file condition that is associated with an input stream. We develop a shortcut technique that C++ provides for testing whether these conditions occur.

As we have noted, C++ collects very specific information about the state of a stream after an operation is performed. From this information, the stream I/O system indicates to a program whether the operation was "successful". The meaning of the term "successful" depends on the operation. For instance, an open() operation flags an error condition when the program attempts to attach a non-existing file for input or attach for output an existing file that is write protected. In these cases, the I/O system specifies that the open() operation was not successful. During input operations, the *end of file (EOF)* flag is set to true when an input stream attempts to read data past the last character of the file. The end of file flag is set to false when data is successfully input from the file. It is possible to directly test the value of the individual status bits. However, it is much easier to test the status of an I/O operation by using a shortcut. C++ allows a program to use the file stream as though it were a Boolean object. After each operation, the stream name may be used in a logical expression that indicates whether the operation is successful (true) or not successful (false).

SYNTAX ▄▄▄

Conditional Statements with Streams

Form: `// test for valid open() or other I/O operation`
            `if (!streamName)`
                `. . .`

            `// read until end-of-file`
            `while (streamName)`
                `. . .`

Action: The logical expression uses the stream name as though it were bool object. Its value is true if the previous I/O operation was successful and false if some error or end-of-file condition is identified.

Example: `fin >> n;`
            `if (fin)`
                `cout << "The input was successful";`
            `else`
                `cout << "The input was unsuccessful";`

Testing for File Open Error. During a stream `open()` operation, the file may not exist (input) or the disk may be full or write-protected (output). When opening an input stream, an error can easily occur when the programmer does not use the correct absolute or relative path name for the file. No matter what the cause, the program should return to the run-time system after detecting the file open error. Error checking using the stream name should be part of the open process. The test is simple. Use an if statement and the stream name to determine whether the `open()` was successful. Assume `streamObj` is the stream object name.

```
streamObj.open(filename);  // attempt to open stream

// if file open fails, return to run-time system
if (!streamObj)
{
   cerr << "Failed to open " << filename << endl;
   exit(1);
}
```

Testing for End-Of-File. A program recognizes when all of the data has been read by testing for the end-of-file condition. When a C++ stream is attached to a disk file, the condition is set to true when the stream attempts to read beyond the last character in the file. This is an important point. Simply reading the last character in the file does not set EOF to true. A subsequent input must be attempted before the stream identifies that no more data is present. For input from the keyboard, EOF is indicated by typing a control character. For instance, `<control D>` is the EOF character on a UNIX system and `<control Z>` is the EOF character on a Windows system.

After each successful input, the stream name has an associated Boolean value of true. The value is false once the EOF condition is true. This fact can be used with a loop to read all of the data in a file. Assume fin is the input stream and item is an object. A while statement reads a series of values until end of file.

```
fin >> item;        // attempt to input a data value
while (fin)         // check for successful input
{                   // enter the loop if successful
    . . .
    fin >> item;    // attempt another input
}
```

PROGRAM 6.7

The program reads a series of string and integer pairs from the disk file "userID". The string is the login name for a computer user and the integer represents the user's access to the system resources. Input terminates on end-of-file. Assume user access value 1 indicates full-access and value 2 indicates Internet-access only.

For output, the program opens the file "accessID". Corresponding to each input pair, the login name, e-mail name, and the access status description are written to the file in the form

```
loginName    loginName@website.net    accessDescription

#include <iostream.h>
#include <fstream.h>
#include <10 manip.h>
#include <stdlib.h>     // for exit()

#include "tstring.h"    // use String class
#include "textlib.h"    // for manipulator setjust()

int main()
{
    // input file specifying user name and access rights
    ifstream accessFile;
    // output file summarizing user status
    ofstream statusFile;
    // used to read login name, access rights from accessFile
    String loginName, emailName;
    int accessNo;

    accessFile.open("userID");      // open "userID"
    if(!accessFile)
    {
        cerr << "Cannot open 'userID' for input" << endl;
        exit(1);
    }

    statusFile.open("accessID");    // open "accessID"
```

```
      if(!statusFile)
      {
         cerr << "Cannot open 'accessID' for output" << endl;
         exit(1);
      }

      // read the information for the first user in the file
      accessFile >> loginName >> accessNo;
      // terminate on end-of-file
      while (accessFile)
      {
         // form the email name
         emailName = loginName + "@website.net";

         // output the descriptive information to statusFile
         // use left justification to line up output data
         statusFile << setjust(Left) << setw(10) << loginName
                    << setw(25) << emailName;
         if (accessNo == 1)
            statusFile << "  Full Access";
         else
            statusFile << "  Internet Access Only";
         statusFile << endl;
         // read the information for next user in the file
         accessFile >> loginName >> accessNo;
      }
      access File.close(); statusFile.close();

      return 0
   }
```

```
   Input file: "userID"

   paxHack    1
   walker     2
   comp101    1

   Run:

   Output file: "accessID"

   paxHack    paxHack@website.net    Full Access
   walker     walker@website.net     Internet Access Only
   comp101    comp101@website.net    Full Access
```

Many systems provide a utility program that reads through a file and outputs the number of characters along with the number of lines in the file. The UNIX version is the word count utility "wc". Application 6-7 emulates such a utility.

The program inputs the name of a text file into the String object `filename`. The object is used to open the file. As the file is read one character at a time, integer objects numchars and numlines are counters that maintain a record of the number of characters and newlines (\n) that are found. We assume that each line of the text file ends with the newline character. After reading EOF, the final count of the number of characters and number of lines in the file are output. The sample run outputs the data for the program source itself, which is contained in the file "apl6_7.cpp."

```cpp
#include <iostream.h>
#include <fstream.h>

#include "tstring.h"    // use String objects

int main()
{
   ifstream fin;        // input stream object
   char c;              // used to read each char from fin
   String filename;
   int numchars = 0, numlines = 0;

   cout << "Enter the name of the file: ";
   cin >> filename;

   // open filename for input
   fin.open(filename.c_str());
   if (!fin)
   {
      cout << "Could not open \"" << filename << '"' << endl;
      return;
   }

   // read a character c
   fin.get(c);
   // loop until EOF
   while (fin)
   {
      numchars++;       // increment character count
      if (c == '\n')
         numlines++;    // increment line count
      fin.get(c);       // read the next character
   }

   // output the results
   cout << "Number of characters: " << numchars << endl;
   cout << "Number of lines: " << numlines << endl;
```

```
        // close the stream
        fin.close();

        return 0;
    }
```

```
    Run:

    Enter the name of the file: ap16_7.cpp
    Number of characters: 867
    Number of lines: 42
```

A stream input statement can be used in Boolean expressions. Its value is true if the input succeeded and false otherwise. For instance, this loop reads a file of integers and doubles each value for output to the screen. The expression "fin >> item" returns false on EOF.

```
    int item;

    while (fin >> item)
        cout << item*item << endl;
```

Technical Note

This loop reads lines of text from the keyboard and echoes the characters to the screen in lowercase. Since "cin.get(ch)" returns false on EOF, the loop will terminate if end of file is typed.

```
    char ch;

    while (cin.get(ch))
    {
        if (ch >= 'A' && ch <= 'Z')
            ch += 32;
        cout << ch;
    }
    cout << endl;
```

Streams as Function Arguments (optional)

In a function, a stream must be passed as a reference argument since any operation will change the state of the stream. C++ implementations will produce a compilation error if you attempt to pass the stream as a value argument.

E X A M P L E   6 . 1 1

The function copyLowerCase() takes both an input stream (ifstream) and an output stream (ofstream) as arguments and uses them to copy the characters from the source file to a destination file with letters in lowercase.

```
// copy source to destination file with lowercase conversion
void copyLowerCase(ifstream& source, ofstream& dest)
{
   char ch;

   fin.get(ch);                          // read first char
   while (fin)                           // continue if successful
   {
      if ('A' <= ch && ch <= 'Z');       // check case
         ch += 32;
      fout << ch;                        // output char
      fin.get(ch);                       // next char
   {                                                          ■
```

Allowing cin/cout Function Arguments. If you wish to define a general function that can take either cin or an ifstream as a run-time argument, you must declare the formal argument in the function to have type istream from the data transfer level. This type is the parent class for both the istream_withassign and ifstream classes. Similarly, a function that performs general output using either cout or an ofstream argument must declare an ostream formal argument. For example,

```
void funcForOutput(ostream& ostr)
{
   ostr << "Output from funcForOutput()" << endl;
}
```

If we declare an ofstream object fout in the main program, we can call the function funcForOutput() using both fout and cout as arguments.

```
ofstream fout;

fout.open("test.dat");
      . . .
funcForOutput(fout);   // writes to "test.dat"
funcForOutput(cout);   // writes to the screen
```

APPLICATION 6-8 ILLUSTRATING STREAM FUNCTION ARGUMENTS

The program illustrates an istream argument in the function, sumInput(). The function reads a text file of integers to end of file, computes the sum of the data, and writes that value to the screen. The main program calls the function with an ifstream argument that is associated with the file "ints.dat" and then with the stream cin. In the latter case, you must type an end of file sequence at your keyboard. For Windows, the sequence is Control Z (^Z).

```
#include <iostream.h>
#include <fstream.h>
#include <stdlib.h>                      // for exit()

// read text file of integers, compute and output their sum
void sumInput(istream& istr);
```

```
int main()
{
   ifstream fin;                    // declare an input stream

   fin.open("ints.dat");            // attach to file "ints.dat"
   if(!fin)
   {
      cerr << "Cannot open 'ints.dat'" << endl;
      exit(1);
   }
   cout << "Calling sumInput() with ifstream argument"
        << endl;
   sumInput(fin);

   cout << endl << "Calling sumInput() with cin argument"
        << endl;
   sumInput(cin);

   return 0;
}

void sumInput(istream& istr)
{
   int item, sum = 0;

   istr >> item;         // read the first item
   while (istr)
   {
      sum += item;       // add the new item
      istr >> item;
   }
   cout << "The sum of the integers is " << sum << endl;
}
```

```
File "ints.dat"
49 35 5
36 27
18 3 55

Run:

Calling sumInput() with ifstream argument
The sum of the integers is 228

Calling sumInput() with cin argument
30 7 21 19
<control Z>
The sum of the integers is 77
```

Stream States and Errors (OPTIONAL)

The ios class provides an integer attribute that indicates the condition of the stream. The attribute consists of a series of binary bits which are set with each I/O operation.

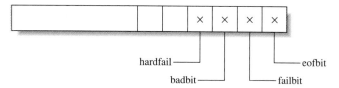

The eofbit is set when an input stream attempts to read beyond the *end-of-file (EOF)*. It provides a stopping condition for a program that must read an unspecified number of data items from a file. The failbit is set when a stream operation produces an error that does not result in any loss of information. For instance, using an incorrect file name to open an input stream will set failbit to true. The badbit and hardfail bits are set when an operation creates a serious system fault that results in loss of information. The hardfail always indicates an unrecoverable error condition.

The ios class provides a set of operations that indicate whether an end-of-file or error condition exists. Operations, like `eof()`, `fail()`, and `bad()`, return specific information about the state bits.

CHAPTER 6 SUMMARY

This chapter looks at advanced selection and loop structures that are important C++ tools for implementing algorithms. A sequence of nested if/else statements can be used to select from among a set of discrete alternatives. However, the switch statement provides a more readable and efficient alternative for approaching this type of problem. In this chapter we use nested if/else statements for even more complex selection problems, where one or both of the alternative actions may involve additional selection.

For good program design, C++ provides enumeration types that allow programs to assign meaningful names to integer values. However, even though such types are very useful, they present problems when used in arithmetic expressions and I/O statements. We solve the problems by introducing an enumeration wrapper class. It encapsulates an enumeration object and provides operations that are normally difficult or impossible to perform with the primitive enumeration type. As a major application of the switch statement and enumeration types, we present the Date class. It makes a variety of date computations easier to implement and will be used throughout the book.

The `while` statement is well-suited for event-controlled loops. For counter-controlled loops, C++ provides the `for` statement that includes efficient syntax for initialization, testing, and updating of control objects. The `for` statement is part of basic loop syntax. The chapter concludes our discussion of control structures by introducing nested loops, generalized `for` statements, break and continue statements and conditional expressions.

In Chapter 3, we introduce pass by value arguments. This chapter introduces pass by reference arguments. Reference arguments have application when a function must update a run-time argument or return more than one value to the calling statement. They are also used as constant reference arguments that avoid costly copying involved with value arguments.

A text file consists of a sequence of ASCII characters that are divided into lines by the newline character \n. In C++, stream objects handle the flow of data between memory and the text file. A stream object is described by a hierarchy of classes that begins at the top with the ios class. The class determines different format settings and monitors the state of the stream. The ifstream and ofstream classes are used to perform I/O with disk files. Objects of type ifstream are used for input, while objects of type ofstream are used for output. The operation `open()` attaches a physical file to a stream object and allows a programmer to use all of the I/O statements that were developed for `cin` and `cout` in the first five chapters. In addition, we learn that the stream can be used as a Boolean object to check for file open errors along with end-of-file. File-stream objects enable us to deal with larger datasets and expand our range of applications.

Classes in the Chapter

Name	Implementation File	Name	System Header File
Date	date.h	ifstream	fstream.h
Days	days.h	ios	iostream.h
PolyShape	polysh.h	istream	iostream.h
String	tstring.h	ofstream	fstream.h
Time24	time24.h		

KEY TERMS

Binary file:
Consists of data items that vary from a single character to more complex structures that include integers, floating-point values, programmer-defined objects, and so forth. These files are used by word processors, graphics programs, and sound and video storage formats.

Break statement (in a loop):
Immediately transfers program control to the first statement following the loop. When a break statement is used as part of an inner-nested loop, program control exits the inner loop but not the outer loop. The break statement is normally used when loop exit conditions are deeply nested within if/else statements in the body of the loop.

Break statement (in a switch statement):
Causes an exit from a switch statement. The next statement following the switch block is executed. Normally, each case statement terminates with a break.

Closing a stream:
Breaking the connection between a stream and a file. C++ provides the member function `close()` for this purpose.

Conditional expression:
An operator containing a condition and two expressions that are delineated by separators "?" and ":," respectively. The condition is tested and if it is true, the conditional

expression returns the value of the first expression; otherwise, it returns the value of the second expression.

Conditional statements with stream objects:

Use a stream name as though it were a bool object. The result is true if the previous I/O operation was successful and false if some error or end-of-file condition is identified.

Constant reference argument:

Efficient method of passing a run-time object that cannot be changed. Use the technique when an object has multiple data members.

Continue statement:

Terminates execution of all remaining statements in the current loop iteration and passes program control to the next iteration. The programmer is responsible for updating control objects, as necessary, before execution continues. The continue statement is normally used if the current iteration should not complete and the program is executing code deeply nested within if/else statements in the body of the loop.

Data transfer level of the stream hierarchy:

Contains the data transfer operations that carry data between memory and the device. The operations are implemented by the classes istream and ostream. The istream class defines input operations like the extraction operator ">>" and the get() member function; the ostream class describes the insertion operator "<<" that is used by cout and cerr.

End-of-file:

A flag that is set to true when the application attempts to read data past the last character of the file. The flag provides a stopping condition to a program that must read an unspecified number of data items from a file.

Enumeration type:

Specifies a list of names that are separated by commas and enclosed in braces. The list of items are names for integer values. The type allows the use of meaningful names in switch statements, function argument lists, and so forth. The equivalent integer values are used when enumeration objects are involved in arithmetic expressions. However, care must be taken to assure that the value of such expressions does not leave the range of the integer values representing the enumeration type.

File identification level of the stream hierarchy:

Contains classes that identify the standard keyboard (cin), screen (cout, cerr) streams, and disk files. The ifstream and ofstream classes are used to define streams that attach to disk files. Objects of type ifstream are used for input, where objects of type ofstream are used for output.

For statement:

Used primarily for counter-controlled loops. Includes three separate parts separated by semicolons. The initialization statement executes only once and initializes control objects. The second part of the for statement is the loop test. When the condition is true, program control passes to the loop body. The third part contains the update expression that is executed at the end of each iteration and alters the loop control objects.

Generalized for statement:

Initialization statement may contain two or more statements separated by commas or a single declaration statement. The update part of a for loop can contain comma-separated expressions that allow the loop to modify more than one object.

ios Level of the stream hierarchy:

A class that describes different format settings and monitors the state of an I/O stream. Member functions set and retrieve attributes.

Multiple selection:

In the simplest case, choosing from among a series of discrete values and taking appropriate action when a value is selected. More complex selection occurs when one or both of the alternative actions at the first level may involve additional selection at a higher level of nesting.

Nested if/else:

One or both of the alternatives in an if statement consists of another if statement.

Nested loops:

A loop whose body contains additional loops.

Opening a stream:

Attaching a stream to a file. The action is provided by the member function `open()` that contains the file name as an argument.

Pass by reference:

An argument-passing method in which a formal argument called a reference argument, becomes another name for the run-time argument. All expressions involving the reference argument use the value of the run-time argument. The run-time argument that is passed by the function call must be a single object name. It cannot be a constant object or an expression involving an operator.

Pass by value:

Describes the action of copying the value of a run-time function argument into its corresponding formal argument, which is called a value argument. When this argument-passing technique is used, a change in the formal argument has no effect on the run-time argument.

Physical file:

A specific device, such as a disk or CD-ROM, which stores information as a sequence of characters (bytes).

Stream buffer:

A block of memory that holds data coming to or from a device.

Stream object:

Handles the flow of data between memory and a physical file. The predefined object, `cin`, is the standard input stream handling data transfer from the keyboard to memory. The objects `cout` and `cerr` are standard output and error streams that write characters to the screen.

Switch statement:

Used to choose alternative actions from a discrete set of values. Execution of the switch statement begins by computing a value for the selector expression. Program control passes to the case statement whose case constant matches the value of the selector expression. The program executes the statements within the switch bock until a break statement is encountered or the end of the block is reached. An optional default case is selected if no case constant corresponds to the value of the selector expression.

Text file:

Consists of a sequence of ASCII characters that is divided into lines by the newline character `'\n'`. A text file can be output to a device that displays text such as a printer.

Wrapper class:

Encapsulates an object of a specified type and provides operations that are normally difficult or impossible to perform with data of that type. Operations often include arithmetic computations and I/O. The Days class in the book serves as a wrapper class for the enumeration type DaysInWeek. Among other operations, it provides successor and predecessor functions and I/O.

REVIEW EXERCISES

1. Trace the nested if statement. What is the output for each value of *t*?

```
if (t < 15)
   if (t > 7)
      cout << "one" << endl;
   else
      cout << "two" << endl;
else
   if (t < 18)
      cout << "three" << endl;

cout << "Finished" << endl;
```

(a) *t* = 9   (b) *t* = 20   (c) *t* = 4   (d) *t* = 7   (e) *t* = 16.

2. Consider the switch statement

```
switch(n)
{
   case 1:
   case 3:
   case 4:   cout << n << endl;
             break;
   case 2:
   case 5:
   case 6:   cout << n*10 << endl;
             break;
   default:  cout << n*100 << endl;
             break;
}
```

(a) What is output for *n* = 5, *n* = 4, and *n* = 8?
(b) Assume the break instructions are removed from the switch statement. What would be the output for *n* = 5, *n* = 4, and *n* = 8?

3. (a) Declare an enumeration type Atm that includes the identifiers quit, cancel, deposit, and withdraw.
   (b) Declare an object called `task` of type Atm whose initial value is deposit.
   (c) Write a statement that outputs "deposit" if task equals deposit.
   (d) What is the output of the following statements?

```
task = withdraw;
cout << task << endl;
```

4. Assume that *d* is a Days object. Write a while loop that cycles *d* through each of the weekdays (Mon through Fri) and outputs the corresponding name of the day.

5. Assume Spring starts on March 21, 2000 and autumn begins September 21, 2000. Declare two Date objects, Spring and Summer, and write a code segment that assigns to the integer object `warmDays` the number of days between the start of Spring and beginning of Autumn.

6. Write the following while loop as a for loop.

```
i = 10;
while (i >= 1)
{
   cout << i << "   ";
   i--;
}
cout << "Blast Off!" << endl;
```

7. Loop statements can contain some tricky syntax or logical errors. Look at the following statements and identify problems as being syntax or logical errors.

(a) `for (i = 1, i <= 5, i++)`   (b) `for(i = 10; i > 0; i++)`
    `cout << i << endl;`   `cout << i << endl;`

8. The object count records the total number of iterations. Trace the nested loops and output the final value of count.

(a) `count = 0;`   (b) `count = 0;`
    `for (i = 1; i <= 5; i++)`   `for (i = 1; i <= 3; i++)`
    `   for (j = 1; j <= 3; j++)`   `   for (j = 0; j < i; j++)`
    `      count++;`   `      count++;`

9. What is the output of the following code?

```
int i,j;

for (i = 1, j = 5; i + 2*j > 9; i++, j--)
   cout << 2*i + 3*j << "   ";
```

10. A free function `readDouble()` prompts for the input of a real number and then reads its value. The function has the String object prompt as a constant reference argument and the double object value as a reference argument.
    (a) Give the function prototype.
    (b) Give the function implementation.
    (c) Declare x as a double object and promptString as a String with value "Enter a real number". Show how to call `readDouble()` with run-time arguments promptString and x.

11. Why use constant reference arguments?

12. Write the conditional expression as an if/else statement

```
ch = distance < 10 ? 'v': 'V';
```

13. (a) Declare fin as a file input stream.
    (b) Write C++ statements that attaches the stream to the file "letter.txt" and does error checking.
    (c) Write a code segment that reads the file one character at a time, terminating at end-of-file. Output each alphabetic character to the screen in lowercase.

Answers to Review Exercises

1. (a) one	(b) Finished	(c) two	(d) two	(e) three
Finished		Finished	Finished	Finished

2. (a) $n = 5: 50$ $n = 4: 4$ $n = 8: 800$

    (b) $n = 5: 50$ $n = 4: 4$ $n = 8: 800$

                   500   40

                              400

3. (a) `enum Atm {quit, cancel, deposit, withdraw};`

    (b) `Atm task = deposit;`

    (c)
```
if (task == deposit)
   cout << "deposit";
```

    (d) 3

4.
```
d = Mon;
while (d.getDay() <= Fri)
{
   d.writeDay();
   cout << "   ";
   d.succ();
}
```

5.
```
Date spring(3,21,2000), autumn(9,21,2000);
int warmDays;

warmDays = autumn.numberOfDays() - spring.numberOfDays();
```

6.
```
for(i=10; i >= 1; i--)
   cout << i << "   ";
cout<< "Blast Off!" << endl;
```

7. (a) Syntax error: The commas should be semicolons.

```
      for (i=1; i <= 5; i++)
```

    (b) Logical error: The control object, *i*, should be decremented.

```
      for(i=10; i > 0; i--)
```

8. (a) 15   (b) 6

9. 17   16

10. (a) `void readDouble(const String& prompt, double& value);`

     (b)
```
void readDouble(const String& prompt, double& value)
{
   cout << prompt;
   cin >> value;
}
```

     (c)
```
double x;
string promptString = "Enter two real numbers";
readDouble(promptString, x);
```

11. A constant reference argument is used for efficiently passing an object that cannot be modified and has more than one data member. The method avoids the overhead of copying data members by value.

12.
```
if (distance < 10)
   ch = 'v';
```

```
     else
        ch = 'V';
```

13. (a) `ifstream fin;`
    (b) ```
        fin.open("letter.txt");
        if (!fin)
        {
            cerr << "Cannot open 'letter.txt'" << endl;
            exit(1);
        }
        ```

    (c) `char c;`

    ```
    fin >> c;        // read first character
    while (fin)      // terminate at end-of-file
    {
        // translate each uppercase char to lowercase
        if (c >= 'A' && c <= 'Z')
            c += 32;
        cout << c;
        fin >> c;   // get next character
    }
    ```

WRITTEN EXERCISES

14. Trace each code segment using integer values x and y. Indicate the output.

    (a) Assume x = 80, y = 60

    ```
    if (x < 100)
        if (y > 50)
            cout << "one";
        else
            cout << "two";
    else
        cout << "three";
    ```

    (b) Assume x = 110, y = 40

    ```
    if (x < 100)
    {
        if (y > 50)
            cout << "one";
    }
    else
    {
        cout << "two";
        cout << "three";
    }
    ```

15. Trace the nested if statements and answer each of the questions.

    ```
    if (a < b)
        if (m > n)
            cout << "Black";
        else
            cout << "Red";
    else
        if (m > n)
            cout << "Green";
        else
            cout << "Blue";
    ```
    ```

(a) What is the output for $a = 3, b = 4, m = 1$, and $n = 5$?
(b) What is the output for $a = 5, b = 3, m = 7$, and $n = 4$?
(c) What is output when a is less than b and m is greater than n?
(d) Write an equivalent nested if statement starting with the comparison

```
if (m > n)
    . . .
else
    . . .
```

16. University admissions uses a student's high school GPA and SAT scores to classify applicants at a level A to D. Assume these two values are given as double objects. Write a nested if statement that outputs the level based on the following conditions.

    For SAT score above 1200 and GPA above 3.5, put student at level A. For SAT score below 900 or GPA below 2.2, put student at level D. When the GPA is above 3.0, put student at level B; otherwise, put the student at level C.

17. Trace the nested if statement and indicate the output for different values of n.

```
if (n <= 10)
    if (n/3 < 2)
        result = "one";
    else if (n/3 >= 3)
        result = "two";
    else
        result = "three"
else if (n > 20)
    result = "four";
else
    result = "five";
```

(a) $n = 17$ (b) $n = 25$ (c) $n = 7$ (d) $n = 0$ (e) $n = 9$

18. (a) What is the role of break in the switch statement?
    (b) What is the action of the default case in the switch statement?

19. Write a switch statement that is equivalent to the following multiple selection statement. Let object a be the switch selector.

```
if (a == 3)
    result = a;
else if (a == 6)
    result = a + 10;
else if (a == 10)
    result = a + 20;
else
    result = a + 30;
```

20. Write the switch statement as a nested if statement.

```
switch(n % 5)
{
    case 0:
    case 2:  cout << "remainder is 0 or 2";
             break;
```

```
case 3:    cout << "remainder is 3";
           break;
default: cout << "remainder is not 0, 2, or 3";
           break;
}
```

21. Write the switch statement as an equivalent if/else statement.

```
switch (intM < 25)
{
    case false:    cout << "first choice" << endl;
                   break;
    default:       cout << "second choice" << endl;
                   break;

}
```

22. (a) Define an enumeration type YearInSchool to represent the classification of a high school student (freshman, sophomore, junior, senior). In the declaration, represent a freshman with the integer value 1.
    (b) Assume John is an object of type YearInSchool. Describe the action of the following C++ statements.

```
John = YearInSchool(2);
John++;
```

    (c) At a high school, any student wishing to participate in athletics must play on a freshman team as a freshman, the junior varsity team as a sophomore, and the varsity team as a junior or senior. Write a switch statement that uses the YearInSchool object, student, as the selector and outputs the type of team designated for the student athlete.

23. Trace the following code.

```
enum Literature {novel, play, poem};

Literature work;
int i;

cin >> i;
work = Literature((i+1) % 3);

switch(work)
{
    case    novel;  cout << "novel";
                    break;
    case    play:   cout << "play";
                    break;
    case    poem:   cout << "poem";
                    break;
}
```

    (a) What is the output for each input $i = 0, 9, 2, 5$?
    (b) What is the output for the input values of part (a) provided that the break statements are removed?

24. (a) What is a wrapper class for an enumeration type?
    (b) Consider a wrapper class, Colors, that includes a ColorType object color as a data member.

    ```
    enum ColorType {red, green, blue};
    ```

    (i) Give the prototype for the constructor.
    (ii) Implement the constructor.
    (iii) Declare a Colors object c with initial value red.
    (iv) Design and implement the member functions succ(), pred(), readColor(), and write Color().

25. Declare a Date object *d* that is initialized to today's date.
    (a) Write a series of C++ statements that output the number of days that still remain in the current month.
    (b) Determine the number of days that still remain in the year. You will need to use the member function isLeapYear().

26. Declare a Date object *d* that is initialized to January 1, 2000. The problem looks at two different ways to output the dates (in long date format) for the first day of each month in the year 2000.
    (a) Write a for loop that uses the control object *i* and the member functions getMonth() and setMonth() to output the dates.
    (b) Write a while loop that outputs the dates by using the member functions incrementDate() and daysInMonth().

27. Convert the for statement into an equivalent while statement.

    ```
    for (i = 1; i < 10; i++)
        cout << (i+5) << endl;
    ```

28. Convert the while statement to an equivalent for statement.

    ```
    i = 1;
    sum = 0;
    while (i <= 15)
    {
        sum += i;
        i += 2;
    }
    cout << sum << endl;
    ```

29. Trace each for statement and give the output.
    (a) `for (i = 1; i < 5; i++)`   (b) `for (i = 5; i > 0; i--)`
        `cout << i * 10 << " ";`   `cout << i*i << " ";`

30. Use a for statement to implement each of the following algorithms.
    (a) Start with integer objects *n* and product. Initialize product = 1 and use the loop to output the powers $n^1 n^2 \ldots n^6$ for exponents 1 to 6.
    (b) With part (a) as a model, compute 2^{20} using long-integer objects. This is the value of "mega" in a megabyte measure.

31. What is the output of this program for each of the values $n = 40, n = 50,$ and $n = 100$? Can you describe, in general, what the program does?

```
#include <iostream.h>

int main()
{
    long n, p;

    cout << "Enter an integer value: ";
    cin >> n;

    for(p=1; p < n; p *= 2)
        cout << p << "   ";
    cout << endl;

    return 0;
}
```

32. Trace the for statement and show its output.

```
for (i = 1; i < 10; i++)

    cout << setw(i)    << '*' << endl;
```

33. Trace the for statement to challenge your understanding of the for syntax.

```
for(n=5; n < 25; n++)
{
    cout << n << endl;
    cin >> n;
}
```

Show the output assuming input 10, 22, 6, 23, 24.

34. In the String class, the length() function returns the number of characters in a String object.
(a) The following loop is designed to take a string and pad it on the right with *'s so that its length is expanded to 15. For example, Short becomes Short**********. Fill in the missing loop test.

```
cin >> str;
for (i = 1; _____ ; i++)        // pad to 15 characters
    str = str + "*";            // add a '*'
```

(b) Modify the for loop in part (a) to take a string and expand it on the left with *'s to a length of 15.

35. The following is a form of an infinite for loop.

```
for(;;)
{ ... }
```

Describe other infinite loop forms using the while and do/while statements.

36. Fill in the missing loop test in each of the following nested loops so that the execution will output 12 asterisks.

```
(a) for(i=1; i <= 3; i++)        (b) for(i=3; i < 5; i++)
        for (j=1; ___; j++)              for (j=6; ___; j--)
            cout << '*';                     cout << '*';
```

(c)
```
for(i=1; i < 8; i += 2)
    for (j=2; ___; j += 3)
        cout << '*';
```

37. How many asterisks are output by each nested loop statement?

(a)
```
int i,j, k;

i = 0;
while (i <= 10)
{
    j = 1;
    while (j < i)
    {
        cout << '*';
        j++;
    }
    i++;
}
```

(b)
```
for (i=0; i < 3; i++)
    for(j=0; j < 3; j++)
        for(k=0; k < 2;k++)
            cout << '*';
```

38. Write a code segment with nested for loops that output the triangle.

```
        1
       12
      123
   .  .  .  .
123456789
```

39. Use the following loop construct.

```
cin >> n;

for (i = 1; i < 10; i++)
{
    if (i % 4 == 0)
        _____        [1]
    else if (i == n)
        _____        [2]

    else
        cout << i << "   ";
}
```

(a) Write a statement [1] that causes an immediate transfer to the next iteration of the loop.

(b) Write a statement [2] that causes an immediate exit from the loop.

(c) Assuming parts (a) and (b), what is output for each of the following input values? *n* = 7, 4, 9.

40. Assume initially *i* = 0 and sum = 0. What is the output of the code segment?

```
while (i < 8)
{
    if (i % 2 ==1)
    {
        i++;
```

```
            continue;
        }
        else
        {
            sum += i;
            i++;
        }
    }
    cout << sum;
```

41. Write a loop that inputs up to 10 integers and processes each one according to the following rules:
   1. Terminate the loop if the input value is 6.
   2. If the input value is divisible by 3, begin the next loop iteration.
   3. If the input value is less than 8, output the square of the number; otherwise, output the number.

42. Give the output for each general for loop statement.
   (a) `for(sum=0,i=0,k=8;  i < k;  i++,k--)`
           `sum += 2*i + k;`
       `cout << sum << endl;`

   (b) `for (i = 0, j = 1; i*j < 100; i++, j *= 10)`
           `cout << i*j << endl;`

43. Trace the function and then give the output.

```
void f(double x, double& y)
{
    x = 2 * y;
    y = y + 3;
}
```

   (a) Assume $a = 2.0$, $b = 3.0$. What are the values of a and b after executing the function call `f(a,b)`?
   (b) Assume $a = 2.0$ and $b = 3.0$. What are the values of a and b after executing the function call `f(b,a)`?
   (c) Does the function call `f(a,7.0)` compile and execute? Explain.

44. Trace the function and then give the output.

```
double f(double& x, double& y)
{
    double t = x;

    x = 2*y;
    y = 3*t;
    return x/y;
}
```

   Assume $q = 3.0$, $r = 5.0$. What are the values of q and r after executing the function call `f(q,r)`? What is the return value?

45. The free function `realParts()` takes a double argument x and computes the whole and fractional part of x. These two values are given as reference arguments.

```
void realParts(double x, double& wpart, double& fpart);
```

Give the implementation for `realParts()`.

46. Write each of the conditional expressions as an if/else statement.

```
bool od;
int x, y, value;
```

(a) `od = value % 2 == 1 ? true : false;`
(b) `value = x > y ? x : y;`

47. The cost of renting a truck is either $45 or $10 plus $0.35 per mile, whichever is larger. Assuming that `mileage` and `rentalCost` are double objects, use a conditional expression to assign the cost of renting a truck to the object `rentalCost`.

48. Convert the if statement to a conditional expression that assigns a value to *c*.

```
if (a < 2 * b)
    c = a;
else
    c = b;
```

49. (a) Declare a file input stream, fin.
(b) Write a code segment that opens the file "int.dat." The code should do error checking.
(c) Assume the file in (b) contains a series of integer values. Write a loop that reads data from the file into object num and outputs the square of each value. The loop should terminate at end-of-file.

50. The file "voters.dat" contains the last name and gender for a series of registered voters.

```
Anderson M
Carlson M
      . . .
Williams F
```

(a) Declare a file-input stream, voters, and use an open() statement to attach it to the data file. Your code should perform error checking.
(b) Declare the following objects:

```
char gender;
String name;
int numMales = 0, numFemales = 0;
```

Create a loop that uses the input stream in part (a) to read the name and gender of each voter. The loop reads until end-of-file and outputs the number of men voters and women voters.

51. Consider the following class description:

DESCRIPTION: Annuity CLASS ▬▬▬▬▬▬▬▬▬▬▬▬▬

An Annuity object maintains and displays the value of a fixed rate savings account.

Attributes: `// amount invested and rate of interest`
                    `double principle, rate;`
                    `// number of years for the annuity`
                    `int nyears;`
                    `// final value of the annuity`
                    `double value;`

Operations:

Annuity   Initialize the data members principle, rate and *nyears* using the constructor arguments. Use these objects to compute the future value of the annuity

                      `Annuity(double p, double r, int y);`

getValue   Return the future value of the annuity.

                      `double getValue();`

displayGrowth   Output the value of the annuity year by year. This operation shows how the annuity grows.

                      `void displayGrowth( );`

(a) Declare an Annuity object named `schoolFund` that has an initial principle of $10,000 invested at 10 percent for 20 years.
(b) Output the future value of the annuity.
(c) Display the growth of the annuity.
(d) Develop the class declaration.
(e) Implement the constructor. Note that the value of the annuity after *nyears* is

$$\text{principle} * (1 + \text{rate})^{nyears}$$

(f) Implement the member function `getValue()`.
(g) Implement the member function `displayGrowth()` using a for loop.

PROGRAMMING EXERCISES

52. Use the results of Written Exercise 6.16. Write a program that inputs the SAT and GPA scores for a student and outputs the level assigned by the Admissions Office.

53. Table 6-3 gives the amount of tax owed by single ('S') and married ('M') taxpayers based on three ranges of income.

TABLE 6-3 Tax Table.

Income range	Single Tax is (%)	For amount over
0–20,000	15	0
20,000–50,000	3,000 + 25	20,000
50,000+	12,500 + 32	50,000

Income range	*Married* *Tax is (%)*	*For amount over*
0–35,000	15	0
35,000–70,000	5,250 + 25	35,000
70,000+	18,750 + 32	70,000

Declare a free function

```
double taxOwed (double income, char taxStatus);
```

that computes the tax owed. Use the function in a complete program that inputs the marital status ('S' or 'M') as well as the income and outputs the tax. Run the program with data that tests four of the possible tax options.

54. Write a program that inputs an uppercase character and looks for its position on a phone pad. For output use a switch statement to display the digit of the corresponding position or an error message indicating the character is not on the phone pad. The characters/digits for phone buttons are

    ABC 2   DEF 3   GHI 4   JKL 5
    MNO 6   PRS 7   TUV 8   WXY 9

    Note: The letters Q and Z do not correspond to a digit.

55. Write a program that uses the StudentAccount class. Declare an object `george("55-3398", "Howard,George,-750)`. To simulate account activity, create a loop containing a switch statement that handles different transactions. For the switch selector, use a character that is input from the keyboard on each iteration. The case statements include:

```
case 'C': Prompt for the amount of the charge, debit the
          account, and then output the resulting balance.
case 'P': Prompt for the amount of the payment, credit the
          account, and then output the resulting balance.
case 'D': Display the account information.
case 'Q': Terminate the transaction loop.
```

    For all other input, output an error message and continue processing. In the run, enter data that will test all of the case options.

56. Write a program that uses the Date class to solve the problems posed in Written Exercise 6.25, parts (a) and (b).

57. Write a program that uses the Date class to solve the problems posed in Written Exercise 6.26, parts (a) and (b).

58. The Fibonacci sequence begins with the terms $1, 1, 2, 3, 5, 8, 13, \ldots$. The first two values are 1. For $n >= 3$, each term in the sequence is the sum of the previous two terms.

$$F_1 = 1, \quad F_2 = 1, \quad F_n = F_{n-1} + F_{n-2}, \quad n \geq 3.$$

Write a complete program that prompts for the value n and then outputs the first n terms of the Fibonacci sequence. Use long integer objects.

59. The infinite series

$$1^3 + (1/2)^3 + (1/3)^3 + (1/4)^3 + (1/5)^3 + \cdots + (1/n)^3 + \cdots$$

gets closer and closer to a real value as n increases. The value is approximately 1.20206. Write a program that uses a for loop and the function `pow()` from **math.h** to approximate the sum of the series. Add the terms through $n = 10,000$ and output the result.

60. Use the results of Written Exercise 6.34(a) to expand a string on the right with *'s.
(a) Write a complete program that enters a sequence of strings from the keyboard stopping with the string "quit." Output each string with expanded length of 15. Run the program using the strings "dog," "Hancock," "rigid," and "quit."
(b) Using the results of Written Exercise 6.34(b), modify your program in part(a) so it expands the input string on the left with *'s.
(c) Create a file consisting of five or more strings. Write a complete program that reads strings from the file, pads them on the right with *'s to 15 characters, and outputs them to the screen. The input stops on an end-of-file. Your program should read the file name as a string and use it to open the input stream.

61. Create a file "students.dat" containing five student records.

<student id>	<units completed>	< grade points earned>
1	45	100
5	100	300
8	124	420
12	50	200
3	145	310

Write a complete program that reads the data until end-of-file and outputs the id and GPA (gradePts/units) for each student.

62. Create the file "picnic.dat" that contains a list of records. Each line includes an employee name and two integers that give the number of adults, and the number of children planning on attending a company picnic.

```
"picnic.dat"
Terry    2    4
Brown    2    3
Dalton   2    0
Perez    4    5
Stein    1    0
Ting     2    5
```

Write a complete program that reads the data until end-of-file. For each employee, echo the input information in the format

```
Employee:   Terry    Adults:   2    Children:   4
```

Output the total number of adults and children planning to attend the picnic.

63. The program copies data from a source file to a destination file, one character at a time. Start the program by prompting for the name of the source file, srcFileName, and the name of the destination file, destFileName. Open the input stream, srcFile, and the output stream, destFile, using the file names. Be sure to perform error checking. Using a loop that terminates at end-of-file, copy each character from the source file to the destination file. Use the `get()` member function to input characters from the source file.

64. Write a program that uses the free function, `realParts()`, developed in Written Exercise 6.45. Develop a loop that inputs a real number from the keyboard until end-of-file (^Z typed in Windows, ^D in Unix). Each iteration of the loop should call `realParts()` and output the whole and fractional part of the input value.

65. Write a program that reads characters one at a time from a file and echoes each character to the screen. In the case of a newline character, output two newlines, which has the effect of double-spacing the text. The program should prompt for the file name and terminate the input on end-of-file. Run the program twice—first selecting the source code of the program itself and then selecting another file from the disk.

66. Implement the class, Annuity, of Written Exercise 6.51 and place it in the file "annuity.h." Write a program that declares an Annuity object, `myChild`, in which $20,000 is invested at 9 percent for 18 years. Output the future value of the annuity and its value for each year.

PROGRAMMING PROJECTS

69. Write a program that uses a nested loop to output the following triangle.

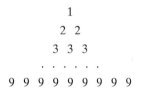

```
         1
        2 2
       3 3 3
      . . . . . .
   9 9 9 9 9 9 9 9 9
```

71. Consider a chessboard whose rows and columns are numbered 0–7. Write a program that accepts an input of the form $i\,j$ ($0 \leqslant i \leqslant 7, 0 \leqslant j \leqslant 7$) and outputs out all the possible positions of a bishop starting at the intersection of row i and column j. For example, when the input is 2 2, the output should be

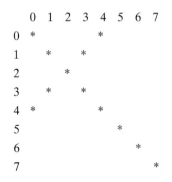

```
    0 1 2 3 4 5 6 7
0   *           *
1     *     *
2         *
3     *     *
4   *           *
5                 *
6                   *
7                     *
```

To help you, let (i_0, j_0) be the starting position. Then, if (I, J) is an arbitrary point on the board, it is on the bishop's path if either

$$J - J_0 = I - I_0 \text{ or } J - J_0 = -(I - I_0).$$

72. Develop free functions

```
void drawMan(double x, double y);
void eraseMan(double x, double y);
```

that draw and erase the following stick man. The man is specified by the point (x,y) on his right shoulder. Write a program that uses drawMan() and eraseMan() to animate motion of the stick man across the screen.

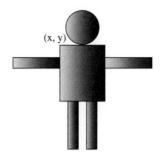

Chapter 7
Arrays

C H A P T E R   C O N T E N T S

7-1 *INTRODUCING ARRAYS*
   Application: Weather Statistics

7-2 *ARRAY STORAGE*
   Array Bounds Checking

7-3 *INITIALIZING ARRAYS*
   Array Initialization in the Date Class

7-4 *ARRAYS AS ARGUMENTS*
   The Statistics Class

7-5 *ARRAYS OF OBJECTS*
   Default Constructor
   Application: Painter's Job Schedule

7-6 *RANDOM NUMBERS*
   Estimating π

7-7 *SEQUENTIAL ARRAY ALGORITHMS*
   Sequential Search
   Removing a List Element
   Application: Removing Duplicates

7-8 *ARRAYS AS CLASS DATA MEMBERS*
   Const Member Functions
   Application: Using the
   FinanceCenter Class
   Implementing the FinanceCenter
   Class

7-9 *GRAPHING DICE TOSSES*
   Graphing Dice Probabilities

7-10 *ARRAY SORTING ALGORITHM*

7-11 *STRING OBJECTS*
   The Index Operator [ ]
   String I/O

7-12 *ADDITIONAL STRING MEMBER
     FUNCTIONS (OPTIONAL)*
   String Search Functions
   Copying Substrings
   Modifying a String
   Analyzing File Names

7-13 *MULTIDIMENSIONAL ARRAYS*
   Two-dimensional Array Arguments
   The SqMatrix Class
   The Storage of Two Dimensional
   Arrays (Optional)

Written Exercises

U p to this point in the book, our applications have used single data objects that consist of numbers, characters, or programmer-defined objects. We now introduce a data structure that consists of a collection of items whose elements have the same object type. The structure, called a C++ one-dimensional array, represents a sequence of consecutive elements. As an example of an array, consider a professional basketball team that maintains a record of attendance at each of its 41 regular-season home games. The data can be organized as a single list called gameAttendance with the individual attendance figures recorded in consecutive elements from the first game through the 41st game. We can perform calculations that determine the total attendance and the average per game attendance. We can also ask questions about individual games such as the attendance on opening night, the attendance when the world-champions came to town, and so forth.

This chapter develops the syntax for one-dimensional arrays and uses them in a variety of applications. Introductory topics include array declaration and initialization, storage of arrays in memory and arrays as function arguments. Arrays of class objects can be declared as long as the class constructor meets special requirements.

Most of the chapter is dedicated to algorithms that use arrays. We develop classical algorithms that search for a key in a list and sort a list in ascending order. An interesting class, FinanceCenter, includes an array of StudentAccount objects as a data member.

The generation of random numbers plays a very important role in the creation of computer games as well as in event simulation. The class, RandomNumber, generates random integer and floating-point numbers. It is used in several programs, including an application that draws a graph depicting the results of tossing two dice 1,000,000 times. The RandomNumber class is used throughout the book as a method to generate test data for searching, sorting, and other types of algorithms.

We defined String objects in Chapter 2 and used them for names, labels, and other text information. Except for simple operations like length() and concatenation ("+"), we have treated strings like primitive number and character types. In this chapter we revisit the String type and use the array index operator "[]" to access the individual characters in the string. We also introduce you to a wide variety of String member functions that do pattern matching and string editing. These operations make the String class one of the most powerful and important object types for applications.

The last section develops multidimensional arrays, which have applications in data processing, engineering and mathematics. We develop the class, SqMatrix, that implements I/O and arithmetic operations for square matrices.

7-1 INTRODUCING ARRAYS

A *one-dimensional array* is a finite sequence of objects of the same data type in which each object has a fixed position. Each item in the sequence is called an *element* of the array. The array is given a name that describes the sequence as a whole and each element has an index that denotes its position in the list.

In this section, we introduce the syntax for a C++ array in two phases. We begin with an example of rainfall totals that a local weather bureau has gathered over the past decade. The data is placed into an array, called rainfall, that consists of 10 floating-point values. The example will allow us to explain how C++ declares an array and uses indices to access an individual yearly rainfall totals. The array elements are used in statistical calculations. After looking at a specific example, we define general arrays of any type.

The declaration for the rainfall array is:

```
const int RAINFALL_PERIOD = 10;
// yearly rainfall is a real number
double rainfall[RAINFALL_PERIOD];
```

The type double begins the declaration and indicates that each element in the array is a real number. The identifier, rainfall, is a programmer-defined name for the array and the integer literal, that is enclosed in square brackets, specifies the number of elements in the array. In our example, the rainfall array contains 10 (RAINFALL_PERIOD) elements.

C++ defines an *index operator* "[]" that allows for indexed access to the elements in the array. The operator uses an integer index in the range 0 to RAIN-FALL_PERIOD-1 in order to store and retrieve an element in the array. The individual elements are referenced using the array name followed by the index enclosed in square brackets. The rainfall totals for the different years are denoted by rainfall[0], rainfall[1], rainfall[2], and so forth. Table 7-1 displays the rainfall totals for each of the 10 years. The top row lists the indices in the range 0 to 9 while the bottom row is the rainfall total for the corresponding years.

```
rainfall[0] = 27.2    rainfall[4] = 30.1    rainfall[8] = 29.8
rainfall[1] = 20.0    rainfall[5] = 21.3    rainfall[9] = 22.5
rainfall[2] = 26.4    rainfall[6] = 34.1
rainfall[3] = 24.8    rainfall[7] = 22.0
```

Each element in the rainfall array is a double object that can be used in C++ statements like any simple double object. The main difference is that an array element is identified by the array name and index.

```
rainfall[index]
```

The following is a varity of C++ statements that use rainfall objects with assignment, I/O, and control structures.

Assignment:

```
rainfall[0] = 27.2;    // 27.2 is rainfall for year 0
t = rainfall[5];       // t is rainfall for year 5
```

I/O:

```
cin >> rainfall[3];    // input rainfall for year 3
cout << rainfall[9];   // output rainfall for year 9
```

TABLE 7-1 10-Year Rainfall Data.

Rainfall Totals (10 year)										
Year	0	1	2	3	4	5	6	7	8	9
Rainfall	27.2	20.0	26.4	24.8	30.1	21.3	34.1	22.0	29.8	22.5

Control Structures:

```
if (rainfall[3] < 28)   // compare 24.8 (rainfall[3] and 28
  . . .                  // result is true
```

Consider the problem of computing the total rainfall over the 10 years. The calculation can be done with a for loop that uses the integer, year, as a control object. Each iteration takes the current value of year as the index and adds the corresponding yearly rainfall to the total.

```
int year;
double totalRainfall = 0;

for (year = 0; year < RAINFALL_PERIOD; year++)
   totalRainfall += rainfall[year];
```

EXAMPLE 7.1 ▬▬▬▬▬▬▬▬▬▬▬▬▬▬▬▬▬▬▬▬▬▬▬▬

A while loop scans the array and identifies the first year in the decade that has a yearly rainfall total exceeding 30 inches. The output statement uses (year+1) to indicate when the heavy rainfall occurred. In this way we associate the first year of the decade with `rainfall[0]`, the second year with `rainfall[1]`, and so forth.

```
int year = 0;     // set control object to 0

// search rainfall list
while (rainfall[year] <= 30.0)
   year++;
// rainfall[year] exceeds 30 inches
cout << rainfall[year] << " inches fell in year "
     << year+1 << " of the decade" << endl;

// Output: 30.1 inches of rain fell in year 5 of the decade
```

General Arrays. The syntax that declares the rainfall array and accesses yearly rainfall totals can be extended to a general array. The word Type is a term that refers to the object type of the elements in the array.

SYNTAX ▬▬▬▬▬▬▬▬▬▬▬▬▬▬▬▬▬▬▬▬▬▬▬▬▬

The Array Data Type

Form: Type arrayName[SIZE]

Action: An array is a sequence of objects of the same data type. The objects in an array are referred to as elements. The declaration consists of the object type for each element, the name for the array, and an integer value SIZE that specifies the number of elements in the array. SIZE must be a constant expression with value greater than 0. The individual elements in the array are denoted by

arrayName[0], arrayName[1], ..., arrayName[SIZE-1].

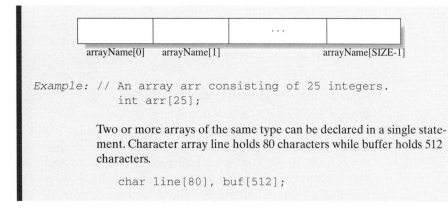

arrayName[0]   arrayName[1]   arrayName[SIZE-1]

Example: `// An array arr consisting of 25 integers.`
`        int arr[25];`

Two or more arrays of the same type can be declared in a single statement. Character array line holds 80 characters while buffer holds 512 characters.

```
char line[80], buf[512];
```

The index allows a program to directly access an element in an array. The element at index i is `arr[i]`. Note that the range of indices is always from 0 to SIZE-1. Thus `arr[0]` is the first element of the array and the literal SIZE is the value of the first index beyond the end of the array.

E X A M P L E 7 . 2

1. The array capletter is declared to hold 26 uppercase letters 'A' - 'Z'

```
char capletter[26];
```

A for loop assigns the letters to the array by using control object i as an offset to the letter 'A'. For instance, when i = 3 letter 'A' + 3 is 'D'.

```
for (i=0; i < 26; i++)
    capletter[i] = 'A' + i;
```

2. The array capletter can also be initialized with a generalized for loop that uses as control objects the integer i and the character ch. The integer is initially set to 0 and serves as an index for the array elements. Character ch moves over the range 'A' to 'Z'.

```
for (i=0, ch = 'A'; ch <= 'Z'; i++, ch++)
    capletter[i] = ch;
```

3. A while loop inputs sales figures from file "sales.dat" and stores them in the array called sales. The loop illustrates how large data sets can be read from a file and stored in an array. Input terminates at end of file.

```
const int MAXSALES = 100;
double sales[MAXSALES], salesAmount;

int count = 0;
ifstream  fin;                        // data read from input file
    ...                               // open the file

fin >> salesAmount;                   // input a sales amount
while (fin)                           // continue until EOF
```

```
      {
          sales[count] = salesAmount;   // assign value to array
          count++;                       // increment the count index
          fin >> salesAmount;            // read next data item
      }   ■
```

Application: Weather Statistics

A great advantage to arrays is that large collections of data are retained in memory and can be used repeatedly in calculations. We again look at the collection of rainfall data over a 10 year period. On a first pass through the data, we compute the average yearly rainfall and then make a second pass to indicate the amount that each yearly rainfall amount varies from the average. The weather bureau refers to a rainfall amount as "above average", "normal", or "below average." These categories are determined by computing the variation from the average.

```
      variation = rainfall[year] - avgRainfall;
```

The relative amount of rainfall is determined by comparing the variation with 0. If less than 0, rainfall is "below average"; if equal to 0, rainfall is "normal"; if greater than 0, rainfall is "above average".

APPLICATION 7-1 ABOVE/BELOW AVERAGE RAINFALL

The program reads the rainfall data from the file "rainfall.dat" using a for loop. The average rainfall is output along with a table that gives the variation from the average for each of the 10 years.

```
#include <iostream.h>
#include <fstream.h>
#include <iomanip.h>              // for setw()
#include <stdlib.h>              // for exit()

#include "textlib.h"
#include "tstring.h"

int main()
{
    double totalRainfall = 0.0;   // objects for the average
    double avgRainfall;
    double variation;            // variation from the average
    int year;                    // array index
    double rainfall[10];         // 10 year rainfall list
    ifstream fin;                // input file

    // open the file
    fin.open("rainfall.dat");
    if (!fin)
    {
        cerr << "Cannot open 'rainfall.dat'" <<, endl;
        exit(1);
    }
```

```
        // read the data and compute totalRainfall in the process
        for (year=0; year < 10; year++)
        {
            // input rainfall for year and add to the total
            fin >> rainfall[year];
            totalRainfall += rainfall[year];
        }

        // compute and output the average rainfall
        avgRainfall = totalRainfall/10;
        cout << "Average rainfall is " << setreal(5,1)
             << avgRainfall << endl << endl;

        // output labels for the table
        cout << setjust(Right) << setw(7) << "Year" << setw(7)
             << "Rain" << setw(22) << "Relative Rain" << endl;

        // scan array for yearly rainfall and output deviation
        // above/at/below average
        for(year=0; year < 10; year++)
        {
            cout << setw(5) << (year+1) << setreal(9,1)
                 << rainfall[year];
            variation = rainfall[year] - avgRainfall;
            // check if deviation is above or below the average
            if (variation > 0.0)
            {
                cout << setreal(7,1) << variation
                     << " inches - above normal" << endl;
            }
            else if (variation == 0.0)
            {
                cout << setreal(7,1) << variation
                     << " inches - normal" << endl;
            }
            else
            {
                cout << setreal(7,1) << -variation
                     << " inches - below normal" << endl;
            }
        }

        return 0;
    }
```

```
    Input file: rainfall.dat
    (data of Table 7-1)

    Run:

    Average rainfall is  25.8
```

```
        Year    Rain            Relative Rain
         1      27.2     1.4 inches - above normal
         2      20.0     5.8 inches - below normal
         3      26.4     0.6 inches - above normal
         4      24.8     1.0 inches - below normal
         5      30.1     4.3 inches - above normal
         6      21.3     4.5 inches - below normal
         7      34.1     8.3 inches - above normal
         8      22.0     3.8 inches - below normal
         9      29.8     4.0 inches - above normal
        10      22.5     3.3 inches - below normal
```

7-2   ARRAY STORAGE

When a program declares an array, the C++ compiler generates code to allocate memory locations and uses a formula to access the individual elements. You need some familiarity with this formula to understand the mechanics of passing arrays as function arguments. This familiarity will also let you understand how undetected errors can occur when the program attempts to access an array element with an index that is out of the range 0 to SIZE-1.

A C++ array is logically stored in consecutive memory locations whose size is specified by the data type of the array elements. The array name is a constant that is assigned the location in memory *(address)* of the first object in the array. Thus, in the declaration

```
Type arr[SIZE];
```

the array name arr is the address of the first element arr[0]. Objects arr[1], arr[2], and so forth occupy consecutive locations in memory.

A compiler provides direct access to the elements of an array by creating an *array access function* that identifies the location of an object in the array. To locate element arr[i], the function uses the index, the size of each array object in bytes, and the starting address of the array.

```
Starting address:        arr
object size in bytes:    m
index:                   i
```

The access function uses the fact that the position of an object in the array can be measured as an offset in bytes from the starting location. The first object, arr[0], has an offset 0, arr[1] has offset 1*m, arr[2] has offset 2*m, and so forth (Figure 7-1).

```
location(arr[i]) = starting location + offset
                 = arr + i*m;
```

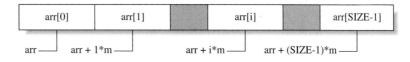

location arr[i] = arr + i*m

FIGURE 7-1
Array Access Function.

EXAMPLE 7.3

1. Assume that a double is stored with 8 bytes (m = 8). The rainfall array declaration allocates 10 * 8 = 80 bytes of storage.

```
double rainfall[10];
```

Assume that the starting address of the array is 1000. At run-time, the identifier rainfall is a constant whose value is the memory address 1000. Element rainfall[3] has an offset of 24 bytes (3*8) and is located at address 1024.

```
// starting address + offset
location(rainfall[3]) = 1000 + 3 * 8
                      = 1024
```

2. Consider an array s of short integers that is stored at location 5012. The size of a short integer is 2 bytes.

```
short s[5];
```

s[0]	s[1]	s[2]	s[3]	s[4]
5012	5014	5016	5018	5020

(a) s[1] is the element at address 5014.

```
location(s[1]) = 5012 + 1*2 = 5014.
```

(b) Location 5020 contains array object s[i]. The index for this element is determined by solving the access equation for i.

$$5020 = 5012 + 2 * i$$

$$i = (5020 - 5012)/2$$

$$i = 8/2 = 4 \quad // \text{ s[4] is at address 5020} \quad \blacksquare$$

Array Assignment. With objects of primitive number or character type or objects of class type, we have used the assignment operator to copy new values into the left-hand operand.

```
int a = 5, b;
Rect r(2,4),s;

b = a;          // value 5 is copied to int b
s = r;          // data members of r are copied to Rectangle s
```

The assignment operator does not apply to arrays even if the sizes of the two lists are the same. The operation is invalid since the array name on the left-hand side represents a constant address.

```
const int SIZE = 20;
int listA[SIZE], listB[SIZE];

listB = listA;                  // listB is a constant
```

The assignment must be done with a loop that copies the individual elements of the right-hand array to the corresponding elements of the left-hand array.

```
for (i = 0; i < SIZE; i++)
    listB[i] = listA[i];        // copy individual elements
```

Programming
Note

The array access function uses the size of an object in its calculation. C++ allows a program access to this value by using the unary operator *sizeof* that takes either a type or an object as its operand:

```
sizeof(Type)
sizeof(object)
```

The operator returns the number of bytes of memory required to store any object of the given type or to store the specific object. For instance:

```
char c;
    sizeof(char) = 1       // char is stored in one byte
    sizeof(c) = 1          // storage of object c

short s;
    sizeof(short) = 2      //  short is stored in two bytes
    sizeof(sh) = 2         //  storage of object sh
```

When the sizeof() operator is applied to an array, it returns the total number of bytes required to store the elements.

For instance, consider the array

```
int arr[3];
```

If sizeof(int) is 2, then sizeof(arr) is 6.

Exploring
Concepts

Consider this array declaration.

```
int arr[8];
```

Write an expression using sizeof() that determines the number of elements in arr. The expression allows a programmer to evaluate the number of elements in an array by knowing the name of the array and the type of its elements.

Array Bounds Checking

The array declaration allocates memory for SIZE number of objects. The program may access any object in the range `arr[0]` to `arr[SIZE-1]`. What about access to objects outside this range? Most C++ compilers do not add machine code that tests whether an index is within the array bounds. For instance, the following declaration provides locations for objects `arr[0]` to `arr[19]`.

```
type arr[20];
```

The objects with indices −1 and 20 are not in the range and are technically out of bounds. Nevertheless, a compiler will use the access function to identify their locations at offsets −m and 20*m. The program can attempt to fetch data from these locations even though they were not allocated by the array declaration.

```
n = arr[-1];        // index out of range
n = arr[20];        // index out of range
```

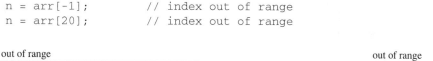

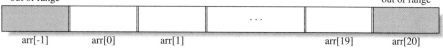

Using an array object with an index that is out of bounds may cause the program to overwrite other data and create serious errors.

Programming Note

Some compilers have an option to perform array bounds checking. The compiler generates run-time code to check that array indices are within bounds. This extra code slows execution. Most programmers use array bounds checking only during program development. Once the code is debugged, the option is turned off and the program is recompiled to produce more efficient code. Chapter 10 develops the Vector class. A Vector object acts like an array in most respects and performs array bounds checking.

7-3 INITIALIZING ARRAYS

In C++, simple objects can be initialized when they are declared. For example, integers u and v are initialized to 2 and 3 in the declaration.

```
int u = 2, v = 3;        // declare objects with initial values
```

The process of initializing objects extends to arrays of primitive data types. An array initialization list is a sequence of values enclosed by braces and separated by commas.

```
Type  arr[SIZE] = {value_0, value_1, …, value_{SIZE-1}};
```

The initialization list assigns initial values to the array elements in the order arr[0], arr[1], and so forth.

```
arr[0]=value_0  arr[1]=value_1    arr[2]=value_2 . . .
```

For instance, the initialization list assigns the integer values 40, 90, 20, 10, and 25 to the array arr.

```
int arr[5] = {40, 90, 20, 10, 25};
```

40	90	20	10	25
arr[0]	arr[1]	arr[2]	arr[3]	arr[4]

Arrays of class type can also be initialized. This topic is discussed in Section 7-5.

C++ allows some variations when initializing an array. One method allows the size of the initialization list to determine the size of the array. The declaration uses the index operator without an explicit array size.

```
// array size is n
Type arr[] = {value_0, value_1, ..., value_{n-1}};
```

The initialization of the integer array arr could be accomplished with the declaration

```
int arr[] = {40, 90, 20, 10, 25};
```

The compiler uses the number of elements in the initialization list to allocate 5 integer locations for the array.

EXAMPLE 7.4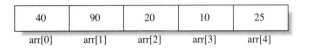

1. The array powerOfTen is initialized to contain powers of the base 10.

```
int   powerOfTen[5] = {1,10,100,1000,10000};
```

2. The items in an initialization can include calculations.

```
int   powerOfTen[5] = {1, 10, 10*10, 10*10*10, 10*10*10*10};
```

3. The array vowel holds five lowercase letters. The size of the array is not given explicitly.

```
char vowel[] = {'a', 'e', 'i', 'o', 'u'};   ■
```

Exploring Concepts

1. How many elements are in each array and what are their values?

```
int arrA[] = {1,2,3,4,5}, arrB[9] = {1,2,3,4,5};
```

2. Give a code segment that declares an array of 20 long integers in which the first 5 elements have the values 10, 20, 30, 40, 50.

3. How would you change your approach so that the 20 element array has values 10, 20, . . . , 200?

4. How would you declare and initialize an array of 50 characters that has its first 49 elements set to a blank and the last element set to the newline character?

A byte is a basic unit of data storage that consists of 8 bits whose values are 0 or 1. When used to store a number, the bits in a byte are numbered from 0 to 7 and have positional values that correspond to increasing powers of two. Reading from right to left, the positional values are $1(2^0), 2(2^1), 4(2^2), \ldots, 128(2^7)$.

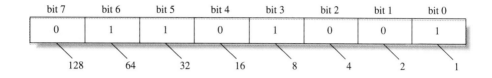

The decimal value of the byte 01101001 is the sum of the positional values for the bits with value 1.

$$01101001 = 64 + 32 + 8 + 1 = 105$$

The application uses a for loop to read the 8 individual bits of a byte. The loop ranges over the bit positions 7 down to 0 so that the bit values can be read from left to right. The array, powerOfTwo, is an initialized array that can be used to identify the positional value of each bit.

```
int  powerOfTwo[8] = {1, 2, 4, 8, 16, 32, 64, 128};
```

For each iteration, the loop body reads a bit value as a character and converts it to the integer value 0 or 1. When the bit is 1, the corresponding positional value is looked up in the array and added to the byte value. The resulting decimal value of the byte is output.

```
#include <iostream.h>
int main()
{
    // used to read an individual bit
    char bitChar;

    // decimal value of bitChar (0 or 1)
    int bitValue;

    // positional values of bits 0 through 7
    int powerOfTwo[8] = {1,2,4,8,16,32,64,128};

    // bit is control object for loop;
    int bit, byteValue = 0;

    cout << "Enter a byte with 8 binary digits: ";
    // read the 8 bits and accumulate the decimal value
    for (bit = 7; bit >= 0; bit--)
    {
        // read bit as character and convert to 0 or 1
```

```
            cin >> bitChar;
            bitValue = bitChar - '0';

            // if bitValue is 1, add positional value of the bit
            if (bitValue == 1)
                byteValue += powerOfTwo[bit];
        }
        cout << "Value is " << byteValue << endl;

        return 0;
    }
```

Run 1:

Enter a byte with 8 binary digits: 00001011
Value is 11

Run 2:

Enter a byte with 8 binary digits: 11111111
Value is 255

C++ allows the programmer to initialize only part of an array whose members have primitive type. The size of the initialization list can be less than the stated array size. The values from the list are assigned in successive index order. The remaining array elements are filled with 0. For instance, the declaration

Programming Note

```
short q[7] = {8, 5, 2};
```

assigns q[0] = 8, q[1] = 5, q[2] = 2, q[3] = 0, . . . , q[6] = 0

An error results when using an initialization list that has more elements than the array size. For example, the following declaration will cause a compilation error.

```
int arr[3] = {1,2,3,4};
```

Array Initialization in the Date Class

In Chapter 6, we declared the Date class that includes the member function numberOfDays(). With array initialization, we can now describe an algorithm that implements the function.

```
Date  d(3,2,2000);              // date 3/2/2000
cout << d.numberOfDays();       // output: 62
```

To compute the number of days from January 1 to the current date, we define the array monthLength, which contains the number of days in each month. The declaration assigns 28 days to February since an extra day will be added to the total by a separate calculation that uses the member function isLeapYear(). The algorithm uses a for loop that scans all of the months prior to the current month and uses `monthLength` to form the sum of the number of days in those prior months. The final calculation adds the day in the current month plus one additional day if the year is a leap year and the month is greater than February. The object, daysToDate, maintains the total number of days. For instance, the number of days to March 2, 2000 is

$$
\begin{aligned}
\text{daysToDate} &= 31(\text{January}) + 28(\text{February}) + 3\,(\text{additional days}) \\
&= 59 + 2(\text{days in March}) + 1(\text{leap year}) \\
&= 62
\end{aligned}
$$

The function numberOfDays() uses an initialization list to declare the array `monthLength`.

```
int monthLength[13] = {0,31,28,31,30,31,30,31,31,30,31,30,31};

// determine the number of days into the year
int Date::numberOfDays()
{
   // assign place holder value of 0 for monthLength[0]
   int monthLength[13] = {0,31,28,31,30,31,30,
                          31,31,30,31,30,31};

   int daysToDate = 0, i;

   // add up all the days in the preceding months
   for (i = 1; i < month; i++)
      daysToDate += monthLength[i];
   // add days in month (day) + 1
   // if year is leap year and month is March or later,
   if (isLeapYear() && month > 2)
      daysToDate += day + 1;
   else
      daysToDate += day;

   return daysToDate;
}
```

7-4 ARRAYS AS ARGUMENTS

C++ allows arrays to be passed as run-time arguments. Since it would be inefficient to copy all of the elements of the array, C++ creates special syntax for a formal array argument that includes the name, the type of its elements, and the index operator (`"[]"`) without an explicit size.

```
// Type is the element type
returnType f(Type arr[], …);
```

For instance, the function arraySum() is passed an integer array and the size of the array as arguments. It computes the sum of the elements and then returns the result.

```
int arraySum(int arr[], int n);
```

The argument n is required since C++ does not retain information about the size of an array. A calling statement passes the run-time array name, which has the effect of copying the address of the array to the corresponding formal argument. The following statements pass integer arrays to the function arraySum().

```
int list[7] = {5, 6, 2, 9, 1, 3, 8};
int score[4] = {92, 85, 80, 72};

// pass list as the array name and 7 as the size
listTotal = arraySum(list,7)      // assign  34 to listTotal

// pass score as the array name and 4 as the size
cout  << arraySum(score,4);       // output: 329
```

Within the function, any reference to an array element is provided by the array access function that uses the array address, the object type, and the index. With this as background, we give an implementation for the function arraySum().

```
int arraySum(int arr[], int n)
{
   int total = 0, i;

   for (i = 0; i < n; i++)
      total += arr[i];
   return total;
}
```

EXAMPLE 7.5 ■■■■■■■■■■■■■■■■■■■■■■■■■■■■■■■■■■

1. To compute the total of the scores, the array name score is passed as the run-time argument to the function arraySum(). Since score is a name for the starting address of the array {92, 85, 80, 72}, the value of arr in the function is the same starting address. Any access to an element arr[i] in the function accesses the element score[i] in the array.

```
int score[4]={92, 85, 80, 72};

arraySum (score, 4)

int arraySum( int arr[], int n)
{
   . . . .
```

```
      total+=arr[i];
   . . . .
}
```

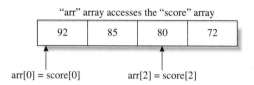

"arr" array accesses the "score" array

| 92 | 85 | 80 | 72 |

arr[0] = score[0]   arr[2] = score[2]

2. Function readList() reads a sequence of n real numbers from the keyboard and stores them in an array. The number of items to read is passed as a argument.

```
void readList(double arr[], int n)
{
   for (int i = 0; i < n; i++)
       cin >> arr[i];              // input array value
}
```

A calling statement uses readList() to input truck weights.

```
double truckWeight[5];

readList(truckWeight,5);    // input 5 truck weights  ■
```

Our examples of array argument passing have used integer and double types. The following is a summary of the key concepts for a general object type.

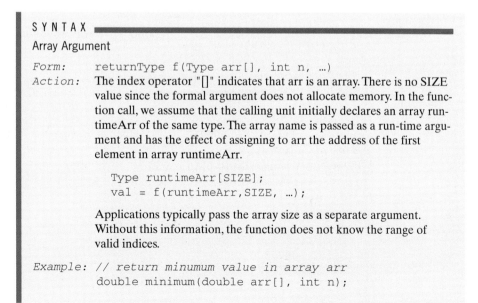

SYNTAX ▬▬▬▬▬▬▬▬▬▬▬▬▬▬▬▬▬▬▬▬▬▬▬▬▬▬▬▬▬

Array Argument

Form: returnType f(Type arr[], int n, …)

Action: The index operator "[]" indicates that arr is an array. There is no SIZE value since the formal argument does not allocate memory. In the function call, we assume that the calling unit initially declares an array run-timeArr of the same type. The array name is passed as a run-time argument and has the effect of assigning to arr the address of the first element in array runtimeArr.

```
Type runtimeArr[SIZE];
val = f(runtimeArr,SIZE, …);
```

Applications typically pass the array size as a separate argument. Without this information, the function does not know the range of valid indices.

Example: `// return minumum value in array arr`
`double minimum(double arr[], int n);`

```
    // calling code
    double table[5] = {3.1, 4.9, 6.3, 2.7, 5.5};
    double min;

    min = minimum(table,5);    // min = 2.7
```

P R O G R A M   7 . 1

The program declares an array of long integers, called homeGames, that lists the attendance at eight home games. A pair of free functions, totalAttendance() and over30000(), compute the total attendance for all of the games and the number of games with attendance greater than 30,000 respectively. Each function is called with the array as an argument and the return values are output.

```cpp
#include <iostream.h>

// computes attendance for n football games
long totalAttendance(long game[], int n);

// computes number of games with attendance
// of more than 30,000
int over30000(long game[], int n);

int main()
{
    // attendance at the 8 home games
    long homeGame[8] = {38000L, 52000L, 28000L, 36000L,
                        58000L, 25000L, 18000L, 59000L};

    cout << over30000(homeGame, 8)
         << " games were attended by over 30,000 people"
         << endl;

    cout << "The total attendance for the season was "
         << totalAttendance(homeGame, 8) << endl;

    return 0;
}

long totalAttendance(long game[], int n)
{
    int i;
    long total = 0;

    // form sum of array elements
    for (i=0;i < n; i++)
       total += game[i];

    return total;
}
```

```
int over30000(long game[], int n)
{
    int i, count = 0;

    // find number of games with attendance
    // over 30,000
    for (i=0;i < n;i++)
        if (game[i] > 30000L)
        count++;

    return count;
}
```

Run

```
5 games were attended by over 30,000 people
The total attendance for the season was 314000
```

The Statistics Class

We conclude this section by developing a simple Statistics class that provides basic statistical information about a list of real numbers. The class returns the count (size) of the list as well as the maximum, minimum and mean (average) of the numbers. What makes the class useful and efficient as a computational tool is the link that is established by the constructor between a Statistics object and the list of numbers. The object does not create a separate copy of the data values. Rather the list is passed as an array argument to the constructor. All of the statistical calculations are carried out on the original list and the results are stored in the class data members. Since we may want the object to be associated with different lists during execution of a program, the class has the member function setData() that passes an array as an argument and computes statistical information for the new list. Before giving an example of a Statistics object in action, we include a declaration of the class.

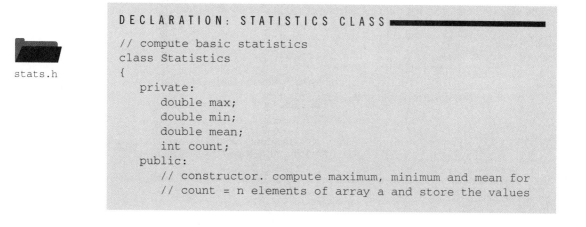

stats.h

```
DECLARATION: STATISTICS CLASS ━━━━━━━━━━━━━
// compute basic statistics
class Statistics
{
    private:
        double max;
        double min;
        double mean;
        int count;
    public:
        // constructor. compute maximum, minimum and mean for
        // count = n elements of array a and store the values
```

```
                // in the class data members
                Statistics(double a[], int n);

                // set attributes corresponding to array a
                void setData(double a[], int n);

                // return the number of elements on which max, min and
                // mean are based
                int getCount();
                // return the maximum
                double getMax();
                // return the minimum
                double getMin();
                // return the mean
                double getMean();
        };
```

EXAMPLE 7.6

The array dataList contains 6 real numbers. The Statistics object listStats returns the number of elements in the list and the maximum, minimum and mean values.

```
double dataList[] = {17.4, 30.8, 16.7, 22.1, 9.7, 14.8};
Statistics listStats(dataList,6);

int i, listSize, average, range;

listSize = listStats.getCount();    // listSize = 6
average = listStats.getMean();      // average = 22.3

// range = 30.8 - 9.7 = 21.1
range = listStats.getMax() - listStats.getMin();
```

PROGRAM 7.2

The program explores statistical information related to employee salaries. The array, empSalary, contains a listing of salaries for all employees at a company.

```
double empSalary[8] = {48250.00, 75500.00, 24750.00, 96100.00,
                       39150.00, 68450.00, 29400.00, 33800.00};
```

Using a Statistics object to do most of the calculations, the program outputs the average salary and determines the ratio between the lowest and highest paid employee. This difference is output in the format

```
"Highest paid earns x.xx times more than the lowest paid."
```

A loop traverses the salary list and outputs relative earnings of the employee compared with the average (mean) salary. The output is given in table form

```
        Salary                  Deviation from the Average
        xxxx.xx                      (+/-)xxx.xx
        . . .                          . . .
```

```cpp
#include <iostream.h>
#include <iomanip.h>

#include "stats.h"
#include "textlib.h"

int main()
{
    // employee salaries
    double empSalary[8] = {48250.00, 75500.00, 24750.00,
                           96100.00, 39150.00, 68450.00,
                           29400.00, 33800.00};
    // to hold the average of the salaries
    double averageSalary;
    // performs the statistical calculations
    Statistics salaries(empSalary, 8);
    // loop control object
    int i;

    // output average salary and ratio of highest to lowest
    averageSalary = salaries.getMean();
    cout << "The average employee salary is $"
         << averageSalary << endl;
    cout << "Highest paid earns " << setreal(1,2)
         << salaries.getMax()/salaries.getMin()
         << " times more than the lowest paid."
         << endl << endl;

    // output table of salaries and deviation of each from mean
    cout << "Salary" << setw(30)
         << "Deviation from the Average" << endl;
    for (i=0; i < 8; i++)
        cout << setreal(1,2) << empSalary[i] << setreal(19,2)
             << (empSalary[i] - averageSalary) << endl;

    return 0;
}
```

```
Run:

The average employee salary is $51925
Highest paid earns 3.88 times more than the lowest
paid.

Salary      Deviation from the Average
48250.00            -3675.00
75500.00            23575.00
24750.00           -27175.00
96100.00            44175.00
39150.00           -12775.00
```

```
68450.00              16525.00
29400.00             -22525.00
33800.00             -18125.00
```

Implementing Member Functions. The function `setData()` is responsible for the statistical calculations. It is called by the construction when a Statistical object is declared. The other member functions simply return values of data members. We give the implementation of `setData()` and then illustrate how it is called by the constructor.

setData():

The mean is the simplest algorithm. A for statement traverses the array and computes the sum of the elements. The mean is the sum divided by the size of the array. Algorithms to compute the maximum or minimum value in the array are similar and present a problem worth noting. To find the maximum, a loop scans the array and checks to see if the current element arr[i] is greater than the maximum of the previous elements. If so, the maximum value is updated.

```
if (arr[i] > max)
   max = arr[i];
```

The algorithm assumes max has an initial value. This is provided by the first element arr[0]. The loop begins its scan with the second element arr[1].

```
// pass the array as an argument; record the maximum, minimum
// and mean for the array
void Statistics::setData(double arr[], int n)
{
   int i;
   double totalSum;

   // set count (array size) to n
   count = n;

   // initially, set minimum and maximum to arr[0]; also
   // set totalSum to arr[0]; loop can then begin at i = 1
   min = max = totalSum = arr[0];

   // compare each arr[i] with min and max; update values
   // if necessary.  add arr[i] to totalSum
   for (i = 1; i < n; i++)
   {
      if (arr[i] < min)          // check min
         min = arr[i];
      else if (arr[i] > max)     // check max
         max = arr[i];
      totalSum += arr[i];        // add to totalSum
   }
}
```

```
    // mean is the value totalSum divided by count
    mean  = totalSum/count;
}
```

Constructor:

A call to setData() initializes the statistical data that is derived from the array arr.

```
// constructor. initialize the attributes
Statistics::Statistics(double arr[], int n)
{
    setData(arr,n);
}
```

7-5 ARRAYS OF OBJECTS

The element type of an array is not limited to primitive number and character types. A program can use class types that create arrays of rectangles, of student accounts, of dates, and so forth. Familiar array syntax allows us to declare the objects.

```
Accumulator iraAccount[30];   // declare 30 Accumulator objects
Rectangle r[10];              // declare 10 rectangles
```

The Rectangle objects are r[0], r[1], ... , r[9]. Each element has the measurement operations `area()` and `perimeter()` and access functions `getLength()`, `getWidth()`, and `setSides()` that deal with the dimensions of a rectangle.

```
cout << r[0].area();            // area of the 1st rectangle

// check if rectangle i is a square
if (r[i].getLength() == r[i].getWidth())
    cout << "Rectangle is a square";
```

With the iraAccount array, a bank can use a loop to post a yearly $35 handling charge to all of the accounts.

```
for (i = 0; i < 30; i++)
    iraAccount[i].addValue(-35);   // debit the account
```

At first glance, all of this looks just like our work with arrays of primitive type. The similarity is real and applies in those cases where the array elements can be created without constructor arguments.

Default Constructor

Our declaration of Rectangle and Accumulator arrays hides a very important fact about constructors. When an array of objects is declared, the constructor is called to initialize each element in the array. It is possible to specify an initialization list that would explicitly assign a value to each element. For instance, we first declare three Rectangle objects and use them to initialize the array rect. We also initialize an array of strings that describe the Rectangle objects.

```
// declare three separate rectangle objects
Rectangle  tag(2,3),  card(3,5),  page(8.5,11);

// array uses existing rectangles for initialization
Rectangle rect[3] = {tag, card, page};
String rName[3] = {"tag", "card", "page"};
```

This process would be very clumsy for a large array. The only sensible way to initialize rect is to declare an array without an initialization list and then use the member function setSides() to assign the dimensions to each element. The following code declares a 100 element array of Rectangle objects and then uses a loop to specify the first rectangle as a 1 by 1 square, the second rectangle as a 2 by 2 square, and so forth.

```
Rectangle rect[100];
int i;

for(i=0; i < 100; i++)
    rect[i].setSides(i+1,i+1);
```

In the declaration, the Rectangle constructor is called for each element in the array rect. The constructor for each object uses the default values for its arguments and sets the length and width to 0.0. Each object in rect starts out as a 0 by 0 square.

```
// Rectangle constructor with default arguments
Rectangle(double len = 0.0, double wid = 0.0);
```

What works for arrays of Rectangles works for any class whose constructor can be called with no arguments. Look at Date examples. The Date class has a constructor whose arguments have default values that initialize an object to January 1, 1600.

```
Date (int mm=1, int dd=1, int yyyy=1600);

// array of 50 Date events, each set to 1/1/1600
Date events[50];
```

Problems occur when a constructor requires that arguments be passed for each object in the array declaration. Consider the MealBill class of Chapter 3. The restaurant name and the local tax rate must be supplied as arguments.

```
// constructor initializes the businessName and tax rate
MealBill(String name, double rate);
```

An attempt to declare a MealBill array without an initialization list is incorrect.

```
MealBill  steakHouse[50];    // constructor called 50 times
```

Constructor arguments are required to create each of the 50 elements.

We have seen that a class may be used in an array declaration if it has a constructor with default arguments. The class may also be used if it has a constructor with no arguments. These two types of constructors are called *default constructors*.

> **Definition** A *default constructor* is a constructor that can be called with no arguments. This occurs when the constructor does not have arguments or each argument has a default value.

When a class has a default constructor, it may be used in an array declaration that does not have an initialization list. The class must have other member functions that allow a program to initialize the data members. Typically these classes have one or more "set" functions to create a run-time update of an object. To use the MealBill class with arrays, we would need to give its constructor arguments default values and add the members functions

```
// default constructor: name is empty, rate is 0.0
Meal Bill (String name="", rate = 0.0);

void setName(String name);   // update value of businessName
void setRate (double rate)   // update value of taxRate
```

Programming Note

When designing a class whose objects may be used in an array, create a default constructor. Either give each constructor argument a default value or to define a constructor with an empty argument list.

The Date and Rectangle classes have a constructor with default arguments. The StudentAccount class has two constructors, one of which is a default constructor. A class may contain *multiple constructors* that provide different forms of initialization. The compiler uses **operator overloading** to distinguish the constructors. This topic is discussed in Chapter 9. In the StudentAccount class, the default constructor assigns the empty string "" to both the student ID and name and sets the starting balance to $0.00.

```
// constructor with arguments (used in previous examples)
StudentAccount(String id, String name, double initbal);

// default constructor allows arrays of StudentAccount
objects
StudentAccount();
```

Anonymous Objects. While discussing the initialization of class arrays, we have an opportunity to introduce an important feature of constructors. The constructor can be explicitly called to build an object for use in assignment statements and other expressions. Since the object is not associated with an identifier in a declaration, it is called an *anonymous object*. For instance, the expression Rectangle(6,4) builds an anonymous object that represents a 6 by 4 rectangle. It is assigned to rect[0], as the first Rectangle in the array.

```
Rectangle  rect[5];

// assign anonymous object to the first rectangle
rect[0] = Rectangle(6,4);
```

A series of these objects can be used to create an array initialzation list.

```
//anonymous objects initialize 4 rooms
Rectangle room[4] = {Rectangle(14,16), Rectangle(9,7),
                     Rectangle(14,21), Rectangle(10,11)};
```

After an anonymous object is used, the compiler discards it.

E X A M P L E   7 . 7

In the year 2002, the first Sunday falls on January 2nd. The example declares a 52 element array, sundayDate, that is designated to contains the date of each Sunday in the year. The expression Date(1,2,2002) builds an anonymous object that represents the date January 2, 2002 and assigns it to sundayDate[0].

```
Date  sundayDate[52];

// assign January 4th as the first sunday
sundayDate[0] = Date(1,2,2002);
```

A for loop uses the member function incrementDate() with argument 7 to assign dates for the remaining 51 Sundays in the year.

```
for (i = 1; i < 52; i++)
{
   // assign dates of previous Sunday and add 7 days.
   sundayDate[i] = sundayDate[i-1];
   sundayDate[i].incrementDate(7);
} ■
```

Application: Painter's Job Schedule

The Date class has a default constructor that initializes an object to January 1, 1600. We use this class to analyze critical job information for a self-employed painter. The array, jobStart, contains the starting dates for up to 10 jobs. A second integer array, jobLength, contains the number of days required to finish each job. The job data in the two arrays is read from the file *jobs.dat* using the stream object jobData. In the process, we determine the number of jobs in the file. As part of the analysis, we use the length of each job to determine its ending date. This information is stored in a separate Date array, jobEnd.

```
jobData >> month >> day > year >> jobDuration;
while (jobData)
{
   // assign data to jobStart and jobLength
   jobStart[i] = Date(month,day,year);
```

```
    jobLength[i] = jobDuration;

    // compute jobEnd
    jobEnd[i] = jobStart[i];
    jobEnd[i].incrementDate(jobLength[i]);
            ...
    jobData >> month >> day > year >> jobDuration;
}
```

We can use the time period between the ending date of one job and the starting date of the next job to determine the painter's idle time. The calculation uses the Date member function `numberOfDays()`. For instance, the idle time between the third and fourth job is

```
idleTime = jobStart[3].numberOfDays()-jobEnd[2].numberOfDays()
```

Table 7-2 displays information for five jobs between April 3, 2000 and June 24, 2000.

TABLE 7-2   Job Schedule.

Job	Starting Date	Ending Date	Length	Idle Time
1	4/03/2000	4/18/2000	15	17
2	5/05/2000	5/17/2000	12	10
3	5/27/2000	6/06/2000	10	2
4	6/08/2000	6/14/2000	6	1
5	6/15/2000	6/24/2000	9	0

APPLICATION 7-3 ANALYZING PAINT JOBS

The file *jobs.dat* contains the data given in Table 7-2. The starting dates and length for the jobs are provided by reading data for the arrays jobStart and jobLength from the file. After building the jobEnd array, the program uses a loop to create the table.

```
#include <iostream.h>
#include <fstream.h>
#include <iomanip.h>        // for setw()
#include <stdlib.h>         // for exit()

#include "date.h"           // use Date class

int main()
{
    // number of jobs processed
    int numberJobs;
    // declare the arrays to contain job starting
    // and ending dates
```

```
            Date jobStart[10], jobEnd[10];
            // to contain length of each job
            int jobLength[10];
            // stream to input job data
            ifstream jobData;
            // loop control object
            int i;
            // used to read job data from the file "jobs.dat"
            int month, day ,year, jobDuration;
            int idleTime;

            jobData.open("jobs.dat");
            if(!jobData)
            {
               cerr << "Cannot open 'jobs.dat'" << endl;
               exit(1);
            }

            numberJobs = 0;
            i = 0;

            // input the initial job data
            jobData >> month >> day >> year >> jobDuration;
            // process job data until end-of-file
            while (jobData)
            {
               // assign data to jobStart and jobLength
               jobStart[i] = Date(month,day,year);
               jobLength[i] = jobDuration;

               // compute jobEnd
               jobEnd[i] = jobStart[i];
               jobEnd[i].incrementDate(jobLength[i]);

               // we have just processed a job
               numberJobs++;

               // increment index i and input new data
               i++;
               jobData >> month >> day >> year >> jobDuration;
             }

            // output formatted job data
            cout << "Job   Starting Date   Ending Date   Length   "
                    "Idle Time" << endl;
            for(i=0;i < numberJobs;i++)
            {
               cout << setw(2) << (i+1) << setw(5) << ' ';
               jobStart[i].writeShortDate();
               cout << setw(5) << ' ';
               jobEnd[i].writeShortDate();
```

```
        cout << setw(8) <<  jobLength[i];

        // no idle time after the last job
        if (i != numberJobs-1)
        {
            idleTime=jobStart[i+1].numberOfDays() -
                    jobEnd[i].numberOfDays();
            cout << setw(10) << idleTime << endl;
        }
        else
            cout << setw(10) << 0 << endl;
    }

    return 0;
}
```

Run:

```
Job    Starting Date    Ending Date    Length    Idle Time
 1        4/03/2000        4/18/2000      15          17
 2        5/05/2000        5/17/2000      12          10
 3        5/27/2000        6/06/2000      10           2
 4        6/08/2000        6/14/2000       6           1
 5        6/15/2000        6/24/2000       9           0
```

7-6 RANDOM NUMBERS

Games are part of most of our lives. Games are also a source of interesting and challenging computer applications. We take a little diversion from the more traditional types of applications in order to look at the world of chance events. By developing random numbers, we have the basic tool that allows a computer to create video and casino games. The same numbers also find important applications in business and scientific simulation models.

Computers represent chance events by generating random real or integer numbers that fall within a specified range. Random integers depend on an argument n and lie in the range 0 to n-1. The numbers are called random because each value in the range has an equal chance or probability of occurring. For instance, integer numbers in the range of 0 to 9 are random when each value has a 1 out of 10 probability of occurring. All random real numbers lie in the interval from 0 to 1. Such a number is random when it has a 1 out of 2 probability of being greater than 0.5, a 1 out of 4 probability of being between 0.25 and 0.5, and so forth.

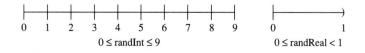

For applications, we provide the RandomNumber class to generate random numbers. Each object of this type is capable of generating a sequence of random numbers.

```
RandomNumber   rnd;          //  rnd is a random number generator
```

The class has a member function random() that takes n as an argument and produces an integer random number in the range 0 to n-1.

```
randInt = rnd.random(n);    // 0 <= randInt <= n
```

A second member function, frandom(), returns a random real number in the inteval 0 to 1.

```
randReal = rnd.frandom();  // 0 <= randReal < 1
```

EXAMPLE 7.8 ▬▬▬▬▬▬▬▬▬▬▬▬▬▬▬▬▬▬▬▬▬▬▬

1. The loop generates 5 random integers in the range 0 to 39.

```
RandomNumber rnd;        // declare random number
int item, i;             // item is assigned random numbers
for (i = 0; i < 5; i++)
   item = rnd.random(40);
```

Possible values for item are: 31 14 25 1 19

2. Each iteration of a do/while loop generates a real random number.

```
double x;
do
   x = rnd.frandom();
while (x < 0.5);
```

Possible values for x are: 0.3458 0.1529 0.498 0.1 0.78136(Stop) ■

Exploring Concepts

Sixty percent of the registered voters in a district actually vote. A name is randomly chosen from the list of registered voters. How would you simulate the event that the randomly selected person votes?

Describing the RandomNumber Class. A computer random number generator is designed to create an unlimited sequence of random values. The generator begins with an initial data value, called the seed, and uses arithmetic calculations to produce the random number. The process is *deterministic* since it is dependent on the initial value of the seed and executes a fixed set of instructions. The resulting sequence of numbers are referred to as *pseudo-random numbers*. In the following class description, the seed is stored as a data member that is initialized by the constructor.

DESCRIPTION: RandomNumber CLASS ━━━━━━━━━━

A RandomNumber object produces a sequence of random integer or real numbers .

Attributes:
 unsigned long randseed;   // large positive long integer

Operations:
 RandomNumber: Initializes the seed with a user supplied value or the current
                  time read from the system clock (s = 0).
                      RandomNumber(unsigned long s = 0);

 random: Takes a positive integer n and generates a random integer in
                  the range 0 to n – 1
                      unsigned short random(unsigned long n);

 frandom: Generates a random real number in the range $0 <= x < 1$
                      double frandom();

When the constructor is passed a non-zero run-time argument, the value provides the initial seed from which the random sequence is generated. If the same value is used with another RandomNumber object, the same random sequence will result. When the default s = 0 is used, the constructor uses the system time as a seed. Since the time is rapidly updated, the RandomNumber object will have a different initial seed each time the program is run and thus produce a different sequence of random numbers. Applications dictate the kind of initialization to use. A business simulation often repeats a random sequence so that the model can be studied with small changes in the organizational structure. Casino games need a different random sequence on each run to insure that a new game is played.

```
// rnd generates random numbers using system time
RandomNumber rnd;

// with seed 75, rnd1 and rnd2 are the same random sequence
RandomNumber rnd1(75), rnd2(75);
```

PROGRAM 7.3

━━━━━━━━━━━━━━━━━━━━━━━━━━━━━━━━━━━

The program illustrates the "randomness" of the numbers generated by a RandonNumber object. A loop looks at one million random integers in the range 0 to 4 and computes the number of times each possible outcome occurs. The count is stored in array intCount where `intCount[0]` is the number of times a 0 occurs, `intCount[1]` is the number of times a 1 occurs, and so forth. Each iteration of the loop also generates a real number and maintains counts for the numbers that are less than 0.25 and greater than 0.60. The integers under25Count and over60Count hold the respective totals. For output, we list the individual counts and their percentage as a fraction of the total number of values (one-million).

In the run, note that each of the five different integer outcomes occurs approximately 20% of the time. A real number is less than 0.25 approximately 25% of the time and greater than 0.60 approximately 40% of the time. The RandomNumber class is found in the file **trandom.h** of the software supplement.

```
#include <iostream.h>
#include <iomanip.h>    // for manipulator setw()

#include "trandom.h"    // for RandomNumber
#include "textlib.h"    // for setreal()

int main()
{
   // random number generator
   RandomNumber rnd;

   // declare counters and set to 0
   long intCount [5] = {0, 0, 0, 0, 0};
   long under25Count = 0, over60Count = 0;

   // control objects in the for loops
   long lint;
   int i;

   // floating point values for percentages
   double pctInt, pctUnder25, pctOver60;

   // object that holds a random number
   double x;

   // generate 1,000,000 integer and real numbers
   for (lint = 0; lint < 1000000L; lint++)
   {
      // value in range 0 to 4 is used as index
      intCount [rnd.random(5)]++;

      // generate real number and test location in an interval
      x = rnd.frandom();
      if (x < 0.25)
         under25Count ++;
      else if (x >= 0.6)
         over60Count++;
   }

   // header for the table
   cout << "Number        Count          Pct" << endl;

   // output array elements as a count and as a percentage
   for (i = 0; i < 5; i++)
```

```
{
    // compute as percentage of 1,000,000
    pctInt = (intCount [i]/1000000.00) * 100;
    cout << setw(3) << i << setw(16) << intCount [i]
        << setreal(13,2) << pctInt << "%" << endl;
}
cout << endl;

// output counts for real numbers along with percentage
pctUnder25 = (under25Count/1000000.0) * 100;
cout << under25Count << " real random numbers <  0.25 "
    << setreal(7,3) << " ("
    << pctUnder25 << "%)" << endl;

pctOver60 = (over60Count/1000000.0) * 100;
cout << over60Count << " real random numbers >= 0.60 "
    << setreal(7,3) << " ("
    << pctOver60 << "%)" << endl;

    return 0;
}
```

```
Run:

Number          Count           Pct
   0            200456          20.05%
   1            200149          20.01%
   2            199693          19.97%
   3            199907          19.99%
   4            199795          19.98%

250786 real random numbers <  0.25        (25.079%)
399204 real random numbers >= 0.60        (39.920%)
```

Interpreting Random Numbers. To define a chance event, a programmer must interpret the value of a random number. For instance, the toss of a coin results in a head or a tail. Assuming the coin is fair, the two outcomes can be represented by the random values 0 and 1. The value rnd.random(2) simulates the toss of a coin.

```
if (rnd.random(2) == 0)
    cout << "Toss is a head" << endl;
else
    cout << "Toss is a tail" << endl;
```

A cafeteria simulation model looks at the work load of a cashier. In the model, customers occupy the cashier for 10 seconds 30% of the time, for 20 seconds 55% of the time, and for 35 seconds 15% of the time. Different customer behavior is simulated by generating a random real number and using it in a nested if statement.

```
x = rnd.frandom();        // x in the range 0<= x < 1.0
if (x <= 0.30)            // outcome has 30% chance
    customerTime = 10;
else if (x <= 0.85)       // outcome has 55% chance
    customerTime = 20;
else
    customerTime = 35;    // outcome has 15% chance
```

A random number is always generated in the range from 0 to randLimit. Many applications require random values in a different range. For instance, the value of a single die is in the range 1 to 6. To simulate the tossing of a die, we can use the random() function with an argument 6. The value of `die.random(6)` has 6 possible outcomes in the range 0 to 5. By adding 1, the values fall in the range $1 - 6$ that corresponds to a die face value.

```
RandomNumber die;                    // die generator
dieface = die.random(6) + 1;         // 1 <= dieface <= 6
```

EXAMPLE 7.9 ◾◾◾◾◾◾◾◾◾◾◾◾◾◾◾◾◾◾◾◾◾◾◾◾◾

At a bridge crossing, the weight of a typical car ranges from 2000 to 3500 pounds. The weight falls in an interval that spans 1500 units, starting at 2000. To simulate a car's weight, a program can use `frandom()` to generate a real number. After multiplying by 1500, the value falls in the expanded interval from 0 to 1500. By adding 2000, the interval shifts to the corresponding car weights.

```
weight = rnd.frandom()*1500 + 2000;   ◾
```

Estimating π

A simulation study uses random numbers to represent a series of events. By using key attributes of each event, the study can model a real world situation. For instance, a bank simulation can model a waiting line for service by its tellers. The model can predict the amount of time an average customer would wait and the workload of the tellers. To illustrate how random numbers are used in simuluation, we provide a interesting way to estimate π. The approach uses the fact that π is the area of a circle of radius 1

```
area = π * radius² = π*1² = π
```

Figure 7-2 illustrates the main components of the simulation. On an x-y axis, the equation $x^2 + y^2 = 1$ represents a circle of radius 1 centered at the origin. The shaded region in the first quadrant of the circle has area $\pi/4$. The quadrant is enclosed in a square with sides of length 1 and with an area of 1.

To estimate the value of π, the study simulates the tossing of 5,000,000 darts into the square region. The landing point, (x,y), is determined by computing x and y as random numbers in the range $0 \ x < 1, 0 \ y < 1$. In some percentage of the cases, the point also lies within the shaded region. A count

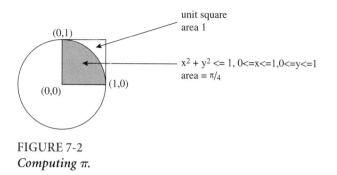

FIGURE 7-2
Computing π.

object, called hits, maintains a record of the number of points that lie in the shaded region.

```
if (x*x + y*y <= 1)
    hits++;
```

An estimate for π is a study in ratios. We know that the ratio of the shaded area to the unit square is $\pi/4$ to 1. This same ratio should apply when comparing the number of hits out of the total number of tosses. A little mathematics creates an equation that approximates π. The symbol $\cong$ means "approximately equal to."

$$\frac{hits}{50000} \cong \frac{\text{area of shaded region}}{\text{area of outer square}} = \frac{\pi/4}{1}$$

$$\pi \cong \frac{4 * hits}{50000}$$

APPLICATION 7-4 ESTIMATING *Π* WITH SIMULATION

The number of tosses is specified by a constant long integer NUMTOSSES with value 5000000L. Running the program with a larger or smaller number of trials simply involves changing the value of NUMTOSSES. A for loop generates a random point in the unit square and increments the long integer called hits whenever the point falls in the shaded area (first quadrant of the circle). The program computes the ratio of hits to NUMTOSSES and uses the value to approximate π. The run gives a result that is not a bad approximation to π.

True Value: π = 3.141592653589793 . . .
Approximate Value: π = 3.14167

```
#include <iostream.h>

#include "trandom.h"    // use RandomNumber class

int main()
{
    // number of times we run the experiment
    const long NUMTOSSES = 5000000L;
```

```
            // a random number generator object
            RandomNumber coordinate;

            // the horizontal and vertical coordinates
            double x, y;

            // hits of points falling in the circle.
            long hits = 0, i;

            // approximation to PI;
            double pi;

            // generate NUMTOSSES random points in the square
            for(i=0; i < NUMTOSSES; i++)
            {
               x = coordinate.frandom();
               y = coordinate.frandom();
               // is the point in the circle?
               if (x*x + y*y <= 1.0)
                     hits++;
            }
            pi = 4.0 * double(hits) / NUMTOSSES;
            cout << "The estimate of PI is "   << pi << endl;

            return 0;
        }
```

Run:

The estimate of PI is 3.14167

7-7   SEQUENTIAL ARRAY ALGORITHMS

Lists are an important design feature in many applications. Databases are designed around tables which are lists of records. Compilers use lists of keywords to parse program source code. A general study of lists belongs to a course in Data Structures and lies beyond the scope of this book. We can, however, look at a small but important set of algorithms that uses arrays as a list structure. In this section, our discussion focuses on the classical sequential search algorithm that enables a program to use a key to find an element in a list. As an application of the sequential search, we develop the function, removeItem(), that deletes an item from a list.

Sequential Search

A search operation looks for an element in a list using a target value called the *key*. The *sequential search* is an algorithm that starts at a specified position in the list and compares each subsequent element with the key. The scan moves sequentially from element to element until it discoveres an object that matches the key or until it reaches the end of the list. The algorithm returns the index of the first element that matches the key or the value −1 when no match occurs.

To design a sequential search function that implements the algorithm, we use four arguments that include: an array, the starting and ending indices for the search, and the key. The prototype assumes a list of integer objects.

```
int seqSearch(int arr[], int start, int end, int key);
```

By using the index start as an argument, the function can implement a generalized search that can identify multiple occurrences of the key in the list. With start defined as 0, the search identifies the first occurrence of the key. By resuming the search with start set to the next array index, the function can locate the second occurrence of the key, and so forth. We illustrate this process with a five element array called list. Three calls to the function seqSearch() look for an occurrence of the key 6 and produce three different return values.

```
int list[5] = {8,3,6,2,6}, index;
```

Call 1: index = seqSearch(list, 0, 4, 6);

> The search scans the five element array from the beginning and identifies the first occurrence of the key 6 at index 2 which becomes the return value.

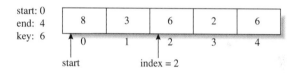

Call 2: index = seqSearch(list, 3, 4, 6);

> The search continues at position 3 (index+1) and scans the tail of the array. The key 6 is located at index 4 which is the next return value.

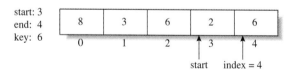

Call 3: index = seqSearch(list, 5, 4, 6);

> To look for the next occurrence of 6, the search begins at position 5 (index + 1). Since this is past the end of the array, seqSearch() returns the value −1 to indicate that the key 6 is not found.

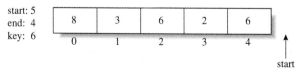

The code for seqSearch() uses a for loop to scan elements beginning at index start and concluding with index end. If the key is found, the function returns the index of the first match. Otherwise −1 is the return value. The definition of the function is found in the header file **seqalgs.h.**

```
// search for key in arr. begin at index start and
// continue through the index end. return the index
// of the first matching element or -1 if key is not found
int seqSearch(int arr[], int start, int end, int key);
{
    int i;                             // scan index
    for(i=start; i <= end; i++)  // scan indices start to end
        if (arr[i] == key)          // compare element with key
            return i;               // immediately return on match
    return -1;                      // otherwise return -1
}
```

Removing a List Element

The remove() function deletes an item from a specified position in the list. The deletion opens a hole in the list and requires a shift to the left of all subsequent elements. This closes up the gap created by removing the element.

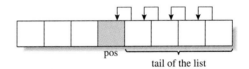

pos

tail of the list

The array, its size, and an index pos are passed as arguments to the function. The position argument designates the element that should be removed and is used in a for loop to shift the subsequent elements in the list to the left one position. Each iteration copies the next item into the current position.

```
arr[i] = arr[i+1];        //  i in the range pos to size-2
```

After removing the item, the size of the list is smaller. By passing size as a reference argument and decrementing its value by 1, the function updates the list size in the calling block. The function is implemented in the header file **seqalgs.h.**

```
// remove the element at index pos from the list
void remove(int arr[], int& size, int pos)
{
    int i;

    // unless pos == size-1, we must shift
    // the tail of the list left one position
    for (i = pos; i < size-1; i++)
        arr[i] = arr[i+1];
    size--;          // decrement the size
}
```

Consider the integer array, arr:

```
int arr[] = {7, 3, 4, 6, 12, 3, 7, 3}, index;
```

1. What is the value of index resulting from the call?
   (i) index = seqSearch(arr, 0, 7, 6);
   (ii) index = seqSearch(arr, 0, 3, 6);
2. For the expression index = seqSearch(arr, start, 7, 7), what range of values for start will return index = 6? What range will return -1?
3. In the remove statements, fill-in values for the index argument so that when the statements execute sequentially they will delete the first and last value of 3 in the list. What is the value of size after each statement?

```
size = 8;
remove(arr, size, index = ?);
remove(arr, size, index = ?);
```

Application: Removing Duplicates

As an application of the seqSearch() and remove() functions, we develop an algorithm that removes all duplicate values from a list. For instance, the array arr starts with 10 elements. After removing duplicates, the array has 4 distinct elements.

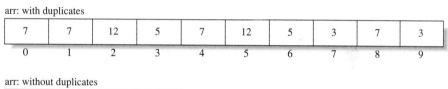

arr: with duplicates

7	7	12	5	7	12	5	3	7	3
0	1	2	3	4	5	6	7	8	9

arr: without duplicates

7	12	5	3
0	1	2	3

We use the data in the array to illustrates how a nested loop defines the main features of the algorithm. The outer loop starts at index 0 and uses the element arr[0] = 7 as a key value. The inner loop carries out a series of sequential searches that start at index 1 and look for other occurrences of 7 (key). When a match is found, the remove() function deletes the duplicate key and shrinks the size of the list. The inner loop terminates when no other 7 is found (return value = −1).

```
i = 0, key = 7;
    Original arr:    7  7  12  5  7  12  5  3  7  3
        Remove 7 at index 1
    Updated arr:     7  12  5  7  12  5  3  7  3
        Remove 7 at index 3
    Updated arr:     7  12  5  12  5  3  7  3
        Remove 7 at index 6
```

```
Updated arr:     7  12  5  12  5  3  3
   Search returns -1 and size = 7
```

After completing the inner loop, the index in the outer loop moves to 1 and the process continues with arr[1] = 12 as the key. In this case, a duplicate is found at index 3.

```
i = 1, key = 12;
   Original arr:     7  12  5  12  5  3  3
      Remove 12 at index 3
   Updated arr:      7  12  5  5  3  3
      Search returns -1 and size = 6
```

With outer index = 2, the inner loop deletes the 5 (arr[2]) at index 3.

```
i = 2, key = 5;
   Original arr:     7  12  5  5  3  3
      Remove 5 at index 3
   Updated arr:      7  12  5  3  3
      Search returns -1 and size = 5
```

With outer index = 3, we continue the process by removing all duplicates of 3.

```
i = 3, key = 3;
   Original arr:     7  12  5  3  3
      Remove 3 at index 4
   Updated arr:      7  12  5  3
      Search returns -1 and size = 4
```

An increment of the outer index to 4 sets it past the end of the list and the process terminates.

The function implementation is found in the header file **seqalgs.h.**

```
// remove duplicate data values from array arr.
// update size
void removeDup(int arr[], int& size)
{
   int i = 0, key, index;

   // search continues until i reaches end of list
   while (i < size)
   {
      // make value at index i the key
      key = arr[i];
      // find and remove all duplicates of key starting
      // at index i+1. terminate when -1 is returned
      while ((index = seqSearch(arr,i+1,size-1,key)) != -1)
         remove(arr, size, index);
      i++;
   }
}
```

Note that the pair of parentheses in the inner loop test are necessary because "!=" has a higher precedence than "=". The return value from seqSearch() is assigned to index and then index is compared to −1.

The main program uses a 15 element array that is assigned random integer numbers in the range 0 to 9. Of course, there will be duplicates. The function writeList() in the file **seqalgs.h** outputs the original array.

```
// output array arr
void writeList(int arr[], int size);
```

The function removeDup() is called to remove all duplicate values and writeList() is again called to output the modified array.

```
#include <iostream.h>

#include "trandom.h"      // use RandomNumber class
#include "seqalgs.h"

int main()
{
   // declare a 15 element array list
   int list[15];
   int i, size = 15;
   RandomNumber rnd;

   // initialize list with random intgers in range 0..9
   for (i = 0; i < size; i++)
      list[i] = rnd.random(10);

   // output intial list with duplicates
   cout << "Initial List: ";
   writeList(list,size);

   // remove all duplicate values. size will be adjusted
   removeDup(list,size);

   // output the list with no duplicates
   cout << "Unique List:   ";
   writeList(list,size);

   return 0;
}
```

```
Run:

Initial List: 3  5  6  3  5  6  1  4  3  8  8  3  9  3  7
Unique List:  3  5  6  1  4  8  9  7
```

The function splice() takes two arrays, arrayA and arrayB, with length sizeA and sizeB respectively. It inserts arrayB into arrayA at index pos. The tail of arrayA that spans the range from pos to sizeA-1 must be shifted to the right sizeB positions to free up room for the insert. The function concludes by updating sizeA to reflect the addition of new elements.

```
void splice(int arrayA[], int& sizeA, int arrayB[], int
sizeB,
                 int pos);
```

*Exploring
Concepts*

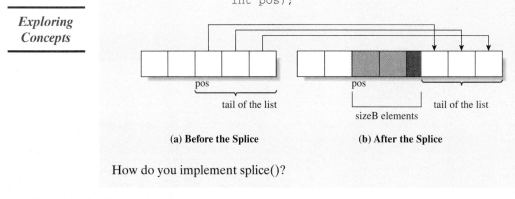

(a) **Before the Splice**   (b) **After the Splice**

How do you implement splice()?

7-8   ARRAYS AS CLASS DATA MEMBERS

In Section 7-7, we introduced arrays as a list-handling structure. We developed the sequential search algorithm and an operation to remove an item from a list. We now use these algorithms in the construction of the FinanceCenter class that handles student records at a university. The class has an array of Student-Account objects as a data member. Each array element maintains the financial records for a particular student. Note that StudentAccount has a default constructor, which is required for the declaration of an uninitialized array.

Data member: acct (list of StudentAccount objects)

The number of elements in the array is determined by the integer constant MAX_ACCOUNTS, whose declaration is placed outside the class. It can be referenced in the declaration of any attribute or in the prototype of a member function. Such global objects are formally discussed in Chapter 8. The number of active records is kept in the integer data member numAcct.

To build and use a FinanceCenter object, we start with a declaration that calls the constructor to create an empty list. StudentAccount records are added to the list using the member function `addAccount()`. Once the accounts are in place, we can use the functions `makeChange()` and `makePayment()` to handle account transactions. Each function requires the student ID as an argument and uses the sequential search algorithm to locate the student's account information in the array. If there is not student in the list with a matching ID, an error message is output. When a student graduates or withdraws, the corresponding account information must be removed. The member function `removeAccount()` accepts the student ID and employs the sequential search algorithm to locate the corresponding StudentAccount object. Once found, the algorithm for deleting a list element is used to remove the account. Given a student ID, the function writeAccount() locates and prints the account information. Since the sequential search algorithm is used frequently by the public member functions, good class design requires that it be coded as a private member function `findAccount()`.

Before giving a class description, we provide an example that illustrates its use.

EXAMPLE 7.10 ▬▬▬▬▬▬▬▬▬▬▬▬▬▬▬▬▬▬▬▬▬▬

Records for John Robinson and Melissa Roberts are added to the FinanceCenter object `financeRecs`. Melissa initially has a $150 negative balance. She makes a payment of $150 on her account and charges supplies at the school book store totaling $50.00. The finance center outputs her new account information. John decides to attend another school and withdraws.

```
StudentAccount john("45-1256","Robinson, John", 0.0),
              melissa("56-9745","Roberts, Melissa",-150.0);

// FinanceCenter list initially has no student accounts
FinanceCenter financeRecs;

// add John and Melissa to the list
financeRecs.addAccount(john);
financeRecs.addAccount(melissa);

// Melissa makes payment of $150 and charges $50
// at book store
financeRecs.makePayment("56-9745",150);
financeRecs.makeCharge("56-9745",50);
// output Melissa's new account information
financeRecs.writeAccount("56-9745");
// John withdraws
financeRecs.removeAccount("45-1256");

Output:
   ID:      56-9745
   Name:    Roberts,Melissa
   Balance: $-50.00  ■
```

We now ready for a presentation of the class declaration and an application that uses the class.

finacct.h

```
DECLARATION: FinanceCenter CLASS ━━━━━━━━━━
const int MAX_ACCOUNTS = 25;

// maintain student records for the finance center
class FinanceCenter
{
   private:
       // number of active student accounts
       int numAcct;
       // acct holds the active accounts
       StudentAccount acct[MAX_ACCOUNTS];

       // locate the StudentAccount object having the given
       // student ID.  return its index or -1 if it does not
       // exist. uses the sequential search algorithm
       int findAccount(const String& studID) const;

   public:
       // constructor.  build an empty list
       FinanceCenter();

       // add a new account to the list
       void addAccount(const StudentAccount& studacct);
       // remove the account with given student ID
       void removeAccount(const String& studID);

       // make a payment or post a charge to an account
       void makePayment(const String& studID, double amount);
       void makeCharge(const String& studID, double amount);

       // output account information for a student
       void writeAccount(const String& studID) const;
};
```

Const Member Functions

Some member functions in the class have the keyword *const* added after the argument list. This specifies that the function does not change any of the data members in the class. The function becomes a *constant member function* and insures that the compiler will generate an error message if the code for the member function attempts to modify a data member. The keyword must also be repeated in the member function implementation after the argument list. Note that a constructor builds an object and can never be declared using const.

Whenever a constant object is declared, the compiler expects that the programmer will select from only the const member functions of that object. If a member function is called that is not specified by const, the compiler will generate a warning or error message. A primary application of const member functions is to support the passing of arguments by constant reference.

The use of const is important for good class design. Use it whenever a member function does not modify data members, and be consistent. We will follow this policy for the remainder of the book.

Application: Using the FinanceCenter Class

To apply the FinanceCenter class in a realistic situation, the StudentAccount data should be read from a file and inserted into the list using addAccount(). The StudentAccount class has a member function, readAccount() that inputs data from the keyboard or a text file.

```
void readAccount(istream& istr = cin);
```

Application 7-6 builds a FinanceCenter object by reading a file and performing interactive list updates.

APPLICATION 7-6 FINANCECENTER TRANSACTIONS

The file `fcacct.dat` contains student account information in the format

<student id>   <lastname,firstname(no blanks)>   <balance>

Using the StudentAccount member function `readAccount()`, the information is read until end-of-file and added to the FinanceCenter object fc. The program then illustrates the class member functions. After reading all of the student account records, a prompt requests a student ID and an amount of a payment on the account. The function `makePayment()` credits the account of the student. It is assumed that the student has purchased $75 in supplies at the bookstore, and makeCharge() posts the charge. To illustrate deletion, the program prompts for a studentID and uses `removeAccount()` to delete the account from the list. A subsequent call to `writeAccount()` results in an error message indicating that the student ID is invalid.

```cpp
#include <iostream.h>
#include <fstream.h>
#include <stdlib.h>

#include "finacct.h"        // use FinanceCenter class

int main()
{
   // build the student records in fc
   FinanceCenter fc;
   // file of student account information
   ifstream students;
   // used to read student information from the file
   StudentAccount studAccount;
   String studID;
   double amount;

   // open the file
   students.open("fcacct.dat");
```

```
       if (!students)
       {
          cerr << "Cannot open 'fcacct.dat'" << endl;
          exit(1);
       }

       // use StudentAccount member function readAccount() to read
       // all the student information from the file
       studAccount.readAccount(students);
       while (students)
       {
          // add records for the current student
          fc.addAccount(studAccount);
          studAccount.readAccount(students);
       }

       cout << "Enter a student ID: ";
       cin >> studID;
       // output account information for the student
       fc.writeAccount (studID);
       cout << endl;

       cout << "Enter a payment amount for student " << studID
            << ": ";
       cin >> amount;
       // make the payment
       fc.makePayment(studID,amount);

       // charge $75
       fc.makeCharge(studID,75);

       // output account information for the student
       cout << "This student charged $75.00 at the bookstore"
            << endl << "Current account information"
            << endl << endl;
       fc.writeAccount(studID);
       cout << endl;

       // prompt for a student to delete.
       // then attempt to write out the account
       cout << "Enter ID of account to delete: ";
       cin >> studID;
       fc.removeAccount (studID);
       fc.writeAccount(studID);

       return 0;
    }
```

```
File fcacct.dat:

45-1256  Robinson,John   0
56-9745  Roberts,Melissa    -150
34-6238  Williams,Thomas   0
54-8263  Bartlett,Rebecca   50
37-2745  Klein,Bob   -500

Run:

Enter a student ID: 56-9745
ID:        56-9745
Name:      Roberts,Melissa
Balance:   $-150.00

Enter a payment amount for student 56-9745: 150
This student charged $75.00 at the bookstore
Current account information

ID:        56-9745
Name:      Roberts,Melissa
Balance:   $-75.00

Enter ID of account to delete: 45-1256
writeAccount(): Invalid ID 45-1256
```

Implementing the FinanceCenter Class

We list the implementation of the FinanceCenter class for selected member functions. We begin with the private member function findAccount() that is called to identify a Student Account.

findAccount():

This function applies the classical sequential search algorithm. It compares the argument against the identification number, `acct[i].getID()`, of each array element. It returns the index of a matching array element or −1 if the student information is not in the array.

```
int FinanceCenter::findAccount(const String& studID) const
{
    int i;

    // perform the sequential search
    for (i = 0; i < numAcct; i++)
        // compare studID with ID of the current object
        if (studID == acct[i].getID())
            return i;
    return -1;
}
```

addAccount():

The array object acct has MAX_ACCOUNTS elements, so if numAcct ==
MAX_ACCOUNTS, there is no space left in the array for another student
record. In this case, the program is terminated. Otherwise, the new student information is added at the rear of the current list. Since the current array elements
lie in the range acct[0] to acct[numAcct-1], the new data is assigned to
acct[numAcct] and numAcct is incremented.

```cpp
// insert studacct at the rear of the list and increment
// numAcct
void FinanceCenter::addAccount(const StudentAccount& studacct)
{
    // if acct is full, the program can't continue
    if (numAcct == MAX_ACCOUNTS)
    {
        cerr << "addAcct(): Account limit exceeded." << endl;
        exit(1);
    }
    else
    {
        // add the new account at the rear of the list
        acct[numAcct] = studacct;
        // increment the number of accounts
        numAcct++;
    }
}
```

removeAccount():

Before attempting to remove an account, the function findAccount() checks
whether an object with a matching student ID is located in the list. If the account is present, the sequential search returns the index that locates the account
in the array. This index is used with the remove algorithm of Section 7-7 to
delete the student account from the finance center records. The algorithm shifts
left one position the accounts from the tail of the list.

```cpp
// locate the student and remove the account
void FinanceCenter::removeAccount(const String& studID)
{
    int i, index;

    // use the sequential search to find the student
    if ((index = findAccount(studID)) == -1)
        cerr << "removeAcct(): Account " << studID
             << " is not removed" << endl;
    else
    {
        // shift acct[index+1]...acct[numAcct-1] to
        // the left one position to fill vacated slot
```

```
        for(i = index; i < numAcct-1; i++)
            acct[i] = acct[i+1];
        numAcct--; // decrement number of student records
    }
}
```

7-9   GRAPHING DICE TOSSES

Casino games often rely on the toss of dice to introduce the element of chance. With a single die, a toss produces one of six equally likely outcomes (1 to 6). When two dice are tossed, the total lies in the range 2 (both dice are 1) to 12 (both dice are 6). The outcomes are not equally likely. Just ask a craps player who sees the dreaded 7 in all too many tosses. The reason for this is that different dice combinations can result in the same total. For instance, a total of 4 can occur in three different ways $(1-3, 2-2, 3-1)$ while a 2 can occur only with $1-1$. Since each die has 6 different faces, the tossing of two dice result in 36 (6*6) different combinations. Table 7-3 gives a count of different combinations that would produce each total and a listing of these combinations.

TABLE 7-3   Tossing Two Dice.

Toss Total	Count	Different Combinations
2	1	1-1
3	2	1-2 2-1
4	3	1-3 2-2 3-1
5	4	1-4 2-3 3-2, 4-1
6	5	1-5 2-4 3-3 4-2 5-1
7	6	1-6 2-5 3-4 4-3 5-2 6-1
8	5	2-6 3-5 4-4 5-3 6-2
9	4	3-6 4-5 5-4 6-3
10	3	4-6 5-5 6-4
11	2	5-6 6-5
12	1	6-6

With fair dice, each of the 36 different combinations is equally likely to occur. This gives rise to a definition for the *theoretical probability* that a toss will produce a specific outcome (total).

Definition The theoretical probability that a total will occur from the toss of two dice is the ratio of the number of combinations that produce the total (com(total)) to the number of possible combinations.

$$thProbability(total) = com(total)/36$$

$$Example: thProbability(2) = 1/36$$

$$thProbability(6) = 5/36$$

The graph in Figure 7-3 plots com(total) for each total in the range 2 to 12. The high point of the graph is 7 which has the highest probability of occuring (6/36).

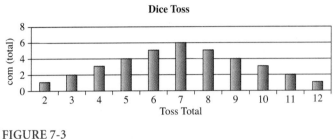

FIGURE 7-3
Dice Toss Frequency Graph.

A theoretical probability is one measure for the likelihood that a dice total will occur. An alternative approach uses a large set of experiments to evaluate another measure of likelihood, called the *empirical probability.*

Definition The *empirical probability* that a total will occur is determined by tossing two dice a great many times and recording the number of times the total occurs (number(total)). The empirical probablity is the ratio of number of times the total occurs to the number of tosses.

empProbability(total) = number (total)/NUMTOSSES

Example: Toss two dice 100,000 times. If a total of 7 occurs 16,423 times

empProbability(7) = 16,423/100000 = 0.16423

Using Simulation for Dice. We build a function that determines the empirical probability of getting each possible total on the toss of two dice. The tossing of the dice is simulated by the member function toss() from the Dice class.

dice.h

DESCRIPTION: Dice CLASS ▬▬▬▬▬▬▬▬

A Dice object simulates the tossing of dice.

Attributes:
   int numberOfDice; // number of dice to toss

Operations:

   Dice: Initialize numberOfDice to n.

                 Dice(int n = 2);

   getNumber: Return number of dice

                 int getNumber();

setNumber:	Set number of dice
	void setNumber(int n);
toss:	Toss the dice and return the total.
	int toss();

The constructor allows a Dice object to toss any number of dice. For our application, the argument is 2, since we are tossing two dice. The class has a simple member function that tosses the dice and returns the total for the n dice.

EXAMPLE 7.11

The example illustrates the declaration of a Dice object and its use in computing the empirical probability that the total 7 will occur on a single toss.

1. Declare two Dice objects and output a possible value from a toss.

```
Dice d(2), e(5);      // d tosses 2 dice and e tosses 5
cout << d.toss();     // outcome in range 2 to 12
cout << e.toss();     // outcome in range 5 to 30
```

2. A for loop uses the Dice object d to toss a pair dice a total of 30,000 times and record the number of sevens. The output displays the empirical probability of tossing a 7.

```
long number7 = 0;    // number of times 7 is tossed

for(i=0;i < 30000;i++)
   // count number of times 7 is tossed
   if (d.toss() == 7)
      number7++;
cout << "7 occurred " << number7
      << " times in 30000 tosses" << endl;
cout << "Empirical probability is "
      << number7/30000.0 << endl;

Sample output:

7 occurred 4935 times in 30000 tosses
Empirical probability is 0.1645
```

3. The Dice class has a default constructor, so it is possible to declare an array of Dice objects. If the objects are not intended to toss 2 dice, use the member function setNumber().

```
Dice diceArr[30];
int i;

// each object in diceArr tosses 3 dice
for(i=0; i < 30; i++)
   diceArr[i].setNumber(3);    ■
```

Computing the empirical probabilities for tossing two dice is implemented by the free function, dieToss(), that takes as arguments the total number of tosses and an array of real numbers that will be assigned the probabilities.

```
// toss two dice numberOfTosses times and return
// the empirical probabilities in the array prob
void diceToss(long numberOfTosses, double prob[])
```

The function uses a Dice object to toss two dice numberOfTosses times and record the outcomes in the locally defined array, tossCount. The value toss-Count[i] (2 ≤ i ≤ 12) is the number of times a total of i appears. The indices 0 and 1 are not used. For instance, if we toss numberOfTosses = 10,000 dice and get 750 fours and 1550 sevens, then tossCount[4] is 750 and toss-Count[7] is 1550.

After completing the simulation, the tossCount values are used to assign the empirical probabilities to the array prob.

```
prob[i] = double(tossCount[i])/ numberOfTosses, 2 < i < 12
```

The following is the implementation of the function. The code uses three for loops for the calculations. The first for loop initializes the elements of toss-Count to 0. The second loop carries out the tossing of the dice and assigns values to each element of tossCount. The final loop computes the empirical probability for the totals 2 through 12.

```
// toss two dice numberOfTosses times and return
// the empirical probabilities in the array prob
void diceToss(long numberOfTosses, double prob[])
{
    // tossCount[i] is number of times i is obtained
    // in numberOfTosses tosses, 2 <= i <= 12
    long toss, tossCount[13];
    int diceTotal;

    // use object that tosses 2 dice
    Dice d(2);

    int i;

    // clear each element of tossCount
    for(i=0; i <= 12; i++)
        tossCount[i] = 0;

    // toss the dice numberOfTosses times
    for(toss = 1; toss <= numberOfTosses; toss++)
    {
        diceTotal = d.toss();
        // increment number of times that diceTotal appears
        tossCount[diceTotal]++;
    }
```

```
    // convert the tossCount to a probability
    for(i = 2; i <= 12; i++)
        prob[i] = double(tossCount[i])/ numberOfTosses;
}
```

Graphing Dice Probabilities

With the function `diceToss()`, we have a method of computing the empirical probabilities that a total will occur when tossing two dice. We now use drawing objects to create a bar graph of these probabilites. If we create probabilities from a large number of tosses, the graph should look very similar to Figure 7-3 that displays theoretical probabilities.

The drawing of the graph is implemented with LineShape objects that draw the axes and RectShape objects that draw the bars. This is your first introduction to the `LineShape` class. Like the other drawing classes, this class has member functions `draw()`, `erase()`, `move()`, and so forth. What is special is the fact that its objects represent line segments specified by endpoints. A LineShape object is initialized by passing the x and y coordinates of each endpoint and the line color to the constructor. We limit our discussion of the class to a declaration of the constructor and a simple example that draws a triangle. The definition of the class is contained in the file **linesh.h** in the supplemental software.

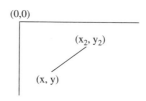

EXAMPLE 7.12

```
// constructor: sets base point (x,y), the
// second point (x2,y2) and the line segment's
// color
LineShape(double x = 0.0, double y = 0.0,
          double x2 = 0.0, double y2 = 0.0,
          ShapeColor c = darkgray);

    // the following code declares three sides of a
    // right triangle by defining their end points.
    // the draw() function creates the triangle
    // with the default color darkgray
    LineShape sideA(2,1,2,4), sideB(2,4,4,4),
              sideC(4,4,2,1);

    sideA.draw();          // side A
```

```
sideB.draw();        // side B
sideC.draw();        // side C
```

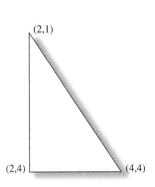

Using LineShape objects, the free function drawAxes() places the axes on the drawing surface. The origin is located at the point (1,5) with the height of the y-axis set to 4.25 and the width of the x-axis set to 4.

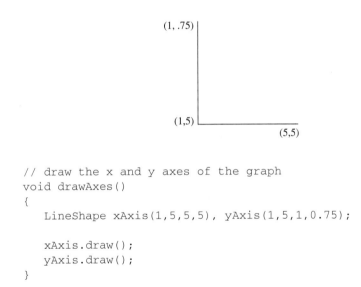

```
// draw the x and y axes of the graph
void drawAxes()
{
    LineShape xAxis(1,5,5,5), yAxis(1,5,1,0.75);

    xAxis.draw();
    yAxis.draw();
}
```

The bar graph is drawn by the function plot() that accepts the array of empirical probabilities as its argument. The function plot() uses the RectShape class to draw the bars in the graph in alternating colors of blue and dark gray. We separate the x span into 23 segments (dx = 4.0/23) so that we can plot the 11 bars and leave equally spaced gaps. We assume that the total 7 will occur approximately 1/6 of the time. A scaling factor Y_SCALE = 24 takes the probabilities and fits them into the 4 unit y-axis span. Note that (1/6)Y_SCALE = 4

The function uses Y_SCALE to set both the barHeight and the y value for the upper left-hand point of the bar.

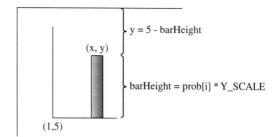

```
// plot the bar graph of empirical probabilities
void plot(double prob[])
{
    const double Y_SCALE = 24;
    double x, dx, y, barHeight;
    int i;
    RectShape bar;

    // now generate the rectangles
    dx = 4.0/23.0;          // 23 equal intervals in the 4 inches
    x = 1.0 + dx;           // set x at origin + dx

    // loop through totals 2 to 12. determine each bar height
    // as a percentage of 4 and then draw the bar
    for(i=2; i<= 12; i++)
    {
        barHeight = prob[i] * Y_SCALE;
        y = 5 - barHeight;
        bar.move(x,y);
        bar.setSides(dx, barHeight);
        if (i % 2 == 0)
            bar.setColor(blue);
        else
            bar.setColor(darkgray);
        bar.draw();
        x += 2*dx;
    }
}
```

APPLICATION 7-7 GRAPH THE DICE PROBABILITIES

The main program uses diceToss() with one-million tosses to compute the empirical probabilities.

```
const long NUMTOSSES = 1000000L;    // total number of tosses
double prob[13];

diceToss(NUMTOSSES, prob);             // toss the dice
```

It then opens the drawing window, draws the axes and plots the graph.

```
#include "dice.h"        // Dice class
#include "rectsh.h"      // RectShape class
#include "linesh.h"      // LineShape class
#include "trandom.h"     // RandomNumber class

// toss two dice numberOfTosses times and return
// the empirical probabilities in the array prob
void diceToss(long tossCount, double prob[]);

// draw the x and y axes of the graph
void drawAxes();

// plot the bar graph of empirical probabilities
void plot(double prob[]);

int main()
{
    const long NUMTOSSES = 1000000L;
    double prob[13];

    diceToss(NUMTOSSES, prob);    // toss the dice

    openWindow();                 // create the drawing surface

    plot(prob);                   // plot the graph
    drawAxes();                   // draw the axes
    viewWindow();                 // wait for a key stroke

    closeWindow();                // close the window

    return 0;
}

/* Code for diceToss(), drawAxes() and plot()
   given in the program discussion */
```

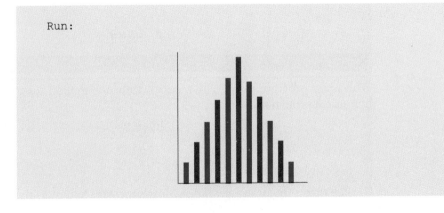

Run:

7-10 ARRAY SORTING ALGORITHM

Searching and sorting are fundamental list handling operations. We have already introduced generalized searching using the function `seqSearch()`. We now look at sorting which arranges items in ascending or descending order. The topic is one of the most heavily researched areas in computer science and involves a variety of techniques. We develop one method, called the selection sort, and look at the exchange sort in the exercises.

The *selection sort* uses an ordering technique that is probably familiar to you from grade school experience. Recall how a teacher might organize children to line up in order from shortest to tallest. Follow the teacher as she starts with the line Tom, Debbie, Mike, and Ron.

Tom Debbie Mike Ron
Starting Line

Step 1: She identifies Ron as the shortest child in the line and asks him to exchange positions with Tom, the first child in the line. The effect is to place the smallest child at the front of the line (Figure 7-4(a)).

Step 2: The line with Debbie, Mike, and Tom remains unordered. The teacher repeats the selection process and identifies that Tom is the shortest child in the group of remaining children and asks him to exchange positions with Debbie (Figure 7-4(b)).

Step 3: With Ron and Tom in position, only the last two children in line must be ordered. The teacher identifies Debbie as the next shortest child and asks her to exchange places with Mike. (Figure 7-4(c)).

After Step 3, the four children in the line are ordered. Mike, the tallest child, is correctly positioned as part of the exchange with Debbie.

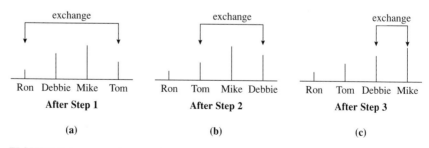

FIGURE 7-4
Selection Sort.

Selection Sort Algorithm. The selection sort algorithm is implemented by a function that takes an array and its size as arguments. The resulting array is sorted in ascending order so that

```
arr[0] <= arr[1] <= . . . <= arr[SIZE-2] <= arr[SIZE-1]
```

The function implementation features a for loop that repeatedly scans smaller and smaller sublists of the array. The selection sort algorithm consists of n-1 iterations that are also called *passes* since they involve a scan over elements in a sublist. The first pass looks at the full list of n elements; the second pass looks at a sublist with n-1 elements, and so forth. Each iteration looks at a sublist of unordered elements. After identifying the smallest element in the sublist, the value is exchanged with the first element in the sublist.

We illustrate the algorithm with a sample array consisting of the n = 5 integer values 50, 20, 40, 75, and 35. Figure 7-5 displays the state of the list after each of the four passes.

Pass 0: Scan the entire list from arr[0] to arr[4] and identify 20 as the smallest element. Exchange 20 with arr[0] = 50, the first element in the list. After completing pass 0, the first element is correcly positioned and the remaining sublist from arr[1] to arr[4] is unordered.

Pass 1: Scan the sublist 50, 40, 75, and 35. Exchange the smallest element 35 with arr[1] = 50. The front of the list (20, 35) is ordered and the sublist from arr[2] to arr[4] remains unordered.

Pass 2: Locate the smallest element in the sublist 40, 75, and 50. No exchange is necessary since 40 is already the first element in the sublist. The sublist from a[3] to a[4] remains unordered.

Pass 3: Two elements remained to be sorted. Scan the sublist 75, 50 and exchange the smaller element with arr[3]. The exchange places 50 in arr[3] and leaves the largest element in arr[4].

The function prototype for the selection sort takes an integer array arr and its size n as arguments.

```
void selectionSort(int arr[], int n);
```

The function implementation consists of nested for loops. The outer loop controls the n-1 passes over the list. The control object is called pass and ranges from 0 to n-2. For each iteration, an inner loop scans the unordered sublist arr[pass] to arr[n-1] and identifies the index of the smallest element. The index, called smallIndex, is used to exchange the smallest element with the first element in the sublist (arr[pass]). The swapping of elements is done by the function exchange() from Chapter 6.

```
void selectionSort(int arr[], int n)
{
    int smallIndex; // index of smallest element in the sublist
    int pass, j;

    // pass has the range 0 to n-2
```

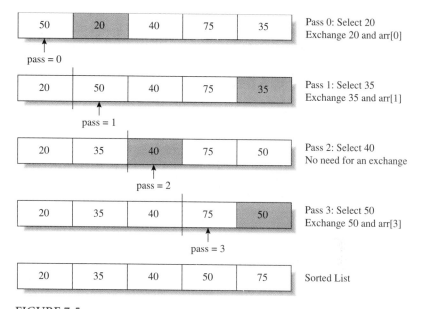

FIGURE 7-5
Sorting an Integer Array.

```
for (pass = 0; pass < n-1; pass++)
{
    // scan the sublist starting at index pass
    smallIndex = pass;

    // j traverses the sublist a[pass+1] to a[n-1]
    for (j = pass+1; j < n; j++)
        // update if smaller element found
        if (arr[j] < arr[smallIndex])
            smallIndex = j;

    // if smallIndex and pass are not the same location,
    // exchange smallest item in the sublist with arr[pass]
    if (smallIndex != pass)
        exchange(arr[pass], arr[smallIndex]);
}
}
```

APPLICATION 7-8 SORTING A LIST

The program uses a list of fifteen random integers in the range 0 to 99 to illustrate the selection sort. The function writeList() from **seqalgs.h** outputs the original list. After calling selectionSort() to arrange the elements of the list in ascending order, function writeList() is again called to display the sorted list.

The implementation of the functions exchange() and selection-Sort() are contained in file **selsort.h** of the supplemental software.

```
#include <iostream.h>

#include "trandom.h"    // generate random integers
#include "selsort.h"    // use selection sort with integer data
#include "seqalgs.h"    // for writeList()

int main()
{
    // list is the array of integers to sort
    int list[15];
    int i;
    // use rnd to generate random integers
    RandomNumber rnd;

    // fill list with random integers in the range 0 to 99
    for (i = 0; i < 15; i++)
        list[i] = rnd.random(100);

    // print original list, sort and print the sorted list
    cout << "Original List" << endl;
    writeList (list,15);
    cout << endl;
    selectionSort(list,15);
    cout << "Sorted List" << endl;
    writeList (list,15);

    return 0;
}
```

```
Run:

Original List
66  20  33  55  53  57  69  11  67  70  81  39  83  13
29

Sorted List
11  13  20  29  33  39  53  55  57  66  67  69  70  81
83
```

7-11 STRING OBJECTS

In this book, we have treated strings as though they were primitive objects. They have been used with the ">>" and "<<" operators for I/O and with operators like "<" and "+" for comparison and concatenation. With our understanding of arrays, we can revisit the String class and introduce indexing that enables us to look at the individual characters in a String object. In the process, we find a wide range of new applications.

The Index Operator []

String objects can be viewed as an array of characters whose size is determined by the length() member function. For instance, the String state = "California" has length 10. The first character is 'C' and the last character is 'a'.

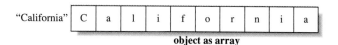

object as array

Using an array model, the String class provides the index operator "[]" that allows the program to access the individual characters.

S Y N T A X

The String Index Operator "[]"

Form:
```
String str;

char chFirst = str[0],              // first char
chLast = str[str.length()-1];       // last char
str[i] = '!';                       // assign '!' to
                                    //   i+1st char
```

Action: The index operator allows access to an individual string character in the range 0 to length() −1. Unlike arrays, strict bounds checking is enforced and any attempt to access a character with an index that is out of range terminates the program after an error message.

Example:
```
// compute length, output 1st and last char
String str = "walk";
int len = str.length();         // len = 4

cout << str[0] << str[len-1];   // print "wk"

// output the string backwards
for(i = str.length() - 1; i >= 0; i--)
    cout << str[i];

str[4] = '!'        // index 4 is out of range
```

String I/O

A String object may be placed in an input (">>") or output ("<<") stream. Like the primitive number and character objects, input uses whitespace separators to distinguish different strings.

```
ifstream fin;
String str1, str2;

// input next two strings
fin >> str1 >> str2;            // input: San Francisco
cout << str1 << "-" << str2;    // output: San-Francisco
```

To input "San Francisco" as a single string, we use the free function `getline()` that takes a stream argument and extracts a sequence of characters terminated by a delimiter. The extracted characters are stored in a String object that is passed by reference.

S Y N T A X ━━━━━━━━━━━━━━━━━━━━━━━━━━━━━━━━━━━━━

The getline Function

Form: `istream& getline(istream& istr, String& s,`
           `char delim);`

Action: The function reads characters from the input stream istr into String s until EOF or the delimiter is reached. The delimiter character is extracted from the stream but is not stored in the string.

           The logical expression `getline(istr,s,delim) != 0` can be used to identify an EOF condition.

Example:
```
// read an entire line of text
// from the keyboard, including  whitespace
getline(cin,str,'\n');

// from stream fin read a string up to ':'
getline(fin,str,':');
// read lines until EOF
while (getline(fin, str, '\n') != 0)
{. . .}
```

The `getline()` function allows for general string input. It is more powerful than the simple `">>"` operator, since it lets the programmer specify the input of all characters up to a delimiter. Successive calls to `getline()` can extract fields of information that are separated by the delimiter. For instance, an operating system password file may use a `':'` delimiter to separate the user name and password.

```
jdoe:v;g&aq#@95<&*     (entry for John Doe)
```

A series of two `getline()` statements extract the information.

```
String userName, userPwd;      // declare String objects
ifstream  fin;                 // declare a stream
    ...
getline(fin, userName,':');    // read user name   jdoe
getline(fin, userPwd,'\n');    // read password    v;g&aq#@95<&*
```

String Palindromes. In the wonderful world of word magic, a palindrome is a string that reads the same forward and backward. Upper and lowercase characters should be considered as equivalent and blanks and punctuation marks (. , ! ? : ; ' ") are not included. For instance, "did," "Madam I'm Adam" and "2442" are palindromes, while "computer" is not a palindrome. Determining whether a string is a palindrome is an excellent problem in string handling.

We restrict our example to palindromes of alphabetic characters. The string to be tested must be adjusted by removing all of its non-alphabetic characters and converting all of its alphabetic characters to lowercase. These actions are performed by the function `stripStr()` that accepts a string input argument and returns a string in the proper format.

```
// return lowercase string with blanks and punctuation
// characters removed
String stripStr()(const String& origStr)
{
    String modifiedString;
    int i;
    char c;

    // cycle through each char of the string
    for(i=0; i < origStr.length(); i++)
    {
        // get character at index i
        c = origStr[i];
        // see if c is alphabetic
        if (c >= 'A' && c <= 'Z' || c >= 'a' && c <= 'z')
        {
            // translate an uppercase character to lowercase
            if (c >= 'A' && c <= 'Z')
                c += 32;

            // add c onto the end modifiedString
            modifiedString += c;
        }
    }
    return modifiedString;
}
```

The function `isPalindrome()` tests whether a string str with lowercase characters and free of punctuation marks is a palindrome. It returns the result as a Boolean value.

```
bool isPalindrome(const String& str);
```

The algorithm uses a while loop and indices lowindex and highindex to perform a pair-wise matching of characters. The indices initially identify the two ends of the string with lowindex = 0 and highindex = str.length() − 1. Each iteration of the loop compares the characters at the respective indices and then updates the indices to move toward the center of the string. The loop continues as long as lowindex < highindex and the characters match. For instance, with str = "level," the algorithm compares `str[0]` = `'l'` with `str[4]` = `'l'` and `str[1]` = `'e'` with `str[3]` = `'e'`. For the next iteration, lowindex = 2 = highindex, and the loop terminates. The string 'level' is a palindrome. For str = "render", the function immediately exits the loop with a return value of false after recognizing that the pair 'n' and 'd' do not match (Figure 7-6).

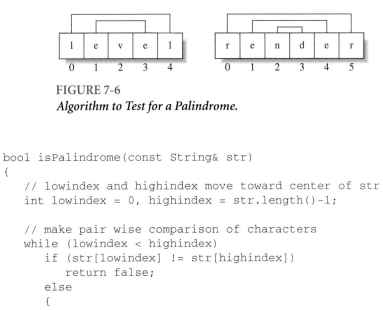

FIGURE 7-6
Algorithm to Test for a Palindrome.

```
bool isPalindrome(const String& str)
{
   // lowindex and highindex move toward center of str
   int lowindex = 0, highindex = str.length()-1;

   // make pair wise comparison of characters
   while (lowindex < highindex)
      if (str[lowindex] != str[highindex])
         return false;
      else
      {
         // move lowindex upward and highindex downward
         lowindex++;
         highindex--;
      }
   return true;
}
```

APPLICATION 7-9 PALINDROMES

The program uses the function `getline()` to read a string that may contain blanks. After calling function `stripStr()` to remove all non-alphabetic characters, the program passes the updated string to `isPalindrome()`. The original string and the result of the test are displayed.

```
#include <iostream.h>

#include "tstring.h"

// return lowercase string with blanks and punctuation
```

```
// characters removed
String stripStr(const String& origStr);

// test whether a lowercase string free of punctuation chars
// is a palindrome
bool isPalindrome(const String& str);

int main()
{
   String origString, modifiedString;

   // read a line of text from the keyboard
   getline(cin,origString,'\n');

   // prepare the string for the palindrome test
   modifiedString = stripStr(origString);

   // call isPalindrome(). output the original string and
   // the result
   if (isPalindrome(modifiedString))
      cout << '"' << origString << "\" is a palindrome"
           << endl;
   else
      cout << '"' << origString << "\" is not a palindrome"
           << endl;

   return 0;
}

/* implementations for stripStr() and isPalindrome() are given
   in the program discussion */
```

```
Run 1:

Yreka Bakery
"Yreka Bakery" is a palindrome

Run 2:

A Man, a plan, a canal, Panama.
"A Man, a plan, a canal, Panama." is a palindrome

Run 3:

C++ programming
"C++ programming" is not a palindrome
```

7-12   ADDITIONAL STRING MEMBER FUNCTIONS (OPTIONAL)

The String class provides a set of string-handling member functions that enable a program to search for characters within a string, extract consecutive sequences of characters called substrings, and modify a string by adding or removing characters. All of the operations use indices to identify positions within the string. Table 7-4 presents a list of selected operations that we will cover in this section. For each operation, the table describes its action and gives a function prototype. Examples illustrate each operation.

TABLE 7-4   Selected String Operations

Operation Name	Action and Prototype
	String Search Functions
find_first_of:	With character c and integer start as an argument, look for the first occurrence of c in the string beginning at index start. Return the index of the match if it occurs; otherwise return -1. By default, start is 0 and the function searches the entire string.
	`int find_first_of(char c, int start = 0);`
find_last_of:	With character c as an argument, look for the last occurrence of c in the string. Return the index of the match if it occurs; otherwise return -1.
	`int find_last_of(char c);`
find:	The search takes String s and index start and looks for a match of s as a substring. Return the index of the first character in the match if it occurs; otherwise return -1. By default, start is 0 and the function searches the entire string.
	`int find(const String& s, int start = 0);`
	String Copy and Update Functions
substr:	The function copies count characters from the string beginning at index start and returns the characters as a substring. If the tail of the string has fewer than count characters or count is -1, the copy stops at end-of-string. By default, start is 0 and the function copies characters from the beginning of the string. Also by default, the function copies the tail of the string.
	`String substr(int start = 0, int count = -1);`
insert:	Place the substring s into the string beginning at index start. The insertion expands the size of the original string.
	`void insert(int start, const String& s);`
remove:	Delete count characters from the string beginning at index start. If fewer than count characters exist or count is -1, delete up to end-of-string. By default, start is 0 and the function removes characters from the beginning of the string. Also by default, the function removes the tail of the string. Note that no arguments at all truncates the string to the NULL string.
	`void remove(int start = 0, int count = -1);`

String Search Functions

The String search functions look for single characters or substrings within a string. The process, referred to as *pattern matching,* is performed by a series of find operations. The member functions `find_first_of()` and `find_last_of()` look for a match with a single character c in the string. The `find_first_of()` search begins at index start in the string and looks for the first occurrence of c starting from that point on. When c is located in the string, the index of the match is the return value. Otherwise the function returns -1. Index start has default value 0 that causes the entire string to be searched. If start is not within the range of the string, the function returns -1. In a similar fashion, `find_last_of()` returns the index of the last occurrence of c in the string. Since the search seeks a match in the tail of the string, no starting index is provided.

```
// begin at index start and find index of c in the string
int find_first_of(char c, int start = 0);

// find the index of the last occurrence of c in the string
int find_last_of(char c);
```

EXAMPLE 7.13 ■■■■■■■■■■■■■■■■■■■■■■■■■■■■■■■■■■■■■■■

1. The string "Mississippi" always provides good pattern matching possibilities.

```
String str = "Mississippi";
int index;

// 's' occurs at indices 2, 3, 5, 6
index = str.find_first_of('s',0);      // index is 2
index = str.find_first_of('s',4);      // index is 5
index = str.find_first_of('s',7);      // index is -1
// find index of last 's' in the string
index = str.find_last_of('s');         // index is 6
```

2. The while loop outputs the index of each 'i' in str = "Mississippi".

```
index = 0;
while ((index = str.find_first_of('i',index)) != -1)
{
    cout << "'i' at index " << index << endl;
    index++;   // restart search at next index
}
Output:
    'i' at index 1
    'i' at index 4
    'i' at index 7
    'i' at index 10   ■
```

Locating a more complex pattern is done using the `find()` member function. The function takes String s and an index start as arguments and looks for match of s as a substring. A return value indicates the index of the first character of the matching substring or −1 if a match fails. Index start has default value 0, which implements a search of the entire list. If start is out of range, the function returns −1.

```
// start search at index start. s can be a C++ string literal
int find(const String& s, int start = 0);
```

EXAMPLE 7.14 ▬▬▬▬▬▬▬▬▬▬▬▬▬▬▬▬▬▬▬▬▬▬▬▬▬▬▬▬▬▬▬▬

Search for several patterns in the string str.

```
int index;
String str = "aabbccbbaa";

index = str.find("bb");        // match substring at index = 2
index = str.find("aabbc");     // match substring at index = 0
index = str.find("cbb", 3);    // match substring at index = 5
index = str.find("abba");      // index is -1 (no match)  ▪
```

Copying Substrings

The String class provides a member function substr() that allows a programmer to copy a substring and return it as a new string. The function creates a string containing a copy of the characters beginning at index start for count characters or until the end of the string. If the index is out of range, an empty string is returned. A second argument of −1 returns the tail of the string. If both default arguments are assumed, the entire string is copied.

```
// copy no more than count characters from
// index start to end of string
String substr(int start = 0, int count = -1);
```

EXAMPLE 7.15 ▬▬▬▬▬▬▬▬▬▬▬▬▬▬▬▬▬▬▬▬▬▬▬▬▬▬▬▬▬▬▬▬

1. ```
String str = "richardson", r;
int index;

r = str.substr(7,3);   // copy 3 chars from index 7; r = "son"

// identify index of "son" in str.
// copy characters before "son" into r
index = str.find ("son", 0);   // index is 7
// extract the substring of characters before "son".
// there are index characters at positions 0 to index-1
r = str.substr(0,index);   // r = "richard"
```

2. ```
String filename, fullpathname = "/directory/file";
index = fullpathname.find_last_of('/');   // index = 10

// filename starts at index+1. copy characters
```

```
// until end-of-string
filename = fullpathname.substr(index+1); // filename is
"file"  ■
```

Modifying a String

The functions `insert()` and `remove()` modify a string by adding and deleting characters. To this point, a programmer could use only concatenation ("+") to add characters onto the end of the string. The insert() member function extends this capability by allowing the addition of a string at an arbitrary index within the bounds of the string. If the index is out of range, the function simply returns.

```
// insert s at position start
void insert(int start, Const String& s);
```

To delete characters from a string, the remove() function extracts count characters beginning at index start. If the tail of the string has fewer than count characters or count is -1, the deletion occurs up to the end of the string. If the default is assumed for both arguments, the string becomes NULL. When start is out of range, the function simply returns.

```
// remove at most count characters from the string
void remove(int start = 0, int count = -1);
```

EXAMPLE 7.16 ■■■

1. Assume String str = "endfile". To create the string "end-of-file", the string "-of-" must be added at index 3 (str[3] = 'f').

```
str.insert(3, "-of-");      // str is "end-of-file"
```

2. Assume String s = "string object type";

```
s.remove(7,7);     // str is "string type"
// remove 4 characters beginning at index 3
s.remove(3,4);
cout << s;         // Output: "strtype"
```

3. With the `find_first_of()` and `remove()` functions, we can delete all blank characters from a string.

```
String str = "a man a plan a canal panama";
int index = 0;

// search for a blank until there are no more left
while ((index = str.find_first_of(' ', index)) != -1)
    str.remove(index,1);   // remove blank at index
cout << str;               // output: amanaplanacanalpanama  ■
```

Analyzing File Names

A program may find it necessary to analyze file names. The required algorithms provide a good application of string handling. A file can be specified by a *pathname* that contains a collection of names distinguished by the separator "/". A pathname may begin with the character '/' that represents the root directory. The sequence of names prior to the last '/' is called the *path*. The last name is the *filename*. For instance, consider files "introcs/string.cc" and "array.cc".

Pathname	introcs/string.cc		Pathname	array.cc
Path	introcs		Path	(none)
File	string.cc		File	array.cc

For our file name analysis, we read a pathname from the keyboard and output the path and the filename. If the filename ends in ".cc", we identify a C++ source file. Otherwise, we merely output the filename.

We outline the structure of the program and indicate the String member functions that apply.

1. Input the pathname and use the function `find_last_of()` to search for the last occurrence of '/' in the string. This character defines the end of the path and the beginning of the filename.
2. The path is the substring of all characters prior to the final '/'. The filename is all characters after the final '/'. Use the index of the last '/' and `substr()` to extract both the path and the filename.
3. The program concludes by analyzing the filename extension. Use the function `find_last_of()` to locate the index of the last "." in the filename. If it exists (return value is not −1), use substr() to extract the characters from "." to the end of the filename and compare the string with ".cc". If a match occurs, output the filename and the message "(C++ source file)"; otherwise, output filename.

```cpp
#include <iostream.h>

#include "tstring.h"

int main()
{
    String pathname, path, filename, extension;
    // index of '/' and '.'
    int slashIndex, dotIndex;

    cout << "Enter the path name: ";
    cin >> pathname;

    //identify index of last '/'
    slashIndex = pathname.find_last_of('/');

    // tail of pathname is the filename
```

```
        filename = pathname.substr (slashIndex +1,
           pathname.length());

        // if '/' was found, pathname is characters prior
        // to the last '/'; otherwise, path is NULL
        if (slashIndex != -1)
           path = pathname.substr(0,slashIndex);
        else
           path = "";

        cout << "Path: " << path << endl;

        cout << "File: " << filename;
        // see if the filename has an extension
        if ((dotIndex = filename.find_last_of('.')) != -1)
        {
           extension = filename.substr(dotIndex,filename.length());
           // check if the filename ends in ".cc"
           if (extension == ".cc")
              cout << "   (C++ source file)";
        }
        cout << endl;

        return 0;
   }
```

```
   Run 1:

   Enter the path name: class/programs/testfile
   Path: class/programs
   File: testfile

   Run 2:

   Enter the path name: /strings/demo.cc
   Path: /strings
   File: demo.cc   (C++ source file)

   Run 3:

   Enter the path name: program.exe
   Path:
   File: program.exe
```

7-13 MULTIDIMENSIONAL ARRAYS

The array type allows a program to access a collection of data using indices. We have focused on one-dimensional arrays that use a single index. C++ allow a program to define multi-dimensional arrays that use two or more indices.

SYNTAX ▬▬▬▬▬▬▬▬▬▬▬▬▬▬▬▬▬▬▬▬▬▬▬▬▬▬▬

Multidimensional Arrays

Form: `Type arrayName[SIZE`$_1$`][SIZE`$_2$`] . . . [SIZE`$_n$`]`

Action: The declaration allocates space for a list of SIZE$_1$*SIZE$_2$*. . .*SIZE$_n$ data items. All of the elements in the list are of the same object type. The individual elements are accessed with the arrayName and index references [i$_1$][i$_2$] . . . [i$_n$]. The range of values for index k is 0 to SIZE$_k$ −1.

Example: `double arr[3][2];`   `// 3 x 2 two-dimensional array`
           `int x[3][3][5];`   `// three-dimensional array`

           `arr[0][1] = 5.3;`
           `x[1][2][4] = 7;`

Two-Dimenisonal Arrays. Our study looks at a two-dimensional array that accesses elements by row and column indices. This is the most commonly used multi-dimensional array and finds important applications in databases and applied mathematics. The restriction to two dimensions does not hinder our learning most of the important concepts.

A two-dimensional array can be viewed as a table consisting of rows and columns of data. The C++ declaration of the two-dimensional array tarr begins with the object type of the elements and then places the number of rows and columns in the table in separate brackets.

```
Type tarr [rowCount][columnCount];
```

For instance, the following statement declares an integer array with three rows and four columns. We refer to tarr as a 3 by 4 array.

```
int tarr[3][4];
```

The array has 12 (3 * 4) elements of type int. The elements are referenced using the array name, tarr, and row and column indices (Figure 7-7).

```
tarr[i][j], 0 ≤ i ≤ rowCount-1, 0 ≤ j ≤ columnCount-1.
```

	COLUMN								
	0	1	2	3		0	1	2	3
0	tarr[0][0]	tarr[0][1]	tarr[0][2]	tarr[0][3]	0	-5	7	-6	-11
ROW 1	tarr[1][0]	tarr[1][1]	tarr[1][2]	tarr[1][3]	1	0	8	3	25
2	tarr[2][0]	tarr[2][1]	tarr[2][2]	tarr[2][3]	2	-20	16	10	6

                    (a)   (b)

FIGURE 7-7

A 3 by 4 Array Displaying (a) *Index References* (b) *Individual Values.*

From the table

```
cout << tarr[1][1];              // output 8
if (tarr[0][1] < tarr[1][0])     // condition is false (7 >= 0)
   . . .
tarr[2][3] = t[0][2] * 3;        // replace 6 with -18 (-6 * 3)
```

Initializing Two-Dimensional Arrays. A program can provide run-time initialization of a two-dimensional array using nested for loops or compile time initialization using an array initializer list. In the process, values are assigned into the table one row at a time. For instance, the following nested loops initialize the three by four array tarr with all 0s.

```
int row, column;

for (row = 0; row < 3; row++)
    for (column = 0; column < 4; column++)
        tarr[row][column] = 0.
```

A two-dimensional array can be viewed as a sequence of rows that are in fact one-dimensional arrays. The number of elements in each row is the value columnCount. A compile-time initialization list contains a sequence of initial row values enclosed in braces. The row values are comma-separated blocks of data using the format for the initialization of one-dimensional arrays. For primitive object type, any missing data values are set to 0. For instance, the following declaration of tarr corresponds to the data in Figure 7-7(b).

```
int tarr[3][4] = {{-5,7,-6,-11},{0,8,3,25},{-20,16,10,6}};
```

EXAMPLE 7.17 ██

1. A school classroom lines up seats in rows and columns. A two dimensional array of strings called seatChart creates a five by six seating chart that lists the students by name. Nested for loops fill the chart by reading names from the keyboard, row by row.

```
const int ROWS = 5;
const int COLUMNS = 6;
String seatChart[ROWS][COLUMNS];
```

Initialization Code:

```
for (i = 0; i < ROWS; i++)
    for (j = 0; j < COLUMNS; j++)
        getline(cin,seatChart[i][j],'\n');
```

2. The table temp is a three by two array of double values where the columns correspond to the low and high temperature of the day.

```
double temp[3][2] = {{38.5, 68.2},{50.0,72.8}};
```

The declaration does not include any values for day three (row 2). These initial values are set to 0.

	Low	High
Day 1	38.5	68.2
Day 2	50.0	72.8
Day 3	0	0

3. C++ stores a two-dimensional array tarr[m][n] as an sequence of one-dimensional arrays whose sizes are each specified by the number of columns n. The language allows a program to use the first index to identify an entire row as a single unit (one-dimensional array).

```
tarr[i]:   list of n data items in row i where 0 <= i < m
```

In Figure 7-7, the rows of tarr are one-dimensional arrays tarr[0], tarr[1], and tarr[2].

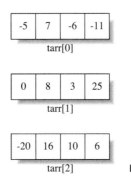

PROGRAM 7.4

In a two-dimensional array, each row can be passed as an argument to a function that handles one-dimensional arrays. In this program, the function writeList() displays a list of integer values. To output the full two-dimensional array, a for loop sequences through the rows and calls `writeList()` on each iteration. The data is taken from Figure 7-7.

```cpp
#include <iostream.h>
#include <iomanip.h>

// display the elements of arr on the screen
void writeList(int arr[], int size);

int main()
{
    int i;

    // declare a 3 x 4 array
    const int ROWS = 3;
    const int COLUMNS = 4;
    int tarr[ROWS][COLUMNS] = {{-5,7,-6,-11},{0,8,3,25},
                               {-20,16,10,6}};
```

```
    // use writeList() to output each row of tarr
    for (i = 0; i < ROWS; i++)
    {
        writeList(tarr[i],COLUMNS);
        cout << endl;
    }

    return 0;
}

void writeList(int arr[],int size)
{
    int i;

    for (i = 0; i < size; i++)
        cout << setw(4) << arr[i];
}
```

```
Run:

 -5    7  -6 -11
  0    8   3  25
-20   16  10   6
```

Two-dimensional Array Arguments

A program may use two-dimensional arrays as function arguments. In the function prototype, the formal array argument must list the number of elements in each column. This is required, since access to array elements depends on knowing the number of elements in each row. Two-dimensional array access is discussed later in this section. Use the notation "[]" for the row dimension, as we did with one-dimensional array arguments. In the following declaration, N is an integer literal or a constant integer object that specifies the number of elements in each column.

```
returnType f (Type tarr[][N], …);
```

For instance, the function maxArray() returns the largest element in a two-dimensional array with 4 columns.

```
// return the maximum of the array elements
// m is the number of rows, and each row has 4 elements
int maxArray(int a[][4], int m)
{
    int i,j;
    int maxValue = a[0][0];              // initialize maxValue

    for(i=0; i < m; i++)                 // scan rows
        for(j=0; j < 4; j++)             // scan columns
```

```
                if (a[i][j] > maxValue)    // if a[i][j] is larger,
                    maxValue = a[i][j];    // update maxValue

            return maxValue;
        }
```

The function, `maxValue()`, can be used only with two-dimensional integer arrays having exactly four columns. In calling the statement, we pass the name for a declared array. For instance, we can call `maxArray()` to find the maximum value of the array tarr in Figure 7-7.

```
    max = maxArray(tarr,3);    // pass array and row count. max = 25
```

Exploring
Concepts

The *transpose* of an n x n square matrix is the matrix obtained by interchanging its rows and columns. We express this mathematically by noting that `transpose[i][j] = arr[j][i]`. Write a function, transpose(), that computes the transpose of a square matrix having three rows and three columns.

```
    // store the transpose of arr in trans
    void transpose(double arr[][3], double trans[][3]);
```

Can you give the prototype for a new version of `transpose()` that changes the original matrix into its transpose?

The SqMatrix Class

A two-dimensional array, often called a *matrix,* is important in engineering and scientific applications. In this section, we explore *square matrices* (same number of rows and columns) whose data items are real numbers. We develop the class, SqMatrix, that handles I/O and basic arithmetic operations for square matrices.

Matrix Operations. A set of operations is defined for square matrices. The sum or difference of two matrices A and B results from adding or subtracting corresponding elements in the matrices. The scalar product of a real number k and a matrix A is a matrix consisting of the elements in A multiplied by k.

Addition: $C = A + B$

C is the matrix with entries $C[i][j]$ whose value is the sum $A[i][j] + B[i][j]$.

Subtraction: $C = A - B$

C is the matrix with entries with entries $C[i][j]$ whose value is the difference $A[i][j] - B[i][j]$.

$$C = \begin{bmatrix} 2 & 1 & 6 \\ 3 & -1 & 2 \\ 0 & 3 & 5 \end{bmatrix} + \begin{bmatrix} 1 & 5 & 4 \\ 2 & 7 & 8 \\ 1 & -9 & 3 \end{bmatrix} = \begin{bmatrix} 3 & 6 & 10 \\ 5 & 6 & 10 \\ 1 & -6 & 8 \end{bmatrix}$$

$$C = \begin{bmatrix} 2 & 1 & 6 \\ 3 & -1 & 2 \\ 0 & 3 & 5 \end{bmatrix} - \begin{bmatrix} 1 & 5 & 4 \\ 2 & 7 & 8 \\ 1 & -9 & 3 \end{bmatrix} = \begin{bmatrix} 1 & -4 & 2 \\ 1 & -8 & -6 \\ -1 & 12 & 2 \end{bmatrix}$$

Scalar Multiplication: $\quad C = kA$

C is the matrix with entries $C[i][j]$ whose value is the product $k*A[i][j]$.

$$C = 2 * \begin{bmatrix} 2 & 1 & 6 \\ 3 & -1 & 2 \\ 0 & 3 & 5 \end{bmatrix} = \begin{bmatrix} 4 & 2 & 12 \\ 6 & -2 & 4 \\ 0 & 6 & 10 \end{bmatrix}$$

The SqMatrix class implements these arithmetic operations along with input and output of square matrices.

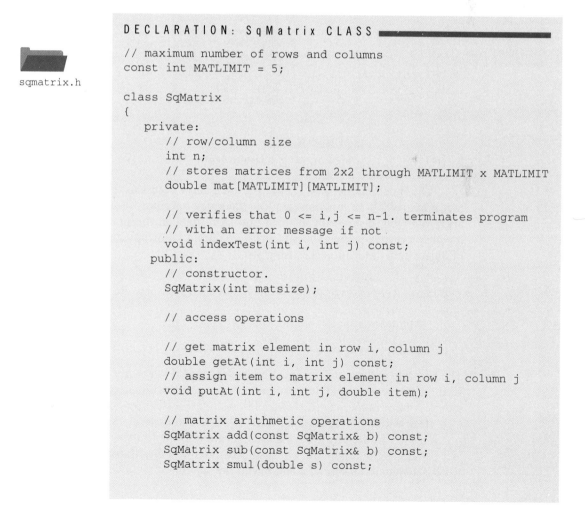

DECLARATION: SqMatrix CLASS ━━━━━━━━━━

sqmatrix.h

```
// maximum number of rows and columns
const int MATLIMIT = 5;

class SqMatrix
{
    private:
        // row/column size
        int n;
        // stores matrices from 2x2 through MATLIMIT x MATLIMIT
        double mat[MATLIMIT][MATLIMIT];

        // verifies that 0 <= i,j <= n-1. terminates program
        // with an error message if not
        void indexTest(int i, int j) const;
    public:
        // constructor.
        SqMatrix(int matsize);

        // access operations

        // get matrix element in row i, column j
        double getAt(int i, int j) const;
        // assign item to matrix element in row i, column j
        void putAt(int i, int j, double item);

        // matrix arithmetic operations
        SqMatrix add(const SqMatrix& b) const;
        SqMatrix sub(const SqMatrix& b) const;
        SqMatrix smul(double s) const;
```

```
        // matrix I/O operations
        void readMatrix();
        void writeMatrix() const;
};
```

The class has a constructor that is passed the row and column size of the matrix which is copied to n. The object mat stores the array elements in its first n rows and columns (Figure 7-8). Since mat is a MATLIMIT × MATLIMIT matrix, we require that n ≤ MATLIMIT.

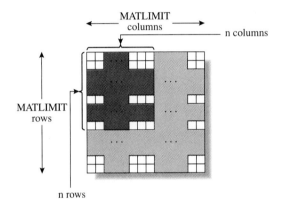

FIGURE 7-8
Using a Subset of a Larger Array.

The functions getAt() and putAt() allow access to the elements of the n × n matrix. These functions act like the index operator for a one-dimensional array, allowing a program to fetch and store data in the matrix. The function getAt() retrieves the element in row i, column j. For update, assign the value of object item at location (i,j) using putAt().

```
SqMatrix twodArray(3);
double item;

// increase the value at (2,3) by 8
item = twodArray.getAt(2,3);
twodArray.putAt(2,3,item+8);
```

The row and column indices must lie in the range $0 \leqslant i \leqslant n - 1, 0 \leqslant j \leqslant n - 1$. Both of the access functions terminate the program with an error message if an index is out of range.

The arithmetic operations add(), sub() and smul() all return a new n × n matrix formed by applying the operation to the Matrix object and the object passed as the argument. For instance, if a and b are Matrix objects, the matrix c is assigned the sum of a and b with the statement

```
c = a.add(b);
```

Input of a matrix is done by entering the data row by row. The first n input values are the elements of row 0, the next n are the elements of row 1, and so forth. Output is also done by row. The first row is output, followed by the second row on the next line, and so forth.

EXAMPLE 7.18

```
SqMatrix a(2), b(2), c(2);    // 2 x 2 matrices
double item;

a.readMatrix();               // enter the rows of a
b.readMatrix();               // enter the rows of b
cout << endl;

c = a.add(b);                 // c = a + b
c.writeMatrix();              // output the sum
cout << endl;
item = c.getAt(1,1);          // get value in row 1, col 1
c.putAt(1,1,item+2);          // update value in row 1, col 1
c.writeMatrix();              // output updated matrix

Input:
1 5
-1 7
3 4
5 8

Output:
   4.00   9.00
   4.00  15.00

   4.00   9.00
   4.00  17.00   ■
```

SqMatrix Class Implementation. We present the implementation of selected member functions. Consult the software supplement for the implementation of the remaining functions.

Access Functions:

In the design of the SqMatrix class, we check that all access functions are passed index values that are in range. Good code design indicates that we should develop a private function to handle the bounds checking. The function indexTest() outputs a message and terminates the program in case of an index error.

```
void SqMatrix::indexTest(int i, int j) const
{
   bool badindex = false;

   if (i < 0 || i >= n)
```

```
    {
        cerr << "row index " << i << " out of range" << endl;
        badindex = true;
    }
    if (j < 0 || j >= n)
    {
        cerr << "column index " << j << " out of range" << endl;
        badindex = true;
    }
    if (badindex)
        exit(1);
}
```

The function getAt() uses indexTest() to verify the indices i, j are valid and then returns the matrix element in row i, column j.

```
double SqMatrix::getAt(int i, int j) const
{
    // verify that i and j are proper indices
    indexTest(i,j);

    // return the element in row i, column j
    return mat[i][j];
}
```

SqMatrix Operations:

The add() operation must return a new matrix that is the sum of the current object and the argument matrix b. For addition to be defined, the dimension of the current object n must equal the dimension of the object b (b.n). We cannot add a 2×2 matrix to a 3×3 matrix! If the dimensions are not the same, the function outputs an error message and terminates the program. Otherwise, it declares a SqMatrix object c with n rows and columns and cycles through c by rows, forming the sum. Object c is the return value.

```
// returns sum of the current object and b.
// current object is not changed.
SqMatrix SqMatrix::add(const SqMatrix& b) const
{
    int i, j;

    if (b.n != n)
    {
        cerr << "add(): matrices have different sizes" << endl;
        exit(1);
    }

    SqMatrix c(n);    // c will be the sum

    // cycle through the rows
    for (i = 0; i < n; i++)
```

```
        // for each row, cycle thru the columns, forming sum
        for (j = 0; j < n; j++)
            c.mat[i][j] = mat[i][j] + b.mat[i][j];
    return c;
}
```

Input/Output for SqMatrix Objects:

It is most natural to perform matrix input one row at a time. Just cycle through the rows and input the elements.

```
// reads matrix elements by rows
void SqMatrix::readMatrix()
{
    double item;
    int i, j;

    for (i = 0; i < n; i++)          // scan rows
        for (j = 0; j < n; j++)      // get row data
        {
            cin >> item;             // read element
            mat[i][j] = item;        // store element
        }
}
```

APPLICATION 7-11 MATRIX OPERATIONS

A program illustrates the SqMatrix class with its I/O and arithmetic operations. The two-dimensional array tarr with three rows and three columns is initialized using an array initialization list. Using the function putAt() in a loop, the 3 × 3 Matrix object arrA is assigned the values in tarr. After displaying arrA using writeMatrix(), the 3 × 3 Matrix object arrB is input using readMatrix(). The matrix operations are tested by computing and displaying the scalar product of 2 and arrA and the difference of arrA and arrB.

```
#include <iostream.h>
#include <iomanip.h>

#include "SqMatrix.h"              // include the SqMatrix class

int main()
{
    double tarr[3][3] = { {1,2,3}, {2,4,5}, {4,7,-9}};
    int i, j;

    // declare three 3 x 3 Matrix objects
    SqMatrix arrA(3), arrB(3), arrC(3);

    // initialize arrA using tarr and putAt().
    // scan the rows
    for (i = 0; i < 3; i++)
        // for each row scan columns
```

```
        for (j = 0; j < 3; j++)
            arrA.putAt(i,j, tarr[i][j]);    // stores the element

    // output matrix arrA
    cout << "Matrix arrA:" << endl;
    arrA.writeMatrix();
    cout << endl;

    // read matrix arrB
    cout << "Enter a 3 x 3 matrix arrB by rows:" << endl;
    arrB.readMatrix();
    cout << endl;

    // compute scalar product of 2 and arrA
    arrC = arrA.smul(2);
    cout  << "Matrix 2 * arrA:" << endl;
    arrC.writeMatrix();
    cout << endl;

    // compute the difference of arrA and arrB
    cout  << "Matrix arrA - arrB:" << endl;
    arrC = arrA.sub(arrB);
    arrC.writeMatrix();
    cout << endl;

    return 0;
}
```

```
Run:

Matrix arrA:
        1.00        2.00        3.00
        2.00        4.00        5.00
        4.00        7.00       -9.00

Enter a 3 x 3 matrix arrB by rows:
 5 6 2
-9 3 7
 2 3 5

Matrix 2 * arrA:
        2.00        4.00        6.00
        4.00        8.00       10.00
        8.00       14.00      -18.00

Matrix arrA - arrB:
       -4.00       -4.00        1.00
       11.00        1.00       -2.00
        2.00        4.00      -14.00
```

The Storage of Two-Dimensional Arrays (Optional)

C++ stores arrays in consecutive memory locations. For a two-dimensional array, the storage occurs by row. The elements in row 0 are followed by the elements in row 1, and so forth. The size of each block is determined by column-Count. The three by four demonstration array, tarr, in Figure 7-9 allocates the 12 consecutive memory locations. The items are stored in the order tarr[0], tarr[1], and tarr[2]

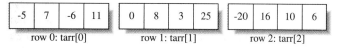

| -5 | 7 | -6 | 11 | | 0 | 8 | 3 | 25 | | -20 | 16 | 10 | 6 |

row 0: tarr[0]   row 1: tarr[1]   row 2: tarr[2]

FIGURE 7-9
Physical Storage for Array tarr.

To locate an element from memory, the compiler uses an access function that returns the location of the element. In addition to the indices, the access function requires information on the starting location of the array, the size of the data type, and the number of columns.

Type tarr [rowCount][columnCount]:

    Starting address: tarr

    Number of columns: columnCount

    Object type size: size = sizeof(Type)

To identify an element in memory, the array access function computes the offset from the start of the array to element tarr[i][j]. The address of tarr[i][j] is tarr + offset.

To understand how the compiler computes the offset, look at an element tarr[i][j] that is located in the i+1st row of the array and the j+1st element of the row. In memory, the offset covers i complete rows with columnCount elements in each row plus j elements into row i. To measure the offset in bytes, multiply the number of elements times the size of the element type.

$$\text{location } T[i][j] = \text{starting location} + \text{offset}$$
$$= \text{tarr} + (i * \text{columnCount} + j) * s$$

EXAMPLE 7.19 ▬▬▬▬▬▬▬▬▬▬▬▬▬▬▬▬▬▬▬▬▬▬▬▬▬▬

Assume array tarr has a starting location of 1000 in memory (Figure 7-10) and the size of an int object is 2.

    Starting address: 1000

    Number of rows: 3

    Number of columns: 4

    Object type size: 2 = sizeof(int)

Address of tarr[1][3] = 1000 + (1 * 4 + 3) * 2
                    = 1014 ■

FIGURE 7-10
Storage of a Two-Dimensional Array.

CHAPTER 7 SUMMARY

This chapter introduces the one-dimensional array that stores a collection of data items using a single identifier. The data items are stored sequentially and are accessed using the index operator "[]".

The array name is a constant and is the address of its first element. The index operator accesses the array elements using an array access formula that depends on the array address, the number of bytes of storage required for the element type and the index. If an array has SIZE elements, care must be taken to assure that an index lies in the range $0 \leq i \leq SIZE-1$. C++ provides no array bounds checking.

An array can be initialized in its declaration by enclosing the initial values in braces ({ }) and separating them by commas. The initialization list can specify all or a subset of the array element values.

When an array is used as a function argument, it is necessary to pass only the address of the array and the element type as arguments. The array access formula is used by the function to read or write the array elements. Since C++ does not attach size information to an array, it is necessary to pass the number of array elements to the function so that the function uses indices that are in range.

Arrays of class objects can be declared, as long as the class has a constructor that does not require any arguments. Most of the classes in the book have these default constructors, including the Rectangle, StudentAccount and Date classes. Arrays of objects are illustrated with the problem of computing a house painter's schedule by using arrays of Date objects.

The generation of random numbers plays a very important role in the creation of computer games and in event simulation. The class, RandomNumber, generates both random integer and random floating point numbers. It will be used throughout the book to generate data for testing algorithms that perform searching, sorting, and so forth. In Section 7-9, it is used in an application that draws a bar graph depicting the results of tossing two dice 1,000,000 times.

Section 7-7 develops two array algorithms. The classical sequential search is used to locate a key in a list. It traverses the list, comparing each element with the key. If successful in locating the key, it returns the key's index. Failure is indicated by returning a value of -1. The section also develops the algorithm to remove an element from an array by shifting the tail of the list to the left. The two algorithms are applied to the problem of removing all duplicate values from a list.

In this book, there are a number of important classes that declare an array as a data member. These include the String class that we have used throughout the book and the Vector class developed in Chapter 10. In Section 7-8 of this chapter, we develop the class, FinanceCenter, that includes an array of StudentAccount objects as a data member. We use the class to show how a college finance center might maintain account information for the student body.

Array sorting is one of the most important and heavily researched topics in computer science. This chapter develops the selection sort, which is relatively easy to understand. The process is similar to the actions of a teacher who orders students from shortest to tallest. Find the shortest student and switch him or her with the first student in line. Find the next shortest student and switch him/her with the 2nd student in line, and so forth. The algorithm is demonstrated by ordering a list of random integers.

Throughout the book, we have used strings like primitive number and character types. In Section 7-11 we revisit the String type and show that the array index operator "[]" can be used to access the individual characters in a string. We also introduce the free function, `getline()`, that allows a program to input a string of characters terminated by a delimiter. The string can include whitespace characters. The index operator and `getline()` are applied to the problem of determining whether a string is a palindrome. In the optional Section 7-12, we introduce you to the a wide variety of String member functions that do pattern matching and string editing.

Section 7-13 develops multidimensional arrays, which have applications in data processing, engineering and science. The concepts are illustrated by the development of the SqMatrix class that implements square matrix I/O and arithmetic operations.

Classes in the Chapter

Name	*Implementation File*
Date	date.h
Dice	dice.h
FinanceCenter	finacct.h
LineShape	linesh.h
SqMatrix	sqmatrix.h
RandomNumber	trandom.h
RectShape	rectsh.h
Statistics	stats.h
String	tstring.h
StudentAccount	studacct.h

KEY TERMS

Address:
The location of data in computer memory.

Anonymous object:
Result of applying a constructor outside a declaration to build an object for use in assignment statements and other expressions. For instance, the construct "d = Date(1,4,1998)" assigns d the date January 4, 1998.

Array access formula: (One-dimensional array)
Uses the index i, the size of each array object, and the starting address of the array to locate element arr[i] in memory.

Array access formula: (Two-dimensional array)
Uses the indices i and j, the size of each array object, the number of columns in the array, and the starting address of the array to locate element tarr[i][j] in memory.

Array bounds checking:
Verifying that an array index, i ,lies in the correct range $0 \leqslant i \leqslant$ SIZE-1. Most C++ compilers do not add machine code that tests whether an index is within the array bounds.

Array function argument:
Method of passing an array to a function without copying all of its elements. The function call passes the run-time array name, which has the effect of copying the address of the array to the corresponding formal argument. When the formal argument is used with the index operator, the array access formula is applied and the elements of the run-time array are accessed.

Array initialization list:
A sequence of values enclosed by braces and separated by commas. The initialization list gives initial values to items in the array in increasing order of their indices.

Default constructor:
A constructor that can be called with no arguments. This occurs when the constructor does not have arguments or each argument has a default value. A default constructor is needed if the programmer declares arrays of the class type.

Index operator:
Operator "[]" that allows for direct access to the elements in an array. The operator uses an integer index in the range 0 to $\text{SIZE} - 1$.

One-dimensional array:
A finite sequence of objects of the same data type in which each object is accessed by using an index. The declaration has the form "Type arrayName[SIZE], . . . ;".

Random number generator:
Returns non-negative integers in a range 0 to n such that each possible number has an equal chance of occurring. A generator may also return real numbers in the range 0 to 1 such that $\frac{1}{2}$ are likely to be greater than 0.5, $\frac{1}{4}$ are likely to be less than 0.25, and so forth.

Selection sort:
Puts an array in ascending order. Find the index, minIndex, of the minimum element in arr[0] to arr[n-1] and exchange arr[minIndex] with arr[0]. Find the index of the minimum element in arr[1] to arr[n−1] and exchange arr[minIndex] with arr[1], and so forth. After n-1 passes, the list is ordered.

Sequential array access:
Beginning at some index i, access the array elements in the order arr[i], arr[i+1], . . . , arr[SIZE−1].

Sequential search:
An algorithm with designated indices start and end. It begins at the start position and successively compares each element with a key until the key is found or the end index is reached. If the key is found in the list, the algorithm returns its index; otherwise the value −1 is returned.

Sizeof operator:
Unary operator that takes either a type or an object as its operand and returns the number of bytes of memory required to store any object of the given type or to store the specific object.

String getline() function:
Reads characters from an input stream into a String object until end-of-line or a delimiter is reached. The delimiter character is extracted from the stream but is not stored in the string. The function allows general string input.

Two-dimensional array:
Describes a table of objects accessed by row and column indices.

REVIEW EXERCISES

1. (a) Declare an array of ten integers whose name is list.
   (b) Identify the item that is the 3rd element in the array.
   (c) Create an assignment statement that copies the 4th element of the array into the 2nd element of the array.
   (d) Write a for loop that will initialize the array to have values 0, 1, 2, . . . , 9

2. (a) Declare and initialize a 5 element integer array arr whose values are 2, −1, 0, 1, 2.
   (b) Declare an integer array daysInMonth and initialize it to contain the number of days in each of the twelve calendar months.

3. What is the output of this code segment?

```
int a[6], i, sum;

for (i=0 ; i < 6; i++)
    a[i] = i+1;

sum = 0;
for(i=5 ; i>=0; i--)
    sum += a[i];
cout << sum << endl;
```

4. The array arr is declared as

```
short arr[5];
```

   (a) How many bytes are allocated for the array?
   (b) If the address of the array is arr = 6000, compute the address of arr[3].

5. Consider the function

```
void f(int a[], int n, int item)
{
    int i;

    for(i=0;i < n;i++)
        if (a[i] < 0)
            a[i] = item;
}
```

   Assume the declaration

```
int q[5] = {-1, 5, 3, -77, -9};
```

   (a) What is the contents of q upon return from the call

```
f(q, 5, 0);
```

   (b) What is the contents of q upon return from the call

```
f(q, 3, 55);
```

6. (a) Declare an array of 10 double values, arr, and use a for loop to give it initial values 90 to 99.

(b) Use the Statistics class from Section 7.4. Declare a Statistics object, statArr, that will compute statistical data for the array arr.

(c) Output the minimum, maximum and mean values for the numbers 90 to 99.

7. The classes One and Two are used as object types in the declaration of arrays a, b, and c.

```
class One                          class Two
{                                  {
    private:                           private:
        int value;                         double fvalue;
    public:                            public:
        One(int v = 0);                    Two(double v);
        int getValue();                    double getValue();
};                                 };
```

```
One a[20];                                      // declaration 1
Two b[20];                                      // declaration 2
Two c[3] = {Two(1.2), Two(3.9), Two(4.5)};      // declaration 3
```

Which declarations are valid?

8. If rnd is a RandomNumber object, what are the ranges for each random number?
(a) int n = rnd.random(100) * 2 + 1;
(b) double x = rnd.fRandom() * 2;

9. (a) What is the return value from seqSearch?

```
int arr[] = {4, 7, -6, 12, 14, 33, 23, 55}, returnVal;
```

(1) returnVal = seqSearch(arr,0,7,33);
(2) returnVal = seqSearch(arr,3,7,23);
(3) returnVal = seqSearch(arr,0,7,17);

(b) What are the contents of arr and size after the statements

```
size = 8;
remove(arr,2);
```

10. The FinanceCenter class has a data member acct that is an array of objects. Declare a FinanceCenter object, fc, and write code to insert into fc a student record with the following information:

```
Student ID:     4567-53
Name:           David Willingstone
Balance:        $-75.00
```

11. Write a code segment that uses a Dice object, d, to determine the empirical probability that a total of 9 occurs when tossing 3 dice. Use 1,000,000 trials.

12. (a) Declare a LineShape object, line, whose endpoints are at (1,2) and (3,4) with color green.
(b) Write a statement to draw the line segment.

13. Show the status of the array arr after each pass of the selection sort.

```
int arr[] = {6, 3, 1, 8, 5};
```

14. (a) Consider the String declarations

```
String s1, s2;
```

and the input statements

```
cin >> s1;
getline(cin,s2,'\n');
```

What is the value of s1 and s2 for input line "George flies!"
(b) What is the value of s1[3] and s1[5]? Of s2[0] and s2[6]?

15. What is the output of this program?

```
#include <iostream.h>

#include "tstring.h"

int main()
{
    String str = "baseball park", s;
    int index;

    index = str.find_first_of('a',0);
    cout << index << endl;

    index = str.find("ball");
    cout << index << endl;

    str.remove(0,4);
    str.insert(0,"foot");
    cout << str << endl;

    s = str.substr(4);
    cout << s << endl;

    str.remove(9,100);
    cout << str << endl;

    str += "stadium";
    cout << str << endl;

    return 0;
}
```

16. Answer the following questions regarding a two-dimensional integer array object table.
(a) Declare the array to have 3 rows and 6 columns.
(b) How many elements does the array contain?
(c) Initialize a second array table2 of the same dimensions so the first row contains 1, 4, 5, 7, 8, 3 and the second row contains 3, 7, 9, 1, 0, 6. What are the values in the third row?
(d) Write a loop that prints table2 with each row on a separate line.

17. (a) Declare a 2 x 2 array of doubles as specified by the figure.

$$arr = \begin{pmatrix} 2 & 1 \\ 3 & 5 \end{pmatrix}$$

(b) Declare 2 x 2 SqMatrix objects marr and tmp.
(c) Using a nested loop, assign marr the same values as arr.
(c) Assign tmp to be the scalar product of marr and 2.0.
(d) Output tmp.

Answers to Review Exercises

1. (a) `int list[10];`
   (b) `list[2]`
   (c) `list[1] = list[3];`
   (d) `for(i=0;i < 10;i++)`
       `list[i] = i;`
2. (a) `int arr[] = {-2, -1, 0, 1, 2};`
   (b) `int daysInMonth[] = {31,28,31,30,31,30,31,31,30,31,30,31};`
3. `21`
4. (a) `5*2 = 10 bytes`
   (b) `Address of arr[3] = 6000 + 3*2 = 6006`
5. (a) `q = {0, 5, 3, 0, 0}`
   (b) `q = {55, 5, 3, -77, -9}`
6. (a) `double arr[10], i;`
       `for(i=0; i < 10; i++)`
           `arr[i] = 90 + i;`
   (b) Statistics statArr(arr, 10);
   (c) Output the minimum, maximum and mean values for the numbers 90 to 99.

```
cout << statArr.getMin() << "  " << statArr.getMax()
        << "  " << statArr.getMean() << endl;
```

7. Declarations 1 and 3 are valid. Declaration 2 fails since class Two does not have a default constructor.
8. (a) `1 to 199`
   (b) `0 ≤ x < 2`
9. (a)   (1) `5`   (2) `6`   (3) `-1`
   (b) `arr = {4,7,12,14,33,23,55}`
       `size = 7`
10. `FinanceCenter fc;`
     `StudentAccount david("4567-53", "Willingstone, David", -75);`

     `fc.addAccount(david);`
11. `const long NTOSSES= 1000000L;`
     `Dice d(3);`
     `long i, number9 = 0;`

     `for(i=0; i < NTOSSES; i++)`

```
        if (d.toss() == 9)
            number9++;
    cout << "Empirical probability = "
            << double(number9)/NTOSSES << endl;
```

12. (a) LineShape line (1, 2, 3, 4, green);

(b) line.draw();

13.
```
Pass 1          1 3 6 8 5
Pass 2          1 3 6 8 5
Pass 3          1 3 5 8 6
Pass 4          1 3 5 6 8
```

14. (a) s1 = "George", s2 = "□flies!" (□ is a blank)

(b) s1[3] = 'r', s1[5] = 'e', s2[0] = ' ', s2[6] = '!'

15.
```
1
4
football park         // removes base adds foot
ball park             // substring starts at 'b'
football              // remove "park"
football stadium      // append "stadium"
```

16. (a) `int table[3][6];`

(b) 18

(c) `int table2[3][6] = { {1, 4, 5, 7, 8, 3},`
`    {3, 7, 9, 1, 0, 6} };`
`    // the last row is {0,0,0,0,0,0}`

(d) `for (i=0;i < 3;i++)`
`    {`
`        for (j=0;j < 6;j++)`
`            cout << table2[i][j] << "  ";`
`        cout << endl;`
`    }`

17. (a) double arr[2][2] = { {2,1}, {3,5}};

(b) Matrix marr(2), tmp(2);

(c) `int i, j;`
`    for(i=0; i < 2; i++)`
`        for(j=0; j < 2; j++)`
`            marr.putAt(i, j, arr[i][j]);`

(c) `tmp = marr.smul(2.0);`

(d) `tmp.writeMatrix();`

WRITTEN EXERCISES

18. Assume the array declaration

```
int a[50];
```

(a) How many elements are in the array?

(b) Give a statement that assigns the last element of the array to the second element of the array.

19. (a) Give a declaration that creates an array, doubleArr, of 25 double objects.
  (b) Declare an array, intArr, of 1000 integer objects.
  (c) Write a statement that assigns the 3rd element of doubleArr to the 6th element of the same array.
  (d) Write a loop that copies the first 10 values from intArr to the first 10 entries of doubleArr.

20. (a) The array arr is declared as

```
short arr[5];
```

  (1) If the size of a short integer is 2 bytes, how many bytes are allocated for array arr?

  (2) If the address of the array is arr = 6000, compute the addresses of arr[1] and arr[3].

  (b) Assume the declaration

```
long larr[] = {30, 500000, -100000, 5, 33};
```

  If a long integer is 4 bytes and the address of larr is 2050,
  (1) What is the contents at address 2066?
  (2) Give statements that double the value of the array elements at addresses 2050 and 2062.
  (3) What is the address of larr[3]?

21. (a) Declare an array b of 3 integers whose initial values are

```
b[0] = 1, b[1] = 5, b[2]  = 8.
```

  (b) Declare an integer array, arr, with 2000 elements. Use a for statement to initialize all elements to 0. Is there a way to use an initialization list that sets all the elements to 0 without listing 2000 zeros?
  (c) Is there anything wrong with this declaration? Explain.

```
char s[4] = {'a', 'b', 'c', 'd', 'e'};
```

22. Write a declaration for an integer array arr with 10 elements, whose first 5 entries are set to 5, 3, 1, 4, 8.

23. (a) Declare an integer array arr with 100 elements.
  (b) Declare a double array x with 5 elements, all of which are 0.0.
  (c) Declare a double array y with 100 elements. Write a loop to initialize all its elements to 1.0. Why isn't compile-time initialization appropriate for this problem?
  (d) Declare the array printChar that consists of 95 characters. Use a loop to initialize it to contain all the printable ASCII characters from ASCII code 32 to 126.
  (e) The enum type Months contains the months of the year.
  Enum months {Jan, Feb, Mar, Apr, May, Jun, Jul, Aug, Sep, Oct, Nov, Dec};
  For the array

```
Months mon[12];
```

  write a code segment that initializes each item to have the corresponding calendar month. For example,

```
mon[3] = Apr;
```

24. What is the output of this program?

```
#include <iostream.h>

int main()
{
    int i, a[10] = {1,5,6,7,8};

    for (i=5; i < 10; i++)
        a[i] = i;
    for(i=0; i < 10; i++)
        if (a[i] % 2 != 0)
            cout << a[i] << "  ";
    cout << endl;

    return 0;
}
```

25. Trace the following program and determine the output.

```
#include <iostream.h>

int f(int a[], int n, int k);

int main()
{
    int c[6] = {1,3,6,5,2}, result;

    result = f(c,5,5);
    if (result != -1)
        cout << result;
    else
        cout << "No!";
    cout << endl;

    return 0;
}

int f(int a[], int n, int k)
{
    int i = 0;

    a[n] = k;
    while(a[i] != k)
        i++;

    if (i < n)
        return i;
    else
        return -1;
}
```

26. Define a function, max(), that finds the maximum value in an n element array of doubles.

```
double max(double arr[], int n);
```

27. Define a function, `avg()`, that returns the average value in an n element array of doubles.

```
double avg(double arr[], int n);
```

28. Write a function that uses reference arguments to return the minimum and maximum of an n element integer array.

```
void minmax(int arr[], int n, int& min, int& max);
```

29. Declare the array arr of doubles containing the initial values 45, 67, 21, 35, 47, 55, 7, 3, 2. Declare a Statistics object, statArr, that computes statistical information for arr. Write statements that output the minimum, maximum and mean of the data values.

30. It can be shown that the sum of the first n integers is given by the formula

$$sum(n) = 1 + 2 + 3 + ... + n = n(n + 1)/2$$

Using this formula, the average value of the first n integers is given by the formula $(n + 1)/2$.
(a) Declare an integer array, arr, with 100 elements.
(b) Input an integer $n \leqslant 100$ and initialize the first n values of arr to be 1, 2, 3, . . . , n.
(c) Declare a Statistics object, statN, that specifies arr as an argument.
(d) Output the average of the first n integers using both the formula and the object statN.

31. Consider the class CL whose declaration has the following outline:

```
class CL
{
    ...
    CL(int m, int n);
    ...
};
```

(a) Explain why this statement is incorrect.

```
CL arr[6];
```

(b) Design the constructor so that the statement in (a) is correct.

32. (a) Declare an array of 3 Rectangle objects and initialize the elements using anonymous objects. The 3 rectangles have dimension $1 \times 2, 3 \times 5$ and 6×7.
(b) Declare an array of 100 Rectangle objects. Explain why you are able to do this and what are the dimensions of each rectangle.

33. (a) June 1, 2040 is Friday. Declare an array, arrDate, of 6 Date objects. Give an assignment statement so that arrDate[0] is set to June 1, 2040.
(b) Declare an array, arrDays, of 6 Days objects. Assign arrDay[0] to be Fri. Recall that the Days class is discussed in Chapter 6.
(c) Using a loop that executes 5 times, initialize the remaining members of the Date array arrDate and the Days array arrDays by adding 30 days to each successive element.

34. What are the ranges for each random number expression?

```
double x;
int n;
```

(a) x = rnd.fRandom()*5 + 2;
(b) n = rnd.random(50) - 8;
(c) n = rnd.random(50) + rnd.random(25);
(d) x = rnd.fRandom() * rnd.fRandom();

35. Use a random number to simulate each situation.

    (a) 1/5 th of automobiles in a state fail to meet smog emission standards. Use `frandom()` to determine if a randomly selected car meets the standards.

    (b) The weight of an individual in a population ranges between 140 and 230 pounds. Use `random()` to select the weight of a person in this population.

    (c) The weather bureau predicts a 10% chance that the baseball game will be canceled, 25% chance it will be delayed, and 65% chance of no interruption. Write C++ statements that use a random number object and a nested if statement to predict the effect of the weather on the game.

36. Implement a function, `toss()`, that simulates the tossing of n coins and returns the number of heads.

```
int toss(int n);
```

37. Consider the integer array, arr:

```
int arr[] = {1, 5, 0, 2, 8, 7, 8, 3, 8}, index;
```

    (a) What is the value of index after the call to the function seqSearch()?

        (i) index = seqSearch(arr, 0, 8, 8);
        (ii) index = seqSearch(arr, 5, 8, 8);
        (iii) index = seqSearch(arr, 0, 3, 8);

    (b) Write a loop that will output the index of each occurrence of 8 in the list.

38. Consider the declaration

```
int arr[] = {1, 3, 5, 1, 6, 1, 7, 9, 11, 1}, size = 10;
```

    (a) Give the contents of arr and size after each call to `remove()`.

        (i) remove(arr, size, 4);
        (ii) remove(arr, size, 3);
        (iii) remove(arr, size, 6);

    (b) Write a loop that removes all values of 1 from the list.

39. Write a function, `insert()`, that places a new value into an array at a specified position. Note that you will need to slide array elements to the right of the position in order to make room for the new element.

```
// insert item at position pos and increment size
void insert(int arr[], int& size, int pos, int item);
```

40. Modify the Selection Sort algorithm so that it sorts in descending order.

41. The following function sorts an integer array arr with n elements using a technique known as the exchange sort.

```
void f(int arr[], int n)
{
    int i, j, temp;

    for (i = 0; i < size-1; i++)
        // locate least of a[i]...a[n-1] at a[i]
```

```
            for (j = i+1; j < size; j++)
               if (arr[j] < arr[i])
                  {
                      temp = arr[i];
                      arr[i] = arr[j];
                      arr[j] = temp;
                  }
        }
```

(a) Trace its execution for `arr = {3, 7, 1, 5, 9}`.

(b) How does it differ from the selection sort? Do you think it is more or less efficient?

42. Assume an array of size n is sorted. If n is odd, the median is the value of the element at the mid-point of the range 0 to n − 1. If n is even, the median is the average of the two middle values. For instance, the median of the 9-element list {0, 1, 3, 4, 7, 8, 10, 14, 19} is 7 and the median of the 6 element list {1, 2, 4, 7, 8, 9} is 5.5. Write a function, `median()`, that computes the median of any sorted array containing n double values.

```
    double median(double arr[], int n);
```

43. Consider the string object declarations

```
    String s1, s2;
```

and the input statements

```
    getline(cin,s1,':');
    getline(cin,s2,'\n');
```

(a) What is the value of s1 and s2 for the input line

```
    Roberts, Larry:345678912
```

(b) What is the value of s1[2] and s1[5]? Of s2[3] and s2[7]?

44. Given the String object str, what is the index of the first and last character in the string?

45. Consider the declarations

```
    String s("abc12xya52cba"), t;
    int index;
```

(a) What is the value of index = s.find_last_of ('c')?

(b) What is the value of s[6]?

(c) What is the value of s[3]?

(d) What is the value of t = s.substr(5,6)?

(e) What is the value of t after executing the statements

```
    t = s;
    t.insert(5,"ABC");
```

(f) What is the value of index = s.find("a52",2)?

46. (a) Implement the free function insert() using only the String member functions `substr()` and "+" by filling in the missing lines.

```
    // insert t into s at position pos
    void insert(String& s, const String& t, int pos)
```

```
{
    String front = s.substr(0,pos), rear = s.substr(pos);

    _____;
    _____;
    _____;
}
```

(b) Using only the String member functions `substr()` and "+", develop the free function `remove()`.

```
// remove count chars from s beginning at pos
void remove(String& s, int pos, int count);
```

(c) Using the free functions `remove()` and `insert()` from parts (a) and (b), write a function that replaces count characters beginning at position pos by a new string.

```
// with String t, replace count chars of s
// beginning at pos.
replace(String& s, int pos, int count, const String& t);
```

47. (a) Declare a two-dimensional array of double values, doubleArr, with 5 rows and 3 columns. How many elements are in the array?

(b) Use compile-time initialization to create an integer array, intArr, with 3 rows and 3 columns. The first row contains all 1's, the 2nd row all 2's and the third row contains all 3's.

(c) Write a nested loop that outputs the rows of doubleArr, one row per line.

(d) Write a nested loop that outputs the columns of intArr, one column per line.

48. What is the output of this program?

```
#include <iostream.h>
#include <iomanip.h>

int main()
{
    int a[2][2] = { {3,5}, {9,8} },
        b[2][2] = { {12,2}, {7,7} },
        c[2][2];
    int i, j;

    for (i=0;i < 2;i++)
        for (j=0;j < 2;j++)
            c[i][j] = a[i][j] + b[i][j];

        for (i=0;i < 2;i++)
        {
            for (j=0;j < 2;j++)
                cout << setw(3) << c[i][j] << "  ";
            cout << endl;
        }

    return 0;
}
```

49. Using the SqMatrix class, create two matrices matrixA and matrixB with the following values:

$$matrix\ A = \begin{pmatrix} 1 & 2 & 3 \\ 4 & 5 & 6 \\ 7 & 8 & 9 \end{pmatrix}, \quad matrix\ B = \begin{pmatrix} 0 & 0 & 0 \\ 1 & 1 & 1 \\ 2 & 2 & 2 \end{pmatrix}$$

Develop code that computes and outputs the sum and difference of the two matrices.

50. The two-dimensional array arr is declared as

    ```
    short arr[5][6];
    ```

    (a) How many bytes are allocated for the array?
    (b) If the address of the array is arr = 1000, compute the addresses of arr[3][2] and arr[1][4].
    (c) What array entry is located at address 1020? At address 1034?

51. Assume T is a two-dimensional array with m rows and n columns. Generate an access function that computes the offset of T[row][col] assuming that the elements are stored by columns.

PROGRAMMING EXERCISES

52. Implement two functions

    ```
    // read n integers into array arr
    void readlist(int arr[], int n);
    // output the n integer values in array arr
    void writelist(int arr[], int n);
    ```

    Write a program that declares an array of 5 integers. After entering the values 2, –3, –4, 6, 5 using readlist(), scan and convert each array element to its negative value. Output the array using writelist().

53. Define an array charCount that reads a text file and counts the number of occurrences for each letter in the range 'a'–'z'. Data is read character by character until end of file. Uppercase characters are converted to lower case. Output the characters and counts, 7 per line in the form

    ```
    <char> [count]     <char> [count]   . . .   <char> [count]
    ```

    Test your program by reading the source code as the text file.

54. Input a list of integers into an array called list. Stop when a 0 is input. Maintain an index n that is incremented after each input. At end of input, n is the total number of array entries. Output the array in reverse order by displaying the element list[n-1], followed by list[n-2], down to list[0]. Initially declare an array of 20 integers.

55. (a) Write a complete program that enters 10 long integer numbers into array arr and outputs the largest and the smallest of the numbers. Your algorithm should declare long integers max and min and update their values with each input. Give max and min initial values using the fact that the range of long integers is

    ```
    -2147483648 <= long integer value < 2147483648
    ```

(b) Use the problem specification from part (a). However, let the input come from random integer values in the range 1000 to 9999. During each iteration, output the value of the random number.

56. Declare an array arr of integers with initial values 1, 2, 7, 12, 16. Implement a function

```
void cummulate(int arr[], int newarr[], int n);
```

to create a second array whose elements newarr[i] are the sum of the elements arr[0]..arr[i]. In our example, the new array has values 1, 3, 10, 22, 38. Write a program that declares an array listA with initial values 2, 7, 3, 12, 16, 8 and an array listB that will hold the cummulative values. Call the function and output the values in listB.

57. Declare the following array in your program.

```
double arr[5] = {2.3, 6.7, -9.6, 5.8, 3.5};
```

Apply the functions max() and avg() from Written Exercises 26 and 27 to output the maximum value in arr and the average of its values.

58. Declare the following array in your program.

```
int intArr[] = {6, 2, -9, 4, 5, 12, 0, 33, 8};
```

Apply the function minmax() from Written Exercise 28 to output the minimum and maximum values in intArr.

59. Implement Written Exercise 7.29 as a complete program.

60. Implement part (d) of Written Exercise 7.30 as a complete program.

61. Write a program that implements Written Exercise 33 and outputs the values in the two arrays arrDate and arrDays.

62. Simulate the playing of the "High-Low Game". Using a random number generator, create a target value in the range 0 to 999. The contestant is given a series of attempts to guess the number. On each attempt, the contestant inputs a number and is told whether the value is higher or lower than the target. The game terminates on a match or after 8 unsuccessful guesses.

63. It can be shown that the theoretical probability of getting n-1 heads when tossing n coins is $(n-1)/2^n$. Use the function, toss(), developed in Written Exercise 36, to simulate the tossing of 8 coins 1,000,000 times and compute the empirical probability of tossing 7 heads. Output the theoretical and empirical probabilities.

64. This program uses the results of Written Exercise 7.39. Declare the integer array

```
int intArr[] = {5, 1, 3, 5, 6, 9, 0, 7};
```

Call insert() to place 4 at index 3, 12 at index 0 and 25 at index 8. Output the new array.

65. We use an array, d, of 50 Dice objects to illustrate how a programmer must compensate for a default constructor that does not appropriately initialize objects in an array. The following is a step-by-step outline of a program that you should create and execute.

1. Declare the array d.
2. Use setNumber() to initialize each object in d to toss five (5) dice.
3. Execute `toss()` for each element in d and record the result in a corresponding 50 element integer array tossResult.

    ```
    tossResult[i] = d[i].toss().
    ```

4. Scan tossResult and output how many times a 15 was thrown.
5. Scan tossResult and find the largest number.
6. Sort tossResult and output the values from the array.
7. Use the remove duplicates algorithm from Application 7-5 to remove all dupli-cate totals from tossResult. Output the modified array.

66. In Written Exerise 7.40, you modified the selection sort so it arranges the array ele-ments in descending order. Write a program that uses your modified function to sort the following array in descending order. Output the array.

    ```
    int arr[] = {1,3,4,2,7,12,16,17,25,12,3,5,13,3,5};
    ```

67. Use the function `median()` developed in Written Exercise 7.42 to compute the me-dian of the values in the array arr given in Programming Exercise 7.66. You must first call selectionSort().

68. Enter the following sequence of words into String str:

    ```
    Arizona   walk   government   C++   beach
    ```

    For each word, output the first and last letter.

69. Input a series of words until end of file, converting each one to Pig Latin. If the word begins with a consonant, move the first character of the word to the last posi-tion and append "ay". If the word begins with a vowel, simply append "ay". For example,

    ```
    Input:    this is simple
    Output:   histay isay implesay
    ```

70. (a) A string of text can be encrypted using an encryption mapping that associates each letter of the alphabet with a unique letter. For example, assume the en-cryption mapping is

    ```
    abcdefghijklmnopqrstuvwxyz → ngzqtcobmuhelkpdawxfyivrsj
    ```

    The letter 'a' is mapped to 'n', 'b' to 'g', and so forth. Under this mapping, "en-crypt" is encrypted as "tdrlpfk"

    Write a program that reads a string, encrypts each alphabetic character and out-puts the result. HINT: Initialize an array with the tabular mapping.
    (b) Write another program that defines the decrypting mapping that reverses the initial Encryption mapping. Using this program, input a string, encrypt it to a second string. Decrypt the second string and output the result.

71. Implement parts (b) and (c) of Written Exercise 47 as a complete program.

72. The trace of an n × n matrix is defined as the sum of the diagonal elements.

    ```
    Trace (arr) = arr[1, 1] + arr[2, 2] + . . . + arr[n, n]
    ```

Write a function that computes the trace of a SqMatrix object.

```
double trace(const SqMatrix& mat);
```

Create a main program to test the function.

PROGRAMMING PROJECTS

73. Allocate an array of 50 string objects. Read the lines from a file, placing each line in an array element. Each line may contain the special symbols '#' and '&'. For example:

```
Dear #

Your lucky gift is available at &. By going to & and iden-
tifying your name, the attendant will give you your prize.
Thank you # for your interest in our contest.

Sincerely,
The String Man
```

Enter a string poundstr that substitutes for all occurrences of '#' in your document. Enter a string ampstring that substitutes for all occurrences of '&' in your document. Traverse the array of strings and perform the substitutions. Print the final document.

74. The Time24 class has a default constructor in which the hour and minute arguments are set to 0. This defines a default time of midnight (00:00). A Time24 array, arrive, specifies the arrival time of the first ten customers at the local clothing store. The first customer arrives at exactly 9:00 AM and then each subsequent customer arrives at some random time within an interval of 2 to 20 minutes. While in the clothing store, a customer takes between 9 and 24 minutes to complete service. Using the random number generator, define an array named depart that lists the departure time for each customer. Do this by developing a function, setDepartures(). Its argument list should contain both arrival and departure arrays, the array sizes, a RandomNumber object, and both the lower and upper bound for the service time. Table 7-5 gives the sample arrival and departure times of four customers.

TABLE 7-5 Arrival and Departure Times of Four Customers.

Customer	Next Arrival	Arrival Time	Departure Time
1		9:00	9:17
2	13	9:13	9:25
3	15	9:28	9:48
4	2	9:30	9:39

The main program must display a table similar to Table 7-5 that gives the customer number, and the arrival and departure times.

75. This exercise develops the class, Sundays, that maintains information about the date for each Sunday in a given year. For the constructor, the argument first Sunday has the date for the first Sunday in January.

```
class Sundays
{
    private:
        int year;
        int numSundays;      // number of Sundays in year
        Date sun[53];        // dates of each Sunday in year
    public:
        // set year. compute numSundays and
        // initialize the array sun
        Sundays(const Date& firstSunday);

        // return the year
        int getYear();

        // return number of Sundays in the year
        int numberOfSundays();
        // return date of 1st Sunday in month
        Date firstSunday(int month);
        // return number of Sundays in month
        int sundaysInMonth(int month);
};
```

(a) Implement the constructor. HINT: Keep incrementing by 7 days until the year changes.
(b) Implement the access member functions getYear() and numberOfSundays().
(c) Implement firstSunday(). HINT: Step through sun until the Date member function getMonth() returns month.
(d) Define sundaysInMonth(). HINT: Step through sun until the Date member function getMonth() returns month. Count Sundays from this point until the month changes.

Implement the class, Sundays, and place it in the file **sundays.h**. The first Sunday in 1998 is January 4. In the main program, for the year 1998 output the number of Sundays, the date of the first Sunday in December, and the number of Sundays in June.

Chapter 8
Program Design and Algorithms

C H A P T E R   C O N T E N T S

8-1 OBJECT COMPOSITION

The Employee Class
UML Representation for Composition
The Constructor in Composition
The Triangle Class

8-2 OBJECT AND PROGRAM DESIGN PRINCIPLES

Object-Oriented Analysis
Object-Oriented Design
Object-Oriented Programming

8-3 CREATING A FULL YEAR CALENDAR

Designing the Calendar Class
Declaring the Calendar Class
Defining the Member Functions
The Calendar Application

8-4 ACCESSING AND STORING OBJECTS

Scope
Storage Class

8-5 RECURSIVE ALGORITHMS

Finding Recursive Algorithms
Developing Recursive Functions
Tracing a Recursive Function

8-6 RECURSION AND PROBLEM SOLVING

The Tower of Hanoi Puzzle
Solving the Tower of Hanoi with Recursion
Traversing a Maze
Using Recursion to Solve a Maze
Comparing Recursive and Iterative Algorithms

Written Exercises

Up to this point in the book, we have introduced computer problem-solving using objects and developed the basic building blocks for C++ programs and classes. For data, a program uses primitive number types and more complex structures like arrays and programmer-defined objects. For problem solving, class member and free functions provide data handling operations, and control structures provide the logic that implement algorithms. You have gained important object-oriented programming background.

We begin this chapter by introducing object composition that occurs when a class includes data members that are objects from other classes. This construct allows a class to use the member functions of another class in its implementation. Composition promotes code reuse that is one of the more important principles of object technology.

In this chapter, we introduce the object-oriented program development cycle, which includes analysis, design, program implementation, and testing. While we have used many of these processes in various discussions and sample programs, we formally show how the program cycle is used to create large applications. We illustrate many of the features of the development cycle in an application that displays a full-year calendar.

In a program, objects are declared in the main program block, a function block, an argument list, or as data members of a class. The same name may be used for different objects in different blocks. The scope of an object is that portion of the program in which it can be accessed. In a program, an object has a lifetime. It comes into existence when it is declared and is normally destroyed when the program leaves its declaration block. In certain cases, the object may persist for the entire program. In this chapter, we discuss the scope and lifetime of an object.

In C++, one function can call another function, even itself. This process, called recursion, is an alternative to iteration (looping) and provides a powerful tool for many algorithms in computer science. Using simple examples, we develop the structure of recursive algorithms and their implementation as recursive functions. A series of applications illustrate many of the key types of recursive algorithms.

8-1   OBJECT COMPOSITION

Class data members may be simple number and character data or arrays. In more complex problems, the data members may be class objects which, themselves, consist of primitive types and programmer-defined object types. For instance, the Division of Motor Vehicles maintains a large amount of information about each licensed driver, including name and date of birth. A Licensed-Driver class could maintain the name as a String object and the date of birth as a Date object.

```
class LicensedDriver
{
   private:
      String name;
      Date  birthday;
       . . . .
};
```

A LicensedDriver object contains programmer-defined objects. This is a principle called object composition.

> **Definition** *Object composition* is a condition that exists when a class contains one or more data members that are objects from other classes. A class that is included by composition is called a *supplier class.* The class that declares the objects is called the *client class.*
>
> ```
> class ClientClass
> {
>    private:
>       SupplierClass obj;
>    public:
>          ...
> ;
> ```

Object composition is a primary example of *code reuse.* The member functions for the supplier class objects do a significant part of the calculations. To study this important topic, we design our discussion around two object composition examples.

The Employee Class

An Employee object maintains personnel records in a small business. For data members, the class includes a String object (empID) as the employee identification and a floating-point value for yearly salary. The data also includes two Date objects that maintain the date of initial hire (hireDate) and the date that ends a probationary period (probationDate). In the language of object composition, Date and String are supplier classes and Employee is the client class.

```
String   empID;                  // String object
double   salary;                 // number of double type
Date     hireDate;               // Date Object
Date     probationDate;          // Date object
```

In the design of the class, the probationary period ends 90 days after the date of initial hire.

75-39	31500	May 19, 1999	August 17, 1999
empID	salary	hireDate	probationDate

The class has a constructor that is used to initialize all of the data members. It is called when an employee is hired and includes the employee ID, the starting salary and the date of initial hire. The probation date is computed to be 90 days after the date of hire. The class has member functions, getSalary() and setSalary(), that allow a program to fetch the current salary and update its value when a change occurs. The member function, getProbDate(), returns the date that specifies an end to the probation period. The class provides an output function called writeEmployee(), that gives a listing of the data with the following format.

```
Employee ID:      <empID>
Yearly salary:    <salary >
Date of hire:     <hireDate with long format >
Probation date:   <probationDate with long format>
```

With this brief description, we give a declaration of the Employee class and include an example to show you how it might be used in an application.

DECLARATION: Employee CLASS ▬▬▬▬▬▬▬▬▬

employee.h

```
// maintain information about an employee
class Employee
{
    private:
        // id number and salary
        String empID;           // employee ID
        double salary;          // yearly salary
        Date hireDate;          // date of initial hire
        Date probationDate;     // date when benefits begin
    public:
        // constructor with five arguments
        Employee(String id, double sal, int mm, int dd,
                 int yyyy);

        // member functions to access data
        double getSalary() const;       // retrieve salary
        void setSalary(double sal);     // set new salary
        Date getProbDate() const;

        // output employee data
        void writeEmployee() const;
};
```

EXAMPLE 8.1 ▬▬▬▬▬▬▬▬▬

1. The following declaration creates an Employee object called tom, who is hired on May 19, 1999 with id "75-39" and starting salary $31,500.

75-39	31500	May 19, 1999	August 17, 1999
empID	salary	hireDate	probationDate

Employee tom("75-39", 31500, 5, 19, 1999);

Note that the constructor has arguments that specify the date of hire. In a separate section, we illustrate how the Employee constructor uses these arguments to initialize the two date objects.

2. Display the employee information for tom

```
tom.writeEmployee();

<output>   Employee ID: 75-39
           Yearly salary $31500.00
           Date of hire: May 19, 1999
           Probation date: August 17, 1999
```

3. To determine when benefits will begin, we first extract the probation date and then output its value in the short date format.

```
Date tomProb = tom.getProbDate();

tomProb.writeShortDate();   // output: 8/17/1999  ■
```

The program further illustrates the use of the Employee class. The Employee object, sara, represents employee "88-72", who begins work on November 5, 2005 at a salary of $38,000.

```
Employee sara("88-72",38000.00,11,5,2005);
```

The initial employee information for sara is output using writeEmployee(). Company policy gives a 5% salary increase after the employee passes a 90-day probationary period. The program uses getProbDate() to identify the probation date and uses getSalary() and setSalary() to post the increase. The program terminates by displaying the final salary for sara.

```cpp
#include <iostream.h>

#include "employee.h"
#include "date.h"

int main()
{
    // sara has id "88-72", a salary of $38,000 and is hired
    // 11/5/2005
    Employee sara("88-72",38000.00,11,5,2005);
    double salary;

    sara.writeEmployee();
    cout << endl;

    salary = sara.getSalary();   // sara's current salary
    salary *= 1.05;              // 5% raise
    sara.setSalary(salary);

    cout << "After ending probation on ";
    (sara.getProbDate()).writeShortDate();
    cout << " Sara earns $" << sara.getSalary() << endl;

    return 0;
}
```

```
Run:

Employee ID: 88-72
```

```
Yearly salary $38000.00
Date of hire: November 5, 2005
Probation date: February 3, 2006

After ending probation on  2/03/2006 Sara earns
$39900.00
```

UML Representation for Composition

UML gives us a simple visual representation of a class. Special links are created in the figure to illustrate composition for data members. An object included by composition is represented by an arrow that connects the *client class* (Employee) to a *supplier class* (Date and String). The arrow is annotated by the name of the corresponding data member in the client class. A private data member is indicated when a "−" appears before the name. A diamond marks the end of the line at the client class and a solid diamond indicates that an actual object is declared. Class composition can also indirectly reference objects through pointers, a topic that is discussed in Chapter 10. Figure 8-1 is the UML representation for Employee.

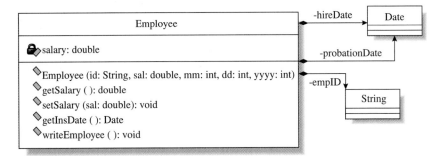

FIGURE 8-1
UML Representation for the Employee Class.

The Constructor in Composition

Implementing a member function for a client class that features composition involves calling member functions from the corresponding supplier class. For instance, the `writeEmployee()` function may use the Date function `write-LongDate()` to output both the hire and probation dates. This is an example of code reuse that we illustrate in the implementation of `writeEmployee()`.

```
// output employee data
void Employee::writeEmployee() const
{
    cout << "Employee ID: " << empID << endl;
```

```
    cout << "Yearly salary $" << setreal(1,2) << salary
        << endl;

    // use writeLongDate() from the Date class for output
    cout << "Date of hire: ";
    hireDate.writeLongDate();
    cout << endl;
    cout << "Probation date: ";
    probationDate.writeLongDate();
    cout << endl;
}
```

The constructor must include arguments that initialize the data members of primitive type and additional arguments that are used to build objects included by composition. We illustrate these ideas with the Employee class constructor. The function has an argument list that includes the String object id and the double value sal that initialize data members, empID and salary, respectively. The argument list also includes the integer values mm, dd, and yyyy that are available to initialize the Date objects hireDate and probationDate.

```
// constructor for the Employee class
Employee(String id, double sal, int mm, int dd, int yyyy);
```

In the implementation of the constructor, an initialization list can be used to assign values to the data members empID and salary. To initialize the hireDate and probationDate objects, we use statements in the function body.

```
// build an Employee object by initializating data members
Employee::Employee(String id, double sal,
        int mm, int dd, int yyyy): empID(id), salary(sal)
{
    // build an anonymous Date object and assign to hireDate
    hireDate = Date(mm,dd,yyyy);

    // assign initial value to probationDate and add 90 days
    probationDate = hireDate;
    probationDate.incrementDate(90);
}
```

Programming Note

When a client-class object is declared, constructors must be called for each supplier-class data member. The supplier-class must have a default constructor, or the objects must appear in the initialization list of the constructor. In the Employee class, the data members hireDate and probationDate are not in the initialization list, and the Date class default constructor is called for each object. Each is initially given the value January 1, 1600. The assignment statements in the constructor body replace these initial values.

C++ provides an alternative method of initializing a supplier-object that must be used when a data member of class type does not have a default constructor.

Place the supplier-object in the constructor initialization list with the appropriate arguments. For instance, the Employee constructor uses the arguments mm, dd and yyyy to initialize hireDate and probationDate.

```
// build an Employee object by initializing its data members
Employee::Employee(String id, double sal, int mm, int dd,
                    int yyyy): empID(id), salary(sal),
                               hireDate(mm,dd,yyyy)
                               probationDate(mm,dd,yyyy)
{
    // initially, probationDate is hireDate.  add 90 days
    probationDate.incrementDate(90);
}
```

*Exploring
Concepts*

Assume the Employee class contains dateOfBirth as a Date object. How would you determine the number of days between the date of hire and the next birthday?

The Triangle Class

A triangle is a three-sided figure that is formed by connecting three points A, B, and C that do not lie on the same line. Using composition, we declare a class, Triangle, that draws triangles specified by the points A, B, and C. The class uses an array of three LineShape objects to draw the sides. For the draw() and erase() member functions, we simply use the corresponding functions for the LineShape objects.

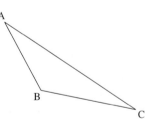

A Triangle object is initialized by two arrays that define the coordinates of the points A, B, and C. The arrays are included as arguments for the constructor. Array x defines the x-coordinates of the three points and array y defines the y-coordinates.

triangle.h

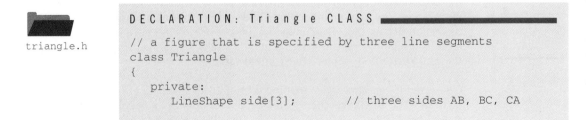

```
DECLARATION: Triangle CLASS
// a figure that is specified by three line segments
class Triangle
{
    private:
        LineShape side[3];          // three sides AB, BC, CA
```

```
    public:
        // point A at (x[0],y[0]), point B at
        // (x[1],y[1]), point C at ((x[2],y[2])
        Triangle (double x[], double y[]Shape Color c =
        darkgray);

        // draw the triangle
        void draw();

        // change a point of the triangle. A(i=0),B(i=1),C(i=2)
        void setPoint(int i, double x, double y);

        // choose color for the triangle
        void setColor(ShapeColor c);

        // erase the triangle
        void erase();
};
```

The program illustrates the declaration of a Triangle object and drawing with the member functions of the class. The initial object t is a right triangle with points A(1,1), B(1,4), and C(6,4). The coordinates are assigned to arrays x and y that are used as arguments for the constructor.

```
double x[3] = {1,1,6}, y[3] = {1,4,4};
Triangle t(x,y);            // pass x and y as the coordinates
```

To illustrate the member functions, we first draw Triangle t (Figure 8-2(a)) in blue. After viewing the figure, we modify its shape by changing the coordinates of point B to (2,3). The change is brought about by the function setPoint() with arguments i = 1 (for B), x = 2, and y = 3 (Figure 8-2(b)). Using setColor() and draw(), the new triangle is displayed in blue.

```
#include "graphlib.h"    // for openWindow(), etc.
#include "triangle.h"    // Triangle class

int main()
{
    double x[3] = {1,1,6}, y[3] = {1,4,4};
    Triangle t(x,y);        // pass x and y as the coordinates

    openWindow();           // open the graphics window

    t.draw();               // draw the triangle
    viewWindow();           // pause to view the first triangle
    t.erase();              // erase the figure
```

```
         // change point B to (2,3), color to blue
         t.setPoint(1,2,3);
         t.setColor(blue);
         t.draw();

         viewWindow();          // pause to view the second triangle
         closeWindow();

         return 0;
}
```

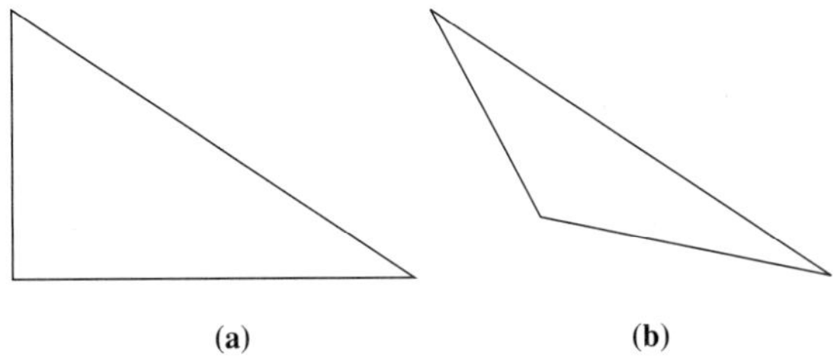

(a)   (b)

FIGURE 8-2
Drawing Triangles in Application 8-2.

Implementing Selected Member Functions of the Triangle Class. The Triangle class is an excellent application of object composition. All of the operations of the class are implemented by the member functions of the LineShape class.

Constructor:

The constructor builds the LineShape objects corresponding to sides AB, BC, and CA. Side 0 is the line AB from (x[0],y[0]) to (x[1], y[1]). Side 1 is the line BC from point (x[1],y[1]) to (x[2],y[2]) and side 2 is the line CA from (x[2],y[2]) to (x[0],y[0]). Notice the pattern for the indices

$$0 \rightarrow 1$$
$$1 \rightarrow 2 \qquad \text{(general: } i \rightarrow (i + 1)\%3)$$
$$2 \rightarrow 0$$

We can initialize side[i] ($0 <= i <= 2$) with a loop that constructs LineShape objects connecting point

$$((x[i],y[i]) \text{ to } (x[(i + 1)\%3],y[(i + 1)\%3])$$

```
// constructor. initialize the lines
Triangle::Triangle(double x[], double y[], Shape Color c)
{
    int i;

    for(i=0;i < 3;i++)
        // side[i] is drawn from (x[i],y[i]) to
```

```
    // (x[(i+1)%3], y[(i+1)%3])
    side[i] = LineShape(x[i],y[i],x[(i+1)%3],y[(i+1)%3]);
}
```

draw():

The function `draw()` for a triangle object simply calls the draw() operation for
each LineShape object.

```
void Triangle::draw() const
{
    int i;

    // draw the lines that form the sides of the triangle
    for(i=0;i < 3;i++)
        side[i].draw();
}
```

*Exploring
Concepts*

How would you generalize the Triangle class to represent a Polyline object? It
draws a sequence of connected lines defined by arrays of x and y coordinates.
Each pair of (x, y) coordinates defines a point. The last point connects to the
first point to form a closed figure.

```
class Polyline
{
    private:
        double xPoints[25],
        double yPoints[25],
        int nPoints;
    public:
        Polyline(double x[], double y[], int n);
        void draw();
};
```

8-2   OBJECT AND PROGRAM DESIGN PRINCIPLES

A computer application begins with a real world problem that somebody (customer) wants solved. One or more programmers are responsible for working
with the customer to understand the problem, to design the application and then
to code and test it. The entire process is called the *object-oriented program development cycle* and includes object-oriented analysis, design, and programming.

Object-Oriented Analysis

In the beginning, the programmer determines the problem that must be solved
and the resulting tasks that an application must perform. This overall view is created during the *object-oriented analysis (OOA)* phase of the cycle and results in
a set of program specifications. In the analysis phase, the programmer investigates objects (attributes and operations), that may be used in the application. In
large commercial applications, the analysis can also involve market studies, cus-

tomer requests for new software features, evaluation of emerging hardware technologies, and so forth.

Object-Oriented Design

Once the initial analysis is complete, a programmer enters into the *object-oriented design (OOD)* phase of the cycle and begins to develop C++ class declarations that describe the structure of the objects. In building a class, the programmer must specify the attributes and operations. This translates into defining the data members with their associated object types and creating prototypes for the member functions. Constructing a UML representation assists in class design.

The design phase of the development cycle not only identifies the individual objects but also specifies their interaction. In object-oriented programming, the three most common forms of object interaction are:

1. Composition
2. Association
3. Inheritance

With *composition,* a class may use other programmer-defined objects as data members. This inclusion allows the programmer to reuse existing code in the implementation of member functions. This was the topic of Section 8-1. In relating objects by *association,* the programmer passes class objects as function arguments, defines a class object as a function return value, or defines a local object in a function. Association creates a type of link between classes that is weaker than composition. The third relationship, called *inheritance,* represents a very important concept in object-oriented programming. A class inherits data and operations from a base (parent) class and adds its own operations. Inheritance is another tool that promotes code reuse. We present a detailed study of this topic in Chapter 12.

EXAMPLE 8.2 ▬▬▬▬▬▬▬▬▬▬▬▬▬▬▬▬▬▬▬▬▬▬▬

To illustrate composition and association, recall the FinanceCenter class from Section 7.8. For convenience, we provide its declaration.

```
const int MAX_ACCOUNTS = 25;

// maintain student records for the finance center
class FinanceCenter
{
   private:
      // number of active accounts and the account list
      int numAcct;
      StudentAccount acct[MAX_ACCOUNTS];

      int findAccount(const String& studID) const;

   public:
      FinanceCenter();
```

```
        void addAccount(const StudentAccount& studacct);
        void removeAccount(const String& studID);

        void makePayment(const String& studID, double amount);
        void makeCharge(const String& studID, double amount);

        void writeAccount(const String& studID) const;
};    ■
```

The StudentAccount class is included by composition, and the String class is used by association as member function arguments. We give the UML representation of the class. Note that the graphical tool representing association is a straight line. The notation 1..* indicates that the object acct is a C++ array.

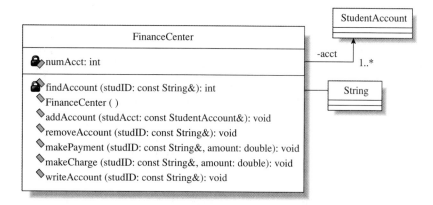

While the program design cycle focuses on classes, it must also deal with a main program and free function units that control class interaction. In object-oriented programming, the main program unit is often called the *agent* of the application.

For large applications, there is a gray area between the OOA and OOD phases of the development cycle. The customer often begins with a partial or fuzzy understanding of the problem. As the programmer moves forward with design, the customer will need to be consulted and allowed to make changes. This may adjust some of the problem specifications and create new design elements. From the very beginning, we must understand that a program development cycle is not a linear series of activities but an interactive process.

Object-Oriented Programming

In object-oriented design, we develop a blueprint for the program. The application is created only after the programmer translates the design into actual code. The activity, called *object-oriented programming (OOP)*, involves implementing algorithms for the class member functions, associated free functions, and the main program.

In creating code for a program unit, a programmer must look for ways to divide an algorithm into pieces that are less complex than the whole. The design strategy, called *code decomposition*, partitions an algorithm into separate tasks that are responsible for part of the job. To create the whole, the action of individual parts combine. This kind of design strategy is used by industry project managers as well as software production teams. Consider the approach of a project manager that is responsible for building a highway between two cities. The manager must break down the phases of the job and insure that tasks are done in the right order.

The project begins by purchasing the land and using heavy equipment to build the road bed with sand and gravel. Once the road bed is prepared, the project is completed by paving the highway and adding signs and road markers. With modern highway construction, tasks are often subcontracted out to firms that have special expertise in one aspect of the job. For instance, a sign shop might be contracted to create the highway signs since it employs graphic designers and painters with specialty skills. The manager breaks the project into hierarchy of tasks that are themselves divided into subtasks, and so forth. In this way, the manager can oversee the entire project while delegating responsibility for most of the tasks to assistant managers and subcontractors.

Good code design follows the model of the highway project. To implement member functions and the main program, the programmer develops private member functions and free functions to subcontract the tasks. In this way, each task is divided into subtasks that are simpler to design and implement (Figure 8-3).

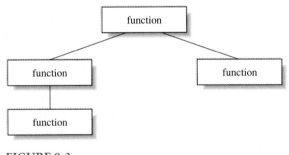

FIGURE 8-3
Code Decomposition.

The design and programming phases of the program development cycle are interactive processes. A programmer will often find that an initial class design needs new data members to specify the state of an object and needs new member functions to access or update the new values. The entire program devel-

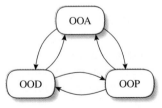

FIGURE 8-4
Interacting Phases of the Program Development Cycle.

opment cycle is a dynamic process that involves a continual interaction between the OOA, OOD, and OOP phases of the cycle (Figure 8-4).

Designing a Main Program. Recognizing objects and then designing and implementing their class types is the dominant feature of the program development cycle. After identifying the object components of an application, however, we must create an algorithm that controls the interaction of objects. The algorithm is typically implemented as the main program unit. The principle of code decomposition applies to the design of this algorithm (Figure 8-5).

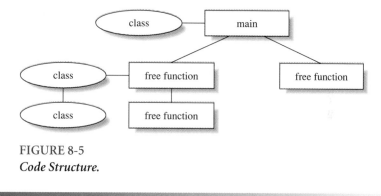

FIGURE 8-5
Code Structure.

8-3 CREATING A FULL YEAR CALENDAR

We illustrate the main concepts in the program development cycle with an application that produces a full year calendar. For the analysis phase, assume we are commissioned by a commercial graphics studio to produce calendars that are enhanced with scenic art. For program specifications, the customer wants the application to prompt for the year and to display a calendar for each month. The display should include a title with the month and year, followed by the table of dates. Figure 8-6 illustrates the desired format for a single month.

July 1776						
Sun	Mon	Tue	Wed	Thu	Fri	Sat
	1	2	3	4	5	6
7	8	9	10	11	12	13
14	15	16	17	18	19	20
21	22	23	24	25	26	27
28	29	30	31			

FIGURE 8-6
Calendar for July, 1776.

After running the application, the customer takes the listing of the individual months, adds graphic art, and markets the calendar.

Designing the Calendar Class

The design phase of the application involves developing class declarations, free functions, and the main program. Our discussion focuses on the design of a Calendar class whose member functions display a calendar for a single month. The main program is responsible for displaying a year-long calendar by simply cycling through the months and outputting the individual calendars.

The Calendar class is designed to display a calendar for a month and year beginning with January, 1600. An object needs to retain a specific month and year as data members and must have a constructor whose integer arguments, initialize these values. To create a default constructor, we give these arguments default values for January, 1600. For operations, the class has a member function, `displayCalendar()`, that outputs the month's calendar. It also should have a series of "get" and "set" functions that allow a programmer to access and update the current value of the month and year. With this information, we can create an initial description of the class.

calendar.h

DESCRIPTION: Calendar **CLASS** ━━━━━━━━━━━━

An object displays a calendar for a specific month and year beginning with January, 1600.

Attributes:
Data items that maintain a value for the month in the range 1 to 12 and a value for the year ≥ 1600.

Operations:

Calendar: Initialize the month and year . Use default values mm = 1 (January) and yyyy = 1600.

Calendar(int mm = 1, int yyyy = 1600);

displayCalendar Display the calendar title and dates.

void displayCalendar();

getMonth Return the current month.

int getMonth();

getyear Return the current year.

int getYear();

setMonth Set the month to mm.

void setMonth(int mm);

setYear Set the year to yyyy.

void setYear(int yyyy);

Designing the displayCalendar() Algorithm. In the Calendar class, an algorithm to display the dates under the correct days in the week poses the most interesting and difficult problem. We need to compute two critical pieces of information. We use April, 1999 as a specific example to illustrate the calculations.

Requirement 1: We require the day of the week on which the first of the month falls.

This information is important, since we must skip space in the first week in order to correctly position the 1st of the month (Figure 8-7).

firstDay

Sun	Mon	Tue	Wed	Thu	Fri	Sat
	Skip to first day			1	2	3
4						
				29	30	

FIGURE 8-7
The Calendar for April, 1999.

Assume that the integer value 0 represents Sunday, 1 represents Monday, and so forth. To find the first day of the calendar year, we set Saturday, January 1, 1600 as the starting point and identify the day corresponding to January 1 for each subsequent year up to the specified calendar year. This calculation simply involves adding either 365 or 366 days to the current day and taking the remainder after division by 7. For instance, year 1600 is a leap year with a total of 366 days. Adding 366 to January 1, 1600 puts the first day of 1601 at Monday

$$(6(Sat) + 366) \% 7 = 1 \text{ (Mon)}$$

By continuing the process, we identify that January 1, 1999 is a Friday (value 5). With this information, we can compute the first day of April by adding the number of days from January 1 to April 1 and taking the remainder after division by 7. In 1999, there are 90 days until April 1. By adding 90 to 5 (Fri) and dividing by 7, the result is 4 (Thu).

Jan. 1, 1600	Jan. 1, 1601		Jan. 1, 1999	Apr 1, 1999
Sat	Mon		Fri	Thu

Requirement 2: We require the number of days in the calendar month.

Once `displayCalendar()` begins placing dates in the calendar grid, it must know when to stop. We must have access to the number of days in each month, including special attention for February. Note that a consideration of leap year is used for both requirement 1 and requirement 2.

Requirement 3: We require a mechanism for placing dates on the calendar.

After identifying the day on which the 1st of the month falls, we will use a loop to output subsequent dates up through the last day in the month. The loop must have a control object that can cycle through the days of the week from Sun to Sat and back to Sun.

Designing Data Members with Composition. To build the Calendar class, we must provide data that represents the month and year. We must also provide operations that satisfy the three requirements we have noted. These needs can be efficiently met by object composition that uses Date and Days objects as data members. The classes were developed in Chapter 6. We define the data members and describe how their operations are involved in the application.

Date member, firstDate:

Stores the date "month 1, year" that is the first day in the specified calendar month.

The object has member functions `getMonth()`, `setMonth()`, `getYear()`, and `setYear()` to access and update the calendar month and year.

The functions `isLeapYear()` and `numberOfDays()` are used in the computation of the day of the week that corresponds to the first of the month (requirement 1).

The return value from `firstDate.daysInMonth()` provides the number of days in the calendar month (requirement 2).

Days member, firstDay:

Stores the day of the week corresponding to "month 1, year".

By starting with Sat January 1, 1600, the function addDay() is used to compute the value of firstDay (requirement 1).

The function succ() provides a control mechanism to display dates on a calendar (requirement 3).

The constructor for the Calendar class has arguments for the month and year that are used to initialize both firstDate and firstDay.

UML for Calendar Class. Having completed a description of the data members and the public member functions, we give a UML representation of the Calendar class (Figure 8-8). The UML also contains a listing of member functions for the supplier classes.

Declaring the Calendar Class

The implementation of the class should use principles of code simplification, duplication, and decomposition. This is accomplished by defining private member functions that handle tasks within the public member functions. For instance, the algorithm for the member function `displayCalendar()` includes displaying the title (month, year, and labels for days of the week) and listing the dates. These are distinct tasks that can be decomposed into separate functions,

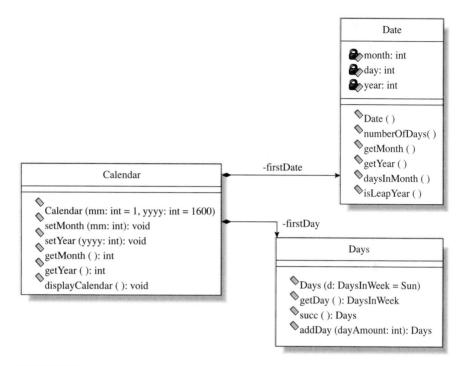

FIGURE 8-8
UML Representation of the Calendar Class.

`displayTitle()` and `displayDates()`. The algorithm to display the dates requires deriving an initial value for the Days object, firstDay. This calculation is performed by the private member function, `firstDayOfMonth()`, that returns the first day of the calendar month as a Days object.

```
firstDay = firstDayOfMonth();
```

Figure 8-9 gives a decomposition chart that includes the public member function displayCalendar() and the related private functions.

The constructor and the member functions `setMonth()` and `setYear()` update the specified calendar month and year. Since, the month must be in the range 1 to 12 and the year must be 1600 or later, we use an error detection func-

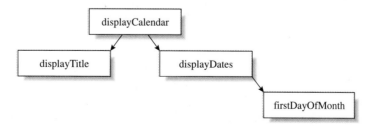

FIGURE 8-9
Decomposition of displayCalendar().

tion, `checkValidDate()`, that checks the run-time values of the arguments mm and yyyy. The use of the error function avoids code duplication since its action is shared by three member functions.

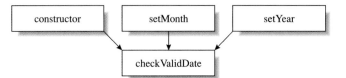

With this framework, we give the full declaration for the Calendar class.

DECLARATION: Calendar CLASS ━━━━━━━━━━

calendar.h

```
class Calendar
{
    private:
        Date firstDate;
        Days firstDay;

        // return day of the week holding first day of month
        Days firstDayOfMonth() const;

        // output month and year followed by labels for days
        // of the week
        void displayTitle() const;

        // output the dates under the correct days of the week
        void displayDates () const;

        // error detection for constructor, setMonth(),
        // and setYear()
        void checkValidDate(int mm, int yyyy) const;

    public:
        Calendar(int mm = 1, int yy = 1600);

        // update the month and year values
        void setMonth(int mm);
        void setYear(int yyyy);

        // access the month and year
        int getMonth() const;
        int getYear() const;

        // display calendar with header and dates
        void displayCalendar() const;
};
```

EXAMPLE 8.3 ▬▬▬▬▬▬▬▬▬▬▬▬▬▬▬▬▬▬▬▬

The example illustrates how Calendar objects can be used in applications.

1. The object, independence, displays the calendar for July, 1776

```
Calendar independence(7,1776);

independence.displayCalendar();

Output:
```

```
                          July 1776
        Sun     Mon     Tue     Wed     Thu     Fri     Sat
                 1       2       3       4       5       6
         7       8       9      10      11      12      13
        14      15      16      17      18      19      20
        21      22      23      24      25      26      27
        28      29      30      31
```

2. With access functions (getMonth(), getYear()) and update functions (setMonth(), setYear()), we can simulate commercial calendars that typically include the next month (in small font) on each page.

```
// calendar objects for the current and next month
Calendar currMonth(month,year), nextMonth;

// display current month
currMonth.displayCalendar();

// set and display next month's calendar
nextMonth = currMonth;

// is month Dec? if so, month is Jan of next year
if (currMonth.getMonth() == 12)
{
   nextMonth.setMonth(1);
   nextMonth.setYear(currMonth.getYear()+1);
}
else
   // increment the month leaving year fixed
   nextMonth.setMonth(currMonth.getMonth()+1);

// display calendar for next month
nextMonth.displayCalendar();   ■
```

Implementing the Member Functions

In the object-oriented design (OOD) phase of the development cycle, we have divided the Calendar class into a constructor and five other public member functions. Four private member functions provide support for the public functions. In this section, we implement selected functions. A completing listing for the Calendar class is contained in the file **calendar.h.**

Implementing the Public Member Functions. For our application, the key public functions are the constructor and `displayCalendar()`. We give the implementation for each function along with code for `setYear()`.

The constructor for the Calendar class is responsible for taking the month and year arguments and initializing the Date member firstDate and the Days member firstDay. An invalid month or year argument is detected by the function checkValidDate().

```
// constructor. check for valid date and initialize attributes
Calendar::Calendar(int mm, int yyyy)
{
    // do error checking before continuing
    checkValidDate(mm,yyyy);

    // assign 1st of month mm in year yyyy
    firstDate = Date(mm,1,yyyy);

    // computation done by the private function
    firstDay = firstDayOfMonth();
}
```

A monthly calendar has a title with month and year and a listing of the dates. Using code decomposition, we break the algorithm for the display into separate functions, `displayTitle()` and `displayDates()`. The implementation of `displayCalendar()` makes calls to these private functions. The following is a graphical display of the decomposition of the function.

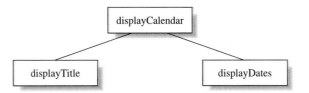

The implementation calls the private member functions displayTitle() and displayDates().

```
void Calendar::displayCalendar() const
{
    displayTitle();     // output the month/year title
    displayDates();     // output the grid of dates
}
```

The function `setYear()` updates the year for the calendar. Like the constructor, the function does error checking and then modifies the objects first-Date and firstDay so that a call to `displayCalendar()` would properly display the month for the new year.

```
// update the current year
void Calendar::setYear(int yyyy)
{
    // verify that yyyy is valid
    checkValidDate(firstDate.getMonth(),yyyy);

    // set firstDate to new year
    firstDate.setYear(yyyy);

    // recompute firstDay
    firstDay = firstDayOfMonth();
}
```

Implementing the Private Member Functions. You have seen how the private member functions are used as tools in the class implementation. The functions, `firstDayOfMonth()` and `displayDates()` use the most interesting algorithms and so we include a completing listing of each function.

firstDayOfMonth():

The function creates a Days object, cday, that is initialized to Sat, since January 1, 1600 was a Saturday. A Date object d is also declared and represents the date January 1, 1600. A for loop begins at year 1600 and moves c day and d forward to the specified calendar year. In each iteration, the value of cday is updated by adding either 365 or 366 days using the `addDay()` function from the Days class. The determination of leap year is handled by using the Date object d. To complete the calculation, we need to add the number of days to the first of the month. This value is provided by executing the Date function `numberOf-Days()` for the object firstDate.

```
// return the first day of the month
Days Calendar::firstDayOfMonth()
{
    int y, year = firstDate.getYear();

    // d is always Jan. 1 for the years y=1600 to the
    // current year. used to check for leap year
    Date d;
    Days cday(Sat);    // set cday to Saturday, January 1, 1600

    for (y = 1600; y < year; y++)
    {
        d.setYear(y);
        if (d.isLeapYear())
            cday.addDay(366);
        else
            cday.addDay(365);
    }
```

```
   // add days from Jan 1 to first of month.  note
   // that we must subtract 1, since Jan 1 is day 1
   cday.addDay(firstDate.numberOfDays()-1);

   return cday;
}
```

displayDates():

With the firstDate and firstDay objects, we have the critical information needed to write the dates under the correct day of the week. The number of days in the month is determined by using the `daysInMonth()` function from the Date class. The Days object d advances through the days of the week, starting with Sun. Before writing the first date, we must skip space to firstDay. Once we start filling the calendar, we move to a new week after writing the date for Saturday. We conclude by skipping any unused days of the last week. These two actions are implemented by putting out a newline.

```
// output dates of the calendar under the correct days of week
void Calendar::displayDates() const
{
   // set number of days in the month
   int monthLength = firstDate.daysInMonth();
   int dayValue = 1;
   Days d(Sun);

   // skip spaces up to the first day of the month
   while (d.getDay() < firstDay.getDay())
   {
      cout << setw(7) << " ";
      d.succ();
   }

   // output the dates 1 .. monthlength
   while (dayValue <= monthLength)
   {
      cout << setw(7) << dayValue;
      dayValue++;
      // is next day Sun of new week, output newline
      if (d.getDay() == Sat)
         cout << endl;
      d.succ();
   }

   // skip unused days in the last week
   if (d.getDay() != Sun)
      cout << endl;
}
```

The Calendar Application

The application displays a calendar for the entire year. Once we know the year, displaying the entire calendar can be implemented with a free function that takes the year as an argument and uses a loop to display the calendar for each month.

APPLICATION 8-3 DISPLAYING A YEARLY CALENDAR

The main program has the task of prompting the user for the desired year and calling the free function displayYearCalendar().

```cpp
#include <iostream.h>

#include "calendar.h"        // use Calendar class


// output a calendar for year
void displayYearCalendar(int year);

int main()
{
    // year entered by user
    int year;

    cout << "Enter the year: ";
    cin >> year;
    cout << endl;
    displayYearCalendar(year);

    return 0;
}

void displayYearCalendar(int year)
{
    // use cal to display each month of year
    Calendar cal;
    // loop control object steps through months 1 to 12
    int month;

    // set year once and set month in each iteration
    cal.setYear(year);
    for(month=1; month <= 12; month++)
    {
        cal.setMonth(month);
        cal.displayCalendar();
        cout << endl << endl;
    }
}
```

```
Run:

Enter the year: 2000

                            January 2000
        Sun     Mon     Tue     Wed     Thu     Fri     Sat
                                                          1
         2       3       4       5       6       7       8
         9      10      11      12      13      14      15
        16      17      18      19      20      21      22
        23      24      25      26      27      28      29
        30      31


                   .    .    .    .

                           December 2000
        Sun     Mon     Tue     Wed     Thu     Fri     Sat
                                                  1       2
         3       4       5       6       7       8       9
        10      11      12      13      14      15      16
        17      18      19      20      21      22      23
        24      25      26      27      28      29      30
        31
```

8-4 ACCESSING AND STORING OBJECTS

In this chapter, we have discussed techniques for program design. In this section we want to consider some technical points on scope and lifetime of objects that will help us better understand code structure. The study will also give us new tools to implement applications.

Scope

In a C++ program, an object is introduced through a declaration. Depending on where the declaration occurs, the object name may be used within a specified region of the program, called its *scope*.

> **Definition** The *scope of visibility* for an object, or simply the *scope* of an object, is the portion of a program in which it can be accessed.

The issue of scope must deal with the fact that C++ is a *block structured language* in which the main program, classes and their member functions, and free functions have a body isolated from the rest of the program with the block delimiters "{" and "}." This requires us to distinguish among local, global, and class scope categories.

Local Scope. An object that is declared within a block has *local scope* that extends from the point of the declaration to the end of the block. The object is not visible outside the block. The formal arguments in a function have local scope within their function body. Their scope begins with the declaration in the argument list and ends with the termination of the function body. Figure 8-10(a) illustrates a formal function argument called value, and Figure 8-10(b) shows a local object of the same name declared in the main program. These two objects are independent of each other. In addition, f() has a local object, temp.

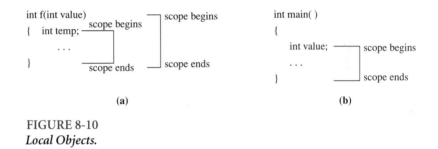

(a)   (b)

FIGURE 8-10
Local Objects.

EXAMPLE 8.4

Functions f and g declare local objects. In addition, f has a formal argument that is local in its body.

```
void f(int n)        // n is local to the body of f()
{
    int x = 5, y;    // x and y are local to the body of f()

    n = 20;          // update value of local object n
    cout << x;
        . . .
}                    // after return, n, x, y are not accessible

void g()
{
    int x;           // x is local within the body of g()

    x = 20;
        . . .
}
```

Any attempt to access the object y outside of function f would result in a compilation error. Both functions declare objects with the same name x. The declarations create two completely separate and unrelated objects. ■

A main program may create nested blocks containing declarations. Any object that is declared in the outer block is visible to statements in the inner block. The reverse is not true. Any object declared in the inner block has scope only within that block. The following example illustrates these points. The problem is somewhat complicated by the fact that object i is declared in both the outer and inner block. In this situation, the inner object i overides the outer i for the duration of its block.

Technical Note

```
int main()
{
    // outer block        // scope of i, j is outer block
    int i = 3, j = 2;

    i += j;                // outer i is 5

    // inner block
    {
        int i = 8;         // scope is inner block

        i += j;            // access inner i and outer j
        cout << i;         // Output: 10
    }

    cout << i;             // Output: 5

    return 0
}
```

We do not use nested blocks with declarations in this book.

Class Scope. Scope is a critical feature of class data members. We discussed the concept when introducing the terms public and private in a class declaration. A private member is local to its class and can be accessed only in a class member function. There is an exception to this rule involving the declaration of a friend that is discussed in Chapter 9.

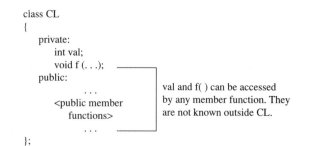

```
class CL
{
    private:
        int val;
        void f (...);
    public:
        ...
        <public member
            functions>
        ...
};
```

val and f( ) can be accessed by any member function. They are not known outside CL.

*Programming
Note*

A class may contain public data members. Of course, such data members can be accessed by any class member function. Furthermore, if a block declares an object of the class, any of its statements can retrieve or modify the public data member. Allowing modification of a data member can be dangerous for program integrity. Good object-oriented programming style keeps data members private and uses member functions to update their values. Recall that this is the principle of information hiding.

Global Scope. An object with *global scope* is declared outside any class or function. Its scope is from the point of declaration to the end of the program. Any function declared below a *global object* can reference the object. Good program design generally avoids nonconstant global objects. They can harm program readability and make debugging difficult. In this book, we declare global objects only when they are named constants. When we use them, they are declared in a group after the include directives and prior to the function prototypes. Named constants are important in good code design. They enhance program readability by attaching meaningful names to numeric, character, or string literals. They make a program easy to modify when critical constant values change. For instance, a government accounting application accesses the local tax rate as a constant. A single change to the named constant updates the rate.

```
const double TAXRATE = 0.0575 0.06; // update from 5.75% to 6%
```

Application 8-4 illustrates an effective use of named constants which are declared as global objects.

APPLICATION 8-4 ILLUSTRATING GLOBAL CONSTANTS

Statistical applications often require the factorial function. The function, denoted by n!, takes a positive integer n and evaluates the series of products

$$n! = n * (n - 1) * (n - 2) * \ldots * 2 * 1$$

For instance,

$$4! = 4 * 3 * 2 * 1 = 24$$

$$6! = 6 * 5 * 4 * 3 * 2 * 1 = 720$$

Before high-speed computers, statisticians would be forced to do hand calculations or use a simple calculator having no factorial key. The task is unrealistic for a large n. As a substitute, Stirling's approximation for n! can be used with results that are remarkably accurate. The following formula defines the approximation as a function of *n* and the constants π and $e = 2.7182818. \ldots$

$$\text{Stirling's Approximation:} \quad \sqrt{2\pi n} \left(\frac{n}{e}\right)^n$$

The program declares two global constants whose values are 2π and e respectively. In keeping with our stated policy, the constants are defined after the include directives and before the function prototypes. The functions factorial() and sterling() provide a direct calculation for n! and its approximation. For $n = 50, 100,$ and 150, we output both results.

```cpp
#include <iostream.h>
#include <math.h>               // used for Stirling formula

// constants used in the program
const double TWOPI = 2.0 * 3.141592653589793;
const double E = 2.718281828459045;

// compute Stirling's approximation to n!
double stirling(int n);

// compute n!
double factorial(int n);

int main()
{
    int n;

    // compute n! and contrast with  Stirling's approximation
    // n = 50, 100 and 150
    for (n=50; n <= 150; n += 50)
    {
        cout << n << "! = " << factorial(n) << endl;
        cout << "Approximation = "  << stirling(n) << endl
             << endl;
    }

    return 0;
}

double stirling(int n)
{
    return sqrt(TWOPI*n)  * pow(n/E,n);
}

double factorial(int n)
{
    double fact = 1.0;
    int i;

    // compute 1 * 2 * 3 * ... * (n-1) * n
    for (i=1;i <= n;i++)
        fact *= i;
    return fact;
}
```

```
Run:

50! = 3.04141e+64
Approximation = 3.03634e+64

100! = 9.33262e+157
Approximation = 9.32485e+157

150! = 5.71338e+262
Approximation = 5.71021e+262
```

*Technical
Note*

Our discussion of local and global scope has focused on objects. The same categories apply to object types. Up to this point in the book, all types have been global. This simply means that the type is known from the point of its declaration and is available for use throughout the remainder of the program. For instance, the istream class is available to the program immediately after including **iostream.h.** The same access is given to the CircleShape and RectShape types once the files **circlesh.h** and **rectsh.h** are included. C++ also allows a programmer to define local types. For instance, the main program outline declares a local enumeration type.

```
int main()
{
    enum Colors {red, green, blue};
    Colors c;
        . . .
    c = blue;
        . . .
}
```

The Colors type would not be available to any program unit outside the main program. In general, programs use global types and do not isolate a type declaration inside the main program or other function.

Storage Class

During program execution, each object has a lifetime that is the period during which its memory is allocated. Some objects exist only temporarily and some exist for the entire program. The lifetime of an object is defined by the storage class that can be either *automatic* or *static*.

> **Definition Automatic Storage Class:** A local object that is declared within a program block is said to be an *automatic object*. The object is allocated when the program enters the block and deallocated when the program exits the block. In a class, an *automatic data member* is allocated when an object is declared and continues to exist until the corresponding object is deallocated.

A function provides a good example of automatic objects. Any argument and any local object that is declared within the function block is automatic. In the following example, objects upper, r, and circ are automatic. The circle object, circ, has a data member called radius that is also automatic. The data member exists so long as the object circ exists.

```
// output area of circles with radii 1, 2, ..., upper
void circleAreas(double upper)
{
    double r = 1.0;   // integer r is automatic
    Circle circ(r);   // circ and c::radius are automatic


        . . .

}
```

To better understand the lifetime of an automatic object, we trace the action of the run-time system during a call to the function circleAreas(). The system is responsible for allocating memory for the objects and assigning initial values.

```
// 10 is the run-time argument corresponding to upper
circleAreas(10);
```

The system first allocates memory for the formal argument upper and copies the value 10 to it (Figure 8-11(a)). Corresponding to the declaration of object r in the function body, the system allocates space for an integer and initializes it with the value 1 (Figure 8-11(b)). With a class object, the system must allocate space for each of the data members and then call the constructor. With circ, a location for data member radius is allocated and the constructor assigns the value of r as its initial value (Figure 8-11(c)).

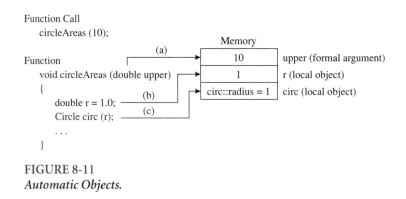

FIGURE 8-11
Automatic Objects.

Upon exiting from the function, memory is deallocated for the objects upper, r, and circ. The object circ is destroyed by deleting memory for its data member, radius.

Static Storage Class. The memory allocated for a static object is permanent. A global object is the simplest example of an object with static storage class. Once it is declared, it remains in existence for the rest of the program and is accessible by all units from the point of its declaration to the end of the program.

A *static local object* is assigned a permanent location in memory and retains its value between function calls. A local object is made static by including the keyword *static* in its declaration.

```
static int lineCount = 0;
```

The Date class member function `writeLongDate()` uses a static array of strings, monthNames.

```
// write date with full month name
void Date::writeLongDate() const
{
    // array begins with empty string corresponding to month 0
    static String monthNames[] =
        {"", "January", "February", "March", "April", "May",
         "June", "July", "August", "September", "October",
         "November", "December"
        };
    // use month as index into monthNames
    cout << monthNames[month] << " " << day << ", " << year;
}
```

The array is initialized only once, prior to the first call of `writeLongDate()`. If monthNames is not declared static, the initialization would occur each time the function is called.

A data member of a class may be declared as static in the class declaration and is known as a *static data member*. There is only one copy of the data member, and it is shared by each object of the class in the program. The data member must be defined outside any program unit, like a global object. The class scope operator must be used to associate the object with the class.

```
class CL
{  ...
    static Type statObj;
};

Type CL::statObj;
```

A static data member is normally private and all of the customary class access rules apply.

EXAMPLE 8.5 ━━━━━━━━━━━━━━━━━━━━━━━━━━━━

In the Dice class, only one random sequence should be shared by all objects. This is done by including a static RandomNumber object in the class declaration.

```
class Dice
{
    private:
```

```
        int numberOfDice;   // number of dice to toss

        // random number generator class used for the dice toss.
        // made static so all Dice objects share the
        // same random sequence
        static RandomNumber rnd;

    public:
        ...
};

// definition for static object rnd
RandomNumber Dice::rnd;   ■
```

*Exploring
Concepts*

In the Dice class, the private data member, rnd, is declared as a static Random-Number object. For a default seed, the RandomNumber class implementation uses a clock time that changes every second. What is the importance of static when two or more Dice objects are used in the same application with a default seed?

For a programming example, we modify the Accumulator class and make the data member total static. We name the new class AccumulatorStatic. Even though a program may declare two or more AccumulatorStatic objects, only one copy of total is shared by all of the objects. Define total immediately after the class declaration using the class scope operator "::" and give the object its initial value of 0.

accstat.h

```
DECLARATION: AccumulatorStatic CLASS ━━━━━━━━
// all objects share one copy of total.  inline code used
class AccumulatorStatic
{
    private:
        // total created by all AccumulatorStatic objects
        static double total;
    public:
        AccumulatorStatic()            // default constructor
        {}

        double getTotal()              // return total
        { return total; }

        void addValue(int value = 1.0) // add value to total
        { total += value;}
};

// declaration of private static data member total
int AccumulatorStatic::total = 0.0;
```

PROGRAM 8.1

The program declares two AccumulatorStatic objects accum1 and accum2 and applies `addValue()` to each object. Note that each call to `addValue()` modifies the shared static data member AccumulatorStatic::total. A call to the `getTotal()` member function of any object will return the shared data value.

```cpp
#include <iostream.h>

#include "accstat.h"        // use AccumulatorStatic class

int main()
{
   AccumulatorStatic accum1, accum2;

   accum1.addValue(3);                // add 3 to shared total
   cout << accum1.getTotal() << endl;
   accum2.addValue(5);                // add 5 to shared total
   cout << accum2.getTotal() << endl;

   return 0;
}
```

```
Run:

3
8
```

8-5   RECURSIVE ALGORITHMS

An algorithm is a sequence of steps that performs a task. In some cases, the algorithm may invoke itself with "smaller" input values. Eventually, the process evolves into trivial cases that can be directly handled. The following situation illustrates the idea of recursion. In an art gallery, a man stares at a picture on the wall. The picture portrays a man in an art gallery staring at a smaller picture that is itself a picture of a man in an art gallery staring at a smaller picture, and so forth. Eventually, the size of the picture gets too small to repeat.

In C++, a recursive algorithm is implemented by a recursive function. In its implementation, a recursive function makes calls to itself.

> **Definition** A *recursive function* is a function that calls itself in its function body. The call uses different arguments that ultimately reach values that will allow the function to return a result.

To illustrate a recursive function, we present a situation that is easier to visualize than the man in the gallery. On a graphics screen, a ring of circles are

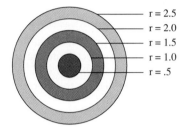

FIGURE 8-12

Ring of Circles.

drawn about a fixed center. The outer circle starts with a radius of r = 3 and in-cludes a series of inner circles whose radius progressively decrease by 0.5 units down to a final radius of 1 (Figure 8-12).

To create the circles with a recursive algorithm, we implement the recursive function called `ringDraw()` that draws a circle of radius r and then calls it-self to draw another circle with a radius reduced by 0.5 units. The following is the skeleton of the function implementation.

```
void ringDraw(CircleShape& circle);
(
    double r = circle.getRadius();

    if (r >= 0)                    // stop when r <= 0
    {
        . . .
        circle.draw();             // draw a circle of radius r
        . . .
        r -= 0.5;
        circle.setRadius(r);

        // call itself for next smaller circle
        ringDraw(circle);
    }
}
```

Note that the function contains an if statement that checks the size of the radius. The recursive process terminates when the radius gets smaller than 1.0. This is called a *stopping condition*. For r >= 1.0, the body of the if statement makes a function call to `ringDraw()`. This is called a *recursive step*. Let's trace the algorithm and see how the function creates the ring of circles. We assume that the main program starts the process by calling ringDraw() with radius 3.0.

Step		Function Call	Action
1	in main:	call ringDraw(circle)	draw circle with r=2.5
2	in ringDraw:	call ringDraw(circle)	draw circle with r=2.0
3	in ringDraw:	call ringDraw(circle)	draw circle with r=1.5
4	in ringDraw:	call ringDraw(circle)	draw circle with r=1.0
5	in ringDraw:	call ringDraw(circle)	draw circle with r=0.5
6	in ringDraw:	call ringDraw(circle)	stop: limit reached

Finding Recursive Algorithms

Recursion can be found in the simple mathematical problem of computing x^n, where x is a real number and n is a non-negative integer. The calculation, called the power function, is usually associated with repeated multiplication

$$x^n = \underbrace{x * x * x * \ldots * x * x}_{n \; x's} \qquad \text{// a product with n x's}$$

For instance, the following products give various powers of 2.

$$2^0 = 1 \qquad \qquad \text{// note! this is a special case}$$

$$2^1 = 2 * 1$$

$$2^2 = 2 * 2 = 4$$

$$2^3 = 2 * 2 * 2 = 8$$

$$2^4 = 2 * 2 * 2 * 2 = 16$$

This process can also be viewed recursively. Think about how you would mentally compute 2^6. Unless you already know the result, you start with smaller powers of 2 and build your answer.

Start with 1

2^1 is $2 * 1 = 2$

2^2 is $2 * 2 = 4$

2^3 is $2 * 4 = 8$

2^4 is $2 * 8 = 16$

2^5 is $2 * 16 = 32$

2^6 is $2 * 32 = 64$

To see the recursion, note that each step in the process uses the results from a previous step as part of the calculation. Successive powers of 2 are just two times the previous value of the function.

$$2^n = 2 * 2^{n-1} \qquad \text{// n > 0. recursive step}$$

$$2^0 = 1 \qquad \text{// n = 0, no recursive call. stopping condition}$$

A similar recursive definition can be used to describe the general power function. For a real number x, x^n is given by

$$x^n = \begin{cases} 1 & n = 0 \\ x * x^{(n-1)} & n > 0 \end{cases}$$

The recursive definition is divided into two parts. For $n > 0$, the value for x^n is obtained by first computing $x^{(n-1)}$ and then multiplying by x. To obtain a value for $x^{(n-1)}$, a similar calculation would multiply $x^{(n-2)}$ and x which in turn assumes a previous calculation with $x^{(n-3)}$ and x, and so forth. The recursive step is executed over and over again with decreasing exponents until we reach the stopping condition that directly evaluates x^0 as 1.

> **Definition** An algorithm is recursive if its definition consists of
>
> 1. One or more *stopping conditions* that can be directly evaluated for explicit data values.
> 2. One or more *recursive steps* which apply the same algorithm to a modified set of data. Eventually, recursive steps must lead to stopping conditions.

Developing Recursive Functions

In the implementation of a recursive algorithm, as a C++ function, the stopping conditions and recursive steps are often distinguished using an if/else statement. In this section, we give examples of recursive functions. The power function that computes x^n is used as the first example.

The Power Function. Recall the recursive formulation of the power function.

$$\text{power}(x,n) = x^n = \begin{cases} 1 & n = 0 \text{ (stopping condition)} \\ x * x^{(n-1)} & n > 0 \text{ (recursive step)} \end{cases}$$

The programmer implements the function with an if/else statement that evaluates the single stopping condition $n == 0$ and returns the value 1 when it is true. The else alternative handles the recursive step and returns the value of the expression $x*x^{(n-1)}$.

```cpp
// compute and return x to the power n
double power(double x, int n)
{
    // stopping condition is n == 0. power(x,0) = 1
    if (n == 0)
        return 1;
    else
        // recursive step: power(x,n) = x * power(x,n-1)
        return x*power(x,n-1);
}
```

PROGRAM 8.2

In a loop with four iterations, the program inputs a base b and exponent n and outputs b^n using `power()`.

```cpp
#include <iostream.h>

#include "textlib.h"

// compute and return x to the power n
double power(double x, int n);

int main()
{
```

```
int i, n;
double b, powerResult;

for (i = 1; i <= 4; i++)
{

    cout << "Enter the base b and exponent n: ";
    cin >> b >> n;
    powerResult = power(b,n);
    cout << "Power is " << setreal(1,3)
         << powerResult << endl;
}

    return 0;
}

/* implementation of power() given in the discussion */
```

```
Run:

Enter the base b and exponent n: 3 6
Power is 729.000
Enter the base b and exponent n: 2 8
Power is 256.000
Enter the base b and exponent n: 2.5 2
Power is 6.250
Enter the base b and exponent n: 10 6
Power is 1000000.000
```

Recursive Ring Draw. We began our discussion of recursion with the ring of circles and the function `ringDraw()`. The following is the recursive implementation of the algorithm and the corresponding C++ implementation.

Recursive algorithm:

stopping condition: stop the drawing when r <= 0
recursive step: draw a circle of radius r.
                     call ringDraw() with radius r-0.5

Recursive function:

To create code for the `ringDraw()` function, we call on our understanding of CircleShape objects. We assume that a main program defines a CircleShape object with a fixed center. The object is passed as a reference argument. The recursive step must draw the circle and then update both its radius and color so that the next figure has a contrasting color.

```
// draw a series of colored rings using recursion
void ringDraw(CircleShape& circle)
```

```
      {
         // used to update color and radius
         ShapeColor cs;
         double r = circle.getRadius();

         if (r > 0)                      // stop when r <= 0
         {
            circle.draw();               // draw circle of radius r

            cs = circle.getColor();      // get current color
            cs++;                        // move to next color
            circle.setColor(cs);         // draw in new color
            r -= .5;                     // decrease the radius
            circle.setRadius(r);         // set the new radius

            ringDraw(circle);            // call with new radius
         }
      }
```

APPLICATION 8-5 CREATING A CIRCLE RING

The program uses the `ringDraw()` function to create a ring of circles.
Note how the main program declares a CircleShape object and then makes the
initial call.

```
#include "graphlib.h"      // graphics functions
#include "circlesh.h"      // CircleShape class

// draw a series of colored rings using recursion
void ringDraw(CircleShap& circle);

int main()
{
   // circle at (5,4), radius 2.5, color purple
   CircleShape circle(5,4,2.5,purple);

   openWindow();           // open the graphics window

   ringDraw(circle);       // call the recursive function

   viewWindow();           // pause to view the circles
   closeWindow();

   return 0;
}

/* implementation of ringDraw() given in the program discus-
sion */
```

```
Run:
```

Tracing a Recursive Function

The relatively simple code that comprises many recursive functions masks the actions that are involved in their execution. To see how the arguments and re-turn values are used in a recursive function, we trace execution of the function, `power()`, for $x = 2$, $n = 4$. The following list gives the sequence of recursive steps when the function is called from the main program.

Step	Fu\nction Call	Action
1	in main: call power(2,4)	evaluate 2 * power(2,3)
2	in power: call power(2,3)	evaluate 2 * power(2,2)
3	in power: call power(2,2)	evaluate 2 * power(2,1)
4	in power: call power(2,1)	evaluate 2 * power(2,0)
5	in power: call power(2,0)	return 1

Note that the first four function calls involve evaluating the expression 2 * power(2,$n - 1$). In each case, the multiplication must be delayed until the call power(2,$n - 1$) returns. Figure 8-13 describes the sequence of function calls. All multiplications are delayed until step 5, when `power()` returns the value 1. This result is then used to evaluate the expression 2 * power(2,0) in step 4. The result is 2, which is the return value that is used in step 3, and so forth.

What is the action of the following recursive function?

```
void f(int n)
{
    if (n > 0)
        f(n/2);
    cout << n%2;
}
```

Exploring Concepts

When run-time arguments are passed to a function, they are stored on the *sys-tem stack*, which is a block of memory allocated by the run-time system. The space for the arguments is not removed until the function returns, which may be a significant amount of time in the case of a large recursive problem. A long series of recursive calls can cause the application to run out of memory and "crash."

Improper coding of a recursive function can also lead to program failure. For instance, show that if the if statement in f() is rewritten as follows, the recursion will continue until memory is exhausted.

```
if (n >= 0)
    . . .
```

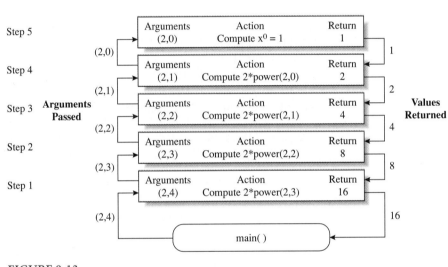

FIGURE 8-13
Power Function Calls.

8-6   RECURSION AND PROBLEM SOLVING

In the previous section, we developed the concept of recursion and its implementation with C++ functions. While the examples use recursion, they can be done more easily using simple looping constructs. This is not always the case. We consider the Tower of Hanoi puzzle and the problelm of solving a maze. There is no simple loop-based algorithm that can be used to solve these problems.

The Tower of Hanoi Puzzle

Tower of Hanoi is one of the most famous recursive algorithims in computer science. It is also a favorite of puzzle fans.

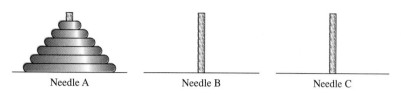

Legend has it that priests in a temple in the Far East were given a brass platform with three diamond needles, labeled A, B, and C. On needle A were stacked 64 golden disks, each one slightly smaller than the one under it. The priests were given the task of moving the disks one at a time from needle to needle. At no time could a larger disk be placed on top of a smaller disk. In the legend, the world ends when the priests complete the movement of disks from needle A to needle C. The Tower of Hanoi is a complex puzzle with a simple recursive solution. The Tower illustrates the power of recursive design that may hide layers of complex operations that occur during execution of the function.

Solving the Tower of Hanoi with Recursion

While the legendary puzzle used 64 disks, we illustrate the problem using a simpler three-disk Hanoi puzzle. Watch the steps as we move disks from needle A to C by way of the intermediate needle B. To illustrate the process, we break up the moves into stages encompassing several steps. These stages will be used later to develop a recursive algorithm.

The first stage uses three moves to shift the top two disks from needle A to needle B.

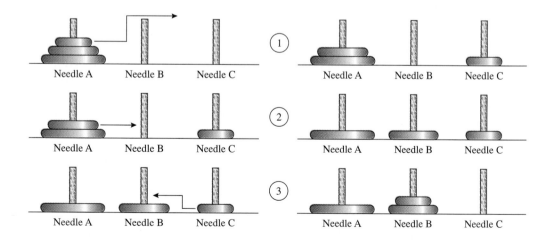

After completing the first stage, only the largest disk remains at needle A. In stage two, a simple move shifts this disk from A to C.

A third stage takes three steps to move the two disks from B to C.

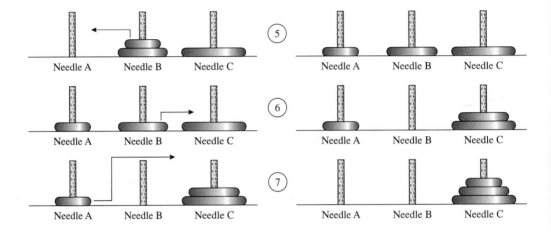

Notice that, in the process, stage 1 and stage 3 describe a Tower of Hanoi problem with 2 disks. The fact that solving the larger algorithm involves using a smaller version of the algorithm makes the solution recursive. In the first stage, two disks move from needle A to needle B and use needle C for temporary storage. In the third stage, two disks move from needle B to needle C with needle A serving as temporary storage.

The recursive process translates into the function called hanoi(). The arguments include n, the number of disks on the tower, and three String arguments that denote the name of the starting needle (initNeedle), the destination needle (endNeedle), and the intermediate needle (tempNeedle) that temporarily hold disks during the move.

```
// move n disks from initNeedle to endNeedle
// using tempNeedle for temporary storage
void hanoi(int n, const String& initNeedle,
                  const String& endNeedle,
                  const String& tempNeedle);
```

Stage 1 is a recursive step. It involves moving n-1 disks from needle initNeedle (needle A) to tempNeedle (needle B) using endNeedle (needle C) for temporary storage.

```
// recursive call for stage 1
hanoi(n-1, initNeedle, tempNeedle, endNeedle);
```

Stage 2 is a stoppping condition that moves a single disk from initNeedle to end-Needle. It transfers the largest disk to endNeedle. Note if n == 1, only Stage 2 is executed.

```
cout << "Move" << initNeedle << " to " << endNeedle << endl;
```

Stage 3 is again a recursive step with n-1 disks moving from tempNeedle to end-Needle using initNeedle for temporary storage.

```
// recursive call for stage 3
hanoi(n-1, tempNeedle, endNeedle, initNeedle);
```

The following is the code for the hanoi() function.

```
// move n disks from initNeedle to endNeedle, using tempNeedle
// for intermediate storage of the disks
void hanoi(int n, const String& initNeedle,
          const String& endNeedle, const String& tempNeedle)
{
    // stopping condition: move one disk
    if (n == 1)
        cout  << "move " << initNeedle << " to "
              << endNeedle << endl;
    else
    {
        // block move takes n-1 disks from initNeedle to
        // tempNeedle using endNeedle for temporary storage
        hanoi(n-1,initNeedle,tempNeedle,endNeedle);

        // move largest disk to endNeedle
        cout  << "move " << initNeedle << " to "
              << endNeedle << endl;

        // block move takes n-1 disks from tempNeedle to
        // endNeedle using initNeedle for temporary storage
        hanoi(n-1,tempNeedle,endNeedle,initNeedle);
    }
}
```

APPLICATION 8-6 SOLVING THE TOWER OF HANOI PUZZLE

The program prompts for the number of disks and uses the hanoi() function to solve the Tower of Hanoi puzzle. The run gives a listing of the moves for *n* = 3 disks.

```
#include <iostream.h>

#include "tstring.h"

// move n disks from initNeedle to endNeedle, using tempNeedle
```

```
                // for intermediate storage of the disks
                void hanoi(int n, const String& initNeedle,
                           const String& endNeedle, const String& tempNeedle);

                int main()
                {
                   // number of disks and the needle names
                   int n;
                   String needleA = "A",
                          needleB = "B",
                          needleC = "C";

                   // prompt for n and solve the puzzle for n disks
                   cout << "Enter the number of disks: ";
                   cin >> n;
                   cout << "The solution for n = " << n << endl;
                   hanoi(n,needleA, needleC, needleB);

                   return 0;
                }

                /* definition of hanoi() given in the program discussion */
```

```
   Run:

   Enter the number of disks: 3
   The solution for n = 3
   move A to C
   move A to B
   move C to B
   move A to C
   move B to A
   move B to C
   move A to C
```

Traversing a Maze

Everyone is familiar with the challenge and frustration of migrating through a maze. Twists and turns down the different hallways in the maze frequently end up in a dead end and force continual retracing of steps. The challenge is to develop a strategy that will ultimately find a path through the maze.

A maze as a numbered set of intersections. As an object moves through the maze, it enters an intersection from one direction and is presented with options to proceed to the left, straight ahead, or to the right (Figure 8-14). To solve a maze, we develop the Maze class that contains a recursive member function. The implementation of this function utilizes a strategy called backtracking.

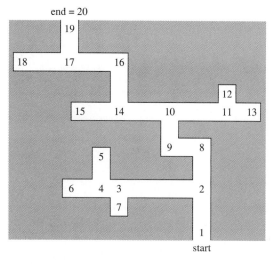

FIGURE 8-14
Traversing a Maze.

Using Recursion to Solve a Maze

To traverse a Maze, an object enters an intersection and then must determine whether it should proceed to the left, straightahead, or to the right. In some cases, one or more of the directions may be blocked. When all of the directions are blocked, the intersection is called a deadend. In Figure 8-15, for intersection A an object that enters from the right may proceed in three directions. If the object proceeds straight ahead, it enters intersection B and finds two directions blocked. It may proceed only to the right. If the object proceeds from intersection A to C (right), it runs into a deadend.

To understand the *backtracking* strategy for moving through a maze, consider the example in Figure 8-16 that has 11 numbered intersections. Passage begins at intersection 1 (start) and ends at intersection 12 (end).

The strategy consists of making specific choices at each intersection. If it is possible to proceed to the left, select this option and enter a new intersection that presents a set of new choices. If the left direction is blocked, attempt to proceed straight ahead. Assuming the first two choices are not available, attempt to proceed to the right. If this fails, you are at a deadend and must backtrack.

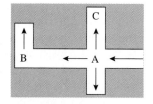

FIGURE 8-15
Maze Intersections.

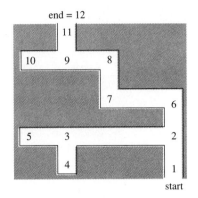

FIGURE 8-16
Backtracking Through a Maze.

Retrace the path to the previous intersection and post a sign that your choice of direction at that intersection ultimately leads to a deadend. Think of this as a "Not a through street" sign. Note that backtracking provides new information. As the backtracking process continues, more and more exits become blocked since they do not provide a path to the finish. Consider the maze in Figure 8-16. We list the first nine choices, including backtracking.

Intersection	Action	Resulting Intersection
At 1	Go straight	Enter 2
At 2	Go left	Enter 3
At 3	Go left	Enter 4
At 4	Deadend; backtrack to 3	Enter 3
At 3	Go straight	Enter 5
At 5	Deadend; backtrack to 3	Enter 3
At 3	Deadend; backtrack to 2	Enter 2
At 2	Go straight	Enter 6
At 6	Go left	Enter 7

A Backtracking Maze Algorithm. Many recursive algorithms use the principle of backtracking. The principle applies only when we are faced with a problem that requires a number of steps with decisions at each step. In an effort to obtain a final solution, we move step by step, creating a partial solution that appears to be consistent with the requirements of the final solution. If, at any step, we create a partial solution that is inconsistent with a final solution, we backtrack one or more steps to the last consistent partial solution. At times backtracking may entail one step forward and n steps backward.

Backtracking can be used to traverse a maze. The problem is to create a path through a series of intersections that leads from the start to the end. At each intersection k, we have a path that leads from the start to k. This path is the "partial solution"; the final solution would be the partial solution for intersection "end." For our analysis, we assume that a maze does not have a cycle that would allow us to wander about in circles. For instance, Figure 8-17 features a maze with a cycle involving intersections 2, 3, 4, and 5.

To create a computer model of a maze, we define the Maze class that includes a list of intersections as a data member. We describe each intersection in the maze as a triple of nonnegative integers that correspond to the three directions left, straightahead, and right. An entry in the triple has value 0 when the corresponding direction is blocked and value k > 0 when choosing that directon would lead to intersection k. To store the intersections, we define a two-dimensional matrix, intsecMat, which has MAX_MAZE_SIZE number of rows and three columns. The following is the C++ declaration of the Maze class that includes the member function `walkFrom()` that implements the backtracking strategy.

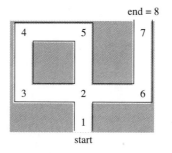

FIGURE 8-17
Maze with a Cycle.

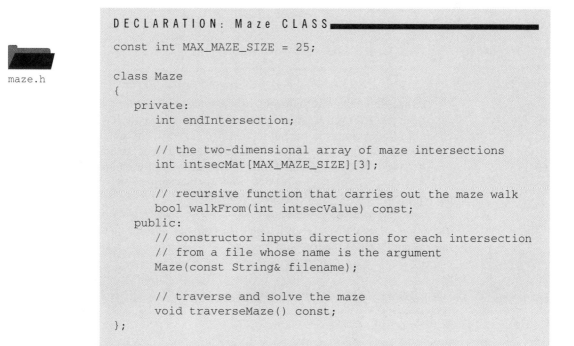

maze.h

```
DECLARATION: Maze CLASS
const int MAX_MAZE_SIZE = 25;

class Maze
{
    private:
        int endIntersection;

        // the two-dimensional array of maze intersections
        int intsecMat[MAX_MAZE_SIZE][3];

        // recursive function that carries out the maze walk
        bool walkFrom(int intsecValue) const;
    public:
        // constructor inputs directions for each intersection
        // from a file whose name is the argument
        Maze(const String& filename);

        // traverse and solve the maze
        void traverseMaze() const;
};
```

In the Maze class, the constructor is passed the name of a disk file that contains an integer triple for each intersection. This disk file has the following format. The first line contains the number of intersections, N; the rest of the file contains N triples that correspond to directions an object may exit at an intersection. The ending intersection has the form N N N. For instance, the input data for the sample maze in Figure 8-18 is:

```
8
0 2 0      (1: proceed straight to 2)
3 5 6      (2: proceed left to 3, straight to 5, right to 6)
0 0 4      (3: proceed right to 4)
0 0 0      (4: 4 is a deadend)
0 0 0      (5: 5 is a deadend)
7 0 0      (6: proceed left to 7)
0 8 0      (7: proceed straight to 8)
8 8 8      (8: ending intersection)
```

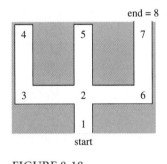

FIGURE 8-18
Sample Maze.

Once the maze is initialized by the constructor, the member function `traverseMaze()` is used to identify a path from start to end. If a path is found, the chain of intersections are output in "reverse" order from the ending intersection back to the starting intersection. If all paths lead to a deadend, the function outputs a message indicating that "There is no path out of the maze."

PROGRAM 8.3
━━

The program uses the Maze class to find a path through the maze in Figure 8-18. Assume that the data is read from file *mazedemo.dat*.

```
#include <iostream.h>

#include "maze.h"         // include the Maze class
#include "tstring.h"

int main ()
```

```
{
    // the file containing the maze parameters
    String mazeFile = "mazedemo.dat";

    // initialize the maze by reading the file
    Maze m(mazeFile);

    // solve the maze and output the result
    m.traverseMaze();
}
```

Run:

Starting the maze!
   Path through the maze is 8 7 6 2 1

Maze Class Implementation. The constructor is responsible for setting up the maze. As such, it opens the input file, reads the number of intersections, reads three integers to represent the directions at each intersection, and assigns a value to endIntersection, as the ending intersection.

```
// build maze by reading the intersection options from file
Maze::Maze(const String& filename)
{
    ifstream fin;
    int numIntSec, i;

    // open filename. terminate if not found
    fin.open(filename.c_str());
    if (!fin)
    {
        cerr << "Cannot open maze data file " << filename
            << endl;
        exit(1);
    }

    // read the number of intersections
    fin >> numIntSec;

    // read the matrix of triples from the file; intersection
    // 1 represented by row 0, 2 by row, etc.
    for (i=0; i < numIntSec; i++)
        fin >> intsecMat[i][0] >> intsecMat[i][1]
            >>intsecMat[i][2];

    endIntersection = numIntSec;

    fin.close();
}
```

The scanning of the maze is handled by the function `traverseMaze()` that calls the private recursive function `walkFrom()`. This private function has the argument, intsecValue, which is the current intersection in the maze walk. The function evaluates the directions at that intersection in the order left, straight, and right and returns the value true or false. For each direction, a value true means that proceeding in that direction provides a path from the current intersection out of the maze. The value false indicates that no such path exists. When the function detects that proceeding in a direction fails to exit the maze, it tries to proceed in the next available direction in order. If all of the directions at the intersection fail, the function itself returns false, which causes a return to a previous intersection. This is the backtracking!

The function `traverseMaze()` initially calls the recursive function `walkFrom()` with argument 1, and the logical return value indicates whether there is or is not a path out of the maze.

```
// call walkFrom() to solve the maze using backtracking
void Maze::traverseMaze() const
{
    cout << "Starting the maze!" << endl;

    if (walkFrom(1) == false)
        cout << "   There is no path out of the maze";
    cout << endl;
}

// find the maze solution or determine there is no solution
bool Maze::walkFrom(int intsecValue) const
{
    // stopping condition.  if intsecValue = 0, the recursive
    // function chose a direction that was blocked.
    // immediately return false
    if (intsecValue == 0)
        return false;
    else
    {
        // stopping condition: have located ending intersection.
        // output the ending intersection number and indicate
        // that a path exists to it by returning true
        if (intsecValue == endIntersection)
        {
            cout << "   Path through the maze is ";
            cout << intsecValue << "   ";
            return true;
        }

        // attempt to go left and ask whether this choice leads
        // to a path that exits the maze
        else if (walkFrom(intsecMat[intsecValue-1][0])== true)
        {
```

```
            // output intersection number and return true
            cout << intsecValue << "   ";
            return true;
        }

        // ask same question about proceeding straight ahead
        else if (walkFrom(intsecMat[intsecValue-1][1]))
        {
            // output intersection number and return true
            cout << intsecValue << "   ";
            return true;
        }

        // left and straightahead are dead ends. go right
        else if (walkFrom(intsecMat[intsecValue-1][2]))
        {
            // output intersection number and return true
            cout << intsecValue << "   ";
            return true;
        }
        // all three directions fail. return false
        else
            return false;
    }
```

APPLICATION 8-7 WALKING A MAZE

The program looks for a path through a maze using the Maze class. For the run, we use the maze A (file *maze1.dat*), maze B (file *maze2.dat*), and the introductory maze in Figure 8-14 (file *intrmaze.dat*). Before looking at the runs, try your own walk.

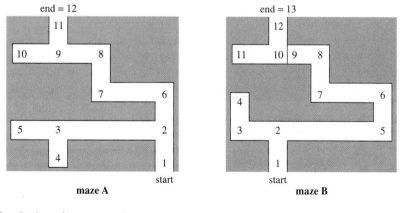

maze A   maze B

```
#include <iostream.h>

#include "maze.h"          // include the maze class
```

```
#include "tstring.h"

int main()
{
    // the file containing the maze parameters
    String mazeFile;

    cout << "Enter the data file name: ";
    cin >> mazeFile;

    // build the maze by reading the file
    Maze  m(mazeFile);

    // solve the maze and output the result
    m.traverseMaze();

    return 0;
}
```

```
Run 1:

Enter the data file name: maze1.dat
Starting the maze!
   Path through the maze is 12  11  9  8  7  6  2  1

Run 2:

Enter the data file name: maze2.dat
Starting the maze!
   There is no path out of the maze

Run 3:

Enter the data file name: intrmaze.dat
Starting the maze!
   Path through the maze is 20  19  17  16  14  10  9
   8  2  1
```

Comparing Recursive and Iterative Algorithms

The run in Application 8-6, the Tower of Hanoi, uses a modest three disks that require seven moves. In general, the solution to the Hanoi problem requires $2^n - 1$ moves. The priests in the temple would need to make $2^{64} - 1$ moves. Working at a rate of one move per second, the priests would require over 584 billion years to complete the task. Despite the number of moves, this algorithm is most easily solved with a recursive function. For many recursive algorithms, there is an alternative implementation that uses iteration.

> **Definition** An algorithm is said to be *iterative* when it is implemented using looping constructs. The number of iterations is determined by conditional expressions that test a count or some event.

The implementation code for an iterative algorithm is more efficient since it uses a loop structure rather than the repeated function calls and argument passing in the recursive form. When a relatively simple iterative algorithm is available, choose it rather than any equivalent recursive algorithm. A case in point is the power() function that has an iterative version to carry out repeated multiplication. The function uses the exponent *n* to specify the number of iterations.

```
// iterative algorithm to compute and return x to the power n
double power (double x, int n)
{
    double product = 1.0;    // holds powers of x
    int i;

    // form x * x * x ... * x (n multiplications)
    for(i=1; i <= n; i++)
        product *= x;

    return product;          // return 1.0 when n is 0
}
```

Some applications must rely on recursion since the underlying structure of the algorithm is recursive and no simple iterative form exists. The Tower of Hanoi puzzle is an example. The recursive algorithm is relatively simple to understand and code. Any iterative version of the function hanoi() would be too complicated to design, implement, and debug. In a situation such as this, a recursive solution is preferred.

CHAPTER 8 SUMMARY

This chapter extends your understanding of object-oriented programming by taking a formal look at object composition. In object composition a class declares objects of other class types in its private section and uses their member functions for its implementation. The technique is illustrated in the Employee and Triangle classes. Object composition promotes code reuse that is one of the basic principles of object technology.

In Chapter 1, we began a discussion of object-oriented analysis, design and programming. These are the elements of the object-oriented program development cycle. We have implicitly used many of the principles in our development of applications. In this chapter, we formally discuss each of these phases of the cycle and apply them to an applications that displays a full-year calendar.

The scope of an object is that portion of the program in which it can be accessed. Each object is either of local, class or global scope. In addition to scope, each object has a lifetime, which is either automatic or static. Most objects are declared in blocks and have automatic storage class. By adding the keyword *static,* a local object is allocated only once and retains its value for the duration of the program. In addition, a class data member can be declared static. In this situation, all objects of the class share the same copy of the data member.

An algorithm is a sequence of steps that performs a task. In some cases, the algorithm may invoke itself with modified data values. Eventually, the process evolves into instances in which the algorithm can be executed with specific data that does not require additional references to the algorithm. These types of algorithms are called recursive algorithms, in contrast to iterative algorithms that create repetition through loops. We described recursive algorithms using stopping conditions and recursive steps. These elements translate into C++ recursive functions. The chapter illustrates recursive algorithms and their implementation with a series of simple examples that include the power function, $power(x,n) = x^n$.

Some problems are naturally solved using recursion and no other simple solution exists. Such examples include the Tower of Hanoi puzzle and the problem of backtracking through a maze. Recursion can cause significant memory overhead because it involves extensive use of the function call and return mechanism. It should only be used when an iterative solution would be too complicated to design, implement, and debug.

Classes in the Chapter

Name	Implementation File
AccumulatorStatic	accstat.h
Calendar	calendar.h
CircleShape	circlesh.h
Date	date.h
Days	days.h
Employee	employee.h
LineShape	linesh.h
Maze	maze.h
Triangle	triangle.h

KEY TERMS

Agent of an application:
The main program that coordinates the activities of objects.

Automatic object:
An object that is declared in a block, is allocated when the program enters the block and is deallocated when the program exits the block. In a class, an automatic data member is allocated when an object is declared and continues to exist until the corresponding object is deallocated.

Backtracking:
Applies in a problem that requires a number of steps, with decisions at each step. Move step by step, creating a partial solution that appears to be consistent with the requirements of the final solution. If, at any step, a partial solution is inconsistent with a final solution, backtrack one or more steps to the last consistent partial solution.

Class association:
Relationship in which class objects are function arguments, are declared locally in a member function, or are used as a return value. Association creates a type of link between classes that is weaker than composition.

Class inheritance:
A relationship in which a class inherits data and operations from a base (parent) class and adds its own operations. Inheritance is one of the most important concepts in object-oriented programming.

Class scope:
Region in which a private data member can be accessed. It includes only the implementation code for class member functions.

Code decomposition:
Dividing an algorithm into pieces that are less complex than the whole. The individual pieces are implemented with functions.

Code reuse:
Using previously developed classes and free functions in the creation of new applications. Class reuse comes about through composition, association, and inheritance. Free functions are made available in function libraries.

Global scope:
Property associated with an object declared outside any class or function. The object can be accessed from the point of declaration to the end of the program.

Iterative algorithm:
An algorithm that accomplishes its goal by using looping constructs. The number of iterations is determined by conditional expressions that test a count or some event.

Lifetime of an object:
The period beginning with the creation of an object and ending when its memory location is deallocated.

Local scope:
Range of statements in a block for which an object can be accessed. The formal arguments in a function have local scope within their function body. Their scope begins with the declaration in the argument list and ends with the termination of the function body.

Object composition:
A condition that exists when a class contains one or more data members that are objects from other classes. A class that is included by composition is called a supplier class. The class that declares the objects is called the client class.

Object-oriented analysis:
Results in a set of program specifications. The programmer investigates the objects that may be used in the application.

Object-oriented design:
Development of classes that describe the structure of the objects. This translates into defining the data members, creating prototypes for the member functions and defining the interaction of classes.

Object-oriented programming:
Implementing algorithms for the class member functions, associated free functions, and the main program.

Program development cycle:
Includes object-oriented analysis, design, and programming.

Recursive algorithm:
Occurs when an algorithm executes by breaking itself into smaller problems of the same type that eventually lead to a solution, called the stopping condition.

Recursive function:

A function that calls itself in its function body. The call uses different arguments that ultimately reach some stopping condition, at which point the function returns a value.

Scope of an object or type:

That portion of the program in which the object or type can be accessed.

Static class data member:

A data member shared by each object of the class in the program. The data member must be defined outside any program unit, like a global object. The class scope operator is used to associate the object with the class.

Static local object:

A local object that is assigned a permanent location in memory and retains its value between function calls.

REVIEW EXERCISES

1. What is meant by the term "object composition"?

2. A square is a special type of rectangle in which the length equals the width. In the declaration for Square class, a Rectangle object is included by composition.

```
class Square
{
    private:
        Rectangle sq; // Rectangle object represents a square
    public:
        // constructor. sides of square have length len
        Square(double len);

        // functions to retrieve and modify private data
        double getLength();
        void setLength(double len);

        // compute and return square measurements
        double perimeter();
        double area();
        double diagonal();
};
```

(a) Implement the constructor for the Square class using
    (i) Assignment with an anonymous object.
    (ii) The initialization list.
(b) Complete the implementation for the member function getLength().

```
double Square::getLength()
{
    return _____;
}
```

(c) Give the implementation for the member function area().
(d) The diagonal of a square is $\sqrt{2} * length$

Give the implementation for the member function, diagonal().

3. Company X offers its employees health insurance that begin on the first day of the month following the end of the probationary period. The insurance begins immediately if the probationary period ends on the first of the month. Assume emp is an Employee object. Write a code segment that will output in long format the date on which the employee's health insurance becomes active.

4. Declare a Triangle object, tri, whose endpoints are (1,1), (1,3), and (4,3). Write a loop that iterates 50 times to simulate the movement of the triangle across the screen. The loop creates a delay of 0.1 seconds for each frame and then sets new vertices for the triangle.

5. What activities are described in the OOD phase of the program development cycle?

6. What is the principle of code decomposition? How is this principle implemented in classes? In the main program?

7. Consider the Calendar class and its object thisMonth. Write a code segment that initializes the Calendar object prevMonth so it will display the previous month's calendar.

8. A calendar year is always 52 weeks plus 1 or 2 additional days, depending on leap year. How can we use this fact to modify the for statement in the Calendar class private member function, getFirstDay()?

9. The program declares an inner block having objects whose names conflict with objects in the outer block. Give the program output.

```
int main()
{   int a = 1, b = 2, c = 3;

    {   int a = b, c = a;
        cout << (a + b + c) << "   ";

        b += 2;
        a += 3;
    }
    cout << (a + b + c) << endl;

    return 0;
}
```

10. The function f() is called five times by the main program using the loop:

```
for (i = 1; i <= 5; i++)
    f(i);
```

What is the output provided by the cout statement in each call?

```
void f(int n)
{
    static int factor = 1;

    cout << factor * n << "   ";
    factor++;
}
```

11. In the Dice class, the private data member, rnd, is declared as a static RandomNumber object. For a default seed, the RandomNumber class implementation uses a clock time that changes every second. Assume the following Dice objects are declared without an argument and the toss() function is executed for each object.

    ```
    Dice a, b, c;    // toss 2 dice
    ```

    ```
    cout << a.toss() << "  " << b.toss() << "  " << c.toss();
    ```

    What would be the likely output if rnd is not declared static in the Random Number class?

12. Consider the following recursive function:

    ```
    int f(int n)
    {
        if (n == 1)
            return 1;
        else
            return 1 + f(n-1);
    }
    ```

    (a) Which of the following mathematical function definitions describes f()?
       (i) $f(n) = 1+2+3+...+n$ (ii) $f(n) = n$
    (b) In part (a), you selected (i) or (ii). Modify the recursive step to generate the other mathematical function.

13. You are given the stopping condition and the recursive step for the computation of arr[0] + arr[1] + . . . + arr[n − 1], where arr is an integer array and n is the number of elements.

    $$sum(arr,n) = \begin{cases} arr[0], & n = 1 (stopping\ condition) \\ sum(arr,n - 1) + arr[n - 1], & n > 1\ (recursive\ step) \end{cases}$$

    Write sum(arr,n) as a recursive function.

14. If a problem can be done recursively, is it always best to use recursion? Give an example to illustrate your point.

Answers to Review Exercises

1. With object composition, a class declares objects of other classes in its private section and uses their member functions for its implementation.

2. (a)

    (i) `Square::Square(double len)`   (ii) `Square::Square(double len):`
    ```
    {                                              sq(len,len)
        sq = Rectangle(len,len);                 {}
    }
    ```

    (b) `double Square::getLength()`
    ```
    {
        return sq.getLength();
    }
    ```

    (c)   `double Square::area()`

```
    {
        return sq.area();
    }
```

(d) `double Square::diagonal()`
```
    {
        return sqrt(2.0)* sq.getLength();
    }
```

3. `Date healthIns = emp.getProbDate();`

```
if (healthIns.getDay() != 1)
{
    if (healthIns.getMonth() == 12)
    {
        healthIns.setMonth(1);
        healthIns.setYear(healthIns.getYear()+1);
    }
    else
        healthIns.setMonth(healthIns.getMonth()+1);
    healthIns.setDay(1);
}
healthIns.writeLongDate();
```

4.
```
int i;
double x[] = {1,1,4}, y[] = {1,3,3}; // triangle
double xposition = 1.0;                // base x-coordinate
Triangle tri(x,y);

    ...
for(i=0;i < 50;i++)
{
    tri.draw();         // draw current triangle
    delayWindow(.1);    // wait 1/10th sec.
    tri.erase();        // erase the triangle

    xposition += .1;   // change base x-coordinate
    // reset the points so triangle moves .1 unit to right
    tri.setPoint(0,xposition,1);
    tri.setPoint(1,xposition,3);
    tri.setPoint(2,3+xposition,3);
}
```

5. In the OOD phase, classes are developed that describe the structure of the objects developed in the OOA phase. This translates into defining the data members, creating prototypes for the member functions and defining the interaction of classes.

6. The principle of code decomposition specifies that an algorithm should be partitioned into pieces that are less complex than the whole. The individual pieces are implemented with functions. In the development of classes, the decomposition is done with private member functions. Free functions are used in the decomposition of the main program.

7.
```
prevMonth = thisMonth;
if (thisMonth.getMonth() == 1)
{
    // month is Dec of previous year
    prevMonth.setMonth(12);
    prevMonth.setYear(thisMonth.getYear()-1);
}
else
    // year the same. go to previous month
    prevMonth.setMonth(thisMonth.getMonth()-1);
prevMonth.displayCalendar();
```

8. Instead of adding 365 or 366 days, add 1 or 2 days.
```
for (y = 1600; y < year; y<==)
{
    d.setYear(y);
    if (d.isLeapYear())
        cday.addDay(2);
    else
        cday.addDay(1);
}
```

9. 6 8

10. 1 4 9 16 25

11. Since the constructors for a, b, and c will execute almost simultaneously, the Random Numbers generators for each object will have the same seed value and thus produce the same random values. When objects a, b, and c toss two dice, each obtains the same total.

12. (a) `f(n) = n`

    (b)
```
int f(int n)
{
    if (n == 1)
        return 1;
    else
        return n + f(n-1);
}
```

13.
```
int sum(int arr[], int n)
{
    if (n == 1)      // stop: 1 element array
        return arr[0];
    else
        return sum(arr, n-1) + arr[n-1];
}
```

14. It is not always best to execute a recursive algorithm. The power function provides a good example. A simple loop can be used to compute x^n. The recursive version of the function involves repeated function calls, with the overhead of argument passing.

WRITTEN EXERCISES

15. The FuelPump class has data member, supply, that is an Accumulator object included by composition. It indicates the available fuel supply at a gas pump. The double object, pricePerGallon, is the cost posted on the pump. The following is a declaration of the class.

```
DECLARATION: FuelPump CLASS ━━━━━━━━━━━━━

class FuelPump
{
    private:
        Accumulator supply;      // available fuel
        double pricePerGallon;   // cost per gallon

    public:
        // sets pricePerGallon and initial fuel supply.
        FuelPump(double price, double initSupply);

        // return the cost of purchasing ga gallons.
        // reduce supply of available fuel
        double buyGas(double ga);

        // add ga gallons to the supply
        void addToSupply (double ga);

        // return available fuel at the pump
        double getSupply();
};
```

(a) Write an implementation of the constructor using an anonymous object.
(b) Write an implementation of the constructor using the initialization list.
(c) Implement the member function buyGas(). If insufficient gas is available, use all of the existing supply.
(d) Give the output from the program.

```
int main()
{
    FuelPump pump(1.25, 35);
    cout << pump.buyGas(24) << endl;

    cout << pump.buyGas(24) << endl;

    pump.addToSupply (25);
    cout << pump.getSupply() << endl;

    return 0;
}
```

(e) The station will replenish the available fuel supply up to 100 gallons. Complete the conditional expression that determines the amount of gas to be added.

```
newAmount = _____ ? _____ : _____;
```

16. Design a class, DisplayYearCalendar, whose objects have the year as a data member. An object outputs a 12-month calendar for the specified year.
(a) What member functions will you declare?
(b) Why is object association useful in developing the class?
(c) Give a class declaration.

17. The class, HiLow, describes objects that can play the "High-Low" game. The game starts with a random target in the range 1 to 1000. The player is challenged to guess the number within n guesses, where typically n <= 10. The player is repeatedly asked to make a quess which is then evaluated as being less than the target, greater than the target, or matching the target. The player wins when a match occurs within the allowed number of guesses.
(a) Using principles of OOA and OOD, design the class so that an object can be reset to compute a new target number and allow for repeated playing of the game. Assume each game is played with the same allowed number of guesses.
(b) What new design features would be required if the number of guesses can vary from game to game?
(c) How would you modify the class design so that two players could alternately make guesses? The first player with a match wins.

18. In the Calendar class, the monthName array is declared as a static object. What are the advantages of this declaration?

19. ClassWithStatic features a static data member, numObjects, that is initially set to 0. The constructor increments the static data member and outputs its current value.

```
class ClassWithStatic
{
   private:
      static int numObjects;
   public:
      ClassWithStatic()
      {
         item++;
         cout << item << endl;
      }
};

_____;
```

(a) Fill-in the blank statement to define item with initial value 0.
(b) Assume the main program declares objects a, b, c and d. What is the output provided by the constructor for the following declaration?

```
ClassWithStatic a, b, c, d;
```

20. The class, StaticData, illustrates the uses of static data. Each object has its own data item while all objects share total and numObjects as common data. At any point, total is the sum of the values for all items stored by existing StaticData objects, and nuMObjects is a count of the number of existing objects. Each time a data object is created (constructor called), a value is assigned to the data member, item. The static member numObjects must be incremented and total must be updated by item. The class has access member functions getItem()and setItem(). The function average() returns the average of the values of all existing objects.

DECLARATION: StaticData CLASS ▬▬▬▬▬▬▬▬

```
class StaticData
{
    private:
        double item;                    //  value held by class
        static double total;            // total of existing
                                        //objects

        static int numObjects;          // number of objects
    public:
        StaticData(double value);       // constructor
        double getItem();               // return current item
        void setItem(double value);     // change item
        double average();               // average of existing
                                        objects

};
                        _____;
```

(a) Declare the blank statement to define static members.
(b) Implement the constructor.

21. The program declares nested blocks having objects with name conflicts. Give the program output.

```
#include <iostream.h>

int main()
{   int a = 1, b = 2, c = 3;
    {   int a = 10;
        cout << (a + b) << endl;

        b += 1;
        a += 2;
        {   int c = 5;

            cout << (a + b + c) << endl;
        }
        cout << (a + b + c) << endl;
    }
    cout << (a + b + c) << endl;

    return 0;
}
```

22. Trace the recursive functions, f(), and give the output for the function calls.

(a)

```
int f(int m, int n)
{
    if (n == 1)
        return m;
    else
        return m + f(m,n-1);
}
```

Calls: `f(3,2)` `f(8,4)`

(b)

```
int f(int m, int n)
{
    if (n < 1 || m > 10)
        return 0;
    else
        return m*n + f(m+1,n-1);
}
```

Calls: `f(8,4)`, `f(5,2)`, `f(5,5)`

23. This function computes a sum of terms.

```
int geometric(int n)
{
    if (n == 0)
        return 1;
    else
        return geometric(n-1) + pow(2,n);
}
```

(a) Give the sum for the call geometric (4).

(b) What is the general sum that results from the call geometric (n)?

24. Trace the function f() and give the return value from each function call.

```
int f(int n, int i)
{
    if (i > n)
        return 0;
    else if (n % i == 0)
        return i;
    else
        return f(n,i+1);
}
```

Calls: `f(40,2)`, `f(35,3)`, `f(37,5)`, `f(99,119)`

25. The factorial of a non-negative integer, written n!, is defined as the product of all positive integers less than or equal to n.

$$n! = n * (n-1) * (n-2) * \ldots 2 * 1$$

(a) Implement the factorial function factIter() using iteration.

```
long factIter(int n);
```

(b) Factorial has a recursive definition that specifies both the stopping condition and the recursive step.

$$n! = \begin{cases} 1, & n = 0 \text{ (stopping condition)} \\ n * (n-1)!, & n > 0 \text{ (recursive step)} \end{cases}$$

Use the definition to implement the function factRecur().

```
long factRecur(int n);
```

26. The Fibonacci sequence 1, 1, 2, 3, 5, 8, 13, 21, 34, . . . has a recursive definition. The terms f(n) are defined for n ⩾ 1. The first two terms are explicitly defined as 1. From that point on, each term is the sum of the previous two terms.

$$fib(n) = \begin{cases} 1, & n == 1 \ or \ n == 2 \\ f(n-2) + f(n-1), & n > 2 \end{cases}$$

(a) Using the recursive definition, implement function fib(n).
(b) Develop an iterative implementation fibIter(n).
(c) There is a formula for the evaluation of fib(n). Write a function fibFormula(n) that evaluates the formula.

$$fib(n) = \frac{2}{\sqrt{5}}\left[\left(\frac{1+\sqrt{5}}{2}\right)^n - \left(\frac{1-\sqrt{5}}{2}\right)^n\right] - 1$$

27. Trace the recursive function.

```
void f()
{
    char c;

    cin.get(c);
    if ( c != '\n')
        f();
    cout << c;
}
```

(a) What is the output if the input is "cat"?
(b) What is the output if the input is "level"?
(c) In general, what does the function f() accomplish?

28. Finding the sum of the digits in a nonnegative integer has a natural recursive formulation.

$$sumdigits = \begin{cases} n\%10, & n/10 == 0 \ (stopping \ condition) \\ sumdigits(n/10) + n\%10, & n/10 \ != 0 \ (recursive \ step) \end{cases}$$

Write the recursive function sumdigits().

29. Write a recursive function that tests whether a string is a palindrome. A palindrome is an alphabetic string containing no blanks that reads the same forward and backward. For instance, the following are palindromes:

```
dad    level    did    madamimadam
```

Use the following declaration

```
int pal(const String& str, int s, int e);
```

where `pal()` determines if the characters in str beginning with index s and ending with index e constitute a palindrome.

```
Stopping Condition:
        s >= e (success)
        str[s] != str[e] (failure)
Recursive Step:
        Is str between indices s+1 and e-1 a palindrome?
```

30. The following is an input file for a maze. Draw the maze and find the solution by tracing the recursive algorithm step by step.

```
11                  // number of intersections
0 2 0               // 1 moves straight to intersection 2
4 3 6               // 2 exits to 4(left), 3(straight), 6(right)
0 0 0
0 0 5
0 0 0
7 0 0
8 11 9
0 0 0
0 0 10
0 0 0
11 11 11            // end at intersection 11
```

PROGRAMMING EXERCISES

31. The Square class is declared in Review Exercise 8.2, and a partial implementation is given in the solutions.
    (a) Give a full implementation of the class in the file *square.h*.
    (b) Write a program that declares a Square object sq of length 2.0 and Circle object circ that will circumscribe the square. The radius of the circle is one-half the diagonal of the square. The program should compute the area of the shaded region in the accompanying figure.

32. The FuelPump class is declared in Written Exercise 8.15. The constructor and the function buyGas() are implemented in parts (a) and (c). Complete the implementation in the file *fuelpump.h* by defining the functions addToSupply() and get-Supply(). Enter and run the program in part (d).

33. In Written Exercise 8.16(c), you developed a declaration of the DisplayYearCalendar class.
    (a) Implement the class and place it in the file *calyear.h*.
    (b) Write a program that declares an object cal with year 2000 as an argument. Display the calendar for the year.

34. The program uses the 10-element integer array arr.

    ```
    int arr[] = {2, 6, 8, 1, 3, 5, 7, 9, 10, 5};
    ```

    Review Exercise 8.13 develops the recursive function sum() that returns the sum of the elements in an array. Use this function to output the sum of array arr.

35. Written Exercise 8.20 declares the StaticData class.
    (a) Give the declaration and implementation of the class in the file *statdata.h*.
    (b) The following is a skeletal program. Complete the statements and run the program.

```
int main()
{
    StaticData a(5), b(10);
    _____    // output average of the objects
    StaticData c(25);
    _____    // output average of the objects
    _____    // double value for object a
    _____    // output average of the objects
    _____    // set c so average is 50
    _____    // output value of c
    _____    // output average of the objects

    return 0;
}
```

36. Write a program that includes the recursive function geometric() from Written Exercise 8.23. The program inputs an integer n and outputs geometric(n). It can be shown that the recursive function evaluates to $2^{n+1}-1$. In a separate output statement, illustrate this fact. Run the program three times with input data n = 5, 8, 10.

37. Written Exercise 8.25 features iterative and recursive functions for the computation of n!. Write a program that includes both functions and outputs the result with the statements

```
cout << "For n = " << n << endl;
cout << "    factIter(n) = " << factIter(n) << endl;
cout << "    factRecur(n) = " << factRecur(n) << endl;
```

Run the program by using a loop with four iterations that input data values n = 3, 0, 5, 10.

38. Develop Written Exercise 8.30 as a complete program that solves the maze. Use Application 8-7 as a model.

PROGRAMMING PROJECTS

39. In Chapter 5, we introduced the Time24 class that handles time with hours in the range 0 to 23. We often refer to this as *military time.* This exercise looks at the more familiar *standard time* and develops the Time12 class that stores hours in the range 12, 1, 2, . . . , 11 for both AM and PM. We could develop the new class "from scratch" by declaring the hour and minute data members and using them in the implementation of the member functions. A simpler design uses composition with a Time24 object to hold the time data. The Time12 class has member functions that are similar to the Time24 class, except that the constructor and I/O operations distinguish between AM and PM units. A private member function, convert12To24(), converts time notation from standard to military time.

DECLARATION: Time12 CLASS ▬▬▬▬▬▬▬

```
// specifies clock time units
enum TimeUnit {AM, PM};
```

```
// maintains clock time
class Time12
{
   private:
      Time24 t;    // store time in 24-hour format

      // build t from standard time
      Time24 convert12To24(int h, int m,
   TimeUnit tunit); public:
      // initialize Time24 data member t
      Time12(int h=12, int m=0, TimeUnit tunit = AM);

      // add m minutes to update current time
      void addTime(int m);

      //I/O member functions use format HH:MM AM (PM)
      void readTime();
      void writeTime() const;
};
```

Example:

```
      Time12 t(8,15,AM);

      t.writeTime();      // Output:   8:15 AM
      t.readTime();       // Input:   12:00 PM
      t.addTime(180);     // add 3 hours to t
      t.writeTime();      // Output: 3:00 PM
```

(a) Implement the class and place it in the file time12.h. Figure 8-19 depicts the algorithm that should be used to implement the private member function convert12To24(). Hint: use % 12.

(b) In Frankfurt, Germany time is 6 hours ahead of the Eastern time zone. Write a program that uses the Time12 class to output the time in Frankfurt that corresponds to midnight on New Year's eve in New York City.

(c) Write a program that inputs the time at which an auto mechanic begins a job. The mechanic asks the customer to pick up the car in 5 hours and 20 minutes. Output the time that the car will be available to the customer.

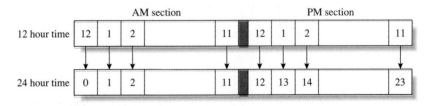

FIGURE 8-19
Conversion between Clock Time and 24-Hour time.

Chapter 9
Operator Overloading and Templates

CHAPTER CONTENTS

9-1 FUNCTION OVERLOADING
Overloading Class Member Functions

9-2 THE RATIONAL NUMBER SYSTEM
Defining Rational Numbers
Rational Number Arithmetic
Number Systems
The Rational Class

9-3 OPERATOR OVERLOADING
Defining Overloaded Operators
Overloading the Stream I/O
Operators

9-4 MEMBER FUNCTION OVERLOADING

9-5 CONVERTING RATIONAL NUMBERS
Mixed Numbers

9-6 TEMPLATE FUNCTIONS
Template Syntax
Template Expansion
Template-based Selection Sort

9-7 GENERALIZED SEARCHING
Binary Search
Comparing Search Algorithms
(Optional)

9-8 TEMPLATE CLASSES
Constructing a Template Class
Declaring Template Class Objects

Written Exercises

C++ allows two or more functions in a program unit to have the same name, provided their argument lists are sufficiently different that the compiler can resolve function calls. The feature, called **function overloading,** simplifies a programmer's task. For instance, an application may need to identify the larger of two integers, the larger of two StudentAccount balances, or the later of two calendar dates. Rather than using names like maxInt(), maxStudentAccount(), and maxDate(), the programmer may define separate functions with the same name max() and let the compiler resolve the differences by distinguishing the int, StudentAccount, and Date argument types. Function overloading applies to both class member functions and free functions. The concept is particularly important for constructors. Programmers often use multiple constructors to provide flexible initialization of data members.

C++ provides a variety of operator symbols that are used with primitive object types. The operators such as +, *, < are used with primitive integer and real types to build arithmetic and logical expressions. C++ allows programmers to redefine most of its operator symbols for use with class and enumeration operands. The process, called *operator overloading,* allows programs to use programmer-defined objects in essentially the same way number and character objects are used in arithmetic and logical expressions. Since operators are a special type of function, operator overloading is simply an extension of function overloading.

To illustrate the full power of operator overloading, we develop the Rational class whose objects are fractions.

$$\frac{2}{3} \qquad \frac{-16}{7} \qquad \frac{8}{2} \qquad \frac{10}{1}$$

You are familiar with fractions from your mathematics training. With the declaration of the class and the implementation of arithmetic and logical operators for Rational objects, you will be able to combine fractions with integer and real numbers in program calculations.

Function overloading allows the programmer to associate the same name with two or more functions. While this simplifies use of the functions in applications, it does not relieve the programmer of the responsibility to write several different function implementations. Three separate versions of max() are required to identify the larger integer, StudentAccount and Date object. C++ provides the capability, with *template functions,* to write a single function with general type arguments. The compiler looks at the types of the run-time arguments and creates a version of the function that matches the types. With template functions, the compiler creates multiple (overloaded) versions of the functions rather than requiring the programmer to write the individual implementations.

The use of templates applies to classes as well as functions. A *template class* has attributes and member function arguments of a generic type that are made explicit when declaring an object of the template class type. The primary application for template classes is in the construction of container classes that store large amounts of data. A study of two such classes is the focus of our work in Chapters 10 and 11. In this chapter we develop a template version of the Accumulator class that holds a single element. The discussion and implementation of the class will provide you with a good understanding of template classes and most of the key template syntax.

9-1 FUNCTION OVERLOADING

A program performing scientific calculations may compute the square of different numeric objects. If the operation is performed with a function, the programmer must write separate versions for each data type since the arithmetic operations are fundamentally different for integers and real numbers. For instance, a programmer may want to square int, long, and double objects. The application requires three separate functions with different argument types and return types.

The programmer may choose to implement the functions as follows:

integer version:	int isqr (int x);
long version:	long lsqr (long x);
double version:	double dsqr (double x);

C++ allows a programmer to give each of the three functions the same function name, `sqr`. This concept is called *function overloading*.

```
// int form          // long form          // double form
int sqr(int x)       long sqr(long x)      double sqr(double x)
{                    {                     {
    return x * x;        return x * x;         return x * x;
}                    }                     }
```

In a function call, the compiler is faced with several implementations of the same function and selects the one whose formal argument list best matches the run-time argument list. For instance, if the run-time argument is a long integer, the compiler selects the version of sqr() whose formal argument x has long type.

```
long  t = 25;
cout << sqr(t);   // Output: 625 (uses sqr(long))
```

When the run-time and formal arguments do not exactly match, as with a float value, the compiler uses type conversion before selecting the function definition.

```
float a = 0.5;   // for sqr(a), compiler converts a to a double
cout << sqr(a); // Output: 0.25 (uses sqr(double))

short r, s;
s = sqr(r);      // uses sqr(int)
```

In some cases, the compiler cannot identify a specific function implementation and creates an error message indicating the presence of an ambiguous reference.

SYNTAX ▬▬▬▬▬▬▬▬▬▬▬▬▬▬▬▬▬▬▬▬▬▬▬▬▬▬▬▬▬▬

Function Overloading

Form: returnType sameName(<argument list$_1$>)
             returnType sameName(<argument list$_2$>)
                 . . . .

Action: Two or more functions may have the same function name provided that the number of items or the data types of items in their argument list differ. It is not sufficient for the functions to differ only in their return type. For a function call, the compiler uses the function whose argument list matches the number and data types of the run-time arguments

Example: Computers distinguish between integer and real number division. Integer division returns the whole number quotient while real number division returns a decimal value. Two definitions of the function divide() implement the different forms of division. In each case, the function is passed two arguments for the dividend and the divisor.

```
// integer division
int divide(int m, int n)
{
    return m/n;
}

// real number division
double divide(double x, double y)
```

```
        {
            return x/y;
        }
```

Function calls must consider the types for two arguments.

1. The compiler calls the function whose prototype is "int divide(int,int)" and returns intval = 3.

$$intval = divide\ (7,2);$$

2. The compiler calls the function whose prototype is "double divide(double,double)" and returns z = 3.5

$$z = divide\ (7.0,2.0);$$

3. The compiler notes that one argument is an int and one is a double. Unable to select between the two versions of divide(), the compiler displays an error message like:

"Ambiguity between 'divide(int,int)' and 'divide(double,double)' in function 'main()'."
realval = divide (7.0,2);

A P P L I C A T I O N   9 – 1   O V E R L O A D I N G   D I V I S I O N

The program illustrates the overloaded divide() function. The definitions display a message ("int divide" or "real divide") to identify which version of `divide()` is being called. The main program calls the function with various combinations of int, short, float, and double arguments.

```cpp
#include <iostream.h>

int divide(int m, int n);              // integer division
double divide (double x, double y);    // real number division

int main()
{
    int   a = 20, b = 6;
    short c = 10;
    float r = 7.5, s = 2.0;
    double x = 7.5;

    cout << divide(a,b) << endl;       // a, b are int
    cout << divide(c,2) << endl;       // c short, 2 int
    cout << divide(r,s) << endl;       // r, s are float
    cout << divide(x,3.0) << endl;     // x, 3.0 are double
    cout << divide(r,x) << endl;       // r float, x double

    return 0;
}
```

```
int divide(int m, int n)
{
    cout << "int divide(" << m << ',' << n << ") ";
    return m/n;
}

double divide(double x, double y)
{
    cout << "double divide(" << x << ',' << y << ") ";
    return x/y;
}
```

```
Run:

int divide(20,6) 3
int divide(10,2) 5
double divide(7.5,2) 3.75
double divide(7.5,3) 2.5
double divide(7.5,7.5) 1
```

Are these two functions unique for the purpose of operator overloading?

```
int f(const Date& d);
double f(const Date& d);
```

When compiling the class CL, will the compiler find any ambiquities?

Exploring
Concepts

```
class CL
{
    . . .
    public:
        CL(int a, int b=0);
        CL(int a);
        . . .
};
```

Overloading Class Member Functions

Up to this point in the chapter, we have focused on the general concept of function overloading. Our examples have used free fractions. In fact, the concept applies equally well to class member functions. This feature is particularly important to programmers who use overloading to create multiple constructors that add flexibility to a class structure. In this section, we introduce multiple constructors and give an example of overloading the addTime() function in the Time24 class.

Multiple Constructors A constructor is a class member that initializes the data members of an object when it is declared. A class may have multiple constructors with different argument lists. This allows a program to use different information when declaring class objects. In Chapter 7 we introduced a default constructor for the StudentAccount class to allow for an array of StudentAccount objects in the FinanceCenter class. The class has multiple constructors.

```
class StudentAccount
{
    .  .  .  .
    public:
        // arguments initialize the data (Chapter 1)
        StudentAccount(String id, String name, double initbal);

        // default constructor with no arguments (Chapter 7)
        StudentAccount();

    .  .  .
};
```

When declaring a StudentAccount object, the compiler uses the argument list to select the appropriate constructor.

```
// the declaration calls the default constructor
StudentAccount stud;              // empty argument list

// use constructor that initializes object with arguments
StudentAccount studTM("97-3418","Murphy,Tom",450);

// default constructor called to build array elements
StudentAccount  studList[25];  // call the default constructor
```

SYNTAX ■■■■■■■■■■■■■■■■■■■■■■■■■■■■■■■■■■■■■■

Multiple Constructors

Form: Class CL and has multiple constructors (overloaded functions)

```
class CL
{
    .  .  .
    public:
        CL ();  // default constructor
        CL (<argument list₁>);
        CL (<argument list₂>);
        .  .  .  .
};
```

Action: Each constructor has the name of the class. Like any overloaded function, the argument lists must be distinct.

Example: Three constructors allow an object to be declared with 0, 1, or 2 arguments.

```
            class CL
            {
                  int dataA, dataB;
                public:
                  CL (int argA = 0);    // default constructor
                  CL (int argA, argB);
            };
```

The compiler selects the constructor that matches the argument list

```
        CL  obj1;           // Default constructor
        CL  obj2(4);        // Constructor with 1 argument
        CL  obj3(1,8);      // Constructor with 2 arguments
```

Overloading a Time24 Member Function. Function overloading can be used with member functions other than constructors. In the Time24 class, the function addTime() takes the integer argument m in minutes and adds the value to the current time. The result is returned as a new Time24 object. For some applications, a programmer may want the addTime() operation to take a Time24 object as the argument. For instance, the length of a movie is 1 hour and 45 minutes and is stored in the Time24 object movieLength. An overloaded version of addTime() would simplify assigning a correct time to the object endMovie.

```
Time24  startMovie(13,45), endMovie, movieLength(1,45);
    . . .
endMovie = startMovie;
EndMovie.addTime(movieLength);
```

If this second version of addTime() were added to the class, its prototype would be:

```
// update time by adding Time24 object
void addTime(const Time24& increment);
```

To implement addTime(), we add the hours and minutes from the object and the argument.

```
void Time24::addTime(const Time24 &t)
{
   // add hour and minute data values
   hour += t.hour;
   minute += t.minute);
   normalizeTime();
}
```

Note that this new version of addTime() is given for illustration purposes only and is not included in time24.h.

9-2   THE RATIONAL NUMBER SYSTEM

In the next three sections, we develop operator overloading as a special case of function overloading. While this concept can apply in a variety of classes, it is best understood with arithmetic classes that implement complex numbers, vectors, matrices, and so forth. For our examples, we will develop the Rational class whose objects are fractions. You have a good understanding of fractions from your mathematics background.

$$\frac{2}{3} + \frac{1}{4} = \frac{11}{12} \qquad \frac{9}{2} \times \frac{3}{5} = \frac{27}{10} \qquad \frac{3}{7} < \frac{1}{2}$$

In this section, we define rational numbers and review the algorithms you use to add, multiply, and compare them. We conclude with a partial listing of the Rational class. We will expand the class in Sections 9.3 and 9.5 as we develop different types of operator overloading.

Defining Rational Numbers

The rational numbers are the set of quotients P/Q where P and Q are integers and $Q \neq 0$. The number P is called the *numerator* and the number Q is called the *denominator.* In mathematics, these are called fractions.

$$\frac{2}{3} \qquad \frac{-6}{7} \qquad \frac{8}{2} \qquad \frac{10}{1} \qquad \frac{0}{5}$$

For each rational number, there is an unlimited number of fractions that have the same ratio. The total collection defines a set of equivalent fractions. For instance, the following rational numbers have the same ratio of numerator to denominator.

$$\frac{2}{3} = \frac{10}{15} = \frac{50}{75}$$

One member in each collection of equivalent fractions has a *reduced form* in which the numerator and denominator have no common divisor. The rational number in reduced form is the most representative value from the collection of equivalent fractions. For instance, 2/3 is the reduced form in the collection 10/15, 50/75, and so forth.

The value of a rational number is positive or negative depending on the signs of its numerator and denominator. Different combinations give rise to equivalent fractions.

$$\begin{array}{cc} \textit{Negative} & \textit{Positive} \\[6pt] \dfrac{-2}{3} = \dfrac{2}{-3} & \dfrac{2}{3} = \dfrac{-2}{-3} \end{array}$$

To distinguish between positive and negative fractions, we represent rational numbers in a *standardized form* with a positive denominator. Thus a positive rational number has a positive numerator and a negative rational number has a negative numerator.

$$\frac{2}{3} \text{ (positive)} \qquad \frac{-2}{3} \text{ (negative)}$$

Rational Number Arithmetic

Algorithms to add and compare two rational numbers rely on the concept of equivalent fractions. First find equivalent forms for the numbers that have the same denominator. Mathematics refers to this activity as "creating like-fractions." Add the numbers by adding the numerators of the like-fractions. Compare the numbers by comparing the numerators.

$$(+) \quad \frac{1}{3} + \frac{5}{8} = \frac{8}{24} + \frac{15}{24} = \frac{23}{24}$$

$$(<) \quad \frac{1}{3} < \frac{5}{8} \text{ is equivalent to the relation } \frac{8}{24} < \frac{15}{24} \text{ The relation is true since } 8 < 15.$$

Multiplication of rational numbers uses different rules. The operation involves creating a new fraction by separately multiplying the numerators and denominators of the numbers.

$$(*) \quad \frac{1}{3} * \frac{5}{8} = \frac{5}{24}$$

Number Systems (Optional)

Mathematics distinguishes different number types by creating a hierarchy of systems that include integer, rational, real, and complex numbers.

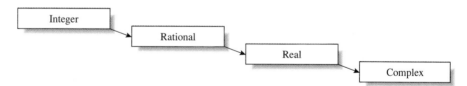

The integers are a discrete set of values consisting of positive and negative whole numbers. The set of rational numbers include the integers as a subset. The representation of an integer as a rational number uses a denominator of 1. Hence

$$(\text{integer}) \quad 25 = \frac{25}{1} \quad (\text{rational})$$

The real numbers are floating point values consisting of a whole part, a decimal point, and an infinite sequence of trailing digits whose positional values are 1/10, 1/100, and so forth.

$$x = w_n w_{n-1} w_1 w_0 . d_1 d_2 d_3 d_4 d_5 \ldots$$

A real number has an infinite decimal expansion. For some real numbers, like π, the trailing digits never repeat. We say these are *irrational numbers.*

$$\pi = 3.141592653589793 \ldots$$

For other real numbers, the trailing digits terminate will 0s or repeat in fixed blocks. Numbers of this type correspond to the rational numbers. As a result, the rationals are a subset of the real numbers.

$$x = 2.50000000 \ldots \qquad \left(\text{terminate with 0s} \quad x = \frac{5}{2}\right)$$

$$x = 0.66666666 \ldots \qquad \left(\text{block 6 repeats} \quad x = \frac{2}{3}\right)$$

$$x = 0.64252525 \ldots \qquad \left(\text{block 25 repeats} \quad x = \frac{6361}{9900}\right)$$

On a computer, it is not possible to store every real number with complete accuracy. While greater accuracy is possible with the double type, we can also approximate a real number with a rational number by rounding off the decimal expansion and writing the result as a rational number.

Real numbers are a subset of the complex numbers. In the programming project, we develop a portion of the Complex class to illustrate how a computer can carry out complex number calculations.

The Rational Class

The rational numbers are represented by objects in the Rational Class whose data members are the long integers num and den. The long object type is used to handle the numerators and denominators that often occur in calculations. The class features a private member function standardize() that stores a rational in standard form (denominator is positive) and a private member function gcd() that is used to compute the reduced form of a number.

To initialize a rational number, we use function overloading and create two forms of the constructor.

```
Rational(int n = 0, int d = 1); // default constructor
Rational(double x);             // rational approximation to x
```

The first form is a default constructor that assigns the numerator and denominator as separate values. The default value is $\frac{0}{1}$. The second form takes a double as input and creates the rational approximation. In each case the constructor calls standardize() so that the rationals are stored in standard form.

```
Rational  r;       // use default constructor   r = 0/1
Rational r(6);     // use default constructor   r = 6/1
```

$$\text{Rational } r(4,-5); \quad \text{// constructor with two arguments} \quad r = \frac{-4}{5}$$

$$\text{Rational } r(2.75); \quad \text{// constructor approximates 2.75. } r = \frac{11}{4}$$

The following is a partial listing of the class. Other than the constructors, only the public member functions getNumerator(), getDenominator(), and reduce() are included. In the next section we begin a study of operator overloading. As this concept is developed, we will expand the declaration of the class. Ultimately, we will have a complete set of arithmetic and comparison operators along with a definition of >> and << for input and output. By adding a conversion operator that converts a rational number to a floating-point number, you will be able to mix integers, rationals, and real numbers in a full range of mathematical expressions.

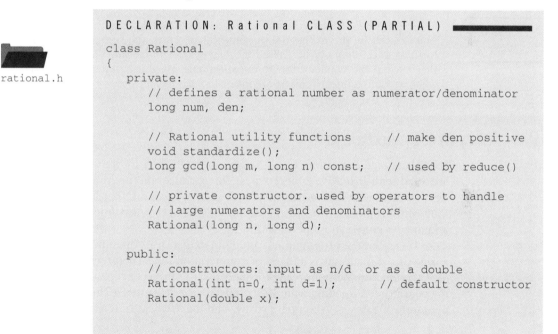

rational.h

```
DECLARATION: Rational CLASS (PARTIAL)

class Rational
{
    private:
        // defines a rational number as numerator/denominator
        long num, den;

        // Rational utility functions      // make den positive
        void standardize();
        long gcd(long m, long n) const;    // used by reduce()

        // private constructor. used by operators to handle
        // large numerators and denominators
        Rational(long n, long d);

    public:
        // constructors: input as n/d  or as a double
        Rational(int n=0, int d=1);        // default constructor
        Rational(double x);


        // data member access functions
        long getNumerator() const;
        long getDenominator() const;

        // convert rational to reduced form
        void reduce();
};
```

EXAMPLE 9.1 ▬▬▬▬▬▬▬▬▬▬▬▬▬▬▬▬▬▬▬▬▬▬▬▬▬

1. The function writeRational() outputs a rational number in the form P/Q.

```
void writeRational(const Rational &r)
```

```
{
    cout << r.getNumerator() << '/' << r.getDenominator();
}
```

2. Declare and then output the rational numbers.

```
Rational r(6,-12), s(0.25), t;
r is stored as -6/12
r.reduce();                    // reduce -6/12
writeRational(r);              // Output:  -1/2

writeRational(s);              // Output:  1/4
writeRational(t);              // Output:  0/1
```

Technical
Note

The class includes the private constructor

```
Rational(long n, long d);
```

This is used by the arithmetic operators that return the sum, product, and so forth, as a Rational object. These objects may have numerators or denominators that exceed the capacity for 16-bit arithmetic. Its use is noted by comments when we define the arithmetic operators in Section 9.3.

9-3   OPERATOR OVERLOADING

In its language definition, C++ specifies over 40 built-in operator symbols that are used with primitive object types. For instance, the operators +, *, !=, and && are used with arithmetic and Boolean expressions. Other less obvious operator symbols include the index operator [ ] for arrays, the function operator ( ), and integer conversion operator int().

C++ allows a programmer to redefine most of its operator symbols as long as one of the operands is of class or enumeration type. The process is called *operator overloading*. Without being formally aware of the concept, you have been using operator overloading with String objects since Chapter 2. The class defines the operators < and == to compare strings and the + operator to combine strings.

```
String str1 = "Smith", str2 = "Johnson", str3;
```

Comparison:
```
str1 < str2                (false since 'S' is greater than 'J')

str2 == str2               (false: "Smith" is not "Johnson")
```

Concatenation:
```
str2 + " and " + str2    (Johnson and Johnson)
```

C++ uses operator overloading for input and output of primitive number and character objects. The stream input operator >> is actually a redefinition of the right-shift operator that shifts the binary bits of an integer. Similarly, the stream operator << is a redefinition of the left-shift operator. The authors extended the overloading of these operators to String objects.

```
String str;
cin >> str;      // input a string with whitespace separation
cout << str;     // output the string
```

Operator overloading is a special type of function overloading. It provides a program great flexibility and simplicity in handling objects. This fact is evident with String objects. You have been able to use strings as though they were another primitive language type.

Defining Overloaded Operators

Operator overloading is carried out by redefining a C++ operator symbol. All but five operators can be redefined. Of those you are familiar with, only the ::(class scope), ?:(conditional expression), and sizeof operators cannot be overloaded. While overloading can apply whenever one of the operands is a class or enumeration object, we look only at class objects and leave enumeration objects for the exercises.

Operators may be overloaded as free functions or as class member functions. The concepts have important differences and so we deal with their syntax separately. Throughout the discussion, examples are drawn from the Rational class.

Overloading with Free Functions To redefine an operator as a free function, we must create a corresponding *operator function.* Its name includes the keyword *operator* followed by the operator symbol. For a binary operator, the two operands are included as arguments. The function form for a unary operator has a single operand. When used in a program statement, however, we use the standard operator/operand format that places a binary operator between its operands and a unary operator before its operand. The compiler takes care of calling the function that implements the overloaded operator.

SYNTAX ▬▬▬▬▬▬▬▬▬▬▬▬▬▬▬▬▬▬▬▬▬▬▬▬▬▬▬

Operator Function

Form: Assume # is a placeholder for a C++ operator symbol. When creating an operator function, replace # by the operator symbol.

```
Function Format:
   // binary operator with operands lhs and rhs
   ReturnType operator# (const ClassName& lhs,
                         const ClassName& rhs);

   // unary operator with operand obj
   ReturnType operator# (const ClassName &obj);

Operator/Operand Format        Function Call
   lhs # rhs  // binary        operator# (lhs, rhs)

   #obj       // unary         operator# (obj)
```

Action: When a statement uses the operator in operator/operand format, the corresponding function is called like any other function. The return type should be consistent with the usual meaning of the operator. For instance, the operator < compares the value of two operands and returns a boolean value.

Example:
```
// the comparison operator < for Rational objects
bool operator< (const Rational& lhs,
                const Rational& rhs);
```
The < operator can be used in two forms. The first form is the familiar binary operator notation. The second form makes an explicit function call.

```
Rational r(1,2), s(3,4);

// form 1
if (r < s)
   . . .
// form 2 (valid but seldom used)
if (operator< (r, s))
   . . .
```

The action of the + operator typically takes two objects and returns a new object that combines the values of the operands. When applied to Rational objects, the return type is Rational.

```
Rational operator+ (const Rational& lhs, const Rational& rhs);
```

With both the < and + operators, use the familiar operator/operand syntax for calculations with Rational objects.

```
Rational r(3,4), s(4,6), t;
t = r + s;                 // add 3/4 + 1/6;  result 11/12
if (s < t)                 // comparison is true 4/6 < 3/4
   cout << "s is less than t";
```

Implementing Operator Functions To overload an operator with free functions, we use the corresponding operator function. Like an ordinary function, this involves creating a function implementation that uses arguments as operands and returns a result. To perform the computation, the operator function needs access to the private data members of the class. For instance, the implementation of the < operator for the Rational class assumes access to the data members num and den. This access is provided by the member functions `getNumerator()` and `getDenominator()`.

Comparison <:

A common divisor for the two operands is the product of the two denominators.

```
commonDen = lhs.getDenominator() * rhs.getDenominator().
```

The resulting equivalent fractions are

$$\text{left operand:} \quad \frac{\text{lhs.getNumerator()*rhs.getDenominator()}}{\text{commonDen}}$$

$$\text{right operand:} \quad \frac{\text{rhs.getNumerator()*lhs.getDenominator()}}{\text{commonDen}}$$

Our implementation of the < operator simply compares the numerators of the equivalent fractions as integer values.

```
// compares numerators for the equivalent fractions
bool operator< (const Rational& lhs, const Rational& rhs)
{
    return  lhs.getNumerator()*rhs.getDenominator()
                <
            rhs.getNumerator()*lhs.getDenominator();
}
```

Implementing operator overloading by using the "get" member functions of a class is inefficient since they involve passing control to a function and obtaining return values. It would be more efficient to directly access the private data members. Unfortunately, ordinary free functions do not have this access which is provided to member functions of a class. C++ recognizes this problem and allows a free function to be declared as a *friend function* of a class. A friend function, which we will simply call a friend, is a free function that has access to the private members of the class. The function is declared in the class by placing the keyword *friend* immediately before its prototype. Despite its access rights, it is not a member function of the class.

```
class ClassName
{
   private:
      Type    dataValue;
      . . . .
   public:
      . . . .
      friend ReturnType operator# (const ClassName& lhs, . . .);

};
```

The keyword friend is used only with the function prototype and not with the function implementation. Since a friend is not a member function, its implementation does not include the class scope operator ClassName::. Any statement in the body of the function may access the private member dataValue.

```
ReturnType operator# (const ClassName& lhs, . . .)
{
    // any statement may access data member lhs.dataValue
        . . .
}
```

If we overload the comparison operation < in the Rational class as a friend, note how this translates to a simpler and more efficient function implementation.

Declaration of < as a friend in the Rational class:

```
friend bool operator< (const Rational& lhs,
                       const Rational& rhs);
```

Implementation of < as a free function:

```
// compares numerators for the equivalent fractions
bool operator< (const Rational& lhs, const Rational& rhs)
{
    return  lhs.num*rhs.den < rhs.num*lhs.den;
}
```

The Rational Class (Extended)

In the Rational class, we use friend functions to overload the four arithmetic operators $+, -, *, /$ and the six comparison operators $==, !=, <, <=, >,$ and $>=$. The following is a partial listing of the class that includes only these operators.

DECLARATION: Rational CLASS (PARTIAL) ━━━━

rational.h

```
class Rational
{
    . . .
  public:
      // binary operators: add, subtract, multiply, divide
      friend Rational operator+ (const Rational& lhs,
                                 const Rational& rhs);
      friend Rational operator- (const Rational& lhs,
                                 const Rational& rhs);
      friend Rational operator* (const Rational& lhs,
                                 const Rational& rhs);
      friend Rational operator/ (const Rational& lhs,
                                 const Rational& rhs);

      // relational operators
      friend bool operator== (const Rational& lhs,
                              const Rational& rhs);
      friend bool operator!= (const Rational& lhs,
                              const Rational& rhs);
      friend bool operator<  (const Rational& lhs,
                              const Rational& rhs);
      friend bool operator<= (const Rational& lhs,
                              const Rational& rhs);
      friend bool operator>  (const Rational& lhs,
                              const Rational& rhs);
      friend bool operator>= (const Rational& lhs,
                              const Rational& rhs);

    . . .
};
```

You have already seen the implementation of the < operator as a friend. A complete listing of all of the friend functions is given in the file *rational.h* of the software supplement. Let us look at the + (addition) and / (divide) operators to reinforce your understanding of how a friend function uses its access rights to the data members.

Implementation of + as a free function:

```
// rational addition
Rational operator+ (const Rational& lhs, const Rational& rhs)
{
return Rational(lhs.num*rhs.den + lhs.den*rhs.num,
                lhs.den*rhs.den);
}
```

Implementation of / as a free function:

```
// rational division
Rational operator/ (const Rational& lhs, const Rational& rhs)
{
// calls the private constructor with long arguments
return Rational(lhs.num*rhs.den, lhs.den*rhs.num);
}
```

In the implementation of /, we let the constructor handle the case where rhs is a negative rational number (rhs.num < 0). When the Rational constructor builds the return value, the denominator argument (lhs.den*rhs.num) is negative. By calling standardize(), the constructor converts the rational number to standard form.

EXAMPLE 9.2 ■

```
Rational a(-4,5), b(0.5), c;   // a is -4/5, b is 1/2

c = a - b;                     // c = -8/10 - 5/10 = -13/10

c = a * b;                     // c = -4/5 * 1/2 = -4/10
c.reduce();                    // c = -2/5

c = b / a;                     // c = 1/2 / -4/5 = 1/2 * -5/4 = -
5/8

b == Rational(3,6)             // comparison is true   ■
```

Overloading the Stream I/O Operators

C++ implements stream I/O by overloading the >> and << operators. The header file **iostream.h** declares versions of the operators allowing integer, real, and character objects to be input from or output to a stream. We will add these operators to the Rational class so that rational numbers can be used with input and output streams. Recall Example 9.1 that includes the function writeRational(). To output a rational number 2/3 as part of the sentence

The attendance was 2/3 of capacity.

a programmer would need three output statements to list the text and the number.

```
Rational  attPct(2,3);

cout << "The attendace was ";  // output first part of sentence
writeRational(attPct);         // call function to output 2/3
cout << " of capacity.";       // output end of sentence
```

By overloading the << operator, the Rational object can be placed in the output stream along with the text strings.

```
cout << "The attendance was " << attPct << " of capacity."
```

Overloaded Stream Operators as Friends To understand the overloading of stream operators, we need to revisit the C++ stream I/O system. The file iostream.h contains declarations for two classes named istream and ostream that provide stream input and stream output, respectively.

The operand on the left is a stream object and the operand on the right is a data object. For output, the operator << takes the value of the object on the right and inserts it into the stream without modifying its value. For input, the operator >> extracts data from the stream and uses it to update the value of object on the right. It is important to note that, like + and <, the stream operators return a value. To understand the value, we must look at more complex expressions that chain together a series of stream operators. Consider the << operator and the cout stream.

```
cout << "The value is " << dataValue;
```

The statement is equivalent to separate cout statements that include the string literal "The value is " in the first statement and the object dataValue in the second.

```
cout << "The value is ";
cout << dataValue;
```

The compiler implements the single statement as

```
(cout << "The value is ") << dataValue;
```

The subexpression, cout << "The value is", is evaluated first and the stream object cout is the return value. That value is then used as an operand in executing the resulting subexpression, cout << dataValue.

With this as background, we are able to describe how a programmer overloads the stream operators to implement input/output of programmer-defined types.

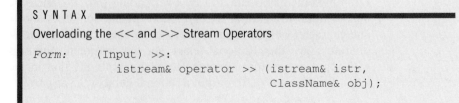

SYNTAX

Overloading the << and >> Stream Operators

Form: (Input) >>:
```
                istream& operator >> (istream& istr,
                                      ClassName& obj);
```

```
         (Output) <<:
            ostream& operator << (ostream& ostr,
                                     const ClassName& obj);
```

Action: The I/O stream object is the left-hand operand in an expression. Like any stream object, it must be passed by reference since its state is changed by the I/O operation. For output, the right-hand side object is passed as a constant reference since it is not changed by the operation. Since the input operation updates the right-hand side object, the argument is passed by reference. The return value is a reference to the same stream that is passed as an argument.

Example: The >> and << operators are overloaded to provide input and output of Rational objects.

```
         istream& operator>> (istream& istr, Rational& r);

         ostream& operator<< (ostream& ostr,
                                const Rational& r);
```

Rational Stream Operators With input, we read a number in the form P/Q where Q is not 0. The number is read as a triple with the '/' extracted as a separator. An exit() statement causes the program to terminate when the denominator is zero. The function, standardize(), stores the rational number in standard form.

```
// overload stream input operator. input in form P/Q
istream& operator >> (istream& istr, Rational& r)
{
    char c;  // reads the separator '/'

    // as a friend, ">>" can access numerator/denominator of r
    istr >> r.num >> c >> r.den;
    // terminate if denominator is 0
    if (r.den == 0)
    {
        cerr << "A Zero denominator is invalid" <<endl;
        exit(1);
    }

    // put r in standard form and return the stream
    r.standardize();
    return istr;
}
```

The overloaded stream output operator << writes a rational number in the form P/Q.

```
// overload stream output operator. output in form P/Q
ostream& operator << (ostream& ostr, const Rational& r)
{
    // output numerator and denominator with / separator
    ostr << r.num << '/' << r.den;
```

```
                    // return the output stream object
                    return ostr;
                }
```

EXAMPLE 9.3 ▬▬▬▬▬▬▬▬▬▬▬▬▬▬▬▬▬▬▬▬▬▬▬▬▬▬▬▬

Input two rational numbers and output the larger.

```
Rational r, s;
cin >> r >> s;        // both r and s use the cin stream object
if (r < s)
    cout << r << " is less than " << s;
else
    cout << s << " is less than " << r;

Input:   7/9   3/4
Output:  3/4 is less than 7/9   ■
```

9-4 MEMBER FUNCTION OVERLOADING

Friend functions are used to overload many class operators. An alternative method declares the operator as a member function. The technique must be used for conversion operators, the index operator, and the assignment operator that we cover in Chapter 10. With the Rational class, we introduce member function overloading for the compound assignment operators $+=$, $-=$, $*=$, and $/=$ along with the unary $-$ (negate) operator. The following is a partial listing of Rational class that includes all of the operations that are overloaded as member functions. The listing also includes the conversion operator double() that is discussed in the next section.

rational.h

DECLARATION: Rational CLASS (PARTIAL) ▬▬▬▬▬▬▬

```
class Rational
{
   . . .
   public:
      // compound assignment operators oveloaded as
      // member functions
      Rational& operator+= (const Rational& rhs);
      Rational& operator-= (const Rational& rhs);
      Rational& operator*= (const Rational& rhs);
      Rational& operator/= (const Rational& rhs);

      // unary minus (change sign)
      Rational operator- () const;

      // conversion operator: Rational to double
      operator double() const;
};
```

You probably note something strange about the declaration of the operators. They seem to be missing an operand. The binary operator += has only one operand while the unary operator has no operands. Member function overloading has one less argument, since the object itself is an operand. In the case of the binary operator +=, the object is the left-hand side (lhs) operand. For the unary − operator, the single operand is the object. This fact is key to your understanding of operator overloading with member functions.

The Negation Operator. Assume r and s are Rational objects. To execute the statement

```
s = -r;
```

The negative of r is created and assigned to s. The negative is created by calling the - operator that is a member function of r.

```
s = r.operator-();
```

Since the negation operator is a member function in the Rational class, it may access the data members num and den. It creates a Rational number with numerator -num and denominator den and returns the object as the value of the function. Its implementation must include the scope operator Rational::, since the operator is declared as a member function.

```
// rational negation
Rational Rational::operator- () const
{
    return Rational(-num, den);

}
```

The += Operator and the Keyword this. The compound assignment statement += provides a good example of a binary operator that is normally overloaded as a member function. To see how C++ views the operation, consider the statement with Rational objects r and s.

```
s += r;
```

The member function of object s is called with r as the argument. The operations is evaluated as

```
s.operator+= (r);
```

Like any assignment operator, it should work in a multiple assignment statement. For instance, it is possible to chain assignment statements that include +=.

```
Rational r(1,2), s(3,4), t;
// first add r to s; then assign the result s = s+r to t
t = s += r;                 // s = 5/4   t = 5/4
```

To allow the use of += in a multiple assignment statement, the overloaded operator must return a reference to its own value. For this and other similar applications, C++ associates with each object the keyword *this,* that represents the address of the object in memory. When a program executes the body of a member function, *this is the object that is executing the function. You will better understand the meaning of this and *this when we study pointers in Chapter 10.

The Rational += operator forms the sum of the current object (*this) and the right hand side, rhs, and then assigns the sum as the new value of the current object (*this).

```
// compound addition assignment operator
Rational& Rational::operator+= (const Rational& rhs)
{
    // *this is the current object.  assign the current
    // object the sum of itself and rhs
    *this = *this + rhs;

    // return reference to the current object
    return *this;
}
```

EXAMPLE 9.4

1.
```
Rational r(-4,8), s(1,3), t; // r = -4/8, s = 1/3, t = 0/1

t = -r;                      // t = r.operator-() = 4/8
t.reduce();                  // Reduce t to 1/2
```

2.
```
t *= s;                      // t.operator+= (s), t = 1/6
r -= t;                      // r.operator-= (t), r = -32/48
cout << r << " " << t;       // Output:  -32/48  1/6  ∎
```

9-5 CONVERTING RATIONAL NUMBERS

The Rational class contains a member function called operator double(). This is a type conversion operator that converts a Rational object into a real number. You have seen this type of converter with primitive number types. For example, the following assignment statements make explicit use of the double(), int(), and char() conversion operators.

```
double x = double(8)/2;   // convert int8 to double
int a = int(6.47);        // convert double 6.47 to int
cout << char(65);         // convert int 65 to char
```

Implicit conversion is also available for primitive types. For instance, in the following statement, the compiler converts the integer literal 4 to the floating-point number 4.0 before performing the addition. The result, 7.5, is assigned to the double y. Before assigning y to sh, 7.5 is implicitly converted to a short value, 7.

```
short   sh;
double  x = 3.5, y;
y = x + 4;              // add 3.5 + 4.0
sh = y;                 // assign 7 to sh
```

The principles of implicit and explicit conversion of types extend to class objects provided the conversion is specified by a constructor or by a type conversion operator. To illustrate these ideas, we focus on conversion between Rational objects and the C++ data types double and int.

Conversion to Rational Type. The Rational class contains two constructors that allow a program to declare a Rational object with either an integer or a real number argument. These constructors serve as type conversion operators from the primitive number types to a Rational type.

The default constructor allows a single integer n to be passed as the argument when declaring an object. The resulting rational number is n/1.

Constructor: Converter from int to rational

```
Rational(int n=0, int d=1);
```

The converter is used when mixing an integer and a rational number in an expression. The following examples illustrate both explicit and implicit conversion. In the first case, the constructor Rational() is explicitly called to convert integer 2 to the rational 2/1

```
Rational r, s;
r = Rational(2);
```

In the second case, the compiler implicitly calls the constructor to convert 5 to the Rational object 5/1.

```
s = 5;
```

Note that the compiler provides the conversion by treating the assignment as

```
S = Rational(5);
```

The implementation of the default constructor simply initializes the attributes and standardizes the number.

```
Rational::Rational(int n, int d): num(n), den(d)
{
   if (den == 0)
   {
      cerr << "A Zero denominator is invalid" << endl;
      exit(1);
   }
   standardize();
}
```

A second constructor, `Rational(double x)`, converts a real number to a Rational object. For instance, the following statements create the rational numbers r = 3/2 and s = 16/5. In the first case, the real number 1.5 is explicitly converted to 3/2 when the constructor creates an anonymous object and uses it to initialize r. In the second case, the real number 3.2 is implicit converted to Rational(16,5) before the assignment to s.

```
Rational r = Rational(1.5), s;
s = 3.2;
```

The implementation of the second constructor is found in the file *rational.h*. The constructor rounds the floating point number to five decimal places and converts this value to a rational number. The resulting rational number may be an approximation to the original real value.

Conversion from Rational to Double A class may contain one or more member functions that convert an object to a new type. In the case of the Rational class, the conversion is from

```
Rational --> double
```

The member function declaration has the form

```
operator double();
```

It takes the current object and returns a value of type double. The real number (decimal) equivalent of a Rational number n/d is obtained by division. For instance

```
3/4 is 3.0/4 = 0.75        4/2 is 4.0/2 = 2.0
```

The declaration of the unary conversion operator does not have a return type since the return type is implicit in the name double. Its implementation simply divides the numerator by the denominator as real numbers. The result is the return value.

```
// convert Rational to a double
Rational::operator double() const
{
    return double(num)/double(den);
}
```

EXAMPLE 9.5

Assume the declarations

```
Rational r(1,2), s(3,5);        // r is 1/2, s is 3/5
double z;

// explicitly convert rational r = 1/2 to double 0.5
z = double(r);

// implicitly convert rational s = 3/5 to double 0.6
z = s;   ▪
```

*Exploring
Concepts*

When using the Time24 class, comparison of two times must be done by converting each time to minutes.

```
Time24 t1(12,35), t2;
   . . .
while (t2.getHours()*60 + t2.getMinutes() <
        t1.getHours()*60 + t1.getMinutes())
   . . .
```

How would you add an int() converter? How will this converter make such comparisons easier?

PROGRAM 9.1

The program illustrates most of properties of the Rational class. The program is devided into five sections that are accompanied by an output statement which describes the actions and the result.

1. Use the constructor to declare a rational number that is equivalent to an integer.
2. Input a rational number with the >> operator and use the double() conversion operator to output its value as a real number.
3. Input two rational numbers and test the arithmetic and relational operators.
4. Demonstrate implicit conversion by reading a floating-point number and assigning it to a rational object. Using the double() conversion operator, convert the rational number back to a real value and output the result.
5. Test the Rational += operator.

```
#include <iostream.h>

#include "rational.h"      // include the rational number class

// each operation is accompanied by output
int main()
{
   Rational r1(5), r2, r3(1,3);
   double f;

   cout << "1. Rational value for integer 5 is " << r1
        << endl;

   cout << "2. Enter a rational number: ";
   cin >> r1;
   f = double(r1);
   cout << "      Floating-point equivalent is " << f << endl;

   cout << "3. Enter two rational numbers: ";
   cin >> r1 >> r2;
   cout << "      Results: " << (r1+r2) << " (+)    "
        << (r1-r2) << " (-)    " << (r1*r2) << " (*)    "
        << (r1/r2) << " (/)    " << endl;
```

```
        if (r1 < r2)
           cout << "        Relation (less than): " << r1 << " < "
                << r2 << endl;
        else if (r1 == r2)
           cout << "        Relation (equal to): " << r1 << " == "
                << r2 << endl;
        else
           cout << "        Relation (greater than): " << r1 << " > "
                << r2 << endl;

        cout << "4. Input a floating-point number: ";
        cin >> f;
        r1 = f;
        cout << "        Convert to Rational " << r1 << endl;
        f = r1;
        cout << "        Reconvert to double " << f << endl;

        r3 += 5;
        cout << "5. Use compound assignment: r += 5"
             << endl;
        cout << "        r = " << r3 << endl;

        return 0;
        }
```

Run:

```
1. Rational value for integer 5 is 5/1
2. Enter a rational number: -1/3
        Floating-point equivalent is -0.333333
3. Enter two rational numbers: 1/2 -7/9
        Results: -5/18 (+)    23/18 (-)    -7/18 (*)
        -9/14 (/)
        Relation (greater than): 1/2 > -7/9
4. Input a floating-point number: 4.25
        Convert to Rational 17/4
        Reconvert to double 4.25
5. Use compound assignment: r += 5
        r = 16/3
```

*Exploring
Concepts*

In grade school, students are often told that π is 22/7. A closer approximation is 3.1416. Explain how the following code segment illustrates a better rational approximation.

```
const double PI = 3.141592653589793;
Rational pi1(22,7), pi2 = 3.1416;
pi2.reduce();
cout << pi1 << "  " << pi2 << endl;
cout << (double (pi1) - PI) << "  " << (double (pi2) - PI);
```

Mixed Numbers

A fraction in which the numerator is greater than the denominator is often written as a mixed number that consists of a whole part and a fractional part that is less than 1. The function `writeMixedNumber()`, writes a fraction as a mixed number.

Fraction	*Mixed Number*
$\dfrac{10}{4}$	$2\dfrac{1}{2}$
$-\dfrac{10}{4}$	$-2\dfrac{1}{2}$
$\dfrac{200}{4}$	50

```
// output a Rational number as a mixed number (+/-)N p/q
void writeMixedNumber (const Rational& x)
{
   // whole part of the Rational number x
   int wholePart = int(x.getNumerator()/x.getDenominator());

   // obtains the fractional part of the mixed number
   Rational fractionPart = x - Rational(wholePart);

   // if no fractional part, output the whole part
   if (fractionPart == Rational(0))
      cout << wholePart << "   ";
   else
   {
      // reduce fractional part
      fractionPart.reduce();

      // output sign with the whole part
      if (wholePart < 0)
         fractionPart = -fractionPart;

      // if the whole part is not 0, output whole and
      // fractional parts; otherwise, output fractional part
      if (wholePart != 0)
         cout << wholePart << " " << fractionPart << "   ";
      else
         cout << fractionPart << "   ";
   }
}
```

APPLICATION 9-2 CONVERTING A RATIONAL ARRAY

The function, `writeRationals()`, outputs an array of rational numbers. It calls the function `writeMixedNumber()` to display each number greater than 1 as a mixed number.

```
#include <iostream.h>
#include <stdlib.h>

#include "rational.h"              // include the Rational class

// output a Rational number as a mixed number (+/-)N p/q
void writeMixedNumber (const Rational& x);

// output each rational number > 1 as a mixed number
void writeRationals(Rational arr[], int n);

int main()
{
    Rational arr[5];
    int i;

    cout << "Enter 5 rational numbers: ";
    for(i=0; i < 5; i++)
      cin >> arr[i];

    cout << "The numbers with values > 1 written as mixed"
            " numbers" << endl;
    writeRationals(arr, 5);

    return 0;
}

/* implementation of writeMixedNumber() given in the program
discussion */

void writeRationals(Rational arr[], int n)
{
    int i;

    for (i=0; i < n; i++)
       if (arr[i] <= Rational(1))
          cout << arr[i] << "  ";        // output as rational
       else
          writeMixedNumber(arr[i]);   // output as mixed number

    cout << endl;
}
```

```
Run:

Enter 5 rational numbers: 1/3 17/5 11/12 47/23 7/6
The numbers with values > 1 written as mixed numbers
1/3   3 2/5   11/12   2 1/23   1 1/6
```

Notes on Operator Overloading. We conclude our treatment of operator overloading by introducing four technical notes and a general discussion of friend versus member function overloading.

1. Operator overloading must use existing C++ operators. For instance, we cannot make up our own operator @ and define it so that x @ y evaluates the expression x * x + y * y.

2. To overload an operator, at least one operand must be of class or enumeration type. As an example, the Days class discussed in Section 6.3 defines the enumeration type DaysInWeek.

```
enum DaysInWeek {Sun, Mon, Tue, Wed, Thu, Fri, Sat};
```

If d is a DaysInWeek object and n is an integer, we can overload the addition operator so that d + n is the day n days from d. For instance, if d is Wed, then d + 5 is Mon.

```
DaysInWeek operator+ (const DaysInWeek& d, int n)
{
    return DaysInWeek( (int(d)+n) % 7);
}
```

3. Overloaded operators obey the same rules of precedence and associativity as the original C++ operators. For instance, if + and * are defined for class ClassName objects, multiplication has higher precedence than addition.

```
ClassName    objA, objB, objC, objD;
objD = objA + objB * objC;    // * is done first
```

4. Some symbols refer to both unary and binary operations. In this case, both operators can be overloaded. For instance, − refers to both negation (unary) and subtraction (binary).

In the Rational class, we implement operator overloading using both friend functions and member functions. In the case of stream operators, friend functions must be used. If the stream operators for the Rational class were overloaded as member functions, the class ostream must be extended to include overloaded versions of >> and << that accept a Rational argument. To understand this fact, consider the example

```
Rational r(3,4);
cout << r;
```

As a member function, the output operator << would be evaluated as

```
cout.<< (r)
```

which implies that we have overloaded the << operator in the class ostream. This is clearly impractical, and so we use friend overloading. In some situations, like type conversion operators and the assignment operator (Chapter 10), member functions must be used. For the other cases, a programmer is free to choose either process. We present general rules that can assist you in making a decision.

Overload a binary operator as a friend if the operator does not modify either operand.

Because both operands are provided as arguments, the compiler can automatically convert either operand to the class type. For instance, our overloaded version of + for the Rational class will handle either of the following assignment statements:

```
Rational a(3,2), b;

b = a + 2;  // b = 3/2 + 2/1 = 7/2
b = 2 + a;  // b = 2/1 + 3/2 = 7/2
```

Suppose we overload Rational addition using the member function

```
Rational operator+ (const Rational& rhs);
```

The second statement, "b = 2 + a", is in error, since the compiler will attempt to evaluate it as follows:

```
b = 2.operator+ (a);
```

The term 2.operator+ has no meaning.

Use member function overloading for a unary operator or a binary operator that modifies its left operand:

Overload operators like unary − for the Rational class as a member function because no implicit type conversion is necessary. For instance, −9 will not be converted to −Rational(9) because unary minus is already defined for integers. Overload compound assignment operators like += and *= for the Rational class using a member function, since these operators update the value of the object itself.

9-6   TEMPLATE FUNCTIONS

In Chapter 7 we introduced the selection sort to order items in a list. Our implementation focused on integer arrays, although the algorithm relies only on a definition of the operator < to compare two objects and the ability to exchange their position in the list. With essentially the same set of instructions, we could have implemented the sort to order real numbers, characters, Rational objects, and so forth. Unfortunately, we could not use the same function for two distinct objects types. Using function overloading, we would have to implement different versions of the function with small changes in the argument list. One version would sort integers, another version would sort real numbers, and so forth. Since the function selectionSort() involves data exchanges, we would need multiple versions of the exchange() function. The following is a listing of the int and double versions for these functions.

Int Version

```
// integer version of exchange()
void exchange(int& a, int& b)
{
   int temp = a;

   a = b;
   b = temp;
}


// integer version of selection sort
void selectionSort(int arr[], int n)
{
   . . . .
   for (j = i+1; j < n; j++)
      if (arr[j] < arr[smallindex])
         smallindex = j;

   exchange(arr[i],arr[smallindex]);

   . . . .
}
```

Double Version

```
// integer version of exchange()
void exchange(double& a, double& b)
{
   double temp = a;

   a = b;
   b = temp;
}


// double version of selection sort
void selectionSort(double arr[],int n)
{
   . . . .
   for (j = i+1; j < n; j++)
      if (arr[j] < arr[smallindex])
         smallindex = j;

   exchange(arr[i],arr[smallindex]);

   . . . .
}
```

This tedious approach is not needed, since C++ allows the programmer to write `exchange()` and `selectionSort()` as template functions that have generic arguments. The compiler has the responsibility to create separate versions of the functions.

Template Syntax

The prototype and implementation of a template function begin with a *template argument list*. Its syntax includes the keyword *template* followed by a non-empty list of formal types enclosed in angle brackets. In the argument list, each type is preceded by the keyword class. In this context, class should be read as type.

```
// argument list with a single template type
template <class T>


// argument list with multiple template types
template <class T, class U, class V, . . . >
```

In the argument list, C++ programmers typically use the letter T to represent the type. This is not required by the language. When the template is used, T is associated with an actual C++ type such as int or char or with a programmer-defined class type. Most applications of templates use a single type T.

Except for the initial template argument list, the declaration and implementation of a template function follow the standard rules of function coding. The template type T must be used as the type for at least one function argument. It may also be used to specify other formal arguments, the function return type, and local objects within the body. For instance, the following is a template version of the exchange() function.

```
template <class T>          // template argument list
void exchange(T& a, T& b)   // start of function implementation
{
    T temp = a;

    a = b;
    b = temp;
}
```

Template Expansion

When a template function is called, the compiler identifies the data types of the run-time arguments and associates an actual C++ type with the template type T. For instance, in the calls to the exchange() function, the compiler recognizes the int type for run-time arguments m and n and the double type for run-time arguments x and y.

```
int m = 20, n = 30;
double x = 4.5, y = 5.5;

exchange(m,n);  // compiler calls the exchange() with T = int
exchange(x,y);  // compiler calls the exchange() with T = double
```

The compiler creates separate instances of the exchange() function for the two types int and double. In effect, the compiler generates two separate implementations for the same function. This is compiler-created function overloading.

Call with int arguments: | **Compiler generated version**

```
int m, n;
. . .
exchange(m,n);
```

```
void exchange(int& a, int& b)
{
    int temp = a;

    a = b;
    b = temp;
}
```

Call with double arguments: | **Compiler generated version**

```
double x,y;
. . .
exchange(x,y);
```

```
void exchange(double& a, double& b)
{
    double temp = a;

    a = b;
    b = temp;
}
```

S Y N T A X ━━━━━━━━━━━━━━━━━━━━━━━━━━━━━━

Template Function

Form:
```
template <class T>
returnType  funcName (T arg, . . . .)
{
    <type T may be used in C++ statements>
}
```

Action: At least one formal argument must reference objects of type T. Assume value is of type ObjType.

```
ObjType  value;
```

From the function call,

```
funcName (value, . . . .)
```

the compiler creates an instance of `funcName()` with T set to the type ObjType. The programmer must check that all operations in the function are valid for the specific type.

Example: The template function `max()` returns the larger of two data items. A template version of the function uses type T for the return value and the arguments.

```
template <class T>
T max (const T& a, const T& b)
{
    return a < b ? b : a;  // return larger of a
                           // and b
}
```

```
Application:

    cout << max(4,5);   // call instance with T = int;

    String s = "template", t = "function";
    cout << max(s,t);   // call instance with String;

    Rectangle r(4,5), s(9,2), t;
    // invalid!  < not defined for Rectangle
    t = max(r,s);
```

Template-based Selection Sort

A template version of the selection sort can be used to order arrays of different object types. The following listing of the function is included in the file **sort.h** of the software supplement. The file includes the template-based exchange() function that is used by selectionSort().

```
template <class T>
void selectionSort(T arr[], int n)
{
    int smallindex; // index of smallest element in the sublist
    int pass, j;

    // pass has the range 0 to n-2
    for (pass = 0; pass < n-1; pass++)
    {
        // scan the sublist starting at index pass
        smallindex = pass;

        // j traverses the sublist a[pass+1] to a[n-1]
        for (j = pass+1; j < n; j++)
            // update if smaller element found
            if (arr[j] < arr[smallindex])
                smallindex = j;

        // when finished, exchange smallest item with arr[pass]
        exchange(arr[pass], arr[smallindex]);
    }
}
```

The function may be used by different array types provided the comparison operator < is defined for the type.

APPLICATION 9-3 GENERIC SELECTION SORT

The program uses the template-based version of the selectionSort() to order an array of integers and an array of String objects and then outputs the ordered lists by calling the template function writeList().

```cpp
#include <iostream.h>

#include "tstring.h"
#include "sort.h"      // generic selection sort

// template function. output the array a of type T
template <class T>
void writeList(const T a[], int n);

int main()
{
    // declare an integer array and a String array
    int list[10] = {5, 9, 1, 3, 4, 8, 2, 0, 7, 6};
    String words[6] = {"john", "rebecca", "sara",
                        "jack", "bob", "joe"};

    // sort and output each array

    cout << "Sorting integer array:  ";
    selectionSort(list,10);
    writeList(list,10);
    cout << endl;

    cout << "Sorting array of strings: ";
    selectionSort(words,6);
    writeList(words,6);
    cout << endl;

    return 0;
}

// template function to output an n element array of type T
template <class T>
void writeList(const T a[], int n)
{
    int i;

    for(i=0;i < n;i++)
        cout << a[i] << "   ";
    cout << endl;
}
```

Run:

Sorting integer array: 0   1   2   3   4   5   6   7   8   9

Sorting array of strings: bob   jack   joe   john   rebecca   sara

Given the template function

```
template <class T>
T f(T x, T y);
```

which calls to f() will create an ambiguity? Explain

*Exploring
Concepts*

```
double x = 5.6, y = 3.7;
float a = 5.8;
int b = 5, d = 3;
long e = 67;

cout << f(x,y) << endl;
cout << f(a,y) << endl;
cout << f(b,d) << endl;
cout << f(e,d) << endl;
```

9-7   GENERALIZED SEARCHING

The sequential search algorithm traverses a list looking item by item for a match with a target. The algorithm applies to any object type for which the comparison operator == is defined. For instance, the algorithm applies to searching arrays of numeric or character objects. It also applies to an array whose element type is a class that overloads the == operator. The function seqSearch() of Section 7.7 is an excellent candidate for implementation as a template function. In the implementation, note that the array is declared to be constant. This prevents modification of any array elements.

```
// perform sequential search for a target
template <class T>
int seqSearch(const T arr[],int start,int end, const T& target)
{
    int i;

    // scan indices start to arraysize-1
    for(i=start; i <= end; i++)
        if (arr[i] == target)    // assume T has the "==" operator
            return i;            // immediately return on a match
    return -1;                   // otherwise return -1
}
```

The function is defined in the file **tsearch.h** of the supplemental software.

EXAMPLE 9.6

A template version of the sequential search can be used to find rational objects in a list since the Rational class provides an overloaded definition of the == operator. Assume rationalList is an array of rational numbers, and that rationalTarget is a specific value.

```
Rational rationalList [25];
Rational rationalTarget;

. . .

   if (seqSearch(rationalList,0,24, rationalTarget) != -1)
      cout << "Found " << rationalTarget << " in the list";
   else
      cout << rationalTarget << " is not in the list";   ■
```

PROGRAM 9.2

The program searches an integer array, looking for the first occurrence of 100. It also searches an array of String objects for the name "Heather."

```
#include <iostream.h>

#include "tsearch.h" // provides access to generic seqSearch()
#include "tstring.h"

int main()
{
   // declare data to use for the generic sequential search
   int list[5] = {5, 3, 100, 89, 27};
   String names[7] = {"Alice", "Linda", "Teresa", "Jacob",
                      "Heather", "Rachel", "Violetta" };
   int index;

   // use generic form of seqSearch() for T = int
   if ((index = seqSearch(list,0,4,100)) != -1)
      cout << "100 occurs at index " << index << endl;
   else
      cout << "100 is not in the list" << endl;

   // use generic form of seqSearch() for T = String
   if ((index = seqSearch(names,0,6,String("Heather"))) != -1)
      cout << "Heather occurs at index " << index << endl;
   else
      cout << "Heather is not in the list of names" << endl;

   return 0;
}
```

```
Run:

100 occurs at index 2
Heather occurs at index 4
```

Binary Search

The sequential search is a general search algorithm that applies to any array. If the list is ordered, however, the *binary search* algorithm provides a significantly improved search technique. For example, when you need a phone number, you do not start at the beginning of the phone book and flip through its pages until you find the name. You use the fact that the names are listed in alphabetical order, jump quickly to the approximate location and start looking for the number. Of course, you have some idea of how names are distributed in the phone book, and this assists you in approximating the location. If you need to search a list of sorted items when you are not familiar with the distribution of values, a good tactic is to start with the value at the midpoint of the list. If the value matches your target, you are done. Otherwise, use the fact that the list is ordered and look for the target in either the lower- or upper-half list. If your target is less than the current midpoint value, look at the midpoint of lower sublist; otherwise, look at the midpoint of the upper sublist. Continue the process with smaller and smaller sublists until you find a match or you run out of data to search. This is the principle behind the binary search.

To understand the binary search algorithm, assume that the list is stored as an array arr with n items and that the search looks for the item called target. The indices for the list fall in the range of low = 0 to high = n − 1.

Compute the index for the midpoint in the array.

```
mid = (low+high)/2;          // midpoint
midvalue = arr[mid];         // midpoint value is arr[mid]
```

Compare midvalue with target and identify three possible outcomes. The action is pictured in Figure 9-1.

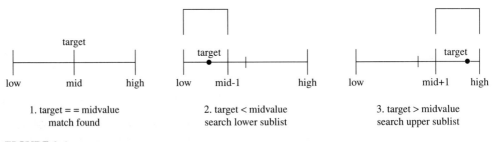

FIGURE 9-1
Illustrating the Binary Search.

1. A match occurs. Return the index mid that locates the target.

```
if (target == midvalue)       // found match
    return mid;
```

2. The value of target is less than midvalue. The search must continue in the lower sublist with indices in the range low to mid-1.

```
else if (target < midvalue)    // search left sublist
    <search in the range low...mid-1>
```

3. The value of target is greater than midvalue. The search must continue in the upper sublist with indices in the range mid+1 to high.

```
else                          // search right sublist
    < search in the range mid+1...high>
```

The process terminates when a match is found or the sublist is empty. An empty sublist occurs when low and high cross each other (low > high).

EXAMPLE 9.7

The example gives a few snapshots of the binary search algorithm as it looks for a target in the integer array arr. The first case finds target = 33 and returns the index 7. The second case looks for target = 4 and returns -1, since the item is not in the array.

	0	1	2	3	4	5	6	7	8
arr	-7	3	5	8	12	16	23	33	55

1. target = 33

```
Iteration 1: low = 0, high = 8, mid = (0+8)/2 = 4,
midvalue = 12
   action: since 33 > 12, search upper sublist with low = 5,
   high = 8
```

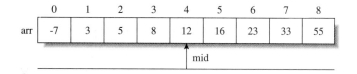

```
Iteration 2: low = 5, high = 8, mid = (5+8)/2 = 6,
midvalue = 23
   action: since 33 > 23, search upper sublist with low = 7,
   high = 8
```

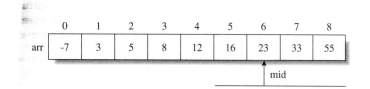

```
Iteration 3: low = 7, high = 8, mid = (7+8)/2 = 7,
midvalue = 33
   action: a match is found and the index mid = 7 is returned.
```

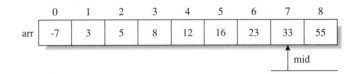

2. target = 4.

```
Iteration 1: low = 0, high = 8, mid = (0+8)/2 = 4,
midvalue = 12
   action: since 4 < 12, search lower sublist with low = 0,
   high = 3.
```

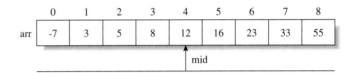

```
Iteration 2: low = 0, high = 3, mid = (0+3)/2 = 1,
midvalue = 3
   action: since 3 < 4, search upper sublist with low = 2,
   high = 3
```

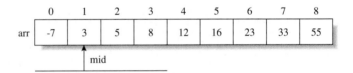

```
Iteration 3: low = 2, high = 3, mid = (2+3)/2 = 2,
midvalue = 5
   action: since 4 < 5, search lower sublist with low = 2,
   high = 1
```

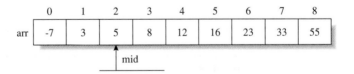

Since low > high, stop and return −1. The target is not found. ■

The binary search algorithm is implemented by the template function binSearch() that requires the definition of the == and < operators for type T. The function has four arguments that identify the array, the lower bound (low) and upper bound (high) for the list, and the target. The function returns the array index when a match is found or −1 if the target is not found.

```
// perform the binary search for a target
template <class T>
int binSearch(const T arr[], int low, int high, const T& target)
{
   int mid;
   T midvalue;               // object that is assigned arr[mid]

   while (low <= high)       // test for nonempty sublist
   {
      mid = (low+high)/2;
      midvalue = arr[mid];
      if (target == midvalue)
         return mid;          // have a match
      // determine which sublist to search
      else if (target < midvalue)
         high = mid-1;        // search lower sublist. reset high
      else
         low = mid+1;         // search upper sublist. reset low
   }
   return -1;                // target not found
}
```

The implementation is found in the file **search.h** of the supplemental software.

A program takes a 10-element array of integers and uses binSearch() to find an item. To insure that the list is ordered, we call the template-based selectionSort() function. The output gives the return index from the search and a message indicating whether the item was found.

```
#include <iostream.h>

#include "tsearch.h"
#include "sort.h"

int main()
{
   int arr[10] = {-7, 12, 5, -1, 7, 2, 3, 55, 8, 33};
   int n, pos;

   selectionSort(arr,10);

   cout <<"Enter an integer target: ";
   cin >> n;

   pos = binSearch(arr,0,9,n);
   if (pos != -1)
      cout << n << " is in the list" << endl;
```

```
        else
            cout << n << " is not in the list" << endl;

        return 0;
    }
```

```
    Run 1:


    33
    33 is in the list


    Run 2:


    6
    6 is not in the list
```

Comparing Search Algorithms (Optional)

For large arrays, the binary search is evidently more efficient than the sequential search. After all, the binary search eliminates one-half of the data items on each iteration, while the sequential search methodically moves through the list element by element.

We can verify this fact empirically by running a program that compares the computation time required by the two search algorithms. For our test, we use a random number generator to initialize two identical 5000 element integer arrays, list1 and list2, with random numbers in the range 0 to 9999. Since the binary search requires a sorted array, the selection sort orders list2. To compare the two search algorithms, we create an array, called targetList, of 5000 targets that consists of random numbers in the same range from 0 to 9999. To evaluate the efficiency of the searches, we separately time the execution of two loops that take each element in targetList and search for it in an array. The first loop uses the sequential search with list1, and the second loop uses the binary search with list2.

The timing process is carried out by declaring a Timer object t, where Timer is a class with the following declaration. They include file, time.h, declares type clock_t, function clock(), and constant CLK_TCK.

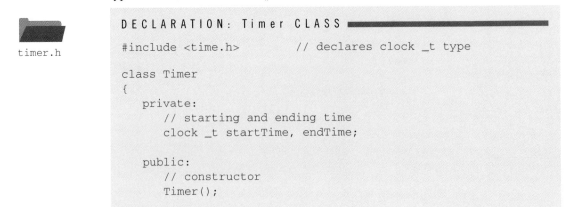

timer.h

```
DECLARATION: Timer CLASS

#include <time.h>            // declares clock _t type

class Timer
{
    private:
        // starting and ending time
        clock _t startTime, endTime;

    public:
        // constructor
        Timer();
```

```
        // start timing an event
        void start();
        // stop timing an event
        void stop();
        // return time the event took in seconds
        double time() const;
};
```

To time an execution of a code sequence, we call the function start() just before beginning the sequence and then call the function stop() immediately after completing it. The function time() returns the time in seconds required for the code sequence.

```
Timer t;
double timeRequired;

t.start();
<code sequence>
t.stop();
timeRequired = t.time();
```

APPLICATION 9-5 SEARCH ALGORITHM EFFICIENCY

The program declares and initializes integer arrays list1, list2, and targetList for the test. After sorting array list2, the Timer object t times the number of seconds we need to carry out a sequential search for each item in the array targetList. The same object times the number of seconds required to use the binary search with the same targets. By displaying these times, we can evaluate the relative efficiency of both algorithms.

```
#include <iostream.h>

#include "tsearch.h" // generic sequential and binary searches
#include "sort.h"    // generic selection sort
#include "trandom.h" // random number generation
#include "timer.h"   // time events

int main()
{
    // two lists for the search and a list of targets
    int list1[5000], list2[5000], targetList[5000];
    int i, matchCount;

    // t used for timing the search algorithms
    Timer t;
    RandomNumber rnd;

    // initialize the lists with random numbers in the
```

```
// range 0 to 9999. initialize the targetList array
// with random numbers in the same range
for (i = 0; i < 5000; i++)
{
   list1[i] = list2[i] = int(rnd.random(10000));
   targetList[i] = int(rnd.random(10000));
}


// sort list2
selectionSort(list2,5000);

cout << "Timing the Sequential Search" << endl;
matchCount = 0;
t.start();        // start timer
// perform search for elements from targetList using the
// sequential search
 for (i = 0; i < 5000; i++)
   if (seqSearch(list1,0,4999,targetList[i]) != -1)
      matchCount++;
t.stop();        // stop timer
cout << "Sequential Search takes " << t.time()
     << " seconds for " << matchCount << " matches."
     << endl;

cout << endl << "Timing the Binary Search" << endl;
matchCount = 0;
t.start();        // start timer
// perform search for elements from targetList using the
// binary search
for (i = 0; i < 5000; i++)
   if (binSearch(list2,0,4999,targetList[i]) != -1)
      matchCount++;
t.stop();        // stop timer
cout << "Binary Search takes " << t.time()
     << " seconds for " << matchCount << " matches."
     << endl;

   return 0;
}
```

```
Run:

Timing the Sequential Search
Sequential Search takes 2.2 seconds for 1976 matches.

Timing the Binary Search
Binary Search takes 0.05 seconds for 1976 matches.
```

Application 9.5 is an empirical test that compares the sequential and binary search algorithms. We can use mathematical analysis to compute the theoretical efficiency of each search algorithm. The expected number of iterations is the average of the number of iterations required for a match when a search is performed many, many times with random data. Assume a search is applied to an element list. After executing the sequential search many times the average position for a match will the midpoint index. Thus we expect n/2 iterations for a sequential search. For the binary search, each sublist has one-half as many elements as the previous sublist. We can only halve the sublist size $\log_2 n$ times before the sublist has one element. The value $\log_2 n$ is the logarithm of n to the base 2. Counting the initial iteration that deals with the entire list, the binary search requires at most $1 + \text{int}(\log_2 n)$ iterations. To see the difference in the performance of the algorithms, look at the case of n = 5000. The expected number of iterations for the two algorithms are:

Technical Note

$$\text{Sequential search:} \quad \frac{n}{2} = 2500$$

$$\text{Binary search:} \quad 1 + \text{int}(\log_2 n) = 13$$

The difference in efficiency is deceptive. Remember that the binary search requires the list to be ordered. If it is not, the sorting time may negate the advantages of the binary search.

9-8   TEMPLATE CLASSES

In the previous section, we saw that an algorithm not depending on a specific data type can be implemented as a template function. As an example, we developed the sequential and binary searches as well as the selection sort. Template types may also be used with classes that store generic data. In this section, we develop a simple template class that stores a single item. The class enables us to understand the syntax and use of template classes. Our class is a template version of the Accumulator class. Its single data member is called total, and member functions include a constructor and operations that add to the total and access its value. For your convenience we repeat the declaration of the Accumulator class for real numbers.

DECLARATION : Accumulator CLASS (DATA OF TYPE DOUBLE)

accum.h

```
class Accumulator
{
    private:
        // total accumulated by the object
        double total;
```

```
   public:
       Accumulator(double value = 0);   // constructor
       double getTotal();               // return total
       void addValue(double value = 1); // add value to total
};
```

By creating a template version of the Accumulator class, we will be able to compute totals for integer, rational and real numbers, and so forth. By using the String type, we will be able to build a long string by adding (concatenating) substrings.

Constructing a Template Class

A template version of a class has a template argument list followed by the class declaration. The data members may use the template type as an object type, and the member functions may use the template type for their arguments and return types.

SYNTAX ▬▬▬▬▬▬▬▬▬▬▬▬▬▬▬▬▬▬▬▬▬▬▬▬

Declaring a Template Class

Form: template <class T>
          class CL
          {
              private:
                  T data;
                  . . .
              public:
                  CL(const T& item);
                  T getValue();
                  . . .
          };

Action: The template argument list is the first item in the declaration. The actual class declaration follows the usual format with private and public sections. All of the data members and functions may reference template type T.

For the Accumulator class, the data member total and each member function references type T.

DECLARATION: Accumulator CLASS (TEMPLATE VERSION) ▬▬▬▬▬▬▬▬▬▬▬▬▬▬▬ •

accum_t.h

```
template <class T>
class Accumulator
{
    private:
        // total accumulated by the object
        T total;
```

```
   public:
      Accumulator(T value);          // constructor
      T getTotal() const;            // return total
      void addValue(const T& value); // add value to total
};
```

In comparing the double and template versions of the Accumulator class, you will note that the template type T replaces the numeric type double for data member total and the member functions. At the same time, note that the member functions in the template class do not have default values. Since the template class may use a variety of types such as double, int, String, and so forth, we cannot define one default value that would apply to different types.

Member functions for a template class can be implemented with inline code or outside of the class body. If inline code is not used, a member function must be treated as a template function that includes the template argument list. In addition, all references to the class as a type must include the class name and the template type T enclosed in angle brackets.

```
Accumulator<T>    (reference to the template class type
                  Accumulator)
```

When implementing a member function outside the class body, the scope operator "::" must be used. For the Accumulator member functions, the scope operator is applied in the form "Accumulator<T>::".

We give the implementation of each member function since it is important to see simple examples of "template mechanics."

Constructor: `Accumulator()`

The constructor has a single argument that is used to initialize the data member total. Note that the constructor still has the class name Accumulator while the type is referred to as Accumulator<T>.

```
// use initialization list to assign total a value
template <class T>
Accumulator<T>::Accumulator(T value): total(value)
{}
```

Access Function: `getTotal()`

The access function getTotal() retrieves the current value of total.

```
// return the current total
template <class T>
T Accumulator<T>::getTotal() const
{
   return total;
}
```

Update Function: `addValue()`

The function addValue() takes an argument whose value is used to update the current total.

```
// add value to total
template <class T>
void Accumulator<T>::addValue(const T& value)
{
    total += value;
}
```

Declaring Template Class Objects

To declare an object whose type is a template class, the compiler needs to create a specific instance of the class for a specified type. To do this, place the type in brackets immediately after the class name.

SYNTAX ████████████████████████████████████

Declaring a Template Class Object

Form: ClassName<type> object(argument list);

Action: The declaration creates an instance of the class with the type used for the data members and operations.

Example: The following declarations create Accumulator objects with different data types.

```
// x is an int accumulator
Accumulator<int> x(5);
// d accumulates double values
Accumulator<double> d(2.7);
// a String instance
Accumulator<String> concatTo("");
```

The following program illustrates how the Accumulator class is used to deal with objects of different types. Since the addValue() member function uses the addition operator, we assume that addition is defined for any class instance that is created.

APPLICATION 9-6 ACCUMULATING DIFFERENT OBJECT TYPES

The program uses the template-based Accumulator class to add integer and rational numbers. An integer Accumulator object, unitCount, maintains a running count for the number of rational values that are input. The Accumulator object rationalTotal computes the sum of the rational values. Input terminates with an end of file after which the getTotal() functions retrieve the totals for the respective objects. An output statement gives the total count and sum.

```
#include <iostream.h>

#include "accum _t.h"    // use template Accumulator class
#include "rational.h"    // use the Rational class

int main()
```

```
{
    // count number of rationals input
    Accumulator<int> unitCount(0);
    // sum the measurements. start with value Rational(0)
    Accumulator<Rational> rationalTotal(Rational(0));
    Rational r, sum;

    cout << "Enter rational numbers. "
         "When done, type end of file." << endl;
    cin >> r;
    // input until end-of-file
    while (cin)
    {
        // count the rational value and add it to the total
        unitCount.addValue(1);
        rationalTotal.addValue(r);
        // input next measurement
        cin >> r;
    }

    // obtain the sum of the rational numbers and reduce
    sum = rationalTotal.getTotal();
    sum.reduce();

    cout << "Total of the " << unitCount.getTotal()
         << " rational numbers is " << sum << endl;

    return 0;
}
```

```
Run:

Enter rational numbers. When done, type end of file.
6/7 22/7 1/9 4/36 14/18
Total of the 5 rational numbers is 5/1
```

CHAPTER 9 SUMMARY

Using function overloading, two or more functions implementations can have the same name, provided their argument lists are sufficiently different that the compiler can distinguish them. This feature is particularly important for constructors, since programmers often use multiple constructors to provide flexible initialization of data members.

C++ allows programmers to overload most of its operators for use with class and enumeration objects. This process allows programs to use these objects in essentially the same way number and character objects are used in arithmetic and logical expressions. Operator overloading is illustrated by developing the Rational class in Sections 9.2 through 9.5. In Section 9.3, it is noted that an operator is just a function with one (unary operator) or two (binary operator) arguments that returns a value. In C++, most operators can be represented using an operator function. An operator function is more efficient if it has access to the private members of the class rather than having to call access functions. C++ provides this access with the concept of a friend function. A friend function is a free function that is not a member of the class but that has access to its private members. The binary arithmetic and relational operators of the Rational class are developed using friend functions. Not all operators can or should be overloaded using a free function. In Section 9.4, member function overloading is discussed. When the operator is executed, the object itself is the left-hand operand. Member function overloading is used to implement the Rational negation and compound assignment operators. The topic of explicit and implicit conversion among object types is discussed in Section 9.5. Conversion to a class type is accomplished by a constructor that converts a single argument to the object type. Conversion from a class type to another type is done by declaring a conversion operator. The concepts are illustrated in the Rational class that converts between integer, rational and real numbers.

C++ provides template functions so the programmer can write a single function with general type arguments. The compiler looks at the types of the run-time arguments and creates a version of the function that matches the types. Template functions are used to develop a generic version of the selection sort that works with any type for which the < operator is defined. In a similar fashion, the sequential search for a target value is developed as a template function and is valid for any type having the == operator. If the data being searched is in ascending order, the binary search is a very fast algorithm for locating a target value in an array. A template function is developed that implements the algorithm for any type having the == and < operators.

A template class has data members of a generic type that are made explicit when declaring an object of the template class type. We will use template classes extensively throughout the remainder of the book in the construction of classes that allow the storage and access of generic data. In this chapter we develop a template version of the Accumulator class that holds a single element.

Classes in the Chapter

Name	Implementation File
Accumulator (Template Version)	accum_t.h
Rational	rational.h
Timer	timer.h

KEY TERMS

Binary search:
A searching technique available for ordered lists. The algorithm compares the target with the midpoint of the list and applies the algorithm to the upper or lower sublist if the target is not matched. The algorithm terminates if the target is located at a midpoint or the sublist size becomes zero.

Conversion from class type:
Implemented by overloading a unary conversion operator as a member function. If the conversion is to type T, declare the converter using the syntax "operator T ()".

Conversion to class type:
Implemented by a constructor that accepts a single argument and builds an object.

Friend function:
A free function that has access to the private members of the class. The function is declared in the class by placing the keyword friend immediately before its prototype. A friend operator function is used to overload most binary operators.

Function overloading:
Allows two or more functions in a program unit to have the same name, provided their argument lists are sufficiently different that the compiler can resolve function calls.

Member function operator overloading:
The operator is declared as a class member. When the operator is applied, the object itself is the left operand. Use this technique for unary operators and binary operators that modify the left operand, such as $+=$.

Multiple constructors:
A form of function overloading in which a class has two or more constructors with distinct argument lists. Multiple constructors make object declaration more flexible.

Operator function:
The free function notation for an overloaded C++ operator. Its name includes the keyword operator followed by the operator symbol. For a binary operator, the two operands are included as arguments, and a unary operator has a single operand.

Operator overloading:
Allows the redefinition of existing C++ operator symbols. Programs can use class objects in essentially the same way number and character objects are used in arithmetic and logical expressions.

Rational number:
the set of quotients P/Q where P and Q are integers and $Q \neq 0$. The number P is called the numerator and the number Q is called the denominator.

Reduced form:
A form for a rational number in which the numerator and denominator have no common divisor.

Standard form:
A form for a rational number in which the sign is attached to the numerator and the denominator is greater than 0.

Template argument list:
Includes the keyword template followed by a non-empty list of formal types enclosed in angle brackets. Each type is preceded by the keyword class. A template argument list must be included before the declaration of any template function or class.

Template class:
Notation used by C++ for creating a class that has attributes, member function arguments, and return values of a generic type. The type is made explicit when declaring an object of the template class type.

Template expansion:
Compiler identifies a template type by looking at run-time arguments. It compiles a version of the function or class for the type.

Template function:
Notation used by C++ for writing a single function with generic type arguments and possibly a generic return value. The compiler looks at the types of the run-time arguments and creates a version of the function that matches the types.

this:
> A keyword that represents the address of the object in memory and may only be used in the code for a member function. The object itself is referenced by the expression *this.

REVIEW EXERCISES

1. C++ allows overloading of function names. Assuming that two functions are declared with the same name, how does the compiler know which function to execute?

2. Two overloaded versions of function f() are defined. For each function call, give the version of f() that is called. Indicate your choice as "version 1", "version 2", or ambiguous. Assume int is represented by 16-bits.

   ```
   double f(double x);   // version 1
   int f(int x);         // version 2
   ```

   Assume declarations

   ```
   short a, b;    int   m, n;    long  r, s;    double x, y;
   ```

   (a) function call: b = f(a);   (b) function call: m = f(x);
   (c) function call: b = f(n);   (d) function call: r = f(s);

3. (a) Declare the Rational number 7 in two different ways.

   (b) Declare the Rational number $\frac{9}{4}$ in three different ways.

   (c) You are given the following declarations:

   ```
   Rational p(3,4), q;
   double z;
   ```

   Explain how the compiler executes the statements
   (i) q = 2 * p   and   (ii) z = p;

4. Suppose that ClassName is a class with structure

   ```
   class ClassName
   {
        . . .
      public:
        . . .
        // overloaded unary negation operator
        ClassName operator- ();
   };
   ```

   Assume a and b are objects of type ClassName. The operation b = −a is implemented as
   (a) b = a.operator-(b)   (b) b = b.operator-()
   (c) b = operator-(a)   (d) b = a.operator-()

5. The following is a declaration of the Time class. The action of each member function is described in a comment.

   ```
   // the time of day is stored in military time (e.g. 22:35)
   class Time
   ```

```
{
    private:
        int hours;        // in the range 0 to 23
        int minutes;      // in the range 0 to 59
    public:
        // constructor. initialize data members.
        Time (int h, int m);

        // constructor for standard time (e.g. 8:15 PM);
        // string tt has values "AM" or "PM";
        // e.g. Time(8,15,"PM") is 20 hours 15 minutes
        Time(int hh, int mm, const String& tt);

        // constructor with a minutes argument; convert to
        // hours and minutes, e.g. 200 is 3 hours 20 minutes
        Time(int min = 0);

        // I/O operators: input and output time
        // in format "hh:mm" e.g. 17:25
        friend istream& operator >> (istream& istr,
                                        Time& t);
        friend ostream& operator << (ostream& ostr,
                                        const Time& t);

        // addition operator Time + Time
        friend Time operator+ (const Time& lhs,
                                 const Time& rhs);

        // comparison operators
        friend bool operator< (const Time& lhs,
                                 const Time& rhs);
        friend bool operator== (const Time& lhs,
                                  const Time& rhs);

        // conversion operator; return time in minutes
        operator int ();
};
```

(a) For each of the three Time objects t1, t2, t3, use a different constructor to initialize the object to have value 1:15.

(b) In the implementation of the overloaded output operator "<<", what is the return value?

(c) For the declaration, give the output.

```
Time t(400);
cout << t;
```

(d) For a Time object t, the following assignment statement is valid.

```
t = 500;
```

Explain the syntax since the statement assigns an integer to a time object.

(e) For the declaration, give the output.

```
Time t(100), u(40);
cout << t + u << "   " << int(t + u);
```

(f) For the output statement in (e), which overloaded functions are called to produce
(i) `cout << t + u;`
(ii) `cout << int(t + u);`

(g) Trace the main program and give the output

```
int main()
{
    Time getUp(6,45), lunch(1,0, "PM"), gotoBed;
    cout << "Get up at " << getUp;
    // Output: 1 _____
    cout << "Class starts at " << getUp + 90;
    // Output: 2 _____
    cout << "Lunch at " << lunch;
    // Output: 3 _____
    cin >> gotoBed;
    // Input: 22:30
    // Output: 4 _____
    cout   << "Go to bed at " << gotoBed << endl;

    return 0;
}
```

(h) Which function gives a conversion from integer to Time?
(i) Which function gives a conversion from Time to integer?

6. Study the function and answer parts (a) and (b).

```
template <class T>
T func(T list[], int n)
{
  T a = list[0], b = list[0];

  for(int i=1; i < n; i++)
  {
     if (list[i] < a)
        a = list[i];
     else if (list[i] > b)
        b = list[i];
  }
  return b-a;
}
```

(a) Consider the array int list[5] = {6, 9 14, 3, 8}. What is the output from the
statement

```
cout << func(list,5); //  _____
```

(b) Consider the String object str = "TRW". The String member function c _str()

coverts a String object to a C++ array of characters. What is the output from the statement

```
cout << int(func(str.c _str(), str.length()));
//  _____
```

(c) What is the action of this template function?
    (i) Returns the minimum and the maximum of the list elements
    (ii) Returns the average of the list elements
    (iii) Returns the range of data values in the list
    (iv) Returns the number with the largest absolute value
(d) Which arithmetic or relational operators must be defined for type T in order to compile func()? _____

7. Consider the integer array

```
int arr[8] = {1, 2, 5, 8, 9, 10, 15, 25};
```

(a) Describe the sequence of iterations and the final return value for the call to the binary search algorithm. Give the values of low, high and mid for each sublist.

```
binSearch(arr, 0, 7, 5);
```

(b) Do the same thing for the call

```
binSearch(arr, 0, 7, 16);
```

Answers to Review Exercises

1. C++ distinguishes between overloaded functions by matching the run-time arguments in the function call with the formal arguments in an overloaded function. In case no match occurs, C++ will use type conversion and look for the best match with the arguments. It is possible that the compiler will find an ambiguity, which results in a compilation error. The return type has no significance in function overloading.

2. (a) Calls version 2.
    (b) Calls version 1.
    (c) Calls version 2.
    (d) Compiler identifies ambiguous call. Truncation to an int may cause loss of digits, and promotion to a double changes internal representation to a floating point number.

3. (a) Rational one(7), two(7,1);
    (b) Rational one(9,4), two($-9,-4$), three (2.25);
    (c) (i) Compiler applies the converter Rational(2) and performs the assignment
            q = Rational(2) * p.
      (ii) Compiler applies the converter double(p) and performs the assignment
            z = double(p).

4. (d) b = a.operator- ()

5. (a) Time t1(1,15), t2(1,15,"AM"), t3(75);
   (b) return ostr;
   (c) Output is 6:40
   (d) Integer 500 is converted to a temporary Time object Time(500) which is then assigned to t. The constructor is used as a converter.
   (e) Output is 2:20 140
   (f) (i) calls overloaded + and <<
       (ii) calls overloaded '+',converter int(), and <<
   (g) Output 1: Get up at 6:45
       Output 2: Class starts at 8:15
       Output 3: Lunch at 13:30
       Output 4: Go to bed at 22:30
   (h) Constructor Time(int min);
   (i) Converter operator int();

6. (a) 11
   (b) int ('W' − 'R') = 5
   (c) (iii) Returns the range of data values in the list.
   (d) <, > and −

7. (a) Low: 0 High: 7 Mid: 3
       Low: 0 High: 2 Mid: 1
       Low: 2 High: 2 Mid: 2   Success.
   (b) Low: 0 High: 7 Mid: 3
       Low: 4 High: 7 Mid: 5
       Low: 6 High: 7 Mid: 6
       Low: 7 High: 7 Mid: 7
       Low: 7 High: 6   Failure.

WRITTEN EXERCISES

8. Consider the following functions for the purposes of overloading.

```
<function 1>                      <function 2>
int f(int x, int y)               double f(int x, int y)
{                                 {
    return x*y;                       return x+y;
}                                 }


<function 3>
int f(int x = 1, int y = 7)
{
    return x+y;
}
```

(a) Are functions 1 and 2 distinct? Explain.

(b) Are functions 1 and 3 distinct? Explain.

9. Function overloading creates two versions for area().

```
// return area of a circle
double area (double radius);
// return area of a rectangle
double area (double length, double width);
```

(a) Which function is executed with the call area(7.5, 2.0);

(b) How does the compiler determine that the function call area(10) should execute the function determining the area of a circle?

(c) If the prototype for the area of a rectangle is modified to be

```
double area (double length = 0, double width = 0);
```

is an ambiguity produced? Explain.

(d) If the prototype for the area of a circle is modified to be

```
double area (double radius = 0);
```

which function is executed with the call area()?

10. Trace the program and determine the output.

```
#include <iostream.h>

char median(char c[], int n);

double median(double f[], int n);

int median(int i[], int n);

int main()
{
    int a[7] = {4,9,13,21,30,33,40};
    cout << median(a,7) << endl;            //Output _____

    double f[4] = {2.0, 3.5, 5.5, 6.0};
    cout << median(f,4) << endl;            //Output _____

    char c[6] = {'a','e','f','h','k','t'};
    cout << median(c,6) << endl;            //Output _____

    int b[] = {9, 13, 17, 24};
    cout << median(b,4) << endl;            //Output _____

    return 0;
}

char median(char c[], int n)
{   return c[n/2];   }
```

```
double median(double f[], int n)
{   int m = n/2;
    return n%2 != 0 ? f[m]  : (f[m-1]+f[m])/2.0;
}

int median(int i[], int n)
{
    int m = n/2;
    return n%2 != 0 ? i[m]  : (i[m-1]+i[m])/2;
}
```

11. The rational number 2/3 cannot be expressed exactly as a real number. Write a code segment that declares a Rational object, twoThirds, and uses it to compute the floating point difference between the rational number and the real number approximation .667.

12. In algebra, a fundamental task is to solve a general fraction equation such as

$$\frac{2}{3}X + 2 = \frac{4}{5}$$

The process involves isolating the X term by moving 2 to the right-hand side of the equation and then dividing both sides of the equation by the rational number 2/3, the coefficient of X.

$$\frac{2}{3}X = \frac{4}{5} - 2 = -\frac{6}{5} \qquad X = \frac{-6}{5} * \frac{3}{2} = \frac{-18}{10} = \frac{-9}{5} \text{ (reduced)}$$

Implement the function, solveEq(), that solves the equation ax + b = c for rational numbers a, b and c. If a == 0, output an error message and return the Rational result 0.

```
// solve the equation ax + b = c
Rational solveEq(const Rational& a, const Rational& b,
                 const Rational& c);
```

13. The class CompactChar stores a character along with its repeat count. For instance, the string "...", can be represented by a CompactChar object with character '.' and repeat count 3.

```
class CompactChar
{
   private:
      char ch;
      int repeatCount;
   public:
      // constructor
      CompactChar(char c, int repeatCnt);

      char getChar();          // return the character
      int getRepeatCount();    // return the repeat count
};
```

(a) Declare two CompactChar objects that correspond to strings of repeating characters "xxxx" and "?"

(b) Add an overloaded version of the relational operator == as a friend of the class. The operator compares only the ch field of two CompactChar objects.

(c) Add an overloaded version of the relational operator < as a friend of the class. The operator compares the repeatCount members of two CompactChar objects and add it to the class declaration.

(d) As a friend, declare an overloaded output operator << that outputs an object in the format ch(repeatCount).

Example: from (a) output is x(4) and ?(1)

(e) The following is a declaration of a conversion operator String() that takes a CompactChar object obj and converts it to a string consisting of the character repeated repeatCount times.

```
operator String();

CompactChar ccObj('a',5); repeatPeriod('.',3);
String s;

s = String(ccObj);    // s = "aaaaa"
s = repeatPeriod;     // s = ". . ."
```

Implement the conversion operator.

14. Give a revised declaration of the Accumulator class with the following features.

(a) Replace the member function addValue() with the overloaded operator += that is declared as a member function. Give its implementation. The argument for the operator has type double.

(b) Add a negation operator to the class as a member function. The operator changes the sign of the current value for total. Give its implementation.

(c) Define an addition operator for the class as a friend function. The operator takes two Accumulator objects and returns an object whose value is the sum of the total values in the two arguments.

(d) What is the output in the following code segment?

```
Accumulator x(5), y(3), z(-9), w;

x += 3;
w = x + y;
z = -z;
cout << w.getTotal() << "  " << z.getTotal();
```

15. The Date class has the output member function, writeShortDate(), that outputs the date in the form "mm/dd/yyyy." Declare an equivalent operator << as a free function. Give an implementation of the operator.

16. Recall that output of an enumeration object displays the integer equivalent by default. To display the actual enumeration values, we can use operator overloading. Consider the enumeration type

```
enum Colors {red, blue, green, yellow, violet};
```

Implement the overloaded operator << that outputs the value of a Colors object as an enumeration value.

```
ostream& operator<< (ostream& ostr, const Colors& obj);
```

17. The class, ModClass, has a single integer data member, dataVal, in the range 0 to 6. The constructor takes any positive integer v and assigns to dataVal the remainder after division by 7.

```
dataVal = v % 7;
```

The + operator adds two objects by summing their data members and finding the remainder after division by 7. For instance,

```
ModClass a(10);     // dataVal in a is 3
ModClass b(6);      // dataVal in b is 6
ModClass c;         // dataVal in c is 0

c = a + b;          // dataVal in c is (3+6)% 7 = 2
```

The following is the class declaration:

```
class ModClass
{
   private:
      int dataVal;
   public:
      ModClass (int v = 0);
      friend ModClass operator+ (const ModClass& x,
                                 const ModClass& y);
      int getValue() const;
};
```

(a) Implement the class member functions.
(b) Declare and implement and operator "*" as friend of ModClass. The operator multiplies the dataVal attributes in two ModClass objects.
(c) Declare an overloaded << operator for ModClass and implement it as a friend.
(d) Replace the function getValue() by overloading the conversion operator int(). The operator converts a ModClass object to an integer by returning dataVal.
(e) (Optional) Write a function

```
ModClass inverse(const ModClass& x);
```

that takes an object such that x.getValue() $\neq$ 0 and returns a ModClass object y such that

```
(x*y).getValue() = 1.
```

The object y is called the inverse of x. HINT: Repeatedly multiply x by objects whose values are 1 to 6. One of these objects is the inverse.

18. Use the template function func for parts (a)–(c). List the value of n and the contents of array b.

```
template <class T>
void func(T A[], int n, T B[], int& m, T key)
{
   int i, j = 0;
```

```
        for (int i=0;i < n; i++)
           if (A[i] != key)
           {
               B[j] = A[i];
               j++;
           }
        m = j;
    }
```

(a) `int arr[5] = {1, 9, 3, 9, 5}, b[5];`
    `int n;`
    `func(arr, 5, b, n, 9);`

(b) `String arr[6] = {"cat", "rat", "bird", "rat", "fish",`
    `                  "rat"}, b[6];`
    `int n;`

    `func(arr, 6, b, n, String("rat"));`

(c) `Rational arr[3] = {Rational(1,5), Rational(2,3),`
    `                   Rational(2,3)}, b[3];`
    `int n;`

    `func(arr, 3, b, n, Rational(2,3));`

19. The code gives a template version of the min() function which is then called by a main program with different data types.

```
template <class T>
T min(const T& a, const T& b)
{
    return (a < b) ? a : b;
}


object declarations:
    int m = 5, n = 6, p;
    Time24 t1(3,11), t2(12,15), t3;
    String str1 = "small", str2 = "large", str3;
```

Evaluate each call and indicate if it will execute correctly (valid) or will execute only if additional operators are available (valid if).
(a) `p = min(m,n);`   `// call is` _____
(b) `str3 = min(str1,str2);` `// call is` _____
(c) `t3 = min(t1,t2);`   `// call is` _____

20. Trace the template function f().

```
template <class T>
int f(T list[], int n, const T& target)
{
    int i, count = 0;

    selectionSort(list, n);
    if ((i = seqSearch(list,0,n-1,target)) != -1)
        while (i < n && list[i] == target)
```

```
                   {
                       count++;
                       i++;
                   }
                   return count;
          }
```

For each array, what is the output of the cout statement?
(a) `int arr[] = {1, 4, 5, 1, 5, 9, 8, 5, 3};`
    `cout << f(arr, 9, 5) << endl;`

(b) `String str[] = {"Glenn", "Holly", "Glenn", "Ann", "Jo"};`
    `cout << f(str, 5, String("Glenn")) << endl;`

21. (a) Which operators must be defined in order for the binary search to be applied for an array of type T?
 (b) Describe the sequence of iterations and the final return value for the call to the binary search algorithm. Give the values of low, high and mid for each sublist.

```
          Rational arr[9] =
              {Rational(1,3),Rational(1,2),Rational(2,3),
               Rational(1),Rational(7,6),Rational(11,7),
               Rational(2),Rational(11,5), Rational(3)
              };

          binSearch(arr, 0, 8, Rational(11,5));
```

22. Write a template class DataStore which has the following member functions:

bool insert(const T& elt);	Insert elt into the private array dataElements having 5 elements of type T. The index of the next available location in dataElements is given by the data member loc, which is also the number of data values in dataElements. Return false if there is no more room left in dataElements; otherwise, return true.
int find(const T& elt);	Search for element elt in dataElements and return its index if it is found and −1 if it is not in dataElements.
int numElts();	Return the number of elements stored in dataElements.
T getData(int n);	Return the element at location n in DataElements. Generate an error message and exit if n < 0 or n >= loc.

PROGRAMMING EXERCISES

23. Write a program that declares the array, arr, of real numbers and the Rational array, r.

```
          double arr[5] = {6.2, 2.5, -3.8, 9.25, -7.75};
          Rational r[5];
```

Copy the elements of arr to r as Rational numbers and use the selection sort to order the array r. Output the sorted rational numbers.

24. The program tests the ModClass developed in Written Exercise 17 by verifying the distributive law for ModClass objects:

```
a*(b+c) = a*b + a*c
```

Define three objects, a, b, and c that have initial values 10, 20, and 30, respectively. Your program should output the value of the expressions a*(b + c) and (a*b + a*c), respectively.

25. Write a free function

```
bool operator < (const Date& x, const Date& y);
```

that compares two Date objects. Use the function in a program that declares the following four Date objects

```
Date d1(6,5,1954), d2(6,8,1954), d3(7,4,1976),
     d4(12,1,1976);
```

Use the template function min() from Written Exercise 19 to separately compare objects d1 and d2, d1 and d3, d3 and d4. In each case, use the overloaded stream operator << from Written Exercise 15 to output the earlier of the two dates.

26. Write a program that uses the function solveEq() from Written Exercise 12 to solve the equation.

$$\frac{2}{3}X + 2 = \frac{4}{5}$$

27. Write a program that uses the CompactChar in Written Exercise 13. Declare two CompactChar objects corresponding to strings "xxxx" and "?". Output the objects using the << operator. Using the String conversion operator, output the objects as Strings.

28. Use the revised Accumulator class from Written Exercise 14 to write a program that implements part(d) of the exercise.

29. This exercise uses the template class DataStore developed in Written Exercise 22.
(a) Write a function writeData() that outputs the data in a DataStore object using the member function getData().

```
template <class T>
void writeData (const DataStore<T>& dat);
```

(b) Write a program that declares a DataStore object, intStore, holding integers. Insert into the object the values 1, 2, 3, . . . until it is full. Search for the value 3 using find() and indicate whether it is found. Declare a second DataStore object, strStore, that contains String objects. Insert the strings "Arizona", "Maine", and "Nevada" into the object. Output the data that is stored in intStore and strStore using writeData().

PROGRAMMING PROJECTS

30. A Complex number is of the form x + iy, where $i^2 = -1$. Complex numbers have vast applications in mathematics, physics and engineering. Complex numbers have an arithmetic governed by a series of rules including the following:

$$\text{Let } u = a + ib, \quad v = c + id$$

$$\text{Magnitude}(u) = \sqrt{a^2 + b^2}$$

Complex number corresponding to real number f is $u = f + i0$

Real Part of $u = a$

Imaginary Part of $u = b$

$$u + v = (a + c) + i(b + d)$$

$$u - v = (a - c) + i(b - d)$$

$$u * v = (ac - bd) + i(ad + bc)$$

$$u / v = \frac{ac + bd}{c^2 + d^2} + i\,\frac{bc - ad}{c^2 + d^2}$$

$$u == v = (a == c) \text{ and } (b == d)$$

(a) Implement the class Complex whose declaration is

```
class Complex
{
    private:
        double real;
        double imag;

    public:
        Complex(double x = 0.0, double y = 0.0);

        double magnitude() const; // return magnitude
        double real() const;      // return real part
        double imag() const;      // return imaginary
                                  // part

        // binary operators
        friend Complex operator+ (const Complex& lhs,
                                  const Complex& rhs);
        friend Complex operator- (const Complex& lhs,
                                  const Complex& rhs);
        friend Complex operator* (const Complex& lhs,
                                  const Complex& rhs);
        friend Complex operator/ (const Complex& lhs,
                                  const Complex& rhs);
        friend bool operator== (const Complex& lhs,
                                const Complex& rhs);
        // negation
        Complex operator- () const;

        //stream I/O operators

        // output in format (real,imag)
```

```
          friend ostream& operator<< (ostream& ostr,
                                       const Complex& x);
          // input Complex number in format (x,y)
          friend istream& operator>> (istream& istr,
                                       Complex& x);
    };
```

(b) To test your work, run the following main program

```
    int main()
    {
        // Complex number i = 0 +1i
        Complex i(0,1), z1, z2;

        // input values
        cout << "Enter two complex numbers: ";
        cin >> z1 >> z2;

        cout << "Test the binary operators:" << endl;
        cout << " z1 + z2 = " << (z1 + z2) << endl;
        cout << " z1 - z2 = " << (z1 - z2) << endl;
        cout << " z1 * z2 = " << z1 * z2 << endl;
        cout << " z1 / z2 = " << z1 / z2 << endl;
        cout << " z1 == z2 = " << z1 == z2 << endl;

        // verify that i*i = -1
        cout << "i*i = " << i * i << endl;

        return 0;
    }
```

(c) Write a function, f(z), that evaluates the complex polynomial function

$$f(z) = z^3 - 3z^2 + 4z - 2$$

Evaluate the polynomial for the following values of z:

$$z = 2 + 3i, \; -1 + i, 1 + i, 1 - i, 1 + 0i$$

Note that the last three values are roots of f().

Chapter 10
Pointers and Dynamic Memory

CHAPTER CONTENTS

10-1 *C++ POINTERS*
Declaring Pointer Objects
Assigning Values to Pointers
Accessing Data with Pointers
10-2 *ARRAYS AND POINTERS*
Pointer Arithmetic
Arrays As Pointer Arguments
Pointers and Class Types
10-3 *DYNAMIC MEMORY*
The Memory Allocation Operator
new
Dynamic Array Allocation
Dynamically Allocated Class Objects
The Memory Deallocation Operator
delete
10-4 *CLASSES USING DYNAMIC MEMORY*
The DynamicDemo Class
10-5 *THE ASSIGNMENT OPERATOR AND COPY
CONSTRUCTOR*
The Assignment Operator for
DynamicDemo Objects
The Class this Pointer
The Copy Constructor for
Dynamic-Demo Objects
10-6 *BUILDING A VECTOR CLASS*
Declaring the Vector Class
Applications Using Vectors
Implementing the Vector Class
10-7 *C++ STRINGS*
C++ String I/O
C++ String Handling Functions
Implementing the String Class
Written Exercises

U p to this point in the book, we have declared primitive and class objects without any consideration for their location in computer memory. In this chapter, we shift focus and declare a new object type, called a pointer, that allows a program to access an object through its address in memory.

The most important use of pointers is managing dynamic memory. A program may request memory at run-time to allocate windows, temporary buffers, data structures, and so forth. When the memory is no longer needed, the program may release it for use by other objects. To implement this feature, we discuss the C++ language operators *new* and *delete*.

When dynamic memory is used to allocate data for a class object, we must identify certain problems that can arise. Sections 10.4 and 10.5 carefully discuss these problems and develop solutions that involve destructor, overloaded assignment operator, and copy constructor member functions. Using dynamic memory, we can design and allocate arrays whose sizes are set by the run-time requirements of the application. These are called *dynamic arrays*. In this chapter, we develop a template-based class that includes a dynamic array as a data member. The class, called Vector, has an overloaded index operator that enables a program to access elements using the familiar [] notation while performing array bounds checking. The Vector class reinforces the concepts of the copy constructor and overloaded assignment operator that are required when dynamic memory is used.

The C++ language defines the primitive C++ string type. A C++ *string* is an array of characters terminated by a NULL character (ASCII value 0). These strings are supported by a series of free functions declared in the system file *string.h*. Historically, the functions were developed for C and are used in millions of lines of C and C++ code worldwide. Despite the fact that the String class can be used, the programmer must have some familiarity with C++ strings to extend and maintain existing application software. For the sake of efficiency, the string functions are implemented using pointers. In Section 10.8, we discuss the C++ string functions and implement some of them.

Pointers have great historical significance in the C programming language and find more selected but important applications in C++. They are part of most professionally written C++ programs. Understanding pointers requires studying them in a variety of applications. The material in this chapter is fundamental to your subsequent study of data structures and advanced C++ programming.

10-1 C++ POINTERS

To understand the concept of a pointer, we must look at the internal storage of data in memory. Memory consists of a sequence of 8-bit locations called bytes. Each byte is defined by its address and the contents at that address.

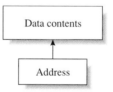

Figure 10-1 provides a physical view of memory as an array of bytes. As a veritcal display, the memory locations resemble numbered lines on a sheet

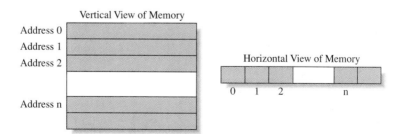

FIGURE 10-1
Vertical and Horizontal View of Memory.

of paper. The horizontal view displays memory as contiguous compartments along a row. This view is used to describe array storage.

C++ objects occupy one or more bytes in memory depending on the size of their type. For instance, a long integer typically requires four bytes of memory, a character one byte of memory, and so forth. The address of the first byte of the object is called the address of the object. For instance, the long integer t (50L) has address 5000 while the short integer s (97) has address 5004.

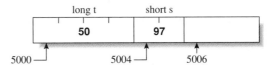

C++ defines an object type called a *pointer* whose values are addresses of data in memory. The term pointer comes from the fact that the object "points at" an item. From our view of memory, a pointer object will have values such as 5000 or 5004 and that are addresses of the long integer t or the short integer s, respectively. To understand a pointer, we must determine how to declare it as an object, how to give it a value so that it actually points at something, and then see how to access the data it points to.

Declaring Pointer Objects

A pointer object is declared by placing a "*" before the object name in an otherwise ordinary declaration. For example,

```
long *ptr;   // pointer to a long integer
```

S Y N T A X ▬▬▬▬▬▬▬▬▬▬▬▬▬▬▬▬▬▬▬▬▬▬▬▬▬▬▬▬

Pointer Declaration

Form: `ObjectType *objPtr;`

Action: objPtr is a C++ object whose value is the address of some ObjectType object in memory. Read the declaration as "objPtr is a pointer to an object of type ObjectType." Two or more pointer objects can be declared in the same statement. The declaration can also include non-pointer objects.

```
ObjectType objValue, *objPtr1, *objPtr2;
```

Example: `// intPtr and charPtr point to int and char data`
`int *intPtr`
`char *charPtr`

The object `intPtr` contains the address of an integer object, and charPtr contains the address of a character object. The figure assumes that intPtr points at integer value 1570 and charPtr points at character 'a'.

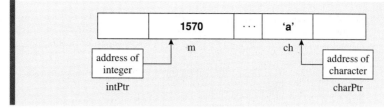

Assigning Values to Pointers

A pointer is designed to hold an address in memory. However, a simple declaration such as

```
ObjectType *objPtr;    // uninitialized pointer
```

does not give the pointer a value and thus it does not initially point at any object in memory. It must be assigned a memory address in order to be used. To initialize a pointer, assign to it the address of an existing object. The address is provided by the *"address-of" operator &*. To see how this works, start with object intData that is declared as an integer with value 250. Next consider the pointer object intPtr that is declared to point at integer data. Initially, the pointer does not point to an object (Figure 10-2 (a)). By using the & operator, we obtain the address of intData which is assigned to intPtr. As a result, `intPtr` points at the object `intData` (Figure 10-2 (b)).

```
int intData = 250, *intPtr;    // pointer is uninitialized
intPtr = &intData;    // &intData is the address of intData
```

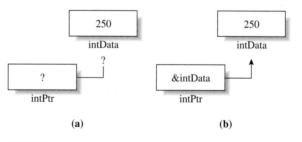

FIGURE 10-2
The Address-of Operator.

SYNTAX ▬▬▬▬▬▬▬▬▬▬▬▬▬▬▬▬▬▬▬▬▬▬

The Address-of Operator &

Form: `// declare an object and a pointer`
`ObjectType obj, *objPtr;`

`// assign &obj, the address of obj, to objPtr`
`objPtr = &obj;`

Action: The & operator returns the memory address of object `obj`. By assigning this value to objPtr, the pointer then points to object `obj`.

Example: The figure identifies the address of the long integer t and the short integer s.

```
// declare a long int and a pointer to a long;
long t = 50, *longPtr;

// declare a short int and a pointer to a short
short s = 97, *shPtr;

// initialize longPtr and shPtr
longPtr = &t;
shPtr = &s;
```

```
            long t        short s
        ┌──────────────┬──────────────┬──────────┐
        │      50      │      97      │          │
        └──────────────┴──────────────┴──────────┘
longPtr = 5000 ─┘    shPtr = 5004 ─┘      5006
```

Accessing Data with Pointers

Once a pointer has a value, a program may use it to access data in memory. This is accomplished with the * operator that is placed in front of a pointer object. When used in this way, *longPtr, is the object pointed to by longPtr. For instance,

```
cout << *longPtr;    // output: 50
*longPtr = 200;      // assign 200 to 50 pointed to by longPtr
```

The * operator is called the *indirection operator* since it enables a program to indirectly access the value of an object from its pointer.

SYNTAX ▬▬▬▬▬▬▬▬▬▬▬▬▬▬▬▬▬▬▬▬▬▬▬▬

The Indirection Operator *

Form: `*objPtr`

Action: The operator * (pronounced "star") is a unary operator that is used with a pointer objPtr to access the object it points to. The following statements combine the * and & operators.

```
// declare pointer and object
ObjectType *objPtr, obj;

// assign objPtr to point at object obj
objPtr = &obj;
```

```
                // output the value pointed to by objPtr
                cout << *objPtr;

Example:    // chPtr is set to point at character ch
            char ch = 'a', *chPtr = &ch;

            cout << *chPtr;    // output:  a

            *chPtr = 'E';      // chPtr points at char 'E'
            cout << *chPtr;    // output:  E
```

Now that we can declare pointers and use them in statements involving the & and * operators, consider a series of examples along with pictures that give a view of memory before and after each statement. Assume the declaration

```
int x = 50, y = 100, *px, *py;
```

Initialize Pointers:

```
px=&x;
py=&y;
```

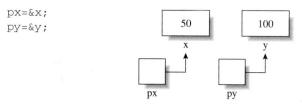

Update Data Values:

```
    x = *py;     // assign x the value 100 from *py (which is y)
  *px = y + 25;  // assign 100+25 to *px (which is x)
  *py = *px * 2  // *px is 125;  assign 125*2 to *py (which is y)
```

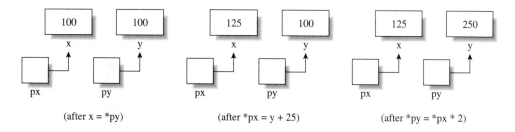

(after x = *py)   (after *px = y + 25)   (after *py = *px * 2)

These examples change the contents pointed to by *px* and *py*. A program can also change the pointers themselves by assigning the value of one pointer to another.

```
py = px;    // py points at the same object as px
```

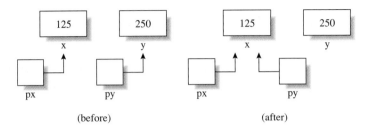

After the assignment, *px and *py access the same values. In our example, y still has value 250.

```
cout << *px << " " << *py;    // output:  125 125
cout << *py << " " << y;      // output: 125 250
```

EXAMPLE 10.1 ■■■■■■■■■■■■■■■■■■■■■■■■■■■■■■■■■■

Assume i and j are integer objects while p and q are pointers to integers. The example uses a series of instructions that illustrate pointer declaration and simple pointer handling using the indirection operator *. The action of each statement is given in Figure 10.3.

1. Integers i and j are initialized with value 15 and 8. Pointers p and q are set to point at i and j using the address-of operator &.

```
int i = 15, j = 8, *p = &i, *q=&j;
```

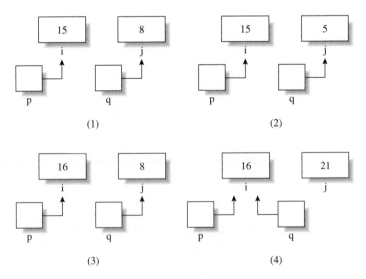

FIGURE 10-3
View the Instructions in EXAMPLE 10.1.

2. The object pointed to by q (integer j) is assigned the value 5.

```
*q = 5;
```

3. The object pointed to by p is increased by 1 using the ++ operator. The object pointed to by q is increased using the += operator.

```
(*p)++;     // value of *p (integer i) is 16
*q += 3;    // value of *q (integer j) is 8
```

4. From the assignment statement, q and p point to the same object (integer i). Integer j is assigned a new value using *q.

```
q = p;          // q points at integer i
j = *q + 5;     // j assigned value 16 + 5 = 21  ∎
```

10-2 ARRAYS AND POINTERS

An array is a collection of data items occupying consecutive memory locations. In the declaration of an array type, the array name is the starting address of the list. In C++, the array name is a pointer constant.

```
int arr[10],  *p;  // both arr and p are pointers to int objects
```

When processing the declaration of arr, the compiler allocates space for 10 integer objects and assigns the starting address of this memory to arr. Since arr has a value, it can be used to initialize other pointer objects. For instance

```
p = arr;   // p  points at arr[0]
```

Pointer Arithmetic

To scan an array, we can use an index to access an element and then update the index value to reference another element in the array. C++ provides an alternative method that uses *pointer arithmetic.* Assume p points to an array whose elements are of type T. The expression p + 1 is the address of the second element in the array, which is *(p + 1) = p[1]. The +1 indicates an offset of 1 array element to the right of p. In general, p + n is the address of the (n + 1)st element in the array which is *(p + n) = p[n]. The +n indicates an offset of n array elements to the right of p. In technical terms, the compiler identifies the address p + n by computing an offset in terms of the size (in bytes) of the data type T.

$$(p + n) = p + n*sizeof (T).$$

Consider an array arr of five long integers and a pointer p that points at the array. Recall that the size of a long is 4 bytes.

```
long arr[5] = {200, -60, 50, 5, 90};
long *p = arr;
```

Assuming that the array begins at address 8500, Table 10-1 gives the address of the first five elements in the array. The table includes the value of the

TABLE 10-1 Pointers and Array Storage.

Address		Array Object	
p	8500	*p	200
p + 1	8504	*(p + 1)	-60
p + 2	8508	*(p + 2)	50
p + 3	8512	*(p + 3)	5
p + 4	8516	*(p + 4)	90

200	-60	50	5	90	

```
      8500      8504      8508      8512      8516
p           p + 1     p + 2     p + 3     p + 4
```

address p + n (0 ≤ n ≤ 4) and the value of the corresponding array element
*(p + n) = p[n].

Pointer arithmetic is used to change the value of a pointer. For instance,
the statements

$$p = p + 2;$$
$$p = p - 4;$$

advances p forward two locations and then backward four locations. The increment operators ++ and −− can be used to move forward or backward one
position.

$$p++; \quad // p = p + 1$$
$$p--; \quad // p = p - 1$$

EXAMPLE 10.2

Consider the seven element array arr of double values and pointers p and q.

```
double arr[7] = {1.2, 4.5, 6.7, 2.3, 7.8, 3.5, 8.9},
       *p = arr, *q;

1. cout << *p << "  " << *(p+2);      // output: 1.2   6.7

2. q = &arr[3];                       // q is address of arr[3]
   cout << *q << "  " << *(q+2)       // output: 2.3   3.5

3. p++;                               // p set to &arr[1]
   q = p;                             // q is address of arr[1]
   q--;                               // q set to &arr[0]
   cout << *q << "  " << *p;          // output: 1.2   4.5  ■
```

Scanning an Array Using Pointers. Use ++ to scan a list in the forward direction and −− to traverse the list from the rear to the front. As we move through a list, we may need to make pointer comparisons. Pointers are compared by treating their values as unsigned integers. For instance, the following code sequence traverses array arr and outputs each element. A loop uses a pointer initialized to arr as its control object. The loop continues until the value of the pointer is arr + 5, which is the memory address after the last array element. A second loop sets the pointer at the last array element and uses the −− operator to move down the list, summing the elements. The loop continues while the pointer is greater than or equal to arr.

```
int arr[5] = {200, -60, 50, 5, 90}, *p, sum = 0;
```

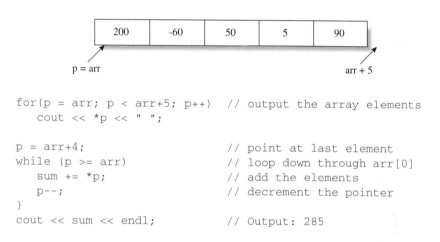

```
for(p = arr; p < arr+5; p++)   // output the array elements
    cout << *p << " ";

p = arr+4;                     // point at last element
while (p >= arr)               // loop down through arr[0]
    sum += *p;                 // add the elements
    p--;                       // decrement the pointer
}
cout << sum << endl;           // Output: 285
```

Assume that arr is an integer array and p is an integer pointer.

```
int arr[10],*p;
```

Exploring Concepts

What is the difference between the statements "p = arr" and "arr = p"? Are both statements valid?

Distinguish the statements "p++" and "arr++".

Arrays As Pointer Arguments

When declaring an array arr as a formal argument in a function, we have used the notation

```
ReturnType functionName(Type arr[], . . .)
```

Within the function body, we have accessed the elements using array index notation.

```
arr[i]
```

A formal array argument can be equivalently specified using a pointer as follows:

```
ReturnType functionName(Type *arr, . . .)
```

The formal pointer argument arr is local to the function body and initially contains the address of the run-time array in memory. The calling statement passes the array name or a pointer value as the run-time argument. For instance, the template function writeList() outputs n items in an array beginning at a starting address specified by a pointer argument.

```
template <class T>
void writeList (T *arr, int n);
```

An array of any type for which << is defined can be passed to writeList(). For example, intList is an array of 25 integers.

```
int intList[25];
```

To output the entire integer list, pass intList as the run-time argument. To output the tail of the list (last 15 items), the address of a[10] can be passed as the argument.

```
writeList(intList, 25);        // output the entire list
writeList(&intList[10],15);    // output tail of list
```

APPLICATION 10-1 REVERSING AN ARRAY

This program demonstrates pointer arithmetic and pointer function arguments. The template free function writeList() outputs the elements of an array. The template free function reverseArray() reverses an array by exchanging arr[0] with arr[n − 1], arr[1] with arr[n − 2], and so forth.

The algorithm used by reverseArray() involves initializing arrRear as the address of the last element of the array. The formal argument arr is a local pointer object in the function and is initially the address of the first array element. In a loop, the pointer arr moves forward (arr++) and the pointer arrRear moves backward (arrRear−−). The array elements *arr and *arrRear are exchanged as long as arr < arrRear. The loop terminates when the two pointers meet in the middle of the array.

```
#include <iostream.h>

#include "tstring.h"

// reverse the elements of arr
template <class T>
void reverseArray(T *arr, int n);

// output the elements of arr
template <class T>
void writeList(const T *arr, int n);
```

```cpp
int main()
{
   double  realArray[6] = {2.3, 6.4, 9.1, 3.5, 2.9, 8.1};
   String  strArray[4] = {"walk", "run", "crawl", "fly"};

   cout << "Real array (before and after)" << endl;
   writeList(realArray,6);
   reverseArray(realArray,6);
   writeList(realArray,6);
   cout << endl;

   cout << "String array (before and after)" << endl;
   writeList(strArray,4);
   reverseArray(strArray,4);
   writeList(strArray,4);

   return 0;
}

template <class T>
void reverseArray(T *arr, int n)
{
   // arrRear scans array from back to front
   T *arrRear;
   T temp;       // used for the exchange

   // no work to do unless n is 2 or more
   if (n > 1)
   {
      arrRear = arr + (n-1);   // arrRear points to arr[n-1]

      // continue exchanging until pointers meet in the middle
      while (arr < arrRear)
      {
         temp = *arr;
         *arr = *arrRear;
         *arrRear = temp;

         // update the pointers
         arr++;          // move arr up the list
         arrRear --;     // move arrRear down the list
      }
   }
}

template <class T>
void writeList(const T *arr, int n)
{
   // arr points at the beginning of the array and end points
```

```
                         // just past last array element
                         T *end = arr+n;

                         while (arr < end)
                         {
                            // output array element and move arr forward
                            cout << *arr << "   ";
                            arr++;
                         }
                         cout << endl;
                      }
```

```
      Run:

      Real array (before and after)
      2.3   6.4   9.1   3.5   2.9   8.1
      8.1   2.9   3.5   9.1   6.4   2.3

      String array (before and after)
      walk   run   crawl   fly
      fly   crawl   run   walk
```

Pointers and Class Types

Most of our examples have featured pointers to primitive number and character types. This was for simplicity while developing the concept of a pointer. In applications, we will want to use pointers to any defined type. Application 10.1 uses the template-based `reverseArray()` and `writeList()` with a String array. String is a programmer-defined class type. As another example, consider the Rectangle class. We define an object called box that is a 2 by 5 rectangle. The object rectPtr is a pointer to a Rectangle and is set to point at box.

```
Rectangle box(2,5);     // a 2 by 5 rectangle
Rectangle *rectPtr;     // unitialized pointer to a rectangle
rectPtr = &box;         // set rectPtr to point at box
```

The expression *rectPtr is the box. We can use it with the "." notation to execute member functions.

```
// (*rectPtr).area() is box.area()
cout << (*rectPtr).area();           // area of the box is 10
```

The use of parentheses with *rectPtr is necessary since the * operator has a lower precedence than the .(dot) operator. Without the parentheses, the result is improperly formed.

```
*rectPtr.area()   <--->   *(rectPtr.area())
```

The (*rectPtr)." notation is somewhat clumsy, and so C++ provides the operator −>. It accesses an object member by using the pointer name and member name as operands. The following statement calls the `area()` function for the Rectangle object box.

```
cout << rectPtr->area();    // output the area 10
```

SYNTAX ▬▬▬▬▬▬▬▬▬▬▬▬▬▬▬▬▬▬▬▬▬▬▬▬▬▬▬▬▬▬▬▬▬▬▬

Class Member Function Selection Using a Pointer

Form: `ptr->f()`   or   `ptr->dataMember`

Action: If ptr is a pointer to a class object, `ptr->f(...)` calls the member function f() for the object pointed to by ptr. The operator includes character − immediately followed by > and can be used only with pointers to class objects.

```
    ptr->f(...)  is equivalent to  (*ptr).f(...)
```

The operator −> can be used to access a data member of the object pointed to by ptr. Since data members are normally in the private section of a class, such access would be available only to a class member function or friend function.

Example: Declare saPtr and timePtr as pointers to StudentAccount and Time24 objects, respectively.

```
    StudentAccount *saPtr;
    Time24 *timePtr;
```

Access public member functions.

```
    // payment of $200 to account *saPtr
    saPtr->payment(200);
    // obtain current balance
    bal = saPtr->getBalance();
    // add 30 minutes to *timePtr
    timePtr->addTime(30);
```

EXAMPLE 10.3 ▬▬▬▬▬▬▬▬▬▬▬▬▬▬▬▬▬▬▬▬▬▬▬▬▬▬▬▬▬

Declare a Calendar object month_11_63 with initial value set to November 1963 and pointer cptr that points at the object. The following are a series of statements that all refer to the same object using the names month_11_63, *cptr or the operator −>.

```
Calendar month_11_63 (11,1963), *cptr = &month_11_63;

cout << month_11_63.getMonth(); // output:  11
cout << cptr->getYear();         // output: 1963
(*cptr).setMonth(9);             // update month to 9
cptr->displayCalendar();         // September 1963 calendar   ■
```

10-3 DYNAMIC MEMORY

For many applications, memory requirements are known only at run time. For such applications, memory should be allocated when the demand is known ("supply on demand") rather than preallocated during the compilation process. For instance, assume a course grading system handles student records. For a course with 500 students, a large array of student records would have to be used whereas a small seminar class would require far fewer records. Rather than allocating a fixed-size list to handle a hypothetically large class, the application should identify the specific class size and then dynamically use this information to allocate storage for the data. This ability requires tools for dynamic memory management. We begin by introducing the C++ operators *new* and *delete* that allocate and deallocate memory.

The Memory Allocation Operator new

When a program is loaded into memory, the system sets aside a block of memory, called the *heap*, that is available for use during execution. To obtain access to a portion of this memory, C++ uses the operator *new* along with pointer objects. The new operator takes an object type as an argument and allocates from the heap an object of this type. The operator returns the address of the allocated memory which can then be assigned to a pointer.

Consider the problem of allocating dynamic memory for a short and a long object. The process begins by declaring a pointer for each type.

```
int  *shPtr;     // assume the size of short is 2 bytes
long *longPtr;   // assume the size of long is 4 bytes
```

The *new* operator makes a request for memory from the heap. If it is available, the system reserves the appropriate number of bytes and returns its starting address. If the memory is not available from the heap, the return value is 0, which is called the *NULL pointer*. The constant NULL is defined as 0 in **iostream.h** and may be used as an initial value for a pointer of any type. NULL is the only integer that can be freely assigned to pointer objects and used in comparison expressions.

The following statements execute the new operator for an int and a long.

```
shPtr = new short;   // a pointer to a short
longptr = new long;  // a pointer to a long
```

Figure 10-4 describes the action of new operator in these statements. Assume the systems provides a heap that starts at address 5000. The new operator directs the system to reserve space for a short int (2 bytes) and returns the address 5000 for assignment to shPtr. A second call to new will obtain memory for a long integer from some other location on the heap. The system maintains a table of heap information that indicates which locations are in use. Assuming that locations 5002 to 5007 are in use, the new operations returns 5008 for assignment to longPtr.

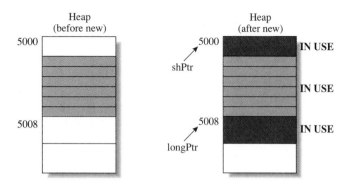

FIGURE 10-4
Requesting Dynamic Memory.

Objects allocated on the heap are not given default values. If the programmer wants to assign an initial value to the object, the new operator can include an initialization list that is enclosed in parentheses immediately after the object type. The following statements allocate a short and a long object on the heap with initial values 3 and 100000L respectively.

```
shPtr = new short(3);
longPtr = new long(100000L);
```

SYNTAX ▬▬▬▬▬▬▬▬▬▬▬▬▬▬▬▬▬▬▬▬▬▬▬▬▬▬▬▬▬▬▬▬▬▬

The new Operator

Form: `new  objType;`
           `new  objType(initvalue);`

Action: The operator requests a block of memory from the heap. The number of bytes is determined by the size of objType. When an initial value is included, the operation assigns the value to the location on the heap. If memory is not available, new returns 0, the NULL pointer.

Example: The example allocates memory for an unitialized object of type double and a string object with initial value "Heap".

```
double *p = new double;
String *str = new String("HEAP");
// test if memory is allocated
if (str == NULL)
{
    cerr << "Memory allocation failure" << endl;
    exit(1);
}
```

Once memory is allocated, the indirection operator * can be used to access the corresponding object. For instance, we can use *shPtr and *longPtr in C++

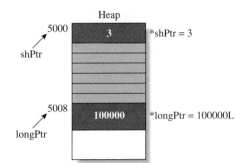

FIGURE 10-5
Dynamic Memory Allocation with Initial
Values.

statements to reference the objects pointed to by shPtr and longPtr. Assume the
data from Figure 10-5.

```
cout << *longRtr;      // output: 100000

*shPtr *= 2;           // double *shPtr to 6
```

Dynamic Array Allocation

The power of dynamic memory allocation is most evident with arrays whose size
requirements are not known until run-time. The new operator can be used to request a block of memory from the heap to hold the array. The syntax is extended
to use the index operator [] with the array size as an argument. For instance, assume arr is a pointer to an object of int type. To dynamically allocate an array of
ARRSIZE = 50 integers, use new with the index operator [].

```
const int ARRSIZE = 50;
int *arr;

arr = new int[ARRSIZE];   // dynamically allocate the array
```

The pointer arr is assigned the starting address of the block of ARRSIZE
integers. The index operator can be used with the dynamic array arr in the same
way it would apply to arr as a static array. For instance, arr[0] is the first array element and `arr[ARRSIZE-1]` is the last element.

EXAMPLE 10.4 ▬▬▬▬▬▬▬▬▬▬▬▬▬▬▬▬▬▬▬▬▬▬▬▬▬▬▬▬

1. A for loop initializes each element to have value 0 in the dynamically allocated array arr.

```
for(i = 0; i < ARRSIZE; i++)
   arr[i] = 0;
```

2. You can check the result of a new operation to ensure that sufficient memory
is available. This code attempts to allocate an array of 1000 doubles. If mem-

ory is not available, the program displays an error message and terminates execution.

```
double *dbl;

dbl = new double [1000];
if (dbl == NULL)                    // check if memory allocated.
{
    cout << "Memory allocation error!";
    exit(1);                         // terminate the program
} ■
```

Dynamically Allocated Class Objects

The new operator can be used to dynamically allocate class objects. The operator causes a constructor to execute when a single object is allocated. Unless the class has a default constructor, arguments must be included. For instance, a Time24 object can be dynamically allocated with or without arguments for the constructor since the class has a default constructor. The following statements dynamically allocate objects for midNight and noon.

```
Time24 *midNight, *noon;

midNight = new Time24;        // time 0:00
noon = new Time24(12, 0);     // time 12:00
```

To allocate a dynamic array of class objects, the class must have a default constructor. The new operator allocates an array of 100 Time24 objects with each initialized to midnight.

```
Time24 *t;

t = new Time24[100];
```

```
                new ClassName[n]
```

Action: An argument list may be passed to the constructor when the Class-
             Name object is allocated. An array of ClassName objects can be de-
             clared only if the class has a default constructor.

Example: ```
            // *startDay is January 1, 1600
            Date *startDay = new Date;

            // *birthday is October 24, 1973
            Date *birthday = new Date(10,24,1973);

            // each object contains the time 00:00 (midnight)
            Time24 *t = new Time24[10];
            ```

## PROGRAM 10.1

The program illustrates the operator new with a GradeRecord object. Memory is dynamically allocated so that grPtr points to student "71-8932" who has a gpa of 2.50 based on
40 units and 100 grade points. The student record is updated by adding 10 units and 30
grade points (B average). The initial and final record are output with the member function `writeGradeInfo()`. Note that the member functions are called using the "→" operator with the pointer grPtr.

```cpp
#include <iostream.h>

#include "graderec.h"
#include "tstring.h"

int main()
{
   GradeRecord *grPtr;

   // dynamically allocate GradeRecord object with
   // ID = "71-8932", 40 units, 100 grade points
   // output the initial record
   grPtr = new GradeRecord("71-8932", 40, 100);
   grPtr->writeGradeInfo();
   cout << endl;

   // update the grade record and output it
   grPtr->updateGradeInfo(10,30);
   grPtr->writeGradeInfo();

   return 0;
}
```

```
Run:

Student:  71-8932  Units:  40  GradePts:  100  GPA:
```
```

```
2.50

Student:  71-8932  Units:  50  GradePts:  130  GPA:
2.60
```

The Memory Deallocation Operator delete

In an application, efficient memory management is the responsibility of the program. Understanding that the heap is a finite resource, the application should request a block of memory (new) and then return it to the heap when it is no longer needed. To allow for a return of memory, C++ provides an operator *delete* that deallocates memory that was previously allocated by the new operator. The syntax is very simple and relies on the fact that the system retains information about the address and the size of memory allocated by each call from the operator new. The delete operator nullifies the action of new by de-allocating the corresponding memory.

To illustrate the operator new, we introduced pointers shPtr and longPtr that were assigned locations 5000 and 5008 from the heap (Figure 10-5). A heap management table not only records the addresses but also the fact that 2 bytes were allocated by "new short" and 4 bytes by "new long."

```
short *shPtr = new short;
long *longPtr = new long;
```

Memory is released by the delete operator that uses the pointers shPtr and longPtr to identify the starting addresses. After using delete, the contents of shPtr and longPtr are invalid and cannot be used to access memory until they are given new values.

```
delete shPtr;    // deallocates 2 bytes starting at 5000
delete longPtr;  // deallocates 4 bytes starting at 5008
```

Figure 10-6 gives a view of the heap immediately after calls to the operator new and calls to the operator delete.

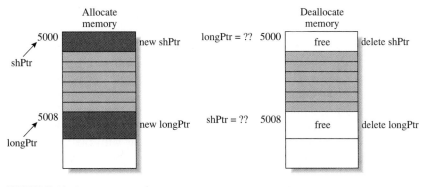

FIGURE 10-6
De-allocating Memory.

When the operator new allocates memory for an array, the operator, delete [], is called to deallocate the memory. Like the simple delete, this operator has a pointer operand. Note that the array delete operator uses [] without any size argument. The amount of memory to deallocate is extracted from information recorded by the initial new operation.

```
int  *arr = new int[ARRSIZE];    // allocate the array arr
delete [] arr;                   // deallocate the array memory
```

SYNTAX

The Delete Operators

Form: `delete objPtr;`   `// deallocate dynamic object`
           `delete [] objPtr;`   `// deallocate dynamic array`

Action: Both operators take a pointer operand that was initialized by a call to new. The corresponding memory that was originally allocated by new is deallocated by delete. For dynamic array storage, use the delete [] operator so that the entire array is deallocated.

Example: `int *p;`
           `long *q;`

```
// p and q are assigned values initialized by new
// allocate memory for a single integer with value 5
p = new int(5);
// allocate memory for 20 long integers.
q = new long[20];

// deallocate the corresponding memory
delete p;           // deallocate a single int object
delete [] q;        // deallocate 20 long integers
```

Resizing a List. Dynamic array management is one of the most important applications of the new and delete operators. Often a program may need to resize an array to expand or contract its number of elements. In this section, we look at a relatively simple function, called `growArray()`, which increases the size of an array by a specified amount. By using template notation, the function can be used for any primitive type or any class with a default constructor. The process saves all of the original data values and leaves any new locations uninitialized. The computer stores an array in contiguous memory, and we cannot simply annex adjacent locations following the array since they may be allocated to other objects in the program. The `growArray()` function must dynamically create a new array by calling the operator new with the larger array size as its argument and copy the original values to the new array (Figure 10-7).

After copying all of the elements from the original array to the new one, a call to delete deallocates the memory for the original array, since it is no longer needed. The function returns the address of the new array.

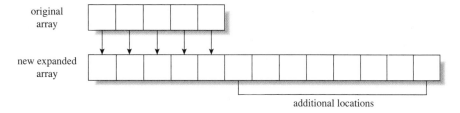

FIGURE 10-7
Expanding a Dynamic Array.

```
// increase the size of the dynamic array
// arraySize is updated to the new array size
template <class T>
T *growArray (T *arr, int& arraySize, int arrayIncrease)
{
   // newsize is the size after adding arrayIncrease elements
   int i, newsize = arraySize + arrayIncrease;
   // use temparr to build the new array
   T *temparr;

   // allocate memory for the new and expanded array
   temparr = new T[newsize];

   // copy elements from original array to new array
   for (i = 0; i < arraySize; i++)
      temparr[i] = arr[i];

   // for demonstration only - set new elements to 0
   for (i = arraySize; i< newsize; i++)
      temparr[i] = 0;

   // delete the old array and update arraySize
   delete [] arr;
   arraySize = newsize;    // size argument is updated
   return temparr;
}
```

APPLICATION 10-2 RESIZING A LIST

To illustrate the action of growArray(), the program prompts the user to input values for arraySize and arrayIncrease. A dynamic array is created with values 0, 1, . . . , arraySize-1. Each of two calls to the function increases the size of the array by the value arrayIncrease. The expanded arrays are output using the function writeArray(). For demonstration purposes, growArray() initializes the new locations to 0. As a result, the newly allocated array elements are identified in the output.

```
#include <iostream.h>

// increase the size of the dynamic arr. both arr and
```

```cpp
// arraySize is updated after array allocation
template <class T>
T *growArray (T *arr, int& arraySize, int arrayIncrease);

//output array arr
template <class T>
void writeArray(const T *arr, int size);

int main()
{
    // dynamic array
    int *arr;
    int i, arraySize, arrayIncrease;

    cout << "Enter original size and desired increase: ";
    cin >> arraySize >> arrayIncrease;

    // allocate the dynamic array and initialize its elements
    // to have values 1, 2, ..., arraySize. output the array
    arr = new int[arraySize];
    for (i = 0; i < arraySize; i++)
        arr[i] = i;
    cout << "Original array: ";
    writeArray(arr, arraySize);

    // increase the array by arrayIncrease elements, which
    // are filled with 0's.  output the new array
    arr = growArray(arr, arraySize, arrayIncrease);
    cout << "Grow by " << arrayIncrease << "      : ";
    writeArray(arr,arraySize);

    // increase the array size again and output the new array
    arr = growArray(arr, arraySize, arrayIncrease);
    cout << "Grow by " << arrayIncrease << "      : ";
    writeArray(arr,arraySize);

    return 0;
}

/* implementation of growArray() is given in the program dis-
cussion */

template <class T>
void writeArray(const T *arr, int size)
{
    int i;

    for (i = 0; i < size; i++)
        cout << arr[i] << "   ";
    cout << endl;
}
```

```
Run:

Enter original size and desired increase: 5 3
Original array: 0  1  2  3  4
Grow by 3      : 0  1  2  3  4  0  0  0
Grow by 3      : 0  1  2  3  4  0  0  0  0  0  0
```

10-4 CLASSES USING DYNAMIC MEMORY

Up to this point in the book, all of our classes have data members whose size is fixed by the compiler. For discussion, we will refer to these as *fixed data members*. Even in the case where a class has contained an array as a data member, the size of the list was fixed. For instance, the FinanceCenter class from Chapter 7 has a list of StudentAccount objects. In the declaration, the size of the list is defined by the constant MAX_ACCOUNTS. This approach was necessary since we did not have the tools to dynamically allocate memory. However, the approach is unrealistic. A state university would need a larger list of student accounts than a small private liberal arts college. To commercially use the class, it must be customized by setting MAX_ACCOUNTS to the appropriate number for each school. With dynamic memory, the class can be redesigned to have the school size as an argument in the constructor. The school size can be used to allocate an array of StudentAccount objects from the heap. To make the class even more flexible, a member function `resize()` could expand or contract the number of accounts as the school population changes.

Classes with dynamically allocated data members are a powerful tool in object-oriented programming. They allow a program to store variable size data collections and use member functions to add, remove, or update items in the collection. When combined with templates, these classes can store and manage objects of different types. In this chapter, we develop a template Vector class whose objects resemble arrays but have additional features. Vector is a wrapper class that contains an a dynamically allocated array as a private data member.

To design a class that uses dynamic memory, we must understand that C++ requires special member functions. The constructor must allocate the dynamic memory used by the object, and the *destructor* must deallocate the memory. Without a destructor, memory on the heap is wasted. By default, when one object is assigned to another, the data members of the right-hand side object are copied to the corresponding data members of the left-hand side object. Unfortunately, when dynamic memory is involved, this default action can lead to disastrous results. The solution is to develop an *overloaded assignment operator* that properly handles the dynamic memory. New objects are created by copying the value of an existing object to another as a result of initialization, call by value argument passing, and generating object return values. As with assignment, the default action of copying corresponding data members leads to fatal program errors. To avoid this problem, the programmer must develop a *copy constructor.* In this section and the next, we learn to implement the required member functions that properly handle the dynamic components of a class.

The DynamicDemo Class

To illustrate concepts, we use a demonstration class called DynamicDemo that has four fixed data members and a dynamic array of integers, arr. The two fixed data members value and arraySize maintain class data. The object id and static data member uniqueObjId maintain information that identifies an object (Figure 10-8). The class has only the member functions that are required to correctly handle dynamic memory. While it cannot be used in any meaningful application, the class presents most of the programming problems that would arise in developing more complex classes that use dynamic memory.

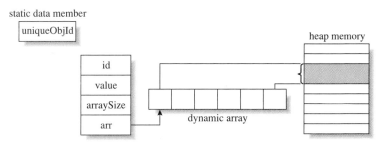

FIGURE 10-8
DynamicDemo Data Members.

The DynamicDemo class has special instructional features that identify each object and the execution of each member function. The data member id contains a unique character value that is assigned when the object is created. To accomplish this, we define uniqueObjID as a static character data member with initial value 'A'. The value of a static data member is shared among all objects of the class (Section 8.4). When a DynamicDemo object is declared, the constructor assigns the current value of uniqueObjID as the id and then increments the value of uniqueObjID. In this way, objects are tagged with the letters A, B, C, and so forth. Each member function in the class outputs its name and a summary of its action. The summary identifies an object by its id and value data members. When DynamicDemo objects are included in a program, the output documents the creation, modification, and destruction of each object.

A partial declaration of the DynamicDemo class includes the constructor and destructor member functions. The purpose for a destructor and its implementation are given after the discussion of the constructor.

DECLARATION: DynamicDemo (PARTIAL LISTING) ▬▬▬▬

```
class DynamicDemo
{
   private:
      // uniquely identifies object for demonstration purpose
      char id;

      // value associated with an object
      int value;

      // dynamic array and number of elements
      int arraySize;
      int *arr;

      // static object used to uniquely identify every
      // DynamicDemo object created by the constructor
      static char uniqueObjId;
      . . .
   public:
      // constructor
      DynamicDemo(int val, int size);

      // destructor
      ~DynamicDemo();
      . . .
};
```

The Constructor in DynamicDemo. The role of a constructor in any class is to initialize the data members. When a data member is a pointer associated with dynamic memory, the constructor is responsible for allocating the memory using the operator new and assigning the address of the memory to the data member. For the DynamicDemo class, the constructor has two arguments that are used to initialize the fixed data members, value and arraySize. The member id is assigned the current character in the object uniqueObjID. The initialization is completed when the constructor calls operator new to allocate the dynamic array of arraySize elements and assign its address to the data member arr. For demonstration purposes, a "cout" statement indicates that the operation is a constructor for object "id/value."

Constructor *DynamicDemo()*:

```
// initialize id, value and arraySize.
// allocate a dynamic array of arraySize integers
DynamicDemo::DynamicDemo(int val, int size)
                  : value(val), arraySize(size)
{
```

```
                // assign id for object and increment uniqueObjId for
                // the next object
                id = uniqueObjId;
                uniqueObjId++;

                // dynamically allocate memory for the array
                arr = new int[arraySize];

                // messsage indicating which object is being created.
                cout << "Constructor for object/value " << id
                     << "/" << value << endl;
        }
```

The Destructor in DynamicDemo. When a program deletes an object, it destroys all of its fixed data members and loses all access to their values. In the case of a DynamicDemo object, the process destroys the character member id, and the integer members value and arraySize. The process also destroys the pointer arr that identifies the associated dynamic array. Therein, lies the problem. Destroying the pointer does not deallocate the corresponding memory for the array on the heap. The system still thinks the memory is reserved. Unfortunately, there is no longer a reference to the address through arr. (Figure 10-9). This situation is referred to as a *memory leak*.

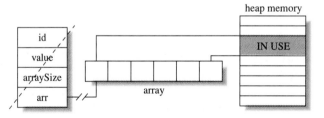

FIGURE 10-9
Incorrectly Destroying a DynamicDemo Object.

Destroying objects that have an associated dynamic array creates a memory management problem for a programmer. If arrays are not deallocated, more and more heap space is reserved but unused. In the extreme, the entire heap could be exhausted and any request for dynamic memory would be denied (new returns the NULL pointer). To handle this problem, every C++ class that uses dynamic memory must have a member function, called the *destructor,* that is automatically called whenever an object is destroyed. The destructor allows a program to deallocate dynamic memory before an object is destroyed. Its name is "~ClassName" and it has no arguments and no return type. The character ~ represents "complement" and so ~ClassName is the complement of the constructor.

In the DynamicDemo class, the destructor deallocates the dynamic array. For demonstration purposes, a message indicates that object "id/value" is being destroyed.

Destructor ~DynamicDemo():

```
// destructor. deallocate the dynamic array
DynamicDemo::~DynamicDemo()
{
   // deallocate memory for the array
   delete [] arr;

   // message indicating which object is destroyed
   cout << "Destructor for object " << id
        << "/" << value << endl;
}
```

APPLICATION 10-3 CALLING THE CONSTRUCTOR AND DESTRUCTOR

The program uses DynamicDemo objects to illustrate two common ways an object is destroyed.

1. An object declared in the main program is destroyed when the program terminates.

2. An object that is dynamically allocated can be destroyed by invoking the operator delete.

All action occurs in the main program. A declaration creates the objects mainObj1 and mainObj2 and the pointer dynCLPtr. After calling new to allocate space for *dynClPtr, the program destroys the object with the delete operator and terminates. This causes the fixed objects to be destroyed.

```
#include <iostream.h>

#include "dynamic.h"

int main()
{
```

```
      cout << "1. Declare  fixed objects in main()" << endl;
      DynamicDemo mainObj1(1,1), mainObj2(2,2);
      cout << endl;

      cout << "2. Declare pointer and allocate a dynamic object"
           << endl;
      DynamicDemo *dynCLPtr = new DynamicDemo(3,3);
      cout << endl;

      cout << "3. Deallocate object with 'delete'" << endl;
      delete dynCLPtr;
      cout << endl;

      cout << "4. Ready to exit program." << endl;

      return 0;
   }
```

```
   Run:

   1. Declare  fixed objects in main()
   Constructor for object/value A/1
   Constructor for object/value B/2
   2. Declare pointer and allocate a dynamic object
   Constructor for object/value C/3
   3. Deallocate object with 'delete'
   Destructor for object C/3
   4. Ready to exit program.
   Destructor for object B/2
   Destructor for object A/1
```

Does the following program create a run-time error? Explain.

```
   int main()
   {
      int arr[4] = {1,2,3,4}, *p = arr;
      int i = 5;

      cout << p[0] << " " << p[3] << endl;

      delete [] p;

      cout << "i = " << i  << endl;

      return 0;
   }
```

*Exploring
Concepts*

10-5   THE ASSIGNMENT OPERATOR AND COPY CONSTRUCTOR

In a program, objects are assigned values when they are initialized during their declaration or when they appear on the left-hand side of an assignment statement. Recall some statements for a primitive object and a class object.

```
int m, n = 30;             // initialize n in the declaration
m = n;                     // assign a value to m

Rectangle r(3,4), s = r, t; // declare s with initial value r
t = r;                     // assign Rectangle r to t
```

Initialization also occurs in functions having a pass by value argument or a return value. For instance, function `doubleSides()` receives a Rectangle object arg by value and returns a Rectangle object.

```
Rectangle doubleSides(Rectangle rect)
{
    // create a temporary Rectangle object whose length and
    // width have twice the dimensions of rect and return it
    return Rectangle(rect.getLength()*2, rect.getWidth()*2);
}

// run-time argument r; assign return value to t
t = doubleSides(r);
```

When the function `doubleSides()` is called, the formal argument rect is a copy of r with length = 3 and width = 4. Before returning, the function creates a temporary object with length = 6 and width = 8 and returns it to the calling statement that then executes an assignment to object t.

While both initialization and assignment have the same effect, the processes are actually quite different. When an object is initialized in a declaration, it is created with data copied from another object. In the example, n is created with initial value 30 and Rectangle s is created with length = 3 and width = 4 from object r. With assignment, however, the object already exists from a previous declaration. Its value is changed by copying the right-hand side value to the object. For instance, m is originally an uninitialized integer and Rectangle t is declared with length = width = 0 using the default constructor. In the assignment, the current value of n is copied to m and the value of each data member in Rectangle r is copied to the corresponding data member in t.

Up to this point, we have relied on the fact that C++ automatically supplies default member functions to implement both initialization and assignment. The functions, called a *copy constructor* for initialization and an *assignment operator* for assignment, have been provided as needed for all of our classes. C++ defines the default versions of these functions to simply make a bit-wise copy of the data members. This works as long as the objects have only fixed data mem-

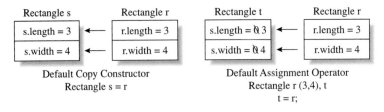

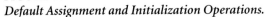

FIGURE 10-10
Default Assignment and Initialization Operations.

bers. For instance, the Rectangle class has fixed data members for length and width. The statement

```
Rectangle r(3,4), s = r, t;  // declare s with initial value r
```

uses the default version of the copy constructor to create s as a duplicate of r. The statement

```
t = r;                       // assign Rectangle r to t
```

uses the default version of the assignment operator to make t another duplicate of r (Figure 10-10).

When objects have dynamically allocated data members, these default operations produce invalid results and may cause the application to terminate with a fatal error. To effectively use objects with dynamic memory, a programmer must explicitly define an assignment operator and a copy constructor that correctly manage dynamic memory. In this section, we look at the operations separately. We use DynamicDemo objects to illustrate why the simple bit-wise copy of data members is incorrect and then develop the syntax and algorithms for the required member functions.

The Assignment Operator for DynamicDemo Objects

A DynamicDemo object has four fixed data members and a dynamic array, arr. The size of the array is determined by the argument arraySize. Consider objects objA and objB whose array sizes are the same and declarations are

```
DynamicDemo objA(5,3), objB(15,3);
```

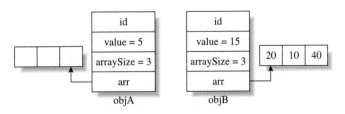

FIGURE 10-11
Dynamic Objects objA(5, 3) And objB(15,3).

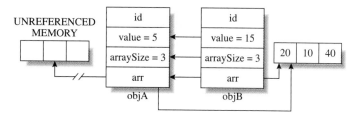

FIGURE 10-12
Incorrect Assignment for DynamicDemo Objects.

Figure 10-11 gives a view of both objects. We assume that objB.arr points at a dynamically allocated array of three integers that currently contains the elements 20, 10, and 40.
Consider the assignment statement

```
objA = objB;
```

If the class uses the default assignment operator that simply copies all fixed data members, objA.value and objA.arraySize become 15 and 3 respectively and the pointer, objA.arr, is assigned the address objB.arr. This is the problem. The pointers objA.arr and objB.arr point to the dynamic array for objB and the link from objA is broken. The corresponding heap memory remains allocated but unusable (Figure 10-12).

Another, even more serious problem occurs if objB is destroyed and the destructor deallocates its dynamic array. The operation would simultaneously deallocate the dynamic array for objA (Figure 10-13). The pointer objA.arr points to memory that was returned to the heap. Any access to the dynamic array objA.arr will likely result in a fatal run-time error.

EXAMPLE 10.5

The function f() has a DynamicDemo reference argument and an integer argument arrSize specifying the size of the array maintained by the object. The DynamicDemo object dobj is declared with value 0 and array size arrSize.

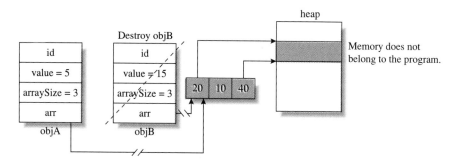

FIGURE 10-13
Destroying Objects Sharing a Common Array.

After assigning obj to dobj using the default assignment operator, the function returns. At that point, the destructor for dobj executes and deallocates its dynamic memory from the heap, which is also the dynamic memory for the run-time reference argument.

```
void f(const DynamicDemo& obj, int arrSize)
{
    DynamicDemo dobj(0,arrSize);

    dobj = obj;     // deletes dynamic memory in obj
}
```

The following code segment calls `f()` twice. The first call deletes the dynamic memory in obj, and the second call attempts to delete already deleted memory. The will likely lead to program failure.

```
DynamicDemo obj(6,3);

f(obj,3);
f(obj,3);    // attempt to delete memory already deleted!  ■
```

Designing the Assignment Operator For DynamicDemo Objects. The previous example illustrates that assigning objects by simply copying their data members will not work with objects that have dynamically allocated data. If the array sizes are the same, the contents of the dynamic array on the right-hand side must be copied to the corresponding array on the left-hand side. With DynamicDemo objects objA and objB, copy the fixed data members value and arraySize from objB to objA and then copy the array elements from objB to objA. In this way, the dynamic arrays for the two objects are kept separate but their individual elements are equal (Figure 10-14). Since the object id is used for demonstration only, its value is not copied so that we can continue to distinguish objects as we trace them in a program.

In the example, the arrays for both objA and objB have three elements. The copying of elements can proceed without making any adjustments. If the sizes of the two arrays are different, deallocate the current array for objA with the operator delete. Allocate another array for objA having objB.arraySize elements. Copy the array elements from objB to objA.

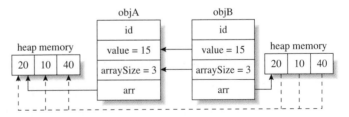

FIGURE 10-14
Correct Assignment Involving Dynamic Data.

```
delete[]  objA.arr;                  // deallocate array
objA.arr = new int[objB.arraySize];  // allocate a new array
```

Implementing the Assignment Operator for DynamicDemo Objects. An over-loaded assignment operator must be implemented as a class member function with the right-hand side operand as the single argument. The function name is "operator=" and the argument is passed as a constant reference, since its value is not changed. A return value must be provided, since C++ allows for a multiple assignment. To understand the return type consider the statement

```
objX = objA = objB;
```

The effect is to assign the value of objB to both objA and objX as though the process were two separate statements.

```
objA = objB;
objX = objA;
```

The compiler implements multiple assignment as one statement by first evaluating (objA = objB) and making objA the return value of the operation. This return value is then assigned to objX.

As a member function, the left-hand operand for the assignment operator is the object itself. Since the left-hand operand is also the return value, the overloaded assignment operator must return its own value. To avoid creating a copy, it returns a reference to itself.

Declaration of the Overloaded Assignment Operator

```
DynamicDemo& operator=(const DynamicDemo& rhs);
```

The function implementation is broken into three parts. First, perform memory management to insure that the size of the dynamic arrays for both objects is the same. If necessary, delete memory for the array on the left-hand side and reallocate new memory. The second task is to copy the data members value and arraySize from the right-hand side. Finally, copy the elements of the dynamic array from the right-hand side. For demonstration purposes, the operator includes output statements that use id/value to identify the operands before and after the assignment is executed.

Overloaded Assignment Operator: operator=():

```
// assignment operator. replace the existing object by
// rhs on the right hand side of "="
DynamicDemo& DynamicDemo::operator= (const DynamicDemo& rhs)
{
    int i;
```

```
            // identify the assignment activity
            cout << "Assign object " << rhs.id << "/" << rhs.value
                 << " to object " << id << "/" << value << endl;

            // check arraySize to see if current array can be used
            if (arraySize != rhs.arraySize)
            {
               // de-allocate existing array and allocate new memory
               delete [] arr;
               arr = new int [rhs.arraySize];
            }

            // copy fixed data members value and arraySize
            value = rhs.value;
            arraySize = rhs.arraySize;

            // copy items from the rhs.arr to current array
            for (i = 0; i < arraySize; i++)
               arr[i] = rhs.arr[i];

            // return a reference to the current object
            cout << "Assignment complete: lhs is object " << id <<
                    "/" << value << endl;
            return *this;          // see next section
         }
```

The Class this Pointer

In the overloaded assignment operator, the expression *this is used to return a reference to the current object. The keyword this can be used in the code for any member function.

> **Definition** The identifier *this* is a pointer that is created by the compiler for any class object and is the address of the object itself. It is a keyword in C++ that can be used only inside a class member function. The full range of pointer syntax may be used.

```
this                // address of the current object
*this               // the current object
return *this;       // return the object itself
this->f();          // call function f() for current object
```

To illustrate the use of the this pointer, consider the Rational class from Chapter 9. An overloaded version of the += operator allows a rational number to take a single operand and add the value to itself.

```
Rational  r(3,4), s(1,2);    // r is 3/4  and  s is 1/2
r += s;                      // action: r = r + s
                             // result: r = 5/4
```

In the implementation of the operator+=, *this is the current object r. The implementation of += includes the expression

```
*this = *this + rhs;
```

The term *this is used on the right-hand side to form the sum of the current object and object rhs. It is used on the left-hand side of the assignment statement to store the sum as the value of the current object. Since C++ allows += to be used in a multiple assignment statement, *this is also the return value of the operation.

```
s = 0.5 + (r += s);     // s = 1/2 + 5/4 = 7/4
```

With our understanding of this, we can give the complete implementation for the Rational += operator.

```
// compound addition assignment operator
Rational& Rational::operator+= (const Rational& rhs)
{
    // *this is the current object.  assign the current
    // object the sum of itself and rhs
    *this = *this + rhs;

    // return reference to the current object
    return *this;
}
```

The Copy Constructor for DynamicDemo Objects

The copy constructor performs object initialization. Much of the analysis for the assignment operator applies to the copy constructor. Consider the declaration

```
DynamicDemo objB(15,3), objA = objB;
```

and assume that the dynamic array for objB has elements 20, 10, and 40. Figure 10.15 illustrates what happens when all of the data members are simply copied from objB to the newly created object objA.

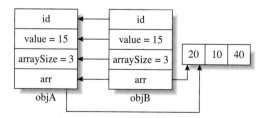

FIGURE 10-15
*Incorrect Copy Constructor for DynamicDemo
Object.*

The two objects point to the same dynamic memory. We have seen in the case of assignment that this can lead to fatal application errors. The copy constructor must allocate new dynamic memory for objA and copy the array elements from objB to objA.

EXAMPLE 10.6 ▄▄▄▄▄▄▄▄▄▄▄▄▄▄▄▄▄▄▄▄▄▄▄▄▄▄▄▄▄▄▄▄▄▄▄

The function f() has a pass by value argument obj. When f() is called, the formal argument obj is created by calling the copy constructor with the run-time object dat as its argument. When f() returns, the destructor for object obj is called, and the dynamic memory in the run-time argument dat is deleted. A second call to f() will attempt to delete the invalid memory.

```
// obj passed by value using DynamicDemo copy constructor
void f(DynamicDemo obj)
{
    // upon return, destructor for obj is called
}

DynamicDemo dat(1,3);

f(dat);    // upon return dat.arr is invalid
f(dat);    // attempt to delete invalid memory   ▄
```

Designing the Copy Constructor For DynamicDemo Objects. The task of the copy constructor is to create a new object, objA, which has its own dynamic array objA.arr. Its data must be a duplicate of the data being copied (objB). In designing the copy constructor, copy the fixed data members value and arraySize from the object obj. Allocate a dynamic array with arraySize elements in the new object and then copy the elements from the existing dynamic array in objB. Since the id is a special member that distinguishes newly created objects, our copy constructor assigns id the character value in the object uniqueObjID. Figure 10-16 describes objA before and after the copy constructor initializes the data.

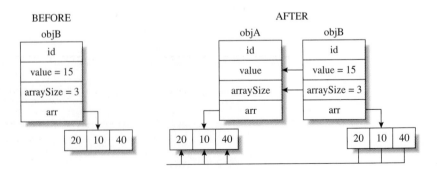

FIGURE 10-16
Correct Copy Constructor for DynamicDemo Objects.

Implementing the Copy Constructor for DynamicDemo Objects. A copy constructor is a constructor and so uses the class name as the function name. The object that provides the initial value is passed as a constant reference argument.

```
ClassName(const ClassName & obj);    // general declaration
```

Like any constructor, the copy constructor has no return value. The following is its declaration in the DynamicDemo class.

```
DynamicDemo(const DynamicDemo& obj);
```

In the implementation, the fixed data members value and arraySize are copied from object obj.

```
value = obj.value;
arraySize = obj.arraySize;
```

Memory is allocated for the dynamic array,

```
arr = new int[obj.arraySize];
```

The elements are copied from the obj array to the new array in the current object. For demonstration, the copy constructor includes output statements that use id/value to identify the new object before and after the initialization occurs.

Copy Constructor `DynamicDemo ( ):`

```
// copy constructor. make the current object a copy of obj
DynamicDemo::DynamicDemo (const DynamicDemo& obj)
{
    int i;

    // set new id for object and increment uniqueObjId for
    // the next object
    id = uniqueObjId;
    uniqueObjId++;

    cout << "Copy constructor for object " << id
         << ". Make copy of " << obj.id << "/" << obj.value
         << endl;

    // copy fixed data members value and arraySize
    value = obj.value;
    arraySize = obj.arraySize;

    // allocate new dynamic memory for the arr array
    arr = new int [arraySize];

    // copy items from the obj.arr to the newly allocated array
    for (i = 0; i < arraySize; i++)
        arr[i] = obj.arr[i];

    cout << "Copy complete: created new object " << id
         << "/" << value << endl;

}
```

Exploring Concepts

1. In the copy constructor, the argument must be passed by reference. C++ compilers will identify a value argument as an error. Why?

2. Suppose you have written a class, WriteFile, for which initialization is not a valid action. For instance, you do not want a programmer to pass a WriteFile object by value since this would create a second object that can write to the same output file. How would you design the class to provide this protection mechanism?

APPLICATION 10-4 TRACING THE COPY CONSTRUCTOR AND ASSIGNMENT OPERATOR

The application allows us to identify different places in a program that call the constructor, destructor, copy constructor, and overloaded assignment operator. When called, each function in the DynamicDemo class displays a brief explanation of its action and the id/value identification of the current object. The copy constructor and assignment operation also identify the right-hand side operand.

The program includes six statements that call one or more of the member functions. The following is a detailed analysis of each statement with the id for each object enclosed in brackets. You can verify the analysis by looking at the corresponding numbered reference in the output.

1. A simple declaration creates `mainObj1<A>` and `mainObj2<B>` with values 1 and 2 and array sizes 1 and 2 respectively. A third object, `mainObj3<C>` has value 0 and array size 0 from the default constructor.

   ```
   DynamicDemo mainObj1(1,1), mainObj2(2,2), mainObj3;
   ```

2. The statement `mainObj3<C> = mainObj2<B>` calls the assignment operator and assigns 2 as the new value.

   ```
   mainObj3 = mainObj2;
   ```

3. When calling function `dynamicF()`, the object `mainObj1<A>` is passed by value. The formal argument `argObj<D>` is initialized by the copy constructor to have value 1.

   ```
   mainObj3 = dynamicF(mainObj1);
   ```

4. In the function, `localObj<E>` is initialized by the constructor.

   ```
   DynamicDemo  localObj(3,3);
   ```

5. The return from the function involves three operations. C++ creates a tempory object with identifier id F that is initialized by `localObj<E>`. Before leaving the function, `localObj<E>` and `argObj<D>` are destroyed since their scope is closed. The temporary object is the return value and has scope in the main program. It is assigned to `mainObj3<C>` with the assignment operator and then is destroyed.

   ```
   return localObj;
   ```

6. At the end of the main program, the three objects that were initially declared are destroyed.

```cpp
#include <iostream.h>

#include "dynamic.h"

// the function has a value argument, a local object
// and a return object of type DynamicDemo
DynamicDemo dynamicF(DynamicDemo argObj);

int main()
{
    cout << "1. Declare objects with constructor" << endl;
    DynamicDemo mainObj1(1,1), mainObj2(2,2), mainObj3;
    cout << endl;

    cout << "2. Execute mainObj3 = mainObj2 " << endl;
    mainObj3 = mainObj2;
    cout << endl;

    cout << "3. Call dynamicF with argument mainObj1;"
         << endl;
    cout << "   Copy constructor initializes argObj"
         << endl;
    mainObj3 = dynamicF(mainObj1);
    cout << endl;

    cout << "6. Ready to exit main program." << endl;

    return 0;
}


// implementation of function
DynamicDemo dynamicF(DynamicDemo argObj)
{
    cout << endl;
    cout << "4. In dynamicF declare local object" << endl;
    DynamicDemo  localObj(3,3);
    cout << endl;

    cout << "5. Create temp object initialized by"
         << "localObj" << endl;
    cout << "   Destroy localObj and return temp" << endl;
    return localObj;
}
```

```
Run:

1. Declare objects with constructor
Constructor for object A/1
Constructor for object B/2
Constructor for object C/0

2. Execute mainObj3 = mainObj2
Assign object B/2 to object C/0
Assignment complete: lhs is object C/2

3. Call dynamicF with argument mainObj1;
   Copy constructor initializes argObj
Call copy constructor for object D. Make copy of A/1
Copy complete: created new object D/1

4. In dynamicF declare local object
Constructor for object E/3

5. Create temp object initialized by localObj
   Destroy localObj and return temp
Call copy constructor for object F. Make copy of E/3
Copy complete: created new object F/3
Destructor for object E/3
Destructor for object D/1
Assign object F/3 to object C/2
Assignment complete: lhs is object C/3
Destructor for object F/3

6. Ready to exit main program.
Destructor for object C/3
Destructor for object B/2
Destructor for object A/1
```

10-6 BUILDING A VECTOR CLASS

The C++ array type from Chapter 7 is a basic structure for handling a list of items of the same object type. In applications we have noted several important limitations for C++ arrays. When an array is declared as a static structure, its size is fixed and cannot be adjusted to meet the run-time demands of an application. The size of a C++ array is not an attribute of the array. Once an array is declared, the compiler "forgets" the size. The program must pass the array size to all functions that deal with the array. Furthermore, a C++ compiler does not normally generate code that checks whether an index is within range. Errors can occur that are difficult to detect. For instance, look at a simple for loop that shifts all elements on the tail of a list one position to the left. The loop begins at index pos and scans to the end of the list.

```
for(i=pos; i < arraySize; i++)
    arr[i] = arr[i+1];
```

The loop accesses the item arr[arraySize], which is not part of the list, and copies it into the array.

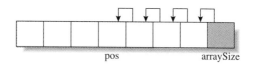

A closer look shows that the loop test should have been "i < arraysize-1".

```
for(i=pos; i < arraySize-1; i++)
    arr[i] = arr[i+1];
```

Some applications may need to create a copy of an array in temporary storage. Unfortunately, C++ arrays cannot be used in an assignment statement and the copy must be performed with a for loop.

```
for(i=0; i < arraySize; i++)
    temparr[i] = arr[i];
```

To deal with the limitations of a C++ array, we use object technology principles and create a template-based class, called *Vector,* that includes an array as a data member. Think of the Vector class as a wrapper class that defines a C++ array as a member and adds constructors and operators to facilitate array handling.

Declaring the Vector Class

The Vector class is a template-based class with a set of three constructors to initialize an object. The constructors contain a size argument that is used to dynamically allocate memory for the vector elements. One constructor includes a C++ array as an argument. By using the array to initialize the vector elements, we can create a Vector object that has the same values as a C++ array. Since the class uses dynamic memory, it has a destructor, copy constructor, and an overloaded assignment operator.

The size of a vector is set when it is declared. For many applications, however, a program may need to expand or contract the size of the vector as run-time conditions change. For instance, a vector may hold airline reservation records. Initially, the program creates a list of N records. If seasonal airline demand produces an unexpectedly large number of customers, the list size will have to expand beyond the N records without losing any existing data. A slack period may require fewer records. To deal with run-time changes in the size of a list, the Vector class has a *resize()* function that dynamically changes the number of elements.

One of the most attractive features of C++ arrays is their access to elements using indices. With operator overloading, this feature applies to Vector objects. C++ allows the Vector class to overload the index operator [] as a member function. Its definition enables a program to access vector elements as though they were array elements. The same operator also provides array-bounds checking.

Having given a general description of the Vector class and its member functions, we now give a declaration of the class.

vect.h

```
DECLARATION: Vector CLASS
const int DEFAULT_VECTOR_SIZE = 50;

template <class T>
class Vector
{
    private:
        // dynamic list containing arraySize elements of type T
        T *arr;
        int arraySize;

        // create general error message and terminate program
        void error(const String& msg) const;

    public:
        // constructors and destructor

        // create uninitialized array with arrsize elements
        Vector(int arrsize = DEFAULT_VECTOR_SIZE);
        // all arrsize elements initialized to value
        Vector(int arrsize, const T& value);
        // initialize with C++ array
        Vector(T a[], int arrsize);
        // copy constructor
        Vector(const Vector<T>& rhs);
        // destructor
        ~Vector();

        // overloaded assignment operator
        Vector<T>& operator= (const Vector<T>& rhs);

        // index operator
        T& operator[] (int n);

        // convert to a C++ array
        T *c_arr() const;
```

```
         // access and update operations
         int size() const;        // return size
         void resize(int sz);     // modify the size
         void clear();            // clear the list
};
```

Vector Class Constructors. The class has three constructors that provide different ways to initialize the array. A default constructor takes a size argument and simply allocates dynamic memory for the vector elements. The default value for the size is VECTOR_SIZE = 50. A second constructor takes a size and a value argument and initializes all of the elements with that value. This enables a program to set the list of elements to zero or to some other initial value. A third constructor allows a program to convert a C++ array to a vector. The array and its size are passed as arguments. After allocating dynamic memory, the constructor initializes the elements from the C++ array. Let's look at a declaration of each constructor and demonstrate their use with examples.

Basic default constructor:

```
   // allocate size number of elements of type T
   Vector (int size = DEFAULT_VECTOR_SIZE);

   Example:
      Vector<int> list(25);      // list of 25 integers
      Vector<double> payroll;    // list of 50 (default) doubles

      // list of 20 StudentAccount objects
      Vector<StudentAccount> stud(20);
```

Constructor with an initial value:

```
   // pass the size and value as arguments
   Vector (int size, const T& value);

   Example:
      Vector<char> line(80, ' ');    // 80 chars set to blanks
```

Constructor with a C++ array argument:

```
   // pass the C++ array and its size as arguments
   Vector (T a[], int size);

   Example:
      int score[5] = {80, 90, 75, 82, 91};

      // vScore is a copy of array score
      Vector<int> vScore(score,5);
```

Vector Index: By creating an overloaded version of the operator[], vector elements may be accessed using an index. The elements may be used as part of an expression or on the left-hand side of an assignment statement. The operator does bounds checking to verify that the index is in the range from 0 to size()-1 where size() is the current number of elements in the vector. The program terminates when a vector index is out-of-bounds.

```
// vector with 10 elements set to 100
Vector<int> v[10, 100];

v[1] = 50;              // assign 50 to second element
cout << v[2] * 2;      // Output: 200

v[10] = v[9] + 1;      // index 10 out of range;
```

Resizing a Vector. The function `resize()` has an argument that is used to change the size of the vector. If the new size is greater than current size, the vector grows and all of the elements are copied to the expanded vector. If the resize() operation shrinks the vector, only the initial elements from the current vector are copied and the remaining elements are discarded. In the example, a Vector object initially has 5 elements. By resizing, it doubles the size to 10 elements and then shrinks the size to 4 elements.

```
int arr[5] = {7, 4, 9, 3, 1};
Vector<int> list(arr,5);    // list initially has 5 integers
list.resize(10);            // list size is doubled
list.resize(4);             // list is contracted
```

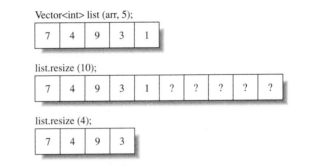

Applications using Vectors

We illustrate the use of the Vector class with two applications. The first application uses the index operator [] and the resize() member function to join two vectors. The algorithm is implemented by the function join() whose code is modeled after the concatenation operation for strings.

The function join() takes vectors vA and vB as arguments. The elements in vB are added to the end of Vector vA after vA is extended by vB.size() number of elements.

```
vA.resize(vA.size() + vB.size());    // combine vector sizes
```

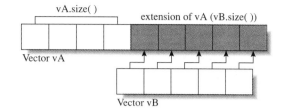

```
template <class T>
void join (Vector<T> &vA, const Vector<T>& vB)
{
    // set szA and szB to the sizes of the two vectors
    int szA = vA.size(), szB = vB.size(), i, j;

    // resize vA to make room for the elements from vB
    vA.resize(szA + szB);

    // use index i to scan vB and index j to scan new elements
    // of vA
    for (i = 0, j = szA; i < szB; i++, j++)
        vA[j] = vB[i];
}
```

The template-based function `writeVector()` outputs the elements of a vector object.

```
template <class T>
void writeVector(const Vector<T>& v)
{
    int i;

    for (i = 0; i < v.size(); i++)
        cout << v[i] << "  ";
    cout << endl;
}
```

APPLICATION 10-5 JOINING VECTORS

In the main program, vector vIntA is a list of five integers initialized by the array intList. We input an integer value readCount and declare a Vector object vIntB that has readCount elements. Initial values for vIntB are input from the keyboard. After combining the vectors with function `join()`, each element in vIntA is output using `writeVector()`;

```
#include <iostream.h>
#include <iomanip.h>

#include "tvector.h"    // use the Vector class

template <class T>
void join (Vector<T>& vA, const Vector<T>& vB);
```

```
template <class T>
void writeVector(const Vector<T>& v);

int main()
{
    // integer list with 5 elements
    int intList[5] = {35, 10, 25, 50, 40};

    // integer vectors with  vIntA initialized by intList
    Vector<int> vIntA(intList,5);

    int readCount, i;

    // enter a size for vIntB
    cout << "Enter size of second vector: ";
    cin >> readCount;

    // declare a vector with readCount elements
    Vector<int> vIntB(readCount);

    // input data into vIntB
    cout << "Enter " << readCount << " integers ";
    for (i = 0; i < readCount; i++)

        cin >> vIntB[i];

    // combine vectors vIntA and vIntB
    join(vIntA, vIntB);

    // output the extended vector vIntA
    cout << endl;
    cout << "Combined list" << endl;
    writeVector(vIntA);

    return 0;
}
/* implementation of join() and writeVector() is given in the
application introduction */
```

```
Run:

Enter size of second vector: 5
Enter 5 integers 75 80 55 60 90

Combined list
35   10   25   50   40   75   80   55   60   90
```

The second application illustrates the use of the Vector class for lists of different data types. It uses Vector objects with integer, Rational, and double data types to measure probabilities.

The program highlights the use of the Vector objects with elements of different data types. A series of 30,000 random numbers are generated in the range of 0 to 9. The total number of 0s, 1s, and so forth are stored in the ten element Vector, randomValue, whose values are integers initially set to 0.

```
Vector<int>  randomValue(10,0);
```

Since the number of random numbers is large, each different possible value should occur approximately one-tenth of the time. The elements in the Rational vector, ratioValue, store the ratio of the number of times each value (0 to 9) occurs out of the 30,000 random numbers. The ratios are converted to real numbers and stored in the double vector, pctValue.

```
Vector<Rational> ratioValue(10);
Vector<Double> pctValue(10);
```

For output, the program creates a table of ratios and percentages.

```
#include <iostream.h>

#include "textlib.h"     // used for setreal()
#include "rational.h"    // Rational class
#include "trandom.h"     // RandomNumber class
#include "tvector.h"     // Vector class

int main()
{
   //Vector to count number of times each value 0 - 9 occurs
   Vector<int> randomValue(10, 0);

   // Vector containing ratio of randomValue[i]/50000
   Vector<Rational> ratioValue(10);

   // Vector of real number equivalents for the ratios
   Vector<double> pctValue(10);

   // rnd produces a total of experimentSize random numbers
   RandomNumber rnd;
   int count;
   int i;

   // generate numbers; count sum of each value
   for (count = 0; count < 30000; count++)
     randomValue[int(rnd.random(10))]++;
```

```
// convert integer count to a fraction and a percent
for (i = 0; i < 10; i++)
{
  ratioValue[i] = Rational(randomValue[i], 30000);
  pctValue[i] = ratioValue[i];
}

// output the results for each number
for (i = 0; i < 10; i++)
  cout << "Number: " << i  << "   Ratio: " << setw(2)
       << ratioValue[i]  << "     Pct: " << setreal(7,4)
       << pctValue[i] << endl;

return 0;
}
```

```
Run:

Number: 0    Ratio: 2959/30000    Pct:  0.1986
Number: 1    Ratio: 3025/30000    Pct:  0.1008
Number: 2    Ratio: 3043/30000    Pct:  0.1014
Number: 3    Ratio: 3013/30000    Pct:  0.1004
Number: 4    Ratio: 3031/30000    Pct:  0.1010
Number: 5    Ratio: 2885/30000    Pct:  0.0962
Number: 6    Ratio: 2982/30000    Pct:  0.0994
Number: 7    Ratio: 2969/30000    Pct:  0.0990
Number: 8    Ratio: 2986/30000    Pct:  0.0995
Number: 9    Ratio: 3107/30000    Pct:  0.1036
```

Implementing the Vector Class

The implementation of the Vector class provides an excellent opportunity to see how a class can use dynamic memory management. The Vector class includes constructors to allocate memory, a destructor to deallocate the memory, a copy constructor, and an overloaded assignment operator. You are familiar with how these functions are defined from the DynamicDemo class. We give a listing of the constructor that passes an array and its size as arguments and creates a Vector object whose elements are initialized from the array.

```
template <class T>
Vector<T>::Vector(T a[], int size): arraySize(size)
{

    if (arraySize < 0)
        // print an error message and terminate the program
        error("Negative Vector size is invalid.");

    else if (arraySize == 0)
    {
```

```
            // if arraySize is 0 assign arr to NULL and return
            arr = NULL;
            return;
        }

        // dynamically allocate memory for the Vector array arr
        arr = new T[arraySize];
        // make sure the allocation succeeded
        if (arr == NULL)
            error("Memory allocation failure.");

        // copy array a to arr
        for(i=0; i < arraySize; i++)
            arr[i] = a[i];


    }
```

Overloading the Index operator [] The C++ index operator [] is used in an expression of the form

$$arrayName[n]$$

where arrayName is the starting address of an array and n is an integer expression. The operator is a function that has two operands, arrayName and n, and returns the element at address arrayName + n.

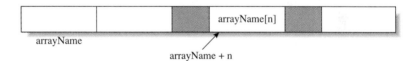

Like most C++ operators, [] can be overloaded but only as a member function. Use the operator when a class has an array as a private data member and an index is to be used to access individual elements in the array. This situation occurs in the Vector class. The array arr is a private data member storing elements of type T. The prototype for the overloaded operator is

```
    T& operator[] (int n);
```

where n is an index. In the operator function implementation, the return value is arr[n]. Note that the return type for the operator involves T&. By specifying a reference, the operator returns an alias for the actual element arr[n] in the vector array. In this way, the index operator may be used on either the right- or left-hand side of an assignment statement. For example

```
    Vector<int> v;
    item = v[2] * 3;    // v[2] used in the right-hand expression
    v[3] = item;        // v[3] is left-hand side of assignment
```

As we have noted, array-bounds checking is not part of the language specification for a C++ array. This feature is part of the Vector class. Since the size of the dynamic array is stored in the data member arraySize, the operator [] checks that the index n is in the range of 0 to arraySize-1. If an index is out of range, the program terminates with an error message after displaying the bad index.

```
// provide access to arr[i] in the array
T& Vector::operator[](int n)
{
    // verify that n is within the proper index range
    if (n < 0 || n > arraySize-1)
    {
        cerr << n << ": Index out of range";
        exit(1);
    }
    // return a reference to the array element at index n
    return arr[n];
}
```

Resizing the Vector The Vector class provides the resize() function that changes the number of elements in the object. If the requested number of elements sz is identical to arraySize, a simple return is executed since no change is required. Otherwise, new memory must be allocated. If resize() contracts the list (sz < arraySize), the first sz number of elements are copied to the new dynamic array and the remaining elements are discarded (Figure 10-17). The new array has size sz and the old array is deleted from the heap.

If the resize operation expands the object, the existing objects are copied to the new dynamic array. This process provides additional uninitialized memory space (Figure 10-18). After copying elements from the original array, the function deletes it from the heap.

resize():
```
// modify the size of the array
template <class T>
void Vector<T>::resize(int sz){
{
    int i, n;
```

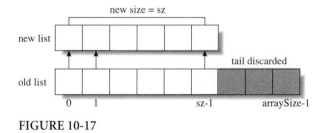

FIGURE 10-17
resize() Contracts the List.

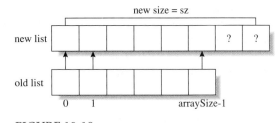

FIGURE 10-18
resize() Expands the List.

```
// handle case of negative size with error message
if (sz < 0)
   error("Negative new size is invalid.");
// handle case of no size change with a return
if (sz == arraySize)
   return;

// handle case of a resize to size 0
if (sz == 0)
{
   delete [] arr;
   arr = NULL;
   arraySize = 0;
   return;
}
// allocate new list with sz elements
T* newlist = new T[sz];

// make sure the allocation succeeded
if (newlist == NULL)
   error("Memory allocation failure.");

// set n to be smaller of new size and current size
if (sz <= arraySize)
   n = sz;
else
   n = arraySize;

// copy n elements from old list to new list
// this may truncate the list
for (i = 0; i < n; i++)
   newlist[i] = arr[i];

// delete original list, set arr to point to newlist,
// update arraySize
delete[] arr;
arr = newlist;
arraySize = sz;
}
```

Vector to Array Conversion With a constructor, the programmer can convert a C++ array to a Vector object. The reverse process is also possible, using the member function, c_arr(). The function returns the address of the dynamic array as a pointer.

```
// convert to a C++ array
template <class T>
T * Vector<T>::c_arr() const
{
    return arr;
}
```

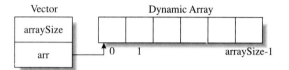

The pointer may be passed as an argument to a function that accepts an ordinary C++ array argument. The effect is to have the function perform calculations using the elements of the dynamic array.

Declarations:

```
Vector<int>  v;

template <class T>
int seqSearch(const T arr[], int start, int end, T key);
```

Function Call:

```
// search the elements of Vector v
seqSearch(v.c_arr(), 0, v.size() -1, 5);
```

The conversion operator allows a program to use C++ array-based algorithms. For instance, the function

```
template <class T>
void selectionSort(T arr[], int n);
```

from Chapter 7 sorts a Vector object by sorting the dynamic array within the vector. A version of selectionSort() for Vector objects is developed in Written Exercise 22.

PROGRAM 10.2

The program illustrates the use of selectionSort() to order a vector. Start with an integer array arr and use it to initialize the Vector object v. After calling selectionSort(), the program uses the function writeArray() to output v.

```
#include <iostream.h>

#include "tvector.h"          // Vector class
#include "sort.h"

// output the n-element C++ array arr
template <class T>
void writeArray(const T* arr, int n);

int main()
{
    int arr[5] = {5, 3, 2, 4, 7};
    // convert C++ integer array to a Vector object
    Vector<int> v(arr,5);

    // sort the array and call writeArray()
    selectionSort(v.c_arr(), v.size());
    writeArray(v.c_arr(), v.size());

    return 0;
}

template <class T>
void writeArray(const T* arr, int n)
{
    for(int i=0;i < n;i++)
        cout << arr[i] << "   ";
    cout << endl;
}
```

Run:

2   3   4   5   7

10-7 C++ STRINGS

Strings are a fundamental data structure in programming. In this book, we use an object-oriented approach that declares a String class to define string objects. Historically, the C programming language defined strings as a simple array of characters and provided a powerful set of utility functions in the system file **string.h**. The array definition of strings was inherited by C++ and woven into the design of many classes that are provided by C++ programming environments. You have experience with this fact in the stream open function that requires the file name be given as a C++ string.

```
ifstream fin;            // input stream
fin.open(<C++ string>); // the C++ string is the filename type
```

Defining a C++ String. A C++ string is a NULL-terminated sequence of characters stored in a C++ array. ASCII 0 designates the NULL character. A *string literal,* which is a sequence of characters enclosed in double quotes, is a C++ string. The following declaration creates a character array and assigns a string literal to the array.

```
char str[9] = "A String";
```

The string is stored in memory as a 9 element character array.

Since the string is stored in an array, its name identifies the address of the first character and the location of NULL identifies the end of the string. For instance, str[0] is A and str[8] is the NULL character. The length of a C++ string is the number of characters preceding the NULL character, so the length of string str is 8

A program has a variety of options for declaring a C++ string. In each case, we must allocate an array of characters and use the NULL character to terminate the string. The size of the array and the length of the string are often different.

```
// the array has 20 characters; the string has 9 characters
char str[20] = "A String";

// str is the NULL string with length 0,    str[0] is the
// NULL character
char str[20] = "";

// compiler allocates 4 characters including NULL character
char str[] = "SOS";       // compiler allocates exactly 4 bytes
```

Since a C++ string name corresponds to the address of the first element in the character array, its value can be assigned to a pointer.

```
char str[] = "Pointers", *s = str;
```

Programming Note

A C++ string literal, such as "Hello World!", is considered to have as its value the address of the first character. This address can be used to initialize a pointer to character constants.

```
const char *hello = "Hello World!";
```

The statement

```
cout << hello;
```

outputs "Hello World!".

Since a C++ string object has as its value the address of a character, we can refer to a C++ string as a char * object. We refer to *char* * as the object type of a C++ string just as double is the object type for a real number.

EXAMPLE 10.7

A character array is not a C++ string until it contains a NULL character that indicates the end of the string.

```
char arr[10], *p = arr;
```

By placing a NULL character in the array, we create a C++ string.

```
arr[0] = 'C';
arr[1] = '+';
arr[2] = '+';
arr[3] = 0;   // arr and p are now the string "C++"  ∎
```

Converting String and C++ string objects. The String class has a constructor that takes a C++ string as an argument. The constructor allows a program to convert a C++ string to a String object.

```
// argument is a C++ string literal
String  strA("Burrito"), strB;

// assigns to strB the object String("Chow Mein")
strB = "Chow Mein";
```

Conversion from a String object to a C++ string is provided by the member function c_str() that returns the address of the equivalent C++ string.

```
String fileName("input.dat");
fin.open(fileName.c_str()); // return fileName as a C++ string
```

C++ String I/O

C++ extends the stream operators "<<" and ">>" to C++ strings. The >> operator extracts the next sequence of characters after skipping whitespace. The output stream displays all of the characters in the string up to the NULL character. For instance,

```
char word1[32], word2[32];

cin >> word1 >> word2; // Input: baseball umpire
```

```
cout << word2;              // Output: umpire

word1[4] = 0;              // insert NULL char after e in baseball
cout << word1;             // Output: base
```

For string input, including whitespace, we use the stream member function `getline()`. The function has three arguments that include a character array, a positive integer n, and a character (delimiter) that terminates input. The delimiter is set to '\n' by default.

```
// function prototype
istream& getline(char *inputBuffer, int count,
                 char delimChar = '\n');
```

The array inputBuffer contains the input string. The operation extracts characters from the input stream until either the character delimiter is found, n − 1 characters are read, or end-of-file occurs. The characters are stored in the array inputBuffer followed by the NULL character. If delimChar is found, the character is extracted from the stream but not stored in the string.

EXAMPLE 10.8

1. Read an entire line from the keyboard by using the delimiter '\n'.

```
char line[81];     // space for 80 chars and NULL
cin.getline(line,81,'\n');
```

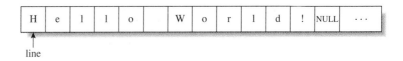

2. The getline() function uses separate count and delimiter conditions to terminate the input of characters. For parts (a) and (b), assume the input is "GETLINE-DEMO".

```
char buffer[25];
```

(a)
```
// read 5 chars. append NULL
fin.getline(buffer,6,'-');
```

(b)
```
// read to - and discard char
fin.getline(buffer,20,'-');
```

3. Read a social security number and a name from a stream fin. The social security number is in the format xxx-xx-xxxx and is followed by a colon (:). The name occupies the rest of the line.

```
char ssn[12], name[51];

fin.getline(ssn,12,':');       // read the ssn and discard ':'
fin.getline(name,51,'\n');     // rest of the line is the name
```

For input: 459-23-4718:Wilson, John

ssn is "459-23-4718"

name is "Wilson, John" ■

The getline() function must be used carefully with other forms of input. Assume input includes an integer followed by a string on the next line. An attempt to read the string with getline() extracts only the newline character (¶), that causes the input string to be NULL. This is a frequent problem when mixing numeric and string input.

```
char inputstr[9];
int n;

// incorrect approach
cin >> n;                       // read integer 25
cin.getline(inputstr,9,'\n');   // read and discard ¶
```

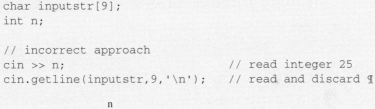

*Programming
Note*

Avoid the problem by extracting the newline character with a simple get(). The input for getline() is then taken from the next line.

```
// correct approach!
char nl;                        // char use by get()

cin >> n;                       // read integer 25
cin.get(nl);                    // extract the newline
                                // from the stream
cin.getline(inputstr,8,'\n');   // read string "Sharon"
```

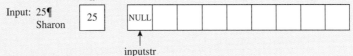

C++ String Handling Functions

Most C++ string handling is performed by functions in the C++ system file
string.h. This section introduces a cross section of functions from the file. For
each function, we include the prototype, a description of its action and an
example.

String Length

Prototype	`int strlen(char* s);`
Action	Returns the length of the C++ string s.
Example	`char s[10] = "Compile";`
	`cout << strlen(s);        // output is  7`

String Compare

Prototype	`int strcmp(char* s, char* t);`
Action	Compares the relative alphabetic ordering of the C++ strings s and t.
	Returns a negative value if s is less than t
	Returns 0 if s is equal to t
	Returns a positive value if s is greater than t
Example	`char *s = "township";`
	`int cmpValue;`

```
// cmpValue is negative (< 0) since
// "township"< "village"
cmpValue = strcmp(s,"village");

// cmpValue is 0 since &s[4] is starting address
//for "ship"
cmpValue = strcmp(&s[4],"ship");

// cmpValue is positive (> 0) since
//"township" > "city"
cmpValue = strcmp(s,"city");
```

Pattern Matching (Single Character)

Prototype	`char *strchr(char* s, char ch);`
Action	Returns a pointer to the first occurrence of ch in the C++ string s. Returns NULL if ch is not in s.
Example	`char *s = "mississippi", *p;`

```
p = strchr(s,'s');      // p is the address of s[2]
p = strchr(s,'t');      // p is NULL

// search for character 'p' in "sippi"
p = strchr(&s[6],'p'); // p is the address of s[8]
cout << p;              // Output: ppi
```

Pattern Matching (Substring)

Prototype	`char *strstr(char* s, char* t);`
Action	Returns a pointer to the first occurrence of string t in the C++ string s. Returns NULL if t is not in s.
Example	`char *s = "division", *t = "vision";`

```
p = strstr(s,t);       // p is the address of s[2]
p = strstr(s,"visor"); // p is NULL
```

String Copy

Prototype	`char *strcpy(char* s, char* t);`
Action	The function copies string t (including the NULL character) into string s and then returns the address of s.
Example:	`char s[255], *t = "Good Morning", *u = "Evening";`

```
// s = t is an invalid statement, since it
// attempts to assign pointer t to constant
// pointer s. C++ strings use strcpy() to copy
// one string to another

strcpy(s,t);          // assigns s = "Good Morning"
strcpy(&s[5],u);      // copies "Evening" at s[5]
cout << s             // output: "Good Evening"
```

String Concatenate

Prototype	`char *strcpy(char* s, char* t);`
Action	Copies string t onto the end of string s and returns the address of s.
Example:	`char s[255] = "Good", *t = "Morning";`

```
strcat(s," ");        // add blank on end of s

strcat(s,t);          // s is "Good Morning"
```

Programming Note

The copy and concatenate functions assume that the program provides sufficient memory for the target string. Since run-time code does not perform array bounds checking, hard to detect errors may occur. For instance, consider these statements.

```
char s[5], t[] = "too big!";
strcpy(s,t);
```

The function copies nine characters to s, but only 5 positions are available. The additional four characters stream into memory, possibly overwriting other program data values. When String objects are used, problems like these do not occur, since the class provides sufficient dynamic memory to hold the result.

```
// String class solution
String s, t = "Not too big!";

s = t;
```

Assume that str is the array of C++ strings

```
char*str[3] = {"ls","-l","-R"};
```

and argv is to be a pointer to str. How will you declare and initialize argv?

What is output by the statement

```
cout<<argv[1]<<" "<<argv[2][1];
```

Implementing the String Class

C++ strings and string functions play an instrumental roll in the implementation of the String class. The class stores the characters in a dynamically allocated C++ string. The number of characters in the string is maintained in the data member size.

tstring.h

```
DECLARATION: String Class   (PARTIAL LISTING)
class String
{
    private:
        // pointer to dynamically allocated string.
        // the string includes the NULL character
        char *str;
        int size;
        . . . .
};
```

To demonstrate the roll of the C++ string functions in the class implementation, we provide the code for the constructor and the function find(). Like many of the member functions in the class, these examples rely heavily on utility functions in **string.h**.

String constructor:

The constructor is passed a C++ string as an argument. The data member size is initialized by using strlen() to determine the length of string. One extra byte is added for the NULL character. After dynamically allo-

cating size number of bytes, the characters from the C++ string argument
are copied into the new space using `strcpy()`.

```
// constructor. allocate memory and copy in a C++string
String::String(char *s)
{
    // length includes the NULL character
    size = strlen(s) + 1;

    // make room for string and NULL char and copy s.
    str = new char [size];
    // terminate program if memory is exhausted.
    if (str == NULL)
        error(outOfMemory);
    strcpy(str,s);
}
```

Pattern matching function find():

Two versions of the `find()` function attempt to match a substring s within
the current object beginning at index start. In one version, the argument is
a C++ string and in the other version it is a String object. To understand
the C++ string version of the function, note that the last valid index in the
dynamic C++ string str is size-2 (str[size-1] is NULL). If the index start is
less then 0 or greater then or equal to size -1, return -1 to indicate an invalid index; otherwise, use the C++ string function strstr() to search for the
pattern s in the beginning at address &str[start]. The return value of
`strstr()` is assigned to the character pointer p. If p is NULL, indicating
that the search was unsuccessful, return -1. If p is not NULL, the pattern is
found and `find()` must return the index where s begins. This index is the
difference between p and str. Consider the example

```
String str = "acbdabcaa";
index = str.find("abc", 0);     // index is 4
```

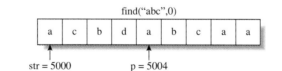

return index 5004 - 5000 = 4

```
// search for s in the string
int String::find(char *s, int start) const
{
    char *p;

    if (start <0    || start >= size-1)
        return -1;
```

```
            p = strstr(&str[start], s);
            if ( p == NULL)
                return -1;
            else
                return int(p-str);
    }
```

When the argument is a String object, the `find()` function simply converts the argument to a C++ string using `c_str()` and applies the version for C++ strings.

```
int String::find(const String& s, int start) const
{
    // execute the find() for C++ string s.c_str()
    return find(s.c_str(), start);
}
```

CHAPTER 10 SUMMARY

In this chapter, we look at a new object type, called a pointer, that contains the address of data in memory. By applying the dereference operator *, the programmer can access the data referenced by the pointer. Operators such as +, ++, and += apply to pointers. Using such operators, pointers can be used for algorithms involving array traversal, but their primary application is in the allocation and maintenance of dynamic memory.

Using dynamic memory, we can allocate arrays whose sizes are set by the run-time requirements of the application. A program can use the operator new to request memory from the heap at run-time for single objects and arrays. When the memory is no longer needed, it is released using the operator delete.

When using dynamic memory for the implementation of a class, the class must define a destructor that removes the dynamic memory from the heap when an object is destroyed. C++ supplies a default assignment operator and copy constructor that simply perform a bitwise copy of data members. When a class uses dynamic memory, the pointers to the dynamic data are copied and not the data itself. This results in two objects pointing at the same dynamic memory. When the destructor for one object is called, the dynamic memory for the other one is invalid. A subsequent reference to the remaining object will most likely result in a fatal application error. These problems are handled by adding an overloaded assignment operator and a copy constructor to the class.

In this chapter, we develop a template-based class whose objects act like an array. The class, called Vector, has an overloaded index operator that enables a program to access elements using the familiar [] notation and be protected by array bounds checking. Since the Vector class uses dynamic memory, it includes a destructor, an overloaded assignment operator and a copy constructor. The member function resize() allows the programmer to increase or shrink the size of the array according to the needs of the application.

The language defines the primitive C++ string type that is an array of characters terminated by a NULL character (ASCII value 0). These strings are supported by a series of free functions declared in the system file **string.h**. The file includes functions for computation of string length, string copy and concatenation, substring matching, and so forth. The String class should be used for most applications. However, the programmer must have some familiarity with C++ strings to maintain existing application software.

Classes in the Chapter

Name	Implementation File
DynamicDemo	dynamic.h
String	tstring.h
Vector	tvector.h

KEY TERMS

Address-of operator (&):

A unary operator that returns the address of an object in memory.

C++ string:

A NULL-terminated array of characters with ASCII 0 designating the NULL character. A string literal is a C++ string.

C++ string functions:

Declared in the C++ system file **string.h.** The functions perform operations with C++ strings, including computing string length, copying and concatenating strings and pattern matching.

Class member selection via pointer operator (−>):

Calls a member function in an object located by a pointer.

Copy constructor:

The default copy constructor simply makes a bit-wise copy of the data members. This works as long as the objects have only fixed data members. When a class uses dynamic memory, the programmer must write a copy constructor that allocates dynamic memory and copies the data from the source object.

Destructor:

A member function that is called whenever an object is about to be destroyed. By defining a destructor, the programmer can deallocate dynamic memory, close file streams, and perform other tasks that properly shut down an object before it is destroyed.

Dynamic array:

Array whose size requirements are not known until run-time. The new operator is used to allocate the array.

Fixed data members:

Data members whose size is fixed by the compiler.

Heap:

Block of memory set aside by the operating system that is available for use during execution. The new operator allocates memory from the heap, and the operator delete returns memory to the heap.

Indirection operator (*):

The unary operator * that is applied to a pointer to access the object it references.

Memory leak:

Created when there is no longer a reference to the address of dynamic memory on the heap. The program cannot call the operator delete to return the memory to the heap.

Operator delete:

Deallocates memory that was previously allocated by the new operator.

Operator new:

Makes a request for memory from the heap. If it is available, the system reserves the appropriate number of bytes and returns its starting address. If the memory is not available, the return value is 0, which is called the NULL pointer.

Operator this:

A pointer that is automatically declared for any class object and is the address of the object itself. It is a keyword in C++ that can be used only inside a class member function.

Overloaded array index operator:

The function "T& operator[] (int i)" that returns the data stored at index i of an array defined as a data member. This operator is defined for the Vector class.

Overloaded assignment operator:

The default assignment operator simply makes a bit-wise copy of the data members. This works as long as the objects have only fixed data members. When a class uses dynamic memory, the programmer must write an overloaded assignment operator that copies the data from the right-hand side object to the dynamic memory allocated for the object.

Pointer arithmetic:

The application of operators such as $+$, $+=$, $++$, and $<$ with pointers.

Pointer conversion operator:

Converts an object to a pointer that is the starting address of a dynamic array. Functions c_arr() and c_str() provide pointer conversion.

Pointer:

An object type whose values are addresses of data in memory.

REVIEW EXERCISES

1. Assume that p is a pointer to a long integer where a long is stored in four (4) bytes.

   ```
   long *p;
   ```

   A memory view includes four long values with pointer p set at location 5000

7000	4500	1000	2500

   5000
   p⎵

   (a) What is the distinction between *p in the declaration and *p in an output statement?

   (b) What is the value of *p + 3?

   (c) What is the value of *(p + 2)?

   (d) What is the value of p+1?

2. Trace the program and give the results of each stream output statement. The array is a C++ string.

```cpp
#include <iostream.h>

int main()
{
    char a[] = "Atlantic", *p = a;

    // 1. what is the value of *(p+8)? _____
    cout << *p;                   output 2: _____
    cout << *p + 1;               output 3: _____
    cout << *(p + 1);             output 4: _____
    p++;
    cout << *p;                   output 5: _____
    p = &a[3];
    cout << *p;                   output 6: _____

    return 0;
}
```

3. Identify the syntax error that occurs in each of the following statements.
   (a) `const int startVal = 100;`
       `int *ptr = &startVal;`
   (b) `int arr[20];`
       `arr++;`
   (c) `int *p = {1,4,9};`
   (d) `int *p;`
       `p = new int[3]{4, 9, 1};`

4. Consider the class DynamicCL that has a single dynamic data member

```cpp
class DynamicCL
{
    private:
        // single dynamic data member
        int *ptr;

    public:
        // constructor: m assigned to dynamic int
        DynamicCL(int m = 0);

        // destructor
        . . . .              //declare the destructor

        // copy constructor
        DynamicCL(const DynamicCL& obj);

        // assignment operator
        . . . .              // declare assignment operator

        // return value of dynamic member
        int getData()const;
```

```
                    // output stream operator << as a friend function
                    friend ostream& operator<< (ostream& ostr,
                                                 const DynamicCl& obj);

        };
```

(a) Declare the destructor for DynamicCl.
(b) Declare the overloaded assignment operator.
(c) Implement the member function getData().
(d) Implement the overloaded operator "<<" as a friend of the class.
(e) The function f() has DynamicCL objects as an argument, a local object, and a return value. Each of these objects involve a constructor or a copy constructor.

```
        DynamicCL f(DynamicCL obj)
        {
            DynamicCL localObj(12+obj.getData());

            return localObj;
        }

        int main()
        {
            DynamicCL  obj1(10), obj2;

            obj2 = f(obj1);                       // call function
            cout << obj2.getData() << endl;

            return 0;
        }
```

   (i)   Indicate the two times that the copy constructor is used when the function is called from the main program.
   (ii) Indicate all of the times that the destructor is called.
   (iii) What is the output value from obj2.getData()?

5. Use the class DynamicCL from review exercise 10.4 and the function new() to dynamically allocate objects pointed to by p.

```
    DynamicCL *p;
```

(a) A single DynamicCL object with an initial data value of 30.
(b) An array with five DynamicCL elements. What is the data value for each object in the array?
(c) Give the delete statements that would deallocate the dynamic memory used in (a) and (b).

6. Consider the class called ClassName.
(a) Explain why you cannot declare a copy constructor as

```
    ClassName (const ClassName obj);
```

(b) Explain why you would not want to use the following declaration for an overloaded assignment operator.

```
    void operator = (const ClassName& rhs);
```

7. What is the meaning of the keyword this? Explain why it is valid only inside a member function.

8. Assume the overloaded operator += is added as a member function in the DynamicCL class.
   (a) Give a declaration of the member function.
   (b) Which of the following statements could be used to implement the operator?
      (i) `this->ptr += rhs->ptr;`
          `return *this;`
      (ii) `*(this->ptr) += *(rhs.ptr);`
          `return this;`
      (iii) `*(this->ptr) += *(rhs.ptr);`
          `return *this;`
      (iv) `this->*ptr += *(rhs.ptr);`
          `return *this;`

9. (a) Declare a Vector object V that stores 30 elements of type double.
   (b) Declare a Vector object V that stores the elements in the array

      ```
      char vowel[] = {'a', 'e', 'i', 'o', 'u'};
      ```

10. Use the C++ strings a, b, c and integer n.

    ```
    char a[20] = "dynamic", b[] = "memory", c[32];
    ```

    (a) How many elements in array a are required to store the string "dynamic".?
    (b) What is the value of a[2]?   b[5]?
    (c) What is the value for n in each statement?

       ```
       n = strlen(a);          // n = _____
       n = strlen(&b[2]);      // n = _____
       ```

    (d) What is the return value from the function strcmp(b,"memorial")?
    (e) What is the output?

       ```
       b[4] = 0;               // 0 is NULL
       cout << b;
       ```

    (f) What is the output?

       ```
       char *tagch = strchr(a,'m');
       cout << strcpy(tagch,"flow");
       ```

Answers to Review Exercises

1. (a) *p in the declaration indicates that p is a pointer; *p in an output statement accesses the contents pointed to by p.
   (b) 7003
   (c) 1000
   (d) 5004

2. 1: 0 (NULL)   2: A   3: B   4: t   5: t   6: a

3. (a) ptr cannot point to a constant integer object. if so, an expression such as *ptr = 99 could modify startVal.

(b) arr is the array name and is a constant address (constant pointer). arr++ would alter a constant and so is not valid.

(c) allocate an array with the initial values and assign its address to p, e.g.

```
int arr[] = {1,4,9}, *p = arr;
```

(d) new operator allocates a dynamic array. The operation cannot be combined with initialization.

4. (a) Destructor:

```
~DynamicCL();
```

(b) Assignment:

```
DynamicCL& operator= (const DynamicCL& rhs);
```

(c) getData():

```
int DynamicCl::getData() const
{   return *ptr;   }
```

(d) operator <<():

```
ostream& operator << (ostream& ostr,
                        const DynamicCl & obj)
{   ostr << *(obj.ptr) << "   ";
    return ostr;
}
```

(e) (i) Initializing the value argument obj
        Initializing the return object in the return statement

   (ii) Destruction of localObj at end of function
        Destruction of local object obj from the argument list.
        Destruction of return object after completing the assignment to obj2
        At the end of the program, the destructor is called for objects obj2 and obj1.

   (iii) 22

5. (a) `p = new DynamicCl(30);`

   (b) `p = new DynamicCl[5];       // each object has value 0`

   (c) `for (a)   delete p;      for (b) delete [] p;`

6. (a) Passing a run-time value to formal argument obj would cause an unending chain of recursive calls to the copy constructor.

   (b) Without a returning a reference to the left-hand side (current object), multiple assignment would not be possible.

7. For each class object, "this" is pointer that references the object. The pointer is an implied data member of the class and can be used only by member functions.

8. (a) `DynamicCL& operator+= (const DynamicCL& rhs);`

   (b) `Code (iii)`

9. (a) `Vector<double> v(30);`

   (b) `Vector<char> v(vowel,5);`

10. (a) 8 (including terminating NULL character)

(b) a[2] = 'n'   b[5] = 'y'

(c) n = strlen(a) = 7   n = strlen(&b[2]) = 4

(d) A positive value since "memory" > "memorial"

(e) "memo"

(f) "dynaflow"

WRITTEN EXERCISES

11. The declaration includes integer and pointer objects. Parts (b) – (e) assume the as-sigment statements from part (a).

```
int x = 6, y, *px, *py;
```

(a) Write two assignment statements that set px and py to point at integers x and y respectively.

(b) Write an output statement using px that displays the contents of x.

(c) Write a statement using py that assigns 20 as the contents of y.

(d) What is the resulting value of *py + *px?

(e) Are the following values equal? Explain
  (i) x+3 and *px + 3   (ii) x+3 and *(px+3)

12. The following statement declares both an array and a pointer.

```
int arr[5] = {9, 2, -3, 5, -1}, *px;
```

(a) Write a statement that sets px to point at array arr.

(b) Write a cout statement using px that outputs the value −3 from the array.

(c) Write a statement that sets px to point at element arr[1]. After executing this statement,
  (i) what is the value of *(px+2)?
  (ii) what is the value of *px+2?

13. Trace the program and give the results of each output statement.

```
# include <iostream.h>
int main()
{
    char word[] = "level", *p=word;
    cout << *p;          // output 1: _____
    cout << *p-1;        // output 2: _____
    cout << *(p+2);      // output 3: _____
    p++;
    cout << *p;          // output 4: _____
    p++;
    cout << p;           // output 5: _____
    p = word;
    *(p+2) = NULL;
    cout << p;           // output 6: _____
    return 0;
}
```

14. What is the result of the following declarations?
(a) `long *p = new long(20);`
(b) `long *p = new long[25];`
(c) Give the delete statements that would deallocate the dynamic memory for parts (a) and (b)

15. Function f() is a member of class DemoCL. Four different implementations of f() include the "this" pointer. Use the different implementations to answer the questions (a) to (c). The declaration for class demoCL is used for each part.

```
class DemoCL
{
    private:
        int data;
    public:
        DemoCL (int d);    // d initializes the data member

        DemoCL f();        // return a DemoCL object
};
```

```
Implementation 1:                Implementation 2:
   DemoCL DemoCL::f()               DemoCL DemoCL::f()
   {                               {
       DemoCL tmp = this;              this->data *= 2;
       tmp.data *=2;                   return *this;
       return tmp;                 }
   }
```

```
Implementation 3:                Implementation 4:
   DemoCL DemoCl::f()               DemoCL DemoCL::f()
   {                               {
       DemoCL tmp = *this;             DemoCL tmp = *this;
       tmp.data *= 2;                  tmp.data *= 2;
       return tmp;                     return *tmp;
   }                               }
```

(a) Identify the implementation for f() that contain syntax errors. Describe the errors.
(b) Identify the implementation for f() that takes the data value of the current object and creates a new object whose data value is twice the original. The function returns the new object.
(c) Identify the implementation for f() that doubles the data value of the current object and returns the current object.

16. Class Dynamic has data members fixedData and ptrData which is a pointer. The constructor takes two integers m and n as arguments. After allocating a dynamic integer pointed to by ptrData, the constructor assigns m to fixedData and n as the contents of the dynamic data. The default value for each arguments is 0. The member function writeDynamic() outputs the values of the data members. For example,

```
Dynamic a(1,3), b;
a.writeDynamic();        // Output:  1   3
b.writeDynamic();        // Output:  0   0
```

```
DECLARATION: Dynamic CLASS ■■■■■■■■■■■■■■■■■■■■■■■■
class Dynamic
{
    private:
      // data members
      int fixedData;        // fixed integer
      int *ptrData;         // pointer to integer
    public:
      // constructor initializes data members
      Dynamic(int m = 0, int n = 0);

      // copy constructor
      Dynamic(const Dynamic& obj);

      // destructor
      ~Dynamic();

      // overloaded assignment operator
       Dynamic& operator= (const Dynamic& rhs);

      // output value of data members
      void writeDynamic();
};
```

(a) Implement the constructor.
(b) Implement a destructor for the class.
(c) Implement the copy constructor.
(d) Assume f() is a free function that takes a Dynamic object as an argument
    and has a Dynamic object as its return value. The function is called in the main
    program.

```
Dynamic f(Dynamic obj)
{  obj = Dynamic(6,8);
   obj.writeDynamic();       // Output 1
   return obj;
}

int main()
{  Dynamic a(1,3), b;
   b = f(a);
   a.writeDynamic();         // Output 2

   return 0;
}
```

(i) What are the values for output 1 and 2.
(ii) Assume Dynamic class does not have a copy constructor. What would be
     the values for the two outputs? Explain.

(iii) Assume Dynamic class does not have an overloaded assignment operator. What would be the values for the two outputs? Explain.

(e) The following statement initializes array arr. In terms of a constructor and a copy constructor, explain how array arr gets its initial values.

```
Dynamic   t[3] = { Dynamic(4,5), Dynamic(-1,4),
                   Dynamic(0,6)};
```

17. The function createArray() has the task of creating a dynamic array whose elements are assigned an initial value. Both size and initValue are passed as arguments and a pointer to the dynamic array is the return value. Implememt the function.

```
double *createArray(int size, double initValue);
```

18. A template version of the swap function can be declared using reference arguments. The same function can also be declared using pointers.

```
Reference Form:       template <class T>
                      void swap(T& a, T& b);
Pointer Form:         template <class T>
                      void swap(T* a, T* b);
```

(a) Implement the pointer version of the swap() function.
(b) Implement a version of swap() that works for C++ strings. HINT: you must use strcpy().

```
void swap (char *a, char *b);    // exchange the strings
```

19. (a) Declare a Vector object v that stores 20 elements of type integer.
(b) Declare a Vector object v that stores the elements in the array.

```
int arr[6] = {9,2,7,1,3,12};
```

20. The function reverseVector() takes a Vector object as an argument and reverses the order of its elements. Implement the function.

```
template <class T>
void reverseVector(Vector& v);
```

21. The function removeDup() takes a Vector object as an argument and removes all duplicate elements. For instance, with integers

```
Initial Vector v:   1  7  2  7  9  1  2  8  9
Revised Vector v:   1  7  2  9  8
```

Implement the function.

```
template <class T>
void removeDup(Vector& v);
```

22. Use the array-based function selectionSort() to implement the function sortVector() that takes a Vector object and rearranges the elements in ascending order.

```
template <class T>
void sortVector(Vector& v);
```

23. C++ strings store characters in an array with a terminating NULL character. Some languages store strings in byte-count format that places the string length in the first byte (char) followed by the actual characters. Consider the string "Hello" and the two formats that both require six elements to store the characters.

C++ String Format: Byte-Count Format

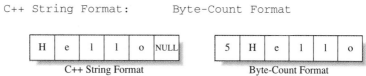

C++ String Format   Byte-Count Format

(a) Implement the function ctob() that converts a C++ string to the equivalent byte-count string.

```
void ctob(char *str);
```

(b) Implement the function btoc() that reverses the process and converts a byte-count string to a C++ string.

```
void btoc(char *str);
```

24. C++ string functions strcpy and strcmp have alternative versions that include a count argument.

```
char* strncpy(char *s1, char *s2, int n);
int   strncmp(char *s1, char *s2, int n);
```

Function strncpy() copies characters from s2 to s1 until either it has copied n characters or it reaches a NULL character in s2. Function strncmp() compares the string s1 to string s2 up to a limit of n characters. It does not compare any characters that follow a NULL character. The return strategy for strcmp is used. Assume

```
char s1[] = "abcd1234", s2[] = "xyz", s3[] = "xyQ";
```

(a) ```strncpy(s1,s2,2);```   // s1 is _____
    ```strncpy(s1,s2,5);```   // s1 is _____
(b) ```n = strncmp(s2,s3,2);```   // n is negative, zero, positive
    ```n = strncmp(s3,s1,5);```   // n is negative, zero, positive

25. Class Demo contains an integer and a string as data members. Three different versions of the class are created by using different formats for the string. For each format, declare and then implement the constructor. Use each constructor to declare the Demo object d:

```
Demo  d(10, "cat");

class Demo
{
   private:
      int item;
      <type> name;
   public
      Demo(. . .);
};
```

(a) <type> is a character array: char name[32];
(b) <type> is a character pointer: char *name;
(c) <type> is a String: String name;

PROGRAMMING EXERCISES

26. Write a program that prompts for the number of rooms in a house. Use the input numRooms to dynamically declare an array of Rectangles. In a loop, input the dimensions for the rooms and then output the total area of the house. Scan the array to identify the room with the largest perimeter and output its dimensions.

27. Written exercise 10.18 discusses a pointer version of the template function swap() and a C++ string version of the function. Use the function in a program that declares integer, real, and C++ string objects. After calling swap(), output the modified values for the objects.

```
int     m = 35, n = 20;
double x = -3.4, y = 100.54;
char strA[32] = "hot", strB[32] = "cold";
```

28. Use the Dynamic class from written exercise 10.16. Declare the class and implement its member functions in file *dynex.h*. Use the class in a program that includes function f().

```
Dynamic f(Dynamic obj)
{   obj = Dynamic(6,8);
    obj.writeDynamic();
    return obj;
}

int main()
{   Dynamic a(1,3), b;
    b = f(a);
    a.writeDynamic();

    return 0;
}
```

29. The function reverseVector() is defined in Written exercise 10.20. In a program declare a Vector v using the integer array list.

```
int list[10] = {9, 12, 6, 24, 16, 8, 3, 19, 11, 4};
```

Use reverseVector() to reverse the order of the elements. Output the elements in the modified vector.

30. Use the function removeDup() for Written Exercise 10.21 to take Vector v and remove all duplicate elements. In the program, declare v using the integer array arr and then output the resulting vector elements after calling removeDup().

```
int arr[] = {1, 7, 2, 7, 9, 1, 2, 8, 9};
```

31. Write a program that stores a list of 15 random integers in the range 0 to 99. Use the function sortVector() from Written Exercise 10.20 to order the elements in the vector and then output their values.

32. Byte-count and C++ string formats are discussed in Written Exercise 10.23. Use the functions ctob() and btoc() to convert between the two formats. Begin by defining a function printBString() that takes a string in byte-count format and outputs the characters.

```
void printBString(char *s);
```

Enter and run the following program.

```
#include <iostream.h>

< declarations of ctob{}, btoc{} and printBString{} >

int main()
{
    char str[] = "C++ and Byte-Count Strings";

    ctob(str);
    cout << "Byte-Count: ";
    printBString(str);
    cout << endl;
    cout << "C++ Format: ";
    btoc(str);
    cout << str << endl;

    return 0;
)

< implementations of ctob(), btoc() and printBString() >
```

PROGRAMMING PROJECTS

33. A *queue* is a list that stores items in their order of arrival. Only two update operations pushRear() and popFront() are allowed. On arrival, a new entry goes to the rear of the list using pushRear(). An item exits a queue from the front using popFront().

```
template <class T>
class Queue
{
    private:
        Vector<T>  queueList; // holds queue elements
    public:
        // constructor
        Queue();

        // add item to the rear of the queue
```

```
    void pushRear(const T& item);

    // remove the first element in the list
    T popFront();

    // return a boolean value indicating if queue empty
    bool empty();

    // clear the queue
    void clear();
};
```

(a) Implement the queue class in the file *myqueue.h.*
(b) Test your work with the following main program

```
#include <iostream.h>

#include "myqueue.h"

// print the Queue q
template <class T>

int main()
{
    Queue<int> posQueue, negQueue;
    int i, item;

    for (i = 0; i < 7; i++)
    {
        cin >> item;
        if (item < 0)
            negQueue.pushRear(item);
        else
            posQueue.pushRear(item);
    }

    cout << "Positive values: ";
    printQueue(posQueue);

    cout << "Negative values: ";
    printQueue(negQueue);

    return 0;
}

template <class T>
void printQueue(Queue<T> q)
{
```

```
    while (!q.empty())
        cout << q.popFront() << "  ";
    cout << endl;
}
```

```
On run 1, input:  9  -4  7  2  -3  -7  4
On run 2, input: 12  80 67 22  19  44 30
```

Chapter 11
The List Class and Linked Lists

CHAPTER CONTENTS

11-1 THE LIST CONTAINER

Creating List Objects
Accessing List Elements
General List Insert and Erase
Operations
Application: Removing Duplicates

11-2 LINKED LISTS

Describing a Linked List
Computer Representation of a
Linked List
The Node Class
Building a Linked List

11-3 BUILDING LINKED LISTS WITH NODES

Creating a Node
Inserting at the Front of a List
Deleting at the Front of a List
Inserting a Node at the Rear of
a List
Clearing a List
Removing a Target Node

11-4 IMPLEMENTING THE LIST CLASS

UML Representation for the List
Class
List Class Private Members
List Iterators
Selected Member Functions
General List Insertion Function

Written Exercises

In Chapter 10, we define the Vector class as a template-based storage structure that uses indices to access its elements. A Vector is an example of a *container* that stores data and provides operations to access and update the data. A course in data structures studies general containers that store and access data in different way. Such a study lies beyond the scope of this book. We choose to focus on a basic storage structure called a sequential list. In Section 11.1, we define this structure and describe its implementation with the List class. As part of the discussion, we develop the concept of an iterator, which is a generalized pointer that facilitates access to the data in the sequential list.

Linked lists are a basic implementation structure for a sequential list container. A linked list is a storage structure that allows for efficient insertion and removal of data. A programmer must master the creation and maintenance of a linked list as a basic "tool of the trade". In sections 11.2 and 11.3, we develop linked lists whose components are Node objects and develop fundamental algorithms for handling such lists.

We conclude the chapter by using linked list to implement the List class. This is an optional section that includes advanced C++ concepts.

11-1 THE LIST CONTAINER

Containers hold data of the same type, but differ in how they access the data. A *sequential list container* stores elements that are ordered by position. There is a first element, a second element, and so forth.

1st item   2nd item   3rd item   · · ·   nth item

A sequential list holds an arbitrary number of elements. The first element occurs at the front of the list and the last element at the rear of the list. Each element except the last element has a unique successor in the next position. Any item can be accessed by starting at the front of the list and moving forward from item to item to the rear of the list

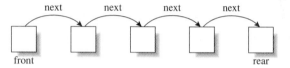

You are familiar with sequential lists in your every day experience. For instance, the bases on a baseball diamond are a sequential list starting at first base and then continuing to second base, third base, and home. Before going to a grocery store, you often create a list of needed items.

In order to design a C++ representation for a sequential list, we declare the List class that features operations to insert and remove items and update values. We develop the class in two phases. The initial phase declares the class attributes and general list management functions. It also declares insert and erase operations that deal only with elements at the extreme ends of the list. This includes the functions insertFront() and eraseFront() that update the first element in the list. To access the value of the first element, the class has the member function front(). Also included in the class is the function insertRear() that adds an element at the end of the list. General insertion and deletion functions that enable us to add or remove an element from any position in the list are discussed in the second phase when we introduce List iterators.

The following is a partial description of the template-based List class. The description of the restricted insertion and deletion member functions are accompanied by an example.

Look at the List member functions carefully so that you can use them in applications. Typical of object technology, you do not have to know or worry about any of the implementation details of the class.

DESCRIPTION: List CLASS (PARTIAL) ▬▬▬▬▬▬

A template-based List object represents a sequential list with elements of type T. For the examples, assume an integer list.

list.h

Attributes:
  A collection of items of the same data type T.
  Objects front and rear that identify the ends of the list.
  The number of elements in the list (listSize).
Operations:
  List: The constructor that
                   builds an empty list.   List<int> intList;
                     List();

  insertFront: Insert item at the front
                   of the list.   intList.insertFront(2);   ⌷ 2 ⌷
                     void insertFront   front rear
                     (const T& item);

  insertRear: Insert item at the rear
                   of the list.   intList.insertRear(5);   ⌷ 2 ⌷   ⌷ 5 ⌷
                     void insertRear   front   rear
                     (const T& item);

  eraseFront: Remove the item at
                   the front of the list.   intList.eraseFront();   ⌷ 5 ⌷
                     void eraseFront();   front rear

  size: Return the number of elements in the list.
                     int size() const;

  empty: Returns true if the list is empty and false if the list contains at least
                   one element.
                     bool empty() const;

  front: Returns the element at the front of the list.
                     T front() const;

  clear: Removes all the list elements.
                     void clear();

Creating List Objects

The type of each data element in a List object is specified using the template notation <T>. The constructor creates an empty list.

```
List<int>    intList;         // list of integers
List<String> name;            // list of String objects
List<StudentAccount> sa;      // list of StudentAccount objects
```

Elements are added by using the member functions insertFront() and in-
sertRear(). At any time, the program may inquire about the current state of the
list using the functions size() and empty(). For instance,

```
intList.insertFront(5);
```

```
intList.insertFront(20);
intList.insertRear(10);      //
```

```
bool listEmpty = intList.empty()    // false since list size =3
cout << intList.size();             // output: 3
```

Items are removed from a list with the functions eraseFront() and clear(). The clear() operation removes all elements and sets the list size to 0.

```
intList.eraseFront();    //
```

```
intList.clear();         // clear the list. list size = 0
```

EXAMPLE 11.1

The object name is a list of strings.

```
List<String> name;
```

1. ```
   name.insertFront("Thomas");
   name.insertFront("Lopez");
   name.insertFront("Schwartz");
   ```

   The resulting list is

                         Schwartz   Lopez   Thomas

   Note that a series of insertFront() operations add elements in reverse order.

2. ```
   name.insertRear("Thomas");
   name.insertRear ("Lopez");
   name.insertRear ("Schwartz");
   ```

   The resulting list is

                         Thomas   Lopez   Schwartz

APPLICATION 11-1 FINDING PALINDROMES

The program uses List operations to determine if each of two string is a palindrome (spells the same forward and backward). After reading the string using getline(), the program scans each character and copies the nonblank ones into separate List<char> objects listInOrder and listRevOrder. The copy to listInOrder uses insertRear() that maintains the same order as the string. The copy to listRevOrder uses insertFront() that reverses the order of the characters. To determine if the string is a palindrome, we compare the first elements in the two lists using front() and then delete them using eraseFront(). The process continues until the characters do not match (no palindrome) or until the lists become empty (palindrome).

The algorithm is applied to two strings. If the first string is not a palindrome (lists not empty), the contents of both lists are deleted using `clear()`.

```cpp
#include <iostream.h>

#include "tlist.h"        // include the List class
#include "tstring.h"

int main()
{
   // declare listInOrder to hold the original nonblank
   // characters and listRevOrder to hold the nonblank
   // characters in reverse order
   List<char> listInOrder, listRevOrder;
   String  str;
   int strCount, i;

   // consider two strings
   for (strCount = 0; strCount < 2; strCount++)
   {
      // input a string
      getline(cin,str,'\n');
      // put the nonblank characters into the two lists
      for (i = 0; i < str.length(); i++)
      {
         if (str[i] != ' ')
         {
            listInOrder.insertRear(str[i]);
            // inserting at front reverses the order
            listRevOrder.insertFront(str[i]);
         }
      }

      // compare and remove characters at the front of the
      // lists until two characters don't match or the lists
      // are exhausted
      while (!listInOrder.empty() &&
             listInOrder.front() == listRevOrder.front())
      {
         listInOrder.eraseFront();
         listRevOrder.eraseFront();
      }

      // if the lists are empty, the string is a palindrome
      if (listInOrder.empty())
         cout << "   This is a palindrome" << endl;
      else
```

```
        {
            cout << "   This is not a palindrome" << endl;
            // clear lists in preparation for the next string
            listInOrder.clear();
            listRevOrder.clear();
        }
    }

    return 0;
}
```

Run:

```
a man a plan a canal panama
    This is a palindrome
walk in the park
    This is not a palindrome
```

Determine the output of this code sequence.

```
List<int> intList;
int n, i;
for(i=6; i >= 1; i--)
{
    intList.insertFront(i);
    intList.insertRear(i+1);
}

n = intList.size() - 2;
for (i=0; i < n; i++)
{
    cout << intList.front() << "   ";
    intList.eraseFront();
}
cout << endl;
if (intList.empty() == false)
    intList.clear();
cout << intList.size() << endl;
```

Exploring Concepts

Accessing List Elements

In our initial description of the List class, we provide member functions that can access elements only at the ends of the list. For general applications, a List object must be able to add or remove elements at any position. It must also have a mechanism to identify the beginning of the list, to move through the list element by element and to update values where appropriate. In order to provide this mechanism, the List class defines an object called a *list iterator*.

> **Definition** A list iterator is an object whose job it is to access the data elements of a List object. It is essentially a pointer (arrow) that is set to the element at the beginning of the list and moves from item to item until the last data element is reached. During the scanning process, the iterator can be used to retrieve or update the value of an item.

List iterators are defined by the class called Iterator. The class is declared inside of the List class and is called a *nested class*. This is an organizational technique that links the Iterator class to the List class. The link is specified by using the List class with the class scope operator "::". The notation List <T>:: Iterator is used to refer to the Iterator nested class.

```
List<int>::Iterator iter;    // declares a list iterator
```

The member functions of the Iterator class include the operator "*" that accesses the value of the item that is pointed to by the iterator and "++" that moves the iterator to the next item in the list. The class also includes the operators == and != that allow a program to compare iterators. These operators are primarily used to determine the end of the list. The following is a description of the Iterator class.

DESCRIPTION: LIST ITERATOR ▬▬▬▬▬▬▬▬▬▬▬▬▬▬▬▬

A list iterator is an object that identifies elements in a List object.

Attributes:
  A pointer to a data value in a List object.

Operations:
  *:   Accesses the value of the item currently pointed to by the iterator

```
*iteratorPtr;
```

  ++:   Moves the iterator to the next item in the list.

```
iteratorPtr++;
```

  ==:   The equal operator takes two iterators as operands and returns true when they both point at the same item in the list.

```
iteratorPtr1 == iteratorPtr2
```

  !=:   The operator returns true when the two iterators do not point at the same item in the list.

```
itratorPtr1 != iteratorPtr2
```

To use an iterator, it must be given a value that points to the beginning of the list. In order to traverse a list, the iterator must know when it has reached the end of the list. These features are provided by the List class member functions begin() and end(). The functions return iterators that are set to the front of the list and just past the rear of the list respectively. The following is a description of these member functions.

list.h

The functions begin() and end() are members of the List class that are used to initialize iterator objects.

Operations:

begin: Return an iterator pointing at the first list element.

```
Iterator begin();
```

end: Return an iterator pointing immediately after the last list element.

```
Iterator end();
```

Examples of List Iterators. Assume inviteList is a List object that contains a sequence of names (Strings). To scan the list, we define an iterator p and initialize it to the first name in the list.

```
List<String> inviteList;   // list of strings for invitation names
List<String>::Iterator p; // iterator for a List<String> object
List object: inviteList
```

The while loop scans the elements to the end of the list and outputs the names.

```
   p = inviteList.begin();       // set p to point at "Tom"
while (p != inviteList.end())    // compare iterator with end of
                                 // list
{
   cout << *p << "  ";           // output name pointed to by p
   p++;                          // increment p to the next name
}

// The output is:  Tom  Sharon  Donna  Mike  Teri  Alex
```

In the while statement, the iterator p is a control object. It acts like a pointer while stepping through the list.

EXAMPLE 11.2

1. The function listAbs() replaces each element of an integer List by its absolute value. The iterator, iter, is used to traverse the elements. After being assigned an initial value with begin(), iter is used in a while loop that continues (iter++) as long as its value is not equal to end(). Each element in the list is accessed by *iter.

```
void listAbs(List<int>& aList)
{
    // declare and initialize iterator
    List<T>::Iterator iter = aList.begin();

    // from beginning to end, update each list element.
    while(iter != aList.end())
    {
        if (*iter < 0)
            *iter = -*iter;
        iter++;
    }
}
```

2. Using an iterator, the example scans a list of StudentAccount objects, looking for the student with ID = "59-2846". When found, the account is updated with a $150.00 payment.

```
// declare a StudentAccount list and list iterator
List<StudentAccount> studentList;
List<StudentAccount>::Iterator studListIter;

        . . .

// initialize the iterator to the start of the list
studListIter = studentList.begin();
while (studListIter != studentList.end())
{
    // test for a match
    if ( (*studListIter).getID() == "59-2846")
    {
        // credit a $150.00 payment and terminate loop
        (*studListIter).payment(150.0);
        break;
    }
    studListIter++;
}   ■
```

Programming Note

When an iterator is used with a constant List object, it must be declared to be of type Const_Iterator. The only difference between Iterator and Const_Iterator objects is that a Const_Iterator object cannot make modifications to list elements. For instance, a Const_Iterator object could not be used in Example 11.2 since both the integer list and the StudentAccount list are updated. The most common use for Const_Iterator is with functions having a constant reference argument. For instance, the function writeList() displays the values in a List object using a Const_Iterator object.

```
template <class T>
void writeList (const List<T>& aList)
{
    // list is constant. use a constant iterator
    List <T>::Const_Iterator iter;
```

```
// from beginning to end, output each element.
iter = aList.begin();
while (iter != aList.end())
{
    cout << *iter << " ";
    iter++;
}
cout << endl;
}
```

General List Insert and Erase Operations

With an understanding of list iterators, we are now in a position to describe the general insert and erase operations for the List class. The member functions add and remove an element at a position that is specified by an iterator.

DESCRIPTION: GENERAL INSERT AND ERASE ━━━━━

The operations insert and erase an item at a specified position and then update the iterator. Since the list is modified, a nonconstant iterator must be used.

Operations:

insert: Insert data value, item, at the location specified by the Iterator object, pos. After insertion, pos is updated to refer to the new data value.

```
void insert (Iterator& pos, const T& item);
```

erase: Erase from the list the data value at the location specified by Iterator object, pos. Update pos to refer to the data value to the right of the erased item. If the erased item is the rear of the list lst, pos has value aList.end().

```
void erase(Iterator& pos);
```

list.h

Figure 11-1 gives a before and after view of the list when integer 4 is added at the position specified by the iterator iter. Initially *iter = 7. The insertion

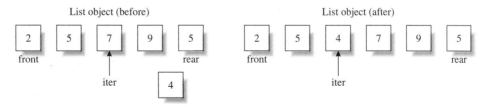

FIGURE 11-1
Insert 4 into a List.

places the new element in the list and positions the iterator at the new element (*iter = 4).

For the erase operation, an item is removed from the list at the current iterator position. After the removal, the iterator is repositioned to the next element in the list. Figure 11.2 gives a before and after view illustrating removal of 7 from the integer list.

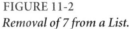

FIGURE 11-2
Removal of 7 from a List.

EXAMPLE 11.3

1. The function, `doubleData()`, takes a list and modifies it to repeat every element. For instance, the integer list 2, 3, 7, 5 becomes 2, 2, 3, 3, 7, 7, 5, 5.

```
template <class T>
void doubleData(List<T>& aList)
{
   List<T>::Iterator p = aList.begin();

   while (p != aList.end())
   {
      // insert current list value at current position
      aList.insert(p,*p);
      p++;                // move forward to the original value
      p++;                // move to the next data value
   }
}
```

2. The function `removeOdd()` erases all odd numbers from an integer list.

```
void removeOdd(List<int>& intList)
{
   List<int>::Iterator intIter = intList.begin();

   while (intIter != intList.end())
      if (*intIter % 2 == 1)
         intList.erase(intIter); // positioned at next integer
      else
         intIter++;                // advance to next integer
}
```

1. After executing the following statements, what is the resulting sequential list?

```
List<char> L;
List<char>::Iterator i;

L.insertFront('t');
L.insertFront('a');
i = L.begin();
i++;
L.insert(i,'m');
L.insert(i,'x');
```

Exploring
Concepts

2. Assume an 11 element list L contains the characters in the string "mathematics." What is the sequence of characters after executing the instructions?

```
List<char> L;
List<char>::Iterator i;

i = L.begin();
i++;
L.erase(i);
i++;
L.erase(i);
L.eraseFront();
```

Application: Removing Duplicates

An algorithm to remove duplicates in a list provides an interesting application of List iterators. After creating a list called aList, begin a scan of the elements. Position an iterator at a list element and record its data value. This provides a target to begin looking for duplicates in the remainder of the list. From this position, scan the tail of the list using a second iterator, erasing all elements whose data values matches the target. Move the original iterator forward and continue the process until reaching the end of the list. For instance, assume the primary iterator is called curr and is positioned at target value 5. A second iterator, p, scans the remaining portion of the list and removes all elements with value 5.

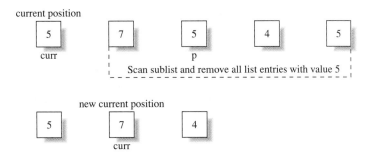

The program implements the algorithm in the template function removeDu-plicates(). An initial list has 15 random integer values in the range 1 to 7. After displaying the list, a call is made to the function. The resulting list with duplicates removed is output using the template function writeList().

```
#include <iostream.h>

#include "list.h"        // include the list class
#include "trandom.h"     // generate random integers

// output list aList
template <class T>
void writeList(const List<T>& L);

// remove all duplicate values from aList. assumes that
// the operator "==" is defined for type T
template <class T>
void removeDuplicates(List<T>& aList);

int main()
{
   List<int> aList;
   int i;
   RandomNumber rnd;

   // insert 15 random integers in range 1-7 and output list
   for(i=0; i < 15; i++)
      aList.insertRear(1+rnd.random(7));
   cout << "Original list: ";
   writeList(aList);
   cout << endl;

   // remove all duplicate data values and output new list
   removeDuplicates(aList);
   cout << "Final list:    ";
   writeList(aList);
   cout << endl;
}

/* definition of writeList() given in the programming note on
page 662 */

template <class T>
void removeDuplicates(List<T>& aList)
{
   // current data value
   T currValue;
   // use two List iterators
```

```
List<T>::Iterator curr, p;

// start at the front of the list
curr = aList.begin();

// cycle through the list
while(curr != aList.end())
{
    // record the current list data value
    currValue = *curr;

    // set p one element to the right of curr
    p = curr;
    p++;

    // move forward until end of list, removing
    // all occurrences of currValue
    while(p != aList.end())
        if (*p == currValue)
            aList.erase(p); // Erase element at p.
        else
            p++;                // move to the next node

    // duplicates of currValue removed. move to the next
    // data value and repeat the process
    curr++;
}
return 0;
}
```

```
Run:

Original list: 5  2  3  1  7  1  4  5  3  2  6  1  2  2
2

Final list:    5  2  3  1  7  4  6
```

11-2 LINKED LISTS

In Section 11.1, we have made extensive use of the List class without any reference to its implementation. Using only the class description, we have been able to develop a range of applications. We have delayed any discussion of implementation since we have lacked the necessary tools to efficiently build the List class.

At this point, the only stuctures we have available to store list elements are C++ arrays and vectors. Of the two, a vector would be more appropriate, since it can be resized to accommodate an arbitrarity large list. Unfortunately, a vector is not appropriate for a List object that may involve a large number of insertions and deletions. To see this, consider the problem of maintaining an integer list. Assume a 7-element integer Vector object holds the values 2, 7, 3, and 10 (Figure 11-3).

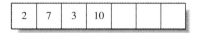

FIGURE 11-3
Integer List.

When an insertion is done, the tail of the list must be shifted to the right to accommodate the new data. For instance, to insert value 5 as the third item, the elements 3 and 10 must be moved.

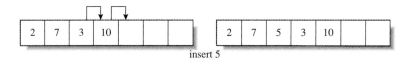

insert 5

Removing an element necessitates shifting the tail of the list to the left. For instance, deleting the first element, 2, requires moving all of the remaining in the list.

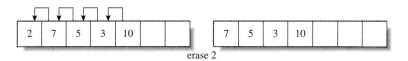

erase 2

A vector-based implementation of a list is too inefficient since insertions and deletions require significant overhead. For a large list, most of the computing time would be dedicated to list reorganization. As the list grows, additional space must be added by using the Vector `resize()` function, that necessitates copying the existing list elements to new memory. As the list decreases in size, either space is wasted or `resize()` is used to reduce the size of the list. This operation also involves copying existing list elements.

Describing a Linked List

The problem with a vector implementation of a list is the fact that the structure stores elements in consecutive memory locations. A better implementation model stores data as independent units that are linked together without being necessarily adjacent in memory. The design of the model treats items in a list as pieces in a pop chain.

The chain can increase without limit by merely adding new pieces. The process involves breaking a connection and reconnecting the chain at both ends of the new piece.

Disconnect   Reconnect

A piece is removed from the chain by breaking its two connections, removing the piece, and then reconnecting the chain.

Disconnect   Reconnect

To use the pop chain as a model for a linear storage structure, we need to view each piece in the chain as an object containing data and a link to the next member. This linear structure, which is called a *linked list,* overcomes many of the limitations we noted with vectors. Our task is to develop a computer implementation for the structure by creating a class whose member functions allow us to connect pieces together into a chain.

Computer Representation of a Linked List

The starting point for a computer representation of a linked list is a *node* that consists of a data value and a pointer to the next node in the list. The pointer is the connection that ties together the individual nodes of the list.

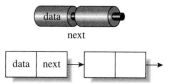

data	next

> **Definition** A linked list consists of a series of nodes whose first element is identified by a pointer called *front.* The nodes are linked together from the first node to successive nodes that end with the last or rear node. The pointer in the last node has value NULL = 0 (the NULL pointer). In a linked list, the symbol ⏚ represents the NULL pointer.

The following chain of nodes is the linked list representation of the integer list 7, 5, 3, and 10.

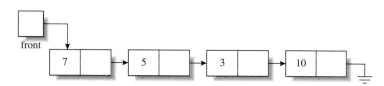

A linked list is a sequential structure. The pointer front identifies the first node in the list. Each element except the last has a unique successor identified

by the next pointer. The last element of the list is identified when next is NULL.
An *empty list* occurs when the front pointer is NULL.

front

The Node Class

The Node class specifies the attributes and actions of one object in a linked list.
Its data members include nodeValue and a pointer to the next node. Before describing the actions of the member functions, we give a class declaration that includes inline code. The description of each class member function follows the declaration and contains a tutorial graphic that illustrates its action.

node.h

```
DECLARATION: Node CLASS

template <class T>
class Node
{
    private:
        T nodeValue;            // data held by the node
        Node<T> *next;          // next node in the list
    public:
        // constructors
        Node(const T& item, Node<T> *nextNode = NULL):
            nodeValue(item), next(nextNode)
        {}

        // access functions
        Node<T> *getNext()
        { return next; }

        T getValue()
        { return nodeValue; }

        // update functions

        // change the current value of the node
        void setValue(const T& item)
        { nodeValue = item; }

        // insert node pointed to by p after the current node
        void linkTo(Node<T> *p)
        {
            // set p to point at successor of current node
            p->next = next;
            // set current node to point at p
            next = p;
        }
```

```
        // unlink the node following the current node and
        // return a pointer to the unlinked node
        Node<T> *unlink()
        {
            // save the location of the next node
            Node<T> *nextNode = next;

            // if no successor, return NULL
            if (nextNode == NULL)
                    return NULL;

            // link current node to successor of the next node
            next = nextNode->next;
            // return the address of the unlinked node
            return nextNode;
        }
};
```

The value of the data member next is a pointer to a Node. The Node class is a *self-referencing* structure in which a pointer member refers to objects of its own type.

Constructor:

A node in a linked list is allocated dynamically and accessed using a pointer. To create a node, first declare a pointer to Node<T> and then use the operator new to allocate the node. The constructor has as arguments the data value of the node and the pointer that identifies the next node. The default value of this pointer is NULL. The following statements link together nodes containing integer values 20 and 10.

```
Node<int> *p, *q;          // declare Node pointer

p = new Node<int> (10);    // create p with value 10

q = new Node<int> (20,p);  // create q with link to p
```

Create p with NULL pointer   Create q with link to p

Data Access Functions:

The member functions getValue() and setValue() allow the retrieval and update of the data value. Assume p points to an integer node whose value is 8.

```
int n = p->getValue();    // n is 8. see part (a)

p->setValue(5);           // change node data value to 5.
                          // see part (b)
```

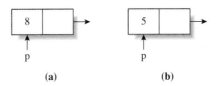

(a)   (b)

Pointer Access Function:

To allow moving from one node to the next in a linked list, the Node class provides the function getNext() that returns the pointer to the following node.

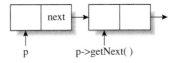

With `getNext()` and `getValue()`, a while loop can scan a linked list and output its data values. The algorithm is written as a template function with the front of the list passed as a argument. The function is available for use in programs by including the header file **nodelib.h**.

```
template <class T>
void writeList(Node<T> *front)
{
    // front points at first node.  curr moves through the list
    Node<T> *curr;

    curr = front;            // set curr to front of the list
    while (curr != NULL)     // continue until end of list
    {
        // output node value and move to the next node
        cout << curr->getValue() << "   ";
        curr = curr->getNext();
    }
}
```

front

50 | next   20 | next   40 | next

curr   curr = curr->getNext()   curr = NULL

Insert After Current Node:

The Node class provides a member function, `linkTo()`, that inserts a new node into a linked list after the current node. The process involves breaking the link to the next node and resetting links to add the new node. Assume curr is pointing at the current node and p is pointing at the new node. Initially, the data member next for the current node identifies the next node in the list. The new node pointed to by p is isolated from the list (Figure 11-4(a)). In order to connect node p to the list, the value of next and p->next must be modified. Node p must link to the next node and the current node must connect to p. The connections are made in two steps (Figure 11-4(b)).

```
p->next = next;    // step 1
next = p;          // step 2
```

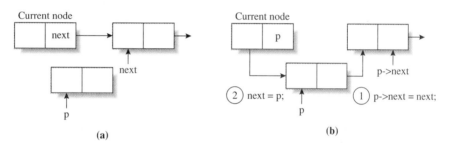

(a)   **(b)**

FIGURE 11-4
Inserting a New Node.

Unlinking the Next Node:

The process of removing the next node involves breaking the links to the node and reconnecting the current node so it points to the successor of the unlinked node. Once the node is unlinked from the list, its address is returned to the calling statement so that it can be reused or deleted. The unlinking process is done by the function unlink() in two steps; first, save the address of the node that will be unlinked and connect the current node to its successor (Figure 11-5).

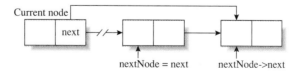

FIGURE 11-5
Unlinking a Node.

```
Node<T> *nextNode = next;    // node to unlink

next = nextNode->next;       // reconnect current node
return nextNode;             // return address of unlinked node
```

If nest is NULL, the node is the last one in the list. In this situation, return NULL as the value of the function.

Building a Linked List

The Node class, with its member functions, provides the tools to build a linked list. To illustrate these tools, we give a sequence of six statements that will ultimately produce the following linked list.

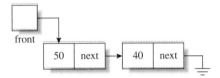

The example is designed to illustrate each of the member functions in the Node class. Some of the effort is redundant, since nodes are added and later deleted. In one case, a data value is modified after the node is in the list. In the next section, we illustrate more structured techniques for building linked lists.

```
Node<int> *front, *p, *curr; // pointers to nodes in our list
```

1. Create an empty list. Figure 11-6(a)
   ```
   front = NULL;
   ```
2. Create node with nodeValue = 20, next = NULL (Figure 11-6(b)). Add the first node by assigning its address to front
   ```
   front = new Node<int>(20);
   ```
3. Insert node p at the rear of the list with nodeValue = 60. (Figure 11-6(c))
   ```
   p = new Node<int>(60);
   curr = front;
   curr->linkTo(p);
   ```
4. Insert new node with nodeValue = 50 at front (Figure 11-6(d)). Pass front as the pointer argument for the constructor
   ```
   curr = new Node<int>(50, front);
   front = curr;
   ```
5. Unlink successor of the front node. (Figure 11-6(e))
   ```
   curr->unlink();
   ```
6. Update value of node p to 40 (Figure 11-6(f))
   ```
   p->setValue(40);
   ```

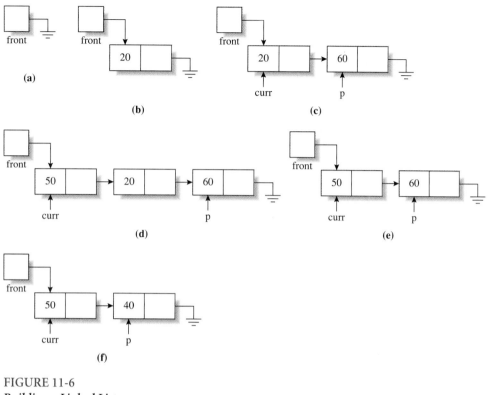

FIGURE 11-6
Building a Linked List.

11-3   BUILDING LINKED LISTS WITH NODES

The previous section illustrates how you can use member functions to hook together nodes that create a linked list much like you might build a jigsaw puzzle.
For applications, this approach is impractical since nodes are added and deleted
using a strategy. For instance, if the list is ordered, new nodes must be added at
the appropriate place to maintain the order. While there are many list handling
situations that may occur, the problem solving strategies often reduce to a relatively small number of algorithms. In this section, we select a series of insertion
and deletion strategies that illustrate key ideas in linked list handling. The algorithms are also used in the implementation of the List class in Section 11.4.

All of the algorithms are translated into free functions are placed in the
header file **nodelib.h.**

Creating a Node

We create a node using the function getNode(), which takes an initial data value and a pointer value and dynamically allocates a new node. By default, the pointer value is NULL. If the memory allocation fails, the program terminates after an error message; otherwise, the function returns a pointer to the new node.

```
// allocate a node with value item and pointer nextPtr
template <class T>
Node<T> *getNode(const T& item, Node<T> *nextPtr = NULL)
{
   Node<T> *newNode = new Node<T> (item, nextPtr);

   // did allocation succeed?
   if (newNode == NULL)
   {
      cerr << "Memory allocation failure" << endl;
      exit(1);
   }

   return newNode;
}
```

Inserting at the Front of a List

Inserting a node at the front of the list requires updating the pointer front since there is a new first node in the list. The problem of maintaining the front of the list is fundamental to list management. If you lose the front, you lose the list!

Assume that newNode is the address of a node to be added to the front of a list. Before updating the pointer front, the new node must point to the original first (front) node in the list. This link is established by creating a new node with the current value of front as the pointer argument. The operation concludes by updating front.

```
newNode = new Node<T>(item, front);
front = newNode;       // update front to point at new node
```

The figures illustrate the algorithm when inserting into a nonempty and an empty list.

Insert at the front of a nonempty list

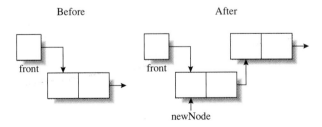

Insert at the front of an empty list

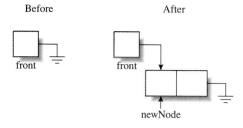

The function `insertFront()` implements the algorithm. For arguments, it has a pointer front and the data item for the new front node. The data is passed as a constant reference argument. Since front is always modified by the operation, it is passed as a reference argument. Read the notation "Node<T> * & front" as "front is a reference to a Node<T> pointer." Using this technique, the function can modify the run-time pointer to the front of the list.

```
// insert a node with value item at the front of the list
template <class T>
void insertFront(Node<T> * & front, const T& item)
{
    // allocate the new node
    Node<T> *newNode = getNode(item, front);

    // update front to point at the new first node in the list
    front = newNode;
}
```

Deleting at the Front of a List

Like an insertion, removing the first node involves updating front. If the list is empty, the operation returns without taking action. For a nonempty list, the new front becomes the value of front->getNext(), which is either NULL for a 1-element list or the address of the second node for a longer list.

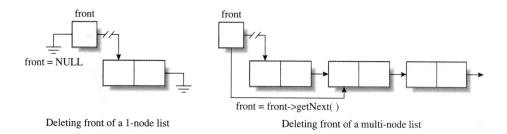

Deleting front of a 1-node list   Deleting front of a multi-node list

The function `eraseFront()` has a pointer front as a reference argument. After the front is removed, the operator delete is called to deallocate its memory.

```
                    // remove the front node of a list
                    template <class T>
                    void eraseFront(Node<T> * & front)
                    {
                        Node<T> *p = front;     // p set to original front pointer

                        if (front != NULL)
                        {
                            // move front to successor node and delete original
                            front = front->getNext();
                            delete p;
                        }
                    }
```

Inserting a Node at the Rear of a List

Inserting a node at the rear of a linked list is an interesting problem in list management. The algorithm must perform an initial test to determine if the list is empty. If so, the operation is implemented by assigning the address of the new node to front. For a non-empty list, we must scan the nodes in the list using the pointer curr to locate the rear node. The rear of the list is identified by curr->getNext() == NULL. The insertion is done by using linkTo() that adds the new node after the current rear of the list. In the figure, part (a) illustrates insertion into an empty list, while part (b) demonstrates insertion into a nonempty list.

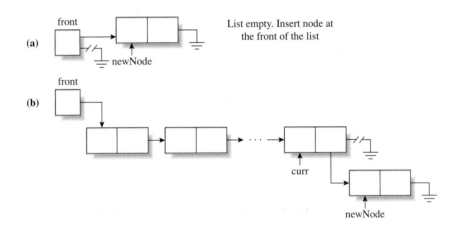

The function insertRear() takes front as a reference argument since its value is changed when the list is empty. The data value is passed as a constant reference argument.

```
                    // insert item at the rear of the list
                    template <class T>
                    void insertRear(Node<T>* & front, const T& item)
                    {
```

```
// new node to insert and the traversal pointer
Node<T>  *newNode = getNode(item), *curr;

// if list is empty, insert item at the front of the list
if (front == NULL)
    front = newNode;
else
{
    // move to the last node in the list
    curr = front;
    while (curr->getNext() != NULL)
        curr = curr->getNext();
    // link newNode after curr.  it becomes the rear
    curr->linkTo(newNode);
}
}
```

Clearing a List

When a program no longer needs a list, the memory occupied by the nodes should be deallocated. An algorithm that clears a list uses eraseFront() to remove the first node in the list. The process is repeated until front = NULL. The implementation is provided by the function clear().

```
//remove each node in list; set front to NULL
template <class T>
void clear(Node<T>* & front)
{
    // repeatedly remove the first node in the list
    while(front != NULL)
        eraseFront(front);
}
```

APPLICATION 11-3 WORD-JUMBLE

In a loop with four iterations, the program inputs a word into the String object called word. In each case, the letters are mixed to create a word-jumble puzzle. Both the original word and the jumbled characters are printed in the format.

Word/Jumbled Word: <original word>   <jumbled characters>

Each successive character word[0] to word[word.length()-1] is inserted at the front or rear of the linked list, jumbleWord, depending on the value of a random integer with value 0 or 1. If the value is 0, the character is inserted at the front of the list (insertFront()); otherwise, it is inserted at the rear (insertRear()). For instance, with input "tank", the random sequence 1 0 0 1 creates the jumbled list of characters n - a - t - k ("natk"). After the jumbled characters for a word are output using writeList(), clear () is called to discard the nodes and create an empty list in preparation for input of the next word.

Note that it is critical for the pointer jumbleWord to have the initial value NULL. In this way, the list is empty prior to the first list operation.

```
#include <iostream.h>

#include "tstring.h"    // use a String object
#include "node.h"       // use the Node class
#include "nodelib.h"    // basic linked list algorithms
#include "random.h"     // use random integers

int main()
{
   // list to hold jumbled characters
   Node<char> *jumbleword = NULL;

   // input string, random number generator and for loop
   // control objects
   String  word;
   RandomNumber rnd;
   int i, j;

   // input four words
   for (i = 0; i < 4; i++)
   {
      cin >> word;
      // use rnd.random(2) to insert char
      // at the front (value = 0) or rear (value = 1) of list
      for (j = 0; j < word.length(); j++)
         if (rnd.random(2) == 1)
            insertRear(jumbleword, word[j]);
         else
            insertFront(jumbleword, word[j]);

      // output the word and its jumbled variation
      cout << "Word/Jumbled Word: " << word << "    ";
      writeList(jumbleword);
      cout << endl << endl;

      // clear the list in preparation for the next word
      clear (jumbleword);
   }

   return 0;
}
```

```
Run:

apple
Word/Jumbled Word: apple   e  l  p  a  p

C++
```

```
Word/Jumbled Word: C++   +   C   +

list
Word/Jumbled Word: list   s   l   i   t

node
Word/Jumbled Word: node   e   d   o   n
```

Removing a Target Node

Up to this point the node insertion and deletion algorithms have focused on the extreme ends of the list. When the operations extend to an intermediate node, a new approach must be used. Consider the problem of locating and deleting a node with a specified target value. We will see that a list scan must identify the address of both the target node and its predecessor.

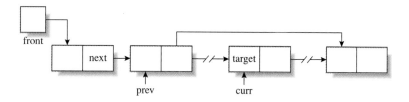

A pointer, called curr, is initially set to the front of the list and is used to scan each successive node until the target is found or curr reaches the end of the list (curr == NULL). A second pointer, called prev, identifies the node just before curr. During the scan of the list, the two pointers curr and prev move in tandem.

```
prev = curr;              // update prev to next position (curr)
curr = curr->getNext();   // move curr to the next node
```

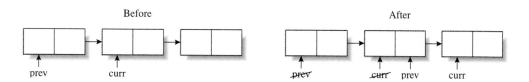

To find the target value, initially set curr to front and prev to NULL since there is no node prior to the first node in the list. The pair curr and prev move through the list looking for the first occurrence of the target. At a match, curr points at the node that must be removed and prev identifies the prior node. There are two possible situations that are determined by the value of prev (Figure 11-7(a) and (b)

The function `eraseValue()` takes the front pointer and a target value as arguments and searches the linked list looking for the first occurrence of the

(a) prev is NULL, and curr is front: remove the first node
from the list by using eraseFront( )

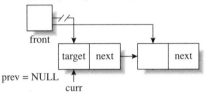

(b) prev is not NULL, and curr is an intermediate node:
remove node at curr using prev->unlink( )

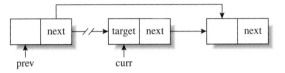

FIGURE 11-7
*Position of Pointers when Deleting a Node from a
Linked List.*

value If a match occurs, the node is removed and the return value is true. Otherwise, no action occurs and the return value is false. Since the function may delete the first node in the list, the front pointer is passed by reference. The function eraseValue() is available in the header file **nodelib.h**.

```cpp
// erase first occurrence of target in list.
// return true or false to indicate if operation occurs
template <class T>
bool eraseValue(Node<T> * & front, const T& target)
{
    // curr moves through list, trailed by prev
    Node<T>  *curr = front, *prev = NULL;

    // scan until item is located or come to end of list
    while (curr != NULL)
        if (curr->getValue() == target)    // match is found
        {
            if (prev == NULL)    // remove the first node
                eraseFront(front);
            else                      // erase intermediate node
            {
                prev->unlink();
                delete curr;
            }
            return true;
        }
        else
        {
            // advance curr and prev
            prev = curr;
            curr = curr->getNext();
```

```
      }
   // search failed; target not found

   return false;
}
```

PROGRAM 11.1

The program takes an array of integers and uses insertRear() to store them in a linked list. A prompt asks for input of a target that is used with eraseValue() to remove all occurrences of the target in the list. The process is done by repeatedly calling the function until it is established that the target is not found (eraseValue() returns false). The final list is output using writeList().

```
#include <iostream.h>

#include "node.h"      // Node class
#include "nodelib.h"   // basic linked list algorithms

int main()
{
   Node<int> *front = NULL;
   int arr[10] = {4,6,2,6,9,4,6,8,1,3};
   bool removedTarget;

   int i, target;

   // insert the 10 integers into the list
   for (i=0; i < 10; i++)
      insertRear(front, arr[i]);

   cout << "Original list: ";
   writeList(front);
   cout << endl;

   cout << "Enter a target: ";
   cin >> target;

   // while last call to eraseValue() removed target,
   // continue. terminate when eraseValue() returns false
   do
   removedTarget = eraseValue(front, target)
   while (removedTarget == true);

   cout << "Revised list:   ";
   writeList(front);
   cout << endl;

   return 0;
}
```

```
Run 1:

Original list: 4  6  2  6  9  4  6  8  1  3
Enter a target: 4
Revised list:  6  2  6  9  6  8  1  3

Run 2:

Original list: 4  6  2  6  9  4  6  8  1  3
Enter a target: 6
Revised list:  4  2  9  4  8  1  3
```

11-4   IMPLEMENTING THE LIST CLASS

This section discusses the implementation of the List class using linked lists. Since the implementation is somewhat complex, we are not able to cover all of the details and must look at only a selected set of member functions. A complete declaration of the class and an implementation of all of its functions can be found in the file **tlist.h** of the software supplement.

Our discussion begins with a UML representation of the List class. This provides a good overview of the class structure and leads into a discussion of the data members and implementation of the class functions.

UML Representation for the List Class

Recall that a List class Iterator object is declared using the syntax

```
List<T>::Iterator iterObj;
```

The Iterator and Const_Iterator types are *nested classes* that are declared locally within the List class. As such, they do not have special access to members of the List class; moreover, the List class has no special access rights to the members of the iterator classes.

```
class List
{
    . . .
    public:
        class Iterator
        {
            . . .
        };
    . . .
};
```

UML provides additional notation to represent a nested class. The basic shape of its icon is a rectangle with the parent class name in parenthesis below the name of the class.

The UML diagram for the complete List class in Figure 11-8 shows the two nested classes.

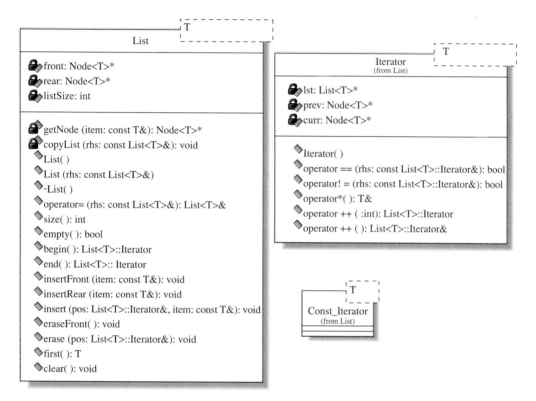

FIGURE 11-8
UML Representation for the List Class.

List Class Private Members

A linked list consists of a set of nodes chained together from the front to the rear of the list. In our previous work with linked lists, we have maintained a pointer to the front of the list and discussed the simple algorithms for inserting and erasing the first element of the list. The List class declares the data member, frontPtr, for this purpose. To insert a value at the rear of a liked list, the algorithm developed in Section 11.3 scanned the list to find the last node and inserted the new node after it. Since inserting an element at the rear of a list is a frequent operation, it should be done more efficiently. For this purpose, the List class maintains a pointer, rearPtr, to the last node of the list. Inserting at the rear involves simply inserting a node after that position. In addition to frontPtr and rearPtr, the class maintains a count, listSize, of the number of elements in the list. It is updated by each insert and erase operation. In keeping with the principle of information hiding, these data members are in the private section of the class. The following is the declaration for the attributes and a view of how they interact with the linked list containing the data.

Private Data Members of the List Class

```
// pointers maintain access to front and rear of list
Node<T> *frontPtr, *rearPtr;

// number of elements in the list
int listSize;
```

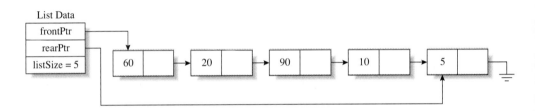

With this as background, we give a listing of the private section of the List class. The declaration includes the private function getNode() that allocates nodes for all of the insert functions. The private function copyList() is used by the copy constructor and the overloaded assignment operator to copy an existing linked list to the current List object.

tlist.h

DECLARATION: List CLASS (PRIVATE SECTION) ━━━

The private part includes a declaration of the Node class.

```
template <class T>
class List
{
    private:

        // pointers maintain access to front and rear of list
        List<T>::Node *frontPtr, *rearPtr;

        // number of elements in the list
        int listSize;

        // allocates a node
        Node<T> *getNode(const T& item);

        // function used by copy constructor and assignment
        // operator to copy List obj to current list
        void copyList(const List<T>& obj);
```

List Iterators

The List class makes iterators available for its objects by declaring Iterator and Const_Iterator as nested classes. The classes are declared in the public section of List so that any program that declares a List object can create a corresponding iterator. Since the Const_Iterator class differs only slightly, we discuss the Iterator class.

All of the data members in the Iterator class are pointers that are used by the iterator. The member listPtr is a pointer to the List object associated with the iterator. The pointer allows the iterator to access the List data members frontPtr and rearPtr, that may be changed by an insert and erase operation.

```
*listPtr           - the List object associated with the iterator
listPtr->frontPtr - address of first element in the linked list
listPtr->rearPtr  - address of rear element in the linked list
```

The pointers curr and prev identify elements in the linked list. The value of curr is the element currently referenced by the iterator and prev is the predecessor node. These pointers are used for retrieval, insert and erase operations. The following is an implementation view of a List object with an iterator attached at data value 90 in the list.

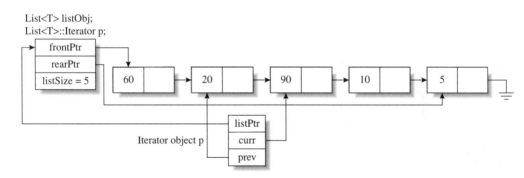

The following is the complete declaration of the Iterator nested class. A discussion of implementation issues follows the listing.

tlist.h

```
DECLARATION: List<T>::Iterator CLASS ■■■■■■■■■

class Iterator
{
   private:
       // used to update front/rear of list traversed by
       // the iterator
       List<T> *listPtr;
       // used for data retrieval, insertion, and deletion
       Node<T> *prev, *curr;
   public:
       friend class List<T>;
```

```
        friend class List<T>::Const_Iterator;

        // constructor
        Iterator();

        // equality for iterators
        bool operator== (const List<T>::Iterator& rhs) const;

        // inequality for iterators
        bool operator!= (const List<T>::Iterator& rhs) const;

        // pointer dereference operator
        T& operator* ();

        // postfix. move prev and curr forward
        // one node
        List<T>::Iterator operator++ (int);

        // prefix. move prev and curr forward
        // one node
        List<T>::Iterator operator++ ();
};
```

The public section declares the List class as a friend. This allows the member functions `insert()` and `erase()` from List to access the private data members of the iterator. The function `insert()` updates its iterator argument to point at the new node, and `erase()` updates its argument to point at the node to the right of the deleted node. For technical reasons described in the file **tlist.h,** the class Const_Iterator must also be a friend of Iterator.

In the Iterator class, the member functions are all overloaded C++ operators.

Operators == and !=:

Compare the pointer value curr for each of the iterator operands. If the values are equal, then both iterators point to the same node in the list and are considered equal. The != operator tests whether the values for curr are unequal and refer to different nodes.

Operator *:

Return the value curr->nodeValue after checking that curr is not NULL. Direct access to the Node class private data member nodeValue is possible because Iterator is a friend of Node.

If obj is an object of a primitive type, the expression ++obj increments obj and returns the new value, whereas the expression obj++ increments obj but returns the original value. The List class overloads both the *prefix* (++obj) and *postfix* (obj++) versions of the operators. Each overloaded function must have a unique argument list so the compiler can determine which version is intended.

The prefix version is overloaded without an argument, as is customary for a unary operator implemented as a member function.

```
List<T>::Iterator operator++ ();
```

Providing two unique argument lists is accomplished by giving the postfix version another argument, that must be of type int. When the operator is called, the value 0 is supplied to this special integer argument. In the declaration, it is necessary to specify that an int argument exists, but it is not necessary to specify a formal argument name.

```
List<T>::Iterator operator++ (int);
```

Operator ++ (postfix):

Save a copy of the current iterator in the object tmp (tmp = *this). Then advance both prev and curr forward one node and return the object tmp as the value of the function. The operator is implemented in line.

```
// postfix. advance prev and curr
template <class T>
List<T>::Iterator operator++ (int)
{
    List<T>::Iterator tmp = *this;

    // if traversal has reached the end of the list
    // or the list is empty, just return
    if (curr != NULL)
    {
        // advance the two pointers one node forward
        prev = curr;
        curr = curr->next;
    }
    return tmp; // return original iterator state
}
```

Technical Note

Care must be taken when two or more iterators are in use with the same List object. An iterator positioned immediately to the right of pos is invalidated when erase() is used at position pos. Of course, any other iterator referencing the location pos is invalid after erase().

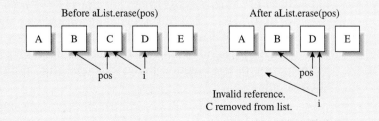

All iterators not pointing to the same data value as pos are in a consistent state after an insertion. If i points to the same value as pos, it is in an inconsistent state.

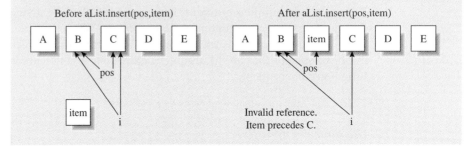

Selected Member Functions

Since the nodes of the linked list are dynamically allocated, in addition to a constructor the class must contain a destructor, copy constructor, and assignment operator.

```
// default constructor
List();

// copy constructor
List(const List<T>& obj);

// destructor
~List();

// assignment operator
List<T>& operator= (const List<T>& rhs);
```

The default constructor creates an empty list with all of the pointer data members set to NULL. In this initial state, the list size is set to 0.

```
template <class T>
List<T>::List(): frontPtr(NULL), rearPtr(NULL),
                 listSize(0)
{}
```

The copy constructor and assignment operator must copy data from a List object, argument, to the current object in order to initialize the elements in the linked list. For this purpose they call the private member function, copyList(), that inserts each of the elements of the List argument at the rear of the current list by using the member function insertRear(). The function copyList() is called only when the current list is empty. We include the implementation of the function that uses a constant iterator to scan the List argument obj.

```
// copy obj to the current list, that is assumed to be empty
template <class T>
```

```
void List<T>::copyList(const List<T>& obj)
{
    // use p to traverse obj
    List<T>::Const_Iterator p = obj.begin();

    // insert each element in obj at rear of current object
    while (p != obj.end())
    {
        insertRear(*p);
        p++;
    }
}
```

Insertion and Removal at the Ends of a List A set of member functions provides access and update operations for the front and rear of a List object. These functions do not require an iterator argument, since the position of the data is fixed for the operation.

```
void insertFront(const T& item);    // insert at front of list
void insertRear(const T& item);     // insert at rear of list

void eraseFront();                  // erase first element
T front() const;                    // return value of the
                                    // first item
```

To implement insertRear(), use the general function insert() to place the item at the end of the list, represented by end().

```
// insert item at rear of list
template <class T>
void List<T>::insertRear(const T& item)
{
    // create iterator pointing at end of list
    List<T>::Iterator iterRear = end();

    // insert before end()
    insert(iterRear, item);
}
```

The function eraseFront() uses begin() to initialize an iterator pointing to the first list element and then calls the general removal function erase().

```
// delete the node at the front of list
template <class T>
void List<T>::eraseFront()
{
    // create iterator pointing at the front
    List<T>::Iterator iterFront = begin();

    erase(iterFront);    // erase the front element
}
```

The List Member Functions begin() and end() The List class functions `begin()` and `end()` return Iterator objects that specify the beginning and end of the list, respectively. In particular, begin() returns an Iterator object whose listPtr data member is set to the address of current List object (this). To position the iterator at the start of the list, the data member prev is set to NULL and curr is set to the front of the list.

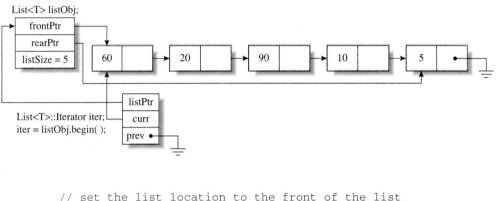

```
// set the list location to the front of the list
template <class T>
List<T>::Iterator List<T>::begin()
{
    List<T>::Iterator iter;

    iter.listPtr = this;    // list iterator traverses is ME
    iter.prev = NULL;       // prev = NULL at front of the list
    iter.curr = front;      // current node is front of the list

    return iter;
}
```

In the case of `end()`, the iterator must be positioned so it reflects a point just past the end of the list. Do this by setting curr to NULL and prev to point at the rear of the list.

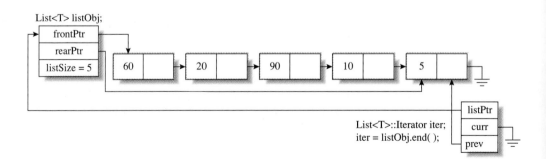

```
// indicates whether have passed the end of the list
template <class T>
List<T>::Iterator List<T>::end()
{
    Iterator iter;

    iter.listPtr = this; // list iterator traverses is ME
    iter.prev = rearPtr; // previous node is rear of the list
    iter.curr = NULL;    // current node is NULL at end of list

    return iter;
}
```

General List Insertion Function

The List class function insert() has an iterator argument, pos, that indicates the position at which the insertion should occur. Its second argument is the data value for the new node.

```
void insert(List<T>::Iterator& pos, const T& item);
```

After calling the private function getNode() to allocate a node, newNode, it performs the insertion, increments listSize by 1, and updates the iterator so that it refers to the new node. To do the insertion, the algorithm must handle two cases.

Insert at the front of the list:

This case occurs when pos.prev is NULL. Add the node to the front of the list and update the List object's front pointer.

```
newNode->next = pos.listPtr->frontPtr;
pos.listPtr->frontPtr = newNode;
```

Insert inside of the list:

Place the new node after pos.prev using the Node member function linkTo().

```
pos.prev->linkTo(newNode);
```

Special attention must be paid to the rear pointer in the List object. When the expression

```
pos.prev == pos.listPtr->rearPtr
```

is true, the insertion is made into an empty list or at the end of a nonempty list, and the value of the List object rear pointer must be updated. Figure 11-9 depicts these two situations.

```
pos.listPtr->rearPtr = newNode;
```

Inserting at the Front of an Empty List

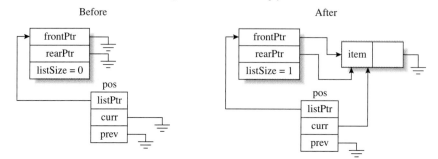

Inserting at the Rear of a Nonempty List

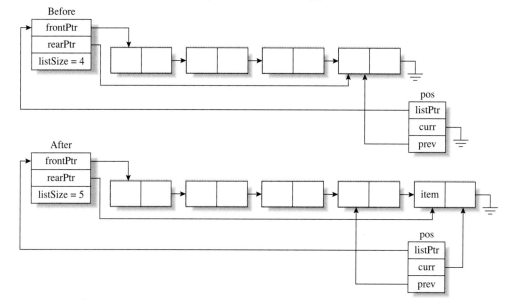

FIGURE 11-9
Updating the List Rear Pointer After an Insertion.

The function concludes by updating the list size and setting the iterator's curr pointer to newNode. The pointer prev remains at its current value.

```
// insert item at the current list position
template <class T>
void List<T>::insert(List<T>::Iterator& pos, const T& item)
{
```

```
Node<T> *newNode;

// create the new node
newNode = getNode(item);

// two cases: inserting at the front or inside the list
if (pos.prev == NULL)
{
   // inserting at the front of the list. also places
   // node into an empty list
   newNode->next = pos.listPtr->frontPtr;
   pos.listPtr->frontPtr = newNode;
}
else
   // inserting inside the list. place node after prev
   pos.prev->linkTo(newNode);

// if prev == rearPtr, we are inserting into empty list
// or at rear of non-empty list; update rearPtr
if (pos.prev == pos.listPtr->rearPtr)
   pos.listPtr->rearPtr = newNode;

// update curr and increment the list size
pos.curr = newNode;
pos.listPtr->listSize++;   // increment list size
}
```

CHAPTER 11 SUMMARY

This chapter introduces the concept of a container class and concentrates on the development of List, a very general sequential list container. Use of the List class depends on understanding the concept of an iterator, which is a generalized pointer that facilitates access to the data in a container. We postpone List class implementation details and discuss how to use its public member functions and iterators to solve problems.

A linked list is a storage structure that allows for efficient insertion and removal of data. The creation and maintenance of a linked list is a somewhat low-level activity but one that a programmer must master. The Node class defines the individual components of a linked list and implements the insertion and removal of data immediately following a list element. The material is developed in Sections 11.2 and 11.3 by presenting fundamental linked list algorithms and implementing them using free functions. This presentation is independent of any previous discussion of the List class.

Section 11.4 discusses elements of the List class implementation using a linked list. The use of a linked list enables a List object to grow or shrink as necessary and facilitates very efficient insertion and removal operations.

Classes in the Chapter

Name	Implementation File
List	tlist.h
Node	node.h

KEY TERMS

Begin() List class member function:
Returns an iterator positioned at the first element of a List object and is used to begin an iterator traversal.

Container class:
Class that stores data and provides operations to access and update the data.

End() List class member function:
Returns an iterator positioned just past the last element of a List object and is used to terminate an iterator traversal.

Iterator:
A generalized pointer that facilitates access to the data in a List object. An iterator has the operations *, ++, ==, and !=. An iterator often moves from item to item until the last data element of a List object is reached. During the scanning process, the iterator can be used to retrieve or perhaps update the value of an item.

Linked list:
Consists of a series of nodes whose first element is identified by a pointer front. Using pointers, nodes are linked together from the start of the list to the last or rear node whose next pointer has value NULL.

Nested class:
A class that is declared inside another class, called the parent class. This is purely an organizational technique. A nested class does not have special access to members of the parent class; moreover, the parent class has no special access rights to the members of the nested class.

Node:
An object consisting of a data value and a pointer to the next node in a linked list. The pointer is the connection that ties together the individual nodes of a list.

Postfix operator "++":
Increment the value of the object but return its previous value.

Prefix operator "++":
Increment an object and return the new value.

Self-referencing structure:
Structure in which a pointer member refers to objects of its own type. The Node class is an example.

Sequential list container:
A container that holds an arbitrary number of elements that are ordered by position. The first element occurs at the front of the list and the last element at the

rear of the list. Each element except the last element has a unique successor in
the next position.

REVIEW EXERCISES

1. Describe a sequential list.

2. Use List<char> objects chList and revList and their member functions.

```
List<char> chList, revList;
```

(a) Give the status of chList after each instruction.

```
chList.insertFront('t');        _____
chList.insertFront('a');        _____
chList.insertRear('j');         _____
chList.eraseFront();            _____
```

(b) Write a code segment with a while loop that deletes the characters from chList
and stores them in revList but in reverse order. Use the member functions
eraseFront(), insertFront(), front(), and empty().

3. Declare tList, amList, and pmList as three List objects holding Time24 objects as elements. Write a code segment that scans tList and inserts the current object at the
front of amList if the time falls in the AM period and at the rear of pmList if the
time falls in the PM period.

4. A *queue* is a list that permits access only at the two ends of the list. Elements are inserted at the rear of the queue and removed from the front of the queue. A waiting
line at a grocery store checkout is an example. In a queue, the element that is first
stored is the first one that is removed and so a queue is called a *first-in, first-out
(FIFO)* structure. To build the Queue class, use the List<T> object, queueList, to
hold the elements. The following is a declaration of the class.

(a) Implement the member function qInsert()

DECLARATION: Queue CLASS

```
template <class T>
class Queue
{
   private:
      // a List object to hold the queue items
      List<T> queueList;

   public:
      // constructor
      Queue();

      // queue update member functions
```

```
        void qInsert(const T& item);
        T qDelete();

        // queue test functions
        bool qEmpty() const;
        void qClear();
};
```

  (b) Implement the member function qDelete()
  (c) Write a code segment that declares the object, queueInt, as a queue of integers.
    With a for loop, input ten integers and insert each item into the queue. With a
    while loop, erase each element from the queue and display its value. The loop
    terminates when the queue is empty.

5. Refer to Review Exercise 4. Declare q as a Queue object storing characters.

```
Queue<char> q;
```

After each statement, specify the order of elements in the queue

```
q.qInsert('t');
q.qInsert('a');
q.qInsert('b');
q.qDelete();
q.qInsert('e');
```

6. Assume the following declarations:

```
List<String> strList;
List<String>::Iterator strIter;
```

and that the list has the following contents:

```
vector   list   begin   insert
```

What are the contents of the list after each statement sequence?

(a) `strIter = strList.begin();`
  `strList.insert(strIter,"template");`
(b) `strIter = strList.end();`
  `strList.insert(strIter,"switch");`
(c) `Assume *strIter is "begin".`
  `strIter++;`
  `strList.erase(strIter);`

7. Trace the function rmItem().

```
template <class T>
void rk(List<T>& tlist, const T& item)
{
    List<T>::Iterator iter;

    iter = tlist.begin();
```

```
        while (iter != tlist.end())
           if (*iter == item)
               tlist.erase(iter);
           else
               iter++;
    }
```

(a) Assume the list

```
    List<int> intList;
```

contains the elements

```
    4  2  7  2  9  3  4  2
```

What are the elements in intList after the function calls

```
       rmItem(intList, 2);
       rmItem(intList, 6);
```

(b) Assume the list

```
    List<char> charList;
```

contains the letters in the string "Mississippi". What are the elements in charList after the function call

```
       rmItem(charList, 'i');
```

8. The loop is used with a linked list of integer nodes. Describe its action.

```
    curr = front;
    while(curr != NULL)
    {
        curr->setValue(curr->getValue() + 7);
        curr = curr->getNext();
    }
```

9. Assume p, q, and r are pointers to character nodes. Initially, the nodes for p and q are dynamically allocated with values 'X' and 'A' respectively. The following three statements are used to build a portion of a linked list. After each statement, describe the resulting chain of nodes.

(a) `r = new Node<char>('M',p);`
(b) `r->linkTo(q);`
(c) `q->unlink();`

10. Trace the function update() that scans a list of integer nodes.

```
    void update(Node<int> * & front)
    {
        Node<int> *curr = front, *prev = NULL, *p;

        while (curr != NULL)
        {
            if (curr->getValue() % 2 == 0)
            {
                if (prev == NULL)
```

```
                          front = curr->getNext();
                    else
                       prev->unlink();
                    p = curr;
                    curr = curr->getNext();
                    delete p;
              }
              else
              {
                    prev = curr;
                    curr = curr->getNext();
              }
         }
    }
```

Consider the linked list 1 2 3 4 5 6 7 8 9 10. What list results from calling update()?

11. (a) In the implementation of the List class, how are the prefix and postfix versions of ++ for iterators distinguished?

(b) Explain why an iterator positioned immediately to the right of pos is invalid after the erase() function is called with pos as an argument.

Answers to Review Exercises

1. A sequential list is a container that holds an arbitrary number of elements that are ordered by position. The first element occurs at the front of the list and the last element at the rear of the list. Each element except the last element has a unique successor in the next position. Elements can be inserted or removed anywhere in the list.

2. (a) t
```
   a t
   a t j
   t j
```

(b)
```
while (chList.empty() == false)
{
    revList.insertFront(chList.front());
    chList.eraseFront();
}
```

3.
```
List<Time24> tList, amList, pmList;
List<Time24>::Iterator tIter;

tIter = tList.begin();
while (tIter != tList.end())
{
    if ((*tIter).getHour() < 12)
       amList.insertFront(*tIter);
    else
       pmList.insertRear(*tIter);
    tIter++;
}
```

4. (a) ```
// inserts item at rear of queue
template <class T>
void Queue<T>::qInsert(const T& item)
{
    queueList.insertRear(item);
}
```

(b) ```
// removes item from front of queue. terminate program
// if the queue is empty
template <class T>
T Queue<T>::qDelete()
{
    // test for an empty queue and terminate
    // program if true
    if (queueList.empty())
    {
        cerr << "Calling qDelete() for an empty queue!"
            << endl;
        exit(1);
    }

    // capture the front of the queue
    T frontElement = queueList.front();

    // erase the front element and return its value
    queueList.eraseFront();

    return frontElement;
}
```

(c) ```
Queue<int> queueInt;
int intValue, i;

for (i=0;i < 10;i++)
{
    cin >> intValue;
    queueInt.qInsert(intValue);
}

while (!queueInt.qEmpty())
    cout << queueInt.qDelete() << " ";
cout << endl;
```

**5.** ```
t
t a
t a b
a b
a b e
```

6. (a) template   vector   list   begin   insert
(b) template   vector   list   begin   insert   switch
(c) template   vector   list   begin   switch

7. (a) 4 7 9 3 4

(b) M s s s s p p

8. The value stored in every node is increased by 7.

9. (a) M   X

(b) M   A   X

(c) M   A

10. Removes all even data values from the list. The resulting list is

1 3 5 7 9

11. (a) An integer argument is added to the postfix version to distinguish the two operators. At run-time, a value of 0 is passed to the argument.

(b) The iterator stores a pointer to the previous node, which no longer exists.

WRITTEN EXERCISES

12. From your experience, give three different examples of a sequential list?

13. Assume strList is a List object that stores a sequence of Strings and that strIter is an iterator for the object. Write a code seqment that scans the elements in the list and outputs only those strings whose length is greater than 4.

14. Use List<char> objects chList and newList

```
List<char> chList, newList;
```

Trace the code.

```
while (chList.size() != 0)
{
    newList.insertFront(chList.front());
    newList.insertRear(chList.front());
    chList.eraseFront());

}
```

(a) Assume chList has the three elements in the string "C++", what is resulting sequence of characters in newList?

(b) What is the sequence if chList has the elements in the string "walk"?

15. The for loop adds elements to the List<int> object intList.

```
for (i = 0; i < 3; i++)
{
    intList.insertFront(arrA[i]);
    intList.insertRear(arrB[i]);
}
```

Describe the elements in arrA and arrB that would store the sequence of values 6   38   22   14   9   5 in intList.

16. A for loop adds elements to the List<int> object intList. After executing the loop, describe the resulting list.

(a)
```
for (i = 1; i <=6; i++)
    intList.insertFront(i);
```

(b)
```
for (i = 1; i <=6; i++)
    if (i % 2 == 1)
        intList.insertFront(i);
    else
        intList.insertRear(i);
```

17. Trace function inList that inserts new items into a list.

```
template <class T>
void inList(List<T> &aList, const T& item)
{
    List<T>::Iterator iter;
    iter=aList.begin();

    while (iter!=aList.end())
    {
        if (item == *iter)
            return;
        iter++;
    }
    aList.insertRear(item);
}
```

(a) Assume List<int> intL is originally an empty list. What are the elements in the resulting list after making six calls to function inList with data values 5 2 4 5 7 2?

(b) Assume List<char> charL is originally empty. Make eleven calls to the list with characters from the string "mississippi"? What are the resulting elements in the list charL?

18. Consider the List objects intList and revList.

```
List<int> intList, revList.
```

Assume intList is an ordered list that may contain duplicate values. For instance

$$2\ 2\ 7\ 8\ 8\ 8\ 15\ 20\ 20$$

Write a code segment that scans intList and copies to revList only the first occurrence of each duplicate value. Use an iterator to scan the list.

19. Implement the function, concatenate(), that sequences through the data in aList2 and inserts each of its items at the rear of aList1. Hint: use a constant iterator for aList2.

```
// add the elements from aList2 onto the end of aList1
template <class T>
void concatenate(List<T>& aList1, const List<T>& aList2);
```

20. A *stack* is a list that permits access at only one end of the list called the top. Elements are inserted and erased from the top of the stack. The insert operation is called push and the erase operation is called pop. A stack of trays in a cafeteria provides a real-world example. With a stack, the element that is last stored becomes the first one that is removed and so a stack is called a *last-in, first-out (LIFO)* structure. The following figure views a stack during a series of push and pop operations.

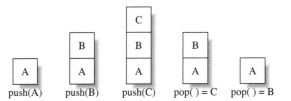

To build the Stack class, use the List<T> object, stackList, to hold the elements. Associate the top of the stack with the front of the list. The following is a declaration of the stack container class.

DECLARATION: Stack CLASS ████████████████████

```
template <class T>
class Stack
{
    private:
        // a List object to hold the Stack items
        List<T> stackList;

    public:
        // constructor
        Stack();

        // stack update member functions
        void push(const T& item);
        T pop();

        // stack test and clear functions
        bool stackEmpty() const;
        void stackClear();
};
```

For parts (a)–(b), implement the Stack member functions push() and pop() using member functions from the List class.

(a) Implement the member function push().
(b) Implement the member function pop().
(c) Write a code segment that declares the object, stackInt, as a stack of integers. With a for loop, input ten integers and insert each item on the stack. With a while loop, erase each element from the stack and display its value. The loop terminates when the stack is empty.

21. Trace the function scanWithIterator() that scans the List<int> object listArg and creates a new list that is provided as a return value.

```
List<int> scanWithIterator(constList<int>& listArg)
{
    List<int> listReturn;
    List<int>::Iterator, iterRtn;
    List<int>::Const.Iterator iterArg;
    int item;

    iterArg = listArg.begin();
    iterRtn = listReturn.begin();
    while(iterArg != listArg.end())
    {
        item = *iterArg;
        if (item > 50)
        {
            listReturn.insert(iterRtn,item);
            listArg.erase(iterArg);
        }
        else
            iterArg++;
    }
    return listReturn;
}
```

(a) Assume List<int> L contains the values   20   30   80   90   75   25   and   10. What are the values in list K after executing the statement

```
K = scanWithIterator(L).
```

(b) Assume List<int> L contains the value   45   90   55   60   80   20   and   95. What are the values in list K after executing the statement

```
K = scanWithIterator(L).
```

22. The following linked list of integer nodes is used for each part. Assume the declaration

```
Node<int> *front, *p, *newNode;
```

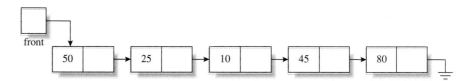

(a) Consider the following statement that adds a new node to the list.

```
front = getNode(30,front);
```

The value of the first node in the list is _____
The value of the second node in the list is _____
The value of the third node in the list is _____

(b) Assume p points at the node having value 10 and the following statement is executed.

```
p->unlink();
```

The integer value stored in node p after the unlink is _____
The value of the node that is deleted from the list is _____

(c) The loop scans the list

```
p = front;
while (p != NULL)
    p = p->getNext();
cout << p->getValue();
```

What is the value of p when the while loop terminates?

(d) Modify the code in part (c) so that value 80 in the last node is output.

(e) Trace the loop

```
int t;
Node<int> *q;

p = front;
while (p->getNext() != NULL)
{
    q = p->getNext();
    t = p->getValue() + q->getValue();
    p->setValue(t);
    p = q;
}
```

What are the data values for each node in the resulting list?

23. Use the list in Written Exercise 11.22. What are the values of the first three nodes in the list after executing the statements?

```
newNode = getNode(30);
front->linkTo(newNode);
```

24. Trace the code for function delFunc().

```
template <class T>
void delFunc(Node<T>* & front)
{
    Node<T> *curr = front, *q;

    if (front == NULL)
        return;

    while((q = curr->getNext()) != NULL)
    {   delete curr;
        curr = q;
    }
    front = curr;
}
```

(a) Assume T is the int type and the list is

$$22 \quad 19 \quad 44 \quad 15 \quad 8 \quad 3$$

What is the resulting list after calling delFunc()?

(b) Assume T is the char type and the list is

LINKED LIST

What is the resulting list after calling delFunc()?

25. The function scanList() traverses the elements in a linked list and deletes some of the nodes. Trace the code and identify the action of the function on sample lists.

```
template <class T>
void func(Node<T> *front)
{   Node<T> *p = front, *q;

    if (front == NULL)
        return;
    while (p != NULL && p->getNext() != NULL)
    {
        q = p->getNext();
        p->unlink();
        p = p->getNext();
        delete q;
    }
}
```

(a) Assume T is the int type and the list is

$$22 \quad 10 \quad 5 \quad 30 \quad 19 \quad 44 \quad 15 \quad 18 \quad 8 \quad 3$$

What is the resulting list after calling scanList()?

(b) Assume T is the char type and the list is

LINKED LIST WITH NODES

What is the resulting list after calling scanList()?

26. The implementation of the List function insert() involves special handling of rearPtr. What situations might affect this pointer in the implementation of the function erase()?

PROGRAMMING EXERCISES

27. Create the template-based function countDuplicates() as a variation of the function removeDuplicates() from Section 11.1. Use an iterator to scan each element in the list. At each current position, define a second iterator that scans the tail of the list, counting each element that matches the current value. Output the number of occurrences of each element in the list.

Write a program that tests countDuplicates() for the integer array arr

```
int arr[10] = {5, 8, 2, 8, 8, 2, 7, 9, 8, 5};
List<int> intList;
```

Output should be:

5(2) 8(4) 2(2) 7(1) 9(1)

28. Implement the class WordFreq with data members that store a word and its frequency.

```
class WordFreq
{
    private:
        String word;
        int freq;
    public:
        // initialize word and set freq to 1;
        WordFreq(String str);
        // equality operator compares the word for the objects
        int operator==(const WordFreq &a, const WordFreq &b);

        // add +1 to the frequency
        int incrementFreq();

        // output an object in the format:  word      freq
        void writeObj();
};
```

(a) Implement class WordFreq in the file **wordfreq.h.**

(b) Implement the function find() that searches a List object for a target. If the target is found in the list, the return value is an iterator pointing to the target. If the target is not in the list, the return value points just past the end of the list.

```
template <class T>
List<T>::Iterator find (const List<T>& alist
                             const T& target);
```

As an example of the find() function, the following statements replace the first occurrence of 7 with 5.

```
Example: List<int> intList;
         List<int>::Iterator iter;
                   . . .
         iter = find(intList, 7);
         if (iter != intList.end())
             *iter = 5;
```

(c) Write a program that inputs each word from a file and stores it in the List<WordFreq> object wf. Use the find() function to determine if the word is already in the list. If so, increment its frequency; otherwise, add the word as a WordFreq object to the list.

(d) Scan the list wf and output each value using writeObj().

29. In a program write a function loadOddEven() that is passed a node pointer front, an integer array arr, and a size parameter n as arguments. The function scans the array and loads each odd integer at the front of the list and each even integer at the rear of the list.

```
void loadOddEven(Node<int>* & front, int arr[], int n);
```

Output the elements from the resulting linked list. For instance, the six element array 6 2 9 8 3 1 translates to the linked list 1 3 9 6 2 8. Use functions from **nodelib.h.**

30. Repeat Programming Exercise 11.29 but with the function loadOddEven() using a List<int> object as an argument.

```
void loadOddEven(List<int>& aList, int arr[], int n);
```

31. In a program, write a function countValue() that counts the number of times an item occurs a linked list.

```
template <class T>
int countValue(const Node<T> *front, const T& item);
```

Generator 20 random numbers in the range 0 to 4. For each number, output its value and insert it into the linked list intPtr using insertRear(). In a loop, call the function countValue() and display the number of occurrences of each value 0 to 4 in the list.

32. Repeat Programming Exercise 11.31 but with the function countValue() using a List<int> object as an argument.

```
template <class T>
int countValue(const List<T>& aList, const T& item);
```

PROGRAMMING PROJECT

33. Define the merge() function for List<int> objects using an iterator. The problem involves merging two sorted lists into a single ordered list. Consider the two List<int> objects, intA and intB, whose elements are already sorted in ascending order. A third List<int> object intC holds all of the elements from the initial two lists.

   Starting at the beginning of each list and use an item-by-item merge of the elements. Compare the values at the current locations and copy the smaller value to intC. When a value from one list is used, move forward to the next value in the list and continue the comparisons. Since the lists are initially ordered, the elements are copied to intC in sorted order. When one list scan is complete, copy the remaining items from the other list to intC. The algorithm is elegantly implemented using three iterators: intAIter, intBIter, and intCIter. Each traverses its respective list. The following figure illustrates the algorithm for a set of five integers.

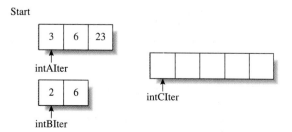

Step 1: Compare 3 and 2. Copy *intBIter = 2. Advance intBIter

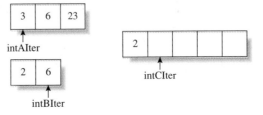

Step 2: Compare 3 and 6. Copy *intAIter = 3. Advance intAIter

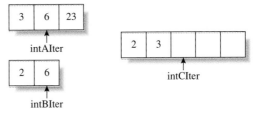

Step 3: Compare 6 and 6. Copy *intBIter = 6. Advance intBIter

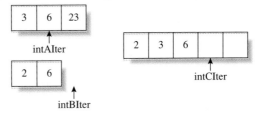

Step 4: intBIter at end of list. Copy remainder of intA.

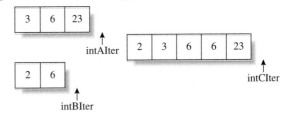

The function merge() implements the algorithm. It is passed two List<int> objects, intA and intB, by constant reference, and a third List<int> object, intC, by reference. The function itself defines three iterators that are set to scan each of the list objects. Test the function with two integer arrays that hold 12 and 8 elements respectively and with three List<int> objects.

```
int arrA[12] = {1,3,6,9,12,23,33,45,55,68,88,95};
int arrB[8]  =  {2,8,12,25,33,48,55,75};
List<int> intListA, intListB, intListC.
```

Insert the elements into intListA and intListB using insertRear(). After calling merge(),output the elements in the sorted list intListC. The run should be

```
Run:
1   2   3   6   8   9   12   12   23   25
33   33   45   48   55   55   68   75   88   95
```

Chapter 12
Inheritance and Virtual Functions

CHAPTER CONTENTS

12-1 INHERITANCE IN C++
Declaring Derived Classes
Declaring the Graphics Hierarchy
Constructors and Derived Classes

12-2 AN EMPLOYEE HIERARCHY
Representing Inheritance Using UML

12-3 ORDERED LISTS
Application: List Insertion Sort
Ordered List Class Implementation

12-4 POLYMORPHISM AND VIRTUAL FUNC- TIONS
Virtual Functions in an Inheritance Hierarchy
Application: Painting Houses using Polymorphism

12-5 GEOMETRIC FIGURES AND VIRTUAL FUNCTIONS
Application: Building a Kaleidoscope

12-6 ADVANCED INHERITANCE TOPICS
Virtual Functions And The Destructor
Abstract Base Classes

Written Exercises

Inheritance is a fundamental concept in object-oriented programming. Like object composition, it enables software reuse. This chapter develops the key features of inheritance using as a demonstration model the graphics classes that are developed in the book. These classes introduce some of the ideas that are found in very large graphics libraries, such as Microsoft Foundation Classes (MFC) and Borland's Object Windows Libraries (OWL).

The first two sections of the chapter combine an intuitive view of inheritance with an introduction to its C++ syntax. With inheritance, a base class provides member functions and data to a derived class. The derived class may choose to add its own member functions or redefine existing ones in the base class. To illustrate the syntax, we discuss the RectShape and CircleShape graphics class that are derived from a common base class named Shape. In Section 12-2, we develop an employee hierarchy as another simple example of inheritance.

Inheritance can be used to extend the functionality of an existing class. In Section 12-3, inheritance is used to develop an ordered list class from the List class.

Polymorphism adds an extra dimension to the use of inheritance. The term polymorphism is derived from ancient Greek and means "many forms." In programming, *polymorphism* means a member function with the same name can be implemented in different classes. When an application needs the function, the particular version is dynamically determined at run-time. In C++, polymorphism is implemented using virtual member functions. Polymorphism is developed in Sections 12-4 and 12-5 and used in a program that draws colored shapes simulating a kaleidoscope.

The chapter concludes with a study of virtual destructors and abstract base classes that are templates, or molds, for the construction of derived classes. A base class can specify the name, argument list, and return value that must be used for selected member functions in a derived class.

12-1   INHERITANCE IN C++

Most of us associate the term inheritance with our parents, grandparents, and so forth. At conception, we inherit important attributes and characteristics from our parents. We become "like them" in very basic ways but have our own uniqueness. Inheritance is also used in biology to describe the subdivision of the animal kingdom. For instance, animals can be identified as cats, dogs, and so forth. The cat family can be further subdivided into lions, tigers, cheetahs and the like. The animal organization can be viewed as a hierarchy tree in which classifications at any level inherit the characteristics of all previous levels. "A cat is an animal", "a tiger is a cat", and so forth. Relationships are valid over multiple levels such as "a tiger is an animal."

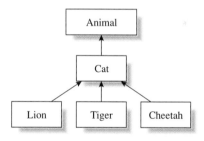

Inheritance exists in C++ classes. A *class hierarchy* begins with a *base* class that defines a set of common attributes and operations that are shared with derived classes. A *derived class* inherits the resources of the base class and overrides or enhances their functionality with new capabilities. For instance, consider objects from the CircleShape and RectShape classes. Each shape is drawn on the screen with a base point to anchor its position. In addition, the shape has a color attribute that specifies the fill color when the shape is drawn. These two attributes are shared by both circle and rectangle objects and define data for a base class called Shape. While base point and color are common to both types of geometric objects, CircleShape and RectShape are derived classes which have attributes that distinguish their objects. A circle is determined by its radius while a rectangle is determined by its length and width (Figure 12-1). In the language of inheritance, both a CircleShape and a RectShape object "is a" Shape.

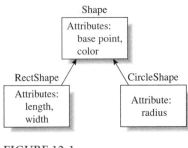

FIGURE 12-1
Shape Hierarchy.

The base class Shape has operations to access and update its data members. The member functions getX() and getY() retrieve the coordinates of the base point while move() repositions the point. The color attribute is referenced by the functions setColor() and getColor(). These operations are used by derived objects to access attributes in the Shape class. However, each derived class has member functions that are unique to itself. The derived class CircleShape has access member functions setRadius() and getRadius() that deal with the radius attribute. Similarly, the derived class RectShape has member functions that deal with the length and width attributes. Each class has the function draw() that displays the specific shape. The relationship between the classes is described in Figure 12-2 that is a partial UML representation of the geometric hierarchy. An open arrow connects the derived class to the base class.

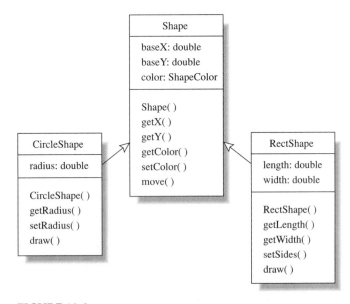

FIGURE 12-2
Geometric Hierarchy UML.

Declaring Derived Classes.

The following discussion develops the syntax to declare a derived class from a base class. The examples use Shape as the base class and CircleShape as the derived class. The base class that starts an inheritance chain has no special designation. The derived class declaration is extended to include a reference to the base class.

Base Class

```
class Shape
{
    ... data and member functions ...
};
```

Derived Class

```
// declare a derived class with reference to its base class
class CircleShape: public Shape
{
    ... data and member functions ...
};
```

Public Inheritance. Shape is the name of the base class that CircleShape inherits. The keyword public specifies the type of access that derived class member functions have to the base class members. The private members in the base class remain private and are accessible only to member functions in the base class. Public members in the base class can be called by any derived object or used in the implementation of any member function in the derived class.

```
int main()
{
    // declare a derived object
    CircleShape circ(1,1,.5,blue);

    // call public derived class function
    circ.draw();

    // call public member function in base class
    circ.move(2,2);

    // invalid. color is private member of base class
    // circ.color = red;

    // valid: calls public member function in base class
    circ.setColor(red);

    return 0;
}
```

In addition to private and public members, C++ defines *protected* members that have special meaning in a base class. When the base class is inherited by a derived class, all of the protected members in the base class may be accessed by the implementation of derived class member functions. However, the protected members may not be accessed by any derived object. They are private as far as a derived object is concerned.

SYNTAX ▬▬▬▬▬▬▬▬▬▬▬▬▬▬▬▬▬▬▬▬▬▬▬▬▬▬▬▬▬▬▬▬

Public Inheritance

Form: `class BaseCL`
                `{ ... members ...};`

                `class DerivedCL: public BaseCL`
                `{ ... members ...};`

Action: All public and protected members of BaseCL are available to the implementation of DerivedCL member functions. Only public members of the two classes are available to a DerivedCL object.

Example: `class Shape`

```
{
    // data accessible to any derived class member
    // function
    protected:
        double baseX, baseY;   // location of base
                               // point
        ShapeColor color;      // fill color

    // functions accessible to derived objects and
    // derived class member functions
    public:
        <members>
};

class CircleShape: public Shape
{
    // may access protected data members
    // baseX, baseY, and color in Shape
    <members>
};
```

Figure 12-3 illustrates a class hierarchy. The arrows on the left specify the access of member functions in the derived class to members of the base class. The functions may access only protected and public members of the base class. The right side of the diagram illustrates the access provided to a derived object. The derived object may access only the public members of the base and derived classes.

C++ also allows derived classes to be defined with *private* and *protected inheritance*. These forms of inheritance modify the access of a derived object to

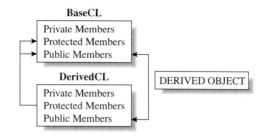

FIGURE 12-3
*Access to Class Members using Public
Inheritance.*

the base class members. Private inheritance is discussed in the exercises. Protected inheritance is little used and is not presented in the book.

Declaring the Graphics Hierarchy

Now that you understand how to declare base and derived classes and have the rules for access to base class members when public inheritance is used, we can illustrate these ideas with the graphics class hierarchy. We give a declaration of the Shape and CircleShape classes and look at inheritance implementation details.

The Shape Base Class. CircleShape member functions must access the coordinates of the base point and the fill color. However, these data members should not be directly accessed by a derived object. For this reason, these attributes are declared as protected data members. The following is a declaration of the Shape class.

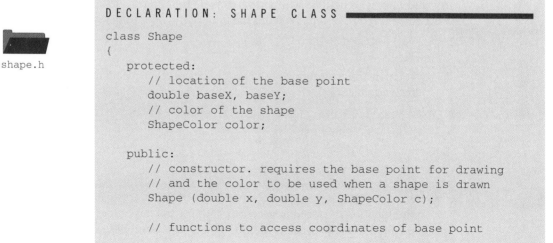

```
DECLARATION: SHAPE CLASS _____
class Shape
{
   protected:
       // location of the base point
       double baseX, baseY;
       // color of the shape
       ShapeColor color;

   public:
       // constructor. requires the base point for drawing
       // and the color to be used when a shape is drawn
       Shape (double x, double y, ShapeColor c);

       // functions to access coordinates of base point
```

shape.h

```
        double getX() const;            // return x coordinate
        double getY() const;            // return y coordinate

        // change base point
        void move(double x, double y);

        // functions to access and update color for the shape
        ShapeColor getColor() const;    // return color
        void setColor(ShapeColor c);    // change color

        // draw shape. must be implemented in a derived class
        virtual void draw() = 0;

        // erase the shape
        virtual void erase();
};
```

The functions draw() and erase() include the keyword *virtual*. This concept is used with polymorphism and abstract base classes that are introduced later in the chapter. The function draw() is designated as a *pure virtual function* by the presence of "=0" after the function argument list. It has no implementation in the Shape class and requires that any class derived from the Shape class must implement (override) its own version of draw(). This makes sense since the draw operation is unique to each graphic figure and are not a general shape operation. Since draw() is a pure virtual function, no objects of type Shape can be declared. The other member functions in the Shape class allow a program to access and update the protected data of the class. The base point is updated by the move() operation that repositions the point at a new location on the drawing surface.

To illustrate the implementation of the Shape class, we define the constructor and move() functions. The virtual erase() function is included in a technical note since it requires support from the underlying operating system.

Shape():

The constructor requires the coordinates of the base point and the color. A derived object can change their values using move() and setColor().

```
// initialize base point coordinates and color
Shape::Shape(float x, float y, ShapeColor c):
     baseX(x), baseY(y), color(c)
{}
```

move():

The function is passed new coordinates for the base point. These values are assigned to the protected data members baseX and baseY.

```
Shape::move(double x, double y)
{
    baseX = x;
    baseY = y;
}
```

Technical
Note

A graphics system such as Windows retains information about each figure that is drawn. An object called a handle provides a reference to the bitmap image for the figure, in the same way that an ifstream object provides a reference to an input file. Graphical operations that access the figure use the handle. In particular, a graphics system provides a low-level operation that erases a figure identified by a handle. Since the operation requires only the handle and does not depend on the particular figure that is drawn, it is implemented in the Shape class and then inherited by all derived classes. The actual code for *erase()* is system dependent and is not listed. If the graphical system does not use a single mechanism to erase shapes, one or more derived classes may require a custom erase() function. For this reason, erase() is declared to be a virtual function in the base class Shape.

The CircleShape Derived Class. The CircleShape class is derived from the Shape class and so it has access to the public and protected members of the base class. In particular, the base point and the color in the Shape class are used when the figure is drawn. The radius is a data member in the CircleShape class and specifies the radius of the circle.

circsh.h

DECLARATION: CircleShape CLASS ━━━━━━━━━

```
// declaration of CircleShape class with base class Shape
class CircleShape: public Shape
{
    private:
        double radius;

    public:
        // arguments for the base point, radius and color
        CircleShape (double x = 0.0, double y = 0.0,
                     double r = 0.0, ShapeColor c = darkgray);

        // radius access functions
        double getRadius() const;
        void setRadius(double r);

        //draw the circle
```

```
            virtual void draw();

};
```

The access member functions, `getRadius()` and `setRadius()` simply retrieve and modify the data member radius. We outline the code for the system dependent function draw(). The constructor is discussed in a separate section since we must develop an understanding of the interaction between base and derived class constructors.

draw()

Since the Shape class members baseX, baseY and color are in the protected section of Shape, `draw()` may reference them. A graphical system provides operations that draw a wide variety of shapes at designated screen coordinates and fill them with prescribed colors. The implementation of `draw()` for CircleShape involves setting the drawing color and calling the appropriate graphics system functions.

Constructors and Derived Classes

The data for a derived class is the combination of the data in the base and derived classes, so the constructor for a derived class must initialize both the base and derived data members of an object. The process resembles construction of a building from the first floor on up to the higher floors. A derived class constructor must first initialize the base class portion of its object and then initialize the derived class data members. The initialization of the base class is done by calling the constructor for the base class. In the graphics hierarchy, a CircleShape object is declared with four arguments. Three are used to initialize the base point and fill color attributes. The fourth argument defines the radius of the circle.

```
// base point (1,1), radius 2, and color blue
CircleShape circ(1,1, 2, blue);
```

In order to initialize its data members and those inherited from the base class, the CircleShape class constructor explicitly executes the Shape class constructor in the initialization list and then initializes the radius. The following is an implementation for the constructor.

CircleShape():

The constructor for the CircleShape class is passed arguments to initialize the base point and color in the Shape class and the data member radius for the CircleShape object.

```
CircleShape::CircleShape(double x, double y, double r,
            ShapeColor c): Shape(x,y,c), radius(r)
{}
```

Assume the constructor for class BaseCL has the prototype

```
BaseCL (int v);
```

and that the class DerivedCL is derived from BaseCL. Assume the DerivedCL constructor has a prototype whose basic form is

```
// v initializes BaseCL
DerivedCL (int v, . . .);
```

The implementation of DerivedCL() has the form

```
DerivedCL:: DerivedCL (int v, . . .) : BaseCL(v), . . .
{ . . .}
```

Programming Note

The BaseCL constructor in the initialization list executes before anything else. You may not omit the call to BaseCL() and initialize base class data members in the body of the derived class constructor.

If the base class has a default constructor and its default values are assumed, the derived class does not need to execute the default constructor explicitly. However, it is good practice to do so.

In an inheritance chain, destructors are called in the opposite order of the constructors. First, the destructor for the derived class is called, followed by the destructors for derived class data members, followed by the destructor for base classes in the reverse order of their appearance. Intuitively, a derived object is created after the base object and so should be destroyed before the base object. If a derived class does not have a destructor but the base class does, a *default destructor* is automatically generated for the derived class. This destructor destroys the derived class data members and executes the base class destructor.

12-2   AN EMPLOYEE HIERARCHY

In Section 1, the graphics hierarchy is used to describe inheritance. The concepts are further illustrated for a company that hires employees who are either salaried or who work on an hourly basis. The Employee class is defined as a base class with the strings name and ssn (social security number) as common attributes that are shared by each of the workers. In order to output this information, the class has a member function, employeeInfo(), that outputs the attributes in the form

```
Name:    <name>
SSN:     <ssn>
```

The function is declared as virtual since each derived class has its own employeeInfo() function that adds salary information. The following is a declaration of the Employee class. The member functions are implemented with inline code and are contained in the file **emphier.h**.

emphier.h

```
DECLARATION: Employee CLASS ━━━━━━━━━━━━━━
// base class for all employees
class Employee
{
   protected:
      // maintain an employee's name and social
      // security number
      String name;
      String ssn;
   public:
      // constructor
      Employee(const String& strName, const String& strSSN):
               name(strName), ssn(strSSN)
      {}

      // output basic employee information
      virtual void employeeInfo() const
      {
         cout << "Name: " << name << endl;
         cout << "SSN:  " << ssn << endl;
      }
};
```

Derived Employee Classes.   Specific information for each type of employee is provided by the derived classes SalaryEmployee and HourlyEmployee. The classes are similar. By giving their separate declarations and looking at selected functions from each class, you can see how inheritance applies.

The SalaryEmployee class has a single data member that stores the monthly salary of the employee. To update this attribute, the class provides the function setSalary(). For output, the function employeeInfo() displays information on the employee's status (salaried) and the monthly salary. By first calling employeeInfo() in the base class, the output function also displays the employee's name and social security number.

```
Name:      <name>
SSN:       <ssno>
Status:    salaried employee
Salary:    <salary>
```

The following is a declaration of the SalaryEmployee class whose member functions are implemented with inline code. Note that the employInfo() member function in the class is declared as virtual. This function overrides the corresponding function in the base class Employee.

```
DECLARATION: SalaryEmployee Classes ━━━━━━━━━━
// salaried employee "is an" employee with a monthly salary
class SalaryEmployee : public Employee
{
```

emphier.h

```
private:
   // monthly salary
   double salary;
public:
   // initialize Employee attributes and monthly salary
   SalaryEmployee(const Strings& strName,
         const String& strSSN, double sal):
         Employee(strName,strSSN),salary(sal)
   {}

   // update the monthly salary
   void setSalary(double sal)
   { salary = sal; }

   // call employeeInfo from base class and add
   // information about the salary
   virtual void employeeInfo() const
   {
      Employee::employeeInfo();
      cout << "Status: salaried employee" << endl;
      cout << "Salary: $" << setreal(1,2) << salary
            << endl;
   }
};
```

In the SalaryEmployee class, the output function employeeInfo() calls a function with the same name and argument list in the base class. The base class function call must be preceded by the base class name and the scope resolution operator.

```
Employee::employeeInfo();    // calls the base class function
```

If the base class and scope operator are not used, the derived class version of the function would be called recursively. This would create an infinite chain of function calls.

The constructor for the Employee base class contains String arguments that initialize the name and ssn attributes. The constructor for the derived SalaryEmployee class must contain these arguments along with arguments for the salary. The strings, strName and strSSN, are passed as arguments to the base class constructor Employee() which is executed in the initialization list. The argument sal is specific to the SalaryEmployee class and is used in the initialization list to set the value for the salary data member.

The HourlyEmployee class has data members that store the hourly payrate and the number of hours worked. To update these attributes, the class provides the functions setHourlyPay() and setHoursWorked(). LikeSalaryEmployee(), this class has an output function, employeeInfo(), that displays the employee's name, social security number, status(hourly), and salary information.

```
Name:        <name>
SSN:         <ssn>
Status:      hourly employee
Hours:       <hoursWorked>
Payrate:     <hourlyPay>
Salary:      <hoursWorked*hourlyPay>
```

The following is a declaration of the HourlyEmployee class whose member functions are implemented with inline code.

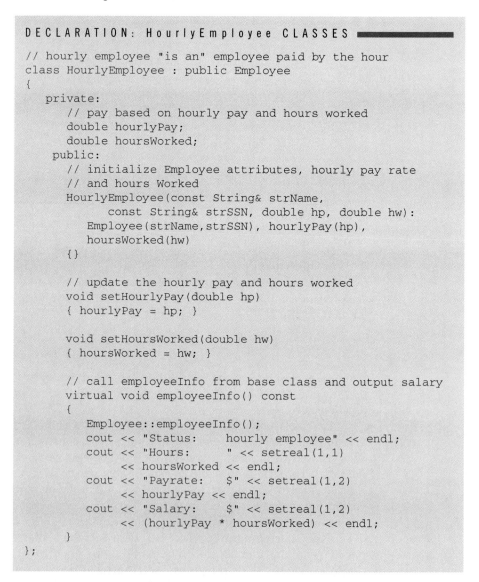

emphier.h

```
DECLARATION: HourlyEmployee CLASSES

// hourly employee "is an" employee paid by the hour
class HourlyEmployee : public Employee
{
    private:
        // pay based on hourly pay and hours worked
        double hourlyPay;
        double hoursWorked;
    public:
        // initialize Employee attributes, hourly pay rate
        // and hours Worked
        HourlyEmployee(const String& strName,
                const String& strSSN, double hp, double hw):
            Employee(strName,strSSN), hourlyPay(hp),
            hoursWorked(hw)
        {}

        // update the hourly pay and hours worked
        void setHourlyPay(double hp)
        { hourlyPay = hp; }

        void setHoursWorked(double hw)
        { hoursWorked = hw; }

        // call employeeInfo from base class and output salary
        virtual void employeeInfo() const
        {
            Employee::employeeInfo();
            cout << "Status:     hourly employee" << endl;
            cout << "Hours:      " << setreal(1,1)
                << hoursWorked << endl;
            cout << "Payrate:    $" << setreal(1,2)
                << hourlyPay << endl;
            cout << "Salary:     $" << setreal(1,2)
                << (hourlyPay * hoursWorked) << endl;
        }
};
```

The program declares objects corresponding to the salaried employee, Mary Dunne, and the hourly worker, Steve Howard. An initial output displays salary information for Mary Dunne using `employeeInfo()` from the derived class SalaryEmployee and basic employee information for Steve Howard using `employeeInfo()` from the base class Employee. Steve is given a raise from $5.00 per hour to $7.00 per hour and his new salary is output.

```cpp
#include <iostrean.h>

#include "tstring.h"
#include "textlib.h"
#include "emphier.h" // include employee hierarchy

int main()
{
    // declare a salaried and an hourly employee
    SalaryEmployee sEmp("Mary Dunne", "234-67-8901",2500);
    HourlyEmployee hEmp("Steve Howard", "896-54-3217",5.00,40);

    // output information for Mary
    sEmp.employeeInfo();
    cout << endl;

    //output only basic information for Steve
    hEmp.Employee::employeeInfo();
    cout << endl;

    // give Steve a raise and output his
    // new employee information
    hEmp.setHourlyPay(7.00);
    hEmp.employeeInfo();

    return 0;
}
```

```
Run:

Name:      Mary Dunne
SSN:       234-67-8901
Status:    salaried employee
Salary:    $2500.00

Name:      Steve Howard
SSN:       896-54-3217

Status:    hourly employee
Hours:     40.0
Payrate:   $7.00
Salary:    $280.00
```

Representing Inheritance Using UML

The UML representation for the employee hierarchy illustrates public inheritance relationships. The following icon specifies that an attribute is a member of the protected section of a class.

In the UML representation for the hierarchy (Figure 12-4), the Employee class data members name and ssn are protected. The attributes in the SalaryEmployee and HourlyEmployee classes are private.

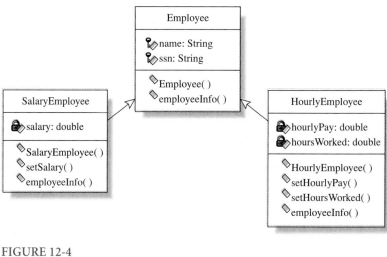

FIGURE 12-4

The Employee Hierarchy.

12-3 ORDERED LISTS

The List class developed in Chapter 11 describes a general sequential list. For many applications, a more restrictive list structure requires that items are stored in order. In this way, the application can scan the list for an item and terminate the search if it encounters a larger value. This makes the sequential search more efficient. By adding order to the list, an application can output the items as a sorted list.

To create an ordered list, we use List as a base class and develop the derived class, OrderedList. The derived class has a member function, insert(), that places items into the list in ascending order using the "<" operator. The base class functions insert(), insertFront(), and insertRear() should not be used, since use of these functions can destroy the list ordering. For instance, if 99 is inserted at the front of the list {2, 5, 7, 8, 12}, the new list {99, 2, 5, 7, 8, 12} is out of order. The prototypes for these functions are duplicated in the private section of the derived class. An attempt to access one of these functions will produce a compiler error. For instance, the sequence

```
OrderedList<int> intList;
        . . .
intList.insertFront(99);
```

may produce the error message

```
insertFront: Cannot access private member declared in class
OrderedList
```

Erase operations are allowed in an ordered list, since removing an element does not affect the list order. An iterator can be used to identify the position of the deletion. Since erasing an item modifies the list, the erase operations use non-constant iterators. For these iterators, the * operator should not be used to modify list elements since this might destroy the ordering. The class also defines a constant iterator for traversal of constant lists.

The following is a delcaration of the OrderedList class.

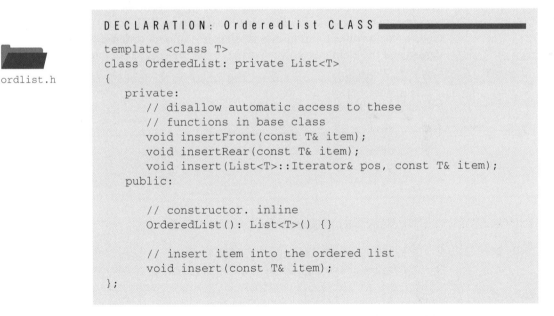

ordlist.h

```
DECLARATION: OrderedList CLASS

template <class T>
class OrderedList: private List<T>
{
   private:
       // disallow automatic access to these
       // functions in base class
       void insertFront(const T& item);
       void insertRear(const T& item);
       void insert(List<T>::Iterator& pos, const T& item);
   public:

       // constructor. inline
       OrderedList(): List<T>() {}

       // insert item into the ordered list
       void insert(const T& item);
};
```

EXAMPLE 12.1

The example includes an ordered list and two types of iterators.

```
OrderedList<int> intOrdList;
OrderedList<int>::Iterator ordIter;
OrderedList<int>::Const_Iterator c_ordIter;
```

1. Create an ordered list using insert().

```
intOrdList.insert(5);    // List: 5
```

```
intOrdList.insert(12);    // List: 5 12
intOrdList.insert(8);     // List: 5 8 12
```

2. Use a nonconstant iterator to delete an element of the list.

```
ordIter = intOrdList.begin();   // initialize iterator
ordIter++;                      // move to element with value 8
intOrdList.erase(ordIter);      // List: 5 12
cout << intOrdList.size();      // Output: 2
```

3. Use a constant iterator to output the list.

```
c_ordIter = intOrdList.begin();
while (c_ordIter != intOrdList.end())
{
    cout << *c_ordIter << "   ";
    c_ordIter++;
} ■
```

Application: List Insertion Sort

The OrderedList class can be used to sort a collection of items, provided the comparison operator < is defined for the data type T. The function listSort() takes a Vector object and inserts its elements into an ordered list. The list is traversed and the elements, now in sorted order, are copied back to the vector.

```
// sort vector v by inserting into an ordered list
template <class T>
void listSort(Vector<T>& v)
{
    OrderedList<T> ordList;
    OrderedList<T>::Const_Iterator iter;
    int i;

    // create an ordered list from the elements of v
    for (i=0; i < v.size(); i++)
        ordList.insert(v[i]);

    // copy the elements of the list back to v
    for(i=0, iter=ordList.begin(); iter != ordList.end(); i++,
        iter++)
        v[i] = *iter;
}
```

APPLICATION 12-2 LIST INSERTION SORT

The program uses the function listSort() to sort a vector of integers and a vector of strings. The vectors are created using initialized C++ arrays. The template function, writeVector(), displays the resulting lists.

```
#include <iostream.h>

#include "ordlist.h"        // use OrderedList class
```

```
#include "tvector.h"      // Vector class
#include "tstring.h"      // String class

// sort vector v by inserting into an ordered list
template <class T>
void listSort(Vector<T>& v);

// output a vector
template <class T>
void writeVector(const Vector<T>& v);

int main()
{
    int intArr[12] = {5, 8, 12, 25, 23, 1, 3, 3, 5, 15, 25, 5};
    Vector<int> vInt(intArr, 12);

    String strArr[5] = {"Maine", "Mississippi", "Arizona",
                        "Massachusetts", "Alabama"};
    Vector<String> vString(strArr, 5);

    // sort the lists
    listSort(vInt);
    listSort(vString);

    // output both lists
    writeVector(vInt);
    writeVector(vString);

    return 0;
}

/*implementation for listSort() given in program discussion */

template <class T>
void writeVector(const Vector<T>& v)
{
    int i;

    for(i=0; i < v.size(); i++)
       cout << v[i] << "   ";
    cout << endl;
}
```

```
Run:

1  3  3  5  5  5  8  12  15  23  25  25
Alabama  Arizona  Maine  Massachusetts  Mississippi
```

A sorting algorithm is said to be *in-place* if all the sorting operations take place within the original array. Unlike an in-place sort such as the selection sort, linkSort() requires additional storage for all n data elements in the ordered list. It also spends time copying elements to and from the list. As a result, it is not as efficient as the selection sort.

Ordered List Class Implementation

A new derived class insert() operation is the major implementation issue. The operation sequentially searches for the insertion point. The function uses a List iterator to search for the first data value that is larger than or equal to the new item. The base class function `insert()` is used to place the new value in the list at the current location. If the new value is larger than all existing values, the data value is appended to the list.

```
template <class T>
void OrderedList<T>::insert(const T& item)
{
    // curr starts at first list element, stop marks end.  use
    // the base class begin() and end()
    List<T>::Iterator curr = begin(),
                      stop = end();

    // find the insertion point, which may be at end of list
    while ((curr != stop) && (*curr < item))
        curr++;

    // do the insertion using base class insert() function
    List<T>::insert(curr, item);
}
```

How would you modify the `insert()` function so that a duplicate data value is placed in the list at the end of the sequence of duplicates? Can you make this modification using < to compare elements?

12-4   POLYMORPHISM AND VIRTUAL FUNCTIONS

Polymorphism is an important feature of inheritance. It allows two or more objects in an inheritance hierarchy to have identical member functions that perform distinct tasks. The computer run-time environment selects a version of the function appropriate to the situation. The concept of polymorphism is fundamental to object-oriented programming. In fact, professionals often refer to object-oriented programming as "inheritance with run-time polymorphism." C++ supports this construct using *dynamic binding* of *virtual member functions*. This contrasts with *static binding* which is the usual way of connecting an object with a member function. We explore these concepts using an example.

A paint contractor accepts jobs for wood, brick and vinyl-sided houses. All of the jobs have common tasks like caulking windows, covering nearby plants, and so forth. These tasks are described in the class House and are invoked with the member function `paint()`. Specific techniques are used to paint each type of house. Painting a wood frame house, for instance, is different than painting a brick house or a vinyl-sided house and so forth. The special painting techniques for each type of house are defined by the operation `paint()` in a derived class that inherits the base class House. Figure 12-5 is a class hierarchy with derived classes WoodFrameHouse, BrickHouse and VinylSidedHouse.

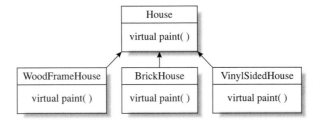

FIGURE 12-5

The paint() Function in the House Hierarchy.

Static Binding. Assume the paint contractor has accepted a job at a wood frame house called bigWoody. The contractor paints the house by explicitly calling the operation `paint()` for the WoodFrameHouse object.

```
bigWoody.paint();
```

This process is an example of *static binding,* since the function `paint()` is called by referencing a specific object by name and using the dot (.) member selection operator. The compiler generates code to call the specific function. As a result, static binding is also known as *compile-time binding.* All function calls up to this point in the book have used static binding.

EXAMPLE 12.2

Declare the RectShape and CircleShape objects rect and circ.

```
RectShape rect(2,2,1,1,blue);
CircleShape circ(5,5,1,red);
```

The appropriate version of the member function `draw()` is called with static binding by using object name and function name. The compiler realizes that the call is made to a specific version of the function.

```
rect.draw();    // calls draw() in RectShape class
circ.draw();    // calls draw() in CircleShape class   ■
```

Dynamic Binding. Assume that the paint contractor has a list of addresses for houses that need to be painted and that he directs his crews to go through the list and paint the houses. A crew has an address for a house but does not know the type of house until it arrives. The crew selects the correct `paint()` operation only when it sees the type of house. This process is known as *dynamic binding.*

```
(Address of house at 3955 S. Oak) -> paint();
```

The specific `paint()` operation that is executed depends on the kind of house at the given address. If the house at address "3955 S. Oak" is a wood frame house, the operation `paint()` from the class WoodFrameHouse is executed.

When static binding is used, the compiler generates the function call. With dynamic binding, the compiler creates machinery that enables the run-time system to make the actual function call. For this reason, dynamic binding is also referred to as *run-time binding.*

Virtual Functions in an Inheritance Hierarchy

Dynamic binding in C++ is invoked by declaring *virtual member functions* in an inheritance hierarchy. Such a function is initially declared in a base class by placing the keyword *virtual* in front of its declaration. To override the virtual function in the base class, derived classes declare a member function with precisely the same name, argument list, and return type. For example, in the Shape class, the function `draw()` is declared to be virtual. The same function is declared in the CircleShape and RectShape derived classes.

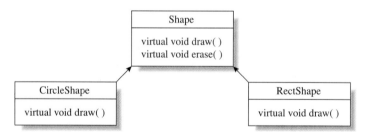

In the derived class, the keyword virtual does not have to be used because the virtual attribute is inherited from the base class. However, it is a good idea to include the word in the derived class declaration. In this way, a programmer who uses the class does not have to look at the base class declaration to determine whether a function is virtual.

Once the inheritance and virtual member functions are implemented, we can implement dynamic binding using pointers to base or derived objects. Consider the declarations:

```
Employee basicDataObj("", "");
SalaryEmployee sharon("Sharon Wallace", "356-68-3355",
                      2900.0);
```

Since SalaryEmployee is derived from Employee (a salaried employee "is an" employee), sharon can be assigned to a base class object. During the assignment, the portion of the SalaryEmployee object's data that is in the Employee class is copied.

```
basicDataObj = sharon;
basicDataObj.employeeInfo (); // Output: Name: Sharon Wallace
                              //         SSN: 356-68-3355
```

At the same time, the assignment of an Employee object to a SalaryEmployee object is not valid since the derived class data may be undefined. For instance, consider the following:

```
sharon = basicDataObj;     // salary in SalaryEmployee not
                           // initialized
```

In the context of pointers, a base class pointer can be assigned the address of a derived object, so the following assignments are legal.

```
Employee *p, *q;

p = &basicDataObj;    // p points at an Employee object
q = &sharon;          // q points at a SalaryEmployee object
```

The statement p-> employeeInfo() calls the employeeInfo() function in the Employee class. The statement q->employeeInfo() illustrates the essence of polymorphism since it calls the function employeeInfo() in the SalaryEmployee class, even though q is an Employee pointer.

> **Definition** *Polymorphism* in an inheritance chain occurs when a virtual function is called using a pointer. The system executes the function for the actual object to which it points.
>
> Example: If empPtr is declared as an Employee pointer but it points to a HourlyEmployee object, then `empPtr->employee-Info()` outputs the name, social security number, pay rate, hours worked, and salary.

EXAMPLE 1 2 . 3

1. The example illustrates polymorphism using the virtual function employeeInfo() of the employee hierarchy. The Employee pointer p is used to reference different derived objects.

```
Employee *p;
SalaryEmployee  glenn("Glenn Rose", "345-83-8287",1600.0);
```

```
HourlyEmployee  rob("Rob Ross", "673-45-1835",7.50,45);

// base class pointer to SalaryEmployee object
p = &glenn;
p=>employeeInfo();     // Output: Name: Glenn Rose
                       // SSN:  345-83-8287
                       // Status: salaried employee
                       // Salary: $1600.00

// base class pointer to HourlyEmployee object
p = &rob;
p->employeeInfo ();    // Output: Name: Rob Ross
                       // SSN:  673-45-1835
                       // Status: hourly employee
                       // Salary: $337.50
```

2. If a programmer wants to execute the function `employeeInfo()` in the Employee class, the class scope operator must be used.

```
// call function employeeInfo() in the Employee class
p->Employee::employeeInfo();   ■
```

*Programming
Note*

Dynamic binding is also used when a virtual function is called using a class reference. Assume the function identify() is written as follows:

```
// pass a reference to an Employee object. use it
// to execute employeeInfo()
void identify (const Employee& p)
{
    // execute the version of employeeInfo()
    // for the object referenced by p
    p.employeeInfo();
    cout << endl;
}
```

In the main program, declare the object

```
SalaryEmployee glenn("Glenn Rose","345-83-8287",1600.0);
```

The program outputs the information for Glenn when this statement executes:

```
identify(glenn);
```

Application: Painting Houses using Polymorphism

To illustrate how polymorphism is used in an application, we return to the paint contractor. Inline code is used in the declaration of the House, WoodFrameHouse, VinylSidedHouse and BrickHouse classes.

The base class House contains the identification string "House" along with a virtual paint() function that displays the string.

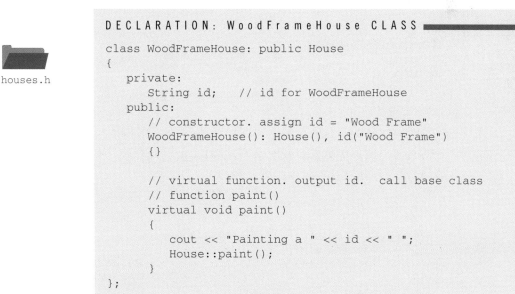

```
DECLARATION: House CLASS
// base class for house painting hierarchy
class House
{
    private:
        String id;            // id for the house
    public:
        // constructor. initialize id to "House"
        House(): id("House")
        {}

        // virtual function. outputs the string "House"
        virtual void paint()
        { cout << id;}
};
```

Each derived class contains a string identifying the type of house. The virtual function paint() overrides paint() in the base class. It outputs the string and calls the base class function paint(). The declaration of the WoodFrame-House is a model.

```
DECLARATION: WoodFrameHouse CLASS
class WoodFrameHouse: public House
{
    private:
        String id;    // id for WoodFrameHouse
    public:
        // constructor. assign id = "Wood Frame"
        WoodFrameHouse(): House(), id("Wood Frame")
        {}

        // virtual function. output id.  call base class
        // function paint()
        virtual void paint()
        {
            cout << "Painting a " << id << " ";
            House::paint();
        }
};
```

houses.h

houses.h

APPLICATION 12-3 PAINTING WITH POLYMORPHISM

The application declares an array, contractorList, that consists of five pointers to the base class House. The array is initialized by dynamically allocating objects whose types are randomly selected from the classes WoodFrameHouse, Brick-House and VinylSidedHouse.

     The program simulates a contractor assigning crews to go to the houses on the list and paint them. The program scans the contractorList array and calls the paint() function for each object. Since an object is referenced by a House pointer, dynamic binding ensures that the appropriate paint() function is executed.

```cpp
#include <iostream.h>

#include "trandom.h"      // include random number generator
#include "houses.h"       // include the painting hierarchy

int main()
{
    // dynamic list of House addresses
    House *contractorList[5];
    RandomNumber rnd;
    int i;

    // construct the list of 5 houses to be painted
    for (i=0;i < 5;i++)
        // randomly choose house type 0, 1, 2, create the
        // object and assign its address in contractorList.
        switch(rnd.random(3))
        {
            case 0: contractorList[i] = new WoodFrameHouse;
                    break;
            case 1: contractorList[i] = new BrickHouse;
                    break;
            case 2: contractorList[i] = new VinylSidedHouse;
                    break;
        }

    // paint houses by calling paint(). since
    // paint() is virtual, dynamic binding is used
    // and the correct function is called.
    for (i=0;i < 5;i++)
    {
        contractorList[i]->paint();
        cout << endl;
    }

    return 0;
}
```

```
Run:

Painting a Vinyl Sided House
Painting a Wood Frame House
Painting a Vinyl Sided House
Painting a Vinyl Sided House
Painting a Brick House
```

Polymorphism in C++ is implemented by using a *virtual function table* that contains the addresses of an object's virtual functions. A pointer to this table is placed in each object. When a virtual function is called by using the address of an object, the run-time system follows the pointer to the table and executes the appropriate function. Consider the statements

```
House *p, *q;

p = new WoodFrameHouse;
q = new BrickHouse;
```

Technical Note

```
p->paint();        // Output: Painting a Wood Frame House
q->paint();        // Output: Painting a Brick House
```

The following figure shows class data members and a pointer to the virtual function table for the objects addressed by p and q.

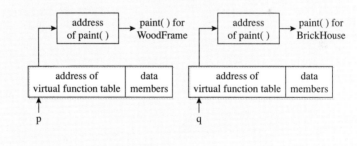

12-5 GEOMETRIC FIGURES AND VIRTUAL FUNCTIONS

We have seen that the Shape class is a base class for a series of derived drawing classes, that include the CircleShape and RectShape classes. In this section, we give the declaration and implementation for the PolyShape class and use it in the same program with Circle to illustrate the use of virtual functions.

The PolyShape class creates regular polygons with the base point at the center of the figure. Like the CircleShape class, PolyShape implements a draw() function to display the polygon. In order to draw a regular polygon with n sides, it is necessary to compute the n vertices (x_0,y_0), (x_1,y_1), ..., (x_{n-1},y_{n-1}) that define the shape. This computation of the vertices is done by the private member function buildPoints() that stores the x and y-coordinates of the points in the Vector<double> objects point_X and point_Y. For instance, Figure 12-6, shows six vertices that are required to define a hexagon. The vertices of the hexagon are stored in point_X = $\{x_0, x_1, x_2, x_3, x_4, x_5\}$ and point_Y = $\{y_0, y_1, y_2, y_3, y_4, y_5\}$.

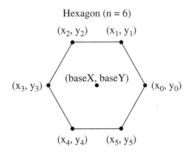

Hexagon (n = 6)

(x_2, y_2) (x_1, y_1)

(x_3, y_3) (baseX, baseY) (x_0, y_0)

(x_4, y_4) (x_5, y_5)

FIGURE 12-6
Points Defining a Regular Polygon.

polysh.h

```
DECLARATION:  PolyShape  CLASS

class PolyShape: public Shape
{
    private:
        int n;              // number of sides
        double length;      // length of each side

        // x and y-coordinates of the vertices
        Vector<double> point_x;
        Vector<double> point_y;

        // construct the vertices
        void buildPoints();

    public:
        // constructor. has arguments for the base point
        // number of sides, the length of each side and the
        // color
        PolyShape(double x = 0.0, double y = 0.0,
                  int numsides = 4, double len = 0.0,
                  ShapeColor c = darkgray);

        // retrieve or set length of a side
        double getLength() const;
        void setLength(double len);

        // retrieve or set number of sides
```

```
    int getN();
    void setN(int numsides);

    // draw the polygon
    virtual void draw();
};
```

Implementation of the PolyShape Class

We discuss the constructor, buildPoints() and draw() member functions. The implementation of the remaining functions can be found in the file **polysh.h.**

PolyShape():

The constructor executes the Shape class constructor and passes it the co-ordinates (x,y) of the base point and the color c. After assigning values for n (number of sides) and length (length of each side), the two Vector objects are initialized to have zero size. Actual memory for the coordinates is allocated by the function buildPoints() when it is called by draw().

```
// initialize base class, the number of sides
// and the length of each side
PolyShape::PolyShape(double x, double y, int numsides,
                  double len, ShapeColor c):
        Shape(x,y,c), n(numsides), length(len),
        point_x(0), point_y(0)
{}
```

buildPoints()

This private member function builds the points that determine the polygon, and its implementation is based on trigonometry. The algorithm is presented for the interested reader. Use Figure 12-7 as a reference.

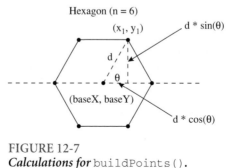

Hexagon (n = 6)

FIGURE 12-7
Calculations for buildPoints().

The distance from the center of the polygon to any vertex is

$$d = \frac{length}{2\,sin(\pi/n)}$$

If the counterclockwise angle at point (x_i, y_i) is θ, then

$$x_i = baseX + d * \cos(\theta) \qquad \text{and} \qquad y_i = baseY - d * \sin(\theta)$$

The loop in `buildPoints()` applies this formula at each point (x_i, y_i) when θ has angle $i*(2\pi/n)$.

```
void PolyShape::buildPoints()
{
    int side;
    double theta, d;
    const double PI = 3.141592653589793,
                 DELTA_THETA = (2.0*PI)/n;

    // allocate space for the n coordinates
    point_X.resize(n);
    point_Y.resize(n);

    d = length/(2.0*sin(PI/n);
    theta = 0.0;
    for(side = 0; side < n; side++)
    {
        point_X[side] = baseX + d*cos(theta);
        point_Y[side] = baseY - d*sin(theta);
        theta += DELTA_THETA;
    }
}
```

draw()

The implementation of `draw()` for the PolyShape class is very similar to draw() for the CircleShape class. Call `buildPoints()` to construct the polygon points. The remaining steps involve technical graphics system details.

APPLICATION 12-4 GEOMETRIC CLASSES AND VIRTUAL FUNCTIONS

This program illustrates dynamic binding and polymorphism for the Shape (base) class, CircleShape (derived) class, and PolyShape (derived) class. Objects one, two, and three are pointers to a Shape object. Using the operator new, these objects are defined to point at dynamically allocated geometric shapes. Using the pointers to call `draw()` will initiate dynamic binding and cause the `draw()` for the derived object to be executed.

```
one:   associated with CircleShape(1.5, 1.75,.25, blue)
two:   associated with PolyShape(3, 1, 9, .5, lightblue)
three: associated with CircleShape(3, 2.5, .5, darkgray)
```

```cpp
#include "graphlib.h"      // for openWindow(), etc.
#include "circlesh.h"      // use CircleShape class
#include "polysh.h"        // use PolyShape class

int main()
{
    // pointers in the Shape (base) class
    Shape *one, *two, *three;

    one = new CircleShape(1.5, 1.75,.25, blue);

    two = new PolyShape(3, 1, 9, .5, lightblue);

    three = new CircleShape(3, 2.5, .5, darkgray);

    // open the drawing window
    openWindow();

    one->draw();     // draw a circle
    two->draw();     // draw a polygon
    three->draw();   // draw a circle

    // pause to view the figures and close the window
    viewWindow();
    closeWindow();

    // delete the objects in dynamic memory before
    // terminating the program
    delete one;
    delete two;
    delete three;

    return 0;
}
```

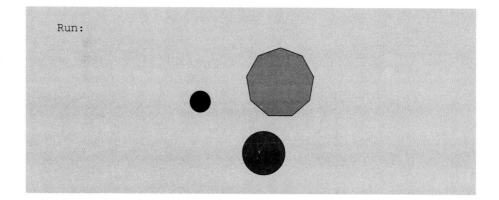

Run:

Application: Building a Kaleidoscope

The geometric drawing classes allow us to draw circles, rectangles and regular polygons. To create the effect of a kaleidoscope, the application dynamically creates a series of random figures and stores their addresses in a vector of pointers to Shape objects. Using polymorphism and random relocations of the base point, the figures are continuously drawn on the screen in an array of colors.

The main object in the application is a Vector object, figure, that stores the pointers to Shape objects. In the function `buildFigures()`, we dynamically allocate a set of CircleShape, RectShape, and PolyShape objects that are pointed to by the elements of figure. To create the kaleidoscope, the function displayFigures() randomly chooses objects pointed to by the vector elements, relocates their base points, assigns fill colors, and uses dynamic binding to draw the corresponding figures on the screen. Let us look at these functions in more detail.

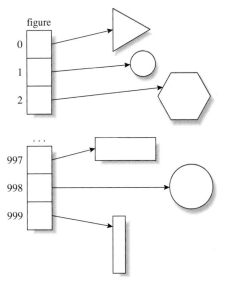

FIGURE 12-8
1000 Random Figures

In the implementation of build Figures(), each figure is created by starting with a random number in the range 0 to 2 and using it to assign the value of currentShape, which is an object of the enumeration type ShapeType. The possible values of currentShape are CircleObj, RectangleObj, and PolygonObj. A switch statement using currentShape directs the dynamic creation of a shape, *figure[i], whose attributes other than base point are assigned randomly. For instance, a circle is given a random radius, a rectangle is given a random length and width, and so forth. Figure 12-8 is a view of 1000 randomly generated graphics figures. The base point is assigned (0,0) and the color is assigned the default value of darkgray.

```
// allocate figure.size() number of random objects
// accessed by a Shape pointer. a switch statement
// oversees the generation of the figures
void buildFigures(Vector<Shape *>& figure, RandomNumber& rnd)
{
    // used to distinguish geometric objects
    enum ShapeType {CircleObj, RectangleObj, PolygonObj};

    ShapeType currentShape;
    double r;                       // radius for CircleShape
    double length, width;           // dimensions for RectShape
    int n;                          // dimensions for PolyShape
    double len;

    int i, size = figure.size();    // loop control objects

    // generate random objects, all with base point (0,0)
    // and default color darkgray
    for (i=0; i < size; i++)
    {
        // convert 0, 1, 2 to circle, rectangle, polygon
        currentShape = ShapeType(rnd.random(3));
        switch (currentShape)
        {
            case CircleObj:
                    // random CircleShape, 0 <= radius < 1.25
                    r = .5 + rnd.frandom() * .75;
                    figure[i] = new CircleShape(0,0,r);
                    break;

            case RectangleObj:
                    // random RectShape, 0 <= length,width <2.25
                    length = .5 + rnd.frandom() * 1.75;
                    width = .5 + rnd.frandom() * 1.75;
                    figure[i] = new RectShape(0,0,length,width);
                    break;

            case PolygonObj:
                    // random PolyShape, 3 <= n <= 6,
                    // 0 <= length of side < 1.25
                    n = 3 + rnd.random(4);
                    len = .5 + rnd.frandom() * .75;
                    figure[i] = new PolyShape(0,0,n,len);
                    break;
        }

    }
}
```

The function `displayFigures()` draws the figures in random order, at random locations on the screen and in colors that cycle through the list of

16 colors. In a continuous loop, that terminates with a keystroke, random coordinates for the base point are chosen in the range $0 \le x < 10$, $0 \le y < 8$.

```
x = rnd.frandom() * 10.0;
y = rnd.frandom() * 8.0;
```

The function randomly selects an index from the Vector of size = figure.size() elements.

```
// generate a random index of a figure
i = rnd.random(size);
```

After moving the base point to (x,y) and assigning a fill color to the figure, it is displayed by using polymorphism to draw the shape pointed to by figure[i].

```
figure[i]->move(x,y);    // move the figure to (x,y)
// set fill color for object
figure[i]->setColor(color);
figure[i]->draw();       // draw the figure
```

Testing for a keystroke is done by calling the function keyPress() declared in the header file **graphlib.h.** This logical function returns the value true if a key has been pressed and false otherwise.

```
// display the figures continuously until a key is pressed
void displayFigures(const Vector<Shape *>& figure,
                    RandomNumber& rnd);
{
   bool continueDraw = true;
   // base point for an object
   double x, y;
   int i, size = figure.size();
   // cycles through all available colors as
   // shapes are drawn
   ShapeColor color = blue;

   // generate a random index into figure. move to random
   // base point (x,y), 0 <= x < 10, 0 <= y < 8, set
   // the color and draw the figure. terminate the loop
   // when a key is pressed
   while (continueDraw)
   {
      // generate a random base point
      x = rnd.frandom() * 10.0;
      y = rnd.frandom() * 8.0;

      // generate a random index of a figure
      i = rnd.random(size);

      figure[i]->move(x,y);       // move the figure to (x,y)
      figure[i]->setColor(color); // set fill color for object
      figure[i]->draw();          // draw the figure
      if (keyPress())             // terminate if key pressed
         continueDraw = false;
```

```
        // advance to next color
        color++;


    }
}
```

The kaleidoscope program uses a vector with NUMBER_OF_FIGURES = 100 Shape pointers. The kaleidoscope is created by calling the functions `buildFigures()` and then `displayFigures()`. Before terminating the program, we delete the dynamically generated geometric objects and then de-allocate the elements of the Vector by calling `clear()`.

```
#include "tvector.h"      // use Vector class
#include "trandom.h"      // use RandomNumber class
#include "circlesh.h"     // use CircleShape class
#include "rectsh.h"       // use RectShape class
#include "polysh.h"       // use PolyShape class
#include "graphlib.h"     // basic drawing operations

// allocate figure.size() number of random objects
// accessed by a Shape pointer. a switch statement
// oversees the generation of the figures
void buildFigures(Vector<Shape *>& figure, RandomNumber& rnd);

// display the figures continuously until a key is pressed
void displayFigures(const Vector<Shape *>& figure,
                    RandomNumber& rnd);

int main()
{
    const int NUMBER_OF_FIGURES = 1000;
    // vector of pointers to derived objects
    Vector<Shape *>  figure(NUMBER_OF_FIGURES);
    // everything generated randomly
    RandomNumber rnd;
    int i;

    // create random figures
    buildFigures(figure, rnd);

    // open the drawing window
    openWindow();

    // display the figures in random order and at random
    // locations
    displayFigures(figure, rnd);

    closeWindow();

    // delete memory for each figure and clear the vector
```

```
            for (i=0;i < NUMBER_OF_FIGURES;i++)
               delete figure[i];
            figure.resize(0);

            return 0;
         }
```

```
   /* implementations of buildFigures() and displayFigures() are
      given in the program discussion */
```

Run:

12-6 ADVANCED INHERITANCE TOPICS

The previous sections introduce the basic concepts of inheritance that apply in most applications. This section introduces two topics that may be of importance in advanced programming situations. When a class uses dynamic memory, a destructor must be implemented to de-allocate the memory. If the class is used as a base class, the destructor should be made virtual or memory leaks may occur. As a second consideration, when a base class defines a pure virtual function, it forces the implementation of the function in a derived class. Such a class is termed an abstract base class and acts like a template in the design of other classes.

Virtual Functions And The Destructor
A subtle but important fact must be considered in base class design. In the following example, the base class dynamically allocates an array of three integers and a non-virtual destructor de-allocates the memory. For demonstration we

include output statements in the constructor and destructor that are used in test programs.

```
class DynBase
{
    protected:
        int *barr;      // pointer to base class dynamic array

    public:
        DynBase ()
        {
            cout << "Allocate 3 element DynBase array" << endl;
            barr = new int[3];
        }

        ~DynBase ()     // not a virtual destructor
        {
            cout << "Delete 3 element DynBase array" << endl;
            delete [] barr;
        }
};
```

The class DynDerived inherits DynBase and allocates its own array of four integers. Figure 12-9 is a view of a DynDerived object.

```
class DynDerived: public DynBase
{
    private:
        int *darr;    // pointer to derived class dynamic array
    public:
        DynDerived (): DynBase ()
        {
            cout << "Allocate 4 element DynDerived array" << endl;
            darr = new int[4];
        }

        ~DynDerived ()
        {
            cout << "Delete 4 element DynDerived array" << endl;
            delete [] darr;
        }
};
```

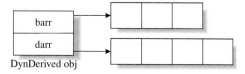

FIGURE 12-9
Object with Dynamic Data in the Base and Derived Class.

To illustrate the problem, Program 12.1 allocates a DynDerived object pointed to by a DynBase pointer and uses the operator delete in an attempt to deallocate the memory. The same test is run in Program 12.2 when the destructor in DynBase is declared as virtual.

PROGRAM 12.1

Declare p as a DynBase pointer and assign it the address of a DynDerived object. The output statements in the constructors illustrate that an array is first allocated for the base class and then one for the derived class.

```
DynBase *p = new DynDerived;   // construct a DynDerived object
```

The destructor of DynBase is not virtual and so the operation delete uses static binding. Only the base class destructor is called.

```
delete p;   // calls the base class destructor
```

The dynamic array that is generated by the derived class is not destroyed.

```
#include <iostream.h>
<insert DynBase and DynDerived classes here>
int main()
{
   DynBase *p = new DynDerived;

   delete p;

   return 0;
}
```

```
Run: (DynBase destructor is not virtual):

Allocate 3 element DynBase array
Allocate 4 element DynDerived array
Delete 3 element DynBase array
```

If the DynBase destructor is declared virtual, the DynDerived destructor is also virtual and the DynDerived destructor is called. This is followed by a call to the base class destructor. The following is the necessary modification to DynBase.

```
virtual ~DynBase ()   // virtual destructor
{
   cout << "Delete 3 element DynBase array" << endl;
   delete [] barr;
}
```

PROGRAM 12.2

The previous program is rerun with the modified base class destructor. Since polymorphism and dynamic binding apply, the derived class destructor is executed first and then C++ calls the destructor for the base class.

```
#include <iostream.h>

<insert DynBase and DynDerived classes here>

int main()
{
    DynBase *p = new DynDerived;

    delete p;

    return 0;
}
```

```
Run (DynBase destructor is virtual):

Allocate 3 element DynBase array
Allocate 4 element DynDerived array
Delete 4 element DynDerived array
Delete 3 element DynBase array
```

If a class is designed to be used as a base class in an inheritance hierarchy, give it a virtual destructor, even if you have to create a destructor that does nothing, such as

```
virtual ~DynBase()
{}
```

This ensures that if a derived class has a destructor, that destructor will always be executed. In the supplemental software, note that the Vector and List classes have a virtual destructor since they may be used to derive other classes.

Abstract Base Classes

Our study of inheritance has led to the use of virtual member functions in the base class, with identical function prototypes appearing in derived classes. Because the base class member function is declared as virtual, dynamic binding is used and the correct version of the function will be called when a pointer or a reference is used. In the Shape class, we declared the virtual member function draw(). This operation is not meaningful for a Shape object that specifies the base point and the color for a shape and so each of the derived geometric classes has its own draw() function that sketches the specific shape. However, by declaring the operation as virtual in the base class, we are assured that dynamic binding will call the correct version for the specific drawing object. We could define draw() in the base class to do nothing.

```
// place holder function implementation in the base class
void Shape::draw()
{}
```

Rather than forcing the programmer to create such place holder implementations, C++ allows the use of pure virtual functions by appending "= 0" to the function prototype.

> **Definition** A *pure virtual function* in a base class is a virtual function that has no implementation in the class. Its prototype forces an implementation of the function in a derived class. A pure virtual function has the form
>
> ```
> virtual returnType func (arguments)= 0;
> ```

The function `draw()` in the Shape class is pure virtual. Each derived geometric class must define a function `draw()` with no arguments and void return type. Shape is said to be an abstract base class.

> **Definition** A class with one or more pure virtual functions is known as an *abstract class*. No objects of its type can be declared. Any class derived from an abstract class must provide an implementation of each pure virtual function, or it is also an abstract class and may not generate objects.

By including a pure virtual function in the Shape class, we ensure that no separate Shape objects can be created. The class can only be used as a base for another class.

```
// Error - no independent Shape object can be declared
Shape shObj(1,1,blue);
```

EXAMPLE 12.4 ▬▬▬▬▬▬▬▬▬▬▬▬▬▬▬▬▬▬▬▬▬▬▬▬▬

The abstract class BaseCL contains two pure virtual functions and hence is an abstract base class.

```
class BaseCL
{
   ...
   public:
      virtual void f() = 0;
      virtual int g() = 0;
};
```

The derived class DerivedCL implements `f()` but not `g()`, and so DerivedCL remains an abstract class.

```
class DerivedCL: public BaseCL
{
   ...
    public:
      // g() not implemented, so class remains abstract
      virtual void f();
};
```

The class DerivedCL can be used as part of a longer inheritance chain that includes a derived class DDerivedCL that implements g() (Figure 12-10). In this case a DDerivedCL object can be declared.

```
DDerivedCL obj;   ■
```

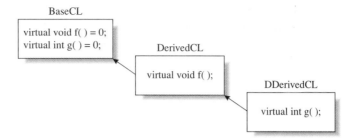

FIGURE 12-10
Inheritance chain defines pure virtual functions.

An abstract class acts like a template for its derived classes. By using pure virtual functions, it provides a prototype for the public member functions that must be implemented by a derived class.

CHAPTER 12 SUMMARY

Inheritance and object composition are the primary techniques for reusing software. Inheritance involves a class hierarchy whose elements are base and derived classes. A base class provides member functions and data to a derived class. The derived class may choose to add its own member functions or redefine existing ones in the base class. To illustrate public inheritance, the book discusses the graphics classes RectShape, CircleShape and PolyShape that are derived from the common base class Shape. Another example is provided by the employee hierarchy. Public inheritance expresses the "is a" relationship. A CircleShape object "is a" Shape and a SalaryEmployee "is an" Employee. Public inheritance is also known as inheritance of the interface.

In Section 12-3, public inheritance is used to develop an ordered list class from the List class. Invalid member functions such as insertFront() are blocked from use by a derived object. The insert() function in the derived class is implemented by using base class functions.

The concept of polymorphism is fundamental to object-oriented programming. In fact, professionals often refer to object-oriented programming as "inheritance with run-time polymorphism." Polymorphism allows two or more objects in an inheritance hierarchy to have operations with the same prototype that perform distinct tasks. When an application calls such a function using a pointer or reference to an object, the required version is dynamically determined at run-time. In C++, polymorphism is implemented by declaring the functions using the keyword virtual. Virtual functions have vast applications in the construction of large graphical libraries and object-oriented database systems.

The chapter concludes with a study of advanced inheritance topics. When dynamic memory is used by a derived class, the base class should have a destructor that is declared as a virtual function. Failure to do this can result in serious memory leaks. As another consideration, a pure virtual function declared in a base class forces the implementation of the function in a derived class. The base class is known as an abstract class which is template, or mold, for the construction of derived classes.

Classes in the Chapter

Name	Implementation File
BrickHouse	houses.h
CircleShape	circlesh.h
Employee	emphier.h
HourlyEmployee	emphier.h
House	houses.h
List	tlist.h
OrderedList	ordlist.h
PolyShape	polysh.h
RectShape	rectsh.h
SalaryEmployee	emphier.h
Shape	shape.h
VinylSidedHouse	houses.h
WoodFrameHouse	houses.h

KEY TERMS

Abstract class:
A class with one or more pure virtual functions. No objects of its type can be declared. Any class derived from an abstract class must provide an implementation of each pure virtual function, or it is also an abstract class and may not generate objects.

Class hierarchy:
A tree of classes. The hierarchy begins with a base class and continues with one or more derived classes.

Dynamic binding:
The process by which a virtual function is called at run-time. A pointer or reference accesses the virtual function table from which the address of the appropriate function is determined.

Polymorphism:
Means that in a system of classes related by inheritance, a member function with the same prototype can be implemented in different classes. The specific action of the member function will vary from class to class. When an application needs the function, the particular version is dynamically determined at run-time. In C++, the function must be declared virtual and be called using a pointer or a reference to an object.

Protected class members:
Section of a base class implementing information hiding. When a base class is inherited by a derived class, all of the protected members in the base class may be accessed by functions in the derived class. The protected members may not be accessed by any derived objects.

Public inheritance:
The most commonly used form of inheritance in which the public and protected members of the base class are available to the implementation of derived class functions. Only public members of the two classes are available to a derived object. Public inheritance should only be used to express the "is a" relationship, also termed inheritance of the interface.

Pure virtual function:
A virtual function in a base class that has no implementation. Its declaration forces an implementation in a derived class.

Static binding:
Occurs when a function is called by referencing a specific object by name and using the dot (.) member selection operator. The code for the function call is generated by the compiler. Static binding is also known as compile-time binding.

Subclass:
Another name for a derived class.

Superclass:
Another name for a base class.

Virtual base class destructor:
Declared so the derived class destructor will be called when an object is deleted using a pointer to the base class. Not declaring the base class destructor virtual can result in memory leaks.

Virtual function table:
Contains the locations of an object's virtual functions. A pointer to this table is placed in each object. When a virtual function is called by using a pointer or reference to an object, the run-time system follows the pointer to the table and executes the appropriate function.

Virtual member function:
Declared by placing the keyword virtual in front of the return type in the function prototype. When a virtual function is called using a pointer or reference to an object, dynamic binding is used.

REVIEW EXERCISES

1. Book is a base class with cover and pageLength defined as protected data members. Textbook is a derived class with the String subjectMatter as a private data member. Each class has the member function describe() along with its constructor.

```cpp
enum CoverType {HardCover, SoftCover};

class Book
{
    protected:
        CoverType cover;
        int pageLength;
    public:
        Book(CoverType ct, int pglen):
            cover(ct), pageLength(pglen)
        {}

        virtual void describe()
        {
            cout << "A " << pageLength << " page";
            if (cover == HardCover)
                cout << " hard covered book" << endl;
            else
                cout << " soft covered book" << endl;
        }
};
```

```
class Textbook: public Book
{
    private:
        String subjectMatter;
    public:
        // constructor
        _____    // (a)

    virtual void describe()
    {
        _____    // (b) describe Book attributes
        cout << "Used for courses in " << subjectMatter
        << endl;
    }
};
```

(a) Implement the constructor for the Textbook class.

(b) Give the statement that outputs a description of the Book attributes.

(c) Give the declaration for the Book object myDictionary that is a 625 page soft covered book.

(d) Give a declaration for the Textbook object courseBook that is a hard covered Computer Science book with 850 pages.

For parts (e) to (h), use the declarations from (c) and (d)

(e) What is output by each of the following statements?

```
myDictionary.describe();
courseBook.describe();
```

(f) Give the statement that would output a description of only the Book attributes of the object courseBook.

(g) Are the following statements valid? Explain.

```
cout << courseBook.pageLength;
myDictionary.cover = HardCover;
```

2. The chart specifies access rights of a derived object and member functions in the base and derived classes to the different types of class members. For instance, the √ indicates that a member function in the base class can access a private member in the base class. Complete the chart assuming that the base and derived classes are related with public inheritance.

Data \ Statement	Private (Base)	Protected (Base)	Public (Base)	Private (Derived)	Public (Derived)
Base	√				
Derived					
Derived object					

3. DerivedCL inherits BaseCL using public inheritance. Both classes have a version of function getValue().

```
class BaseCL
{
    protected:
        int a;
    public:
        BaseCL(int m)  : a(m)
        {}

        int getValue()
        { return a; }
};

class DerivedCL:  public BaseCL
{
    private:
        int b;

    public:
        DerivedCL(int v, int w)  : BaseCL(v),b(w)
        {};

        int getValue()
        { return a + b; }
};
```

Assume the following declarations for objects one and two. Give the output for each valid statement. If a statement is not valid, indicate that as the output.

```
BaseCL one(3);
DerivedCL two(2,3);
```

(a) cout << one.getValue();   // Output: _____
(b) cout << two.getValue();   // Output: _____
(c) cout << two.BaseCL::getValue();   // Output: _____
(d) Assign a derived object to a base object

```
        one = two;
        cout << one.getValue() << endl;  // Output: _____
```

(e) Assign a base object to a derived object

```
        two = one;
        cout << two.getValue() << endl;  // Output: _____
```

(f) cout << two.a;   // Output: _____

4. In a for statement, data is entered into an ordered list from an array. Trace the code and indicate the resulting list.

```
OrderedList<int>  alist;
int i, arr[] = {28, 45, 90, 17, 22, 87, 82, 38, 77, 50};

for (i  = 0; i < 10; i++)
{
    if (!alist.empty() && arr[i] > alist.front())
        alist.eraseFront();
    alist.insert(arr[i]);
}
```

5. What is polymorphism? Give an example of its use.

6. This question uses the classes Book and Textbook discussed in Review Exercise 1. Assume the following function definitions:

```
void identify(Book b)
{
    b.describe();
}
```

```
void identify(Book *b)
{
    b->describe();
}
```

Declare the objects:

```
Book cookBook(HardCover, 150), *p, *q;
Textbook poetry(SoftCover, 500, "English");
```

What are the outputs?
(a) `p = &cookBook;`
    `identify(cookBook);`
    `identify(p);`
(b) `q = &poetry;`
    `identify(q);`
    `identify(poetry);`

7. In the Shape class, explain why
   (a) move() is not a virtual function.
   (b) draw() is a pure virtual function.

8. What is a pure virtual function? How does the concept relate to an abstract base class? What are the applications for abstract base classes?

Answers to Review Exercises

1. (a) `Textbook::Textbook(CoverType ct, int pglen,`
                         `const String& subject):`
           `Book(ct, pglen), subjectMatter(subject)`
        `{}`
   (b) `Book::describe();`
   (c) `Book myDictionary(SoftCover, 625);`
   (d) `Textbook courseBook(HardCover, 850, "Computer Science");`
   (e) A 625 page soft covered book
       A 850 page hard covered book
       Used for courses in Computer Science
   (f) `courseBook.Book::describe();`
   (g) No. Each object is a protected data member of the Book class. The objects can only be accessed by member functions of the Book and Textbook classes.

2.

Data Statement	Private (Base)	Protected (Base)	Public (Base)	Private (Derived)	Public (Derived)
Base	√	√	√		
Derived		√	√	√	√
Derived object			√		√

3. (a) 3   (b) 5   (c) 2   (d) 2   (e) not valid   (f) not valid

4. Resulting list is 50 77 82 87 90

5. In a system of classes related by inheritance, a member function with the same prototype can be implemented in different classes. The specific action of the member function will vary from class to class. When an application needs the function, the particular version is dynamically determined at run-time. In C++, polymorphism is implemented using virtual member functions. The draw() operation in the graphics hierarchy is a virtual function. When it is called using a Shape pointer or reference to a derived object, the version of draw() in the derived object is called.

6. (a) A 150 page hard covered book
     A 150 page hard covered book

   (b) A 500 page soft covered book
     Used for courses in English
     A 500 page soft covered book

7. (a) The function move() changes the base point for the figure. There is no need for it to be overridden in a derived class.

   (b) The Shape class maintains the base point and color for the figure. There is no viable definition for draw() in the base class. However, declaring it as a pure virtual function assures that each derived class will implement draw() to display the figure on the drawing surface.

8. A pure virtual function is a virtual function in a base class that has no implementation. Its declaration forces an implementation in a derived class. An abstract base class is a class with at least one pure virtual function. An abstract base class is used as a template for the construction of derived classes and cannot generate objects.

WRITTEN EXERCISES

9. Assume the strings represent names of C++ classes.

```
SuperBowl, Television, Movies, Comedy, ActionThriller
```

Draw a hierarchy of base and derived classes from this list.

10. Consider the class hierarchy structure

```
class BaseCL
{
   private:
      int m;
   protected:
      int n;
   public:
      BaseCL();
      virtual void demoFunc();
};

class DerivedCL: public BaseCL
{
   private:
      int r;
   public:
      DerivedCL();
      virtual void demoFunc ();
};
```

(a) Which of the data members m, n, and r can be accessed by a member function in the derived class?
(b) Which of the data members m, n, and r can be accessed by a member function in the base class?
(c) Consider the declarations

```
BaseCL bObj;
DeriveCL dObj;
```

Which of the objects bObj and dObj may exectute demoFunc() in the base class? Give the C++ statements that provide the call.
Which of the objects bObj and dObj may execute demoFunc() in the derived class? Give the C++ statements that provide the call.

11. Consider the following outline for a base and derived class:

```
class BaseCL
{
   protected:
      int data;
   public:
      // constructors
      BaseCL(int a): data(a)
      {}

      BaseCL(): data(0)
      {}
};

class DerivedCL
{
   private:
      int x;
   public:
```

```
             // constructors
             DerivedCL(int a, int b);    // constructor ONE
             DerivedCL(int a);           // constructor TWO
    ...
};
```

(a) Use inline code to implement constructor ONE that assigns a to the derived class and b to the base class.

(b) Use inline code to implement constructor TWO that assigns a to the derived class and uses the default constructor for the base class.

12. When a class is derived from a base class using *private inheritance*, the public members of the base class become private members of the derived class. The public and protected members of the base class are available only to the derived class member functions and not to a derived object. The base class member functions are used for implementing the member functions of the derived class. Private inheritance is referred to as *inheritance of the implementation*.

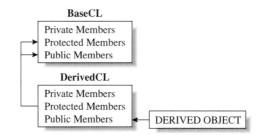

Look at Review Exercise 12.2. Fill in the chart assuming that the base and derived classes are related by private inheritance.

Statement \ Data	Private (Base)	Protected (Base)	Public (Base)	Private (Derived)	Public (Derived)
Base	√				
Derived					
Derived object					

13. You are given the outline of a base class BaseCL. Explain what is wrong syntactically or otherwise with each derived class declaration.

```
class BaseCL
{
   private:
      int bData;
   public:
      BaseCL(int a);
      ...
};
```

(a) class DCL1 public BaseCL   (b) class DCL2: BaseCL

```
(a) class DCL1 public BaseCL          (b) class DCL2: BaseCL
    {                                     {
       private:                              private:
          int dData;                           ...
       public:                               public:
          DCL1(int z): dData(z)                 // DCL2 has no
          {}                                    // constructor
          ...
    };                                          int getData()
                                                { return bData; }
                                          };
```

14. The program illustrates the order in which constructor and destructor calls are made in a class hierarchy. What is the output of the program?

```cpp
#include <iostream.h>

class BaseCL
{
   public:
      BaseCL() { cout << "BaseCL constructor" << endl; }
      ~BaseCL() {cout << "BaseCL destructor" << endl;}
};

class DerivedCL: public BaseCL
{
   public:
      DerivedCL: BaseCL
      {
        cout << " DerivedCL constructor" << endl;
      }
      ~ DerivedCL
      {
        cout << " DerivedCL destructor" << endl;
      }
};

int main()
{
   BaseCL bObj;
   DerivedCL dObj;

   return 0;
}
```

15. What is the output of the program?

```cpp
#include <iostream.h>

#include "tstring.h"

class BaseCL
{
   private:
      String msg;
```

```
        protected:
           int n;
        public:
           BaseCL(String s, int m = 0): msg(s), n(m)
           {}

           void output()
           {  cout << n << "   " << msg << endl; }
    };

    class DerivedCL: public BaseCL
    {
        private:
           int n;
        public:
           DerivedCL(int m = 1):BaseCL("Base",m-1),n(m)
           {}

           void output()
           {  cout << n << endl;
              BaseCL::output();
           }
    };

    int main()
    {
        BaseCL bObj("Base Class",1);
        DerivedCL d1Obj(4), d2Obj;

        bObj.output();
        d1Obj.output();
        d2Obj.output();

        return 0;
    }
```

16. Use the Employee, SalaryEmployee, and HourlyEmployee inheritance chain of Section 12.2 for this question. For each statement, determine if the assignment is legal. Draw a picture supporting your answer.

```
    Employer generic Employee("",""); //NULL arguments
    HourlyEmployee ron("Ron Karl","867-49-3985",8.00,45);
```

(a) genericEmployee = ron;
(b) ron = genericEmployee;

17. Assume the *median* value in an array is the element at the mid-index(n/2) of the list if it is sorted. For instance, consider the two integer arrays

```
    int arr1[5] = {5, 8, 1, 3, 6},
        arr2[4] = {6, 12, 3, 9};
```

The median of arr1 is 5, and the median of arr2 is 6. Write a function

```
template <class T>
T median (T arr[], int n);
```

that returns the median of array arr. Use an OrderedList object in the implementation.

18. (a) Implement a function mode() that takes an OrderedList object and returns the
element that occurs most frequently in the list and the number of times it occurs. If two or more elements occur with the same frequency, return the first element.

```
template <class T>
T mode(const OrderedList<T>& aList,int& numOcc);
```

(b) Define a function freq() that takes an OrderedList object and displays the number of times each element occurs in the list. The output order is from most frequent to least frequent.

```
template <class T>
void freq(const OrderedList<T>& aList);
```

For instance, freq() takes the list 2, 2, 6, 6, 6, 6, 9, 12, 12, 12
and produces the output:

```
6(4)   12(3)   2(2)   9(1)
```

HINT: Copy aList to another OrderedList object. By repeatedly calling mode(),
search the list for the most frequently occurring element and execute a series or
erase() operations until all occurrences are removed from the list.

19. The SquareShape class is derived from the RectShape class using public inheritance.

```
// declaration of SquareShape class
class SquareShape: public RectShape
{
   private:
      // length of each side
      double side;
   public:
      // constructor.
      SquareShape(double x = 0.0, double y = 0.0,
                  double side = 0.0,
                  ShapeColor c = darkgray);

      // SquareShape data access and update functions
      double getSide() const
      { return side; }

      void setSides(double s)
      { side = s; }

};
```

(a) Implement the constructor SquareShape() using inline code.
(b) Explain why the derived class does not need a draw() function?

(c) Declare a SquareShape with a length of 8, a base point at (20, 20) with red as the fill color.

20. Use the Employee hierarchy and the following statements.

```
Employee boss("Mr. Boss", "555-33-5555"), *p;
SalaryEmployee
   karen("Karen Ross", "567-23-8357", 3300.0), *q = &karen;
HourlyEmployee
   will("William Johns", "463-38-4712", 6.5, 40),
   *r = &will;

p = &karen;
```

(a) Give the output for the employeeInfo() functions.

```
r->employeeInfo();
q->employeeInfo();
q->Employee::employeeInfo();
p->employeeInfo();
```

(b) Consider the three functions.

```
void identify1(Employee p)
{
    p.employeeInfo();
    cout << endl;
}

void identify2(Employee *p)
{
    p->employeeInfo();
    cout << endl;
}

void indentify3(const Employee& p)
{
    p.employeeInfo();
    cout << endl;
}
```

What is the output for the instructions?

(1) `identify1(boss);`
(2) `identify1(karen);`
(3) `identify2(&boss);`
(4) `identify2(r);`
(5) `identify3(will);`
(6) `identify3(*p);`

21. Consider the following classes:

```
class BaseCL
{
    protected:
        int one;
```

```
   public:
      BaseCL(int a): one(a)
      {}

      virtual void identify()
      {cout << one << endl;}
};

class DerivedCL: public BaseCL
{
   protected:
      int two;
   public:
      DerivedCL(int a, int b): BaseCL(a), two(b){}

      virtual void identify()
      {cout << one << "  " << two << endl;}
};
```

The following functions are used to identify the classes.

```
void announce1(BaseCL x)
{
   x.identify();
}

void announce2(BaseCL *x)
{
   x->identify();
}
```

(a) Give the output from the code segment.

```
BaseCL A(7), *p;
DerivedCL B(1,2);

announce1(A);
announce2(&B);
p = &B;
p->identify();
```

(b) Give the output from the code segment:

```
BaseCL *p, *arr[3];
DerivedCL B(3,5);
int i;

announce1(B);
announce2(&B);
for(i=0;i < 3;i++)
   if (i == 1)
      arr[i] = new BaseCL(7);
   else
```

```
        arr[i] = new DerivedCL(i,i+1);
    for(i=0;i < 3;i++)
        arr[i]->identify();
```

PROGRAMMING EXERCISES

22. Use the inheritance hierarchy for classes Book and TextBook from Review Exercise 12.1. Declare the following Book and TextBook objects.

```
Book bk1(HardCover, 250), bk2(SoftCover, 360);
TextBook econ101(HardCover, 725, "Economics");
```

Write a program that outputs the Book descriptions for bk1, bk2 and econ101 and the TextBook description for econ101.

23. Use the SquareRect class from Written Exercise 12.19 to draw a series of 5 nested squares in different colors about the point (5,4).

24. Use the function median() that is declared in Written Exercise 17. Write a program that inputs an integer n and allocates a vector of n integer objects.

```
cin >> n;
Vector<int> arr(n);
```

Input n integers and find their median value. Note that you will have to apply the Vector class member function c_arr() when passing arr to median().

25. Use the functions mode() and freq() that are developed in Written Exercise 12.18. Write a program that takes the integer array

```
int arr[10] = {2,2,6,6,6,6,9,12,12,12};
```

and outputs the frequency for each element in the array.

26. A company office processes print jobs using a priority status. The class printJob describes the job using the data member priority to rank the job and data member time to measure its length. When comparing two jobs, the one with the lower value for priority is considered the most important. The class declares an overloaded < operator that compares the priority ranks. The class declaration is included.

DECLARATION: PrintJob CLASS ■■■■■■■

```
class PrintJob
{
    private:
```

```
        int priority;
        int time;
    public:
        PrintJob(int pty=0, int t=0);
        int getPriority() const;
        int getTime() const;
        void setPrintData(int pty,int t);
        friend bool operator<(const PrintJob &a,
                              const PrintJob &b);
};
```

Implement the class and write a program that reads print job data from the file printjob.dat and assigns them to an OrderedList object pjList and then outputs them in their order of priority.

```
Data File          Output List
3   9              1   5
2   8              1   4
1   9              1   9
3   5              2   7
1   4              2 12
2  12              2   8
3  10              3   7
2   7              3 10
1   5              3   5
3   7              3   9
```

PROGRAMMING PROJECT

27. Implement the class, GenVector, that generalizes the Vector class to create a safe array with general starting and ending indices. For instance,

    ```
    GenVector <int> a(1,10), b(-1,8);
    ```

    creates safe array objects a and b with index ranges $1 \leq i \leq 10$ and $-1 \leq i \leq 8$, respectively. GenVector objects can indexed within their defined range. For instance,

    ```
    int i;
    for(i=-1; i <= 8;i++)    // initialize all elements to 0
        b[i] = 0;
    ```

    Derive GenVector from the Vector class using public inheritance. Override the index operator so it accepts indices in the correct range. Implement a derived class resize() function that resizes the vector and resets the ending index. These actions prevent references to the Vector class index operator and resize() function unless the class scope operator :: is used.

DECLARATION: GenVector CLASS ▬▬▬▬▬▬▬

```
template <class T>
class GenVector: public Vector<T>
{
   private:
      int lower;
      int upper;

   public:
      // array has high-low+1 elements
      GenVector(int low, int high);
      // operator checks bounds
      T& operator[] (int i);
      void resize(int sz);    // resize vector
};
```

Write a program that declares the following objects:

```
GenVector<char> ucLetter(65,90);
GenVector<double> tempVector(-10,25);
```

Initialize ucLetter so ucLetter[65]='A', ..., ucLetter[90]='Z'. Initialize tempVector so tempVector[t] is the Fahrebnheit equivalent of Celsius temperature t. Recall that

```
F=9.0/5.0*C+32
```

Output the contents of each vector.

Appendix A
Computer Data Storage

The electronics of a computer stores data using a series of switches, called bits (binary digits), in the ON or OFF position. The two-states of each bit are represented by 0 and 1. For instance, the bits in Figure A.1 represent the number 1001. Its value in a computer is determined by its base-two (binary) representation that is modeled on our familiar decimal or base-10 system. A number has both a positional and an expanded notation representation. Let's explore these ideas by starting with decimal numbers and then relating the concepts to binary numbers.

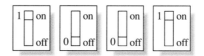

FIGURE A-1
Binary Number 1001 Represented by Bits.

Binary Numbers

Decimal numbers are stored in positional notation as a set of digits d_k, d_{k-1}, ... , d_1, d_0 with each digit in the range 0 to 9. The position of each digit corresponds to a power of 10 that starts on the right with 1 (10^0) and progressively increases in value through the range 10 (10^1), 100 (10^2), 1000 (10^3), and so forth A number has an equivalent **expanded notation representation** that gives its value as a sum of powers of ten. For instance, 365 is a three digit number in positional notation with the following expanded notation representation. The subscript 10 indicates that 365 is a decimal (base-10) number.

$$365_{10} = 3(10^2) + 6(10^1) + 5(10^0)$$

In general, a k-digit decimal number N has the following representations:

Positional decimal notation

$$N_{10} = d_{k-1}d_{k-2}...d_2d_1d_0 \qquad (0 <= d_i <= 9)$$

Expanded decimal notation

$$N_{10} = d_{k-1}(10^{k-1}) + d_{k-2}(10^{k-2}) + \ldots + d_i(10^i) + \ldots + d_1(10^1) + d_0(10^0)$$

Binary numbers use digits 0 and 1 with positions corresponding to powers of 2 (1, 2, 4, 8, 16, and so on). These powers of 2 are used in the expanded binary representation of the number. For instance, the bits in Figure A.1 correspond to the binary number 1001_2 in positional notation. The subscript 2 indicates a number is given in binary. The expanded binary representation shows that the number is equivalent to the decimal number 9.

$$1001_2 = 1(2^3) + 0(2^2) + 0(2^1) + 1(2^0) = 9_{10}$$

In general, a k-digit binary number has representations

Positional binary notation

$$N_2 = b_{k-1}b_{k-2} \ldots b_2 b_1 b_0 \qquad (b_i = 0 \text{ or } 1)$$

Expanded binary notation

$$N_2 = b_{k-1}(2^{k-1}) + b_{k-2}(d^{k-2}) + \ldots + b_i(2^i) + \ldots + b_1(2^1) + d_0(2^0)$$

Like decimal numbers, binary numbers are unchanged if you add leading zeros. For instance, $1001_2 = 01001_2 = 001001_2 = 9$.

Converting Binary and Decimal Numbers

Converting numbers between their equivalent decimal and binary representation is easily done using expanded notation. For instance, the value of the binary number 101010_2 is computed directly from its expanded representation by adding up the terms in the sum.

$$101010_2 = 1(2^5) + 0(2^4) + 1(2^3) + 0(2^2) + 1(2^1) + 0(2^0) = 42_{10}$$

Equivalently,

$$101010_2 = 1(32) + 0(16) + 1(8) + 0(4) + 1(2) + 0(1) = 42_{10}$$

EXAMPLE A.1

The example converts the value of a binary number to the equivalent decimal value using the expanded binary representation of the number.

1. $110101_2 = 1(32) + 1(16) + 0(8) + 1(4) + 0(2) + 1(1) = 53_{10}$
2. $10000110_2 = 1(128) + 0(64) + 0(32) + 0(16) + 0(8) + 1(4) + 1(2) + 0(1)$
$= 134_{10}$
3. $11111_2 = 1(16) + 1(8) + 1(4) + 1(2) + 1(1) = 31_{10}$ ∎

When converting from decimal to binary, find the largest power of two that is less than or equal to the number. Starting with that power, build the expanded binary representation of the number. For instance, with decimal number

75, the largest power of two less than or equal to 75 is 64. The binary expansion begins at 64 and includes all smaller powers 32, 16, 8, and so forth.

$$75^{10} = 1(64) + 0(32) + 0(16) + 1(8) + 0(4) + 1(2) + 1(1) = 1001011_2$$

EXAMPLE A.2 ▰▰▰▰▰▰▰▰▰▰▰▰▰▰▰▰▰▰▰▰▰▰▰▰▰▰▰▰▰▰▰▰▰▰▰▰▰

The example converts a decimal value to a binary number with expanded representation and positional notation.

1. $35_{10} = 1(32) + 0(16) + 0(8) + 0(4) + 1(2) + 1(1)$
   $= 100011_2$
2. $148_{10} = 1(128) + 0(64) + 0(32) + 1(16) + 0(8) + 1(4) + 0(2) + 0(1)$
   $= 10010100_2$ ▪

Storing and Retrieving Numbers in a Computer

A general discussion of binary numbers makes no reference to their size, since we assume larger and larger powers of two can be used in the expanded representation. The implementation of binary numbers on a computer, however, does not have this freedom. Computer arithmetic is performed on data stored in fixed-length memory locations. The basic unit of storage is 8-bits or a **byte.** For instance, the byte with decimal number 148 is stored as

$$148_{10} = 1(128) + 0(64) + 0(32) + 1(16) + 0(8) + 1(4) + 0(2) + 0(1)$$
$$= 10010100_2$$

1	0	0	1	0	1	0	0
7	6	5	4	3	2	1	0

The individual bits in each byte are labeled with the corresponding power of two in the expanded representation. Stored as a byte, the decimal number 75 would be filled with a 0 on the left.

$$75_{10} = 1(64) + 0(32) + 0(16) + 1(8) + 0(4) + 1(2) + 1(1)$$
$$= 01001011_2$$

0	1	0	0	1	0	1	1
7	6	5	4	3	2	1	0

Data in computer memory is stored in a consecutive sequence of bytes. Each byte has a location, or **address,** in memory. The first byte in memory has address 0, the second has address 1, and so forth. The data in each byte is called the **contents.** Figure A-2 gives a view of memory with value 75_{10} stored at address 2.

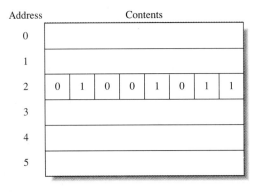

FIGURE A-2
View of Memory.

The size limitation of a byte restricts the size of any number in a memory location. Positive numbers must fall in the range 0 to 255

$$0 = 00000000_2 \leq N \leq 255 = 11111111_2$$

For larger numbers, a computer uses two or more consecutive bytes to store the data. Typically, numbers using 16-bits (2 bytes) or 32-bits (4 bytes) are available to the programmer and are part of the basic definition of a programming language. Most computers have hardware that will access 16 or 32-bit integers in one operation. If larger numbers are needed, the programmer must call on supplemental software or the support of additional hardware.

EXAMPLE A.3

The number 855_{10} can be stored as a 16-bit number. Its binary representation requires higher powers of 2, namely 256 (2^8) and 512 (2^9).

855_{10} = 1(512) + 1(256) + 0(128) + 1(64) + 0(32) + 1(16) + 0(8) + 1(4) + 1(2) + 1
= 1101010111_2.

Figure A-3 gives a view of 855 as a 16 bit number in adjacent bytes. A million is stored in 32 bits or 4 bytes.

Note that in each case leading zeros are added to fill each possible bit position. ∎

FIGURE A-3
Numeric Storage.

Primitive Data Types

The **int** type is the most commonly used C++ language-defined type and as such is the workhorse of C++ programming. An int object has a natural size supported by the machine architecture. Normally, the size of an integer is either 16 or 32 bits. For some applications we want more control over the size of an integer value and other number types are provided.

The Object Type char

A char object is at least 1 byte in size and holds any item from the designated character set. In most cases, the character set is ASCII and the size of a character is 1 byte. In such a case, the range of positive integers represented by a char object is 0 to 127.

The Object Type short

An object of type **short** is an integer whose value is defined to use at least 16-bits. On most systems, the short type uses exactly 16-bits. The standard integer operators are available for short objects, including stream input and output. Since the range for short integers is normally $-32,768$ to $32,767$, the user must carefully avoid **overflow** that would discard significant digits. Integer overflow occurs when an arithmetic operation produces a result that cannot be stored using the number of bits allocated to the object. Consider the following example that uses short integers a, b and c. The product a*b creates overflow and assigns the wrong result in object c. The fact that the product of two positive numbers is negative stems from the fixed length storage of integers and a special format **(twos-complement)** for negative numbers.

```
short a = 10000, b = 6, c;      // c is uninitialized
c = a * b;                      // c is -5536
```

Overflow is also possible for char and int objects.

The Object Type long

The **long** type guarantees the widest range of integer values and is used when numeric calculations may result in large values. A long integer always uses at least 32 bits. The long object has all of the standard int operations, including stream input and output.

Storage of Real Numbers

Internal storage of real numbers typically uses a standard known as IEEE floating point format. It specifies storage for a sign, an exponent and the mantissa. The IEEE format is more complex than integer formats and we give only a brief overview.

In the IEEE format, a real number is stored in either 32, 64 or 96 bits. The high order bit holds the sign (0 = positive, 1 = negative), while the remaining bits store the exponent as a power of 2 and the mantissa (significant digits).

$$X = \pm \text{ significant digits} \times 2^{\text{exp}}$$

A float object is normally represented using 32-bit IEEE format(Figure A-4). The sign of the number is stored in bit 31 while the exponent is stored in the next 8 bits. The low-order bits of the number store the mantissa that represents the significant digits of the numbers.

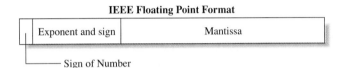

IEEE Floating Point Format

FIGURE A-4
IEEE Floating Point Format

For instance,

$$12.25_{10} = 1(8) + 1(4) + 0(2) + 0(1) + 0(1/2) + 1(1/4)$$
$$= 1100.01 \qquad // \text{ binary positional notation}$$
$$= +1.10001 \times 2^3$$

The sign is +(0), the exponent is 3, and the mantissa is 1.10001.

Real numbers lie on a line in the approximate range from -10^{38} to 10^{38}. A more precise calculation indicates both the range of the numbers and their limits near 0. The IEEE format for 0 is a special case.

Negative Numbers   *Positive Numbers*
$-1.7 \times 10^{+38}$ to -0.29×10^{-38} 0.29×10^{-38} to $1.7 \times 10^{+38}$

IEEE format also includes 64-bit numbers that have accuracy to 15 decimal digits. This representation is normally used for objects of type double. The range of a 64-bit number in IEEE format is

Negative Numbers   *Positive Numbers*
$-0.9 \times 10^{+308}$ to -0.86×10^{-308} 0.86×10^{-308} to $0.9 \times 10^{+308}$

Arithmetic with floating point numbers is much more time-consuming than integer arithmetic. Most modern systems are equipped with an auxiliary processor called an **floating point unit** (FPU) that performs all calculations with floating point numbers at hardware speed. The alternative is to write software that emulates floating point operations. Typically, software emulation runs 10–20 times slower than computations using an FPU.

The C++ sizeof Operator

C++ has a unary operator **sizeof** that takes either a type or an object as its operand:

```
int sizeof(type)
int sizeof(object)
```

The operator returns the number of bytes of memory required to store any object of the given type or the specific object. For an array argument, sizeof returns the number of bytes of memory used by the array.

EXAMPLE A.4

1. Consider the declarations

```
char c;
short s;
```

We assume that a character is stored using one byte of memory and a short is stored using two bytes (16-bits) of memory. Each type and object may be an argument for the sizeof() operator.

```
sizeof(char) = 1          sizeof(short) = 2
sizeof(c) = 1             sizeof(s) = 2
```

2. On most machines a long integer is 32 bits or 4 bytes, so sizeof(long) = 4. Since an int object is compiler and system dependent, sizeof(int) = 2 or sizeof(int) = 4.

3. Let arr be the integer array

```
int arr[5];
```

and assume that sizeof(int) = 4. Then, sizeof(arr) = 20 (5*4). ■

PROGRAM A.1

The program uses the sizeof() operator to output the sizes of the primitive C++ types, of two arrays and of an object of type Date. In the case of an object of a class, sizeof returns the number of bytes used by the attributes. The output was obtained by running the program using Microsoft Visual C++ 5.0.

```
#include <iostream.h>

#include "tstring.h"
#include "date.h"
```

```
// output size information for a type of object
void outputSize(const String& str, int size);

int main()
{
   // the 20 elements of arr1 contain 0. arr2 is
   // completely initialized
   int arr1[20] = {0}, arr2[] = {2, 5, 3, 7, 15, 33};
   Date d(12, 25, 2080);

   outputSize("char", sizeof(char));
   outputSize("short", sizeof(short));
   outputSize("int", sizeof(int));
   outputSize("long", sizeof(long));
   outputSize("float", sizeof(float));
   outputSize("double", sizeof(double));
   outputSize("Date", sizeof(Date));
   outputSize("arr1", sizeof(arr1));
   outputSize("arr2", sizeof(arr2));

   cout << "The number of elements in array arr2 = "
        << sizeof(arr2)/sizeof(int) << endl;

   return 0;
}

void outputSize(const String& str, int size)
{
   cout << "sizeof(" << str << ") = " << size << endl;
}
```

```
Run:

sizeof(char) = 1
sizeof(short) = 2
sizeof(int) = 4
sizeof(long) = 4
sizeof(float) = 4
sizeof(double) = 8
sizeof(Date) = 12
sizeof(arr1) = 80
sizeof(arr2) = 24
The number of elements in array arr2 = 6
```

Appendix B
Character Representations

Since the memory of a computer contains only binary numbers, we must develop numeric codes to represent characters such as 'A', '5' and '?'. The predominant code in use is ASCII, but some applications use the EBCDIC character representation. Due to global communications, the computer community has created the Unicode character set that defines characters in many languages.

ASCII Character Set

In the early 1960's, the computer industry adopted the ASCII standard (American Standard Code for Information Interchange) to represent characters.

The ASCII code for a character uses 7 bits that is stored in an 8-bit number. The $2^7 = 128$ different codes are divided into 95 printable characters and 33 control characters that are used in data communications. Table B-1 shows the printable ASCII character set. The blank character, represented by □, is the first printable character with ASCII value 32. The code for each character is given in decimal and can be obtained by combining the left and right digits for the character. For instance, the character T has ASCII value 84.

TABLE B-1 Printable ASCII Character Set

		0	1	2	3	4	5	6	7	8	9
						Right Digit					
	3			□	!	"	#	$	%	&	'
	4	(	)	*	+	,	-	.	/	0	1
	5	2	3	4	5	6	7	8	9	:	;
Left Digit	6	<	=	>	?	@	A	B	C	D	E
	7	F	G	H	I	J	K	L	M	N	O
	8	P	Q	R	S	T	U	V	W	X	Y
	9	Z	[	\	]	^	_	`	a	b	c
	10	d	e	f	g	h	i	j	k	l	m
	11	n	o	p	q	r	s	t	u	v	w
	12	x	y	z	{	|	}	~			

Control Codes

Control codes lie at the extreme ends of the ASCII range. They consist of values 00 – 31 and "Del" with value 127. Table B-2 lists noteworthy control characters, along with a description of their effect on a typical peripheral device.

TABLE B-2 Control Characters

Symbol	Decimal	Meaning
BS	8	Backspace — move cursor back one character
HT	9	Horizontal tab — advance cursor to next tab setting
LF	10	Line Feed — advance cursor down one line
FF	12	Form Feed — advance printer to the top of the next page
CR	13	Carriage return — move cursor to start of the line

Printable Characters

Within the printable ASCII character set, decimal digits, and alphabetic characters fall within well-defined ranges. The ranges are illustrated by Table B-3.

TABLE B-3 ASCII Character Ranges

ASCII Characters	Decimal
Blank space	32
Decimal digits ('0' – '9')	48 – 57
Uppercase letters ('A' – 'Z')	65 – 90
Lowercase letters ('a' – 'z')	97 – 122

Note that the ASCII codes for the digits are consecutive values, beginning at 48. By subtracting 48 from the code for a digit, the corresponding binary number is obtained ('0' − 48 = 0, '5' − 48 = 5).

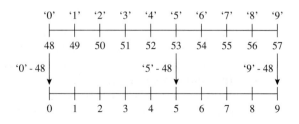

Similarly, the upper and lowercase letters are stored in blocks of consecutive codes, beginning at 65 and 97, respectively. Corresponding letters differ by 32, so that conversion between cases is done by adding or subtracting 32 ('A' + 32 = 'a', 'q' − 32 = 'Q').

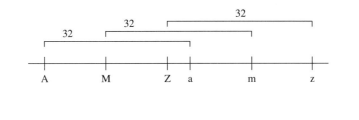

EXAMPLE B.1

1. The ASCII representation for characters in the string "C++" is given by

   67   43   43

2. The following sequence of ASCII codes transmits to the screen two backspace characters followed by a carriage return and line feed.

   08   08   13   10

3. Assume the declarations

```
char ch1 = 'A', ch2 = '8', ch3;
int v;
```

   The assignments

```
ch3 = ch1 + 5 + 32;    // ch3 = 'A' + 5 + 32 = 'F' + 32 = 'f'
v = ch2 - 48;          // v = '8' - 48 = 56 - 48 = 8
```

   give e the value 'f' and v the value 8. ■

EBCDIC Character Set

The EBCDIC (Extended Binary-Coded Decimal Interchange Code) character set is of historical value and has applications in certain environments. EBCDIC is a true 8-bit code, with most characters having an integer value greater than 127 (Table B-4). The alphabetic characters and digits are not represented by consecutive integers, so simple addition and subtraction cannot be used for conversion between uppercase and lowercase letters. Characters corresponding to 00 through 63 and 250 through 255 are nonprintable.

TABLE B-4 Printable EBCDIC Character Set

Left Digit	Right Digit 0	1	2	3	4	5	6	7	8	9
6					□					
7					¢	.	<	(	+	|
8	&									
9	!	$	*	)	;	¬	-	/		
10							^	'	%	_
11	>	?								
12			:	#	@	'	=	"		a
13	b	c	d	e	f	g	h	i		
14						j	k	l	m	n
15	o	p	q	r						
16			s	t	u	v	w	x	y	z
17								\	{	}
18	[	]								
19				A	B	C	D	E	F	G
20	H	I								J
21	K	L	M	N	O	P	Q	R		
22							S	T	U	V
23	W	X	Y	Z						
24	0	1	2	3	4	5	6	7	8	9

Unicode Character Set

Unicode is multilingual character-coding system. It is a comprehensive character set organized as a table of 16-bit values that allows for 65,536 characters including alphabetic, syllabic (American Indian languages) and ideographic (Chinese) language symbols with ample space for standard scientific and mathematical notations as well. Encompassing the principal languages of the world, the Unicode standard provides the foundation for the internationalization and localization of software.

The familiar ASCII code is a subset of Unicode. It is the first 128 characters in the Unicode system. Thus characters like 'a' (ASCII 97) and '1' (ASCII 49) are valid Unicode characters. Some versions of C++ support Unicode characters.

Appendix C
C++ Operator Summary

Symbol	Meaning	Associativity	Usage
::	Class scope resolution	L	class_name :: member
::	Global scope	R	:: name
.	Class member selection (name)	L	object.member
->	Class member selection (pointer)	L	pointer -> member
[]	Indexing	L	pointer [expr]
()	Function call	L	expr (expr_list)
()	Explicit type conversion	L	type (expr)
sizeof	Size of object	R	**sizeof** (expr)
sizeof	Size of type	R	**sizeof** (type)
++	Post increment	R	lvalue++
++	Pre increment	R	++lvalue
—	Post decrement	R	lvalue—
—	Pre decrement	R	—lvalue
~	Complement	R	~expr
!	Not	R	!expr
-	Unary minus	R	-expr
+	Unary plus	R	+expr
&	Address of	R	&lvalue
*	Dereference	R	*expr
new	Allocate dynamic memory	R	**new** type
delete	Deallocate dynamic memory	R	**delete** pointer
delete []	Deallocate dynamic array	R	**delete** [] pointer
()	Cast (type conversion)	R	(type)expr
.*	Pointer to class member using name	L	object.*member_pointer
->*	Pointer to class member using pointer	L	pointer->*member_pointer
*	Multiply	L	expr * expr
/	Divide	L	expr / expr
%	Remainder	L	expr % expr
+	Add	L	expr + expr
—	Subtract	L	expr - expr

Symbol	Meaning	Associativity	Usage
<<	Shift left	L	expr << expr
>>	Shift right	L	expr >> expr
<	Less than	L	expr < expr
<=	Less than or equal to	L	expr <= expr
>	Greater than	L	expr > expr
>=	Greater than or equal to	L	expr >= expr
==	Equal	L	expr == expr
!=	Not equal	L	expr != expr
&	Bitwise AND	L	expr & expr
^	Bitwise exclusive OR	L	expr ^ expr
|	Bitwise inclusive OR	L	expr ! expr
&&	Logical AND	L	expr && expr
||	Logical inclusive OR	L	expr || expr
?:	Conditional expression	L	expr ? expr : expr
=	Simple assignment	R	lvalue = expr
*=	Multipy and assign	R	lvalue *= expr
/=	Divide and assign	R	lvalue /= expr
%=	Remainder and assign	R	lvalue %= expr
+=	Add and assign	R	lvalue += expr
-=	Subtract and assign	R	lvalue -= expr
<<=	Shift left and assign	R	lvalue <<= expr
>>=	Shift right and assign	R	lvalue >>= expr
&=	Bitwise AND and assign	R	lvalue &= expr
|=	Bitwise inclusive OR and assign	R	lvalue |= expr
^=	Bitwise exclusive OR and assign	R	lvalue ^= expr
,	Comma operator (sequencing)	L	expr , expr

class_name is the name of a class, *member* is a class member name, *object* is an expression yielding a class object, *pointer* is an expression yielding a pointer, *expr* is an expression, and *lvalue* is an expression denoting a non-constant object. Lines separate blocks of operators that have the same precedence.

Appendix D
Stream Formatting

C++ output streams such as cout use the operator "<<" to display integer, real, and character data on the screen. There are default rules that apply to the format of the output. For many applications, however, a programmer needs the ability to specify the format of the output. To address this issue, C++ provides formatting functions that alter character spacing and decimal precision.

Format Flags

Each output stream inherits a set of format flags that specify how data is formatted. The flags are defined in the class ios as enumeration items whose values are used to set or clear the flags. A flag specifies a bit of an integer. The bit value is 1 if the flag is set and 0 if the flag is cleared. The following is a partial listing of output flags along with a brief description of their action when they are set (active).

Output Justification:

left: output is left justified in the field

right: output is right justified in the field (default setting)

Example: Assume □ represents a blank and that output occurs in a field of 10 characters.

```
cout << setw(10) << "String";   // Output (left): String□□□□
cout << setw(10) << "String";   // Output (right): □□□□String
```

Number Bases for Numeric Values

dec: output value in decimal (default setting)

oct: output value in octal or base-8

hex: output value in hexadecimal or base-16

Example: 35 is output as: 35 (decimal)   43 (octal)   23 (hexadecimal)

Base/Decimal Point/Sign Format   *(by default the flags are cleared)*

showbase: causes base of the numeric value to be shown

Example: (hex) 2D is output as Ox2D   (oct) 116 is output as O116

showpoint: always include a decimal point and trailing zeros with each floating-point output.

Example: float x = 4;

```
cout << x;      // Output (showpoint set):   4.00000
```

showpos: display a leading '+' sign before positive values

Example: int x = 2, y = -3;

```
cout << x << " " << y;   // Output (showpos set):   +2 -3
```

Real Number

scientific: outputs floating-point numbers in scientific notation.

fixed: outputs floating-point numbers in the standard notation.

The number bases octal and hexadecimal are not discussed in this book. Format flags that specify these items are included in this appendix for completeness.

EXAMPLE   D.1   ▬▬▬▬▬▬▬▬▬▬▬▬▬▬▬▬▬▬▬▬▬▬▬▬▬▬▬▬▬

1. By default, real numbers are output with six significant digits. If the whole number part has 6 or fewer digits, the output is in fixed format; otherwise, the output is in floating point format. Trailing zeros are not printed.

```
Assume x = 1234.56789,  y = 123456789.0552
cout << x;           // Output 6 digits:   1234.57
cout << y;           // Output 6 digits:   1.23457e+08
cout << 3.100;       // Output with no trailing zeros:   3.1
```

2. Assume showpos and showpoint are set.

```
double x = 5;
cout << x;           // Output (fixed):          +5.000000
cout << x;           // Output (scientific): +5.000000e+00   ■
```

Handling Format Flags

Format flags are internally stored in the least significant 16 bits of a long word. A flag is set if the corresponding bit is 1 and cleared if the corresponding bit is 0.

The ios class provides member functions setf() and unsetf() to set and clear the format flags. The member function setf() has two forms.

One Argument Form of setf()

The member function returns sets the flags specified by the argument and then returns the original value of the integer containing the flags: No other flags are changed.

```
long setf(long flags);
```

C++ allows the argument to reference the flag using the form ios::<flag>. Since the format flags are specified in the ios class at the top of a class inheritance hierarchy (See Chapter 12), the scope operator "ios::" must be used in the argument. For instance, to set the showpoint flag for the cout stream, use the statement.

```
cout.setf(ios::showpoint);
```

When two or more flags are to be set, the flags can be combined using the | (bitwise OR) operator.

```
cout.setf(ios::showpoint | ios::showpos);
```

EXAMPLE D.2

1. The member function setf() must be associated with a specific stream.

```
ofstream fout;
fout.setf(ios::showpoint); // sets showpoint for stream fout
setf(ios::showpos);        // invalid; no stream object is
                           //    specified
```

2.
```
int m = 14;
cout.setf(ios::showpos);
cout << m;                 // Output:  +14
```

3.
```
float x = 3;
cout.setf(ios::showpoint | ios::showpos);
cout << x;                 // Output:  +3.00000  ■
```

Two Argument Form of setf()

This form of setf() uses a second argument.

```
long setf(long flags1, long flags2);
```

The flags specified by the second argument are first cleared and then the flags in the first argument are set. For instance:

```
// clear the showpos flag and set the showpoint flag
cout.setf(ios::showpoint, ios::showpos);
```

For justification, number bases, and real number values, two or more conflicting flags can be simultaneously set. Consider the following setf() statement assuming that the default justification of right is set.

```
cout.setf(ios::left);
```

The statement sets the bit corresponding to left and the stream now has both left and right set simultaneously. A similar ambiguity would occur with the statement.

```
// if default dec is set, the statement sets both hex and dec.
cout.setf(ios::hex);
```

For these situations, the ios class defines special flags that can be used as the second argument in setf().

```
adjustfields          // used with left, right
basefield             // used with dec, oct, hex
floatfield            // used with scientific, fixed
```

These special flags cause all of the bits in the corresponding flag group to be cleared before setting the flag in the first argument. For instance:

```
// clear the dec, oct, and hex flags and set the hex flag
cout.setf(ios::hex, ios::basefield);
// clear the left and right flags and set the right flag
cout.setf(ios::right, ios::adjustfields);
// clear the scientific and fixed flags and set the fixed flag
cout.setf(ios::fixed, ios::floatfield);
```

EXAMPLE D.3

The example looks at the output of real numbers by first using the default flags and then setting the fixed and scientific flags.

1. Default values

```
cout << 3.14159265;    // Fixed with 6 significant digits
                       // 3.14159
cout << 3141592.65;    // Scientific with 6 digits
                       // 3.14159e+06
```

2. Set to fixed representation

```
cout.setf(ios::fixed, ios::floatfield);
cout << 3.14159265;    // Fixed, 6 decimal places
                       // 3.141593
cout << 3141592.65;    // Fixed, 6 decimal places
                       // 3141592.650000
```

3. Set to floating point representation

```
cout.setf(ios::scientific, ios::floatfield);
cout << 3.14159265;    // Scientific, 6 decimal places
                       // 3.141593e+00
cout << 3141592.65;    // Scientific, 6 decimal places
                       // 3.141593e+06    ■
```

Clearing Flags with unsetf()

The member function unsetf() is the complement of setf() and has the effect of clearing flags.

```
long unsetf(long flags);
```

The function clears the format flags specified in the argument. The original value of the integer containing the flags is returned.

EXAMPLE D.4

```
double x = 35;
cout.setf(ios::showpoint);
cout << x;                     // Output (showpoint set):    35.0000
cout.unsetf(ios::showpoint);
cout << x;                     // Output (showpoint clear):  35  ■
```

Accessing Flag Values

The ios class provides two versions of the flags() member function to access and set the format flags for a stream.

```
// returns the current value of the flags
long flags();
// uses the long flagValue to set the value of the flags.
// returns the original value of the flags.
long flags(long flagValue);
```

EXAMPLE D.5

1. With only the showpos and showpoint flags set, the internal value of the integer that stores the flags is 1280.

```
float x = 100;
```

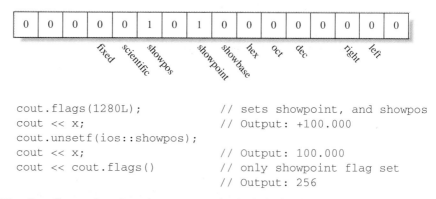

```
cout.flags(1280L);            // sets showpoint, and showpos
cout << x;                    // Output: +100.000
cout.unsetf(ios::showpos);
cout << x;                    // Output: 100.000
cout << cout.flags()          // only showpoint flag set
                             // Output: 256
```

2. The flags() member functions are particularly helpful when a program needs to temporarily set flags and then return the stream to its initial state. Consider for instance writeHex() that outputs an integer in hexademical.

```
void writeHex(long n)
{
    long currentflags = cout.flags();      // save flags
    cout.setf(ios::hex, ios::basefield);   // set hex flag
    cout << n;                             // output argument n
    cout.flags(currentflags);             // restore original
                                          // flags
} ■
```

A programmer can technically set flags knowing the bit value of the format flags. This is highly prone to error and we suggest that the flags be set using the more familiar names.

Adjusting the Width of Output

To control the separation of output on the line, the stream I/O system provides the width() member function that specifies the minimum number of characters for the next output operation.

```
cout.width(n);    // next output uses a minimum of n characters
```

The next output item is aligned in a field of n character positions. By default, output is right-aligned. If n is not large enough to accommodate the item, the data is output fully starting at the current output position. We emphasize that the width parameter applies only to the next output value. Subsequent output returns to the default status, which is to output the data immediately after the last character sent to the stream. Assume □ denotes the space character.

```
cout << '*';
cout.width(10);
cout << 12345 << '*';      // output *□□□□□12345*
cout.width(4);
cout << 9 << "**";         // output □□□9**
```

Adjusting the Fill Character

Normally, output fills spaces in an n character field with the blank character. The fill() function allows the program to designate any character to fill empty space.

```
cout.fill('#');                         // fill character is now '#'
cout.width(10);
cout << 12345;                          // output      #####12345
cout.setf(ios::left, ios::adjustfield);
cout.width(10);
cout << 12345;                          // output      12345#####
```

Setting Decimal Point Precision

When fixed or scientific mode is in effect, exactly 6 digits will be output to the right of the decimal point, including trailing zeros. When default mode is used, a maximum of 6 significant digits are output. You can control the number of digits in these cases by using the function precision().

```
cout.precision(n);          // output n decimal places
```

For fixed or scientific mode, n decimal places are printed, including trailing zeros. The format specification applies to all subsequent real numbers.

EXAMPLE D.6

```
1. // set to fixed point mode
   cout.setf(ios::fixed, ios::floatfield);
   cout.precision(7);
   cout << 3.14159265;    // Output (7 digit precision): 3.1415927
   cout.precision(3);
   cout << 3.14159265;    // Output (3 digit precision): 3.142
   cout << 7.1;           // Output (3 digit precision): 7.100
```

2. Currency output can be handled using the function precision() and the flag fixed. For instance,

```
   double amount = 5.5;
   cout.precision(2);
   cout.setf(ios:fixed, ios::floatfield);
   cout << "amount = $" << amount;    // amount = $5.50  ■
```

I/O Manipulators

Formatting can be done using the width(), precision(), and setf() functions in a series of separate statements. In some cases this can be tedious. For instance, a programmer may have a series of data values that should be output with different field widths and precision.

```
cout.width(10);
cout << customerid;
cout.width(5);
cout << checkcount;
cout.width(8);
cout.precision(2);
cout << checktotal;
```

For some applications, the programmer may want to change a format for an operation and then return to the original format immediately after the output. The change requires a series of separate statements.

```
cout.precision(1);                // initial setting
. . . . . .
cout.precision(2);                // set precision for currency
cout << balance;
cout.precision(1);                // return to initial setting
```

When written as separate statements, formatting can be clumsy. C++ addresses this problem by implementing **manipulators** that allow format directives such as width and precision to be inserted directly into the stream.

Width Manipulator: setw(n)

The setw manipulator is placed in the stream to specify the number of characters in the output field for the next item. The manipulator replaces the statement cout.width(n) and affects only the next item in the output stream. The manipulator can be used as many times as desired in a stream statement. For instance, if ☐ represents the blank character,

```
cout << setw(3) << 12 << setw(5) << 123 << endl;
```

creates the output

```
☐12☐☐123
```

Precision Manipulator: setprecision(n)

The manipulator is placed in the stream and sets the number of significant digits to the right of the decimal point in fixed or scientific output. It has the same effect as cout.precision(n). The setting remains in effect until precision is given a new value. For instance

```
cout.setf(ios::fixed, ios::floatfield);
cout << setprecision(4) << 19.28 << "   "
     << setprecision(1) <<  19.28
     << "   " << 5.85 << endl;
```

creates the output

```
19.2800   19.3   5.9
```

Note that the manipulators setw() and setprecision() are provided by the system header file <iomanip.h>. The program must include this header file along with <iostream.h> to use any manipulators requiring an argument. Since the manipulator endl does not have an argument, the header file is not required.

```
#include <iostream.h>
#include <iomanip.h>
```

EXAMPLE D.7 ▬▬▬▬▬▬▬▬▬

1. Using manipulators, output that requires five separate statements when using member functions can be replaced by two statements. In each case the output is /*##3##*/

Using member functions	Using manipulators
`cout.fill('#');`	`cout.fill('#');`
`cout << "/*";`	`cout << "/*" << setw(3) << 3`
	`          << setw(4) << "*/";`
`cout.width(3);`	

```
cout << 3;
cout.width(4);
cout << "*/";
```

2. Consider the statements

```
const double e = 2.71828;
cout.setf(ios::fixed, ios::floatfield);
cout << setprecision(3) << e << "   ";
cout << setprecision(8) << e << "   ";
cout << 5.3569 << endl;        // precision 8 remains

Output:    2.718  2.71828000  5.35690000  ∎
```

PROGRAM D.1

The program inputs a series of real numbers from the data file "acct.dat". Using format flags, it outputs each number with two decimal places preceded by the label "Credit" for a number greater than 0 and "Debit" for a number less than 0. Using the setw() manipulator and fill(), a line ("-----") separates this output from the sum of the data.

```
#include <iostream.h>
#include <fstream.h>
#include <iomanip.h>
#include <stdlib.h>

int main()
{
   ifstream fin;
   double value, total = 0.0;

   // open the input file
   fin.open("acct.dat");
   if (!fin)
   {
      cerr << "Error opening file 'acct.dat'" << endl;
      exit(1);
   }

   // flags for real numbers; fixed with 2 decimal points
   cout.setf(ios::fixed, ios::floatfield);
   cout.precision(2);

   // read real numbers until end of file
   fin >> value;
   while (fin)
   {
      total += value;

      // label justified left in 8 character positions
      cout.setf(ios::left,ios::adjustfield);
      cout.width(8);
```

```
        if (value < 0)
           cout << "Debit";
        else
           cout << "Credit";

        // reset justification to right (default)
        cout.setf(ios::right, ios::adjustfield);
        cout.width(7);
        cout << value << endl;
        fin >> value;
     }

     // draw line (fill '-') beneath numbers and record total
     cout << setw(9) << "";                // skip space for label
     cout.fill('-');                       // set fill to '-'
     cout << setw(7) << "" << endl;        // draw the line
     cout.fill(' ');                       // reset fill to space
     cout << setw(15) << total << endl;    // record total

     return 0;
}
```

```
/*
File "acct.dat":

200.56
-40.86
-90.00
100.45
-50.59
-25.08

Run:

Credit    200.56
Debit     -40.86
Debit     -90.00
Credit    100.45
Debit     -50.59
Debit     -25.08
          ------
           94.48
*/
```

Appendix E
The C++ Preprocessor

The C++ preprocessor reads through the program source code and identifies directives that supply information to the compiler. A preprocessor directive begins with #, and is followed by the directive identifier. Whitespace may precede the #. A directive is not a C++ statement and thus does not end with a semicolon (;). It is fully handled before compilation.

This appendix discusses only a limited subset of available C++ preprocessor directives. We look at the include, define and simple conditional compilation directives.

#include Directive

The #include preprocessor directive is used throughout the text, beginning with Chapter 1. It causes a specified file to be inserted into the source code in place of the directive. The directive assumes one of two forms:

```
#include <filename>
#include "filename"
```

The two forms differ in the method used by the compiler to search for the file. When the file is enclosed in angle brackets (<...>), the preprocessor searches one or more directories supplied by the compilation environment. These are known as system directories. When the file is enclosed in double quotes ("..."), the preprocessor first searches the directory that contains the source file and then checks system-specified directories.

This book uses #include directives for system-supplied header files such as **iostream.h, stdlib.h,** and **iomanip.h.** All classes are developed in separate header files and included in the program using the second form for #include

```
#include <iostream.h>

#include "date.h"          // use Date class
```

In some cases, free function prototypes and implementations are placed in header files so they can be easily included into programs.

```
#include "graplib.h"        // basic drawing functions
```

#define Directive

The **#define** directive specifies an identifier and a character string that is substituted for the each occurrence of the identifier. Its simplest form is

```
#define      IDENTIFIER      CharacterString
```

Once the directive is defined, the identifier can then be used in the program since the compiler substitutes the equivalent character string into the source code. The following use of the directive defines the newline character.

```
#define      NL       '\n'
```

```
Program Statement:     cout << value << NL;
Expanded Statement:    cout << value << '\n';
```

EXAMPLE E.1

The directive approximates the constant π.

```
#define PI       3.14159265
         ...
double  radius, area;

area = PI * radius * radius;
```

Note that it is better in a C++ program to define a constant object rather an using this form of the #define directive. A constant object declaration provides more information and assures that the compiler will be able to perform type checking at each use of the constant.

```
const double PI = 3.14159265;   ∎
```

A #define statement can be parameterized. The form of the statement is

```
#define  IDENTIFIER(arg₁, arg₂,.., argₙ)   CharacterString
```

When the preprocessor encounters the identifier followed by the parenthesized list of actual arguments, it substitutes the character string with all occurrences of the argument names replaced by the actual arguments.

EXAMPLE E.2

1. Consider the parameterized define

```
#define PRINT(I)       cout << "Value " << (I) << endl
```

   (a) The line

```
PRINT(175);
```

   expands to the statement

```
cout << "Value " << 175 << endl;
```

During execution, the output is "Value 175".

(b) The line

```
PRINT(Q+3);
```

expands to the output statement.

```
cout << "Value " << Q+3 << endl;
```

2. Arguments in a #define statement must be used with care. Consider the statement

```
#define  SQR(X)    X * X
```

In the situation

```
double A,B,C
C = SQR(A+B);
```

The assignment statement expands to

```
C = A + B * A + B
```

which is not the intended result since the higher precedence of multiplication causes the expression to be evaluated as

```
C = A + (B*A) + B
```

A simple remedy is to place the argument X in parentheses.

```
#define  SQR(X)    (X) * (X)
```

The assignment statement then correctly expands to

```
C = (A + B) * (A + B);  ■
```

The parameterized #define directive creates inline expansion. This is the only way to do inline expansion in the C programming language. C++, however, has inline functions that implement inline expansion and cause the compiler to provide strong type checking at each function call. The inline function should be used in C++ in preference to #define.

PROGRAM E.1

A parameterized #define is used to output a truth table for the logical operators OR (||), AND (&&) and NOT (!). The defined name OUTPUT with argument x displays "FALSE" if x is 0 and "TRUE" otherwise. Note that a preprocessor directive can be continued to another line by placing the character \ at the end of the line.

```
#include <iostream.h>

#define OUTPUT(x)    if ((x) == false) cout << "FALSE    "; \
                     else cout << "TRUE    ";
```

```
int main()
{
    bool p, q;

    // create a truth table
    cout << "  P        Q      P AND Q   P OR Q   NOT P" << endl
         << endl;
    p = false; q = false;
    OUTPUT(p); OUTPUT(q); OUTPUT(p&&q); OUTPUT(p||q);
    OUTPUT(!p); cout << endl;
    p = false; q = true;
    OUTPUT(p); OUTPUT(q); OUTPUT(p&&q); OUTPUT(p||q);
    OUTPUT(!p); cout << endl;
    p = true; q = false;
    OUTPUT(p); OUTPUT(q); OUTPUT(p&&q); OUTPUT(p||q);
    OUTPUT(!p); cout << endl;
    p = true; q = true;
    OUTPUT(p); OUTPUT(q); OUTPUT(p&&q); OUTPUT(p||q);
    OUTPUT(!p); cout << endl;

    return 0;
}
```

Run:

P	Q	P AND Q	P OR Q	NOT P
FALSE	FALSE	FALSE	FALSE	TRUE
FALSE	TRUE	FALSE	TRUE	TRUE
TRUE	FALSE	FALSE	TRUE	FALSE
TRUE	TRUE	TRUE	TRUE	FALSE

Conditional Compilation

A conditional compilation directive allows the programmer to control which source code is compiled. The #ifndef (if undefined) directive tests the state of a preprocessor identifier provided by the #define directive. This book uses only one form of conditional compilation, which is outlined as follows:

```
#ifndef PREPROCESSORIDENTIFIER
#define PREPROCESSORIDENTIFIER
C++ code for classes or free functions
#endif
```

You will note that each class or free function library in the supplemental software header files contains this sequence of preprocessor directives. For instance, the String class header file tstring.h is structured as follows:

```
#ifndef STRING_CLASS
#define STRING_CLASS
```

```
#include <iostream.h>
#include <string.h>      // C++ string library
#include <stdlib.h>      // for exit()


class String
{
   ...
};
...


#endif  // STRING_CLASS
```

The first time the tstring.h header file is included (#include "tstring.h"), STRING_CLASS is not defined. The #define directive makes STRING_CLASS defined, and the C++ code is compiled up to the #endif directive. If the header file is included again in the same compilation, STRING_CLASS is defined and the code is not compiled again. This avoids compiling the String class a second time and obtaining error messages that String is multiply defined.

EXAMPLE E.3 ■■■■■■■■■■■■■■■■■■■■■■■■■■■■■■■

The String class is included by both the Days and Date classes. If a main program uses both of these classes, the String class is only compiled once.

```
#include <iostream.h>

#include "date.h"       // date.h includes tstring.h
#include "days.h"       // days.h includes tstring.h

int main()
{
   Days day(Mon);
   Date d(1,1,2000);
         ...
} ■
```

Appendix F
Namespaces and the ANSI/ISO C++ Standard Library

A NSI (American National Standards Institute) and ISO (International Standards Organization) are cooperating to develop a worldwide standard for the language called the ANSI/ISO C++ Standard. The object type bool is one of the features of this standard. Another important feature, called namespaces, is currently implemented by most C++ compilers.

The **namespace** mechanism, creates a collection of classes, free functions, constant declarations and so forth that are qualified by a name. The syntax for a namespace declaration is:

```
namespace Name
{
    declaration and implementations of classes, functions,
    constants, etc.
}
```

Two namespaces may contain classes or functions of the same name. In a program, the elements of a namespace can be accessed by using the "::" operator. For instance, the namespace MathConstants contains the definitions of two mathematical constants.

```
namespace MathConstants
{
    const double PI = 3.141592653589793;
    const double E = 2.718281828459045;
}
```

Namespaces permit the programmer to bundle a variety of C++ constructs in a named collection.

PROGRAM F.1   *Declaring and using Namespaces*

This short program declares a namespace MathConstants and accesses the constants in the function main().

```
#include <iostream.h>

#include "textlib.h"

namespace MathConstants
{
    const double PI = 3.141592653589793;
    const double E = 2.718281828459045;
}

int main()
{
    cout << setreal(1,8) << MathConstants::PI << endl
         << setreal(1,10) << MathConstants::E << endl;

    return 0;
}
```

```
Run:

3.14159265
2.7182818285
```

The Keyword using

The Keyword *using*. The keyword *using* allows the elements of a single namespace to be referenced without the "::" operator. All elements of any other namespace must use the operator. The syntax for the keyword is

```
using namespace Name;
```

For instance, consider the two namespaces MathConstants and ShortConstants.

```
namespace MathConstants
{
    const double PI = 3.141592653589793;
    const double E = 2.718281828459045;
}

namespace ShortConstants
{
    const double PI = 3.14159;
    const double E = 2.71828;
    const double ROOT2 =  1.41421;
}
```

If the statement

```
using namespace MathConstants;
```

is provided, the code segment

```
cout << E << "  " << ShortConstants::ROOT2
     << endl;
```

outputs the value of E from MathConstants and ROOT2 from ShortConstants. Any reference to a constant in the namespace ShortConstants must use the "::" operator.

The C++ Standard Library

The ANSI/ISO C++ Standard defines a new C++ library that includes classes inherited from the original C++ library (e.g. iostream.h) and the original C library (e.g. math.h). The standard library also includes new components such as the Standard Template Library (STL) of container classes and a string class that extends the operations available in the String class (tstring.h). The library bundles the components in a namespace called std. The C++ Standard library provides 32 C++ header files, as shown in Table F-1. Note that many of the file names look familiar, except that the suffix ".h" is omitted.

TABLE F-1 Library Headers.

<algorithm>	<iomanip>	<list>	<queue>	<typeinfo>
<bitset>	<ios>	<locale>	<set>	<utility>
<complex>	<iosfwd>	<map>	<sstream>	<valarray>
<deque>	<iostream>	<memory>	<stack>	<vector>
<exception>	<istream>	<new>	<stdexcept>	
<fstream>	<iterator>	<numeric>	<streambuf>	
<functional>	<limits>	<ostream>	<string>	

The Standard Library also includes 18 additional headers that implement the key facilities of the original Standard C Library. The headers are provided in Table F-2:

TABLE F-2 C++ Headers for C Library Facilities.

<cassert>	<ciso646>	<csetjmp>	<cstdio>	<cwchar>
<cctype>	<climits>	<csignal>	<cstdlib>	<cwctype>
<cerrno>	<clocale>	<cstdarg>	<cstring>	
<cfloat>	<cmath>	<cstddef>	<ctime>	

To use the components of the standard C++ library, include the necessary header files and add the statement

```
using namespace std;
```

to the program. For instance, to use the new I/O library and the extended string class, include the following statements:

```
#include <iostream>        // accesses new I/O stream classes
#include <string>          // new string class

using namespace std;       // reference components without using
                           // std::
```

PROGRAM F.2   *Illustrating Namespace std*

The program declares the string objects first and last and uses them to input first and last names. Using string concatenation, the two parts are combined in an object fullname that contains the last name followed by a comma and the first name. The full name is output. The program concludes by using sqrt() from <math> to output the square root of a number that is input from the keyboard.

```
#include <iostream>
#include <string>
#include <cmath>

using namespace std;

int main()
{
    string first, last, fullname;
    double x;

    // I/O using the stream classes
    cout << "Enter a first and last name:  ";
    // operations from the ANSI string class
    cin >> first >> last;
    fullname = last + ", " + first;
    cout << "The full name is " << fullname << endl;

    cout << "Enter a number: ";
    cin >> x;
    // sqrt() comes from <cmath>
    cout << "The square root of " << x << " is "
        << sqrt(x) << endl;

    return 0;
}
```

```
Run:

Enter a first and last name:  Standard Ansi
The full name is Ansi, Standard
Enter a number: 5
The square root of 5 is 2.23607
```

Index

A

Abstract class, 750
Accumulator class (accum.h), 112, 213
Accumulator class (template-based) (accum_t.h), 556
AccumulatorStatic (accstat.h), 474
Actions, 3
Address, 346, A-3
Address-of operator &, 579
Agent, 3, 453
Algorithm, 10
 array
  removing a list element, 376
  removing duplicates, 377
 date and time
  creating a calendar, 455
  normalizing time, 223
 efficiency, 556
 graphics
  building a kaleidoscope, 742
  graphing dice tosses, 387
  jack-in-the-box, 186
  shooting star, 300
 iterative, 495
 list
  removing duplicates, 665
 node
  deleting at front of list, 677
  inserting at front of list, 676
  inserting at rear of list, 678
  removing a target node, 681
 recursive, 475, 478
  maze traversal, 486
  power function, 477
  ring draw, 229, 475, 479
  Tower of Hanoi, 482
 search
  binary search, 548
  sequential (integer data), 374
  sequential (template-based), 546
 sort
  list insertion sort, 728
  selection (integer data), 395
  selection (template-based), 544
AND operator, 152
Animation, 185, 300
Anonymous object, 363
ANSI (American National Standards Institute), F-1
Argument, 8
Array
 access function, 346
 as class data member, 380
 as pointer argument, 585
 assignment, 347
 bounds checking, 349
 data type, 342
 element, 340
 function argument, 355
 index operator, 341
 initialization, 349
 multidimensional, 410
 one-dimensional, 340
 two-dimensional, 410
 two-dimensional array storage, 421
 two-dimensional function argument, 413
ASCII
 character set, 54, B-1
 control code, B-2
 escape code, 51
 printable character, B-2
Assembly language, 23
Assignment
 compared with initialization, 605
 compound assignment, 71
 conversion, 70
 implementing, 609
 multiple assignment, 42
 syntax, 41
Associativity of operator, 67
Attributes, 3
Automatic
 data member, 471
 object, 471
 storage class, 471

B

Backtracking, 488
Base class, 713
Binary
 bit, A-1
 digit, A-1
 file, 306
 number, 36, 351, A-1
 operator, 40
Binary search, 548
Bit, 36, A-1
Block, 157
Block structured language, 466
Bool type, 165
Boole, George, 150
Borland Object Windows Library (OWL), 712
Break statement, 257, 259, 288
BrickHouse class (houses.h), 734
Buffer, 306
Buffered input, 46
Byte, 54, 350, A-3

C

C programming language, 23
C++ string
 definition, 630

functions
  strcat(), 635
  strchr(), 634
  strcmp(), 634
  strcpy(), 635
  strlen(), 634
  strstr(), 635
Calendar class (calendar.h), 456, 460
Calling
  a free function, 121
  a member function, 97
  an operation, 12
Case sensitive, 11
Cast, 69
Char type, 51
Character
  ASCII character set, 54, B-1
  backslash, 51
  backspace, 51, B-2
  carriage return, B-2
  cin.get(), 54
  control, 51, 55, B-2
  EBCDIC character set, 56, B-3
  escape code, 51
  line feed, B-2
  literal, 51
  newline, 46, 51, 307
  operations, 56
  printable, 51, 55, B-2
  tab, 51, B-2
  type, 51
  unicode character set, 56, B-4
  whitespace, 47, 53
Cin, 14, 46
Circle class (circle.h), 230
CircleShape class (circlesh.h), 116, 719
Class
  abstract, 750
  anonymous object, 363
  assignment operator, 605
    implementing, 609
  association, 452
  body, 104
  composition, 442, 452
  constant member function, 382
  constructor, 95
    implementation, 206
    overloading, 515
  constructor in object composition, 446
  constructor initialization list, 206, 207
  copy constructor, 600, 605
    implementation, 613
  declaration, 104, 105
  default constructor, 363
  destructor, 599, 602
    virtual, 746
  header, 104
  header file, 210
  hierarchy, 713
  inheritance, 452
  member function

    implementation, 204, 205
    prototype, 94
  member function default arguments, 111
  member function selection using a pointer->, 589
  multiple constructors, 363
  nested, 660
  overloaded assignment operator, 599
  pointer, 588
  private inheritance, 759
  private member function, 219
  private section, 106
  public section, 106
  pure virtual function, 750
  scope, 468
  scope resolution operator ::, 205
  template class, 556
  virtual function table, 737
  virtual member function, 732
  wrapper class, 265
Class Scope
  resolution operator ::, 205
Classes in the book
  declaration
    Accumulator (accum.h), 112
    Accumulator (template-based) (accum_t.h), 556
    AccumulatorStatic (accumstat.h), 474
    Calendar (calendar.h), 460
    Circle (circle.h), 231
    CircleShape (circlesh.h), 719
    Date (date.h), 271
    Days (days.h), 265
    DormRoom (dormroom.h), 107
    DynamicDemo (dynamic.h), 601
    Employee (base) (emphier.h), 722
    Employee (employee.h), 444
    FinanceCenter (finacct.h), 382, 452
    GradeRecord (graderec.h), 114
    HourlyEmployee (emphier.h), 724
    House (houses.h), 735
    Iterator (tlist.h), 687
    List (tlist.h), 686
    Loan (loan.h), 226
    Maze (maze.h), 489
    MealBill (mealbill.h), 108
    Node (node.h), 670
    OrderedList (ordlist.h), 727
    PolyShape (polysh.h), 738
    Rational (rational.h), 521, 526, 530
    Rectangle (rect.h) (UML), 104
    SalaryEmployee (emphier.h), 722
    Shape (shape.h), 717
    ShapeColor (shape.h), 20
    SqMatrix (sqmatrix.h), 415
    Statistics (stats.h), 357
    String (tstring.h), 636
    StudentAccount (studacct.h), 105
    Time24 (time24.h), 221
    Timer (timer.h), 552
    Triangle (triangle.h), 448
    Vector (tvector.h), 618
    WoodFrameHouse (houses.h), 735

description
    Calendar, 456
    CircleShape, 116
    Const_Iterator, 662
    Date, 270
    Dice, 388
    DormRoom, 98
    Iterator, 660
    LineShape, 391
    List, 655
    PolyShape, 281
    RandomNumber, 369
    Rectangle, 18, 101
    RectShape, 21
    Shape, 714
    StudentAccount, 8, 93, 95
    TextShape, 125
implementation
    Accumulator, 213
    Accumulator (template-based) (accum_t.h), 557
    AccumulatorStatic, 474
    Calendar, 461
    Circle, 231
    CircleShape, 720
    Date, 272, 353
    Days, 267
    DynamicDemo, 601, 603, 609, 613
    Employee, 446
    Employee (base), 722
    FinanceCenter, 385
    HourlyEmployee, 724
    House, 735
    Iterator, 688
    List, 690
    Loan, 228
    Maze, 491
    Node, 670
    OrderedList, 730
    PolyShape, 739
    Rational, 525, 529, 531
    Rectangle, 208
    SalaryEmployee, 722
    Shape, 718
    SqMatrix, 417
    Statistics, 360
    String, 636
    StudentAccount, 205
    Time24, 223
    Triangle, 450
    Vector, 624
    WoodFrameHouse, 735
reference
    BrickHouse (houses.h), 734
    ShapeColor (shape.h), 20, 125, 281, 301, 744
    VinylSidedHouse (houses.h), 734
Client class, 442
    and UML, 446
Closing a stream, 310
Code
    decomposition, 453
    reuse, 441

simplification, 120, 129
Command line environment, 17
Comment, 13
Compiler, 11, 16
Compile-time binding, 731
Complex number, 573
Compound assignment operator, 71
Conditional expression, 304
Const_Iterator class (tlist.h), 662
Constant
    declaration, 64, 302
    member function, 382
    reference argument, 302
Constructor, 9, 95
    implementation, 206
    in object composition, 446
    initialization list, 206, 207
Continue statement, 289
Control
    code, B-2
    flow, 146
    looping, 149
    selection, 147
Conversion
    assignment conversion, 70
    binary to decimal, A-2
    decimal to binary, A-2
    double to Rational, 534
    int to Rational, 533
    operator, 532
    overloading conversion operator, 532
    Rational to double, 534
    String to C++ string, 308
    String to char *, 631
    Vector to array, 628
Copy constructor, 600
    implementation, 613
Counter, 42
    controlled loop, 173
Cout, 14, 42

D

Dangling else, 253
Date class (date.h), 269, 353
Days class (days.h), 265, 458
Debugger, 16
Default
    by default, 36
    constructor, 363, 721
    function arguments, 111
    real number output, 61
    value, 111
Define preprocessor directive, E-2
Delete operator, 595
Derived class, 713
Design
    main program, 455
    object-oriented, 118
    structured analysis, 119, 120

Destructor, 599, 602
  virtual, 746
Deterministic process, 368
Dice class (dice.h), 388
Discrete type, 58
Do/while loop, 179
DormRoom class (dormroom.h), 98, 107
Double
  storage format, A-6
  type, 59
Duplicates (removing), 665
Dynamic
  array, 592
  memory, 590
Dynamic binding, 731
DynamicDemo class (dynamic.h), 600

E

EBCDIC character set, 56, B-3
Editor, 16
Empirical probability, 388
Employee (base) class (emphier.h), 721
Employee class (employee.h), 443
Endl manipulator, 15, 44, 52
End-of-file (EOF), 311
Enter key, 46
Enumeration type, 262
Event-controlled loop, 173, 176
Exceptions, 219
Exchange(), 298
Exclusive OR, 155
Executable code, 16
Exit(), 218
Expanded
  binary notation, A-2
  decimal notation, A-2
Exponent, 59, A-6
Expression, 41
  arithmetic, 66
  conditional, 304
  logical, 150
    as a numeric value, 169
    false, 150
    short-circuit evaluation, 154
    true, 150

F

Factor of an integer, 279
False (logical value), 150
Fatal error, 218
File
  binary, 306
  buffer, 306
  filename, 408
  path, 408
  pathname, 407
  physical, 306
  text, 306

Fill() stream member function, D-6
FinanceCenter class (finacct.h), 380, 452
Fixed
  data member, 599
  point format, 59
  real number output, 61
Flags() stream member function, D-5
Float
  storage format, A-6
  type, 59
Floating point
  format, 59
  unit (FPU), A-7
Flow of control, 146
Flowchart, 147
For statement, 276, 286
Frame (in animation), 185
Free function, 120
  body, 127
  implementation, 127
Friend function, 525
Front pointer, 669
Fstream class, 308
Function
  array argument, 355
  body, 127
  call, 97
  calling a free function, 121
  constant reference argument, 302
  formal argument list, 94
  free, 120
  friend function, 525
  implementation, 127
  overloading, 512, 541
    stream operators, 528
    using member function, 531
  prototype, 94, 121
  reference argument, 294
  return statement, 128
  run-time argument, 97
  two-dimensional array argument, 413
  value argument, 292

G

Geometric class hierarchy, 714
Getline()
  stream member function, 632
  String function, 400
Global
  object, 469
  scope, 469
GradeRecord class (graderec.h), 113
Graphics library (graphlib.h), 117
  closeWindow(), 124
  delayWindow(), 124
  eraseWindow(), 125
  openWindow(), 125
  viewWindow(), 125
Graphing dice tosses, 387

H

Handle, 719
Header file, 14, 104, 210
Heap, 590
HourlyEmployee class (emphier.h), 722
House class (houses.h), 735

I

I/O, 42
  buffer, 306
  buffered input, 46
  cin, 14, 46
  class hierarchy, 307
  close() member function, 310
  conditional statement, 312
  cout, 14, 42
  end-of-file, 319
  errors, 319
  fill() stream member function, D-6
  fixed point format, 59
  fixed real number output, 59
  flags() stream member function, D-5
  fstream class, 308
  function arguments, 316
  get() operation, 54
  getline() member function, 632
  ifstream class, 308
  input conversion, 57
  input operator >>, 47
  iomanip.h header file, 45
  ios class, 307
  istream class, 307
  istream_withassign class, 308
  manipulator, 44, D-7
    endl(), 15, 44, 52
    setjust(), 262
    setreal(), 61
    setw(), 45, 74
  numeric base
    decimal, D-1
    hexadecimal, D-1
    octal, D-1
  object, 42
  ofstream class, 308
  open() member function, 308
  ostream class, 307
  ostream_withassign class, 308
  output justification
    left, D-1
    right, D-1
  output operator <<, 43
  precision() stream member function, D-6
  right justified output, 45
  scientific format flag, D-2
  setf() stream member function, D-3
  setprecision() manipulator, D-8
  setw() manipulator, D-8
  showpos format flag, D-2
  states, 319
  String, 74, 399
  textlib.h header file, 61
  unsetf() stream member function, D-5
  width() stream member function, D-6
Identifier, 11
IEEE format, A-5
If statement, 147
Ifndef preprocessor directive, E-4
Ifstream class, 308
Include preprocessor directive, E-1
Inclusive OR, 155
Increment operator, 72
Index operator, 341
Indexing a Vector object, 620
Indirection operator *, 580
Infinite loop, 288
Information hiding, 107
Inheritance, 452
  abstract class, 750
  base class, 713
  CircleShape class, 719
  compile-time binding, 731
  default constructor, 721
  derived class, 713
  dynamic binding, 731
  Employee class, 722
  HourlyEmployee class, 724
  OrderedList class, 727
  polymorphism, 712, 730, 733
  PolyShape class, 738
  private, 716, 759
  protected, 716
  protected member, 715
  public, 715
  pure virtual function, 718, 750
  SalaryEmployee class, 722
  Shape class, 714, 717
  static binding, 731
  UML representation, 726
  virtual destructor, 746
  virtual function table, 737
  virtual keyword, 718
  virtual member function, 732
Initialization, 38, 605
Inline code
  class, 230
  free function, 234
In-place sorting algorithm, 730
Input conversion, 57
Int type, 14, 36
Integer
  addition (+), 39
  division (/), 39
  int type, 36
  literal, 36
  long type, 37
  multiplication (*), 39
  number, 36
  object declaration, 37
  remainder (%), 39

short type, 37
  subtraction (-), 39
Integrated environment (IDE), 17
Iomanip.h header file, 45
Ios class, 307
Iostream.h header file, 14, 36
Irrational number, 520
ISO (International Standards Organization), F-1
Istream class, 307
Iteration, 172
Iterative algorithm, 495
Iterator
  initialization, 661
  List, 659
Iterator class (tlist.h), 660, 687

J

Jack-in-the-box animation, 186
Java programming language, 120

K

Kaleidoscope (building), 742
Key in search, 374
Keyword, 14
  bool, 165
  break, 257, 259, 288
  case, 256
  char, 51, A-5
  class, 104
  const, 64, 302
  continue, 289
  default, 256
  delete, 595
  do, 179
  double, 59
  else, 159
  enum, 262
  false, 150
  float, 59
  for, 276, 286
  friend, 525
  if, 147
  inline, 234
  int, 14, 36, A-5
  long, 37, A-5
  namespace, F-1
  new, 590
  operator, 523
  private, 106
  protected, 715
  public, 106
  return, 128
  short, 37, A-5
  sizeof, 348, A-7
  static, 473
  switch, 256
  template, 542
  this, 531, 610
  true, 150

using, F-2
virtual, 718
void, 94
while, 171

L

Leap year computation, 273
Left
  associative operator, 67
LineShape class (linesh.h), 391, 448
Linked list
  array implementation, 667
  building, 674
  clearing a list, 679
  creating a node, 676
  deleting at front of list, 677
  describing, 668
  front pointer, 669
  inserting at front of list, 676
  inserting at rear of list, 678
  node, 669
  NULL pointer, 669
  removing a target node, 681
  Vector class implementation, 667
Linker, 16
List class (tlist.h), 655, 685, 686
  erase operations, 656, 663
  insertion operations, 656, 663
  iterator, 659, 687
    initialization, 661
  status operations, 656
  UML diagram, 685
List insertion sort, 728
Loan class (loan.h), 226
Local scope, 467
Local type, 471
Logical
  expression, 150
  operator, 152
Long
  double type, 59
  type, 37
Loop
  body, 171
  control object, 172
  counter-controlled, 173
  do/while, 179, 180
  event-controlled, 173, 176
  iteration, 172
  postloop conditions, 172
  preloop conditions, 172
  structure, 149
  test, 171
  while, 171
Looping, 149

M

Machine instructions, 11
Main program

design, 455
unit, 12
Manipulator, D-7
Mantissa, 59, A-6
Mascitti, Rick, 23
Mathematics library (math.h)
ceil(), 122
cos(), 122
exp(), 122
floor(), 122
log(), 122
pow(), 122
sin()], 122
sqrt(), 122
Matrix, 414
operations
addition, 414
scalar multiplication, 415
subtraction, 414
Maze class (maze.h), 489
Maze traversal, 486
solution, 487
MealBill class (mealbill.h), 108
Median, 761
Member function
constant, 382
constructor
implementation, 206
implementation, 204
operator overloading using, 531
private, 219
Memory
address, A-3
byte, A-3
leak, 602
Merging sorted lists, 709
Microsoft Foundation Class Library (MFC), 712
Mixed
number, 537
type conversion, 68
Mode, 762
Multidimensional array, 410
Multiple
assignment, 42
constructors, 363
selection, 148, 161

N

Named constant, 64
Namespace, F-1
Nested
class, 660, 684
if statement, 251
loop, 283
New operator, 590
Newline charcter, 307
Node, 669
Node class (node.h), 670
insert after current node, 673
unlink following node, 673

Node library
clearing a list, 679
creating a node, 676
deleting at front of list, 677
inserting at front of list, 676
inserting at rear of list, 678
removing a target node, 681
NOT operator, 152
NULL
character, 630
pointer, 590, 669
string, 73
Number
exponent, A-6
mantissa, A-6
sign, A-6
significant digit, A-6
systems, 519

O

Object, 3
actions, 3
association, 452
attributes, 3
code, 16
composition, 442, 452
composition and UML, 446
declaration, 11
inheritance, 452
initialization, 49
library, 16
scope, 466
temporary, 68
type, 7
uninitialized, 38
Object-oriented
analysis (OOA), 451
design (OOD), 452
program development cycle, 451, 454
programming (OOP), 453
Ofstream class, 308
One-dimensional array, 340
One-way selection, 148, 155
Opening a stream, 308
Operation (of object type), 8
Operator
-- and pointers, 584
++ and pointers, 584
address-of operator &, 579
associativity, 67
character arithmetic, 56
class member selection using a pointer ->, 589
conversion
overloading, 532
Rational to double, 534
Vector to array, 628
delete, 595
exclusive OR, 155
function, 523

inclusive OR, 155
index []
      overloading, 625
indirection operator *, 580
integer arithmetic, 39
keyword, 523
left-associative, 67
logical, 152
      AND, 152
      NOT, 152
      OR, 152
new, 590
      allocating class objects, 593
      dynamic array allocation, 592
overloading, 511, 522
      rules for, 539
      this pointer, 531
      using friend function, 525
      using member function, 531
postfix increment, 688
precedence, 66
      arithmetic and logical operators, 154
      of each C++ operator, C-1
prefix increment, 688
real arithmetic, 59
relational, 151
right-associative, 67
sizeof(), 348, A-7
stream input >>, 47
stream output <<, 42
ternary, 304
Operator
      class scope resolution ::, 205
OR
      exclusive, 155
      inclusive, 155
      operator, 152
Ordered list, 726
OrderedList class (ordlist.h), 726
Ostream class, 307
Overflow, 70, A-5
Overloading
      assignment operator, 599, 609
      class member functions, 515
      constructors, 515
      stream operators, 528
      using member function, 531

P ▬▬▬▬▬

Palindrome, 180, 401, 657
Pass
      by reference, 294
      by value, 292
Physical file, 306
Pointer
      arithmetic, 583
      object, 578
      to class type, 588

Polymorphism, 712, 730, 733
PolyShape class (polysh.h), 280, 738
Positional
      binary notation, A-2
      decimal notation, A-1
Postfix increment operator, 688
Postloop conditions, 172
Precedence of operators, 66, 154
      addition +, C-1
      address of &, C-1
      allocate dynamic memory new, C-1
      class member selection by name . (dot), C-1
      class member selection by pointer ->, C-1
      class scope resolution ::, C-1
      compound assignment +=, -=, *=, /=, %=, C-2
      conditional expression ?:, C-2
      deallocate dynamic memory delete, C-1
      decrement --, C-1
      division /, C-1
      increment ++, C-1
      indexing [], C-1
      integer division remainder %, C-1
      logical AND &&, C-2
      logical NOT !, C-1
      logical OR ||, C-2
      multiplication *, C-1
      pointer dereference *, C-1
      relational operators ==, !=, C-2
      relational operators >, >=, <, <=, C-2
      size of object or type sizeof, C-1
      stream input >>, C-2
      stream output <<, C-2
      subtraction -, C-1
      unary minus -, C-1
Precision() stream member function, D-6
Prefix increment operator, 688
Preloop conditions, 172
Preprocessor, 16
      #define directive, E-2
      #ifndef directive, 215, E-4
      #include directive, E-1
      conditional compilation, E-4
Principle of code duplication, 224
Printable character, B-2
Private
      inheritance, 716, 759
      member function, 219
      section of a class, 106
Probability
      empirical, 388
      theoretical, 387
Problem
      analysis, 2
      design, 2
Program design tool, 9
Prompt, 12
Protected
      inheritance, 716
      member, 715
Pseudo-random number, 368

Public
    inheritance, 715
    section of a class, 106
Pure virtual function, 718, 750

Q

Quadratic equation, 163
Queue, 651, 697, 701

R

Random number, 367
RandomNumber class (trandom.h), 368
Rational
    arithmetic, 519
    class declaration, 521
    denominator, 518
    number, 518
    numerator, 518
    reduced form, 518
    standardized form, 519
Rational class (rational.h), 520, 526, 530
Real number, 58
    default output, 61
    double type, 59
    exponent, 59
    fixed output, 61
    fixed point format, 59
    float type, 59
    floating point format, 59
    long double type, 59
    mantissa, 59
    operator
        *, 59
        /, 59
        +, 59
        −, 59
    scientific notation, 59
    scientific output, 61
Rectangle class (rect.h), 17, 101
RectShape class (rectsh.h), 20, 713, 731
Recursion
    backtracking, 488
    recursive step, 476
    stopping condition, 476
Recursive
    algorithm, 475, 478
    developing recursive functions, 478
    function, 475
    function examples
        hanoi(), 485
        Maze class, 489
        power(), 478
        ringDraw(), 479
    tracing recursive functions, 481
Reference argument, 294
Relational
    expression, 151

    operator, 151
Removing duplicates, 665
Reserved word, 14
Resizing
    a Vector object, 620, 626
    an array, 596
Return
    statement, 128
    value, 8
Return key, 46
Right
    associative operator, 67
    justified output, 45
Ritchie, Dennis, 23
Run-time
    environment, 14
    function argument, 97

S

Safe array, 766
SalaryEmployee class (emphier.h), 722
Scientific
    notation, 59
    real number output, 61
Scientific format flag, D-2
Scope, 466
    class, 468
    global, 469
    local, 467
    resolution operator ::, 205
Search algorithms
    binary search, 548
    sequential search
        integer data, 374
        template-based, 546
Selection, 147
Selection sort
    integer data, 395
    template-based, 544
Self-referencing structure, 671
Sequential list container, 655
Sequential search
    integer data, 374
    template-based, 546
Setf() stream member function, D-3
Setprecision() manipulator, D-8
Setreal() manipulator, 61
Setw() manipulator, 45, 74, D-8
Shape class (shape.h), 713
ShapeColor class (shape.h), 20, 125, 281, 301, 744
Shooting star animation, 300
Short type, 37, A-5
Short-circuit evaluation, 154
Showpos format flag, D-2
Sign of a number, A-6
Significant digit, A-6
Simple selection, 156
Sizeof operator, 348, A-7

Smalltalk programming language, 120
Sort algorithms
   selection sort
      integer data, 395
      template-based, 544
Sorting, 298
Source code, 14, 16
   design
      alternatives for, 215
      classes, 210
      main program, 211
SqMatrix class (sqmatrix.h), 414
Square matrix, 414
Stack, 704
Standard
   library, F-3
   template library, F-3
Statement
   assignment
      compound assignment, 71
      multiple, 42
      syntax, 41
   block, 157
   break, 257, 259, 288
   conditional expression, 304
   continue, 289
   dangling else, 253
   declaration, 156
   do/while, 179
   for, 276
   generalized for, 286
   if, 147
   multiple selection, 148, 161
   nested if, 251
   nested loop, 283
   one-way selection, 148, 155
   simple, 156
   switch, 256
   two-way selection, 147, 158
   while, 171
Static
   data member, 473
   local object, 473
   storage class, 471, 473
Static binding, 731
Statistics class (stats.h), 357
Stirling's approximation for n!, 469
Storage format
   double, A-6
   float, A-6
Stream I/O (see I/O), 42
String
   class, 73, 74
   function
      assignment, 75
      c_str(), 308
      concatenation, 76
      find(), 404, 406
      find_first_of(), 404
      find_last_of(), 404
      getline(), 400

      insert(), 404, 407
      length(), 76
      remove(), 404, 407
      substr(), 404, 406
   I/O, 74, 399
   index operator, 399
String class (tstring.h), 36, 73, 636
String literal, 630
Stroustrup, Bjarne, 23
StudentAccount class (studacct.h), 8, 93, 105, 205
Supplier class, 442
   and UML, 446
Switch statement, 256
   default case, 256
   selector expression, 256

T

Template
   argument list, 542
   class, 556
   class object, 558
   expansion, 542
   function, 542
Ternary operator, 304
Text file, 306
Textlib.h header file, 61
TextShape class (textsh.h), 125
Theoretical probability, 387
This pointer, 531, 610
Thompson, Ken, 23
Time24 class (time24.h), 219
Timer class (timer.h), 552
Tower of Hanoi puzzle, 482
   solution, 483
Transpose of square matrix, 414
Triangle class (triangle.h), 448
True (logical value), 150
Two-dimensional array, 410
Twos-complement, A-5
Two-way selection, 147, 158
Type, 36
   bool, 165
   cast, 69
   char, 51, A-5
   char *, 631
   conversion, 67
      assignment, 70
      explicit, 68
      implicit, 67
      mixed, 68
   discrete, 58
   double, 59, A-6
   enumeration, 262
   float, 59, A-6
   int, 14, A-5
   long, 37, A-5
   long double, 59
   pointer, 578
   short, 37, A-5

U

UML (Unified Modeling Language), 18, 103
  and object composition, 446
  client class, 446
  supplier class, 446
Unary operator, 41
Unicode character set, 56, B-4
Unix, 23
Unsetf() stream member function, D-5
Using keyword, F-2

V

Value argument, 292
Vector class (tvector.h), 617

VinylSidedHouse class (houses.h), 734
Virtual
  destructor, 746
  function table, 737
  keyword, 718, 732
  member function, 732

W

While loop, 171
Whitespace, 53
Width() stream member function, D-6
WoodFrameHouse class (houses.h), 735
Wrapper class, 265

End-User License Agreement for Microsoft Software

MICROSOFT VISUAL C++, Learning Edition

IMPORTANT—READ CAREFULLY: This Microsoft End-User License Agreement ("EULA") is a legal agreement between you (either an individual or a single entity) and Microsoft Corporation for the Microsoft software product identified above, which includes computer software and may include associated media, printed materials, and "online" or electronic documentation ("SOFTWARE PRODUCT"). By installing, copying, or otherwise using the SOFTWARE PRODUCT, you agree to be bound by the terms of this EULA. If you do not agree to the terms of this EULA, do not install, copy, or use the SOFTWARE PRODUCT; you may; however, return it to your place of purchase for a full refund.

SOFTWARE PRODUCT LICENSE

The SOFTWARE PRODUCT is protected by copyright laws and international copyright treaties, as well as other intellectual property laws and treaties. The SOFTWARE PRODUCT is licensed, not sold.

1. **GRANT OF LICENSE.** This EULA grants you the following rights:

   a. **Software Product.** Microsoft grants to you as an individual, a personal, nonexclusive license to make and use copies of the SOFTWARE for the sole purposes of designing, developing, and testing software application(s). Except as provided in Section 2(a), you may install copies of the SOFTWARE PRODUCT on an unlimited number of computers provided that you are the only individual using the SOFTWARE PRODUCT in the manner provided above.

   b. **Electronic Documents.** Solely with respect to electronic documents included with the SOFTWARE PRODUCT, you may make an unlimited number of copies (either in hardcopy or electronic form), provided that such copies shall be used only for internal purposes and a re not republished or distributed to any third party,

   c. **Storage/Network Use.** You may also store or install a copy of the SOFTWARE PRODUCT on a storage device, such as a network server, used only to install or run the SOFTWARE PRODUCT on your computes over an internal network; however, you must acquire and dedicate a license for each separate computer on which the SOFTWARE PRODUCT is installed or run from a storage device. A license for the SOFTWARE PRODUCT may not be shared or used concurrently on different computers.

   d. **Sample Code and Microsoft Foundation Classes.** In addition to the rights granted in Section 1(a), Microsoft grants you the right to use and modify the source code version of those portions of the SOFTWARE PRODUCT that are identified: (i) as the Microsoft Foundation Classes ("MFC"); and (ii) as sample code in the documentation and/or listed in the subdirectory DevstudiolVC\Samples located in the SOFTWARE PRODUCT (collectively, "SAMPLE CODE"), for the sole purposes of designing, developing, and testing your software applications(s), provided that you comply with Section 1(f), below.

   e. **Redistributable Files.** Provided that you comply with Section 1(f), in addition to the rights granted in Section 1(a), Microsoft grants you a nonexclusive, royalty-free right to reproduce and distribute the object code version of the following portions of the SOFTWARE PRODUCT (collectively, the "REDISTRIBUTABLES"): (i) SAMPLE CODE (including any modifications you make): (ii) MFC (including any modifications you make); and (iii) the files identities in the Redistrb.wri file located in the SOFTWARE PRODUCT. For the purposes of this section, "modifications" shall mean enhancements to the functionality of the MPC or Sample Code.

f.   **Redistribution Requirements.** If you redistribute the REDISTRIBUTABLES, you agree to (i) distribute the REDISTRIBUTABLES in object code only in conjunction with and as a part of a software application developed by you that adds significant and primary functionality to the REDISTRIBUTABLES and that is intended solely for noncommercial use of distribution ("Application"); (ii) not use Microsoft's name, logo, or trademarks to market your Application; (iii) include a valid copyright notice on your Application; (iv) indemnify, hold harmless, and defend Microsoft from and against any claims or lawsuits, including attorney's fees, that arise or result from the use or distribution of your Application; (v) not permit further distribution of the other terms of the REDISTRIBUTABLES by your end user. The following exception applies to Subsection (f)(v), above; provided that your end users comply with all the other terms of this EULA, you may permit your end users to reproduce and distribute the object code version of the files listed below ("COM Redistributables") only in conjunction with the redistribution of a Component Object Model (COM) object (e.g., an ActiveX control) designed or use or development of an Application and/or Web page that adds significant primary functionality to the COM Redistributables and that is intended for noncommercial use or distribution. COM Redistributables: Msvrt.dll, Mfc42.dll, Atl.dll, Msstkprp.dll, and Axdist.exe.

2.   DESCRIPTION OF OTHER RIGHTS AND LIMITATIONS.

a.   **Academic Edition Software**. If the SOFTWARE PRODUCT is identified as "Academic Edition" or "AE," you must be a "Qualified Educational User" to use the SOFTWARE PRODUCT. To determine whether you rae a Qualified Educational User, please contact Microsoft Sales Information Center/One Microsoft Way/Redmond, WA 98052-6399 or the Microsoft subsidiary serving your country,

b.   **Not for Resale Software.** If the SOFTWARE PRODUCT is labeled "Not of Resale" or "NFR," then notwithstanding other sections of this EULA, you may not resell, or otherwise transfer for value, the SOFTWARE PRODUCT.

c.   **Limitations on Reverse Engineering, Decompilation, and Disassembly.** You may not reverse engineer, decompile, or disassemble the SOFTWARE PRODUCT, except and only to the extent that such activity is expressly permitted by applicable law notwithstanding this limitation.

d.   **No Separation of Components.** The SOFTWARE PRODUCT is licensed as a single product and neither the software programs making up the SOFTWARE PRODUCT nor any UPDATE may be separated for use by more than one user at a time.

e.   **Rental.** You may not rent or lease the SOFTWARE PRODUCT.

f.   **Support Services.** Microsoft may provide you with support services related to the SOFTWARE PRODUCT ("Support Services"). Use of SUpport Services is governed by the Microsoft policies and programs described in the user manual, "online" documentation and/or other Microsoft-provided materials. Any supplemental software code provided to you as part of the Support Services shall be considered part of the SOFTWARE PRODUCT and subject to the terms and conditions of this EULA,. With respect to technical information you provide to Microsoft as part of the Support services, Microsoft may use such information for its business purposes, including for product support and development. Microsoft will not utilize such technical information in a form that personally identifies you.

g.   **Software Transfer.** You may permanently transfer all of your rights under this EULA, provided that you retain no copies, you transfer all of the SOFTWARE PRODUCT (including all component parts, the media and printed materials, any upgrades, this EULA, and, if applicable, the Certificate of Authenticity), and the recipient agrees to the terms of this EULA. If the SOFTWARE PRODUCT is an upgrade, any transfer must include all prior versions of the SOFTWARE PRODUCT.

h.   **Termination.** Without prejudice to any other rights, Microsoft may terminate this EULA if you fail to comply with the terms and conditions of this EULA. In such event, you must destroy all copies of the SOFTWARE PRODUCT. In addition, your rights under this EULA that pertain to the Microsoft Internet Explorer software shall terminate upon termination of your Microsoft operating system product EULA

3. **UPGRADES.** If the SOFTWARE is labeled as an upgrade, you must be properly licensed to use a product identified by Microsoft as being eligible for upgrade in order use the SOFTWARE PRODUCT. A SOFTWARE PRODUCT labeled as an upgrade replaces and/or supplements the product that formed the basis for your eligibility for the upgrade. You may use the resulting upgraded product only in accordance with the terms of this EULA. If the SOFTWARE PRODUCT is an upgrade of a component of a package of software programs that you licensed as a single product the SOFTWARE PRODUCT may be used and transferred only as part of that product package and may not be separated for use on more than one computer.

4. **COPYRIGHT.** All title and copyrights in and to the SOFTWARE PRODUCT (including but not limited to any images, photographs, animations, video, audio, music, text, and "applets" incorporated into the SOFTWARE PRODUCT), the accompanying printed materials, and any copies of the SOFTWARE PRODUCT are owned by Microsoft or its suppliers. The SOFTWARE PRODUCT is protected by copyright laws and international treaty provisions. Therefore, you must treat the SOFTWARE PRODUCT like any other copyrighted material except that you may install the SOFTWARE PRODUCT on a single computer provided you keep the original solely for backup or archival purposes. You may not copy the printed materials accompanying the SOFTWARE PRODUCT.

5. **DUAL MEDIA SOFTWARE.** You may receive the SOFTWARE PRODUCT in more than one medium. Regardless of the type or size of medium you receive, you may use only one medium that is appropriate for your single computer. You may not use or install the SOFTWARE PRODUCT on a single computer provided you keep the original solely for backup or archival purposes. You may not copy the printed materials accompanying the SOFTWARE PRODUCT.

6. **U.S. GOVERNMENT RESTRICTED RIGHTS.** The SOFTWARE PRODUCT and documentation are provided with RESTRICTED RIGHTS. Use, duplication, or disclosure by the Government is subject to restrictions as set forth in subparagraph (c)(1)(ii) of the Rights in Technical Data and Computer Software clause at DFARS 252.227-7013 or subparagraphs (c)(1) and (2) of the Commercial Computer Software-Restricted Rights at 48 CFR 52.227-19, as applicable. Manufacturer is Microsoft Corporation/One Microsoft Way/Redmond, WA 98052-6399.

7. **EXPORT RESTRICTIONS.** You agree that you will not export or re-export the SOFTWARE PRODUCT to any country, person, entity or end user subject to U.S.A. export restrictions. Restricted countries currently include, but are not necessarily limited to Cuba, Iran, Iraq, Libya, North Korea, Syria, and the Federal Republic of Yugoslavia (Serbia and Montenegro, U.N. Protected Areas and areas of Republic of Bosnia and Herzegovina under the control of Bosnian Serb forces). You warrant and represent that neither the U.S.A. Bureau of Export Administration nor any other federal agency has suspended, revoked or denied your export privileges.

MISCELLANEOUS

If you acquired this product in the United States, this EULA is governed by the laws of the State of Washington.

If you acquired this product in Canada, this EULA is governed by the laws of the Province of Ontario, Canada. Each of the parties hereto irrevocably attorns to the jurisdiction of the courts of the Province of Ontario and further agrees to commence any litigation which may arise hereunder in the courts located in the Judicial District of York, Province of Ontario.

If this product was acquired outside the United States, then local law may apply.

Should you have any questions concerning this EULA, or if you desire to contact Microsoft for any reason, please contact the Microsoft subsidiary serving your country, or write: Microsoft Sales Information Center/One Microsoft Way/Redmond, WA 98052-6399.

LICENSE AGREEMENT AND LIMITED WARRANTY

READ THE FOLLOWING TERMS AND CONDITIONS CAREFULLY BEFORE OPENING THIS SOFTWARE PACKAGE. THIS LEGAL DOCUMENT IS AN AGREEMENT BETWEEN YOU AND PRENTICE-HALL, INC. (THE "COMPANY"). BY OPENING THIS SEALED SOFTWARE PACKAGE, YOU ARE AGREEING TO BE BOUND BY THESE TERMS AND CONDITIONS. IF YOU DO NOT AGREE WITH THESE TERMS AND CONDITIONS, DO NOT OPEN THE SOFTWARE PACKAGE. PROMPTLY RETURN THE UNOPENED SOFTWARE PACKAGE AND ALL ACCOMPANYING ITEMS TO THE PLACE YOU OBTAINED THEM FOR A FULL REFUND OF ANY SUMS YOU HAVE PAID.

1. **GRANT OF LICENSE:** In consideration of your purchase of this book, and your agreement to abide by the terms and conditions of this Agreement, the Company grants to you a nonexclusive right to use and display the copy of the enclosed software program (hereinafter the "SOFTWARE") on a single computer (i.e., with a single CPU) at a single location so long as you comply with the terms of this Agreement. The Company reserves all rights not expressly granted to you under this Agreement.

2. **OWNERSHIP OF SOFTWARE:** You own only the magnetic or physical media (the enclosed media) on which the SOFTWARE is recorded or fixed, but the Company and the software developers retain all the rights, title, and ownership to the SOFTWARE recorded on the original media copy(ies) and all subsequent copies of the SOFTWARE, regardless of the form or media on which the original or other copies may exist. This license is not a sale of the original SOFTWARE or any copy to you.

3. **COPY RESTRICTIONS:** This SOFTWARE and the accompanying printed materials and user manual (the "Documentation") are the subject of copyright. The individual programs on the media are copyrighted by the authors of each program. Some of the programs on the media include separate licensing agreements. If you intend to use one of these programs, you must read and follow its accompanying license agreement. You may not copy the Documentation or the SOFTWARE, except that you may make a single copy of the SOFTWARE for backup or archival purposes only. You may be held legally responsible for any copying or copyright infringement which is caused or encouraged by your failure to abide by the terms of this restriction.

4. **USE RESTRICTIONS:** You may not network the SOFTWARE or otherwise use it on more than one computer or computer terminal at the same time. You may physically transfer the SOFTWARE from one computer to another provided that the SOFTWARE is used on only one computer at a time. You may not distribute copies of the SOFTWARE or Documentation to others. You may not reverse engineer, disassemble, decompile, modify, adapt, translate, or create derivative works based on the SOFTWARE or the Documentation without the prior written consent of the Company.

5. **TRANSFER RESTRICTIONS:** The enclosed SOFTWARE is licensed only to you and may not be transferred to any one else without the prior written consent of the Company. Any unauthorized transfer of the SOFTWARE shall result in the immediate termination of this Agreement.

6. **TERMINATION:** This license is effective until terminated. This license will terminate automatically without notice from the Company and become null and void if you fail to comply with any provisions or limitations of this license. Upon termination, you shall destroy the Documentation and all copies of the SOFTWARE. All provisions of this Agreement as to warranties, limitation of liability, remedies or damages, and our ownership rights shall survive termination.

7. **MISCELLANEOUS:** This Agreement shall be construed in accordance with the laws of the United States of America and the State of New York and shall benefit the Company, its affiliates, and assignees.

8. **LIMITED WARRANTY AND DISCLAIMER OF WARRANTY:** The Company warrants that the SOFTWARE, when properly used in accordance with the Documentation, will operate in substantial conformity with the description of the SOFTWARE set forth in the Documentation. The Company does not warrant that the SOFTWARE will meet your requirements or that the operation of the SOFTWARE will be uninterrupted or error-free. The Company warrants that the media on which the SOFTWARE is delivered shall be free from defects in materials and workmanship under normal use for a period of thirty (30) days from the date of your purchase. Your only remedy and the Company's only obligation under these limited warranties is, at the

Company's option, return of the warranted item for a refund of any amounts paid by you or replacement of the item. Any replacement of SOFTWARE or media under the warranties shall not extend the original warranty period. The limited warranty set forth above shall not apply to any SOFTWARE which the Company determines in good faith has been subject to misuse, neglect, improper installation, repair, alteration, or damage by you. EXCEPT FOR THE EXPRESSED WARRANTIES SET FORTH ABOVE, THE COMPANY DISCLAIMS ALL WARRANTIES, EXPRESS OR IMPLIED, INCLUDING WITHOUT LIMITATION, THE IMPLIED WARRANTIES OF MERCHANTABILITY AND FITNESS FOR A PARTICULAR PURPOSE. EXCEPT FOR THE EXPRESS WARRANTY SET FORTH ABOVE, THE COMPANY DOES NOT WARRANT, GUARANTEE, OR MAKE ANY REPRESENTATION REGARDING THE USE OR THE RESULTS OF THE USE OF THE SOFTWARE IN TERMS OF ITS CORRECTNESS, ACCURACY, RELIABILITY, CURRENTNESS, OR OTHERWISE.

IN NO EVENT, SHALL THE COMPANY OR ITS EMPLOYEES, AGENTS, SUPPLIERS, OR CONTRACTORS BE LIABLE FOR ANY INCIDENTAL, INDIRECT, SPECIAL, OR CONSEQUENTIAL DAMAGES ARISING OUT OF OR IN CONNECTION WITH THE LICENSE GRANTED UNDER THIS AGREEMENT, OR FOR LOSS OF USE, LOSS OF DATA, LOSS OF INCOME OR PROFIT, OR OTHER LOSSES, SUSTAINED AS A RESULT OF INJURY TO ANY PERSON, OR LOSS OF OR DAMAGE TO PROPERTY, OR CLAIMS OF THIRD PARTIES, EVEN IF THE COMPANY OR AN AUTHORIZED REPRESENTATIVE OF THE COMPANY HAS BEEN ADVISED OF THE POSSIBILITY OF SUCH DAMAGES. IN NO EVENT SHALL LIABILITY OF THE COMPANY FOR DAMAGES WITH RESPECT TO THE SOFTWARE EXCEED THE AMOUNTS ACTUALLY PAID BY YOU, IF ANY, FOR THE SOFTWARE.

SOME JURISDICTIONS DO NOT ALLOW THE LIMITATION OF IMPLIED WARRANTIES OR LIABILITY FOR INCIDENTAL, INDIRECT, SPECIAL, OR CONSEQUENTIAL DAMAGES, SO THE ABOVE LIMITATIONS MAY NOT ALWAYS APPLY. THE WARRANTIES IN THIS AGREEMENT GIVE YOU SPECIFIC LEGAL RIGHTS AND YOU MAY ALSO HAVE OTHER RIGHTS WHICH VARY IN ACCORDANCE WITH LOCAL LAW.

ACKNOWLEDGMENT

YOU ACKNOWLEDGE THAT YOU HAVE READ THIS AGREEMENT, UNDERSTAND IT, AND AGREE TO BE BOUND BY ITS TERMS AND CONDITIONS. YOU ALSO AGREE THAT THIS AGREEMENT IS THE COMPLETE AND EXCLUSIVE STATEMENT OF THE AGREEMENT BETWEEN YOU AND THE COMPANY AND SUPERSEDES ALL PROPOSALS OR PRIOR AGREEMENTS, ORAL, OR WRITTEN, AND ANY OTHER COMMUNICATIONS BETWEEN YOU AND THE COMPANY OR ANY REPRESENTATIVE OF THE COMPANY RELATING TO THE SUBJECT MATTER OF THIS AGREEMENT.

Should you have any questions concerning this Agreement or if you wish to contact the Company for any reason, please contact in writing at the address below.

Robin Short
Prentice Hall PTR
One Lake Street
Upper Saddle River, New Jersey 07458

LICENSE AGREEMENT
AND LIMITED WARRANTY

By opening the sealed software package, you accept and agree to the terms and conditions printed below and in the full printed license agreement. If you do not agree, do not open the package.

The software is distributed on an "AS IS" basis, without warranty. Neither the authors, the software developers, nor Prentice Hall make any representation, or warranty, either express or implied, with respect to the software programs, their quality, accuracy, or fitness for a specific purpose. Therefore, neither the authors, the software developers, nor Prentice Hall shall have any liability to you or any other person or entity with respect to any liability, loss, or damage caused or alleged to have been caused directly or indirectly by the programs contained on the media. This includes, but is not limited to, interruption of service, loss of data, loss of classroom time, loss of consulting or anticipatory profits, or consequential damages from the use of these programs. If the media itself is defective, you may return it for a replacement.

SYSTEM REQUIREMENTS

To run Visual C++, Learning Edition, you need:

- *PC with a 486DX/66 MHz or higher processor (Pentium 90 recommended)*
- *Microsoft Windows 95 operating system or WIndows NT® Workstation operating system version 4.0 or later*
- *20 MB of RAM (24 MB recommended)*
- *Hard-disk space required:*
  - *Typical installation: 175 MB*
  - *Minimum installation: 120MB*
  - *CD-ROM installation: (tools run from the compact disc): 50 MB*
  - *Total tools and information on the disc: 650MB*
- *CD-ROM drive*
- *32-bit protected mode CD-ROM driver*
- *VGA or higher-resolution monitor (Super VGA recommended)*
- *Microsoft Mouse or compatible pointing device*

CD KEY:
636-6824537

Don't Lose This Number!
You must use it every time you install this software.
